# THE CONTENT AND SETTING
# OF THE GOSPEL TRADITION

# The Content and Setting of the Gospel Tradition

*Edited by*

Mark Harding and Alanna Nobbs

WILLIAM B. EERDMANS PUBLISHING COMPANY

GRAND RAPIDS, MICHIGAN / CAMBRIDGE, U.K.

Published 2010 by

Wm. B. Eerdmans Publishing Co.

2140 Oak Industrial Drive N.E., Grand Rapids, Michigan 49505

Printed in the United States of America

22 21 20 19 18 17 16      10 9 8 7 6 5 4

**Library of Congress Cataloging-in-Publication Data**

The content and setting of the Gospel tradition /
edited by Mark Harding and Alanna Nobbs.
p.      cm.
Includes index.
ISBN 978-0-8028-3318-1 (pbk.: alk. paper)
1. Bible. N.T. Gospels — Introductions.
I. Harding, Mark.   II. Nobbs, Alanna, 1944-

BS2555.52C66   2010
226′.061 — dc22
2010033370

www.eerdmans.com

*To our colleagues in teaching*

"To the one who gives wisdom I will give glory."

Sirach 51:17

# The Content and Setting of the Gospel Tradition

## Jesus' Life and Ministry

# FOREWORD

This book has its genesis in the strong connections forged over the years between the Ancient History Department of Macquarie University and the Australian College of Theology (ACT), many of whose teachers are graduates of the Ancient History Department at Macquarie and still retain links as honoraries.

The Ancient History Department at Macquarie has long had a focus on the Greco-Roman background of the New Testament. Its Ancient History Documentary Research Centre series, New Documents Illustrating Early Christianity (nine volumes to date), now published by Eerdmans, discusses evidence for the background of the New Testament in published inscriptions and papyri. The Society for the Study of Early Christianity, also based in the Research Centre, funds annual conferences, seminar series and an international Visiting Scholar in the field. The Centre has had a long term interest too in the papyri from Egypt which bear on the history of Christianity. Many of the essays included in this volume demonstrate the fruits of the historical enquiry fostered there.

The ACT, a major provider of theological education since its establishment by the General Synod of the Anglican Church of Australia in 1891, operates nationally as a network of affiliated colleges. Each college has its own well-qualified faculty teaching a range of disciplines, including the New Testament and its Greco-Roman and Jewish background. Eight of the 16 contributors to this volume are ACT academic staff members.

Whereas many introductory books on the New Testament and its background continue to be written, they tend to concentrate almost exclusively on the content of the books of the New Testament, and deal with issues such as authorship, date and provenance. This work is a serious attempt to tackle the social setting and textual tradition of the New Testament, in a way that provides a distinctly Australian contribution and shows the degree of scholarship in this area. It is aimed as a resource primarily for undergraduates in theology or history but the bibliographies and wider setting of the issues will we hope make it useful to scholars beyond those years. A Macquarie PhD graduate and current principal of an ACT affiliated college (the Queensland Theological College), Dr Bruce Winter, edited a pioneering six volume series on the *Book of Acts in its First Century Setting*, which serves as something of a model for the present volume.

In view of our understanding of the prime readership of this volume, and to maximize its benefits, we have retained Greek quotations but transliterated Hebrew ones.

All contributions have been refereed, and thanks are owed both to those who generously gave their time, and to the contributors who rewrote and adapted sometimes in several drafts.

Both editors used their contacts to invite the contributors, and discussed the overall plan and details with them, but by far the larger share of the burden was shouldered by Mark Harding, and it is fitting that his name come first not merely for alphabetical reasons.

For the detailed work of subediting we are indebted to Philip Harding and Meredith Walker, both ACT graduates in theology.

We wish to thank Eerdmans publishing house for their ready endorsement of this project, and our families for support over its duration.

Alanna Nobbs
Professor of Ancient History
Macquarie University
16 February 2010

# CONTRIBUTORS

## Mark Harding

Mark Harding is an Honorary Associate of Macquarie University. Since 1996 he has been the Dean of the Australian College of Theology. He has postgraduate degrees from London University, Macquarie University, and Princeton Theological Seminary where he completed a PhD in New Testament in 1993. He is the author of *Tradition and Rhetoric in the Pastoral Epistles* (Peter Lang, 1998) and *Early Christian Life and Thought in Social Context* (T. & T. Clark, 2003).

## Alanna Nobbs

Alanna Nobbs is Professor of Ancient History and deputy Director of the Ancient Cultures Research Centre at Macquarie University. Her teaching, research interests and publications are in Greek and Roman historiography (including New Testament background), and in the history of Christianity especially as seen through the papyri.

## Evelyn Ashley

Evelyn Ashley has been lecturing at Vose Seminary (previously known as the Baptist Theological College of Western Australia), an affiliated college of the Australian College of Theology, since 2003. She is a graduate of the Seminary and Murdoch University where in 2006 she completed a PhD entitled "Paul's Paradigm for Ministry in 2 Corinthians: Christ's Death and Resurrection."

## Scott D. Charlesworth

Scott Charlesworth holds an MA in Early Christian and Jewish Studies from Macquarie and a PhD in Greek from the University of New England (Armidale, NSW). His doctoral thesis will be published in 2010 as *Early Christian Gospels: their Production and Transmission* in the European series Papyrologica Florentina. He currently teaches biblical languages and theology at Pacific Adventist University in Papua New Guinea.

## Johan Ferreira

Johan Ferreira is Principal of the Bible College of Queensland, an affiliated college of the Australian College of Theology. Johan is a graduate of the Reformed Theological College, the University of Queensland, and Princeton Theological Seminary. He is the author of *Johannine Ecclesiology* (Sheffield Academic Press, 1998), *The Hymn of the Pearl: The Syriac and Greek Texts with Introduction, Translations, and Notes* (St Pauls, 2002), and Chinese language grammars of Biblical Hebrew and Greek. He has published several articles in biblical studies and missiology. Johan is completing a book on Tang Christianity based on extensive study of original Chinese documents and inscriptions.

## Chris Forbes

Chris Forbes is a Senior Lecturer in Ancient History at Macquarie University, where he teaches New Testament history, Hellenistic history and Greco-Roman history of ideas. He completed his PhD in Ancient History at Macquarie University under the supervision of Professor E. A. Judge in 1987. His thesis was published by Mohr Siebeck in 1995 as *Prophecy and Inspired Speech in Early Christianity and its Hellenistic Environment*. He has published various articles on the intellectual and cultural context of the early Christians and is a regular contributor to the conferences of the Society for the Study of Early Christianity held annually at Macquarie University.

## Greg W. Forbes

Greg Forbes is the head of the Department of Biblical Studies at the Bible College of Victoria, an affiliated college of the Australian College of Theology, where he has taught for 18 years. He currently lectures in Greek, New Testament, and Hermeneutics. After completing an undergraduate degree and a research Masters degree in Theology with the Australian College of Theology, he was awarded a PhD from Deakin University for a thesis on the parables in Luke's Gospel. Greg's published works include *The God of Old: The Role of the Lukan Parables in the Purpose of Luke's Gospel* (Sheffield Academic, 2000) and a commentary on 1 Peter in the Asia Bible Commentary Series (Asia Theological Association, 2006).

## Timothy J. Harris

Tim Harris is Dean of Bishopdale Theological College in Nelson, New Zealand. He has degrees from Macquarie University and the Australian College of Theology, and was awarded his PhD by Flinders University (South Australia) for a thesis entitled "The Subversion of Status: Pauline Notions of Humility and Deference in Graeco-Roman Perspective" which is in the process of being prepared for publication. He is New Testament Moderator for the Australian College of Theology, and has lectured at a number of Australian theological colleges.

## James R. Harrison

James Harrison, Head of Theology at Wesley Institute (Sydney), completed his PhD in Ancient History at Macquarie University under the supervision of Professor E. A. Judge and Chris Forbes in 1997. His book *Paul's Language of Grace in Its Graeco-Roman Context*, published by Mohr Siebeck, was the 2005 Winner of the Biblical Archaeology Society Publication Award for the Best Book Relating to the New Testament published in 2003 and 2004. He is the editor of the forthcoming Mohr Siebeck collection of papers by Professor E. A. Judge, *The First Christians in the Roman World: Augustan and New Testament Essays*. James is an Honorary Associate at Macquarie University and a regular contributor to the conferences of the Society for the Study of Early Christianity held annually at Macquarie University.

### Theresa Yu Chui Siang Lau

Theresa Yu Chui Siang Lau was a lecturer in the Chinese Department of the Bible College of Victoria from 1998 to 2009. She is a graduate of Sydney Missionary and Bible College, the Australian College of Theology, and the University of Melbourne where in 2007 she completed a PhD entitled "Reading the Gospel of Matthew as a Gospel of the Jerusalem Council." She is currently lecturing in New Testament at the Chinese Biblical Seminary in Barcelona, Spain.

### Erica A. Mathieson

Erica Mathieson has been the Rector of Holy Cross Anglican Church, Hackett, in the Australian Capital Territory, since 2008. She is a visiting lecturer in pastoral theology at St Mark's Theological College, Charles Sturt University and an Honorary Associate at Macquarie University. Prior to her current appointment she was Research Assistant at Macquarie University in the fields of papyrology, early Christianity and women in antiquity. Her doctoral studies in Ancient History were undertaken at Macquarie and explored the writings of Jewish and Christian women in the early centuries of the Christian Era. Publications are in process on early literacy, "Signed with Love: Literacy and Subscription in Personal Letters among the Papyri," and "Perspectives of the Greek Papyri of Egypt on the religious lives of Jewish and Christian Women 100-400 CE."

### Robert K. McIver

Robert McIver is an associate professor, specializing in Biblical Studies at Avondale College (Cooranbong, NSW) and Dean of the Faculty of Theology. He has degrees from Canterbury University (NZ), Avondale College, the University of London, and Andrews University where he completed a PhD in New Testament and Archaeology in 1989. He is a contributor to the conferences of the Society for the Study of Early Christianity held annually at Macquarie University. He is the author of a number of books, including *The Four Faces of Jesus* (Pacific Press, 2000).

### Brian Powell

Brian Powell is the Vice Principal for Academic Administration and Senior Lecturer in New Testament at Morling College, the Baptist Theological and Bible College of New South Wales, a college affiliated with the Australian College of Theology. He has taught at Morling since 1983, initially in Systematic Theology and in New Testament since 1992. He completed a PhD in Paul's character ethics in 1996 at Macquarie University under the supervision of Professor E. A. Judge. Brian was Head of the Department of Bible and Languages of the Australian College of Theology from 1997 to 2006.

### Van Shore

Van Shore was the head of New Testament Studies at Garden City College of Ministries (Brisbane, Queensland) from 2003 until 2008. He has a PhD degree from the University of Queensland for a thesis entitled "Ears to Hear in the Book of Revelation." He completed an extensive teaching ministry on the Gospels in the United Kingdom, Atlanta, and Brasil in 2007. He is currently involved in teaching New Testament Greek with ALPHACRUCIS College, heading up an evening college course affiliated with Hillsong International Leadership College, Brisbane, as well as, exercising a Pastor of Spiritual Formation role as a staff member at Hillsong Church, Brisbane.

### Ian K. Smith

Ian Smith was appointed Principal of the Presbyterian Theological Centre (Sydney), an affiliated college of the Australian College of Theology, in 2010. He has been a lecturer in New Testament at the Centre since 1995. He also serves as the Head of the Department of Bible and Languages in the College. He has postgraduate degrees from the University of New England, the Australian College of Theology, and the University of Sydney where he completed a PhD in New Testament in 2002. He is the author of *Heavenly Perspective: A Study of the Apostle Paul's Response to a Jewish Mystical Movement at Colossae* (T. & T. Clark, 2006).

### Murray J. Smith

Murray Smith lectures in Biblical Studies at the Presbyterian Theological Centre (Sydney), and previously taught on Jesus & the Gospels at Macquarie Christian Studies Institute. He has Masters degrees from the University of Sydney (Reformation History) and Macquarie University (Early Christian and Jewish Studies). He is currently completing a PhD in Ancient History at Macquarie University on "the logic of Jesus' future advent in earliest Christianity."

### Stephen Voorwinde

Steve Voorwinde has taught at the Reformed Theological College (Geelong, Victoria), an affiliated college of the Australian College of Theology, since 1985. He was awarded the Doctor of Theology degree of the Australian College of Theology in 2003. His doctoral dissertation was published by T. & T. Clark in 2005 under the title *Jesus' Emotions in the Fourth Gospel – Human or Divine?* He also contributes regularly to *Trowel & Sword* and *Vox Reformata*. Some of his articles have been published in the *Reformed Theological Review* and the *Westminster Theological Journal*.

Details of all papyri referred to in this volume (especially chapters 2, 3 and 5) can be accessed in: John F. Oates et al., *Checklist of Editions of Greek, Latin, Demotic and Coptic Papyri, Ostraca and Tablets*, 5th ed., BASPSup 9 (Oakville: American Society of Papyrologists, 2001).

Note also the regularly updated on-line resource of: John F. Oates, Roger S. Bagnall, Sarah J. Clackson, Alexandra A. O'Brien, Joshua D. Sosin, Terry G. Wilfong, and Klaas A. Worp, *Checklist of Greek, Latin, Demotic and Coptic Papyri, Ostraca and Tablets*: http://scriptorium.lib.duke.edu/papyrus/texts/clist.html, May, 2008.

Details of inscriptions referred to in this volume (especially chapters 3 and 5) can be accessed at the on-line resource sponsored by the American Society of Greek and Latin Epigraphy: http://www.bbaw.de/forschung/ig/ectypa/1syllabus.html, May, 2008.

For abbreviations of works not listed below, see: Siegfried M. Schwertner, *Internationales Abkürzungsverzeichnis für Theologie und Grenzgebiete*, 2nd ed (Berlin: de Gruyter, 1992).

| | |
|---|---|
| *1 Apol.* | Justin, *First Apology* |
| *1 Clem.* | *1 Clement* |
| *1 En.* | *1 Enoch* |
| 11QMelch | *Melchizedek*, from Qumran cave 11 |
| 11QT | *Temple Scroll*, from Qumran cave 11 |
| 1QH | *Thanksgiving Hymns*, from Qumran cave 1 |
| 1QM | *War Scroll*, from Qumran cave 1 |
| 1QpHab | *Pesher Habbakuk*, from Qumran cave 1 |
| 1QS | *Rule of the Community*, from Qumran cave 1 |
| 1QSa | *Rule of the Congregation*, from Qumran cave 1 |
| *2 Bar.* | *2 Baruch* |
| *2 Clem.* | *2 Clement* |
| 4QMMT | *Some Observances of the Law*, from Qumran cave 4 |
| 4QpNahum | *Pesher Nahum*, from Qumran cave 4 |
| *ABD* | David Noel Freedman, ed. *The Anchor Bible Dictionary*. 6 vols. New York: Doubleday, 1992 |
| ABRL | Anchor Bible Reference Library |
| *AE* | *Année épigraphique*. Paris: Presses universitaires de France, 1888- |
| *Ag. Ap.* | Josephus, *Against Apion* |
| *Ann.* | Tacitus, *Annals* |
| *ANRW* | *Aufstieg und Niedergang der römischen Welt: Geschichte und Kultur Roms im Spiegel der neueren Forschung*. Edited by H. Temporini and W. Haase Berlin: de Gruyter, 1972- |
| *Ant.* | Josephus, *Jewish Antiquities* |

| | |
|---|---|
| ASV | American Standard Version |
| *Aug.* | Suetonius, *Augustus* |
| *b. 'Erub.* | *Babylonian Talmud, Eruvin* |
| *b. Ber.* | *Baylonian Talmud, Berakhot* |
| *b. Pesah.* | *Babylonian Talmud, Pesahim* |
| *b. Sanh.* | *Babylonian Talmud, Sanhedrin* |
| *b. Shabb* | *Babylonian Talmud, Shabbat* |
| BAGD | Bauer, W., W. F. Arndt, F. W. Gingrich, and F. W. Danker. *Greek-English Lexicon of the New Testament and Other Early Christian Literature*, 2$^{nd}$ ed. Chicago: University of Chicago Press, 1979 |
| *Barn.* | *Barnabas* |
| BASPSup | Bulletin of the American Society of Papyrologists: Supplement |
| BDAG | Danker, Frederick W, ed. *A Greek-English Lexicon of the New Testament and Other Early Christian Literature.* 3$^{rd}$ edn. Chicago: University of Chicago Press, 2000 |
| *Bell. civ.* | Appian, *Civil War* |
| *Ben.* | Seneca, *De beneficiis* |
| BETL | Bibliotheca ephemeridum theologicarum lovaniensium |
| BGU | *Aegyptische Urkunden aus den Königlichen Staatlichen Museen zu Berlin, Griechische Urkunden.* 15 vols. Berlin, 1895-1983 |
| *BibInt* | *Biblical Interpretation* |
| *CBQ* | *Catholic Biblical Quarterly* |
| CBQMS | Catholic Biblical Quarterly Monograph Series |
| CD | Cairo Genizah copy of the *Damascus Document* |
| *Cher.* | Philo, *On the Cherubim* |
| CII | *Corpus inscriptionum judaicarum.* Edited by J. B. Frey. 2 vols. Rome: Pontificio Istituto di Archeologia Cristiana, 1936-1952 |
| CIJ | *Corpus inscriptionum judaicarum* |
| CIL | *Corpus inscriptionum latinarum* |
| *Claud.* | Suetonius, *Claudius* |
| col. | column |
| *Comm. Isa.* | Jerome, *Commentariorum in Isaiam libri XVIII* |
| *Comm. Matt.* | Jerome, *Commentariorum in Matthaeum libri IV* |
| Contempl. | Philo, *On the Contemplative Life* |
| CPJ | *Corpus papyrorum judaicarum.* Edited by V. Tchericover. 3 vols. Cambridge: Harvard University Press, 1957-1964 |
| *DDBDP* | *Duke Databank of Documentary Papyri* |
| *Dial.* | Justin, *Dialogue with Trypho* |
| *Did.* | *Didache* |
| *Diogn.* | *Diognetus* |
| DJG | *Dictionary of Jesus and the Gospels.* Edited by J. B. Green and S. McKnight. Downers Grove: InterVarsity, 1992. |
| *DSD* | *Dead Sea Discoveries* |
| eap | Gospels, Acts & Catholic Epistles, Pauline Epistles |
| eapr | Gospels, Acts & Catholic Epistles, Pauline Epistles, Revelation |
| *Ebr.* | Philo, *On Drunkenness* |
| *Ecl.* | Stobaeus, *Eclogues* |

| | |
|---|---|
| *Ep.* | Pliny the Younger, *Epistles* |
| *Eph.* | Ignatius, *To the Ephesians* |
| ET | English translation |
| fr. | fragment |
| FRLANT | Forschungen zur Religion und Literatur des Alten und Neuen Testaments |
| *Geogr.* | Strabo, *Geography* |
| Gr. | Greek |
| *Haer.* | Irenaeus, *Adversus haereses* |
| *Hist.* | Dio Cassius, *Roman History* |
| *Hist.* | Tacitus, *Histories* |
| *Hist. eccl.* | Eusebius, *Ecclesiastical History* |
| *IEJ* | *Israel Exploration Journal* |
| *IG.* | *Inscriptiones graecae.* Editio minor. Berlin, 1924- |
| imp. | Imperial |
| *j. Ta'an.* | *Jerusalem Talmud, Ta'anit* |
| *J.W.* | Josephus, *Jewish War* |
| *JBL* | *Journal of Biblical Literature* |
| *JECS* | *Journal of Early Jewish Studies* |
| *JJS* | *Journal of Jewish Studies* |
| JPTSup | Journal of Pentecostal Theology Supplement Series |
| *JSJ* | *Journal for the Study of Judaism in the Persian, Hellenistic, and Roman Periods* |
| *JSNT* | *Journal for the Study of the New Testament* |
| JSNTSup | Journal for the Study of the New Testament Study: Supplement Series |
| *JSOT* | *Journal for the Study of the Old Testament* |
| JSPSS | Journal for the Study of the Pseudepigrapha: Supplement Series |
| *JTS* | *Journal of Theological Studies* |
| *Jub.* | *Jubilees* |
| *Jul.* | Suetonius, *Julius Caesar* |
| KJV | King James Version |
| *Legat.* | Philo, *On the Embassy to Gaius* |
| *Let. Aris.* | *Letter of Aristeas* |
| LXX | Septuagint |
| m. | hand (*manus*) |
| *m. 'Abot* | *Mishnah, Avot* |
| *m. 'Ohal.* | *Mishnah, Ohalot* |
| *m. Ber.* | *Mishnah, Berakhot* |
| *m. Gitt.* | *Mishnah, Gittin* |
| *m. Hag.* | *Mishnah, Hagigah* |
| *m. Kelim* | *Mishnah, Kelim* |
| *m. Ketub.* | *Mishnah, Ketubbot* |
| *m. Pea.* | *Mishnah, Pe'ah* |
| *m. Pesah.* | *Mishnah, Pesahim* |
| *m. Tehar.* | *Mishnah, Teharot* |
| Macc. | Maccabees |
| *Magn.* | Ignatius, *To the Magnesians* |

| | |
|---|---|
| *Marc.* | Tertullian, *Adversus Marcionem* |
| *Mart. Pol.* | *Martyrdom of Polycarp* |
| MM | Moulton, James H., and George Milligan. *The Vocabulary of the Greek Testament Illustrated from the Papyri and Other Non-Literary Sources* London: Hodder & Stoughton, 1930 |
| *Mor.* | Plutarch, *Moralia* |
| *Mos.* | Philo, *On the Life of Moses* |
| MT | Masoretic Text |
| *Nat.* | Pliny the Elder, *Natural History* |
| *Neot.* | *Neotestamentica* |
| NICNT | New International Commentary on the New Testament |
| NIDNTT | *New International Dictionary of New Testament Theology.* Edited by Colin Brown. 3 vols. Grand Rapids: Eerdmans, 1975-1978 |
| NIDOTTE | *New International Dictionary Old Testament Theology and Exegesis.* Edited by W. A. VanGemeren. 5 vols. Grand Rapids: Zondervan, 1997 |
| NIGTC | New International Greek Testament Commentary |
| NovTSup | Novum Testamentum Supplements |
| NRSV | New Revised Standard Version |
| *NTS* | *New Testament Studies* |
| *OGIS* | *Orientis graeci inscriptions selectae.* Edited by W. Dittenberger. 2 vols. Leipzig: S. Hirzel, 1903-1905 |
| *Or.* | Dio Chrysostom, *Orations* |
| parr. | parallels |
| *Phaedr.* | Plato, *Phaedrus* |
| *Phil.* | Polycarp, *To the Philippians* |
| *Phld.* | Ignatius, *To the Philadelphians* |
| pll. | plates |
| Ps. Philo | Pseudo-Philo |
| Ps.-Phoc. | Pseudo-Phocylides |
| *Pss. Sol.* | *Psalms of Solomon* |
| *Rom.* | Ignatius, *To the Romans* |
| *Ruth Rab.* | *Rabbah Ruth* |
| *Sat.* | Juvenal, *Satires* |
| *SB* | *Sammelbuch griechischer Urkunden aus Aegypten.* Edited by F. Preisigke et al. Vols. 1-, 1915- |
| SEG | *Supplementum epigraphicum graecum* |
| *Sen.* | Cicero, *De senectute* |
| *Sib. Or.* | *Sibylline Oracles* |
| SIG | *Sylloge inscriptionum graecarum.* Edited by W. Dittenberger. 4 vols. 3$^{rd}$ ed. Leipzig: S. Hirzel, 1915-1924 |
| Sir. | Sirach |
| *Smyrn.* | Ignatius, *To the Smyrnaeans* |
| SNT | Studien zum Neuen Testament |
| SNTSMS | Society for New Testament Studies Monograph Series |
| *Spec.* | Philo, *On the Special Laws* |
| *Strom.* | Clement of Alexandria, *Stromata* |

| | |
|---|---|
| *SVTQ* | *St. Vladimir's Theological Quarterly* |
| t. Ber. | *Tosephta, Berakhot* |
| T. Iss. | *Testament of Issachar* |
| T. Jos. | *Testament of Joseph* |
| T. Jud. | *Testament of Judah* |
| t. Meg. | *Tosephta, Megillah* |
| t. Menah. | *Tosephta, Menakhot* |
| T. Reu. | *Testament of Reuben* |
| *TD* | *Theology Digest* |
| TDNT | Kittel Gerhard, and Gerhard Friedrich, eds. *Theological Dictionary of the New Testament.* 10 vols. Translated by Geoffrey W. Bromiley. Grand Rapids: Eerdmans, 1964-1976 |
| TDOT | *Theological Dictionary of the Old Testament.* Edited by G. J. Botterweck and H. Ringgren. Translated by J. T. Willis, G. W. Bromiley, and D. E. Green. 8 vols. Grand Rapids: Eerdmans, 1974- |
| *Tg. Isa.* | *Targum Isaiah* |
| *Tg. Onq.* | *Targum Onqelos* |
| *Tib.* | Suetonius, *Tiberius* |
| *Tim.* | Lucian, *Timon* |
| *Tim.* | Plato, *Timaeus* |
| *TJ* | *Trinity Journal* |
| Tob. | Tobit |
| *Tract. ep. Jo.* | Augustine, *Tractates on the First Epistle of John* |
| *Trall.* | Ignatius, *To the Trallians* |
| TU | Texte und Untersuchungen |
| *TynBull* | *Tyndale Bulletin* |
| *TZ* | *Theologische Zeitschrift* |
| UBS | United Bible Societies |
| *Vir. ill.* | Jerome, *De viris illustribus* |
| *VR* | *Vox reformata* |
| *WTJ* | *Westminster Theological Journal* |
| WUNT | Wissenschaftliche Untersuchungen zum Neuen Testament |
| *ZNW* | *Zeitschrift für die neutestamentliche Wissenschaft* |
| *ZPE* | *Zeitschrift für Papyrologie und Epigraphik* |

# 1. The Archaeology of Palestine from the Maccabees to the Second Jewish Revolt (167 BC–AD 135)

*Robert K. McIver*

It was with considerable amusement that I recently overheard one conference participant say to another, "People are most interested in sex, but aside from that they are most interested in archaeology." The conference was the yearly meeting of ASOR (the American Society for Oriental Research) and both partners in the conversation were archaeologists, so the comment probably overstates the interest in archaeology experienced by the general public. Nevertheless, the remark does capture the fascination that archaeology has for many people. By examining the foundations of buildings, pottery (mostly broken), bones, and even pollen from ancient towns and cities, and drawing on the knowledge of a whole range of experts—including ceramicists, botanists, zoologists, physicists, historians, linguists, anthropologists— archaeologists attempt to reconstruct civilizations long dead. The whole process involves the lively cooperation and interaction of a whole range of people, and can provide interesting insights into such texts as the New Testament (NT), spiced with the entertainment derived from observing the larger-than-life characters that archaeology seems to attract.

Archaeology, of course, deals with artifacts, while NT studies deals with texts. It is important to recognize that the two disciplines form separate endeavors, and illuminate each other more or less by happenstance. Nevertheless, archaeology does have much to offer NT studies, and this chapter will provide a brief survey of some of the discoveries and theories of archaeologists most relevant to the study of the gospels. It begins with two sections that give a general overview of the societies found in Palestine between 167 BC and AD 135. The first section deals with the frequent traumatic changes that overtook such societies, and the second the continuities surviving those changes. It then looks at the regions of Galilee, Judea and Samaria, stopping along the way to comment on some of the significant town and cities.

## A. They Were Interesting Times

Archaeologists call them destruction layers. Most civilizations before the Romans usually rebuilt their cities on top of the ruins of a city that had previously occupied the site. Archaeologists are pleased to discover destruction layers as they mark the boundaries between the different layers (or strata) that represent the various time periods that an individual site was occupied. Almost all of the cities of Palestine have several clear destruction layers in the period 167 BC–AD 135.

Historians, on the other hand, describe destruction layers as evidence of wars, or conquests, or revolts. But for those living when they were formed, destruction layers represent times of great trauma associated with the loss of loved ones, loss of dwelling painstakingly built up over years, and the unavoidable witnessing or experiencing torture, wanton murder, rape and other atrocities.

Nor were wars the only disasters that regularly overtook those living in Palestine during this period. Periodic crop failures resulted in famines, occasional earthquakes leveled most dwellings over large areas, and the threat of devastating disease pandemics was ever present.[1] Life was precarious. Indeed it is no surprise that of every 100,000 babies born, only about 45,830 were still alive at age ten, or less than 50 percent. Those who survived to ten years of age had a life expectancy of approximately thirty-five further years (or a total life expectancy of forty-five years), while a mere 5,400 (or 5 percent) of the most hardy and lucky would be alive at age seventy.[2] Life was short, sometimes violent, and marked by frequent losses of those most important in the lives of individuals.

Yet curiously enough, despite all of the uncertainties of life, the period 167 BC–AD 135 enjoyed sufficient stability that it was one of rising prosperity. The late Hellenistic, Roman and early Byzantine periods are marked by increasing population levels and the establishment or expansion of significant cities.[3] Compared to other periods of human history, these were "good times" as well as "interesting times." There are worse things that can happen to a population than to fall into the hands of an exploitative and oppressive government such as the Roman Empire, if that Empire brings relative stability in its train![4]

---

[1] In the early Roman period, Palestine suffered from two major famines, the first in 29 BC and the second sometime in 41–54 (the reign of Claudius); there was a major earthquake in 31 BC that killed many people and cattle, and other quakes in 24 BC and AD 19, 30, 33, 37 and 48. See David A. Fiensy, *The Social History of Palestine in the Herodian Period* (Lewiston, Queenston, Lampeter: Edwin Mellen Press, 1991), p. 99.

[2] These figures are taken from Bruce Frier, "Roman Life Expectancy: Ulpian's Evidence," *Harvard Studies in Classical Philology* 86 (1982), pp. 213-51.

[3] For example, see figures 102 and 103 in Ze'ev Safrai, *The Economy of Roman Palestine* (New York: Routledge, 1994), pp. 438-39, which graphs the demographic expansion and contraction of Palestine at different time periods.

[4] In this regard it is instructive to consider the evaluation of Herod the Great made by Donald E. Gowan: "Yet, as we attempt to evaluate the man, a more balanced estimate may be that although as a person he was despicable, as Hellenistic kings went he was one of the most

The following table outlines some of the major changes that took place during this time period.

| Dates | Ruling Elite | Major personalities and events | Archaeological Period |
|-------|--------------|-------------------------------|----------------------|
| 167–64 BC | Hasmoneans | Under leadership of Mattathias and his sons John, Simon, Judas, Eleazar and Jonathan, a long and bitter war (the Maccabean Revolt) results in establishment of the Hasmonean kingdom | Late Hellenistic |
| 64 BC onwards | Romans | 64 BC<br>The Roman general Pompey establishes pro-Roman rulers, and reduces area of Jewish influence to Judea, and Galilee.<br><br>37–4 BC<br>Herod the Great, by war and diplomacy is established as "King" over large territory<br><br>4 BC–AD 66<br>Herod's kingdom divided into three:<br>*Judea-Samaria* under Archelaus to AD 6, then under Roman Procurators, including Pilate (26–36).<br>*Galilee-Perea* under Herod Antipas (4 BC–AD 39).<br>*Northern Transjordan* including Decapolis under Philip (4 BC–AD 34).<br><br>AD 66–70<br>First Jewish Revolt.<br><br>AD 132–125<br>Second Jewish Revolt (the Bar Kokhba revolt). | Early Roman |

## B. The More Things Change the More they Stay the Same

On the other hand, from the perspective of the majority of the population—those belonging to the families of peasant farmers living in small villages—the conditions of life, though tough, were relatively constant between 167 BC and AD 135. It is estimated that the governing elite and their retainers made

able of them all. The Jews had done worse before Herod appeared, and would do worse after he died. True, they suffered under heavy taxation to pay for his buildings, but he did provide for the country a badly-needed harbor at Caesarea and made it possible for the Jews to live in relative peace and stability for 30 years. Morton Smith has estimated that some 200 campaigns were fought in Palestine between 232 and 63 BC, so 30 years without a war was a gift of some value."
Donald E. Gowan, *Bridge Between the Testaments: A Reappraisal of Judaism from the Exile to the Birth of Christianity* (Pittsburgh: Pickwick Press, 1976), p. 128.

up only 6 percent of the population during this period, and that fewer than 10 percent of the total population lived in the cities.[5] Later in the first century, as Christianity began to spread, cities became much more important to Christians. Aside from Jerusalem, however, Jesus and his disciples had very little, if anything, to do with cities but were found amongst the rural villages of Galilee, an environment that changed little with the changing of political elites, because the basic realities of life for peasant farmers changed little.

Robert Coote describes the economic facts of life in Palestine where everybody was dependent on the production of grain for bread, the principal food. He writes:

> [E]verybody engaged in the struggle to keep or take as large a share as possible of the annual grain pile. As a rule, if one worked on the land, one's share was small; if one did not work, one's share was often large. The struggle for a share of food brought the residents of palace, town, village, homestead, tent and cave together in the struggle against weather, birds, insects, and human predators, and in political and social interaction rooted in violence, which all abhorred and none evaded.[6]

What is striking about these words is that Coote is describing the basic economics of Palestine at the moment of transition between Canaanites and Israelites, over a millennium earlier than the time of Jesus. But every word is true also of the time of Jesus, and for most of the next millennium as well! The technologies of food production that made life possible for the settlers from the early tribes of Israel in the Judean highlands—plastered cisterns for water, and plastered pits for the storage of grain, terracing, animal-drawn iron-tipped ploughshares, careful selection of crops—all changed very little for the next two millennia.

This is not to say that there had been no changes for peasant farmers between the time of the kings of Israel and Judah and the time of the Roman Empire. Societal changes and technological innovations did make farming slightly more efficient, as did the monetization of the economy and improvements in road and other transport systems. But it is hard to see how the lot of a peasant farmer was improved by any of them, as Gerhard Lenski points out as he traces the impact that technological advances have had on social organization.

Lenski notes the importance to a society of surpluses beyond that needed for survival. In a hunter-gatherer society there is no surplus, and such societies often cannot support the elderly and ill. In such societies there is little to differentiate a leader from the small group that live together. But as technological innovations begin to generate surpluses of food, and weapons and the art of war are unavailable to the majority of the population as they become more expensive and technical, then a ruling elite is able to use force

---

[5] These figures are true of most agrarian societies, as is pointed out by Gerhard Lenski, *Power and Privilege* (New York: McGraw-Hill, 1966), pp. 200, 246.

[6] Robert Coote, *Early Israel: A New Horizon* (Minneapolis: Fortress Press, 1990), p. 10.

to take any surplus for its own purposes. Of course, except in the all too frequent times of war, enough must be left for the peasant farmer to survive. But in all societies up to and including the time of the Roman Empire, peasant farmers were kept at subsistence level only. Any surplus generated was taken from them by the ruling elite who controlled the means to compel obedience to their demands for taxes.[7] Indeed the lot of peasant farmers may have become worse between the times described by Coote and the period 167 BC–AD 135.

It is possible to understand 1 Sam. 8:11-17 to suggest that at the very beginning stages of the Israelite monarchy, the taxes exacted by the king and his retainers may well have comprised only about 10 percent of the rural produce. This, together with the tithe given to the priests (Deut. 14:22-29), would mean that the ruling elites and their retainers would consume about 20 percent of the increase in crops and animals. By the Roman period, this percentage was close to 50 percent.[8] Given that crop yields at the time were of the order of a four or fivefold increase in that which was sown in a good year,[9] once enough seed grain had been set aside to plant crops for the following year, the peasant farmer was left very little to live on. A poor crop, which happened all too frequently, would leave the farmer and his family in desperate straits indeed.

Yet, for all their interest in exacting strict taxation, the interference of the ruling elite in the day-to-day life of the villages in which the peasant farmers lived was minimal. Taxes must be paid, but beyond that, the villages were free to organize themselves.[10] Indeed, at a national level, Roman government itself tended to leave local arrangements in place in their client and conquered territories. Thus, alongside of the Roman government, one could also find many traditional institutions of Jewish government, such as the Sanhedrin, still operating in the time of Jesus (Matt. 26:59 and parallels).

The items that made up a villager's diet also changed little in the millennia between the time described by Coote and the period 167 BC–AD 135. The bulk of a peasant's diet consisted of bread, made palatable by olive oil. It was supplemented by vegetables and some fruits, especially grapes, and only rarely meat or fish. Sheep and goats provided some milk products.[11] Clothing continued to be mainly made from rough woolen cloth. Although some of the more affluent peasants might possess finer clothes that were made

---

[7] Lenksi, *Power and Privilege*, pp. 1-296 (*passim*).

[8] Safrai, *Economy*, p. 342; Lenski, *Power*, p. 228. Fiensy, *Social History*, p. 81, mentions that a landowner might demand two-thirds of a crop, or percentages of 50 percent, 33 percent (1/3) or 25 percent. The suggestion that two-thirds of a crop might go to the landowner as rent and other taxes does not appear to be economically viable for the farmer.

[9] See Robert K. McIver, "One Hundred-Fold Yield—Miraculous or Mundane?: Matt. 13.8, 23; Mark 4.8, 20; Luke 8.8," *New Testament Studies* 40 (1994), pp. 606-8, for the evidence supporting crop yields of four to five-fold in first-century Palestine.

[10] Again, this is typical of all societies ruled by elites, as is pointed out by John H. Kautsky, *The Politics of Aristocratic Empires* (Chapel Hill: University of North Carolina Press, 1982), e.g. pp. 118-27, 251-52, 257-58, 273-74.

[11] Oded Borowski, "Eat, Drink and Be Merry: The Mediterranean Diet," *Near Eastern Archaeology* 67 (2004), pp. 96-107.

of linen, multiple changes of clothes made of linen were more typical of the ruling elite and wealthy in society.

In one area, though, there are differences between the time described by Coote and the Roman period: the area of religion and its impact on daily life. The Old Testament period is marked by a constant struggle amongst the ruling elite over religious observance (e.g. 1 Kings 18–19; 2 Kings 9–10, etc). Religious pluralism is also reflected in the archaeological record of villages during the time of the monarchy. Religious practices and beliefs, though, became more homogeneous after the Maccabean revolt, at least in Judea and Galilee.

## C. The Villages of Galilee

The origins of the ethnic and religious nature of the first-century Galilean villages may be traced to the time of the Maccabean revolt and subsequent Hasmonean kingdom. This observation demonstrates why the Maccabean revolt makes such a suitable historical starting-point from which to consider first-century Galilee and Judea. The revolt itself was provoked by the decision of the Seleucid ruler Antiochus Epiphanes to insist on the integration of Judea into the wider Seleucid Empire. In the words of 1 Macc. 1:41 (NEB), "The king then issued a decree throughout his empire: his subjects were all to become one people and abandon their own laws and religion." In Judea, Antiochus made it illegal to circumcise children, and set in train a process whereby all those living in the land had to take part in what many Jews would consider to be sacrifices outlawed by the law of Moses.

The beginnings of the resulting revolt are to be found in a dramatic scene, described in 1 Macc. 2:15-28, that took place in the small village of Modein. Antiochus had decreed that altars should be erected in every village, and in the course of time a representative of the king arrived at Modein to ensure that sacrifices were offered on it, and to enrol those who so sacrificed as friends of the king. An elderly priest named Mattathias refused to sacrifice, and went so far as to strike down and kill a citizen of the village who was prepared to do so in his place. He then slew the officers of the king. Thereupon Mattathias and his five sons fled, and formed the leadership of a revolt which had the preservation of their religion as a crucial goal. Many years of bitter fighting ensued which resulted in the deaths of Mattathias in 166 BC, and his sons Judas Maccabeus (i.e. Judas "the hammer") in 161 BC, Jonathan in 143 BC, and Simon in 134 BC. It was the grandson, John Hyrcanus, who was able to negotiate a truce, and then take advantage of the collapse of the Seleucid Empire to establish "Judea [as] the most important military power in the area."[12] A kingdom, let it be said, whose ruling elite had its origins amongst those who were religiously conservative in Judea.

It is the conservative religious motivation of the Maccabean revolt that resulted in a strongly Jewish settlement of Galilee. One of the goals of the

---

[12] Gowan, *Bridge*, p. 114.

early Hasmonean leaders was the purification of the land, by which they meant that only Jews should be permitted to live in it. This explains why John Hyrcanus forced the Idumeans (who lived in the area between Judea and the desert to the south) to become circumcised, and why he destroyed the Samaritan temple. In this way, the Judaism of those who returned from Babylonian exile—at least as it was understood in the second century BC— came to be the dominant religion and culture of Judea, and indeed of the whole Hasmonean kingdom.

This is important for Galilee because most of the villages still occupied at the time of Jesus were established during the Hasmonean period. True, Galilee had remained settled, if only sparsely, following the destruction of Israel and the widespread deportations by the Assyrians in 722/721 (2 Kings 17:1-6, 24-34), and the destruction of Judah and subsequent deportations of the Babylonians in 587 (2 Kings 24:20–25:26). But these villages tended to fall into disuse. From an archaeological perspective, late Hellenistic is the earliest settlement detectable in the majority of Galilean villages still occupied in the time of Jesus.[13] The population of Galilee from the time of the Hasmoneans onwards is marked archaeologically by increasing finds into the Roman and Byzantine periods. The peak expansion of population occurred in the late Roman and early Byzantine eras,[14] periods later than those considered in this chapter. In other words, the villages of Galilee were all established by those in tune with the religiously conservative policies of the Hasmoneans.

At the time of Jesus this was reflected in the complete absence of many of the otherwise regular features of life in the Greco-Roman world. Of course, villages would not in any case have constructed such Greco-Roman amenities as a theater or a hippodrome. But the villages of early Roman Galilee lack the small idols and other cult objects found elsewhere in the Roman Empire. Indeed, there is a marked boundary between villages which have temples established in the first century BC and those that do not, a boundary that matches that of the geographic region of Galilee.[15]

---

[13] This observation tends to make unlikely the argument of Richard Horsley that ". . . most of the Galileans must have been descendants of the northern Israelite tribes." Richard Horsley, *Archaeology, History and Society in Galilee: The Social Context of Jesus and the Rabbis* (Valley Forge: Trinity Press International, 1996), p. 173.

[14] See table 2.2, Jonathan Reed, *Archaeology and the Galilean Jesus* (Harrisburg: Trinity Press International, 2000), p. 33.

[15] In his chapter entitled, "Borders Between Jews and Gentiles in the Galilee," Mordechai Aviam points out that Greco-Roman temples are not found in early Roman Galilee, but are found in neighboring territories. He notes that these temples were largely built in two periods: the first century BC, and the second century AD. He concludes (p. 20): "Determination of the boundaries between Jews and Gentiles is important as it reveals that no mixed communities existed in the rural areas. Unlike cities, where a diversity of beliefs and faiths was very common, small villages were closed societies, especially during periods when deep antagonism existed." See also later discussion of Sepphoris and Tiberius. While it is known pagan temples were built in those cities, it is not usually thought that these date as early as the first century BC/AD. See Mordechai Aviam, *Jews, Pagans and Christians in the Galilee* (Rochester: University of Rochester Press, 2004), pp. 9-21

Jonathan Reed identifies four further features as indicators of Jewish religious identity: 1. chalk (i.e. stone) vessels, 2. *miqvaot*, 3. ossuaries, and 4. bone profiles that do not include pork.[16]

The use of the more expensive stone vessels is thought to relate to Jewish purity laws. Plates and storage jars made of stone were probably used because stone cannot become unclean from a religious perspective (see Leviticus 11–15 for laws relating to cleanness and uncleanness), whereas plates and storage jars made of clay (i.e. ceramics) could become unclean. Food served on an unclean plate would become unclean, and because it was not possible to make a ceramic dish clean from a religious perspective, an unclean plate must be discarded. It is thought that several collections of clay pots and other ceramics that appear to have been deliberately damaged (with a small hole placed in jugs, for example), are pottery vessels that have been rendered unusable because they had become unclean. Stone vessels have been found in the early Roman sites from Jerusalem to Galilee. A quarry and workshops have been discovered just outside Jerusalem, and there are at least two further quarries and workshops known from Galilee.[17] Reed is no doubt correct is seeing most of these stone vessels as indicators of the presence of law-observant Jews.

A *miqveh* is a distinctive small pool of water widely found in many Roman 1 archaeological sites. It was used as part of the cleansing ritual for persons who had become unclean (e.g. Lev. 14:9; 15:7, 16-18, 21).[18] A *miqveh*, then, is a feature that represents distinctive Jewish religious practices of the time. Ossuaries are small boxes in which the bones of the dead were collected—something practised by Jews and not others at this time period.[19] The prescription against eating pork is again related to the question of purity—pork was unclean meat (Lev. 11:7), although it is possible that absence of pig bones may be the least useful indicator of the four outlined by Reed.[20]

Reed makes a strong case that these four indicators have been found in all early Roman Galilean villages that have been excavated to date. More

---

[16] Reed, *Archaeology*, pp. 43-49.

[17] Yitzhak Magen, *The Stone Vessel Industry in the Second Temple Period* (Jerusalem: Israel Exploration Society, 2002), pp. 1-3, 148-62.

[18] Ronny Reich, "They *Are* Ritual Baths: Immerse Yourself in the Ongoing Sepphoris Miqveh Debate," *Biblical Archaeology Review* (March/April 2002), pp. 50-55.

[19] Steven Fine, "Why Bone Boxes?: Splendor of Herodian Jerusalem Reflected in Burial Practices," *Biblical Archaeology Review* (September/October 2001), pp 39-44, 57.

[20] There are other reasons that might lie behind the absence of pig bones from the archaeological reports. I know of at least one archaeologist who was debating whether or not to publish bone finds precisely because pig bones are well represented among them, although admittedly the site concerned is of a later period. Reed himself, while arguing for the avoidance of pork in a certain place in Sepphoris writes, "Over 450 animal bone fragments have been found in the kitchen area alone, of which only four are possibly pork, statistically considered nil." Reed, *Archaeology*, p. 127. The debate as to the Jewish or otherwise character of Sepphoris will be canvassed later, but it is hard to say that there are no pig bones, when in fact there were some. James F. Strange, in a private communication, and also in James F. Strange, Thomas R. W. Longstaff and Dennis E. Groh, *Excavations at Sepphoris* (Leiden: Brill, 2006), confirms that there is a small percentage of pig bones found in the Sepphoris remains from the early Roman period, a percentage that increases in later periods.

importantly, these four indicators are absent from other villages that have been excavated outside of Galilee. His conclusion that "the term Jews is thoroughly appropriate for the inhabitants of Galilee in the first century, as is the characterization of the Galilee as Jewish,"[21] appears to be inescapable.

Yet, a Jewish Judea and a Jewish Galilee is not the whole picture in first-century Palestine. Between them was a region that most pious Jews would have considered to be dominated by Gentile influences, a state of affairs that goes back to the arrival of the Romans. In the first century BC, a Roman army under the leadership of Pompey arrived in Syria. From there Pompey led his army to Jerusalem to enforce a decision he had made in favor of one of two Hasmoneans vying for the throne. Jerusalem opened her gates to him, but the temple resisted throughout a three-month siege, finally succumbing in 63 BC. From this moment onwards, Rome became the crucial source of patronage for any ruler of any territory in Palestine.

While in the area, Pompey also reorganized the political geography at the expense of the Hasmoneans, considerably diminishing the influence of the kingdom of Judea, and strengthening the Greek cities that had been established in the area. Noteworthy was his establishment of a league of 10 cities, the Decapolis, and the restoration of a number of Greek cities along the plains. Doing so effectively divided the Jewish areas of Judea and Galilee.[22] These "Greek" or Greco-Roman areas eventually came under the control of Herod the Great, but Herod did not change their Greco-Roman character. Furthermore, it will emerge that two of the cities in which Herod did a considerable amount of construction, Sebaste (Samaria) and Caesarea, were largely devoted to the worship of the gods other than Yahweh, and the cities of the Decapolis had always been Greco-Roman. Thus, Judea and Galilee continued to be two "Jewish islands" surrounded by people of other religious faiths and customs. The culture of the Greco-Roman world, while absent in the Galilee in which Jesus grew up and within whose borders spent much of his ministry, was very close at hand.

This, then, is a general overview of the character of the land at the time of Jesus. Many of the crucial villages and cities associated with Jesus have been investigated by archaeologists, and it is to a consideration of some of these that attention will be given for the bulk of the rest of this chapter.

## 1. Capernaum: A Galilean Village

The town most important to the Galilean ministry of Jesus is Capernaum, a small village on the northern shores of the sea of Galilee, and the place identified as the center of his activities by the gospels (e.g. Matt. 4:13; Mark 2:1).

---

[21] Reed, *Archaeology*, p. 55.

[22] Michael Avi-Yonah, *The Holy Land: A Historical Geography from the Persian to the Arab Conquest (536 B.C.–A.D. 640)* (Jerusalem: Carta, 2002), pp. 77-84.

At its greatest extent, during the Byzantine period, the village of Capernaum extended along the lake shore some 800 meters, and inland by some 300 meters, an area of some twenty-four hectares. But archaeological finds dating to the early Roman period, the time that Jesus was living there, are confined to an area of approximately six hectares. This would mean that the village known to Jesus would have had between 600 and 1500 inhabitants.[23]

*Figure 1.*
*First-century Capernaum:*
*Remains from rooms*
*clustered around paved*
*courtyards.*
*Photograph by the author.*

The village already possessed a seawall and paved promenade along the lakeshore at the time of Jesus. This was linked to several piers against which boats could be moored.[24] Behind this promenade, the village consisted almost entirely of single-storied rooms built around courtyards. Often a household would make use of only one room found in a courtyard, so each courtyard could be shared by two or more households. The photograph in figure 1 shows two of these "rooms" or "houses" with small windows made up of long stones opening into a courtyard paved with stones. Although two-storied houses were not uncommon in the first century,[25] the walls of the houses at Capernaum were not thick enough to support a second story. Figure 2 shows a reconstruction drawn by the archaeologists responsible for excavating this part of the site.

---

[23] The population estimate is that of Reed, *Archaeology*, p. 153, and close to that of one of the archaeologists who dug the site, Stanislao Loffreda, *Recovering Capharnaum* (Jerusalem: Franciscan Printing Press, 1993), p. 18. Cf. the estimate of 1,200-1,500 by Horsley, *Archaeology, History and Sociology*, p. 114.

[24] In Mendel Nun, "Ports of Galilee: Modern Drought Reveals Harbors from Jesus' Time," *Biblical Archaeology Review* (July/August 1999), pp. 19-31, 64, Nun writes that he usually looks for evidence of a harbor by the presence of rocks. But Capernaum was so rocky that he needed to look for an absence of rocks—where the rocks have been removed to make piers. He found several piers linked to a promenade: "Along the shore ran a 2,500-foot-long [760 m.] promenade, or paved avenue, supported by an 8-foot-wide [2.4 m.] seawall" (p. 26). See also the artist's reconstruction showing the piers that form the harbor on pp. 24-25. Nun also notes that the river Jordan exits Lake Galilee at a different place than it did at the time of Jesus, which has resulted in the lake level being raised about 3 feet.

[25] Katharina Ualor, "Domestic Architecture in Roman and Byzantine Galilee and Golan," *Near Eastern Archaeology* 66 (2003), pp. 44-58.

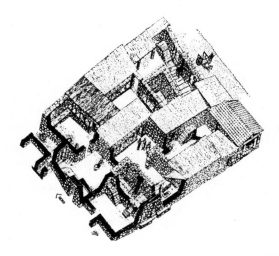

*Figure 2.*
*Reconstruction of part of*
*first-century Capernaum*
*(from Loffreda, Recovering*
*Capharnaum, p. 25).*
*Used by permission of*
*Franciscan Printing Press,*
*Jerusalem.*

What is missing from the reconstruction in figure 3, of course, is people. Two or more families would usually share a courtyard. Many of the two to six rooms (between 4.8 by 3.4 m. to 4.5 by 5.6 m. in size) surrounding the courtyard was used by one complete family, which averaged six people in number.[26] Thus between twelve and thirty-six adults and children are likely to have shared the space of the courtyard, along with their animals.

Today the remains of a large synagogue built using well shaped limestone dominates the site. Over 30,000 coins were found beneath the floor of this synagogue, all dating to the late Roman Period, and confirming other evidence that this synagogue was built late in the fourth century. It is not unlikely that some foundations and a first-century pavement discovered under the floor are all that remain of the synagogue at Capernaum mentioned as part of the gospel accounts of Jesus' activities (e.g. Mark 1:21; John 6:59).[27]

The other large structure from antiquity visible on the site is the foundation of an eight-sided Christian church built in the time of Constantine (d. AD 337), supposedly over the house of Peter in which Jesus stayed while at Capernaum. The archaeologist Stanislao Loffreda makes a case that the first-century room underneath this church was used as a first-century Christian church, which would make it one of the very earliest Christian churches that are known. He further suggests that the church was made out of enlarging a room that actually belonged to Peter's house. Nothing can be known for

---

[26] Fiensy, *Social History*, pp. 119-33.

[27] John S. Kloppenborg traces some of the debates concerning the existence or otherwise of actual buildings associated with first-century synagogues at such sites as Gamla, Herodium, Masada, Magdala, Jericho, Kiryat Sepher and Capernaum in his article, "The Theodotos Synagogue Inscription and the Problem of First-Century Synagogue Buildings," in James H. Charlesworth, ed., *Jesus and Archaeology* (Grand Rapids: Eerdmans, 2006), pp. 236-82, esp. pp. 248-51. Kloppenborg himself argues that not only are these first-century buildings synagogues, but that the Theodotos synagogue inscription should be dated to the first century, and provides evidence of at least one further synagogue in first-century Jerusalem.

certain, of course, but if this room was not part of Peter's house, he lived in one very like it and close by.

Capernaum, then, gives us a very good feel for how Jesus and his first disciples lived. They would have spent some of their nights sitting on the roof of the house, or around a fire in the courtyard. It might be imagined that Jesus took the opportunity to share some of his teachings with them during such occasions.

## 2. Nazareth

Less is known of Nazareth than Capernaum. Little is said about it in the literary sources. While Jesus spent his childhood and early adulthood there (Matt. 2:23; 4:13; Luke 2:39-40, 51), almost nothing is said about this time of his life in the gospels, and the town is not mentioned in either Josephus or the Talmud.[28] Furthermore, because there have been no less than five major church structures built on the site of ancient Nazareth, there are also far fewer archaeological remains at Nazareth than at Capernaum. Nevertheless, it is possible to gain some picture of what Nazareth might have looked like in the first century.

*Figure 3.*
*Nazareth areas 40 and 41. Note walls defining a courtyard and gate outside of the large cave.*
*Bagatti,* Nazareth, *fig. 28.*
*Used by permission of Franciscan Printing Press, Jerusalem.*

Because graves were situated outside of towns and cities at least in law-observant villages in Judea and Galilee—it is possible to estimate the approximate extent of first-century Nazareth from their location. From the graves in the area, it can be determined that the town was less than 400 by 100 meters in extent.[29] Later quarrying has meant that little remains above the

---

[28] Josephus mentions forty-five towns in Galilee and the Talmud sixty-three. Neither source mentions Nazareth. So Jack Finegan, *The Archeology of the New Testament: The Life of Jesus and the Beginning of the Early Church*, rev. ed. (Princeton: Princeton University Press, 1992), p. 43; Merrill F. Unger, *Archaeology and the New Testament* (Grand Rapids: Zondervan, 1962), p. 119.

[29] Clemens Kopp, "Beitrage Zur Geschichte Nazareths," *Journal of the Palestinian Oriental Society* 18 (1938), pp. 187-229; Finegan, *Archaeology*, p. 58.

limestone bedrock, although at least three *miqvaot* are known. There are a number of caves, some of which show evidence they were used as homes. Figures 3 and 4 show a photograph and plan of a cave labeled by the archaeologist Bellarmino Bagatti as areas 40 and 41.[30] This large cave, just over two meters high, and measuring about three by six meters, would have formed an ideal dwelling: cool in summer and warm in winter. The bases of some walls outside the cave have survived which appear to have defined a small courtyard in front of the cave, and a gateway. An oven for cooking purposes was found inside the entrance. Other caves in the area were apparently modified to make them suitable for inhabiting as well (e.g. Area 48). It is probably also noteworthy that the contemporary Church of the Annunciation, like all four that had been on the site before it, is built over a cave that was also apparently used as a dwelling place. This cave is reputedly the home of Mary the mother of Jesus, and the place to which the angel came to announce to her that she would bear a child (Luke 1:26-38).

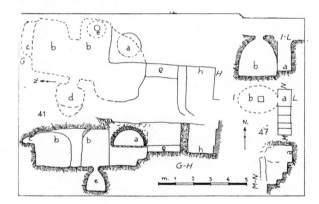

*Figure 4. Bagatti fig. 16, giving dimensions of area 41, a roomy cave with an outside courtyard formed by a wall and a door. Archaeological remains indicate that it had been used as a dwelling. Used by permission of Franciscan Printing Press, Jerusalem.*

Other caves were apparently used for storage purposes. One (grotto 37) even has a regular pattern of indentations on the floor which correspond to the type of pattern formed by the bases of amphorae, which were pottery vessels used to store wine. Amphorae had pointed bases rather than flat bases, as the irregular flooring in the first century meant that it was more stable to set them firmly on their pointed base, and lean them against a wall, or other amphorae, than to try and put a flat-bottom vessel on the floor. A wine press was located near this cave. Another wine press has been discovered less than 800 meters from Nazareth, along with terraces and three towers: all the necessary components of a vineyard.[31] The parable of Jesus which begins with a man establishing a vineyard by building a wall and a tower (Mark 12:1-12 and

---

[30] B. Bagatti, *Excavations in Nazareth*, volume one (Jerusalem: Franciscan Press, 1969), pp. 60-65.

[31] James H. Charlesworth, "Jesus Research and Archaeology: A New Perspective," in James H. Charlesworth, ed., *Jesus and Archaeology* (Grand Rapids: Eerdmans, 2006), p. 38.

parallels) could be illustrated by many such vineyards found in first-century Palestine, including one very close to Nazareth itself.

What, then is to be made of this evidence? What was first-century Nazareth like? Despite the best evidence of habitation that survives from first-century Nazareth being found in the caves, it is unlikely that everybody in Nazareth lived in caves. At the very least, the *miqvaot* would have been associated with above-ground dwellings. On the other hand, it also appears unlikely that Nazareth was settled with anything like the density of Capernaum, let alone nearby Sepphoris. Such density would quickly give a population too large for a town as obscure as Nazareth. If Nazareth had been a large town so close to Sepphoris, the sometime capital of Galilee and important to Josephus, as well as the center of much important Rabbinic activity during the compilation of the Mishnah, it must surely have deserved mention. But Nazareth is absent from both Josephus and the Mishnah. Thus, it appears likely that the town of Nazareth consisted of a few scattered dwellings, many of them utilizing existing caves. Figure 6 shows one possible reconstruction of first-century Nazareth.[32]

*Figure 5.*
*First-century Nazareth.*
*Reconstruction by McIver & Collis.*

## 3. Sepphoris

Although not mentioned in the Bible, Sepphoris was almost certainly visited by Jesus and it is most probable that he and his father worked there. Sepphoris

---

[32] I have presented the arguments for this reconstruction in more detail in "First-century Nazareth," in Bernhard Oestreich, Horst Rolly and Wolfgang Kabus, eds., *Glaube und Zukunftsgestaltung: Festschrift zum hundertjährigen Bestehen der Theologischen Hochschule Friedensau: Aufsätze zu Theologie, Sozialwissenschaften und Musik* (Frankfurt am Main: Peter Lang, 1999), pp. 139-59; the reconstruction may be found on p. 155. See John Dominic Crossan and Jonathan L. Reed, *Excavating Jesus* (San Francisco: HarperSanFrancisco, 2001), plate 3 between pp. 170-1, and the key on p. 37; and Willibald Bösen, *Galiläa: Lebensraum und Wirkungsfeld Jesu* (Basel: Herder, 1998), pp. 105-9 for other possible reconstructions of Nazareth.

was the capital of Galilee for most of the time Jesus lived at Nazareth, and at 6 km. distance, was within easy reach. Destroyed after the death of Herod the Great in the suppression of a short-lived insurrection, and chosen as the new capital of Galilee by Herod's son, Herod Antipas, Sepphoris would thus have been in need of skilled builders such as Jesus and his father Joseph, who are each described as a *tektōn* in separate places in the gospel accounts (τέκτων; Matt. 13:55; Mark 6:3). A *tektōn* was somebody skilled with wood and stone, and able to build houses and other structures. The closest modern equivalent would be a builder or carpenter; not, let it be noted, a cabinet-maker or joiner. It is hard to see the small village of Nazareth providing sufficient work for two builders, especially when the large building projects taking place nearby at Sepphoris were in such need of their services.

Sepphoris has been excavated extensively, with at least three teams working on the site in the last few decades. A considerable number of *miqvaot* have been discovered, showing that significant portions of the population of the town were observant Jews. This is supported by the low number of pork bones found. Another prominent feature of the site, though, is definitely Greco-Roman. Dominating part of the city was a Greco-Roman theater, and there is considerable debate as to when the theater was added to the city, although part of it is likely to have been built during the time of Jesus.[33] Perhaps one should not expect a city to have the same social uniformity as one of the local villages. Certainly at a later time the city was both a very active centre of rabbinic Judaism—significant work was done on the Mishnah in the city—as well as a Gentile administrative center, complete with magnificent Greco-Roman mansions decorated with mosaics with cultic themes.[34] Such a mixture of cultures is not unlikely in the first century as well.[35]

The establishment of the cities of Sepphoris and (slightly later) Tiberias had, perforce, a considerable impact on the local economy. The population of these cities (probably between 8,000 and 12,000 inhabitants[36]) provided a market for local produce and other goods, as well as a closer supervision of the collecting of taxes. The population of the Galilee region continued to increase during and after the building of these two large cities.

---

[33] Eric M. Meyers, Ehud Netzer and Carol L. Meyers, *Sepphoris* (Winona Lake: Eisenbrauns, 1992), p. 33, argue that the Jewish character of the city in the first century, shown by the large number of miqvaoth and the absence of depictions of humans and statues, means that a theater is unlikely to have been built during that time period. On the other hand, James F. Strange, "Six Campaigns at Sepphoris: The University of South Florida Excavations, 1983–1989," in Lee I. Levine, ed., *Galilee in Late Antiquity* (New York: Jewish Theological Seminary, 1992), p. 342, argues that the theater was in fact built in two stages, the first stage being already built in the first century. See also Richard A. Batey, "Did Antipas Build the Sepphoris Theatre?" in Charlesworth, ed., *Jesus and Archaeology*, pp. 111-19.

[34] For example R. Talgam, R. and Z. Weiss, *The Mosaics of the House of Dionysus at Sepphoris: Excavated by E. M. Meyers, E. Netzer and C. L. Meyers* (Jerusalem: Institute of Archaeology, Hebrew University of Jerusalem, 2004).

[35] This point has been argued at greater length in Robert K. McIver, "Sepphoris and Jesus: Missing Link or Negative Evidence?" in David Merling, ed., *To Understand the Scriptures: Essays in Honor of William H. Shae* (Berrien Springs: Andrews University Press, 1997), pp. 221-32.

[36] Reed, *Archaeology*, pp. 77-80.

Sepphoris, Capernaum and Nazareth may serve is samples of cities, villages and hamlets from the region of Galilee. These three sites have been discussed with only one passing mention of Herod the Great. However, his imprint is unavoidable in the archaeological remains of Judea and Samaria

## D. Herod the Great

Herod must have been an extraordinary individual. He played the game of kings, always a highly lethal game for the losers, and for the most uncertain early stages of his career, during a very turbulent time. Rome was in transition between republic and principate. During Herod's time, power in the east passed in turn from Caesar to Cassius to Anthony to Octavian (Augustus). Several of these were enemies, and Anthony and Octavian were on opposite sides of a civil war. But Herod managed to gain favor with each of them in turn! His big opportunity came when the Parthians installed a Hasmonean as king (Antigonus). Herod went to Rome, and was appointed King over Judea. All he had to do was to take his kingdom by force from Antigonus, which he then set about doing. By 37 BC, Herod was in power. He reigned with total ruthlessness from then until his death in 4 BC.

Herod's reign lasted for over 30 years, and during that time he embarked on many magnificent building projects. As well as the complete rebuilding of the temple at Jerusalem, he built an important palace there. He established the port city of Caesarea Maritima, rebuilt Samaria (and called it Sebaste), and constructed magnificent palace fortresses at Masada, Herodium and Machaerus. He built a sumptuous palace at Jericho, and one of the best preserved first-century monumental buildings whose walls have survived nearly intact—the building over the cave of Machpela, the traditional place of the burial of Abraham (Gen. 29:8-9).

## E. Jerusalem

The Jerusalem that Jesus visited, and where he eventually met his death, was a city significantly shaped by the architectural achievements of Herod the Great. Herod's palace with its three tall towers dominated the main city gate. The most prominent architectural feature of the city itself was the temple that Herod rebuilt. The so-called second temple was destroyed by the Romans in AD 70, but even today the surviving foundations of the temple dominate the old city of Jerusalem.

Josephus describes what must have been a very interesting conversation between Herod the Great and the priests in charge of the temple.[37] Herod explained that he wished to re-build the temple, but met with opposition, because of fears that the job would not be completed. As a measure of good faith, Herod gathered the necessary supplies to rebuild the temple, and trained some of the priests to do the necessary work in places only priests were

---

[37] Josephus, *Ant.* 15.380-425.

permitted to go. He enlarged the area of the temple mount, and, as well as rebuilding the temple, built a two storied colonnade across the south of the temple mount, the so-called royal portico. Josephus says that "the thickness of each column [of the royal portico] was such that it would take three men with outstretched arms touching one another to envelop it; [and] its height was twenty-seven feet [8 m.]"[38] In fact, archaeologists have discovered some of the columns from this portico, and they are of an impressive size. They also discovered steps from the second temple outside the southern wall, as well as evidence for entry doors. A reconstruction of this area of the temple may be found in figure 6.[39]

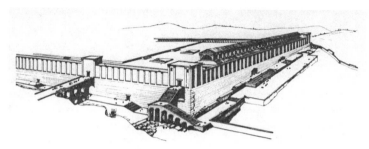

*Figure 6. Reconstruction of south-western corner of Herod's Temple Mount*
*[for publication details see n. 39].*
*Used by permission of the Israel Exploration Society, Jerusalem.*

Two disasters occasioned by war have enabled the archaeological reconstruction of much of first-century Jerusalem. The first was the destruction of the city by the Romans in AD 70. The next city was rebuilt over the ruins of the city destroyed in 70, and thus many of the foundations and the bottoms of walls of the earlier city were preserved under a clearly discernible destruction layer. An opportunity for archaeological investigation of parts of Jerusalem arose in 1967. Large parts of the city had been destroyed in bitter fighting between 1948 and 1967, thus allowing access to the various layers of remains from earlier cities long buried. While most of this area has now been rebuilt, several of the finds made by archaeologists have been made accessible to the public. In one of these places, the so-called burnt house, the burnt remains of a female arm were found, as well as a spear propped in a corner.

---

[38] Josephus, *Ant.* 15:413.

[39] This reconstruction of the south-west corner of Herod's temple mount is reproduced in several places, e.g., Benjamin Mazar, "Excavations Near the Temple Mount Reveals Splendors of Herodian Jerusalem," *Biblical Archaeology Review* 6, no. 4 (July/August 1980), pp. 56-67 and Y. Yadin, ed., *Jerusalem Revealed* (Jerusalem: Israel Exploration Society, 1975), p. 27; D. F. Payne, "Jerusalem," in J. D. Douglas, ed., *The Illustrated Bible Dictionary: Part 2* (Leicester: InterVarsity Press, 1980), p. 757. See also David Jacobson, "Herod's Roman Temple," *Biblical Archaeology Review* (March/April 2002), pp. 19-27, 60-61 for a more recent color reconstruction of this part of Herod's temple complex, and W. Harold Mare, *The Archaeology of the Jerusalem Area* (Grand Rapids: Baker, 1987), pp. 140-59, for a summary of what is known of the construction techniques used in its building.

Some named weights allowed the identification of the owner of this particular house as belonging to one of the high priestly families, which may well explain why more stone vessels were found in it than pottery vessels (as noted earlier, from a religious perspective stone plates and bowls do not become unclean as can pottery plates and bowls). Many of the more sumptuous excavated houses in Jerusalem also contained a *miqveh*.

*Figure 7. The Holy land Hotel model of Jerusalem just before its destruction in AD 70 by the Romans. Note the way the temple dominates the city. The so-called third wall in the foreground was not built at the time of Jesus. Photograph by the author.*

Several other landmarks associated with the gospel accounts of Jesus have been investigated archaeologically, including the Siloam pool. This pool is connected to the Gihon spring by a tunnel that goes back to the time of king Hezekiah (715 to 647/6 BC). The steps of the actual pool have been partially exposed in recent years.[40] The place of the crucifixion of Jesus has occasioned great interest throughout the centuries, and deserves separate consideration.

## F. The Place of the Crucifixion

The period of the first Christian Emperor, Constantine the Great (ruled 306–337), marks the emergence of Christian architecture throughout the Mediterranean and Palestine. On a pilgrimage to Palestine, his Christian mother (Empress Helena) naturally was curious to know the place of the crucifixion, and a site was pointed out to her. She thereupon arranged for a church to be built over it. As the workmen were digging the foundations for the new church, they received remarkable confirmation of the correctness of its location when they found the true cross on which Jesus had been crucified,

---

[40] Hershel Shanks, "The Siloam Pool where Jesus Cured the Blind Man," *Biblical Archaeology Review* (Sept/Oct 2005), pp. 16-23.

or so the story goes. The Constantinian church, inaugurated, but not yet complete in 335, was the first of a number of structures built on the site, culminating in the Church of the Holy Sepulcher which today may be visited in the old city of Jerusalem. The vicissitudes of history have left the Greek Orthodox, Roman Catholic, Armenian, Syrian Orthodox and Coptic churches with control over various parts of the building, and visitors find the different sections in various stages of restoration and using various styles of religious iconography. If visiting at the appropriate time of day, visitors may also be treated to several different liturgies all taking place at the one time.

It is no surprise, then, that many find the so-called garden tomb—with its large rolling stone, just to the north of the old city behind a rock formation which has the appearance of a skull[41]—a more congenial place to imagine the burial of Jesus. For all that is uncertain about the location of the actual tomb of Jesus, one thing is certain: the garden tomb is from the wrong time period, and is definitely *not* the tomb of Jesus.[42] The major objection to the Church of the Holy Sepulcher as the location of Golgotha is that it is found within the walls of the old city proves to be groundless. It lies outside of the "second" wall of Jerusalem, the wall that existed at the time of Jesus. When the third wall was completed just before the revolt of 66–70, the bones of the graves found in the area on which the Church of the Holy Sepulcher now stands were moved outside of the new city boundaries.

The various buildings built on the site have damaged much of the crucial archaeological evidence. What survives, though, shows that the place was originally a stone quarry. Empty tombs were also found there. Some remains survived from the temple to Venus that the Emperor Hadrian (117–138) built there. This temple was demolished on the orders of Constantine to make way for the new Christian church.[43] Nothing was found that would contradict the supposition that this was the place where Jesus was crucified and where he was buried, but little more can be said with confidence.

---

[41] The Garden tomb is built into a hill now described as Gordon's Calvary. While visiting Jerusalem in 1883–84, Charles G. Gordon accepted an earlier suggestion by Otto Thenius that a rocky outcrop to the north of the old city wall which appeared somewhat like a skull is the most likely place for Golgotha (a photograph of the rocky outcrop as it would have appeared to him which was taken before most of the modern building that has obscured the site, may be found in Shimon Gibson, *Jerusalem in Original Photographs 1850–1920* [Winona Lake: Eisenbrauns, 2003], p. 144).

[42] Investigated in 1974 by Israeli archaeologist, Gabriel Barkay, the style of tomb is that of the First Temple period (eighth or seventh century BC), and thus far too early to be that used for Jesus (Hershel Shanks, *Jerusalem: An Archaeological Biography* (New York: Random House, 1995), p. 200). Matt. 28:59-60, Luke 23:53 and John 19:41 all insist that Jesus was buried in a newly excavated, unused tomb, which must therefore date to the first century AD.

[43] Shimon Gibson and Joan E. Taylor, *Beneath the Church of the Holy Sepulchre Jerusalem* (London: Palestine Exploration Fund, 1994), *passim*. See, e.g. the time line on p. xix.

## G. The Archaeology of Crucifixion

Curiously enough, although many are known to have been crucified in Palestine during the Roman era, only one surviving skeleton can be identified as belonging to a man who met his death by crucifixion. His bones were amongst those found in some tombs near Mount Scopus, north of Jerusalem. There archaeologists excavated four cave tombs, and from pottery found in them were able to determine that the skeletons that were found dated from between the second century BC and AD 70. Bones from thirty-five individuals were discovered, and their manner of death reveals much about the violent conditions that prevailed in first-century Palestine. Three children appear to have died from starvation, and another child of four died after an arrow penetrated the occipital bone of his skull. A woman in her early twenties died in a fire. A young man of about seventeen years likewise burned to death, but the pattern of charring on his bones suggest that he was deliberately burned to death on a rack. A woman of about sixty died from a massive wound to the head, of the type that would be inflicted by a mace. A woman in her early thirties died in childbirth. We know death resulted from an unsuccessful attempt to give birth because the unborn fetus was discovered still wedged in her pelvis. These are the type of deaths that left evidence on the bones from which inferences can be drawn. The other bones are from individuals who died through illnesses or accidents the nature of which cannot so far be identified. These bones illustrate once more that in first-century Palestine, health was generally poor amongst the populace and that life was often short and brutal.

For Christians, though, the most interesting bones from those found on Mount Scopus are those of a young male of between twenty-four and twenty-eight years called Jehohanan, who was crucified. Those that crucified him apparently had trouble removing the nail through his ankles into the cross, and his feet were cut off from the body to make it easier to free the nail. This much can be inferred from the severed ankle bone with the nail still in place, together with the knot in the wood in which it was embedded. There is also a groove in the lower third of Jehohanan's right radial bone, which was apparently caused by a nail put through the forearm to fix his arms to the cross beam of the cross.[44]

There is some debate as to how to interpret the evidence of the remains of Jehohanan. Although different suggestions have been made, my preference is still for the one published with the original 1973 article reproduced in figure 10.[45]

---

[44] The details of the thirty five sets of bones are conveniently gathered by J. H. Charlesworth, in his article, "Jesus and Jehohanan: An Archaeological Note on Crucifixion," *Expository Times* 84 (1972–73), pp. 147-48.

[45] The diagram in figure 10 is taken from Charlesworth, "Jesus and Jehohanan," p. 149. Other suggestions may be found in Vilhelm Møller-Christensen, "Skeletal Remains from Giv'at ha-Mivtar," *Israel Exploration Journal* 26 (1976), p. 36; and Joseph Zias and Eliezer Sekeles, "The Crucified Man from Giv'at ha-Mivtar: A Reappraisal," *Israel Exploration Journal* 35 (1985), p. 27.

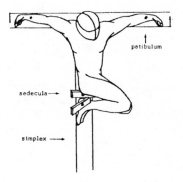

*Figure 8.*
*Reconstruction of method of crucifixion.*
*Reproduced with permission from James H.*
*Charlesworth, "Jesus and Johanan: An*
*Archaeological Note on Crucifixion,"*
*©Expository Times 1972–73, by permission of*
*Sage Publications Ltd..*

By the time the victim was finally mounted on the cross, he would usually have been considerably weakened by the pain and loss of blood occasioned by his scourging before crucifixion, and by the violence associated with positioning him on the cross. The blood would attract flies to the naked body of the victim, and with pinned limbs it would be impossible to brush them away. Death, interestingly enough, was most frequently by asphyxiation. It is impossible to breathe properly while hanging from the arms, so the victim would have to push up with the feet to be able to breathe. The nails through the feet made this supremely painful. The victim would attempt to sit on the half seat (*sedecula*), but would slip off, painfully jarring his wounds. Then he would struggle to stand upright, or sit on the half seat, and the process would continue on. Eventually, he would become so weakened that he could not push himself up, and would die from lack of oxygen. This process could take some days if the victim was strong and healthy. If, for some reason, it was wished to hasten death, the legs of the victim could be broken, so that being unable to struggle for breath, the victim would die fairly quickly.[46] The whole procedure was designed to provide the most horrifying death imaginable.

## H.  The Greco-Roman Cities of Caesarea Maritima, Samaria, Nablus and the Decapolis

Herod, the rebuilder of the magnificent Jewish temple at Jerusalem, also rebuilt or established a number of large Greco-Roman cities, prominent amongst which were the port city of Caesarea Maritima and the inland city of Sebaste (Samaria).

Caesarea has been extensively explored by archaeologists, who have revealed many of the important features of the city which Herod built on the remains of the earlier port of Strato's Tower. Much of the breakwater of Herod's city survives, and has been examined by underwater archaeologists, who discovered the fascinating building technique used in its formation. The

---

[46] The medical cause of death is explored in the article, by William D. Edwards, Wesley J. Gabel, and Floyd E. Hosmer, "On the Physical Death of Jesus Christ," *Journal of American Medical Association* 255 (1986), pp. 1455-63.

Romans used a form of concrete built up of layers of lime and sand in which large lumps of rock (aggregate sized 100-300 mm.; or 4-12 in.[47]) were placed. It could be strengthened and made waterproof by the addition of volcanic sand (*pozzolana*) and/or crushed pottery or tiles. Techniques had been developed to form concrete in underwater locations. For Caesarea, five large (7 by 14 by 4 m.) watertight boxes were constructed of imported wood, floated out to where they were to be positioned, and gradually filled with concrete until they sank. Not only was the wood for the barges imported, much of the materials for the concrete used at Caesarea was also imported. The *pozzolana*, for example, was imported from Vesuvius in Italy.[48] The design of the harbor breakwater survived Herod, and lasted till the end of the first century, before being eroded by the sea, whereupon the harbor became unusable in the second century AD.

Three colossal statues stood at the entrance to the harbor, marking the city as a non-Jewish Greco-Roman city, a fact quickly confirmed to somebody arriving by sea by the very large temple dedicated to the goddess Roma and to Caesar Augustus that dominated the foreshore.[49] Sea travelers could also, no doubt, see the large Roman theater that was built further along the seashore. The theater has been restored by modern archaeologists. A notable discovery on a stone re-used in a fourth-century repair of one of the staircases of theater was an inscription that named Pontius Pilate,[50] who previously had only been known from literary sources. The Roman procurators made Caesarea the center of their administration, rather than Jerusalem. The city also possessed a hippodrome / amphitheater which was used to stage chariot races, athletic competitions, gladiatorial games and wild animal fights.[51]

Samaria, which Herod renamed Sebaste in honor of Caesar Augustus (*Sebastos* is the Greek equivalent of Augustus), was another distinctively Greco-Roman city rebuilt by Herod. As well as Roman-style houses with atriums and colonnaded gardens, and a theater, the city was dominated by a magnificent temple which had within it a colossal statue of Augustus, remains of which have been found by archaeologists.

---

[47] Modern concrete uses lime, clay, metallic salts, sand and aggregate about 25 mm in diameter.

[48] Christopher Brandon, Stephen Kemp and Martin Grove, "*Pozzola*, lime, and singe-mission barges (area K)," in K. G. Holum, A. Raban and J. Patrick, eds., *Caesarea Papers 2* (Portsmouth: Journal of Roman Archaeology, 1999), pp. 169-78.

[49] Kenneth G. Holum, "Caesarea's Temple Hill," *Near Eastern Archaeology* 67 (2004), pp. 184-99.

[50] Four lines of Latin text are legible on the stone, and enough survives that it is possible to reconstruct the inscription with some certainty: [CAESARIEN] S (IBUS) TIBERIEVM [PON] TIUSPILATUS [PRAEF]ECTVSIVDA[EA]E, which may be translated: "To the people of Caesarea Tiberieum Pontius Pilate Prefect of Judea." Jack Finegan, *The Archaeology of the New Testament: The Life of Jesus and the Beginning of the Early Church* (Princeton: Princeton University Press, 1992), pp. 138-39.

[51] Useful aerial photos showing the extent of modern excavations and the restored theatre, as well as the site as it was in 1917 may be found pp. 166-67 of Benjamin Z. Kedar, *The Changing Land Between the Jordan and the Sea: Aerial Photographs from 1917 to the Present* (Jerusalem: Yad Izhak Ben-Zvi Press, 1999).

The original ten cities of the Decapolis established by Pompey consisted of Damascus, Philadelphia, Raphana, Scythopolis, Gadar, Hippus, Dium, Pella, Gerassa and Canatha. Several of these cities have been excavated, and show all the typical features of a Greco-Roman city. Space permits only a brief discussion of Scythopolis and Pella.

By the time of Jesus, the only city of the Decapolis west of the Jordan River, Scythopolis (today called Bet Shean), had become the chief city. The presence of ample supplies of water and a geographic location at key crossroads enabled this city to grow. Excavations have been taking place at Bet Shean periodically since the 1920s, and much of the ancient city, at least its foundations, is visible to the modern visitor. The city had the typical accoutrements of a Greco-Roman city—paved streets flanked by colonnades for shops, a theater, temples to various gods, and, from the second century AD onwards (i.e. just after our time period), a hippodrome.[52]

Pella is not mentioned in the Bible, but is important in early Christian history as the reputed place to which early Christians fled as they escaped Jerusalem just before its destruction by the Romans.[53] The city is located in the foothills of the eastern side of the Jordan valley, 30 km. (18 miles) south of the Sea of Galilee. A reliable spring, winter rains and a warm winter all made the site desirable. It was destroyed by the Hasmoneans, presumably because of its cultic character, but restored by Pompey. Its archaeological investigation reveals that in the first century it was a small city. It continued to grow during the late Roman and Byzantine periods. At all times it had a distinctive Greco-Roman appearance and culture.[54]

The importance of this list of Greco-Roman cities can be readily ascertained by reference to a map. Judea and Galilee were Jewish in their culture. But they were surrounded by Greco-Roman cities, which were also incorporated into the kingdoms controlled by Herod and by his successors. What is remarkable is that these two relatively small geographic areas dominated by Jewish culture should provide so many migrants to other parts of the Roman world. They swelled the numbers of previous Jewish migrants to such an extent that many cities of the eastern Mediterranean, and even

---

[52] The street layout, theater and hippodrome are clearly visible in the aerial photograph of Bet Shean on p. 181 of Kedar, *Aerial Photographs*. The aerial photograph in Ariel Lewin, *The Archaeology of Ancient Judea and Palestine* (Los Angeles: J. Paul Getty Museum, 2005), p. 92, while not including the hippodrome, allows a closer inspection of the central part of the site; while those found in Richard Cleave, *The Holy Land Satellite Atlas* (Nicosia: Rohr Productions, 1994), pp. 117-19, gives other panoramic views of the site.

[53] John J. Gunther, "The Fate of the Jerusalem Church: The Flight to Pella," *Theologische Zeitschrift* 29 (1973), pp. 81-94; Gerd Lüdemann, "The Successors of Pre-70 Jerusalem Christianity: A Critical Evaluation of the Pella-Tradition," in E. P. Sanders, ed., *Jewish and Christian Self-Definition*, Volume One (Philadelphia: Fortress Press, 1980), pp. 161-73; S. Sowers, "The Circumstances and Recollection of the Pella Flight," *Theologische Zeitschrift* 26 (1970), pp. 305-20.

[54] Robert Houston Smith, "Pella," in Ephraim Stern, ed., *The New Encyclopaedia of Archaeological Excavations in the Holy Land*, volume three (Jerusalem/New York: Israel Exploration Society & Carta/Simon and Schuster, 1993), pp. 1172-80.

Rome itself, developed very large Jewish minorities that remained true to their cultural and religious identity.

## I. Manuscript Discoveries

In 1947 some scrolls turned up in the antiquities market at Jerusalem, which upon further investigation turned out to have been discovered in some caves near the ruins at Khirbet Qumran not far from the Dead Sea. The finds came to be known as the Dead Sea Scrolls. The British mandatory government had come to an end on 15 May 1948, after which the country was plunged into civil war. So the archaeological investigations and early work on the scrolls took place under extraordinary circumstances. The caves and nearby ruins were explored by archaeologists, and the documents discovered in them have enriched our understanding of the breadth of ideas circulating in first-century Palestine.[55]

Other document discoveries have been made that are of considerable significance for the study of the gospels and early Christianity. Of great importance are a set of documents found in 1945, buried in jars near Nag Hammadi in Egypt. The Nag Hammadi documents were bound in codices (i.e. books, rather than scrolls), and consist of some fifty-two tractates (short works) dating from the third and fourth centuries, most of which are of great interest to historians of early Christianity. They included such documents as the *Gospel of Truth*, the *Gospel of Thomas*, and the *Gospel of Philip*. The works contain several different viewpoints—which have been loosely described as forms of Gnosticism[56]—viewpoints quite distinctive from those contemporaneously developing into mainstream, catholic Christianity.[57] Other

---

[55] There are a number of translations of the Qumran documents available. For example, Geza Vermes, *The Complete Dead Sea Scrolls in English* (London: Penguin, 2004); Florentino García Martínez, *The Dead Sea Scrolls Translation: The Qumran Texts in English* (Leiden: Brill, 1994). Even the casual reader can gain a "feel" of the Qumran community, its organization and its ideology from reading translations such as these.

[56] There are many different philosophical and religious ideas in the writings which have been described as gnostic, so much so that the usefulness of the term has been challenged by Karen King and Michael Williams. See Karen L. King, in *What is Gnosticism?* (Cambridge/London: Belknap, 2003), and more specifically in *The Gospel of Mary of Magdala: Jesus and the First Woman Apostle* (Santa Rosa: Polebridge Press, 2003), e.g. pp. 155-60, where she argues that the *Gospel of Mary* is not gnostic, because ". . . there was no religion in antiquity called Gnosticism" (p. 155); cf. Michael Allen Williams, *Rethinking "Gnosticism": An Argument for Dismantling a Dubious Category* (Princeton: Princeton University Press, 1996), *passim*. However, the term Gnosticism is not disappearing from academic discourse. For example, it is used freely by Fred Lapham, in *An Introduction to the New Testament Apocrypha* (New York: T. &T. Clark, 2003). The book by Elaine Pagels, *The Gnostic Gospels* (New York: Vintage Books, 1979), provides a very useful summary of ideas shared by many of the groups found within Gnosticism.

[57] By far the best introduction to the Nag Hammadi discoveries is that of James M. Robinson, ed., *The Nag Hammadi Library in English* (San Francisco: Harper and Row, 1977). It begins with a brief account of the actual discoveries, followed by an English translation of the documents together with a brief introduction to each. Although the *Gospel of Mary* was not found at Nag Hammadi, a translation of that gospel is also provided in Robinson, ed., *Nag*

important manuscript finds were made amongst the rubbish heaps at Oxyrhynchus. The uniquely dry conditions have preserved literally heaps of papyrus documents and fragments of documents from the Ptolemaic and Roman periods of Egyptian history. As well as literary works and fragments of some very early copies of the NT writings, these documents include such things as tax assessments, court documents, contracts, sales, wills, and private letters, which taken together enable the reconstruction of much of the detail of life as it was lived in what was the third-largest city of Egypt for much of the time period represented in the documents.

## J. Archaeology, Jesus and the Twelve

Archaeology uses different data and methodologies than does the interpretation of the NT. Yet despite their dissimilarities, archaeology does in fact have much to offer the study of the gospels. Christianity is a historical religion in the sense that its founder and his earliest followers lived and worked in specific locations. At the very least archaeology has allowed those with even limited imagination to place the events narrated in the gospels in their historical environment. But archaeology provides more important clues to the meaning of the gospel accounts than just a background against which to picture the action of the story. It allows a parallel reconstruction of first-century Palestine that provides significant information by noting what is missing in the gospel accounts. The Galilee revealed by archaeology has two major centers of population: Sepphoris and Tiberias. Sepphoris does not appear in the gospels at all, and Tiberias is only mentioned as a place from which some boats arrived carrying people looking for Jesus (John 6:23). The gospels place Jesus' ministry in the smaller villages of Galilee, not in its large urban centers. The only city that Jesus is recorded as visiting is Jerusalem, and he meets his death there.

That John the Baptist met his death at the hand of Herod Antipas, may alone be sufficient to explain why Jesus may well have wanted to avoid Sepphoris and Tiberias during the time of his ministry. Whatever the reason, he is not recorded as being present in either city. Rather, his ministry is pictured in villages such as Nain, Bethsaida, Capernaum, and in the surrounding countryside. The illustrations in his teachings are drawn from the everyday life of the farmer and fisherman. What is perhaps even more remarkable is that between the time of the earthly ministry of Jesus and the writing of the first documents of the NT, a village-based, Aramaic-speaking[58]

---

*Hammadi Library.* One should also perhaps mention the recently published partial manuscript of the *Gospel of Judas,* also discovered somewhere in Egypt, most easily accessed in English in Rodolphe Kasser, Marvin Meyer, and Gregor Wurst, eds., *The Gospel of Judas* (Washington, DC: National Geographic, 2006).

[58] Despite the occasional protest to the contrary (e.g. Stanley E. Porter, "Jesus and the Use of Greek in Galilee," in Bruce Chilton & Craig A. Evans, eds., *Studying the Historical Jesus: Evaluations of the State of Current Research* (Leiden: Brill, 1998), pp. 123-54), the majority of those who have considered the matter conclude that Galilee was almost entirely Aramaic-

movement made up exclusively of ethnic Jews, had transformed into a largely Greek-speaking, city-based movement in which an increasing number of Gentiles joined Jewish followers of Jesus.

## Bibliography

Avi-Yonah, Michael. *The Holy Land: A Historical Geography from the Persian to the Arab Conquest (536 B.C.–A.D. 640)*. Jerusalem: Carta, 2002.

Chancey, Mark A. *Greco-Roman Culture and the Galilee of Jesus*. Cambridge: Cambridge University Press, 2005.

Crossan, John Dominic and Jonathan L. Reed. *Excavating Jesus*. San Francisco: HarperSanFrancisco, 2001.

Fiensy, David A. *The Social History of Palestine in the Herodian Period*. Lewiston, Queenston, Lampeter: Edwin Mellen Press, 1991.

Horsley, Richard. *Archaeology, History and Society in Galilee: The Social Context of Jesus and the Rabbis*. Valley Forge: Trinity Press International, 1996.

Kloppenborg, John S. "The Theodotos Synagogue Inscription and the Problem of First-Century Synagogue Buildings." In *Jesus and Archaeology*, edited by James H. Charlesworth, pp. 236-82. Grand Rapids: Eerdmans, 2006.

Lenski, Gerhard. *Power and Privilege*. New York: McGraw-Hill, 1966.

Levine, Lee I., ed. *Galilee in Late Antiquity*. New York: Jewish Theological Seminary 1992.

Lewin, Ariel. *The Archaeology of Ancient Judea and Palestine*. Los Angeles: J. Paul Getty Museum, 2005.

Loffreda, Stanislao. *Recovering Capharnaum*. Jerusalem: Franciscan Printing Press, 1986.

Mare, W. Harold. *The Archaeology of the Jerusalem Area*. Grand Rapids: Baker, 1987.

Yadin, Yigael, ed. *Jerusalem Revealed*. Jerusalem: Israel Exploration Society, 1975.

McIver, Robert K. "First-century Nazareth." In *Glaube und Zukunftsgestaltung: Festschrift zum hundertjährigen Bestehen der Theologischen Hochschule Friedensau: Aufsätze zu Theologie, Sozialwissenschaften und Musik*, edited by Bernhard Oestreich, Horst Rolly and Wolfgang Kabus, pp. 139-59. Frankfurt am Main: Peter Lang, 1999.

————. "Sepphoris and Jesus: Missing Link or Negative Evidence?" In *To Understand the Scriptures: Essays in Honor of William H. Shae*, edited by David Merling, pp. 221-32. Berrien Springs: Andrews University Press, 1997.

Meyers, Eric M., Ehud Netzer, and Carol L. Meyers. *Sepphoris*. Winona Lake: Eisenbrauns, 1992.

Reed, Jonathan. *Archaeology and the Galilean Jesus*. Harrisburg: Trinity Press International, 2000.

Safrai, Ze'ev. *The Economy of Roman Palestine*. New York: Routledge, 1994.

Shanks, Hershel. *Jerusalem: An Archaeological Biography*. New York: Random House, 1995.

---

speaking, with Sepphoris and Tiberias the only possible exceptions. See pp. 122-65 of his book *Greco-Roman Culture and the Galilee of Jesus* (Cambridge: Cambridge University Press, 2005) where Mark A. Chancey surveys the currently known inscriptions to determine the extent of the "Use of Greek in Jesus' Galilee." See also Hayim Lapin, "Palestinian Inscriptions and Jewish Ethnicity in Late Antiquity," in Eric M. Meyers, ed., *Galilee Through the Centuries* (Winona Lake: Eisenbrauns, 1999), pp. 239-68. Lapin notes that while inscriptions in Galilee are found in Aramaic, Hebrew and Greek, most dedicatory inscriptions are in Aramaic, literary inscriptions (i.e. those quoting the OT) tend to be in Hebrew, while Greek inscriptions are largely confined to cities (p. 245).

Stern, Ephraim, ed. *The New Encyclopaedia of Archaeological Excavations in the Holy Land*. Jerusalem/New York: Israel Exploration Society & Carta/Simon and Schuster, 1993.

Strange, James F., Thomas R. W. Longstaff and Dennis E. Groh. *Excavations at Sepphoris*. Leiden: Brill, 2006.

Talgam, R. R., and Z. Weiss. *The Mosaics of the House of Dionysus at Sepphoris: Excavated by E. M. Meyers, E. Netzer and C. L. Meyers*. Jerusalem: Institute of Archaeology, Hebrew University of Jerusalem, 2004.

Ualor, Katharina. "Domestic Architecture in Roman and Byzantine Galilee and Golan." *Near Eastern Archaeology* 66 (2003): 44-58.

Zias, Joseph. and Eliezer Sekeles. "The Crucified Man from Giv'at ha-Mivtar: A Reappraisal." *Israel Exploration Journal* 35 (1985): 22-27.

# 2. The Gospel Manuscript Tradition

*Scott D. Charlesworth*

## A. Introduction

Contrary to the assumption of many New Testament (NT) scholars, the *text* of the four canonical gospels cannot be found in the most commonly used edition of the Greek NT, the Nestle-Aland *Novum Testamentum Graece* (NA[27]).[1] This is because the gospel text exists mainly in *manuscripts* (MSS) and the printed text of NA[27] does not correspond to that of any single MS (not to mention the fact that no two MSS are identical in every respect).[2] Instead, NA[27] consists of a hypothetical text reconstructed by comparing the texts of the most important of the more than 2300 MSS containing the four gospels or parts thereof. In addition, while NA[27] aims to provide the reader with an "appreciation of the whole textual tradition" through its critical apparatus,[3] it cannot hope to distil and yet present in a coherent manner the individual characteristics of the many gospel MSS. That is to say, the gospel textual tradition involves *individual* MSS and not simply the variant readings listed conveniently on each page of NA[27].

This chapter is intended to be an introduction to gospel MSS and NT textual criticism generally. But it is the "early" gospel MS tradition that will be the primary focus, i.e., gospel MSS dated up to the end of the third or beginning of the fourth century (III/IV). The importance of these MSS can hardly be overestimated because in some cases they take us back into the second century. It will be argued that they can help us "bridge the gap between the originals and the earliest extant evidence and thus afford a basis for inferences about the original text."[4] They are also at the center of current

---

[1] See B. Aland, K. Aland, et al., eds., *Novum Testamentum Graece*, 27th rev. ed. (Stuttgart: Deutsche Bibelgesellschaft, 2001).

[2] The gospel text in the early versions (Coptic, Latin, Syriac, etc.) and patristic quotations will not be considered here. On the versions see B. M. Metzger, *The Early Versions of the New Testament: Their Origin, Transmission, and Limitations* (Oxford: Clarendon, 1977). On the use of patristic quotations see G. D. Fee, "The Use of the Greek Fathers for New Testament Textual Criticism," in B. D. Ehrman, M. W. Holmes, eds., *The Text of the New Testament in Contemporary Research: Essays on the Status Quaestionis. A Volume in Honor of Bruce M. Metzger* (Grand Rapids: Eerdmans, 1995), pp. 191-207.

[3] See NA[27], p. 45*.

[4] G. Zuntz, *The Text of the Epistles: a Disquisition upon the Corpus Paulinum* (London: Oxford University Press, 1953), p. 11.

scholarly perspectives on the gospel MS tradition which will be discussed in section G. However, later gospel MSS will not be neglected entirely; there will be some discussion of the majuscule and minuscule MSS in section C.

## B. Materials and Formats

"Manuscripts" as a term designates texts written on papyrus and parchment.[5] Papyrus takes its name from a fibrous reed (βύβλος, πάπυρος) that grew in the Nile delta and valley.[6] According to Pliny the Elder (*Nat.* 13.74-82), the tall stem was sectioned, the outer rind removed, and the pith sliced lengthwise into very thin strips. These were placed slightly overlapping in a single layer on a flat surface so that the strips ran vertically. A second layer of horizontal strips was laid at right-angles on top of the first and the two pressed and hammered together. Natural juices mixed with acted as an adhesive. After drying, the sheets were polished to minimize surface irregularities and trimmed to size. They were then glued together to form rolls usually measuring between 23-30 cm in height and ranging from 3-15 m in length.[7] In a well-made roll the joins were easily detectable only from the back or verso, the side of the roll with vertical fibers (↓), which was usually left blank.[8] The inside or recto of the roll had horizontal fibers (→) down its length. At each join the edge of the left-hand sheet was above that of the right-hand sheet, so that when copying a Greek text the scribe wrote "downhill" over the joins and *along* the fibers.[9] The lines (being parallel to the length of the roll) were arranged in consecutive columns of 5-10 cm width (including inter-columnar space). When read it was unrolled with the right hand and rolled up with the left.

The papyrus roll was the preferred format for Greek literary works, but it was clearly technology in need of upgrade. Its unwieldy nature, which adversely affected usability and portability, also made finding specific passages difficult. Amongst other things, these were probably factors motivating the remarkable Christian preference for the codex (the ancient prototype of the modern book).[10] Of the early papyrus MSS of the canonical

---

[5] The use of paper only began to increase in popularity from the twelfth century: K. Aland and B. Aland, *The Text of the New Testament*, trans. E. F. Rhodes, 2nd. ed. (Grand Rapids: Eerdmans, 1989), p. 77.

[6] The standard works are E. G. Turner, *Greek Papyri: An Introduction*, rev. ed. (Oxford: Clarendon, 1980) and N. Lewis, *Papyrus in Classical Antiquity* (New York: Oxford University Press, 1974).

[7] W. A. Johnson, *Bookrolls and Scribes in Oxyrhynchus* (Toronto: University of Toronto Press, 2004), pp. 143-52, esp. p. 149.

[8] Occasionally the text continued on to the back of the roll. Such rolls are called opisthographs, from ὀπισθόγραφος meaning written on the back.

[9] In practice, however, the scribe often wrote "at a slight angle to the fibres" which tended "to mask defects in straightness and regularity": T. C. Skeat, "Early Christian Book Production," in P. R. Ackroyd et al., eds., *The Cambridge History of the Bible*, vol. 2 (3 vols; Cambridge: Cambridge University Press, 1963–70), p. 57.

[10] For a comprehensive introduction to Christian book culture see H. Y. Gamble, *Books and Readers in the Early Church: A History of Early Christian Texts* (New Haven: Yale University

gospels discovered to date, only one certainly comes from a roll ($\mathfrak{P}^{22}$). When constructing a codex, sheets cut from a papyrus roll were usually laid on top of each other with the $\rightarrow$ sides facing upward (i.e., the sides with the horizontal fibers). They were then folded in half left to right to make a quire or gathering. For example, a four sheet quire would have eight leaves and sixteen pages. In this way, the left-hand side of the back of the bottom sheet in the stack would become the first right-hand page of the quire. In terms of the fiber direction of the pages, therefore, the usual arrangement was $\downarrow\rightarrow\downarrow\rightarrow$ to the center of the quire, and then $\rightarrow\downarrow\rightarrow\downarrow$ to its end.[11] Some early papyrus codices of the gospels are single quire (e.g., $\mathfrak{P}^{75}$, Luke and John), while others contain multiple quires (e.g., $\mathfrak{P}^{66}$, John). Finally, the codex was stitched and often bound with leather and tied with string.

Vellum or (as it was later called) parchment (περγαμηνή, μεμβράνα[12]) codices were made in the same way, except that animal hides instead of papyrus were used. The hide, generally that of a sheep or goat, was not tanned but softened in a lime solution before the hair was scraped off. It was then polished with pumice stone, dressed with chalk, and cut to size. Because the hair side was somewhat darker than the flesh (and retained the ink better), the sheets were often arranged so that like faced like in an aesthetically pleasing way when the codex was open. While the horizontal fibers of papyrus codices provided guidelines for writing, parchment codices were marked out with pin pricks. The indents made when lines were ruled between these pricks with a blunt metal stylus are often still visible today.[13] A sharpened reed (κάλαμος) was used for writing, usually in black carbon ink (μέλαν). Parchment was stronger and more durable than papyrus, but it was also much more expensive. An average parchment codex containing a number of NT writings required the hides of 50-60 sheep or goats, and a larger MS like Codex Sinaiticus or one with high quality parchment would have been even more expensive.[14] Parchment use began to increase in Egypt from the third century, but the reasons why it had largely displaced papyrus by the seventh century are obscure.

In addition to the strong preference for the codex (particularly for writings regarded as sacred texts[15]), another distinguishing feature of early Christian MSS is the unique system known as *nomina sacra*. By convention, the Greek words for the divine names and/or titles, "God" (Θεός), "Lord" (Κύριος),

---

Press, 1995).

[11] See E. G. Turner, *The Typology of the Early Codex* (Philadelphia: University of Pennsylvania Press, 1977), pp. 43-71.

[12] The Latin *membranae* became a technical term for the parchment notebook that had no Greek counterpart: see C. H. Roberts, T. C. Skeat, *The Birth of the Codex* (London/New York: Oxford University Press, 1985), pp. 19-23.

[13] The lines were ruled "on the flesh side, so that they appear as raised lines on the hair side", so Skeat, "Early Christian Book Production," p. 78.

[14] Aland and Aland, *Text*, p. 76.

[15] L. W. Hurtado, *The Earliest Christian Artifacts: Manuscripts and Christian Origins* (Grand Rapids: Eerdmans, 2006), pp. 43-61, esp. pp. 57-60, has updated the figures of Roberts and Skeat for Christian and non-Christian use of the roll and codex.

"Jesus" ('Ιησοῦς), and "Christ" (Χριστός), were contracted by retaining only the first and last letters and overstroked with a supralinear line (the lunate *sigma* ϲ is used in all early papyrus and parchment MSS). For example, 'Ιησοῦς in its various case endings was usually written as ῑϲ, ῑν, ῑυ, and ῑυ (dative).[16] Words like "spirit," "cross," "father," "man," "son," and a number of others, were similarly treated. To some degree the convention probably emulated Jewish regard for the Tetragrammaton (יהוה, Yahweh). The presence of a single *nomen sacrum*, even on a small papyrus or parchment fragment, is generally sufficient reason to designate the MS as Christian.

## C. Gospel Majuscule (and Minuscule) MSS

In 1908 Gregory re-classified the MSS of the NT with the aim of sorting out the system used in Wettstein's edition (1751–52).[17] He added a new category, papyri, to the latter's majuscules, minuscules, and lectionaries. Papyri were indicated by an initial 𝔓 (𝔓[1], 𝔓[2], etc.), the majuscules by an initial 0 (while retaining the use of capital letters A, B, etc. through to 045), the minuscules with Arabic numerals (1, 2, etc.), and the lectionaries with a prefixed *l* (*l*1, *l*2, etc.).[18] After Gregory's death E. von Dobschütz continued his work, and then K. Aland revised and supplemented the list.[19] In 1908 Gregory catalogued 14 papyri, 161 majuscules, 2292 minuscules, and 1540 lectionaries.[20] By 2007 118 papyri, 318 majuscules, 2877 minuscules, and 2433 lectionaries had been catalogued. While only 3 majuscule (ℵ 01, A 02, C 04) and 56 minuscule MSS contain all or most of the NT, the four gospels or parts thereof are preserved in c. 2361 MSS. In comparison with the scant remains of other ancient texts, this is truly an abundance of riches.

Most of the majuscule MSS are dated between Constantine and the transition to minuscule MSS in the tenth century.[21] Between the ninth and the sixteenth centuries (the period of virtually all of the minuscules) the

---

[16] As far as the name Jesus is concerned, there are also instances of long contraction in which the first, second and last letters are overstroked, as well as some cases of the suspension ῑη: see C. H. Roberts, *Manuscript, Society and Belief in Early Christian Egypt* (London: Oxford University Press, 1979), pp. 36-37. For recent discussion of the *nomina sacra* see Hurtado, *Earliest Christian Artifacts*, pp. 95-134, including consideration of possible Jewish instances (pp. 101-10).

[17] C. R. Gregory, *Die griechischen Handschriften des Neuen Testaments* (Leipzig: J. C. Hinrichs, 1908).

[18] The lectionaries contain liturgical lessons with biblical selections to be read on specific days of the church year. For introductory material see K. Junack, "Lectionaries," in D. Freedman et al., eds., *Anchor Bible Dictionary*, vol. 4 (6 vols; New York: Doubleday, 1992), pp. 271-73 (= ABD); and C. D. Osburn, "The Greek Lectionaries of the New Testament," in Ehrman, Holmes, *Text*, pp. 61-74.

[19] See K. Aland et al., eds., *Kurzgefasste Liste der griechischen Handschriften des Neuen Testaments*, 2nd ed. (New York: de Gruyter, 1994). Updated at *http://www.uni-muenster.de/NTTextforschung/KgLSGII06_12_12.pdf* (accessed 10 Dec. 2007).

[20] Cf. Aland and Aland, *Text*, p. 74.

[21] Unless otherwise indicated this paragraph is based on D. C. Parker, "The Majuscule Manuscripts of the New Testament," in Ehrman and Holmes, *Text*, pp. 22-42.

majuscules were scarcely used, as the paucity of medieval corrections and marginalia indicate. They only began to attract scholarly attention in the sixteenth and seventeenth centuries; and in the nineteenth century finds and collations of MSS greatly augmented their numbers. Formerly known as uncials, the majuscules are characterized by a large bilinear script (i.e., written between two notional parallel lines), the use of parchment, and a continuous text.[22] Majuscule MSS written in the fourth century or later feature a script or hand commonly known as biblical majuscule.[23] Turner gives it as one of three types of formal, round hands: "each letter (ι only excepted) occupies the space of a square (ε θ ο c being broad circles) and only φ and ψ reach above and below the two lines" while "υ regularly and ρ often reach below the two lines."[24]

In the introduction to NA[27] the editors provide a list of consistently cited gospel witnesses of the first order.[25] Since they do not start to appear until the ninth century, the only minuscules listed are 33, 2427, and $f^1$ and $f^{13}$ (two groups of MSS which share a "family" resemblance).[26] Although earlier (that is, older) readings and text-types can be found in individual minuscule MSS,[27] most have a "Byzantine" type of text (text-type) because they were copied when the use of Greek was virtually confined to the Byzantine Empire.[28] In contrast, the great majority of the earlier gospel papyri have none of the characteristics of the Byzantine text.[29] Moreover, the Byzantine text-type is not "widely diffused" throughout the earliest Greek MSS, the early versions, and the Church Fathers. Instead, as far as early witnesses are concerned, the Byzantine text "did not *exist* in the first four centuries."[30] This effectively rules out the possibility that the "original" text is Byzantine in form, even though the majority (about 90%) of extant MSS have a Byzantine type of text.

For that reason the Alands rank the papyrus, majuscule and minuscule

---

[22] Parker, "Majuscule Manuscripts," pp. 22-23.

[23] The definitive work on the script known as biblical majuscule is by G. Cavallo, *Ricerche sulla Maiuscola Biblica* (Firenze: Le Monnier, 1967).

[24] E. G. Turner, *Greek Manuscripts of the Ancient World*, rev. P. J. Parsons (London: Institute of Classical Studies, 1987), p. 21. See also G. Cavallo and H. Maehler, *Greek Bookhands of the Early Byzantine Period A.D. 300–800* (London: Institute of Classical Studies, 1987), p. 5 and pll. 13, 18, 24, 24a, 25, 29, 43a, 48b, 56.

[25] NA[27], p. 58*; cf. Aland and Aland, *Text*, pp. 244-45. The other widely used edition, the United Bible Societies' *Greek New Testament*, is unsuitable for text-critical work by virtue of its less extensive critical apparatus. See B. Aland et al., eds., *The Greek New Testament*, 4th ed. (Stuttgart: United Bible Societies, 2001).

[26] For a descriptive list of important minuscules see Aland and Aland, *Text*, pp. 129-42.

[27] See B. M. Metzger, "The Bodmer Papyrus of Luke and John," *Expository Times* 73 (1961/62), pp. 201-20.

[28] B. M. Metzger and B. D. Ehrman, *The Text of the New Testament: Its Transmission, Corruption, and Restoration*, 4th ed. (New York: Oxford University Press, 2005), p. 220.

[29] Only several later papyrus MSS have been influenced by the Byzantine text (see Aland and Aland, *Text*, pp. 96-102): 𝔓[63] (dated c. 500), 𝔓[84] (VI), and possibly 𝔓[73] (VII).

[30] D. B. Wallace, "The Majority Text Theory: History, Methods, and Critique," in Ehrman and Holmes, *Text*, p. 311. See also G. D. Fee, "The Majority Text and the Original Text of the New Testament," in E. J. Epp and G. D. Fee, *Studies in the Theory and Method of New Testament Textual Criticism* (Grand Rapids: Eerdmans, 1993), pp. 183-208.

MSS according to their distance from the "late and normal forms of the Byzantine [textual] tradition."[31] If a MS has a higher number of variations from the Byzantine text, there can be some certainty that it preserves a relatively early form of the gospel text. They assign each MS to one of five categories which are reproduced below with minor changes for the sake of brevity.[32]

- *Category I:* MSS of "very special quality which should always be considered in establishing the original text" (e.g., the Alexandrian text). "The papyri and uncials[/majuscules] through the third/fourth century belong here automatically. . . because they represent the text of the very early period."
- *Category II:* MSS of "special quality", but which contain "alien influences (particularly of the Byzantine text), and yet are of importance for establishing the original text" (e.g., the Egyptian text[33]).
- *Category III:* MSS of "distinctive character with an independent text, usually important to establishing the original text (e.g., $f^1, f^{13}$)."
- *Category IV:* MSS of "the D ["Western"] text."
- *Category V:* MSS "with a purely or predominantly Byzantine[/Koine] text."

Apart from the proportion of Byzantine readings, these categories are also based on the proportion of early and special readings found in each MS.[34] Early readings are identified by their presence in the majority of those MSS which have the fewest Byzantine text readings. Each MS is compared in a high number of test passages with "the ancient text, presumably the original text."[35] It is noteworthy that these test passages correspond with the text of NA[27] which creates some potential for circular reasoning.[36] But this is offset by the fact that *categories I* and *II* also "include those MSS that vary most

---

[31] B. Aland and K. Wachtel, "The Greek Minuscule Manuscripts of the New Testament," in Ehrman and Holmes, *Text*, p. 49. In specific terms, the Byzantine text is "the text of the majority of late Byzantine" MSS, i.e., it is characterized by "a special kind of late majority readings": K. Wachtel, "Early Variants in the Byzantine Text of the Gospels," in J. W. Childers and D. C. Parker, eds., *Transmission and Reception: New Testament Text-Critical and Exegetical Studies* (Piscataway: Gorgias Press, 2006), p. 29.

[32] See Aland and Aland, *Text*, p. 106.

[33] "A form of text which developed from the Alexandrian tradition, clearly preserving its original core, but with an admixture of Byzantine influence. Here as elsewhere the basic rule of New Testament textual transmission is apparent, that the Byzantine text exerted a constantly increasing influence on all the other text types", so Aland and Aland, *Text*, p. 335, cf. p. 56.

[34] The statistical data for the categories (arranged under the designations 1, ½, 2, and S) provide more detailed information. See Aland and Aland, *Text*, pp. 334-37.

[35] Aland and Aland, *Text*, p. 333.

[36] See the objections of E. J. Epp, "New Testament Textual Criticism Past, Present, and Future: Reflections on the Alands' "Text of the New Testament," *Harvard Theological Review* 82 (1989), pp. 225-56; and B. D. Ehrman, "A Problem of Textual Circularity: The Alands on the Classification of New Testament Manuscripts," *Biblica* 70 (1989), pp. 378-80.

strikingly in their special readings" from both NA[27] and the Byzantine text.[37] Special readings are defined as readings that are neither ancient/early nor Byzantine. So checks and balances are built into the system of classification, which in any case only purports to be an initial or preliminary means of sorting through the huge number of NT MSS.[38]

NT textual criticism has traditionally traced the history of the text backwards from later to earlier MSS. In this respect, the value of the minuscule MSS lies in their ability to enable methodological advances that are more difficult to make solely on the basis of the papyri and majuscules. Genealogical relationships can be established "with relative ease, both for distinct MS groups and broader groups within the tradition" and can then be traced "back into the time of the majuscules. Thus they allow one to draw lines of development [stemmata] that reach into the early period and that help to clarify how the solitary representatives of the earlier tradition are related to one another."[39]

Aland and Wachtel contend that the earlier "papyri and majuscules are for the most part individual witnesses: despite sharing general tendencies in the form of their texts, they differ so widely from one another that it is impossible to establish any direct genealogical ties between them."[40] This is correct, although a number of broad textual trajectories can be drawn from the early papyri to the major majuscules of the fourth century and beyond.[41] Consistently cited gospel majuscules of the first order are listed below by date in Table 1 below.[42] Most are *category II* or *III* but there are also a few *category I* witnesses.[43] In summarizing the content of each MS the following abbreviations are used: e = Gospels; a = Apostolos, i.e., Acts and Catholic letters; p = Pauline letters; r = Revelation; and † = in some respects the preserved text is defective or incomplete.

---

[37] Aland and Wachtel, "Greek Minuscule Manuscripts," p. 49, n. 16 (emphasis theirs).

[38] Rather than undermining traditional text-critical methodology, Aland and Wachtel claim their use "facilitates and confirms the analysis of manuscripts in text types and their subdivisions" (Aland and Wachtel, "Greek Minuscule Manuscripts," p. 49).

[39] Aland and Wachtel, "Greek Minuscule Manuscripts," pp. 46-47; cf. M. W. Holmes, "From Nestle to the *Editio Critica Maior*: A Century's Perspective on the New Testament Minuscule Tradition," in S. McKendrick and O. O'Sullivan, eds., *The Bible As Book: The Transmission of the Greek Text* (London: The British Library, 2003), pp. 123-137.

[40] Aland and Wachtel, "Greek Minuscule Manuscripts," p. 46.

[41] See E. J. Epp, "The Significance of the Papyri for Determining the Nature of the New Testament Text in the Second Century: a Dynamic View of Textual Transmission," in W. L. Petersen, ed., *Gospel Traditions in the Second Century: Origins, Recensions, Text, and Transmission* (Notre Dame: University of Notre Dame Press, 1989), pp. 92-99.

[42] See NA[27], pp. 58*-59*. I follow K. Aland's dating here. For editions and fuller descriptions see also K. Aland, *Repertorium der griechischen christlichen Papyri, vol. 1: Biblische Papyri: Altes Testament, Neues Testament, Varia, Apokryphen* (New York: de Gruyter, 1976); and J. van Haelst, *Catalogue des papyrus littéraires juifs et chrétiens* (Paris: La Sorbonne, 1976).

[43] For recent discussion of the major majuscule codices Alexandrinus, Sinaiticus, Vaticanus and Bezae see the first four essays in McKendrick and O'Sullivan, *The Bible As Book*, pp. 1-50.

| IV | ℵ 01 | Codex Sinaiticus, London, British Library, Add. 43725; eapr; written in four columns; discovered in 1844 at St. Catherine's monastery by Constantine Tischendorf; inferior to B, but with B and 𝔓[75] represents the Alexandrian text; *category I.* |
| --- | --- | --- |
| | B 03 | Codex Vaticanus, Rome, Vatican Library, Gr. 1209; eap†; three cols.; provenance and early history unknown; catalogued in the Vatican Library about 1475; the most valuable of the majuscules; *I.* |
| | 058 | P.Vindob. G. 39782, Österreichische Nationalbibliothek, Vienna (Mk. 18:18-19, 22-23, 25-26, 28-29); *III?* |
| | 0188 | P.Berlin inv. 13416, Staatliche Museen, Berlin (Mk. 11:11-17); *III.* |
| | 0231 | P.Ant. 1.1, Papyrology Rooms, Sackler Library, Oxford (Mt. 26:75; 27:1, 3-4); *III.* |
| | 0242 | Cairo, Egyptian Museum, 71942 (Mt. 8:25-9:2; 13:32-38, 40-46); *III.* |
| | 059 | P.Vindob. G. 39779, Österreichische Nationalbibliothek, Vienna (Mk. 15:29-38); *III.* |
| IV/V | 0160 | P.Berlin inv. 9961, Staatliche Museen, Berlin (Mt. 26:25-26, 34-36); *III.* |
| | 0181 | P.Vindob. G. 39778, Österreichische Nationalbibliothek, Vienna (Lk. 9:59-10:14); *II.* |
| | 0214 | P.Vindob. G. 29300, Österreichische Nationalbibliothek, Vienna (Mk. 8:33-37); *III.* |
| | A 02 | Codex Alexandrinus, London, British Library, Royal 1 D.VIII; eapr†; two cols.; from 1098 kept in the Patriarchal Library of Alexandria; presented to Charles I of England in 1628; Gospels, *III*; elsewhere, *I.* |
| | C 04 | Codex Ephraemi Syri Rescriptus, Paris, Bibliothèque Nationale, Gr. 9; eapr†; one col.; palimpsest,[44] erased in the twelfth century and rewritten with a Greek translation of 38 treatises of Ephraem; *II.* |
| | D 05 | Codex Bezae Cantabrigiensis, Cambridge, University Library, Nn. 2.41; ea†; one col.; Greek-Latin bilingual/diglot; given to the University of Cambridge by Beza in 1581; "no known manuscript has so many and such remarkable variations";[45] principal witness of the "Western" text; *IV.* |
| V | T 029 | Codex Borgianus, New York: Pierpont Morgan Library, M 664A; Paris, Bibliothèque Nationale, 129.7-10; Rome, Vatican Library, Borg., Copt. 109 and T. 109; parts of Lk.-Jn.; two cols.; Sahidic Coptic-Greek diglot; Egyptian text, quite close to B; *II.* |
| | W 032 | Codex Freerianus (Washington, D.C., Smithsonian Institution, Freer Gallery of Art 06.274); e†; one col.; text varied as though copied from a number of MSS;[46] *III.* |
| | 068 | London, British Library, Add. 17136 (Jn. 13:16-27; 16:7-19); double palimpsest, the two top texts are in Syriac; *III.* |
| | 069 | P.Oxy. 1.3, Chicago, Oriental Institute, 2057 (Mk. 10:50-51; 11:11-12); *III.* |
| | 0182 | P.Vindob. G. 39781, Österreichische Nationalbibliothek, Vienna (Lk. 19:18-20, 22-24); *III.* |

---

[44] The term comes from πάλιν and ψάω and means "to rub away again."
[45] Metzger and Ehrman, *Text*, p. 71.
[46] See the discussion in Metzger and Ehrman, *Text*, p. 80.

| | 0216 | P.Vindob. G. 3081, Österreichische Nationalbibliothek, Vienna (Jn. 8:51-53; 9:5-8); *III.* |
| | 0217 | P.Vindob. G. 39212, Österreichische Nationalbibliothek, Vienna (Jn. 11:57-12:7); *III.* |
| | 0218 | P.Vindob. G. 19892 B, Österreichische Nationalbibliothek, Vienna (Jn. 12:2-6, 9-11, 14-16); *III.* |
| | 0274 | Cairo, Coptic Museum, 6569/6571 (Mk. 6-10†); *II.*[47] |

*Table 1. Consistently cited Gospel majuscules by date.*

## D. Gospel Papyrus MSS

Almost all early gospel papyri dated up to third/fourth century (III/IV) are assigned to *category I*, apart from a few which have a predominantly "Western" text-type (discussed below in section F.1). When grouped by century their early dating in comparison with the majuscules is obvious.[48] Although some papyrus gospel MSS were written in early or formative biblical majuscule, the majority were copied in a variety of other hands— ranging from documentary (rapid, non-literary hands found in the many kinds of ancient documents) through so-called reformed documentary (the careful documentary hands of many Christian texts) to semi-literary (approaching book/literary) hands. The early (dated up to III/IV) gospel MSS are listed below in Table 2. All are from papyrus codices with the exception of $\mathfrak{P}^{22}$ (and perhaps $\mathfrak{P}^{7}$) and two parchment codices at the end of the list.

| II (6 MSS) | $\mathfrak{P}^{52}$ | P.Ryl. 3.457, John Rylands University Library, Manchester, P.Ryl.Gk. 457; Jn. 18:31-33, 37-38. |
| | $\mathfrak{P}^{77}$ | P.Oxy. 34.2683 + 64.4405, Papyrology Rooms, Sackler Library, Oxford; Mt. 23:30-34, 35-39. |
| | $\mathfrak{P}^{90}$ | P.Oxy. 50.3523, Papyrology Rooms, Sackler Library, Oxford; Jn. 18:36–19:7. |
| | $\mathfrak{P}^{103}$ | P.Oxy. 64.4403, Papyrology Rooms, Sackler Library, Oxford; Mt. 13:55-56 and 14:3-5. |
| | $\mathfrak{P}^{104}$ | P.Oxy. 64.4404, Papyrology Rooms, Sackler Library, Oxford; Mt. 21:34-37, 43, 45(?). |
| | $\mathfrak{P}^{64+67}$ | Gr. 17, Magdalen College, Oxford (Mt. 26:7-8, 10, 14-15, 22-23, 31-33) + P.Barc./Montserrat inv. 1, Abadia de Montserrat (Mt. 3:9, 15; 5:20-22, 25-28)[49] |

---

[47] For later consistently cited majuscule witnesses see NA[27], p. 58*. For frequently cited gospel witnesses of the second order see p. 59*.

[48] For editions, descriptions and bibliography see Aland and Aland, *Text*, pp. 83-102; Aland, *Repertorium*; van Haelst, *Catalogue*. For further bibliography see J. K. Elliott, *A Bibliography of Greek New Testament Manuscripts*, 2nd ed. (Cambridge: Cambridge University Press, 2000); and J. K. Elliott with contributions by J. N. Birdsall, "Supplement 1 to *A Bibliography of Greek New Testament Manuscripts*," *Novum Testamentum* 46 (2004), pp. 376-400; J. K. Elliott, "Supplement II to J. K. Elliott, *A Bibliography of Greek New Testament Manuscripts*," *Novum Testamentum* 49 (2007), pp. 370-401.

[49] P.Barc. inv. 1, now housed in the Abadia de Montserrat near Barcelona, has received a new inventory number based on its old designation.

| | | |
|---|---|---|
| II/III<br>(2 MSS) | $\mathfrak{P}^4$ | Suppl. Gr. 1120 (2), Bibliothèque Nationale, Paris; Lk 1:58-59, 62-80; 2:1, 6-7; 3:8, 38; 4:1-2, 29-32, 34-35; 5:3-8, 30-39; 6:1-16.[50] |
| | $\mathfrak{P}^{66}$ | P.Bodmer 2 (Bibliotheca Bodmeriana, Geneva) + P.Beatty (Chester Beatty Library, Dublin) + P.Köln 5.214 (Universität zu Köln, Institut für Altertumskunde, inv. 4274/4298); Gospel of John†.[51] |
| III<br>(17 MSS) | $\mathfrak{P}^1$ | P.Oxy. 1.2, University Museum of Archeology and Anthropology, Egyptian Section, University of Pennsylvania, Philadelphia, E. 2746; Mt. 1:1-9, 12, 14-20. |
| | $\mathfrak{P}^5$ | P.Oxy. 2.208 + 15.1781, British Library, London, inv. 782 (P.Oxy. 208) and inv. 2484 (P.Oxy. 1781, formerly referred to as P.Lit.Lond. 213); Jn. 1:23-31, 33-40, 16:14-30, 20:11-17, 19-20, 22-25. |
| | $\mathfrak{P}^{22}$ | P.Oxy. 10.1228, Special Collections, Glasgow University Library, Glasgow, Ms. General 1026/13; two columns from a roll preserving Jn. 15:25-27, 16:1-2, 21-32. |
| | $\mathfrak{P}^{28}$ | P.Oxy. 13.1596, Palestine Institute Museum, Pacific School of Religion, Berkeley, Pap. 2; Jn. 6:8-12, 17-22. |
| | $\mathfrak{P}^{39}$ | P.Oxy. 15.1780, formerly held at Ambrose Swabey Library, Colgate Rochester Divinity School, Rochester, inv. 8864; sold June 2003; location unknown; Jn. 8:14-22. |
| | $\mathfrak{P}^{45}$ | P.Beatty 1 (Chester Beatty Library, Dublin) + P.Vindob. G. 31974 (Österreichishe Nationalbibliothek, Vienna); fragmentary codex of the Gospels and Acts†.[52] |
| | $\mathfrak{P}^{53}$ | P.Mich. inv. 6652, University of Michigan, Ann Arbor; Mt. 26:29-40; Acts 9:33-38, 9:40–10:1. |
| | $\mathfrak{P}^{69}$ | P.Oxy. 24.2383, Papyrology Rooms, Sackler Library, Oxford; Lk 22:41, 45-48, 58-61. |
| | $\mathfrak{P}^{70}$ | P.Oxy. 24.2384, Papyrology Rooms, Sackler Library, Oxford + PSI inv. 3407 fr. A (= CNR 419) and 3407 fr. B (= CNR 420), Instituto Papirologico «G. Vitelli», Università degli Studia di Firenze, Florence; Mt. 11:26-27; 12:4-5; 2:13-16, 2:22-3:1; 24:3-6, 12-15. |
| | $\mathfrak{P}^{75}$ | P.Bodmer 14-15, Biblioteca Apostolica Vaticana, Rome; Luke and John†.[53] |
| | $\mathfrak{P}^{95}$ | P.Laur. II/31, Biblioteca Medicea Laurenziana, Florence; Jn. 5:26-29, 36-38. |
| | $\mathfrak{P}^{101}$ | P.Oxy. 64.4401, Papyrology Rooms, Sackler Library, Oxford; Mt. 3:10-12, 3:16–4:3. |
| | $\mathfrak{P}^{106}$ | P.Oxy. 65.4445, Papyrology Rooms, Sackler Library, Oxford; Jn. 1:29-35, 40-46. |
| | $\mathfrak{P}^{107}$ | P.Oxy. 65.4446, Papyrology Rooms, Sackler Library, Oxford; Jn. 17:1-2, 11. |

---

[50] Aland (*Kurzgefasste Liste*, p. 3), Turner (*Typology*, p. 145), and Roberts and Skeat (*The Birth of the Codex*, pp. 40-41) all date the codex to III or perhaps III/IV, but because $\mathfrak{P}^{64+67}$ and $\mathfrak{P}^4$ were written by the same scribe, the latter must be of a closely similar date: see my article "T. C. Skeat, $\mathfrak{P}^{64+67}$ and $\mathfrak{P}^4$, and the problem of fiber orientation in codicological reconstruction," *New Testament Studies* 53 (2007), pp. 582-604.

[51] For details of the extant text see Aland, *Repertorium*, pp. 296-98.

[52] For details of the extant text see *ibid.*, p. 269.

[53] For details of the extant text see *ibid.*, p. 309-11.

37

| | | |
|---|---|---|
| | $\mathfrak{P}^{108}$ | P.Oxy. 65.4447, Papyrology Rooms, Sackler Library, Oxford; Jn. 17:23-24, 18:1-5. |
| | $\mathfrak{P}^{109}$ | P.Oxy. 65.4448, Papyrology Rooms, Sackler Library, Oxford; Jn. 21:18-20, 23-25. |
| | $\mathfrak{P}^{111}$ | P.Oxy. 66.4495, Papyrology Rooms, Sackler Library, Oxford; Lk. 17:11-13, 22-23. |
| III/IV (3-7 MSS) | $\mathfrak{P}^{37}$ | P.Mich. 3.137, University of Michigan, Ann Arbor, inv. 1570; Mt. 26:19-52. |
| | $\mathfrak{P}^{102}$ | P.Oxy. 64.4402, Papyrology Rooms, Sackler Library, Oxford; Mt. 4:11-12, 22-23. |
| | 0171 | P.Berlin inv. 11863, Staatliche Museen, Berlin (Mt. 10:17-20, 21-23, 25-27, 28-32) + PSI 2.124, Biblioteca Medicea Laurenziana, Florence (Lk. 22:44-56, 61-63); 2 cols.; parchment.[54] |
| | [0162] | P.Oxy 6.847, Metropolitan Museum of Art, New York, 09.182.43 (Jn. 2:11-22); parchment.[55] |
| | [$\mathfrak{P}^{62}$] | P.Oslo. inv. 1661, University Library, Oslo; Mt. 11:25-30.[56] |
| | [$\mathfrak{P}^{80}$] | P.Barc. inv. 83, Fundación San Lucas Evangelista, Barcelona; Jn. 3:34.[57] |
| | [$\mathfrak{P}^{7}$?] | Kiev, Ukrainian National Library, F. 301 (KDA), Petrov 553; Lk. 4:1-2.[58] |

[Later gospel papyri—IV: $\mathfrak{P}^{6}$, $\mathfrak{P}^{25}$, $\mathfrak{P}^{35}$(?), $\mathfrak{P}^{71}$, $\mathfrak{P}^{86}$, $\mathfrak{P}^{88}$, $\mathfrak{P}^{110}$; IV/V: $\mathfrak{P}^{19}$, $\mathfrak{P}^{21}$, $\mathfrak{P}^{82}$; V: $\mathfrak{P}^{93}$.]

*Table 2. Early Gospel MSS by date.*

There is general agreement that these MSS are of highest importance for establishing and understanding the transmission and history of the early text prior to the major majuscules of the fourth century. But until fairly recently the early papyri were described and classified in terms of the later major majuscule MSS and the text-types they represent: Alexandrian (B and ℵ), "Western" (D and Old Latin Gospels), Caesarean (W and Θ), and Byzantine (A E [07] and the Majority [𝔐]).[59] That is, the earlier evidence was wrongly

---

[54] See the survey of studies in Parker, "Majuscule manuscripts," pp. 28-29.

[55] 0162 is probably later than the III/IV dating of Aland (*Kurzgefasste Liste*, p. 33). It is dated to IV by B. P. Grenfell and A. S. Hunt (*P.Oxy.* 6 [1908], p. 4), van Haelst (*Catalogue*, no. 436), Turner (*Typology*, p. 159). See also Parker, "Majuscule Manuscripts," pp. 29-30.

[56] $\mathfrak{P}^{62}$ is dated early IV by L. Amundsen, "Christian papyri from the Oslo collection," *Symbolae Osloenses* 24 (1945), pp. 121-40; IV, Aland and Aland (*Text*, p. 100), van Haelst (*Catalogue*, no. 359); IV(?), Turner, *Typology*, p. 148.

[57] The remains of interpretative comments on both sides show that this MS was probably used for fortune-telling purposes instead of functioning as a gospel MS: see B. M. Metzger, "Greek manuscripts of John's Gospel with 'hermeneiai,'" in T. Baarda et al., eds, *Text and Testimony: Essays on New Testament and Apocryphal Literature in Honour of A. F. J. Klijn* (Kampen: Kok, 1988), pp. 162-69; D. C. Parker, "Manuscripts of John's Gospel with *hermeneiai*," in Childers and Parker, *Transmission and Reception*, pp. 48-68; cf. O. Stegmüller, "Zu den Bibelorakeln im Codex Bezae," *Biblica* 34 (1953): 13-22; Aland, *Repertorium*, p. 316.

[58] K. Aland, "Neue neutestamentliche Papyri," *New Testament Studies* 3 (1957), pp. 262-65. Gregory dated this MS IV-VI, but it was never photographed and has been lost, so the hand cannot be dated or the original format (roll or codex) determined. Cf. van Haelst (*Catalogue*, nos. 1224, 1225).

[59] See the discussion of text-types in section F.1 below.

treated as derivative instead of primary. Since the 1950s there has been a reappraisal and a number of studies have examined the relationship between the papyri and majuscules.[60] Instead of imposing the later majuscules "upon the period which antedates their origin," Zuntz contended, the task is to describe the later MSS "in terms of this primitive stage."[61] The need for the same kind of approach was subsequently affirmed by Clark: "We require a new mental approach, wherein we . . . approach these earliest material *de novo*";[62] and then by Birdsall: "The task of present-day criticism is to inaugurate an era in which we begin from the earlier evidence and on the basis of its interpretation discuss the later."[63]

## E. Provenance and Transmission of Early Gospel MSS

The secretive nature of the antiquities trade makes establishing the provenance of MSS notoriously difficult. In 1934 the Chester Beatty papyri including $\mathfrak{P}^{45}$ were reported to have been found near At'fih (Aphrodotipolis) in the Fayum.[64] However, Roberts following Turner thought that together with the Bodmer papyri they might have come from Panopolis.[65] The Bodmer papyri which include $\mathfrak{P}^{66}$ and $\mathfrak{P}^{75}$ were found at Dishna (12 km east of Nag Hammadi), and it was assumed that they were part of an archive of the nearby Pachomian monastery buried for safe-keeping in the seventh century.[66] But it is more likely that some of the Bodmer papyri were copied at a Christian school at Panopolis whose curriculum included religious and literary works, and that the gospel MSS were acquired from Christian copying centers (in any case, $\mathfrak{P}^{66}$ and $\mathfrak{P}^{75}$ antedate the monastery).[67] As for other gospel MSS, only the provenance of those known to be from Oxyrhynchus and the Fayum is

---

[60] See J. N. Birdsall, "The Recent History of New Testament Textual Criticism (from Westcott and Hort, 1881, to the Present)," in H. Temporini and W. Hasse, eds., *Aufstieg und Niedergang der römische Welt* 2.26.1 (New York: de Gruyter, 1992), pp. 103-9. He provides a full survey of the century following the critical watershed initiated by Westcott and Hort.

[61] Zuntz, *Text*, p. 11.

[62] K. W. Clark, "The Manuscripts of the Greek New Testament," in M. M. Parvis and A. P. Wikgren, eds., *New Testament Manuscript Studies: the Material and the Making of a Critical Apparatus* (Chicago: University of Chicago Press, 1950), pp. 20-21.

[63] J. N. Birdsall, *The Bodmer Papyrus of the Gospel of John* (London: Tyndale, 1960), p. 7.

[64] C. Schmidt, "Die neuesten Bibelfunde aus Äegypten," *Zeitschrift für die neutestmentliche Wissenschaft* 30 (1931), pp. 292; 32 (1933): 225. For details of the Chester Beatty and Bodmer publications see A. Pietersma, "Chester Beatty Papyri," in *ABD*, vol. 1, pp. 901-3; A. Pietersma, "Bodmer Papyri," *ABD*, vol. 1, pp. 766-67.

[65] Roberts, *Manuscript*, p. 28, n. 1; Turner, *Greek Papyri*, pp. 52-53.

[66] J. A. Robinson, *The Pachomian Monastic Library at the Chester Beatty Library and the Bibliothèque Bodmer* (Claremont: Institute for Antiquity and Christianity, 1990).

[67] On the first point see J. van Haelst in A. Carlini, ed., *Papyrus Bodmer XXXVIII, Erma: Il Pastore (Ia-IIIa visione)* (Cologny-Genève: Fondation Martin Bodmer, 1991), pp. 105, n. 5, 118-19; cf. R. Cribiore, *Gymnastics of the Mind: Greek Education in Hellenistic and Roman Egypt* (Princeton: Princeton University Press, 2001), p. 200. Robinson thinks the Greek literary works and quality gospel MSS like $\mathfrak{P}^{66}$ and $\mathfrak{P}^{75}$ may have been gifted to the library (*Pachomian Monastic Library*, pp. 4-5).

certain.[68] But quite clearly all are from Egypt where the dry conditions are conducive to preservation.[69] Given their common derivation, this raises the question of whether the papyri are representative of the early history of the gospel text as found throughout the second and third-century Christian world.

Some idea of the extent and interactivity of Egyptian Christianity in the second century is helpful in this regard. $\mathfrak{P}^{52}$ (John), P.Oxy. 1.1 (*Gospel of Thomas*), and Egerton Papyrus 2 (the so-called Egerton Gospel) are variously dated c. 150–200 and were found in the Oxyrhynchus and Fayum areas. So by the first half of the second century Christianity was established in Middle Egypt 240-320 km from Alexandria.[70] Close ties were also maintained between Alexandrians and their relatives and friends in the provinces.[71] We know that members of the Alexandrian museum had country estates, and that scholars in Oxyrhynchus obtained literary works from Alexandria.[72] A tax register for Philadelphia in the Fayum lists 64 of 325 villagers living elsewhere as resident in Alexandria.[73] The small number of Christian texts found at Oxyrhynchus with scholarly markings might also indicate contact with the Alexandrian catechetical school.[74] There is nothing, therefore, that would prevent Christian MSS finding their way from Alexandria to Middle Egypt in the second century.

Furthermore, although it was previously assumed that NT MSS of Egyptian provenance originated in Egypt and were examples of local text-types,[75] the papyri in general evince a healthy two-way flow of people, letters and literature between Alexandria and the Mediterranean world in the early centuries. Non-Christian written material was carried into Egypt from places such as Ravenna, Macedonia, Asia Minor, Seleucia, Ostia, Rome and Constantinople.[76] The state postal service in the Hellenistic and Roman periods was reserved for official and military purposes. But the Hellenistic

---

[68] Around 40% of NT papyri are from Oxyrhynchus: cf. E. J. Epp, "The New Testament Papyri at Oxyrhynchus in Their Social and Intellectual Context," in W. L. Petersen, J. S. Vos, and H. J. de Jonge, eds., *Sayings of Jesus: Canonical and Non-Canonical: Essays in Honour of Tjitze Baarda* (Leiden: Brill, 1997), pp. 47-68.

[69] For an up-to-date summary of provenances see E. J. Epp, "Issues in New Testament Textual Criticism: Moving from the Nineteenth to the Twenty-First Century," in D. A. Black, ed., *Rethinking New Testament Textual Criticism* (Grand Rapids: Baker, 2002), pp. 62-64.

[70] Epp, "Significance," p. 78.

[71] Roberts, *Manuscript*, pp. 3-4.

[72] Turner, *Greek Papyri*, pp. 86-87. See also his "Scribes and Scholars of Oxyrhynchus," in H. Gerstinger, ed., *Akten des VIII. Internationalen Kongresses für Papyrologie, Wien 1955* (Vienna: R. M. Rohrer, 1956), pp. 141-46.

[73] Roberts, *Manuscript*, p. 4. Tax registers of Karanis in the Fayum also list a number of Alexandrian Greeks and citizens. The latter were probably absentee landlords (Turner, *Greek Papyri*, pp. 80-81).

[74] Roberts, *Manuscript*, p. 24. According to Eusebius, the catechetical school developed under Pantaenus in the last quarter of the second century and subsequently under Clement and Origen (*Hist. eccl.* 5.10.1; 6.3.3; 6.4.19).

[75] See, for example, K. W. Clark, *The Gentile Bias and Other Essays* (Leiden: Brill, 1980), p. 127: "All the manuscripts so far discovered, including the most sensational of recent discoveries, may enable us to recover no more than the early text in Egypt."

[76] Turner, *Greek Papyri*, pp. 50-51, 96.

evidence shows that despite some difficulties (delivery times might increase exponentially if a letter carrier was unreliable or a boat unavailable), private senders were able to find carriers and letters frequently moved with relative ease.[77] In the same way gospel MSS could have found their way to Egypt from elsewhere.[78] $\mathfrak{P}^{52}$, for instance, demonstrates that the Gospel of John, though apparently written in western Asia Minor (Irenaeus, *Haer.* 3.1.1) was circulating in Egypt in the first half of the second century. Thus, the relatively easy transit of documents (until the Diocletianic persecution of III/IV) means that the early gospel papyri found in Egypt are very likely representative of textual traditions from around the Mediterranean world.[79]

To some extent "the coherence of the early church" must have depended on the efficient movement of communications and literature.[80] Roberts thought that the pervasive use of the *nomina sacra* convention[81] and the remarkable Christian preference for the codex (particularly for writings regarded as sacred text[82]) added up to a strong case for there having been "a degree of organization, of conscious planning, and uniformity of practice" in the early church.[83] This is confirmed by codicological features common to nearly all of the early gospel MSS.[84] From the MS evidence we may infer that Christians favored standard sized gospel codices in the second and third centuries.[85] Other conventional approaches to MS production—hands in the semi-literary to (formative) biblical majuscule range and the use of "reader's aids" (punctuation and text division) to facilitate easy public reading—support the idea that some early gospels were produced in small copying centers

---

[77] See S. R. Llewelyn, *New Documents Illustrating Early Christianity*, vol. 7 (Macquarie University: The Ancient History Documentary Research Centre, 1994), pp. 1-57; S. R. Llewelyn, "Sending letters in the ancient world," *Tyndale Bulletin* 46 (1995), pp. 337-56; E. J. Epp, "New Testament Papyrus Manuscripts and Letter Carrying in Greco-Roman Times," in B. A. Pearson et al., eds., *The Future of Early Christianity: Essays in Honor of Helmut Koester* (Minneapolis: Fortress Press, 1991), pp. 35-56, esp. pp. 43-51.

[78] On the movement of communications and MSS between early Christian groups see Gamble, *Books*, pp. 108-32; and M. B. Thompson, "The Holy Internet: Communication between Churches in the First Christian Generation," in R. J. Bauckham, ed., *The Gospels for all Christians: Rethinking the Gospel Audiences* (Grand Rapids: Eerdmans, 1998), pp. 49-70; L. Alexander, "Ancient Book Production and Circulation of the Gospels," in Bauckham, *The Gospels for all Christians*, pp. 71-105.

[79] Epp, "Letter Carrying," p. 56; Epp, "The Papyrus Manuscripts of the New Testament," in Ehrman and Holmes, *Text*, p. 9.

[80] C. H. Roberts, "Books in the Graeco-Roman World and the New Testament," in Ackroyd, ed., *The Cambridge History of the Bible*, vol. 1 (Cambridge: Cambridge University Press, 1970), p. 64.

[81] Of around 300 Christian MSS earlier than 300 the number without *nomina sacra* "can be counted on the fingers of our two hands": L. W. Hurtado, "$\mathfrak{P}^{52}$ (P.Rylands Gk. 457) and the *nomina sacra*: Method and Probability," *Tyndale Bulletin* 54 (2003), p. 5.

[82] See Hurtado, *Earliest Christian Artifacts*, pp. 57-60.

[83] Roberts, *Manuscript*, p. 41.

[84] For detailed discussion of what follows see my "Public and Private: Second- and Third-Century Gospel Manuscripts," *Buried History* 42 (2006), pp. 25-36.

[85] These sizes correspond to the Turner Groups 9.1 (W11.5-14 × H at least 3 cm higher than W) and 8.2 (W12-14 × H not quite twice W) in the second and third centuries respectively: cf. Turner, *Typology*, pp. 13-25.

comprised of two or more scribes.[86] It is reasonable to suggest that such copying centers existed in the second century in cities like Antioch, Alexandria, Caesarea, Jerusalem and Rome.[87] This appears to be verified by the wholesale contraction of *nomina sacra* in early gospel MSS.[88] The presence of the same approach in all of the larger continuous MSS is a strong indication that most were copied in copying centers where "policy" dictated some aspects of production. All of this suggests a higher degree of communication and collaboration between early Christian communities than has often been allowed.

## F. Text-Critical Impact of the Chester Beatty and Bodmer Gospels

Since their discovery, $\mathfrak{P}^{45}$ (P.Beatty 1), $\mathfrak{P}^{66}$ (P.Bodmer 2) and $\mathfrak{P}^{75}$ (P.Bodmer 14-15), the longest of the early gospel MSS (all others are small and fragmentary by comparison), have inspired major advances in text-critical scholarship. In this section we will trace some of those advances and propose ways that these important MSS might illuminate the early history of the gospel MS tradition.

### 1. Text-types

The Byzantine text developed slowly from the fourth century—its earliest witness in the gospels is the fifth-century Codex Alexandrinus (A)—by incorporating and combining existing textual traditions. Thus, its primary characteristic is completeness, including the tendency to harmonize parallel synoptic passages. In contrast, the "Western" text has difficulty qualifying as a text-type and might better be described as a "free genre" whose representatives "are distinct from all other types, but puzzlingly unlike each other."[89] Scribes in "Western" witnesses (the most important are Codex Bezae [D] and the Old Latin MSS) are unconstrained by any need to transmit the text accurately, and freely paraphrase, omit, and add, to the extent of sometimes changing the original meaning. However, it would be wrong to characterize the early transmission of the gospel text as generally free or undisciplined. At

---

[86] Gamble, *Books*, pp. 120-21. It is reasonable to assume that early copying centers were small and not to be compared with the large number of assistants used by Origen early in the third century (see Eusebius, *Hist. eccl.* 6.23.2).

[87] See G. Zuntz, "The Text of the Epistles," in his *Opuscula Selecta: Classica, Hellenistica, Christiana* (Manchester: Manchester University Press, 1972), pp. 252-68, esp. pp. 266-68; Zuntz, *Text*, pp. 271-75; Turner, *Greek Papyri*, p. 92; Roberts, *Manuscript*, p. 24; Gamble, *Books*, pp. 121-23.

[88] Certain *nomina sacra* were contracted across the board without regard to the referent, meaning or (the "sacred" or "non-sacred") context in which the word was found. This comprehensive approach to contraction sought to bring an end to earlier, incorrect application of the convention: see my "Consensus Standardization in the Systematic Approach to *nomina sacra* in Second- and Third-Century Gospel Manuscripts," *Aegyptus* 86 (2006), pp. 37-68.

[89] D. C. Parker, *Codex Bezae: an Early Christian Manuscript and its Text* (New York: Cambridge University Press, 1992), p. 284.

Alexandria "a very ancient line of text was copied and preserved" with a view to accurate transmission.[90] While scribes still made some changes to the text they copied, the Alexandrian text-type is characterized by a strict approach to transmission, as demonstrated by the very close relationship between the third-century $\mathfrak{P}^{75}$ and the fourth-century Codex Vaticanus (B). Finally, mention should be made of the Caesarean text which mixes Western and Alexandrian readings and is more developed in later witnesses (its witnesses include W, $\Theta$, $f^{1,13}$). According to Metzger and Ehrman, it is "the most mixed and the least homogeneous" of any of the text-types.[91]

Prior to the publication of the Chester Beatty and Bodmer papyri, text-critical scholarship was focussed on identifying and establishing the priority of either the Alexandrian/B-text or "Western"/D-text. But study of the papyri constituted "the turning point from confidence to skepticism about early text-types."[92] Colwell concluded that "very few, if any, text-types were established" before 200,[93] while Aland went further in arguing that since the papyri with their various distinctive characteristics all come from Egypt, that "is the best argument against the existence of any text-types, including the Alexandrian and Antiochian[/Byzantine]" prior to the fourth century.[94] For K. Aland, $\mathfrak{P}^{75}$ was not proof that the Alexandrian text-type existed at an earlier date, but an example of the kind of good MSS that were selected and revised in various ecclesiastical centers in the fourth century.[95] While textual mobility (the relative ease with which MSS could move around) undermines some of the rationale for this argument, it does not completely destroy its force. It is difficult to fit the early papyri into the later text-types.

In contrast, Epp was concerned to defend the historical-documentary method, which seeks to organize MSS into text-types and then to identify trajectories of textual transmission. This method of textual criticism focuses primarily on external criteria such as the provenance and age of MSS, scribal characteristics, and the quality of the text. While acknowledging the complexities involved, Epp expressed a North American perspective: "many textual critics. . . are convinced that this is the path that must be followed and that the isolation of the earliest text-types must be our goal."[96] When dealing with the individualistic early papyri, he argues that a text-type should be understood as a textual "cluster or constellation" with a distinct textual

---

[90] Metzger and Ehrman, *Text*, p. 278.

[91] Metzger and Ehrman, *Text*, p. 312. For the main witnesses for each text-type see pp. 306-13.

[92] E. J. Epp, "Textual Criticism," in E. J. Epp and G. W. McRae, eds., *The New Testament and its Modern Interpreters* (Atlanta: Scholars Press, 1989), p. 98.

[93] E. C. Colwell, *Studies in Methodology in Textual Criticism of the New Testament* (Leiden: Brill, 1969), p. 55.

[94] K. Aland, "The Significance of the Papyri for Progress in New Testament Research," in J. P. Hyatt, ed., *The Bible in Modern Scholarship* (Nashville: Abingdon, 1965), p. 336.

[95] Aland, "Significance," p. 336.

[96] Epp, "Textual Criticism," pp. 93-94: "It was in this spirit and with these goals that the International Greek New Testament Project was developed and that much postwar text-critical work was pursued, including the extensive studies in quantitative measurements of manuscript relationships."

complexion.[97]

The questions generated by the papyri were and are profound.[98] It had been thought that text-types developed in different localities. But textual "mixture" in the papyri and their common provenance appeared to seriously challenge or even rule out the existence of early text-types. For example, in the Gospel of Mark $\mathfrak{P}^{45}$ is nearer to the Caesarean family than to the B-text or D-text, while in the other gospels that papyrus is intermediate between those text-types.[99] As used here, the word "mixture" again describes the papyri in terms of (the text-types of) later majuscules. But it also encapsulates quite well the idiosyncrasies of the Bodmer and Chester Beatty Gospels. Textual or MSS mobility would have been one factor in promoting textual admixture. But after noting that "the distinctiveness of a local text tended to become diluted and mixed with other texts," Metzger adds, "on the whole, however, during the earliest centuries the tendencies to develop and preserve a particular type of text prevailed over the tendencies leading to a mixture of texts."[100] So the early development of text-types cannot be ruled out.

To avoid classification through the lens of the great majuscules, textual clusters are identified by first classifying papyri based on textual differences and then looking for later partners.[101] Epp argues that three textual "groupings" already existed in the second century which form trajectories forward in time through other witnesses:[102]

1. *B-text:* $\mathfrak{P}^{75}$ and B, including $\mathfrak{P}^{66}$ and $\aleph$ (not in John), with a trajectory forward through L and 33.
2. *D-text:* 0171 and perhaps $\mathfrak{P}^{69}$ can be connected with D.
3. $\mathfrak{P}^{45}$ and W in Mk. 5:31-16:20 (in the rest of the gospels W is halfway between B and D),[103] transmitting through, for example, $f^{13}$.

He also argues that different "textual complexions can be identified in the various papyri, even in the fragmentary ones." If this process "were to result

---

[97] Epp, "Papyrus Manuscripts of the New Testament," pp. 16-17. '

[98] See J. H. Petzer, "The Papyri and New Testament Textual Criticism—Clarity or Confusion," in J. H. Petzer and P. J. Hartin, eds., *A South African Perspective on the New Testament: Essays by South African New Testament Scholars Presented to Bruce Manning Metzger* (Leiden: Brill, 1986), pp. 18-32.

[99] Metzger and Ehrman, *Text*, p. 54.

[100] B. M. Metzger, *A Textual Commentary on the Greek New Testament: a Companion Volume to the United Bible Societies' Greek New Testament (Fourth Revised Edition)*, 2nd ed. (Stuttgart: Deutsche Bibelgesellschaft, 1994), p. 5*.

[101] Epp, "Papyrus Manuscripts," p. 18.

[102] These are drawn from Epp, "Significance," pp. 92-99. The Byzantine text has no early papyrus representatives, but includes A in the Gospels and the later $\mathfrak{P}^{84}$ (VI) and $\mathfrak{P}^{42}$ (VII/VIII).

[103] The text of Mark in $\mathfrak{P}^{45}$ and W cannot strictly be described as either "Caesarean" or "pre-Caesarean." It constitutes its own textual group and lacks significant connections to putative "Caesarean" MSS like Codex Θ. See L. W. Hurtado, "P[45] and the Textual History of the Gospel of Mark," in C. Horton, ed., *The Earliest Gospels: the Origins and Transmission of the Earliest Christian Gospels. The Contribution of the Chester Beatty Gospel Codex P⁴⁵* (London: T. & T. Clark, 2004), pp. 145-46.

in the identification of only one very early cluster, succeeded by one or more later clusters, then readings belonging to that earliest cluster might legitimately be identified as those closest to the original and as most plausibly the original readings."[104] However, it is important to recognize that quantifying the agreements of early witnesses with a third and fourth century control group of MSS risks treating text-types "as fixed and closed entities rather than open and changing entities," and has difficulty explaining how the early MSS "fit into the earlier developmental phases of these text-types."[105] Nevertheless, the possibility remains that a text-type in general or in particular books and/or chapters might be very close to the "original" text.[106]

## 2. Quantitative Method

Besides threatening the Caesarean text,[107] $\mathfrak{P}^{45}$ "revealed broader problems in practically all efforts to determine textual relationships of manuscripts."[108] Prior to that time, neither "an adequate definition of a text-type relationship," nor "an adequate method for discovering such a relationship between two or more witnesses" had been formulated.[109] Rather than examining every place of variation in MSS, scholars merely counted the number of non-Byzantine readings. But then $\mathfrak{P}^{45}$ appeared with many readings that had been considered "Byzantine," in a MS written long before that text-type was thought to have been produced.

Colwell led the way in improving methodology, and subsequent scholars have continued to refine the criteria he proposed. In short, his method involved examining the textual affiliations of a MS "in a substantial amount of text at significant places of variation" against control witnesses representing major text-types.[110] Quantitatively, a textual group of MSS should agree more than 70% of the time and be separated from its neighbors by about a 10% gap.[111] This relationship exists between $\mathfrak{P}^{75}$ and B in John, and $\mathfrak{P}^{45}$ and W in Mark.[112] Thus early fragmentary papyri can become types

---

[104] Epp, "Textual Criticism," pp. 98, 93.

[105] J. H. Petzer, "The History of the New Testament Text—its Reconstruction, Significance and Use in New Testament Textual Criticism," in B. Aland and J. Delobel, eds., *New Testament Textual Criticism, Exegesis, and Early Church History: a Discussion of Methods* (Kampen: Pharos, 1994), p. 29.

[106] As J. N. Birdsall ("The New Testament Text," in Ackroyd, ed., *The Cambridge History of the Bible*, vol. 1, p. 317) observes: "Although the main lines of groupings of witnesses into text-types can be seen, no one text-type can be shown to be superior to the others in its readings in every respect."

[107] Birdsall, "Recent History," pp. 149-53.

[108] Hurtado, "Textual History," p. 141.

[109] L. W. Hurtado, *Text-critical Methodology and the Pre-Caesarean Text: Codex W in the Gospel of Mark* (Grand Rapids: Eerdmans, 1981), p. 5.

[110] T. C. Geer Jr., "Analyzing and categorizing New Testament Greek manuscripts: Colwell revisited," in Ehrman and Holmes, *Text*, p. 256. See Colwell, *Studies*, pp. 26-44, 56-62, esp. pp. 57-59.

[111] Colwell, *Studies*, p. 59.

[112] Colwell's approach was refined by Fee. See G. D. Fee, "Codex Sinaiticus in the Gospel

for later MSS as witnesses are grouped from "corpus to corpus," "book to book," and even from section to section.[113]

## 3. Recension

Closely tied to the existence of text-types is the concept of "recension." In strict terms, a recension is a critical edition produced by an editor or editors; however, it is often used loosely to refer to families of MSS.[114] We have already seen that the "Western" text is more genre than text-type, so it can hardly be a fourth or fifth century recension. Along similar lines, the final form of the Byzantine text-type "represents a slowly developing tradition, not . . . a textual recension created by a single person or community."[115] As for the possibility of an Alexandrian recension, it seemed to be confirmed by $\mathfrak{P}^{66}$. Evaluation of that papyrus, which was deemed pre-recensional or proto-Alexandrian, appeared to show that a fluid transmission process ended in a fourth-century recension of the Alexandrian or B-text.[116] But when the very close textual affinity between $\mathfrak{P}^{75}$ and B was identified, it immediately put paid to any such notion.[117] The proposition that agreement between $\mathfrak{P}^{75}$ and B ℵ is a strong case for the original reading has continued to the present day.

This overarching methodology of $NA^{26,27}$ resembles that of the very influential Westcott and Hort;[118] but does it simply push the problem of recension back to the second century? Fee argues that *both* $\mathfrak{P}^{75}$ and B are "faithfully preserving textual phenomena which are anterior to them, which in turn means that $\mathfrak{P}^{75}$ is not itself the recension."[119] He also adduces evidence for the non-recensional nature of their common ancestor, and concludes that comparison of $\mathfrak{P}^{75}$ B with other MS traditions reveals that they "represent a 'relatively pure' form of preservation of a 'relatively pure' line of descent from the original text."[120] Therefore, "Hort was basically correct, that the Egyptian [= Alexandrian] text-type is a *carefully preserved* tradition (= careful copying) and not a recension at all."[121] As a result, the editorial

---

of John: A Contribution to Methodology in Establishing Textual Relationships," in Epp and Fee, *Studies*, pp. 221-44; G. D. Fee, *Papyrus Bodmer II (P66): Its Textual Relationships and Scribal Characteristics* (Salt Lake City: University of Utah Press, 1968); Hurtado, *Text-Critical Methodology*, pp. 63-66, 88-89, 94.

[113] Colwell, *Studies*, p. 55.

[114] Metzger and Ehrman, *Text*, p. 161 n. 58; cf. p. 165.

[115] Metzger and Ehrman, *Text*, p. 279; cf. Colwell, *Studies*, pp. 45-55.

[116] G. D. Fee, "P$^{75}$, P$^{66}$, and Origen: The Myth of Early Textual Recension in Alexandria," in Epp and Fee, *Studies*, pp. 248-51.

[117] See C. M. Martini, *Il problema della recensionalità del codice B alla luce papiro Bodmer XIV* (Rome: Pontifico Istituto Biblico, 1966); and Fee, "P$^{75}$, P$^{66}$, and Origen."

[118] "Where the two ultimate witnesses agree [B ℵ], the text will be as certain as the extant documents can make it": B. F. Westcott and F. J. A. Hort, *The New Testament in the Original Greek*, including vol. 2: *Introduction* [and] *Appendix*, vol. 2 (London: Macmillan, 1881), p. 41. When they disagree, B should be followed (p. 32).

[119] Fee, "P$^{75}$, P$^{66}$, and Origen," p. 268.

[120] Fee, "P$^{75}$, P$^{66}$, and Origen," p. 272.

[121] Fee, "P$^{75}$, P$^{66}$, and Origen," p. 256 (emphasis his). Cf. J. N. Birdsall, "Rational

activity in $\mathfrak{P}^{66}$ is not of the scholarly, text-critical type associated with recension, but in a directly opposite fashion tends to smooth out grammar in the interests of readability.[122]

## 4. Reasoned vs. Rigorous Eclecticism

Questions concerning text-type, recension and quantitative method all derive from the "traditional" *external* focus of textual criticism. In contrast, "rigorous" or thoroughgoing eclecticism attempts to solve "textual variation with an appeal primarily to *internal* considerations."[123] Internal criteria were divided by Hort into two types "which cannot be too sharply distinguished from each other."[124] "Intrinsic probability" concerns "what an author is likely to have written" and includes consideration of vocabulary, theology and style, immediate context, harmony with other parts of the book, and the historical context of writing. "Transcriptional probability" concerns "what copyists are likely to have made him seem to write," and considers palaeographical details and scribal tendencies, such as the more difficult reading is to be preferred (the *lectio difficilior potior* principle), harmonization to parallels, and scribal changes including the occasional tendency to bring the Greek into conformity with the norms of fourth century BC Attic Greek.[125]

In its concentration on these criteria rigorous eclecticism appears to ignore "the problems of the history of the tradition and the relationships of manuscripts."[126] Rigorous eclectics counter that charge by arguing that most textual variants were created by 200. Therefore, regardless of date, all readings go back "into a period from which virtually no MSS survive. Thus external evidence as such is of little relevance."[127] But as a result of minimizing external criteria such as the date and geographical distribution of

---

Eclecticism and the Oldest Manuscripts: A Comparative Study of the Bodmer and the Chester Beatty Papyri of the Gospel of Luke," in J. K. Elliott, ed., *Studies in New Testament Language and Text: Essays in Honour of George D. Kilpatrick on the Occasion of his Sixty-Fifth Birthday* (Leiden: Brill, 1976), pp. 39-51.

[122] Fee, "P[75], P[66], and Origen," pp. 256-59. See also Fee, *Papyrus Bodmer II*, pp. 36-75. Cf. Colwell, *Studies*, pp. 106-24.

[123] See J. K. Elliott, "Thoroughgoing Eclecticism in New Testament Textual Criticism," in Ehrman and Holmes, *Text*, pp. 321-35, here p. 321 (emphasis mine). See also J. K. Elliott, "In Defence of Thoroughgoing Eclecticism in New Testament Textual Criticism," *Restoration Quarterly* 21 (1978), pp. 95-115; G. D. Kilpatrick, *The Principles and Practice of New Testament Textual Criticism: Collected Essays of G. D. Kilpatrick*, J. K. Elliott, ed. (Leuven: Leuven University Press, 1990).

[124] Westcott and Hort, *The New Testament*, vol. 2, p. 20.

[125] Westcott and Hort, *The New Testament*, vol. 2, p. 20; Metzger and Ehrman, *Text*, pp. 302-4; cf. Epp, "Textual Criticism," p. 94; Birdsall, "Recent History," p. 157. On Atticism in particular see G. D. Kilpatrick, "Atticism and the Text of the Greek New Testament," in J. Blinzer et al., eds., *Neutestamentliche Aufsätze: Festschrift für Prof. Josef Schmid zum 70. Gerburtstag* (Regensburg: Pustet, 1963), pp. 125-37. Contrast G. H. R. Horsley, "*Koine* or Atticism—a Misleading Dichotomy," in his *New Documents Illustrating Early Christianity*, vol. 5 (Sydney: Macquarie University Documentary Centre, 1989), pp. 43-44.

[126] Birdsall, "Recent History," pp. 156-58.

[127] Elliott, "Thoroughgoing Eclecticism," p. 331.

witnesses, and the genealogical or textual relationship of texts and families of witnesses,[128] rigorous eclectics "have accredited scores" of Byzantine readings.[129] This approach is predicated not only on assumptions about the emergence of variants, but effectively also on a belief that the early history of the text cannot be reconstructed,[130] perhaps another "consequence" of questions raised by the papyri. But to marginalize historical-documentary criteria could hardly be described as thoroughgoing when part of the data is ignored.[131] Quite clearly it is not simply a question of *either* internal *or* external criteria, as the qualified language of rigorous eclecticism sometimes seems to suggest.[132]

In practice, the majority of textual critics give weight in varying degrees to both external and internal criteria in an approach known as "reasoned" eclecticism,[133] the principles of which are outlined, for example, in Metzger's *Commentary*.[134] In response, Elliott has repeatedly objected to editors of NA[26,27] inconsistently abandoning "their own principles of internal criteria if they, or a majority of them, did not approve of the MS support for the reading that the internal criteria pointed to as original."[135] Such criticism is salient because it highlights deficiencies in current knowledge.[136] Fifty years ago Clark expressed hope that the "secondary and tentative method" of eclecticism might be abandoned: "The eclectic method, by its very nature, belongs to an age like ours in which we know only that the traditional theory of the text is faulty but cannot yet see clearly to correct the fault."[137] Epp is also hopeful that "the eclectic method can be replaced by something more permanent—a confidently reconstructed history and a persuasive theory of the text," which would furnish us with "more objective methods."[138] However, even with such advances (which would be greatly aided by discoveries of earlier MSS), because we can never be absolutely sure that the MSS we have

---

[128] Metzger and Ehrman, *Text*, p. 302. For example, the "age, prestige or popularity" of MSS is of no value in making textual decisions: J. K. Elliott, "Can We Recover the Original New Testament?" *Theology* 75 (1972), p. 352.

[129] Epp, "Textual Criticism," p. 95.

[130] Cf. Petzer, "The Papyri," p. 25.

[131] Cf. Epp, "Interlude," p. 99.

[132] Consider the implied caveats in: "Thoroughgoing text critics prefer to edit a text by solving textual variation with an appeal primarily to purely internal considerations"; "Thoroughgoing eclecticism is the method that allows internal considerations for a reading's originality to be given priority over documentary considerations" (Elliott, "Thoroughgoing Eclecticism," p. 321).

[133] Epp, "Issues," p. 43. See G. D. Fee, "Rigorous or Reasoned Eclecticism—Which?" in Epp and Fee, *Studies*, pp. 124-40; E. J. Epp, "The Eclectic Method in New Testament Textual Criticism," in Epp and Fee, *Studies*, pp. 141-73; M. W. Holmes, "Reasoned Eclecticism in New Testament Textual Criticism," in Ehrman and Holmes, *Text*, pp. 336-60.

[134] Metzger, *Commentary*, pp. 11*-14*; cf. Aland and Aland, *Text*, pp. 279-82.

[135] Elliott, "Thoroughgoing Eclecticism," p. 325.

[136] Cf. J. K. Elliott, "Can We Recover the Original New Testament? An Examination of the Rôle of Thoroughgoing Eclecticism," in his *Essays and Studies in New Testament Textual Criticism* (Cordoba: Ediciones El Almendro, 1992), p. 37.

[137] Clark, "Effect," pp. 37-38.

[138] Epp, "Textual Criticism," pp. 102, 103. Cf. Clark, *Gentile Bias*, p. 129.

are the same as the autographs, intrinsic probabilities (eclecticism) will continue to play a part in deciding what is "original."[139] In the meantime, different ideas about the early history of the text will also continue to affect evaluation of variant readings.[140]

## 5. Scribal Tendencies

The basic criterion for evaluating variant readings is to "choose the reading that best explains the origin of the others," followed closely by "the reconstruction of the history of a variant reading is prerequisite to forming a judgment about it."[141] The second task will generally involve some analysis of scribal tendencies. It is fundamental that knowledge about scribes both in general and in particular can help guard against subjectivity in deciding between variants.[142] Therefore, if considerations of "transcriptional probability are to be soundly based, they must rest upon a knowledge of scribal habits."[143] Because of the manifold MS attestation for the gospels, scribal profiles have traditionally been developed by analyzing the singular readings of individual MSS (i.e., unique readings found only in a single MS). The assumption has been that singular readings should derive from individual scribes. Scribes share certain tendencies, but they also have idiosyncrasies, so text-critical generalizations can be misleading in the absence of knowledge about particular scribes.

In his analysis of the gospel papyri $\mathfrak{P}^{45}$, $\mathfrak{P}^{66}$ and $\mathfrak{P}^{75}$ Colwell found that all three featured scribal leaps (parablepsis), i.e., after looking away from their exemplar the scribes looked ahead three times as often as they looked back, so all three tended to omit more text than they added.[144] On the basis of similar findings Royce called into question the "the shorter reading is to be preferred" criterion.[145] As well, all of the scribes tended to harmonize much more to immediate context (83/104 instances) than to remote parallels or general usage.[146] But while increased understanding of scribal practice can help refine

---

[139] See the valuable discussion of Holmes, "Reasoned Eclecticism," pp. 346-49.

[140] Holmes, "Reasoned Eclecticism," p. 350. For a useful discussion of the various reconstructions of the history of the text see Petzer, "History," pp. 11-36.

[141] Metzger and Ehrman, *Text*, pp. 300-301.

[142] "Colwell's explicit goal is to isolate the tendencies of particular scribes, as a prerequisite to finding the original text": J. R. Royse, "Scribal Tendencies in the Transmission of the Text of the New Testament," in Ehrman and Holmes, *Text*, p. 245. For a survey of scribal errors see Metzger and Ehrman, *Text*, pp. 250-71.

[143] Colwell, "Scribal Habits," p. 107.

[144] Colwell, "Scribal Habits," p. 112. On scribal leaps see J. R. Royse, "The Treatment of Scribal Leaps in Metzger's *Textual Commentary*," *New Testament Studies* 29 (1983), pp. 539-51.

[145] See Royse, "Scribal Tendencies," p. 246. On the basis of his analysis of fourteen small fragments of the gospels, P. M. Head also concluded omission was more common than addition: "Observations on Early Papyri of the Synoptic Gospels, Especially on the 'Scribal Habits,'" *Biblica* 71 (1990), pp. 240-47.

[146] Colwell, "Scribal Habits," p. 113.

text-critical criteria,[147] it is more important to "establish the particular habits and preferences evident in particular witnesses, instead of invoking generalizations blindly."[148]

The scribe of $\mathfrak{P}^{45}$ copied phrases and words (idea-content) rather than syllables (as did the scribe of $\mathfrak{P}^{66}$) or letters (so the scribe of $\mathfrak{P}^{75}$).[149] Moreover, he felt no need to reproduce exactly his exemplar, and freely culled words and recast the text in the interests of conciseness, clarity and style. Clarification also motivated the scribe of $\mathfrak{P}^{75}$, but most of the time his priority was the disciplined desire to make an exact copy.[150] In contrast, the copying in $\mathfrak{P}^{66}$ is careless, but numerous corrections against a second exemplar are indicative of conscientious efforts to produce a good final copy.[151] Today $\mathfrak{P}^{66}$ is seen as a wild member of the $\mathfrak{P}^{75}$ B text,[152] and is most useful for the insights it provides into the early transmission process.[153] Generally speaking, apart from the copyist of $\mathfrak{P}^{75}$, scribes in the early period were not as careful as their later counterparts.[154] But as noted above, it would be wrong to stereotype the second century as a period of wild textual variation.[155] Clearly, "scribes made changes in style, in clarity, in fitness of idea, in smoothness, in vocabulary."[156] But the papyri provide evidence of several types of copying, a "free" approach that would have produced many variants, "strict" or careful copying, and a "normal" approach to transmission. A "strict" text transmits "the text of an exemplar with meticulous care," while a "normal" text is "a relatively faithful tradition which departs from its exemplar only occasionally."[157]

Three kinds of scribal intervention in the transmission process can be

---

[147] E. J. Epp, "The New Testament Papyrus Manuscripts in Historical Perspective," in M. P. Horgan and P. J. Kobelski, eds., *To Touch the Text: Studies in Honor of Joseph A. Fitzmeyer, S.J.* (New York: Crossroad, 1989), p. 288.

[148] L. W. Hurtado, "Beyond the Interlude? Developments and Directions in New Testament Textual Criticism," in D. G. K. Taylor, ed., *Studies in the Early Text of the Gospels and Acts: the Papers of the First Birmingham Colloquium on the Textual Criticism of the New Testament* (Birmingham: Birmingham University Press, 1999), p. 37.

[149] This is clear from what is omitted when the scribe's eye jumps forward.

[150] "In P[75] the text that is produced can be explained in all its variants as the result of a single force, namely the disciplined scribe who writes with the intention of being careful and accurate" (Colwell, "Scribal Habits," p. 117).

[151] G. D. Fee, "The Corrections of Papyrus Bodmer II and Early Textual Transmission," *Novum Testamentum* 7 (1964/65), pp. 247-57; J. R. Royse, *Scribal Habits in Early Greek New Testament Papyri* (Leiden: Brill, 2008), pp. 413-15.

[152] Fee, "P[75], P[66], and Origen," pp. 258-59.

[153] Fee, *Papyrus Bodmer II*, pp. 35, 56, 76-83; Epp, "Historical Perspective," p. 283.

[154] Royse, "Scribal Tendencies," p. 248.

[155] Cf. "*The story of the manuscript tradition of the New Testament is the story of progression from a relatively uncontrolled tradition to a rigorously controlled tradition . . .* The general nature of the text in the earliest period (to AD 300) has long been recognized as 'wild,' 'uncontrolled,' 'unedited'": Colwell, *Studies*, pp. 164, 166, n. 3 (emphasis his).

[156] Colwell, "Scribal Habits," 118.

[157] Aland and Aland, *Text*, p. 64. In contrast, a "free" text treats its exemplar in "a relatively free manner" (pp. 59, 93-5); and there are few examples of the "paraphrastic" text which is similar to the D-text (pp. 64, 93-5; cf. 69). Cf. the use of these four classifications as regards the papyri (pp. 94-95).

identified: (1) limited stylistic smoothing; (2) interpretative change aimed at more clearly expressing the existing sense; and (3) interpretative change that alters the meaning of the text.[158] Types (1) and (2) are characterized by changes to minor details that do not affect the essential meaning of the text, and type (3) changes are very rare. This means that although scribes made minor detail changes the early textual tradition was transmitted accurately *en bloc*. This calls into question the common assumption that the first 150 years of transmission were characterized by heightened textual fluidity in comparison with subsequent decades and centuries.

## G. Contemporary Perspectives on the Early Gospel Text

Nonetheless, the notions of instability and fluidity underlie a number of contemporary perspectives on the second-century gospel text. For Koester the "assumption that the reconstruction of the best archetype for the manuscript tradition is more or less identical with the assumed autograph is precarious."[159] He claims the MS archetypes represented by the papyri are "substantial revisions of the original texts" which occurred during the first hundred years of transmission, and that the lack of second-century MSS evidence for the gospels[160] means that an older gospel must be sought in the Apostolic Fathers and early apologists[161] (both of which are thought to have depended on the same pre-synoptic oral and/or written tradition).[162] Behind these assertions lie assumptions about a diverse and primarily oral early Christianity and a concomitant "very unstable" second-century gospel text.[163]

While Koester sidesteps the implications of the predominance of the B-text in the early period, this did not escape Petersen.[164] In his view, the papyri cannot contribute new readings or move us any closer to the original text, "for the vast majority of the papyri belong to the B-ℵ recension and . . . their chief function is to take the manuscript evidence for that recension back to the third century." They merely "confirm the *status quo*—in other words, they confirm our biases."[165] But "bias" is a word that is most applicable when part of the evidence is discounted. Early conventional features—the use of the codex and *nomina sacra*—permit the "claim that our very earliest New Testament papyri

---

[158] See B. Aland, "Die Münsteraner Arbeit am Text die Neuen Testament und ihr Beitrag für die frühe Überlieferung des 2. Jahrhunderts: Eine methodologische Betrachtung," in Petersen, *Gospel Traditions*, pp. 55-70.

[159] H. Koester, "The text of the Synoptic Gospels in the second century," in Petersen, *Gospel Traditions*, p. 19. The word "autograph" means the first or original copy of a text.

[160] See the objections of Hurtado ("Interlude," pp. 40-41), and see Table 2 above for second-century gospel MSS.

[161] Koester, "Text of the Synoptic Gospels," pp. 37, 19.

[162] See H. Koester, *Synoptische Überlieferung bei den apostolischen Vätern* (Berlin: Akademie Verlag, 1957).

[163] Koester, "Text of the Synoptic Gospels," p. 37.

[164] W. L. Petersen, "What Text can New Testament Textual Criticism Ultimately Reach?" in Aland and Delobel, *New Testament Textual Criticism*, pp. 136-52.

[165] Petersen, "What Text," p. 140.

had antecedents or ancestors as much as a century earlier than their own time."[166] Furthermore, if $\mathfrak{P}^{75}$ is non-recensional, it may take us back into the third quarter of the first century.

Petersen also asks why textual criticism largely ignores early patristic and versional evidence in favor of the MS tradition.[167] Against the Alands who argue that an established NT text did not emerge until c. 180,[168] but at the same time limit the versions and Apostolic Fathers to no more than a supplementary role because of the difficulties inherent in their use,[169] Petersen contends "there *was* a "fixed" manuscript tradition before 180."[170] He proffers several examples using multiple, second-century patristic and versional sources ("*widely dispersed*" by language and geography) to recover readings from "other recensions *prior to 180*."[171] This ancient text, he argues, can be recovered with great effort "here and there."[172]

Certainly, it would be rash to assert that "proto-orthodox" (see below) scribes were "immune" from altering texts to suit their doctrinal positions.[173] But what is most interesting about the latter proposal is that it assumes that pre-180 recensions will exhibit the theological/philosophical hallmarks of their day; i.e., they will be the products of later Christian communities and not of the apostolic church—that (textual) traditions will be framed in terms of the present experience of the church.[174] This assumption which reaches back to the early form critics is attracting increasing criticism.[175]

Hurtado has raised a number of salient objections to views of this kind.[176]

1. Evidence for the historical developments, influential figures, or centers that might have produced second century recensions is wanting.
2. Despite the dominance of the B-text, the different textual complexions and scribal approaches in the papyri speak against early recensions "so completely successful as to have thoroughly reformulated" the gospel

---

[166] Epp, "Significance," pp. 101-02.

[167] Petersen, "What Text," pp. 139-40. "*Only* when a Patristic reading is supported by the uncials does it enter the critical text" (emphasis his).

[168] Aland and Aland, *Text*, pp. 54-55.

[169] "The primary authority for a critical textual decision lies with the Greek manuscript tradition, with the versions and Fathers serving no more than a supplementary and corroborative function, particularly in passages where their underlying Greek text cannot be reconstructed with absolute certainty" (Aland and Aland, *Text*, p. 280). On the problems unique to patristic texts see G. D. Fee, "The Use of the Greek Fathers for New Testament Textual Criticism," in Ehrman and Holmes, *Text*, pp. 191-207.

[170] Petersen, "What Text," p. 149.

[171] Petersen, "What Text," pp. 149-50 (emphasis his).

[172] Petersen, "What Text," p. 150.

[173] Birdsall, "New Testament Text," p. 329.

[174] Cf. W. L. Petersen, "The Genesis of the Gospels," in A. Denaux, ed., *New Testament Textual Criticism and Exegesis: Festschrift J. Delobel* (Leuven: Leuven University Press, 2002), pp. 33-65.

[175] See Gamble, *Books*, pp. 14-41.

[176] On points (1) and (2) see Hurtado, "Interlude," pp. 40-43. On points (3) and (4) see Hurtado, "The New Testament in the Second Century: Text, Collections and Canon," in Childers and Parker, *Transmission and Reception*, pp. 13-19.

text. In addition, the early dating of $\mathfrak{P}^{75}$ does not allow sufficient time for evolution from text-forms in the Apostolic Fathers and early versions to the B-text.[177]

3. Second century citation technique was free and flexible (interpretative/adaptive). This was normal literary practice for Paul and his Greco-Roman and Jewish counterparts (perhaps involving the use of personal collections of excerpts),[178] and there is no reason to think that the Apostolic Fathers and early apologists were different in this regard. However, "limited flux" in line with accepted scribal practice—more limited in the context of strict as against free copying—rather than citation technique, should be seen to characterize the transmission of the gospel text.[179]

4. Public familiarity deriving from regular public reading of gospel MSS in worship gatherings would tend to guard against "wild" textual transmission.[180]

Scholars are also rethinking the actual meaning of "original text" and the goal of NT textual criticism.[181] For example, without questioning the need to recover early text-forms, Parker questions the goal and importance of recovering the original text.[182] Working from the presupposition of a free MS tradition in the first 150 years,[183] he declares that the recovery of an original text is incompatible with the development of a "living" text: the Jesus traditions were handed on in "an interpretative rather than exact fashion";[184] therefore, the "recovery of a definitive "original" text that is consequently "authoritative" cannot be presumed to be an attainable target."[185] This is

---

[177] Birdsall, "New Testament Text," pp. 340-42.

[178] See C. D. Stanley, *Paul and the Language of Scripture: Citation Technique in the Pauline Epistles and Contemporary Literature* (New York: Cambridge University Press, 1992). See also B. Aland, "Die Rezeption des neutestamentlichen Textes in den ersten Jahrhunderten," in J.-M. Sevrin, ed., *The New Testament in Early Christianity* (Leuven: Leuven University Press, 1989), pp. 1-38, who argues that accuracy in citation increased in the second half of the second century in response to heretical threats and repeated liturgical use of some texts.

[179] Cf. S. Talmon, "The Textual Study of the Bible—a New Outlook," in F. M. Cross and S. Talmon, eds., *Qumran and the History of the Biblical Text* (Cambridge: Harvard University Press, 1975), pp. 321-400, esp. p. 326; B. Aland, "The Significance of the Chester Beatty Papyri in Early Church History," in Horton, ed., *The Earliest Gospels*, pp. 108-21; B. Aland, "Sind Scheiber früher neutestamentlicher Handschriften Interpreten des Textes?" in Childers and Parker, *Transmission and Reception*, pp. 114-22.

[180] Cf. H. Y. Gamble, "Literacy, Liturgy, and the Shaping of the New Testament Canon," in Horton, ed., *The Earliest Gospels*, pp. 27-39.

[181] See E. J. Epp, "The Multivalence of the Term 'Original Text' in New Testament Textual Criticism," *Harvard Theological Review* 92 (1999), pp. 245-81. Cf. B. D. Ehrman, "The Text as Window: New Testament Manuscripts and the Social History of Early Christianity," in Ehrman and Holmes, *Text*, p. 361 n. 1.

[182] D. C. Parker, *The Living Text of the Gospels* (New York: Cambridge University Press, 1997), pp. 3-7, 45-8, 91-4, 203-13.

[183] Parker, *Living Text*, pp. 70, 88, 200, 209.

[184] D. C. Parker, "Scripture is Tradition," *Theology* 94 (1991), p. 15.

[185] Parker, *Living Text*, p. 91. This perspective has been endorsed by E. J. Epp, "It's all about Variants: A Variant-Conscious Approach to New Testament Textual Criticism," *Harvard*

because early Christians—based on variation between the Synoptic Gospels (as regards oral tradition) and between the MSS (as regards written tradition) —did not attempt to remember or transmit the sayings of Jesus "with perfect accuracy."[186] In emphasizing this variation Parker contends that textual critics have fundamentally misunderstood the term "original text" and early transmission. "The concept of a gospel that is fixed in shape, authoritative, and final as a piece of literature has to be abandoned," he argues.[187] All credible variants make up the living gospels, and "the people of God" will have to decide on the best reading without an authoritative text.[188]

For Epp "every intentional, meaningful scribal alteration to a text— whether motivated by theological, historical, stylistic, or other factors— creates a new Textform, a new original."[189] But while this is true in a relative sense, it is debatable whether "multiple 'originals'" or "dimensions of originality" really capture the essence of the new perspectives.[190] For Parker, the original text never existed or ceased to exist as soon as it was copied. In deference to such views, Epp has suggested the terms *predecessor*, *autographic*, *canonical* and *interpretive text-form* be used. An autographic text-form is defined as "the textual form as it left the desk of Paul or a secretary, or of other writers of portions of what became our New Testament. Whole books in this dimension of originality would normally be close in form to the New Testament writings as we possess them."[191]

The basic position of Walter Bauer, that "heterodoxy" was the dominant force in the early church, also informs the text-critical perspectives of a number of scholars, in particular that of Ehrman.[192] But what if second-century orthodoxy was not as marginal as Bauer thought? Wisse argues cogently that third and fourth-century orthodoxy and heresy cannot be projected back on to the earlier period and its texts.[193] He contends that Christianity before 200 was generally "heterodox," in that diversity was tolerated (as, e.g., in the Pauline churches), rather than partisan (i.e., orthodox

---

*Theological Review* 100 (2007), pp. 275-308.

[186] Parker, *Living Text*, pp. 199-200. Fundamental to his thesis is the proposition that there are as many differences between the Synoptic Gospels as there are between MS readings (pp. 46, 197).

[187] Parker, *Living Text*, p. 93.

[188] Parker, "Scripture is Tradition," pp. 102, 212.

[189] Epp, "Issues," pp. 74-75. He argues this is true "in a *real* sense" (emphasis mine).

[190] So Epp, "Multivalence," p. 276. He notes that the positions of Parker and Ehrman repeat emphases of Lake, Harris, and the Chicago School from the earlier twentieth century (pp. 271-74).

[191] Epp, "Multivalence," p. 276.

[192] See W. Bauer, *Orthodoxy and Heresy in Early Christianity*, edited by R. A. Kraft and G. Krodel, 2nd ed. (Philadelphia: Fortress Press, 1971). Cf. B. D. Ehrman, *The Orthodox Corruption of Scripture: the Effect of Early Christological Controversies on the Text of the New Testament* (New York: Oxford University Press, 1993), pp. 3-46. Petersen ("The Diatessaron and the Fourfold Gospel," in Horton, ed., *The Earliest Gospels*, pp. 50-68) and Parker (*Living Text*, 22, 70) also endorse Bauer's position.

[193] F. Wisse, "The Use of Early Christian Literature as Evidence for Inner Diversity and Conflict," in C. Hedrick and R. Hodgson, Jr., eds., *Nag Hammadi, Gnosticism, and Early Christianity* (Peabody: Hendrickson, 1986), pp. 177-90.

and heretical). This is the reason many writings from this period are not as overtly polemical as later writings. He coins the term "orthocracy" to describe the early period. As the forerunner of orthodoxy, "orthocracy" developed on the basis of apostolic authority and church leadership; while orthodoxy only arose out of the increasing conflict between extreme heterodoxy (Gnosticism) and orthocracy. While this construct needs qualification in a number of areas (local variation is overemphasized and the mobility and interrelatedness of the early church unappreciated), it has much to recommend it. "Heterodoxy" as a term also carries too much baggage from the later period to encapsulate adequately the general naïveté of the earliest period. Clearly, fourth-century orthodoxy is at several removes from proto-orthodoxy or nascent "orthodoxy." But proto-orthodoxy seems to have preceded what was later termed heresy in Egypt and Syria,[194] and the idea that the church at Rome was able to stamp other centers with its particular form of Christianity cannot be substantiated.[195] As far as Egypt is concerned, Pearson observes, the "earliest papyri provide absolutely no support for Bauer's view that Gnosticism was the earliest and, for a long time, most dominant form of Christianity."[196]

Wisse, in affirming the position of the Alands, also restores some balance to the question of transmission. Working back from later evidence,[197] he objects to the idea that late second century orthodoxy imposed "an extensively interpolated 'standard' text," and successfully suppressed "all non-interpolated copies." He argues as follows.

1. If scribes had made changes freely before texts were considered "apostolic and authoritative," we might expect that NT writings for which "canonical status was long in doubt would have suffered more extensive and more serious textual corruption, but this is not the case."[198]

2. It appears interpolations for which there is textual evidence "increase

---

[194] Roberts, *Manuscript*, pp. 26-48; D. Bundy, "Christianity in Syria," in *ABD*, vol. 1, pp. 970-79. See also T. A. Robinson, *The Bauer Thesis Examined: the Geography of Heresy in the Early Christian Church* (Lewiston: Mellen, 1988). For further bibliography see D. J. Harrington, "The Reception of Walter Bauer's *Orthodoxy and Heresy in Earliest Christianity* During the Last Decade," *Harvard Theological Review* 73 (1980), pp. 289-98; M. R. Desjardins, "Bauer and Beyond: on Recent Scholarly Discussions of *hairesis* in the Early Christian Era," *Second Century* 8 (1991), pp. 65-82.

[195] L. W. Hurtado, *Lord Jesus Christ: Devotion to Jesus in Earliest Christianity* (Grand Rapids: Eerdmans, 2003), p. 521.

[196] B. A. Pearson, *Gnosticism and Christianity in Roman and Coptic Egypt* (New York: T. & T. Clark International, 2004), pp. 13-14. Cf. B. A. Pearson, "Pre-Valentinian Gnosticism in Alexandria," in B. A. Pearson et al., eds., *The Future of Early Christianity: Essays in Honor of Helmut Koester* (Minneapolis: Fortress Press, 1991), pp. 455-66; Pearson, "Christianity in Egypt," in *ABD*, vol. 1, pp. 954-60.

[197] F. Wisse, "The Nature of Redactional Changes in Early Christian Texts: The Canonical Gospels," in Petersen, *Gospel Traditions*, pp. 39-53. "Since there is no basis to assume that the early, poorly attested history of the transmission of the text was governed by factors different from those operative in the canonical period, the existing textual evidence may be taken to be indicative of the nature and purpose of redactional activity from the beginning" (p. 47).

[198] Unless otherwise indicated, what follows is based on Wisse, "Redactional Changes," pp. 44-45.

rather than decrease after the second century," and the main reason for that is frequency of copying.

3. "Long after the third century" the church was still not placed to "establish and control the biblical text, let alone eliminate rival forms of the text."

4. If there had been extensive redaction and interpolation, the "tenacity" of the textual tradition would both indicate that and ensure that the original readings were preserved.

According to the Alands, whenever a change was made to the NT text "there always continued to be a stream of the tradition (sometimes broad, sometimes narrow) that remained unaffected." On this basis they propose two reliable rules of transmission: (1) "every reading ever occurring in the New Testament textual tradition is stubbornly preserved, even if the result is nonsense"; and (2) when a major disturbance in transmission has occurred a profusion of variants will attest to that. Therefore, major disturbances in transmission "can always be identified with confidence." This leads to a further important conclusion: "where such a profusion of readings does *not* exist the text has not been disturbed but has developed *according to the normal rules*."[199]

Two major and several dozen minor interpolations to the gospels— defined as alterations to the text by the later addition of material—are discussed in Metzger's *Commentary*.[200] The two major additions are very well-known: the *pericope de adultera* (John 7:53–8:11) and the long ending of Mark (16:9-20). The former is the reading of D and the Byzantine text but is omitted by most other witnesses including $\mathfrak{P}^{66}$ $\mathfrak{P}^{75}$ ℵ B L N T Θ (and probably A C), the whole Syriac tradition and most Coptic MSS. The passage was known in the second century. According to Eusebius (*Hist. eccl.* 3.39.17), Papias recounted a story about a woman who was reproached for many sins before the Lord, a story that was also found in the *Gospel according to the Hebrews*. But the number of different places where the *pericope de adultera* is inserted in various MSS also supports the case for its exclusion.[201] In contrast, the long ending of Mark is found in the vast majority of Greek as well as some Latin, Syriac and Coptic MSS, and there is definite second century attestation in Irenaeus. But Mark ends at 16:8 in B and ℵ (and hypothetically, therefore, in the Alexandrian text represented by $\mathfrak{P}^{75}$); and Eusebius states that accurate copies of Mark which constitute the vast majority of MSS

---

[199] Aland and Aland, *Text*, pp. 295-96 (their emphasis). Cf. K. Aland, "Glosse, Interpolation, Redaktion und Komposition in der Sicht der neutestmentlichen Textkritik," in his *Studien zur Überlieferung des Neuen Testaments und seines Textes* (Berlin: de Gruyter, 1967), pp. 35-57.

[200] Mark 16:9-20 and John 7:53–8:11; Matt. 5:44; 6:13; 17:21; 18:11; 19:9; 20:16, 22-23; 21:44; 23:14; 25:13; 26:39; 27:35, 49; Mark 1:34; 2:16; 3:14; 7:7-8, 16; 9:44, 46; 10:21, 40; 11:26; 14:65; 15:28; Luke 1:28; 4:4; 8:43, 45; 10:22; 11:2-4, 11, 33; 12:21, 39; 15:21; 17:24, 36; 18:24; 22:19b-20; 23:17, 38, 53; 24:1-2, 12, 36, 40; John 1:51; 3:20, 31b-32; 8:59; 13:26. Some of these passages are also discussed by the Aland and Aland, *Text*, pp. 292-305.

[201] After John 7:36, 7:44, 21:25; Luke 21:38, 24:53: Metzger, *Commentary*, p. 221; Parker, *Living Text*, pp. 96, 100.

contain the short ending (the Eusebian sections also end at v. 8).[202] The difficulties created by the short ending—the post-resurrection appearance is only foretold, and the women flee in fear and say nothing to anyone (which has led some to suggest the autograph was damaged and broke off at this point)—apparently generated uncertainty that the long ending was designed to resolve.

There is also an intermediate ending, various combinations of all three endings, and one instance of an *even longer* long ending in W.[203] The fact that the short ending is also preserved in the Sinaitic Syriac syr[s], the Old Latin k (IV-V), at least one Sahidic MS (V), the earliest Georgian and many Armenian MSS, and the minuscule 304 (XII), while its originality is questioned in critical or marginal notes up to the sixteenth century, "is a striking example" of tenacity in the gospel MS tradition. Church tradition came to favor the long ending, but the short ending "could not be eradicated. It persisted stubbornly."[204] The long ending contains a summary account of resurrection appearances from the other gospels, a more radical admonition to evangelize than Matt. 28:19-20, and an ascension account. The non-Marcan vocabulary and style, the use of ἀναστὰς δέ at the beginning of v. 9 (more fitting for the beginning rather than the continuation of a narrative), and the repeated rhetorical emphasis on the disciples refusal to believe (not a significant preoccupation of 1:1–16:8) suggest that the passage was inserted in its entirety.[205]

It should be noted, however, that about 75% of interpolations are harmonizations to synoptic parallels, and their relatively low incidence is again indicative of "the conservative nature of the transmission process."[206] There is also a small group of readings that may be oral tradition and a number of interpretative glosses.[207] However, in comparison with the number of theologically motivated changes to the NT text estimated by Ehrman, Wisse lists only about a score of the more obvious with respect to the gospels.[208] Most are corrected by change or omission, not by interpolation. However, the Alands' assertion that "every reading ever occurring in the New Testament textual tradition is stubbornly preserved," should be qualified by reason of variants once widely attested but now poorly represented in the NT

---

[202] Parker, *Living Text*, p. 134.

[203] See Metzger, *Commentary*, pp. 122-26; Parker, *Living Text*, pp. 124-47.

[204] Aland and Aland, *Text*, p. 292.

[205] Metzger, *Commentary*, p. 125. For detailed analysis of the passage see J. A. Kelhoffer, *Miracle and Mission: the Authentication of Missionaries and their Message in the Longer Ending of Mark* (Tübingen: Mohr, 2000).

[206] This paragraph is based on Wisse, "Redactional Changes," pp. 48-51, unless otherwise noted.

[207] The *pericope de adultera* might also be a piece of oral tradition: see Metzger, *Commentary*, p. 188; Parker, *Living Text*, p. 101. According to Wisse, the verses in the latter category are Matt. 10:23; Mark 8:26; 9:49; 10:24; Luke 10:38; 22:62; John 2:3; 3:13; 7:46.

[208] Matt. 27:9; Mark 1:2; 3:21; 8:31; 10:13; 13:32; Luke 2:33, 41, 43, 48; 5:39; 22:43-44; 23:32; 24:51-52; John 7:8; 8:53. Ehrman argues that hundreds of changes may have resulted from christological debates (*Orthodox Corruption*, p. 46 n. 124), and "several hundred" from theological controversies generally ("Text as Window," p. 365).

MS tradition.[209] Occasionally as well, a variant widely attested in the Fathers may have been "removed" from the MS tradition.[210] Apart from this minor caveat, it still remains true that the gospel papyri "contribute virtually no new substantial variants."[211]

## H. Conclusion

This suggests that (1) virtually all variants "are preserved somewhere in our extant manuscript tradition"; and (2) they preserve "representatives of virtually all textual complexions."[212] However, as already mentioned, it is difficult to explain the early MSS against later developed text-types.[213] Instead of focussing on elusive textual clusters, the Alands differentiate between tendencies in transmission prior to the third/fourth century when they think text-types developed.[214] Though their "strict" ($\mathfrak{P}^{75}$), "normal," "free" ($\mathfrak{P}^{45}$, $\mathfrak{P}^{66}$), and "paraphrastic" (similar to the D-text)[215] classifications have been criticized,[216] they derive from thorough acquaintance with early gospel MSS. Because the early period was a developmental phase, B. Aland argues that individual readings of early MSS need to be analyzed for their reception of original readings rather than compared quantitatively to later MSS. This is a promising avenue for research, but it should not be conducted in isolation from early text-forms, particularly the Alexandrian text. A few more relationships like $\mathfrak{P}^{75}$ B might even indicate orderliness.[217] Furthermore, $\mathfrak{P}^{75}$ has confirmed Westcott and Hort's assessment of the quality of the B-text.

In the absence of conclusive proof it is methodologically unsound to assume that the first 150 years of textual transmission were characterized by heightened fluidity.[218] Scribes made changes, but the early gospel text was transmitted accurately *en bloc*. "Normal" and "strict" approaches to copying gainsay the contention that the high fluidity of early gospel MSS renders impossible the recovery of the "original" text. Instead, the earliest attainable gospel text should generally be very close to the autograph or "original" text as it existed at the end of the composition process and the beginning of the transmission process. Likewise, a few examples do not prove the existence of

---

[209] Aland and Aland, *Text*, pp. 295-96; M. W. Holmes, "The 'Majority Text Debate': New Form of an Old Question," *Themelios* 8 (1983), pp. 13-19, esp. p. 17.

[210] See, for example, the discussion of Heb. 2:9 in Zuntz, *Text*, pp. 34-35.

[211] Epp, "Significance," p. 101.

[212] Epp, "Significance," p. 101.

[213] Petzer, "History," p. 29.

[214] Aland and Aland, *Text*, pp. 50-51, 59, 64.

[215] For examples of "paraphrastic" (similar to the D-text) texts see Aland and Aland, *Text*, pp. 64, 93-95; cf. p. 69.

[216] See E. J. Epp, "New Testament Textual Criticism Past, Present, and Future: Reflections on the Alands' *Text of the New Testament*," *Harvard Theological Review* 82 (1989), pp. 224, 226.

[217] Epp, "Significance," p. 93.

[218] So Epp, "Variants," p. 295; Parker, *Living Text*, pp. 70, 88, 188, 200, 209; Koester, "Text of the Synoptic Gospels," p. 37.

"recensions" that antedate the gospel MS tradition;[219] and the Bauer hypothesis of a marginal proto-orthodoxy is undermined by the early gospel MSS themselves. Conventional approaches to MSS production, in terms of codex size and shared codicological features including a comprehensive approach to the contraction of *nomina sacra*, are indicative of both "standard" textual practices by c. 175 (when the importance of the written gospels for the life and faith of the church had already been recognized);[220] and also of an interconnected "catholic" church in the second half of the second century.

Finally, as regards text-critical methodology, there is "a remarkable degree of consensus,"[221] but a methodological impasse is evident in the lack of interest in textual theory.[222] Indeed, leading NT textual critics seem to have abandoned the possibility of theoretical advance. Clearly, further refinements in criteria are desirable and achievable. But there is also cause to be hopeful that a correct history of the early text can inform methodology and evaluation of readings; and there is no reason to believe that the gospel papyri have been exhausted in this regard. They may still be our "best hope of 'cracking' the textual "code" and breaking through to the original text"; but the question remains "exactly *how* are we to use them?"[223] The answer, in part at least, is to approach each *individual* MS holistically, as something much more than a source of readings. This will provide a wider frame of reference for making assessments about the textual worth of potential witnesses to the "original" text.

## Acknowledgements

I would like to thank M. W. Holmes, G. H. R. Horsley and W. F. Warren for their comments on drafts of this chapter.

---

[219] *Contra* Petersen, "What Text," pp. 149-50. See again the points marshaled against this view by Hurtado in section G.

[220] See my "Public and Private." Cf. G. N. Stanton, "The Early Reception of Matthew's Gospel: New Evidence from Papyri?" in D. A. Aune, ed., *The Gospel of Matthew in Current Study: Studies in Memory of William G. Thompson, S.J.* (Grand Rapids: Eerdmans, 2001), pp. 42-61.

[221] The key points and aspects of methodology can all be found in Zuntz: Holmes, "Reasoned Eclecticism," p. 344. Cf. M. W. Holmes, "*The Text of the Epistles* Sixty Years After: an Assessment of Günther Zuntz's Contribution to Text-Critical Methodology and History," in Childers and Parker, *Transmission and Reception*, pp. 89-113, for discussion of Zuntz's view of the history of the text in comparison with that of Westcott and Hort.

[222] Holmes, "Reasoned Eclecticism," p. 344. Most critics, with the notable exceptions of Epp and Petzer, are focussed on using methodology and not "analyzing or developing it" (p. 345).

[223] Epp, "Textual Criticism," p. 106.

# Bibliography

Aland, Kurt, and Barbara Aland. *The Text of the New Testament*. Translated by E. F. Rhodes, 2nd. edn. Grand Rapids: Eerdmans, 1989.

Aland, Barbara, and J. Delobel, eds. *New Testament Textual Criticism, Exegesis, and Early Church History: a Discussion of Methods*. Kampen: Pharos, 1994.

Black. D. A. ed. *Rethinking New Testament Textual Criticism*. Grand Rapids: Baker, 2002.

Cavallo G., and H. Maehler. *Greek Bookhands of the Early Byzantine Period A.D. 300–800*. London: Institute of Classical Studies, 1987.

Childers, J. W., and D. C. Parker, eds. *Transmission and Reception: New Testament Text-Critical and Exegetical Studies*. Piscataway: Gorgias Press, 2006.

Colwell, E. C. *Studies in Methodology in Textual Criticism of the New Testament*. Leiden: Brill, 1969.

Denaux, A. ed. *New Testament Textual Criticism and Exegesis: Festschrift J. Delobel*. Leuven: Leuven University Press, 2002.

Ehrman, Bart D. *The Orthodox Corruption of Scripture: The Effect of Early Christological Controversies on the Text of the New Testament*. 4th ed. New York: Oxford University Press, 2005.

Ehrman, Bart D., and M. W. Holmes, eds. *The Text of the New Testament in Contemporary Research: Essays on the Status Quaestionis: A Volume in Honor of Bruce M. Metzger*. Grand Rapids: Eerdmans, 1995.

Elliott, J. K. *Essays and Studies in New Testament Textual Criticism*. Cordoba: Ediciones El Almendro, 1992.

————. *A Bibliography of Greek New Testament Manuscripts*. 2nd edn. Cambridge: Cambridge University Press, 2000.

Epp, Eldon J., and G. D. Fee. *Studies in the Theory and Method of New Testament Textual Criticism*. Grand Rapids: Eerdmans, 1993.

Gamble, Harry Y. *Books and Readers in the Early Church: A History of Early Christian Texts*. New Haven: Yale University Press, 1995.

Horton, Charles, ed. *The Earliest Gospels: The Origins and Transmission of the Earliest Christian Gospels. The Contribution of the Chester Beatty Gospel Codex P45*. London/New York: T. & T. Clark International, 2004.

Hurtado, Larry W. *The Earliest Christian Artifacts: Manuscripts and Christian Origins*. Grand Rapids: Eerdmans, 2006.

Kilpatrick, G. D. *The Principles and Practice of New Testament Textual Criticism: Collected Essays of G. D. Kilpatrick*. Edited by J. K. Elliott. Leuven: Leuven University Press, 1990.

McKendrick S., and O. O'Sullivan, eds. *The Bible as Book: The Transmission of the Greek Text*. London: The British Library, 2003.

Metzger, Bruce Manning. *The Early Versions of the New Testament: Their Origin, Transmission, and Limitations*. Oxford: Clarendon Press, 1977.

————. *A Textual Commentary on the Greek New Testament: A Companion Volume to the United Bible Societies' Greek New Testament (Fourth Revised Edition)*. 2nd edn. Stuttgart: Deutsche Bibelgesellschaft/United Bible Societies, 1994.

Metzger, Bruce Manning, and Bart D. Ehrman. *The Text of the New Testament: Its Transmission, Corruption, and Restoration*, 4th edn. New York: Oxford University Press, 2005.

Parker, David C. *The Living Text of the Gospels*. Cambridge/New York: Cambridge University Press, 1997.

Petersen, William L. ed. *Gospel Traditions in the Second Century: Origins, Recensions, Text, and Transmission*. Notre Dame: University of Notre Dame Press, 1989.

Roberts, Colin H. *Manuscript, Society and Belief in Early Christian Egypt*. London/New York: Oxford University Press, 1979.

Roberts, Colin H., and T. C. Skeat. *The Birth of the Codex*. London/New York: Oxford

University Press, 1987.

Taylor, D. G. K. ed. *Studies in the Early Text of the Gospels and Acts: the Papers of the First Birmingham Colloquium on the Textual Criticism of the New Testament.* Birmingham: Birmingham University Press, 1999.

Westcott B. F., and F. J. A. Hort. *The New Testament in the Original Greek.* 2 vols. London: Macmillan, 1881.

# 3. The Language of the Gospels: Evidence from the Inscriptions and the Papyri

*Erica A. Mathieson*

Study of the language of the gospels, as of the rest of New Testament (NT), has a long history.[1] The oldest surviving lexica coincide with the development of the printing press. The first NT lexicon to include a number of English glosses to its Latin text was Edward Leigh's *Critica sacra*, published in 1639. Greek-English NT lexica, revisions and new editions of old works have appeared regularly from the 1800s to the present.[2] The history of the study of NT grammar tells a similar story, from G. Pasor's *Grammatica Græca sacra Novi Testamenti* of 1655 to contemporary contributions including works that focus on specific aspects of the language of the NT and those that offer a complete grammatical overview.[3]

Interest in the language of the gospels, witnessed by the rich scholarly output, derives from their status among Christians as sacred texts which, for many, are determinative of faith. Study of their grammar, that is, exploring the relationships among terms, and study of their vocabulary, that is, examining the terms themselves, are aspects of the quest for greater understanding of the meaning of the texts. Such critical analysis has sometimes sat in tension with belief in the divine inspiration, and in some Christian circles verbal inspiration, of the texts. Yet such study has produced a new appreciation of

---

[1] For the history of lexical study of the NT, see G. H. R. Horsley, "The Inscriptions of Ephesos and the New Testament," *Novum Testamentum* 34.2 (1992), pp. 105-68, here pp. 112-16; J. A. L. Lee, *A History of New Testament Lexicography* (New York: Peter Lang, 2003), pp. 3-190.

[2] For a chronological list of Greek NT lexica to 2000, see Lee, *New Testament Lexicography*, pp. 321-26. For useful NT lexica for students, see the bibliography of this chapter. See the bibliography also for texts which are not lexica but which draw on the papyri and inscriptions for NT vocabulary analysis.

[3] For a list of useful NT grammars, see the bibliography of this chapter. Some examples of specific studies include: Kenneth L. McKay, "Syntax and Exegesis," *Tyndale Bulletin* (1972), pp. 39-57; S. E. Porter, *Verbal Aspect in the Greek of the New Testament, with Reference to Tense and Mood* (New York: Peter Lang, 1989); Stanley E. Porter and D. A. Carson, *Biblical Greek Language and Linguistics: Open Questions in Current Research* (Sheffield: JSOT Press, 1993). A number of grammatical studies appear in G. H. R. Horsley and S. R. Llewelyn, *New Documents Illustrating Early Christianity* (Sydney: Ancient History Documentary Centre, Macquarie University, 1983–1997). Useful material for the study of NT grammar is contained in F. T. Gignac, *A Grammar of the Greek Papyri of the Roman and Byzantine Periods*, 2 vols. (Milan: Istituto Editoriale Cisalpino, 1976, 1981).

the nature of the language of the gospels and brought new insights into its meanings.

This chapter will explore the contribution of the documentary papyri and inscriptions to the study of the language of the gospels. My aim is to introduce readers to the field and provide a review of scholarship in both lexicography and grammatical analysis as it relates specifically to the gospels. The chapter also provides examples of the illustrative and elucidatory contribution of documentary texts drawing from contemporary and past research. Analysis of the contribution of documentary texts is set within the context of recent debates about the nature of the language of the gospels.

The documentary papyri are texts written in ink on parchment, wood, cloth, ostraca, wax tablets and other moveable items as well as papyrus. The documentary papyri are distinguished from literary papyri by their occasional nature.[4] Documentary papyri include personal, business and official letters; legal and commercial texts such as contracts, leases and loan agreements, marriage and divorce papers with details about dowry arrangements; and administrative documents such as petitions, the registration of births, deaths and landholdings, and tax receipts. The majority of papyri come from Egypt, surviving because of the dryness of the climate. A relatively few documentary papyri have also been found in Palestine, Herculaneum and Britain. Inscriptions are texts carved in stone, jewels or on lead, and include public notices, decrees, honorary and epigraphic texts. Inscriptions are drawn from all over the Mediterranean world and have proved invaluable in demonstrating the essential homogeneity of the *koine*[5] across the wide geographic, ethnic and cultural diversity of the Roman Empire.

Given that this chapter examines the contribution of documentary texts to an understanding of the language of the gospels, the focus is on texts written in the period from the third century BC to the third century AD. This period gives priority to synchronic evidence for language usage[6] and recognizes, on the one hand, the developments in the Greek language from the classical to the Hellenistic periods, and, on the other, the greater likelihood of influence from the gospels and other NT writings on the language of documentary texts following the accession of Constantine in the early fourth century. For this reason, too, the evidence of texts that are classified as "Christian" is generally excluded from analysis. In such texts it is uncertain whether the language of

---

[4] On the papyri in general, see E. G. Turner, *Greek Papyri: an Introduction* (Princeton: Princeton University Press, 1968); R. S. Bagnall, *Reading Papyri, Writing Ancient History* (New York: Routledge, 1995). For texts that focus on the interrelation between the language of the papyri and the gospels and NT, see the bibliography of this chapter.

[5] The *koine* refers chronologically to all Greek language from late IV BC and Alexander the Great through to the end of VI AD at which time Byzantine Greek dominates.

[6] This synchronic methodology does not to deny the value of diachronic studies in language study. Indeed there is a recognition among modern linguists of the potential value of analyzing Greek usage in both earlier and later periods in determining the meaning of words and syntactical forms in the gospels; see, for example, G. P. Shipp, *Modern Greek Evidence for Ancient Greek Vocabulary* (Sydney: Sydney University Press, 1979). On synchronic and diachronic methodologies in lexicography, see F. de Saussure, *Cours de linguistique général* (Paris: Payot, 1915), pp. 141-260, who first made the distinction.

the gospels has influenced the writers' linguistic choices.

The value of inscriptional evidence to study of the language of the gospels and other NT writings was realized early[7] but has received little attention in more recent years.[8] A problem that regularly limits its usefulness is the difficulty in dating epigraphic texts. The results of the early studies in this field have been incorporated into MM and BDAG.

Study of the contribution of the documentary papyri to an understanding of the language of the gospels owes much to the work of Adolf Deissmann[9] who wrote at the turn of the nineteenth and twentieth centuries in the years immediately after the first systematic publication of the papyri.[10] Deissmann recognized the potential of the papyri to illustrate gospel, NT and Septuagint (LXX) language. His approach found fresh expression in the work of J. H. Moulton and G. Milligan.[11] Other scholars have incorporated the methodology to different extents in their writings.[12] The documentary texts and their relationship to the language of the gospels and the rest of the NT are the focus of the *New Documents* series. The vast number of new papyri published since MM, offering new examples of NT vocabulary, led G. H. R. Horsley and J. A. L. Lee to embark on the production of a new lexicon of NT Greek of which *New Documents* is a forerunner.[13]

---

[7] E. Nachmanson, *Laute und Formen der magnetischen Inschriften* (Uppsala: Almqvist & Wiksells, 1903); P. E. G. Thieme, *Die Inschriften von Magnesia am Mäander und das Neue Testament* (Gottingen: Vandenhoeck und Ruprecht: 1906; J. Rouffiac, *Recherches sur les caractères du grec dans le Nouveau Testament d'après les inscriptions de Priène* (Paris: Ernest Leroux, 1911).

[8] But see F. W. Danker, *Benefactor: Epigraphic Study of a Graeco-Roman and NT Semantic Field* (St Louis: Clayton, 1982); Horsley, "The Inscriptions of Ephesos and the New Testament," pp. 105-68.

[9] A. Deissmann, *Bible Studies: Contributions Chiefly from Papyri and Inscriptions to the History of the Language, the Literature, and the Religion of Hellenistic Judaism and Primitive Christianity* (Edinburgh: T. & T. Clark, 1901); A. Deissmann, *Light from the Ancient East: The New Testament Illustrated by Recently Discovered Texts of the Graeco-Roman World* (London: Hodder & Stoughton, 1927).

[10] The first papyrus was published in Europe in 1778, re-edited as *SB* 1.5124 (AD 193). Systematic publication began at the end of nineteenth century, for example B. P. Grenfell and A. S. Hunt, *Oxyrhynchus Papyri*, vol. 1 (London: Egypt Exploration Fund, 1898).

[11] For example, J. H. Moulton, *Grammar of New Testament Greek*, vol. 1 (Edinburgh: T. & T. Clark, 1908); J. H. Moulton, "Grammatical Notes from the Papyri," *Expositor* 6th series, vol. 3 (1901), pp. 271-82; vol 7 (1903), pp. 104-21; vol. 8 (1904), pp. 423-39; *Classical Review* (1901), pp. 31-37; 434-41; (1904), pp. 106-12; 151-55; MM.

[12] For example, James Barr, *The Semantics of Biblical Language* (Oxford: Oxford University Press, 1961); BAGD/BDAG.

[13] For a preliminary statement of the form, scope and need for a new lexicon see G. H. R. Horsley "The Greek Documentary Evidence and NT Lexical Study: Some Soundings," in Horsley and Llewelyn, eds., *New Documents*, vol. 5, pp. 67-93; J. A. L. Lee and G. H. R. Horsley, "A Lexicon of the New Testament with Documentary Parallels: Some Interim Entries, I" *Filologia Neotestamentaria* 10 (1997), pp. 55-84; G. H. R. Horsley and J. A. L. Lee, "A Lexicon of the New Testament with Documentary Parallels: Some Interim Entries, 2," *Filologia Neotestamentaria* 11 (1998), pp. 57-84; G. H. R. Horsley, "Towards a Lexicon of the New Testament with Documentary Parallels," in I. Andorlini et al., eds., *Atti del XXII congresso internazionale di papirologia*, vol. 1 (Florence: Istituto Papirologico G. Vitelli, 2001), pp. 655-67. See also C. J. Hemer, "Towards a New Moulton and Milligan," *Novum Testamentum* 24

The work of these scholars indicates that the contribution the documentary papyri and inscriptions make to gospel-language study is multifaceted. It demonstrates that the language of the gospels is an integral part of the *koine* and not, as some have thought, a "special" dialect of it. The documentary texts confirm the importance of taking account of "register" in language, that is, the way language varies according to its social setting and purpose. They reveal that the *koine* exists along a continuum from a literary level of language to the vernacular with no clear division between them. Indeed, both literary texts and documentary texts show variation in linguistic register in themselves. The papyri and inscriptions exhibit the full range of linguistic registers. The recognition of registers has proved useful in analyzing the language of the gospels which also use a range of registers, from Matthew and Luke's more literary style to Mark and John's greater use of more vernacular features. The construction of different registers within each of the Gospels has been found to function to make theological points. It is a mistake to think that the language of the gospels, as of the documentary texts, is a unity.

Analysis of the contribution of the documentary papyri and inscriptions to an understanding of the language of the gospels has been facilitated by the computerized publication of the *Duke Databank of Documentary Papyri (DDBDP)*.[14] Its published texts are supplemented by *Wörterlisten aus den Registern von Publikationen griechischer und latinischer dokumentarischer Papyri und Ostraka* (WL).[15] Inscriptions can be searched on CD-ROM <PHI 7> and on the Cornell University's epigraphical database.[16] These electronic sources enable searches of published documentary texts for Greek words and word groups. The availability of the gospels in Greek on the *Thesaurus Linguae Graecae*[17] and a number of web sites[18] makes the kind of language analysis involved in this chapter and in the works of recent scholars possible.

The strand of scholarship emphasizing documentary texts as a source for gospel-language study and represented by such writers as Deissmann, Moulton and Horsley stands alongside the understanding of the language of the gospels as unique or special Greek. Nigel Turner, for example, considers papyrology and epigraphy to have only a small and marginal contribution to make to study of the gospels in comparison to Semitic influences.[19] Turner

---

(1982), pp. 97-123.

[14] http://www.perseus.tufts.edu/Texts/papyri.html. Also available as CD-ROM <PHI 7> produced by the Packard Humanities Institute. The CD-ROM includes most inscriptions published to 1996 as well as the Duke Database of Documentary Papyri. The original published editions of papyri are consulted because of minor errors in the DDBDP and because it is not always clear what is reconstructed text and what survives on the papyrus.

[15] http://www.iaw.uni-heidelberg.de/hps/pap/WL/WL.pdf (accessed 5 May 2008).

[16] http://epigraphy.packhum.org/inscriptions/search_main.html (accessed 5 May 2008).

[17] M. C. Pantella, ed., *Thesaurus Linguae Graecae* (1999), CD ROM E.

[18] For example, http://www-users.cs.york.ac.uk/~fisher/gnt/; and http://stephanus.tlg.uci.edu/inst/fontsel (accessed 5 May 2008).

[19] N. Turner, *Grammatical Insights into the New Testament* (Edinburgh: T. & T. Clark, 1965); N. Turner, *Grammar of New Testament Greek*, vols. 3, 4 (Edinburgh: T. & T. Clark, 1963, 1976); N. Turner, "The Quality of the Greek of Luke-Acts," in J. K. Elliott, ed., *Studies in*

consistently refers to the language of the gospels and other NT books as "special Greek" and "Jewish Greek."[20] This position had a major influence on linguistic study for much of the twentieth century,[21] determined more perhaps by theological considerations than linguistic ones.[22] It is not the argument of this chapter that Semitic influence did not occur but that it did not give rise to a distinct "NT Greek." With renewed interest in the approach of Deissmann and Moulton, the weight given to Greco-Roman and Semitic influences on the Evangelists has achieved a greater balance. Documentary evidence has brought the gospels and the NT in general out of the linguistic isolation that has dominated the field in much of the twentieth century.[23]

In his *Bible Studies*, Deissmann was among the first to examine critically supposed Semitisms[24] in the Greek Bible, specifically Hebraisms. He notes a problem with the theory of Semitic influence in that so-called Semitic irregularities are widely scattered in the gospels and in texts with no Semitic connection. He finds documentary parallels for numbers of these "irregularities,"[25] thereby locating them in the *koine*, as does Horsley in the

---

*New Testament Language and Text: Essays in Honour of George D. Kilpatrick on the Occasion of his Sixty-fifth Birthday*, (Leiden: Brill, 1976), pp. 387-400.

[20] Turner, *Grammatical Insights*, pp. 174-88; Turner, *Grammar of NT Greek*, vol. 3, pp. 1-9. A similar trend is evident in R. E. Brown, ed., *New International Dictionary of New Testament Theology*, 3 vols. (Grand Rapids: Zondervan, 1975–1978) which gives little place to the evidence of documentary texts and greater emphasis to Semitic influences. The same is true of TDNT.

[21] For example A. D. Nock, "The Vocabulary of the New Testament," *Journal of Biblical Literature* 52, nos. 2, 3 (1933), pp. 131-39; Moule, *An Idiom Book of New Testament Greek*, pp. 171-91; M. Black, *An Aramaic Approach to the Gospels and Acts* (Oxford: Clarendon, 1967); E. E. Ellis and M. Wilcox, eds., *Neotestamentica et semitica: Studies in Honour of Matthew Black* (Edinburgh: T. & T. Clark, 1969).

[22] Horsley and Llewelyn, eds., *New Documents*, vol. 5, p. 40.

[23] See G. H. R. Horsley, "The Fiction of Jewish Greek," in Horsley and Llewelyn, eds., *New Documents*, vol. 5, pp. 5-40.

[24] Semitisms refer to words and constructions that do not reflect normal Greek usage but can be explained by normal Semitic usage.

[25] Examples from the gospels include ὑποζύγιον, meaning "ass," borrowed from the LXX (Matt. 21:5) in P.Flind. Petr. 2.22 (Ptolemaic) [= P.Petr. 3.26.5 (c. 240 BC)]; P.Flind. Petr. 2.25.d [= P.Petr. 2.25.Fr.D.3] (late III BC), Deissmann, *Bible Studies*, pp. 160-61, also in P.Cair.Zen. 1.59075.4 (257 BC), Deissmann, *Light from the Ancient East*, p. 162, and since Deissmann, for example P.Hib. 1.34.Fr.A-B.3, 5 (243–242 BC); 1.73.9 (243-242 BC); εἰς for the purpose of donations and expenditure instead of a dative (Mark 8:19-20) in BGU 1.34.10, 30 (? [IV AD]); PER 1.11 (AD 83-84); IPergamon 553 (early II AD); 554 (after AD 105), Deissmann, *Bible Studies*, pp. 195-96, and since Deissmann, for example, P.Amh. 2.55.4 (176 or 165 BC); P.Oxy. 2.275.19 (AD 66); ἐρωτάω, meaning "request," (for example, Matt. 15:23; Luke 7:3; 14:32; John 4:31; 12:21; 14:16) in SIG 328.5 (84 BC); P.Oxy. 2.292.7 (AD 25); BGU 1.50.9 (AD 115); BGU 2.423 (II AD) [= Chres.Wilck. 480.11 (AD 139/40)]; BGU 2.417.2-3 (II/III), *Bible Studies*, pp. 195-96, and since Deissmann for example, SIG 2.705.58 (112 BC); P.Oxy. 4.744.6,13 (1 BC); P.Oxy. 2.292.7 (AD 25); P.Ryl.2. 229.8 (AD 38); ἐνώπιον, as a preposition meaning "in the presence of," (for example Luke 5:18; 13:26; 24:43 and nineteen other occurrences; John 20:30) in P.Hib. 1.30.25 (before 271 BC); P.Tebt. 1.14.18 (AD 114); BGU 2.578 (AD 189), [= Chres.Mitt. 227.1), Deissmann, *Bible Studies*, p. 213, and since Deissmann, for example, P.Cair.Zen. 1.59073.14 (257 BC); P.Grenf. 1.38.11 (170 BC); P.Oxy.4. 658.9 (AD 250).

*New Documents* series.[26] E. C. Colwell also has questioned the hypothesis of "Jewish Greek" as an explanatory device for some peculiarities of the language of the gospels.[27] For example, he has examined the use of ῥακά, "fool," in Matt. 5:22. The word has long puzzled scholars and has been explained by a majority as the Greek transliteration of an Aramaic word *reqa* (רקא) meaning "empty" and "vain"[28] although the vocalization of the word is problematic. Colwell notes that C. C. Edgar, in editing the Zenon papyri, identified a letter from Amyntas to Apollonios, 2.7-8 (257 BC)[29] stating ἐὰν οὖν οἱ περὶ Ἀντίοχον τὸν ῥαχᾶν ἐνοχλῶσίν σε, "so, if the associates of Antiochus, the braggart, annoy you. . ." Amyntas is known for his colorful language. Edgar comments on the similarity of ῥαχά to ῥακά in Matt. 5:22, and the similarity in function and denotation as an uncomplimentary epithet. A problem in accepting this as a parallel occurrence in a documentary text is the difference in spelling, but a majority of the earliest manuscripts spell the word in Matt. 5:22 with *chi*, and given the shifts between *chi* and *kappa* in the *koine*,[30] the Greek ῥαχά appears likely to be the same word, and its appearance in the Zenon papyrus to be an illustrative example from the papyri of the use in Matthew's Gospel. In Horsley's essay, "The Fiction of 'Jewish-Greek,'"[31] he, like Deissmann before him, does not deny the influence of Aramaic and Hebrew on the Greek of the gospels but argues that it can be attributed to Greek/Aramaic bilingualism in Palestine of the Roman period and to the "interference" of one language on another, but without constituting a separate "NT Greek" dialect.

Deissmann also begins the critical discussion of the emphasis placed by some commentators on supposed *hapax legomena* in the gospels even of terms without religious reference, as witness to the "specialness" of the

---

[26] For example, οὐρανός "heaven" as a periphrasis for god/the gods, Luke 15:18, 21 and the frequent βασιλεία τῶν οὐρανῶν, "kingdom of heaven," for example Matt. 13:11, 24, 31, explained as a Semitism, occurs in the non-Jewish and non-Christian epigraph *Belleten* 42 (1978), pp. 402-5 (III or IV AD) and republished in Horsley and Llewelyn, eds., *New Documents*, vol. 3, pp. 49-50; the imperative use of ἵνα in Mark 5.23, explained as a Semitism, has a documentary parallel in P.Oxy. 46.3314.16 (IV AD) republished in Horsley and Llewelyn, eds., *New Documents*, vol. 3, p. 148. B. G. Mandilaras, *The Verb in the Greek Non-literary Papyri* (Athens: Ministry of Culture and Sciences, 1973), pp. 585-89, lists earlier examples, P.Hib. 1.207.16 (260–245 BC); P.Petr. 2.4.1.5-6 (255–254 BC) [= *SB* 18.13881]; P.Oxy. 14.1762.11-13 (II-III C). Similarly Horsley and Llewelyn, eds., *New Documents*, vol. 6, p. 183 notes a documentary occurrence of εἰ introducing a direct question, once taken as a Semitism in Matt. 12:10; 19:3; Mark 8:23; Luke 13:23; 22:49, in P.Nag.Ham. 72.12 (AD 348). The text is a letter from Proteria to two monks asking for chaff. The date is late but construction is unlikely to reflect biblical influence. See also Index 3, Horsley and Llewelyn, eds., *New Documents*, vol. 5, p. 175, s.v. "Semitisms" for other examples of proposed Semitic influence now located in the *koine*.

[27] E. C. Colwell, "Has *raka* a Parallel in the Papyri," *Journal of Biblical Literature* 53, no. 4 (1934), pp. 351-54.

[28] For example, MM, ῥακά, s.v.

[29] *A New Group of the Zenon Papyri* (repr. from the *Bulletin of the John Rylands Library*, vol. 18.1 [1934]) (Manchester: John Rylands Library, 1934).

[30] Gignac, *A Grammar of the Greek Papyri*, vol. 1, p. 86.

[31] Horsley and Llewelyn, eds., *New Documents*, vol. 5, pp. 5-40.

language. He demonstrates, for example, that ὀφειλή, "debt," once considered peculiar to "NT Greek",[32] is regularly used in the papyri with the sense of indebtedness that is found in Matt. 18:32.[33] For example, BGU 1.112, l.11 (c. AD 60) uses the phrase καθαρὰ ἀπό τε ὀφιλῆς, "free from debt."[34] An example of σουδάριον, "handkerchief," in Luke 19:20; John 11:44; 20:7, occurs in PER 21.19 (AD 230), a marriage contract detailing the contents of a dowry.[35] Horsley lists fifteen words from the gospels among sixty across the NT, treated in the previous volumes of the series, for which documentary parallels have been found[36] in addition to the approximately 5,100 for which parallels already exist in MM, leaving only some 500 words for which documentary parallels are yet to be recorded.

To illustrate the contribution a documentary text can make to study of the language of the gospels, I now turn to P.Oxy. 46.3313 (II AD) which offers both lexical and grammatical parallels to gospel texts. The text supports the argument that shared language between the gospels and documentary texts is to be expected as parts of the one *koine*, and that documentary occurrences serve to illustrate and elucidate the meanings of terms and constructions in the gospels.

```
1     Ἀπολ[λώνι]ος καὶ Σαραπιὰς Διονυσίᾳ
                          (vac.)              χαίρειν
      χαρ[ᾶς ἡμ]ᾶς ἐπλήρωσας εὐαγγελισαμένη
      τὸν γ[άμον] τοῦ κρατίστου Σαραπίωνος καὶ εὐθέως
5     ἂν ἦλθ[ομ]εν διακονήσοντες αὐτῷ ὡς ἐν εὐκταιστάτῃ
      ἡμῖν ἡμ[έ]ρα καὶ συνευφρανθησόμενοι, ἀλλὰ διὰ τὸν
      δι[αλο]γισμὸν καὶ ὅτι ἀναλαμβάνομεν ἀπὸ νωθρείας
      οὐκ ἠδυνήθημεν ἐλθεῖν. ῥόδα πολλὰ οὔπω γέγο-
      νεν ἐνθάδε, ἀλλὰ σπανίζει, καὶ ἐκ πάντων
10    τῶν κτημάτων καὶ παρὰ πάντων τῶν στεφανη-
      πλόκων μόλις ἠδυνήθημεν συλλέξαι ἃ ἐπέμ-
      ψαμέν σοι διὰ Σαραπᾶ χείλια, τρυγηθέντων καὶ
      ὧν ἔδει αὔριον τρυγηθῆναι. νάρκισσον ὅσην ἤθε-
      λες εἴχομ‘εν’, ὅθεν ἀντὶ ὧ ἔγραψας δισχειλίων
15    τετρακισχειλίαν ἐπέμψα‘μεν’. οὐ βουλόμε‘θα’ δέ σε
      οὕτως κ[ατ]αγεινώσκειν ἡμῶν ὡς μεικρολόγων
```

---

[32] For example, H. Cremer, W. Urwick, trans., *Biblico-theological Lexicon of New Testament Greek*, 4th ed. (Edinburgh: T & T Clark, 1895), p. 737.

[33] The word also occurs in Rom. 13:7; 1 Cor. 7:3.

[34] The same phrase occurs in BGU 1.184.25 (AD 72); PER 220.10 (I); BGU 2.536.6-7 (II/III [81-96]), Deissmann, *Bible Studies*, p. 221. See also BGU 4.1158 18 (9 BC); P.Oxy. 2.286.18 (AD 82). Other documentary parallels are given in MM, s.v.

[35] Again in a marriage contract, PER 27.7-8 (AD 190), reconstructed, Deissmann, *Bible Studies*, p. 223; also in a magical text, P.Lond. 1.121.826 (III AD).

[36] Horsley and Llewelyn, eds., *New Documents*, vol. 5, pp. 87-89. For example, ἄγρα "catch/draught" Luke 5:4, 9, in P.Oxy. 46.3269.1 (III) (Horsley and Llewelyn, eds., *New Documents*, vol. 3, pp. 16-17); αἰών "age" Matt. 12:32 with 29 additional occurrences across all gospels, in P.Oxy. 42.3065.8 (III) (Horsley and Llewelyn, eds., *New Documents*, vol. 4, p. 58). Horsley notes that it is not possible to determine whether the omission of the approximately 500 NT words from MM was because of a lack of documentary parallels or through oversight.

ὥστε καταγελῶσαν γράψαι πεπομφέναι τὴν
τιμήν, ὁπότε καὶ ἡμεῖς ἔχομεν τὰ παιδία
ὡς ἴδια τέκνα καὶ πλέον τῶν ἡμῶν τιμῶμεν
20     καὶ ἀγαπῶμεν αὐτὰ καὶ οὕτως χαίρομεν ἴσα
σοι καὶ [τ]ῷ πατρὶ αὐτῶν. περὶ ὧν ἄλλων θέλεις
γρ[ά]ψο[ν ἡμ ]ῖν. ἄσπασα[ι] ᾿Αλέξανδρον τὸν
κράτιστον καὶ τοὺς ἀβασκάντους ῾αὐτοῦ᾿ Σαραππίωνα
καὶ Θέωνα καὶ ᾿Αριστόκλειαν καὶ τὰ τέκνα
25     ᾿Αριστοκλείας. μαρτυρήσει σοι Σαραπᾶς περὶ τῶν ῥόδων ὅτι πάντα πεποίηκα εἰς τὸ
ὅσα ἤθελες πέμψαι σοι, ἀλλὰ οὐχ εὕρο[[ν]]μεν.
         (m.2) ἐρρῶσθαί σε εὐχόμεθα, κυρία.
verso (m.1) Διονυσίᾳ γυναικὶ (vac.) ᾿Αλεξάνδρου

Apollonios and Sarapias to Dionysia, greeting. You filled us with joy when
you announced the good news of the marriage of the most noble Sarapion and
immediately we wanted to come to render some service to him as on a day
very much prayed for by us and join in rejoicing. But because of the judicial
inquiry and since we are recovering from sickness we were not able to come.
There have not been many roses here yet; on the contrary they are scarce.
Indeed from all the estates and from all the garland-weavers we could only
just gather the thousand we sent to you by Sarapas' hand; some even of what
we picked ought to have been picked the next day. We had as much narcissus
as you wanted whence instead of the two thousand you wrote for we sent four
thousand. And we do not want you to condemn us as tight-fisted so that you
write mocking that you have sent their value, when we also hold the young
ones as our own children and esteem and love them more than ours and so
rejoice equally as you and their father. About the other things you want, write
to us. Greet the most noble Alexander and—may the evil eye not touch
them—his Sarapion and Theon and Aristoklia and Aristoklia's children.
Sarapas will testify to you about the roses that I have done everything in
order to send you as many as you wanted but we could not find them.

(m.2) We pray you be well, lady.
Verso (m.1) To Dionysia wife of Alexander.[37]

     This personal letter from Apollonios and Sarapias to Dionysia contains a
number of words and phrases that are significant in the gospels. It has raised
the possibility that this text may be an early Christian letter[38] but given its date
the common words are not sufficient to allow such a classification. Further
there are no overtly Christian elements in the letter, and the use of
ἀβάσκαντος in 1.23, while not excluding a Christian classification, argues
against it.[39]

---

[37] Author's translation.
[38] E. A. Judge, *Rank and Status in the World of the Caesars and St Paul* (Christchurch:
University of Canterbury, 1982), pp. 24-26, notes the possibility and argues against it.
[39] The *abaskantos* formula occurs in certainly Christian letters, e.g. P.Mich. 8.519 (IV) with
χμγ; PSI 8.972 = *SB* 12.10841 (IV) with *nomina sacra*; P.Wisc. 2.76 (IV) with ἐν θεῷ "in

Apollonios and Sarapias refer to χαρ[ᾶς ἡμ]ᾶς ἐπλήρωσας "having been filled with joy," l.3. The phrase offers a documentary parallel to similar expressions in John's Gospel, most notably John 3:29, where John the Baptist says, in recognition of Jesus the bridegroom, ἡ χαρὰ ἡ ἐμὴ πεπλήρωται "my joy has been fulfilled," that is, in the context of a wedding[40]: the phrase has no parallels in the Synoptic Gospels but occurs elsewhere in the NT five times.[41] The phrase is not attested elsewhere in the papyri in the period although a similar expression μετὰ τῆς πλείστης ⟦χαρᾶς⟧ σπουδῆς ⟦προθυμίας τε⟧ καὶ χαρᾶς "with the greatest zeal and joy" is found in an official document, BGU 8.1768.7 (I BC), and parallel phrases occur in literary texts.[42] The pattern of occurrences suggests that the expression belongs to a relatively high register of language and, at the same time, that "fullness of joy" and "being filled with joy" are not unknown in common language. It is noteworthy that in John's Gospel, ἡ χαρὰ ἡ ἐμὴ πεπλήρωται and similar phases occur exclusively in relation to Jesus, either in his own speech or in reference to him. The focused use supports the findings of J. A. L. Lee on the use of language in Jesus' speech in Mark's Gospel, that the writers of the gospels give Jesus language of a relatively high register as is appropriate to his identity.[43] With the hyperbolic protestations of affection and the banter about payment and miserliness in Apollonios and Sarapias' letter, the choice of χαρ[ᾶς ἡμ]ᾶς ἐπλήρωσας may be part of the affectionate "status games" suggested in it.

The occurrence of χαρ[ᾶς ἡμ]ᾶς ἐπλήρωσας (l.3) in the letter indicates the context in common life, already signaled in John 3:29, which provides the content for the nature of the joy being discussed in John's Gospel: the joy of a wedding. The gospels' frequent use of weddings as a metaphor for the kingdom of God, with Jesus as the bridegroom, find their imaginative *locus* in documentary texts such as this.

Of interest also from the letter in relation to the language of the gospels is the verb εὐαγγελίζομαι, "announce good news." Apollonios and Sarapias write that their fullness of joy arises because Dionysia "has announced the good news of the wedding of the most noble Sarapion" (εὐαγγελισαμένη τὸν γάμον του κρατίστου Σαραπίωνος, ll.3-4).[44] The middle verb occurs in the gospels only in Luke's Gospel and there, eight times,[45] always in reference to

---

God"; P.Oxy. 20.2276 (III/IV) with ἐν κυρίῳ θεῷ "in the Lord God." See M. Naldini, *Il cristianesimo in Egitto: lettere private nei papiri dei secoli II-IV*, 2nd ed. (Florence: Le Monnier, 1968, 1998), p. 279; Horsley and Llewelyn, eds., *New Documents*, vol. 1, p. 70.

[40] Reference to being filled with joy occurs elsewhere in John's Gospel at 15:11, "so that my joy may be in you and your joy may be fulfilled" (ἵνα ἡ χαρὰ ἡ ἐμη ἐν ὑμῖν ᾖ καὶ ἡ χαρα ὑμῶν πληρωθῇ); also 16:24; 17:13.

[41] Acts 13:52; Phil. 2:2; 2 Tim. 1:4; 1 John 1:4; 2 John 12.

[42] Josephus, *Ant.* 15.421; *Diogn.* 10.3; *Let. Arist.* 261, 294; Philo, *Mos.* 1.177.

[43] J. A. L. Lee, "Some Features of the Speech of Jesus in Mark's Gospel," *Novum Testamentum* 27, no. 1 (1985), pp. 1-26. Lee argues that the formal aspects of Jesus' speech are not due to later Atticizing correction but were chosen by the writers to reflect Jesus' status.

[44] The phrase τὸν γάμον εὐηγγελίζετο occurs in Longus, *Daphnis and Chloe* 3.33.

[45] Luke 3:18; 4:18, 43; 8:1; 9:6; 20:1.

the "good news" of salvation, for example, in Luke 1:19 and 2:10 to announce the good news of the birth of John the Baptist and Jesus. With reference also to salvation, the passive occurs in Matt. 11:5; Luke 7:22; 16:16. The verb is absent from the other gospels although the word group occurs elsewhere in the NT.[46] The verb is infrequent in documentary texts. It occurs in the period, in addition to this letter, only in *IGRR* 4.1756 (I BC) of Augustus' son attaining manhood[47] and in P.Giss. 27 = P.Giss.Apoll. 9 (c. AD 115) of the announcement of victory during the Jewish revolt.[48] The noun is more frequent in both singular and plural forms in documentary texts where it is used of the announcement of imperial benefactions and victories.[49] The pattern of occurrences in the documentary texts suggests that the word group belongs in contexts that use a higher register of language as is consistent with Apollonios and Sarapias' exalted style. In the gospels, the pattern discernable in the documentary material suggests that the writers chose a word they considered of suitably high style for the announcement of salvation won by Christ, particularly with his connotations of kingship which parallel the documentary use of εὐαγγελίζω / εὐαγγελίζομαι in relation to imperial matters.

Apollonios and Sarapias refer to Sarapion and his father Alexander as κράτιστος, ll.4, 22–23. The adjective functions as an honorific title of respect, "most noble / most excellent," that is extremely frequent among documentary texts in the period AD 100–300, occurring more than 1,000 times. It does not occur qualifying people or gods, but only things, in the period BC but appears in the first century twenty-four times describing people of high status and occurs always with a title, for example, the ἡγεμών "ruler/prefect" in BGU 1.112.7 (AD 60/1), the ἐπίτροπος ("governor") in P.Hib. 2.215.FrA.4 (AD 17–130) and the ἀρχιπροφήτης ("chief prophet") in P.Gen. 1.7.5 (AD 86).[50] It occurs with a name and no title only once, in a formal document, P.Oxy. 45.3240.10 (c. AD 88/89), with a reference to Vegetos, but he is otherwise known to be a prefect. The use then in this text with a name and no title is unusual but offers a parallel to Luke 1:3. Evidence from inscriptions about the use of the word is difficult to evaluate with few instances being securely dated in the period. However, in I.PrusiasHyp. 22.1.7 Agrippa is called κράτιστος. Given the apparent status of the characters in P.Oxy. 46.3313, use of the word

---

[46] The middle εὐαγγελίζομαι is regular, also, in the rest of the NT, particularly frequent in Acts occurring thirteen times, fourteen times in the Pauline corpus and twice in 1 Peter but not elsewhere; see BDAG, s.v. The noun εὐαγγέλιον occurs in Matthew and most frequently in Mark but not otherwise in the gospels.

[47] In the passive, εὐαγγελίσθη ἡ πόλις ("the city received the good tidings").

[48] τιν[ὶ] παιδαρίῳ ἐρχομένῳ εὐαγγελίζοντι τὰ τῆς νείκης αὐτοῦ καὶ προκοπῆς ("to whichever child comes and receives the good news of his victory and progress" l.6).

[49] εὐαγγέλιον, for example, I.Priene 105.40-41 (9 BC); *SB* 1.421.2 (c. AD 240); εὐαγγέλια, for example, *SEG* 1.362.7-8 (306 BC); *IG* II 1224 (c. 166 BC); *IG* VII 417.68 (1 BC); *IGRR* 4 860 (I AD).

[50] A number of inscriptions use κράτιστος of benefactors, doctors, virginal women, imperial officers and as a status marker, possibly the equivalent of a *vir egregius* but the date of these inscriptions is uncertain; see *I.Klaudiop* 23.4; 29.5, both referring to women; *I.Eph.* 27A.76 (AD 104) where the word occurs with "benefactor."

by Apollonios and Sarapias conforms to its reference to someone of high status but not necessarily an official. It confirms Theophilus (see Luke 1:3) of whom the superlative adjective is used—σοι γράψαι, κράτιστε Θεόφιλε, "to write to you, most excellent Theophilos"—as also of high status, but his rank as an official remains uncertain. Κράτιστος comes to be used of people of lower or indeterminate status towards the end of the period, for example, in P.Oxy. 40.2925.3 (AD 270–275) and P.Stras. 1.6.3 (AD 255–261), where the adjective is again attached to a personal name of unknown or lower status, but such use is a later debasement of the word.

Also of interest in this letter is Apollonios and Sarapias' use of the verb ἀγαπάω in the phrase τιμῶμεν καὶ ἀγαπῶμεν αὐτά, "we esteem and love them," ll.19f. The ἀγαπάω / ἀγάπη word group is frequent in the gospels[51] as in the rest of the NT following its regular appearance in the LXX (II/I BC). In his *Bible Studies* Deissmann discusses ἀγάπη under the heading "So-called 'Jewish-Greek', 'Biblical' or 'New Testament' Words or Constructions."[52] He argues against the hypothesis that the word is a specifically "biblical" one in either its construction or meaning. The papyri published throughout the twentieth century confirm Deissmann's contention. The verb's appearance in this letter to denote Apollonios and Sarapias' love for the wedding couple witnesses to the word group's regular place in the *koine* and supports the thesis that the word group ἀγαπάω / ἀγάπη was in the process of replacing φιλέω / φιλία.[53] The noun and adjective form the basis of names attested in Greek from 505–500 BC,[54] names which occur regularly in inscriptions from 300 BC[55] and point to the currency of ἀγαπάω / ἀγάπη in the *koine*. Interesting examples of the non-Jewish and non-Christian use of ἀγάπη occur in two documentary texts: on the Rosetta stone, OGI 90.4 (196 BC) where

---

[51] Matt. 5:44; 22:37; Mark 10:21; 12:30; Luke 10:27; 11:42, 43; John 3:19, 35; 5:42; and twenty other occurrences including most notably John 21:15-17. In the sense in this letter of affection / warm regard between human beings, see Matt. 5:43, 46; 6:24; 19:19; 22:39; Mark 12:31, 33; Luke 6:27, 32, 35; 7:5, 42, 47; 16:13; John 13:34; 15:12, 17.

[52] *Bible Studies*, p. 198.

[53] The synonymous use of ἀγαπάω and φιλέω is evident in Xenophon, *Mem.* 2.7.9 and 2.7.12. On ἀγαπάω / ἀγάπη see A. Ceresa-Gastaldo, "'ΑΓΑΠΗ" nei documenti anteriori al Nuovo Testamento." *Aegyptus* 31 (1951), pp. 269-306; A. Ceresa-Gastaldo, "ΑΓΑΠΗ nei documenti estranei all'influsso biblico," *Rivista di filologia* 31 (1953), pp. 347-56; C. Spicq, "Le lexique de l'amour dans les papyrus et dans quelques inscriptions de l'époque hellénistique," in *Mnemosyne*, series 4, 8 (1955), pp. 25-33; R. Joly, *Le vocabulaire chrétien de l'amour est-il original? φιλεῖν et ἀγαπᾶν dans le grec antique* (Brussels: Brussels University Press, 1968) cited in Horsley and Llewelyn, eds., *New Documents*, vol. 3, p. 15; MM, s.v.

[54] See J. D. Beazley, *Attic Red-Figure Vase Painters*, vol. 1 (Oxford: Clarendon, 1963), p. 16 cited in Horsley and Llewelyn, eds., *New Documents*, vol. 4, pp. 258-59 where Ἀγάπη occurs as a name.

[55] For example, Ἀγάπα *I.Thess.* I.82 (Thessaly VI/V BC); Ἀγαπήτα *IG* V(2) 92 (Tegea IV BC); Ἀγάπων *IG* VII.220.10 (Megaris 190–175 BC); Ἀγαπίς *IG* II (2) 10564 (Athens III BC); Ἀγαπήτος *IG* XII (3) 668b, 711.5 (Thera imp.); *IG* V (1) 1467.3 (Messeme I AD). Also Ἀγάπη *Script* 361 (Athens 515–510 BC); *CIL* X 3674 (Misenum imp.) and ὑπὲρ μνήμης τῆς γυν(αικὸς) αὐτοῦ Ἀγαπῆς *IG* IX 1(2) 2.446 (dated I BC by G. Kraffenbach, ed. *IG* IX. Christian symbols apparently added by a later hand. He notes a later opinion that it should be dated IV AD).

Ptolemy is ἠγαπημένου ὑπὸ τοῦ Φθᾶ, "beloved by Phtha," and in P.Oxy. 11.1380 (early II AD) where Isis is referred to as ἀ[γά]πην θεῶν, "love of the gods", ll.109-110.[56] The earliest occurrences in the papyri are P.Cair.Zen 4.59580.3 (III BC) and PSI 6.577.16 (248/247 BC) with a trickle of examples from then until the fourth century AD[57] when the frequency of the word group increases under Christian influence. Among the papyri ἀγαπάω / ἀγάπη carries a range of meanings that includes family love and friendship, as here, and divine love. Documentary evidence locates the word group securely within the *koine*.

Apollonios and Sarapias express their desire to be with Sarapion on his wedding day, "rendering some service to him" (διακονήσοντες αὐτῷ, 1.5). The expression διακονεῖν γάμους occurs in Posidippus 26.19 (III BC) and raises the possibility that some formal function is intended by its use but whether this is the case, and what it may be, is not clear. It is more likely that διακονέω τινι here denotes more generally "render assistance to / serve" someone. In this sense the use illustrates occurrences in the gospels where the expression is used of women supporting Jesus and the twelve, αἵτινες διηκόνουν αὐτοῖς ἐκ τῶν ὑπαρχόντων αὐταῖς, "(women) who used to serve them from their own possessions"[58]; and Jesus' description of his work in relation to human beings, ὥσπερ ὁ υἱὸς τοῦ ἀνθρώπου οὐκ ἦλθεν διακονηθῆναι ἀλλὰ διακονῆσαι, "just as the Son of Man did not come to be served but to serve,"[59] although here the use is absolute rather than constructed with the dative. Διακονέω τινι denotes service rendered to friends in a letter from Thermouthas to Apolinarios, BGU 1.261.26-27 (II/III AD), ἵνα διακονήσει ἡμῖν.[60] An interesting example of the absolute use of διακονέω occurs in an apprenticeship agreement of the period. In P.Wisc. 1.4.9-10 (AD 53) Pausiris apprentices his son, Dioskous, to Ammonios, the fuller. Pausiris undertakes on his son's behalf a whole-hearted service, διακονοῦντα καὶ ποιοῦντα πάντα τὰ ἐπιτασσόμενα αὐτῶι, "serving and doing all the things commanded him."[61] The verb does not denote a condition of slavery but indicates a service that is all-embracing.[62]

---

[56] The reading is accepted by Griffiths after examination of the papyrus, rejecting Manteuffel's, and West's, ἀ[γα]θὴν Θεόν. See J. G. Griffiths, "Isis and 'The Love of the Gods,'" *Journal of Theological Studies* NS 29 (1978), pp. 147-51; Horsley and Llewelyn, eds., *New Documents*, vol. 4, pp. 257-59, here p. 259.

[57] P.Münch. 3/1.45.12 (221–205 BC); P.Oxy. 50.3555.6 (I/II AD); CPR 1.30.Fr.2.20 (AD 184); P.Mert. 1.22.8 (II AD); P.Oxy. 47.3345.2.77, 3.86 (AD 209); P.Giss.Univ. 3.25.13 (III AD); P.Ross.Georg. 3.4.28 (III AD).

[58] Luke 8:3. Also Matt. 8:15; 25:44; 27:55; Mark 1:31; 15:41; Luke 4:39; 12:37; 17:8; John 12:2, 26.

[59] Matt. 20:28; Mark 10:45.

[60] In the papyrus, ἵνα διακονέσσι ἱμιν.

[61] The same wording occurs in SB 10.10236.13-14 (36); P.Oxy. 2.275.10 (AD 66) pointing to a stock phrase.

[62] A similar idea appears in UPZ 1.18.23 (163 BC) not in the context of an apprenticeship agreement, but linked to settlement of a family dispute, ἡμᾶς δέξασθαι ἵνα διακονῆι ἡμῖν τὸν υἱὸν αὐτῆς Παγχράτην, ". . . us to receive her son Panchrates so that he might serve us"; also UPZ 1.19.25 (163 BC)

The construction in the letter, ἤλθομεν διακονήσοντες . . . καὶ συνευφρανθησόμενοι, ll.5f, using a participle rather than an infinitive to express purpose, parallels the phrase, ἀνέστη ἐκπειράζων αὐτόν, "stood up to test him," in Luke 10:25. The construction finds parallels in P.Oxy. 1.113.13 (II AD) and 20.2276.29, 30 (III/IV AD).[63]

The capacity of documentary texts to illuminate gospel language contributes to an understanding of the gospels' philosophical, ethical and social context in which their teachings find meaning. For example, in Luke 12:19, the parable of a rich man tells how, having accumulated vast wealth, the man says ψυχή, . . ἀναπαύου, φάγε, πίε, εὐφραίνου, "soul, . . . relax, eat, drink, be merry." A similar expression occurs in 1 Cor. 15:32 citing Isa. 22:13.[64] W. Ameling provides eighteen examples of phrases he describes as *carpe diem* maxims from grave inscriptions which include the words ἐσθίω and πίνω[65] used in a way similar to the gospel text to express the "good life" as eating, drinking and taking pleasure. Ameling records a further fourteen epitaphs that include εὐφραίνω in this sense.[66] One stele, erected for a student dying away from home, is a close parallel to the Lukan saying, πίε, φάγε, τρύφησον, ἀφροδισίασον, "drink, eat, revel, engage in sexual pleasure."[67] In the papyri expressions with ἐσθίω and πίνω are less frequent, occurring three times in the period.[68] The regular occurrence of the phrase indicates that the writer of the Gospel has chosen an epithet that is well-known if not part of common language, and Ameling concludes that the Lukan saying is dependent on neither Isaiah nor Paul but reflects the maxim's prevalence. The documentary evidence illustrates the attitude the parable aims to question, an enjoyment of life now through pleasure without any broader perspective. The maxim indicates a lack of belief in an after-life or belief in an after-life that is a shadow of present existence.

In a similar vein, as illustrated in the *New Documents* series, documentary texts provide valuable information on such matters as the status, work and possible gender of an ἰατρός, "doctor/physician"[69] (Matt. 9:12; Mark 2:17;

---

[63] See Mandilaras, *The Verb*, sections 912-17.

[64] φάγωμεν καὶ πίωμεν, αὔριον γὰρ ἀποθνήσκομεν, "let us eat and drink, for tomorrow we die."

[65] W. Ameling, "φάγωμεν καὶ πίωμεν." *ZPE* 60 (1985), pp. 35-43. For example, *AP* XI 56; *TAM* IV 1. 324; *GVI* 1363, 1956; *AP* X 47 reads, ἔσθιε, πῖνε similarly *AP* XI 38. Ameling also records twelve inscriptions including the words παίζω, γελάω, τρυφάω.

[66] For example *GVI* 1987; *AP* XI.62.

[67] J. Nollé, "Grabepigramme und Reliefdarstellungen aus Kleinasien," *ZPE* 60 (1985), pp. 117-35, here pp. 121-26; also Horsley and Llewelyn, eds., *New Documents*, vol. 8, p. 119.

[68] *SB* 6.9636 (AD 136), a personal letter, the context of which is unclear but appears to assure the recipient that once they eat and drink what they have φάγε τὰ σὰ καὶ πῖε, l.21, the writer will provide for them; a negative form of the phrase occurs twice, with a sense of threat: P.Oxy. 1.119.14-15 (III AD) of an urgent request from Theon to his father, ἄμ(= ἄν) μὴ πέμψῃς οὐ μὴ φάγω, οὐ μὴ πείνω (= πίνω)· ταῦτα, ". . . if you do not send (the lyre), I will not eat and I will not drink. So there!"; similarly P.Wash.Univ. 2.71.2. 6 (II AD). In P.Mert. 2.81.37 (II AD), Epoeris warns her son, Demetrius, about to sail up the Nile, about μεθ' ὧν δὲ ἐσθίεις κε πίνεις, "with whom you eat and drink."

[69] Horsley and Llewelyn, eds., *New Documents*, vol. 2, pp. 10, 19-20, 22-23; vol. 4, p. 23, 140.

5:26; Luke 4:23; 5:31); the possible age and chastity requirements of a παρθένος, "virgin," about to marry[70] (Matt. 1:23; Luke 1:27); the social status including literacy of an ἁλιεύς "fisherman"[71] (Matt. 4:18-19; Mark 1:16, 17; Luke 5:2); δοῦλος, "slave," as a metaphor for a disciple[72] (Matt. 24:45, 49; 25:21, 23); and the work of a τελώνης, "tax-collector"[73] (Matt. 9:10-11; 11:19; 18:17; Mark 2:15; Luke 5:30; 7:34).

The value of the documentary texts for the study of the language of the gospels is acknowledged by B. G. Mandilaras in his essay "New Testament and Papyri," part of his study of the grammar of the verb in documentary papyri.[74] He argues that the closest parallels to the language of the gospels are in the papyri[75] and discusses their usefulness for understanding a number of features of the gospels. The papyri provide the background for numbers of phonetic changes evident in the gospel manuscripts—the shift from ει to ι,[76] from αι to ε, οι to υ, the interchange of η and ι, and the loss of distinction between long and short vowels are all evidenced in documentary texts as developments in the *koine*; the inflection of nouns ending in -ρα like those ending in -σσα and -λλα; use of the accusative -ην in third declension nouns ending in -ης and use of -αν for -α in σάρκαν, σάλπιγγαν, χεῖραν, γυναῖκαν; the accusative plural of vowel stem nouns follows the pattern of consonantal stems, for example ἰσχύας (*sic*, ἰχθύας) Matt. 14:17; βόας John 2:14; confusion of cases; use of un-augmented forms of compound verbs especially those beginning ευ- and οι-; use of new present tense formations based on the aorist of verbs, for example κρύβω and νίπτω; use of first aorist ending with second aorist forms, for example εἶπα, ἔβαλα and ἔλαβα; verbs ending in -μι tend to take -ω forms; the rare occurrence of the optative and mainly in stereotyped phrases, for example μὴ γένοιτο, "may it not be." Documentary examples of all these developments are set out in F. T. Gignac, *A Grammar of the Greek Papyri*.[77]

A different perspective on the contribution that the documentary papyri and inscriptions make to the study of the language of the gospels is offered by a text that falls outside the time-frame generally adopted in this chapter. A clearly Christian fourth-century inscription, Gibson, no.19 = *SEG* 1100, among the "Christians for Christians" series from Phrygia,[78] opens with Χρηστιανοὶ Χρηστιανοῖς, ll.1-2. The orthography of "Christian" reflects changes in the phonetics of the *koine* whereby ει, η and ι come to have nearly

---

[70] Horsley and Llewelyn, eds., *New Documents*, vol. 1, pp. 71-72; vol. 4, pp. 221-29, 239.

[71] Horsley and Llewelyn, eds., *New Documents*, vol. 4, 18-19; vol. 5, pp. 95-107.

[72] Horsley and Llewelyn, eds., *New Documents*, vol. 2, p. 53; vol. 8, pp. 1-46.

[73] Horsley and Llewelyn, eds., *New Documents*, vol. 8, pp. 47-76.

[74] Mandilaras, *The Verb*, sections 21-35, pp. 49-53.

[75] 53. Mandilaras, *The Verb* does not include the inscriptions in his work.

[76] In P.Oxy. 46.3313.15 the interchange is from ι to ει in Apolonios and Sarapias' misspelling μεικρολόγων.

[77] Vol. 1 gives examples of the philological changes listed.

[78] E. Gibson, *The "Christians for Christians" Inscriptions of Phrygia*, Harvard Theological Studies 32 (Missoula: Scholars Press, 1978). Nos. 3, 5, 19 and 22 are re-edited in Horsley and Llewelyn, eds., *New Documents*, vol. 3, pp. 128-34.

completely identical sounds. The interchange occurs regularly in papyri and inscriptions dating from II AD.[79] The similarity between Χριστός and χρηστός led to the frequent assumption in the early Christian era that χριστιανός, χρηστιανός and χρειστιανός derive from χρηστός.[80] Some early Christian writers use the similarity to generate plays-on-words. This phenomenon led Gibson to suggest that such a play on words may operate in Luke 6:35 where the writer has Jesus say, ἔσεσθε υἱοὶ ὑψίστου, ὅτι αὐτὸς χρηστός ἐστιν ἐπι τοὺς ἀχαρίστους καὶ πονηρούς, "you will be sons of the Most High, because he is kind to the ungrateful and wicked."

The contribution of the papyri and inscriptions to gospel language study is limited by the chance and non-systematic nature of the survival of texts. It requires that certain words and constructions survive in the documentary texts to enable comparisons to be made. This is not always the case. For example, in the field of textual criticism, an assumption in the assessment of evidence about disputed texts is that Atticism is a secondary feature of the language of the gospels and other books of the NT, an attempt by later scribes to "improve" their language by presenting the gospels at a higher register.[81] It is argued that where *koine* and Atticistic variants occur, the *koine* form is more likely to be original and is to be preferred,[82] presuming that the writers of the gospels were less likely to use linguistic forms of a literary register and more likely to use vernacular forms. A problem is identifying the Atticistic elements. G. D. Kilpatrick uses the example of ζήσομαι / ζήσω, "I will live," textual variants in John, to argue the case for the later correction of texts to Atticistic forms.[83] Kilpatrick prefers readings with ζήσομαι because it is the *koine* form, to ζήσω which he argues is the Atticistic. The papyri and inscriptions of the period attest too few occurrences of the words to allow an assessment of the hypothesis. The papyri attest two possible occurrences of the middle future form: κατ' ἔτος ἐφ' ὃν ζήσεται χρόνον, "every year for the time he will live," in P.Oxy. 6.907.23 (AD 276) and a similar phrase is reconstructed in P.Hamb. 1.73.9 (II AD). A search of the inscriptions yields no non-Jewish and non-Christian occurrences in the period. Literary sources, however, attest both forms. J. A. L. Lee[84] concludes that ζήσομαι is an

---

[79] See Gignac, *Grammar of the Greek Papyri*, vol. 1, pp. 239-42. Note also Suetonius, *Claud.* 25 which speaks of riots among the Jewish population of Rome during the reign of Claudius that were instigated by a certain Chrestus. "Chrestus" may be a reference to "Christus."

[80] Tertullian, *Apol.* 3.5; Lactantius, *Inst.* 4.7.5; F. Blass, "Χρηστιανοὶ Χρηστιανοῖς," *Hermes* 30 (1895), pp. 465-70, here pp. 468-70.

[81] G. D. Kilpatrick, "Atticism in the Text of the Greek New Testament," in J. Blinzler et al., eds., *Neutestamentliche Aufsätze, Festschrift für Prof. J. Schmid* (Regensberg: Pustet, 1963), pp. 125-37; G. D. Kilpatrick, "The Greek New Testament Text of Today and the *Textus Receptus*," in H. Anderson and W. Barclay, eds., *The New Testament in Historical and Contemporary Perspective. Essays in Memory of G. H. C. Macgregor* (Oxford: Blackwell, 1965), pp. 189-208.

[82] G. D. Fee points out that "it is hypothetically equally probable. . . that a Christian scribe in the second century altered a less common form (= the alleged Atticism) to a more common, if less literary, form," cited by G. H. R. Horsley, "Koine or Atticism—A Misleading Dichotomy," in Horsley and Llewelyn, eds., *New Documents*, vol. 5, p. 44.

[83] Kilpatrick, "Atticism," p. 132-33.

[84] J. A. L. Lee, "The Future of ζάω in Late Greek," *Novum Testamentum* 22.4 (1980), pp.

innovation of the *koine*, displacing βιώσομαι the preferred Attic future where ζήσω also occurred. He argues that the *koine* later opts for ζήσω, not as a return to the Attic use but as part of the tendency of the *koine* to replace middle future verbs with active forms.[85] The supposed Atticistic form, therefore, is ζήσομαι, and ζήσω is the reading in John's Gospel most likely to reflect the everyday *koine*. The documentary evidence does not assist in establishing this result, but the one certain documentary example of ζήσεται in P.Oxy. 6.907.23 (AD 276) occurs in the copy of a will belonging to Aurelius Hermogenes, a president of the *boule* and a wealthy and educated man. The fact that P.Oxy. 6.907 is a copy means the date of the original is an unknown time before AD 276 but at least in mid-III AD since Hermogenes is known from a register, P.Oslo 3.111.258-263 in AD 235. The nature of the text suggests ζήσομαι is at home in a formal level of language.

The documentary papyri and inscriptions provide illustrative examples of lexical and grammatical usage in the gospels that serve to locate the language as integral to the *koine* and to identify different registers of language both within and between them. The documentary texts further demonstrate the background thought and illustrate the contexts within which the philosophy, ethics and theology of the gospels become grounded.

## Bibliography

*NT Lexica*

Danker, Frederick W, ed. *A Greek-English Lexicon of the New Testament and Other Early Christian Literature*, 3rd ed., Chicago: University of Chicago Press, 2000. (BDAG)
Lampe, G. W. H., ed. *A Patristic Greek Lexicon*, Oxford: Clarendon Press, 1961.
Louw, Johannes P., and Eugene A. Nida, eds. *Greek-English Lexicon of the New Testament: Based on Semantic Domains*. New York: United Bible Societies, 1988.
Kittel, Gerhard, and Gerhard Friedrich, eds. *Theological Dictionary of the New Testament*. 10 vols. Translated by Geoffrey W. Bromiley. Grand Rapids: Eerdmans, 1964–1976.

*NT Grammars*

Blass, Friedrich, Albert Debrunner and Robert W. Funk. *A Greek Grammar of the New Testament and Other Early Christian Literature*. Chicago: University of Chicago Press, 1961.
McKay, Kenneth L. *A New Syntax of the Verb in New Testament Greek: an Aspectual Approach*. New York: Peter Lang, 1994.
Moule, C. F. D. *An Idiom Book of New Testament Greek*. Cambridge: Cambridge University Press, 1953.
Moulton, James H., Wilbert F. Howard and Nigel Turner. *A Grammar of New Testament Greek*, Vol. 1 *Prolegomena*, Vol. 2 *Accidence and Word Formation*, Vol. 3 *Syntax*, Vol. 4 *Style*. Edinburgh: T. & T. Clark, 1906–1976.
Porter, Stanley E. *Idioms of the Greek New Testament*. Sheffield: Sheffield Academic Press, 1992.
————. "The Greek Language of the New Testament." In *Handbook to Exegesis of the New Testament*, edited by Stanley E. Porter, pp. 99-130. Leiden/New York: Brill,

---

289-98.

[85] Moulton, *Grammar of NT Greek*, vol. 1, pp. 154-55; Mandilaras, *The Verb*, p. 367.

1997.

Robertson, A. T. *A Grammar of the Greek New Testament in the Light of Historical Research.* 4th edn. Nashville: Broadman Press, 1934.

Voelz, James W. "The Language of the New Testament." *Aufstieg und Neidergang der römischen Welt* II 25.2 (1984): 893-977.

*Works Drawing on the Papyri and Inscriptions*

Deissmann, A. *Bible Studies: Contributions Chiefly from Papyri and Inscriptions to the History of the Language, the Literature, and the Religion of Hellenistic Judaism and Primitive Christianity.* Edinburgh: T. & T. Clark, 1901.

————. *Light from the Ancient East: the New Testament Illustrated by Recently Discovered Texts of the Graeco-Roman World.* London: Hodder & Stoughton, 1927.

Hunt, Arthur S, and C. C. Edgar. *Select Papyri: With an English Translation.* 2 vols. Cambridge: Harvard University Press, 1932–1934.

Horsley, G. H. R., and Stephen R. Llewelyn, eds. *New Documents Illustrating Early Christianity.* 9 vols. North Ryde/Grand Rapids: Ancient History Documentary Research Centre/Eerdmans, 1981–2002.

Moulton, James H., and George Milligan. *The Vocabulary of the Greek Testament Illustrated from the Papyri and Other Non-Literary Sources.* London: Hodder & Stoughton, 1930.

White, John L. *Light from Ancient Letters.* Philadelphia: Fortress Press, 1986.

# 4. The Political Context of the Gospels[1]

*Murray J. Smith*

The recognition of a hard and fast distinction between "politics" and "religion" is a peculiarity of the modern western world. To the Roman emperors of the first century, who accepted divine honors; to the Jewish revolutionaries of the same era, who sought to establish the "sole rule of God" by the sword (Josephus, *Ant.* 18.23); and to Jesus of Nazareth, who claimed that "all authority in heaven and on earth has been given to me" (Matt. 28:18), the distinction simply would not have made sense. In the ancient world, "politics" and "religion" were deeply intertwined, embedded together in the concrete forms of social life. An appreciation of the "political context"[2] of the gospels is, therefore, essential for anyone who wishes to understand the meaning of these ancient texts; and crucial for anyone who desires to know something of the prophet-messiah whose history they narrate. This chapter introduces the political world of Jesus and the first disciples via a narrative history of Palestine[3] centered on the period 37 BC–AD 70.

## A. The Advent of Roman Rule in Palestine

In whichever direction one chooses to look out from the gospels, the political horizon is dominated by the Roman Empire. It was the Roman client King Herod I who threatened the life of the infant Jesus (Matt. 2:13). The principates of the Roman Emperors Augustus and Tiberius circumscribed the world in which Jesus came to maturity (Luke 1:5; 2:1-2; 3:1-2). And the propriety of paying taxes to Caesar engaged Jesus and others in serious debate during his active years as a teacher (Matt. 22:15-22/Mark 12:13-17/Luke 20:20-26). Moreover, it was of sedition against his Roman overlords that

---

[1] I am grateful to Dr Stephen Llewelyn, whose generous and expert advice significantly improved this chapter.

[2] "Politics" is here understood in a relatively narrow sense as "those activities with a direct relation to government." See O. O'Donovan, *The Ways of Judgment* (Grand Rapids: Eerdmans, 2005), pp. 55-56.

[3] The term Palestine was first coined by the Romans under Hadrian (AD 117–138) after the Second Jewish Revolt (AD 132–135). In the absence of a better alternative for our period, however, the term is used here loosely to refer to that narrow strip of land bordered by the Lebanon mountains in the north, the Sinai desert in the south, the Arabian desert in the east and the Mediterranean in the west.

Jesus' enemies accused him (John 19:12). It was under the Roman prefect Pontius Pilate that he was tried and condemned (Matt. 27:2/Mark 15:1/Luke 23:1). And it was by a Roman method of execution that he met his death.

In the first century Roman rule was a relatively recent development in the history of Palestine. The region had, however, long been dominated by foreign powers. Assyrian rule from the eighth century BC was followed, without intermission, by that of Babylon (598/7–539 BC), Persia (539–333 BC) and finally—following the conquests of Alexander III of Macedon ("the Great")—the hellenistic kingdoms of the Ptolemies (c. 301–200 BC) and Seleucids (c. 200–143/42 BC). It is true that under the Persians and the hellenistic kingdoms Jerusalem and the small surrounding area of Judea enjoyed a significant degree of autonomy as a temple state, being administered in part by the Jewish high priest. And certainly at the time of Jesus, local Jewish authorities still exercised considerable influence. Nevertheless, their powers were always subject to those of the foreign overlords, and so the claim of the "Jews" at John 8:33 to have "never been slaves to anyone" is deeply ironic: political subjugation had in fact characterized the history of their ancestors for centuries. When Rome first insinuated herself in Palestine in the first century BC she was merely the most recent of the great ancient empires to do so (see *Table 1*).

| 722 BC | Assyrian conquest and rule. |
|---|---|
| 597/586 BC | Babylonian rule: destruction of first temple and exile. |
| 539 BC | Persian rule: return of exiles and building of second temple. |
| 334–23 BC | Conquests of Alexander the Great. |
| 301–167 BC | Hellenistic kingdoms rule Palestine. |
| 167–63 BC | Maccabean revolt and Hasmonean rule of Palestine. |
| 63 BC | Roman conquest of Palestine under Pompey. |
| 6–4 BC | Birth of Jesus. |
| AD 6 | Roman annexation of Judea as a Roman province. |
| AD 26–36 | Pontius Pilate, governor of Judea. |
| AD 30 or 33 | Death and resurrection of Jesus. |
| AD 66–70 | First Jewish War with Rome and destruction of second temple. |

*Table 1. Some important dates in the history of Palestine.*

## 1. Rome on the Horizon: The Hasmonean Period

The advent of Roman rule in Palestine was preceded by a brief and remarkable period of political independence. Beginning with the Maccabean Revolt of 167 BC, the Jewish people wrested control of Palestine from their Seleucid masters and established an autonomous Jewish state under the

Hasmonean Priest-Kings (143/42–63 BC).[4]

The era of Hasmonean rule was a uniquely formative period for Second Temple Judaism. All of the most important Jewish religio-political parties (Sadducees, Pharisees and Essenes) trace their decisive years—if not their absolute origins—to this time. And, more particularly, the Maccabean revolt left an indelible mark on the Jewish psyche. The Seleucid king Antiochus IV Epiphanes had given worship at the Jerusalem temple over to the cult of Olympian Zeus (167 BC).[5] To many of his outraged Jewish subjects, this was nothing less than a βδέλυγμα τῆς ἐρημώσεως—an "appalling sacrilege"; an "abomination of desolation."[6] Judas ὁ Μακκαβαῖος (the Maccabean = "the Hammer"), however, recaptured the temple and rededicated it to the worship of YHWH (164 BC).[7] He thereby laid the foundations for the subsequent rule of his family over the Jews. The echoes of this crisis rang down through the centuries: they could still be clearly heard two hundred years later when Jesus drove out of the temple those who had polluted it,[8] and then spoke of an "abomination of desolation" (βδέλυγμα τῆς ἐρημώσεως) being set up in the "holy place."[9]

## 2. Roman Conquest: From Pompey to Herod

The success of the Hasmoneans was, however, short lived. In 63 BC the steady eastward march of the Roman legions brought Pompey "the Great" to Palestine. Having been invited by the Hasmoneans Aristobulus II and Hyrcanus II to settle their dispute over the Jewish throne, the Roman general decided to invade. After a three-month siege Pompey took the city of Jerusalem. He established Judea as a vassal state of the Roman Empire, and reinstated Hyrcanus II to rule, no longer as king, but as Jewish ἀρχιερεύς (high priest).[10]

The following turbulent years were dominated by civil war in the Roman Empire, and the fortunes of the East were closely tied to the vicissitudes of Roman politics.[11] In this new political landscape, where the favor of Rome meant everything, Hyrcanus II was quickly out-maneuvered by a new player on the political scene—Antipater II, an Idumean general (from the region

---

[4] The most comprehensive treatment of this and subsequent periods of Jewish history is still E. Schürer, *The History of the Jewish People in the Age of Jesus Christ (175 BC–AD 135)*, 3 vols. (Edinburgh: T. & T. Clark, 1973); see chapter 6 of the present volume.

[5] 1 Macc. 1:29-32, 38, 41-64; 2 Macc. 5:22-26; 6:1-11, 17; Dan. 7:25; 8:11; 11:31, 39; 12:11; Josephus, *Ant.* 12:251-53, 265-86; cf. Tacitus, *Hist.* 5.8.4.

[6] 1 Macc. 1:54, 59; Dan. 9:27; 11:31; 12:11.

[7] 1 Macc. 4:36-59; 2 Macc. 10:1-8; Josephus, *Ant.* 12:316-26.

[8] Matt. 21:12-13/Mark 11:15-17/Luke 19:45-46; cf. John 2:14-17.

[9] Matt. 24:15/Mark 13:14; cf. Luke 21:20. It is perhaps also significant that it was during the Feast of the Dedication, which commemorated Judas Maccabeus' actions, that the Jews questioned Jesus about his messianic identity (John 10:22).

[10] Josephus, *Ant.* 14.29-79; 20.244; *J.W.* 1.120-58.

[11] For an introduction to the turbulent events of Roman politics in this period, see e.g. H. H. Scullard, *From the Gracchi to Nero: A History of Rome from 133 BC to AD 68* (New York: Routledge, 1982), pp. 154-71.

south of Judea) whose family had risen to prominence under the Hasmoneans. While cleverly feigning support for Hyrcanus II, Antipater II courted the favor of the successive Roman generals who marched through the region.[12] Although Antipater II did not live to see it, his stratagem worked, and in 40 BC the Roman senate appointed his son, Herod, as king of Judea.[13] Jerusalem had been momentarily taken by the Parthian Empire—based in modern day Iran—and the Hasmonean Antigonus had been installed on the throne as its puppet.[14] Under the patronage of Mark Antony, however, and with two Roman legions, Herod was able to expel Antigonus and recapture Jerusalem. Thus, by 37 BC, Herod the Idumean, with the aid of Roman troops, had established himself as king of the Jews.[15] Roman rule had come to Palestine in a new and decisive way.

## B. The Realities of Roman Rule in Palestine 37 BC–AD 70

### 1. A complex and changing "political map"

First century Palestine under Roman rule was home to a complex and frequently changing political map. The region was populated by a variety of ethnic groups (Jews, Greeks, Samaritans) and encompassed a diverse conglomeration of districts. Moreover, in the years which followed Herod I's appointment as king of Judea, the Romans governed Palestine by a variety of methods (see *Table 2* below). In what follows we will examine first the "client kingdoms" of Herod and his sons, through which the Romans indirectly ruled much of Palestine well into the first century AD (section B.2). Then, we will consider the rule of the Roman governors of the province of Judea, through whom Rome ruled more directly (section B.3). These two systems of government provide the immediate political context of the gospels. It is worth noting, however, that a number of Greek cities, including the ten cities of the "Decapolis," retained a form of autonomy under Roman supervision throughout the entire period.[16]

---

[12] Josephus *Ant.* 14.137, 143, 156-58, 163-64, 301-03, 324-29; 15.182; cf. *J.W.* 1.201-03, 242-47.

[13] Antipater was murdered in 43 BC (Josephus, *Ant.* 14.281; *J.W.* 1.226). On the appointment of Herod as king, see: Josephus, *Ant.* 14.381-89; *J.W.* 1.282-85; cf. Strabo, *Geogr.* 26.2.46; Appian, *Bell. civ.* 5.74; Tacitus, *Hist.* 5.9.

[14] Josephus, *Ant.* 14.330-69; 20.245; *J.W.* 1.248-73; cf. Tacitus, *Hist.* 5.9.

[15] Josephus, *Ant.* 14.394-491; 20.246; *J.W.* 1.286-358.

[16] The Δεκάπολις (Decapolis) was a league of ten Greek cities located to the east of the Jordan and the Sea of Galilee, which first gained impetus from Pompey's settlement of the region. It is mentioned in the gospels at Matt. 4:25; Mark 5:20; 7:31; cf. Pliny, *Nat.* 5.18, 74. On the Greek cities see A. Kasher, *Jews and Hellenistic Cities in Eretz-Israel: Relations of the Jews in Eretz-Israel with the Hellenistic Cities during the Second Temple Period (332 BCE–70 CE)* (Tübingen: Mohr [Siebeck], 1990).

| | Palestine | | |
|---|---|---|---|
| | Judea, Samaria and Idumea | Galilee and Perea | North and East of Galilee |
| 37–4 BC | Kingdom of Herod I. | | |
| 4 BC–AD 41 | Ethnarchy of Archelaus | Tetrarchy of Antipas (to 39). | Tetrarchy of Philip (to 34). |
| | Roman province under prefects: "Judea" (from AD 6). | | |
| 41–44 | Kingdom of Agrippa I. | | |
| 44–70 | Roman province under procurators: "Judea." | | |

*Table 2. Roman Rule in Palestine 37 BC–AD 70.*

## 2. Indirect Roman Rule: The Herodian Client Kingdoms

### (a) Rome and the Client Kingdoms

The Herodian client kingdoms of Palestine were similar to those of the various other client kings around the empire.[17] Quite simply, it was often safer and easier for Rome to entrust newly conquered regions to local elites who could bear the burdens of the early stages of Roman rule. Herod I received official recognition as a φίλος καὶ σύμμαχος (friend and ally) of the Romans early in his career, and his relationship with Rome set the pattern for the subsequent Herodian dynasts.[18]

Relations of this kind between Rome and her client rulers were symbiotic,

---

[17] The title "client king" is a modern construction used to describe those rulers whom the Roman Senate formally recognized as *rex sociusque et amicus* (king and ally and friend). See D. C. Braund, *Rome and the Friendly King: The Character of Client Kingship* (New York: St. Martin's Press, 1984).

[18] Josephus, *Ant.* 17.246; cf. the coin of Agrippa I declaring his συμμαχία (friendly alliance) with Rome (Y. Meshorer, *A Treasury of Jewish Coins* (New York/Jerusalem: Amphora Books/Yad Ben-Zvi Press, 2001), pp. 100-101 (coin 124).

if unequal, in nature. On the one hand, client kings received Roman support for their position. All things being equal, they could count on the intervention of the Roman legions in their favor, if required. They also received various other privileges that helped to buttress their rule. The Herods of Palestine, for example, were granted Roman citizenship, and allowed to mint (bronze) coins, raise taxes, maintain a small army, and administer capital punishment.[19] To be sure, they held their various titles only by Roman permission, could not form alliances with other kings or wage war independently of Rome, and were reliant on Rome's approval for any succession plans they may devise. But the powers they did have were sufficient for them to maintain their positions in a somewhat hostile environment.[20]

In exchange, client kings were expected to meet the demands of the empire. These typically included paying tribute to Rome,[21] ensuring the frontiers against external threats, and providing auxiliaries upon request.[22] Moreover, although it is difficult to establish a conscious and deliberate policy to the effect, client kingdoms often served the useful purpose of hellenizing the people of a province before full scale provincialization and direct Roman rule took place.[23] The efforts of the Herods to hellenize the people of Palestine (outlined below) are, therefore, at least partially explicable as a necessity placed upon them by their Roman masters.

Significantly, the Herodian client kingdoms formed the immediate political context for Jesus' proclamation of the "kingdom of God." Of course, for both Jesus and his hearers the biblical vision of the coming kingdom of the God of Israel, the creator, was foundational. And, indeed, any mention of a coming kingdom must have also evoked the imperial shadow cast by Rome. Nevertheless, there is no doubt that Jesus' announcement of the coming kingdom of God was also intended—and received—as a direct challenge to the "kingdoms" of the sons of Herod.

---

[19] Antipas' soldiers are mentioned at Luke 23:11; cf. Luke 3:14 where the στρατευόμενοι (those serving as soldiers) could be Jews in the service of Antipas, or Gentiles enlisted in the Roman *auxilia*.

[20] On the administrative structures employed by the Herods, see H. W. Hoehner, *Herod Antipas* (Grand Rapids: Zondervan, 1980), p. 102; cf. Mark 6:21; Josephus, *Ant.* 20.159.

[21] It is unclear whether Herod I was granted exemption from paying tribute from 30 BC onwards (Josephus, *Ant.* 14.137; *J.W.* 1.194; cf. A. H. M. Jones, *The Herods of Judea* (Oxford: Clarendon, 1967), pp. 64-65; Hoehner, *Herod Antipas*, pp. 298-300). Such a privilege was certainly not enjoyed by his sons.

[22] The client-kingdoms of Palestine formed part of a long line of client kingdoms and πόλεις (city-states) which acted as a kind of buffer-zone between the eastern Roman provinces newly organized by Pompey, and Rome's major rival in the East, the kingdom of Parthia (see Scullard, *History of Rome*, pp. 103-04).

[23] Suetonius, *Aug.* 59-60 lists as typical the activities of the client kings (unnamed) in building temples, holding five-yearly games and otherwise generally "Greco-Romanizing" their kingdoms. Cf. Jones, *Herods of Judea*, pp. 66-67; P. W. Barnett, *Jesus and the Rise of Early Christianity: A History of New Testament Times* (Downers Grove: InterVarsity Press, 1999), p. 72.

## (b) Herod I (37–4 BC)

Herod I ("the Great") appears only a handful of times in the gospels (Luke 1:5; Matt. 2:1-18), but his presence in the background casts a long and ominous shadow over the story of Jesus.[24] Although Herod himself died not long after Jesus was born, he gave his name to the dynasty that ruled over significant parts of Palestine for more than a century (see *Figure 1*).[25]

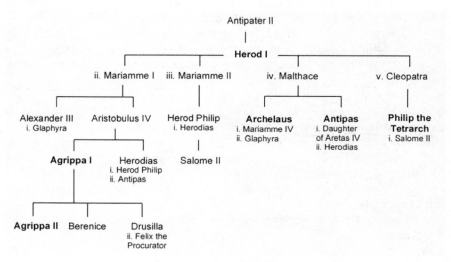

*Figure 1. The Herodian dynasty.*

Herod I was, above all, a <u>faithful client king</u> of the Roman Empire, and in winning and maintaining Roman favor he had remarkable success. He faithfully supported Roman military aims, and became the champion of Greco-Roman culture in Palestine, integrating his kingdom with the wider Roman Empire at every level. Most importantly, Herod embarked on a <u>stupendous program of construction</u>, building cities and fortresses which gave his territories a more Greco-Roman face than they had ever had before, and also accelerated the development of Greco-Roman institutions in the region.[26] Pride of place here belonged to the impressive maritime city of Caesarea

---

[24] Of the studies on Herod I, see especially A. Schalit, *König Herodes: der Mann und sein Werk* (Berlin: de Gruyter, 1969); and P. Richardson, *Herod: King of the Jews and Friend of the Romans* (Columbia: University of South Carolina Press, 1996).

[25] Herod's family was large and complicated: he married ten wives and had numerous children. (cf. Josephus, *Ant.* 14.300; 17.19-22; 18.109, 130-42; *J.W.* 1.562-63, and the more extensive genealogical table in Schürer, *History of Jewish People*, vol. 1, p. 614). On the Herodian dynasty, see now N. Kokkinos, *The Herodian Dynasty: Origins, Role in Society and Eclipse* (Sheffield: Sheffield Academic Press, 1998).

[26] E.g. Herod's renovations in Jerusalem (Josephus, *Ant.* 15.267-81) and Sebaste = Samaria (Josephus, *Ant.* 15.292-98; *J.W.* 1.403; Strabo, *Geogr.* 16.760). The πραιτώριον (praetorium) referred to in the gospels (Matt. 27:27; Mark 15:16; John 18:28, 33; 19:9) was one of the string of fortresses Herod built or renovated throughout his kingdom.

(completed 10/9 BC): centered as it was around a gleaming marble temple—dedicated to the worship of Caesar Augustus and Rome—it advertised to the world Herod's devotion and loyalty to his masters.[27] Not surprisingly, such loyalty was rewarded: Herod was granted vast tracts of land in Palestine,[28] and even enjoyed the personal friendship of the emperor.[29]

In winning the loyalty and respect of his subjects, however, Herod had less success, though not for lack of trying. The client king, indeed, made deliberate attempts to buttress the legitimacy of his rule and to mitigate the odium his program of hellenization had attracted in certain quarters: he married the Hasmonean Princess Mariamme I;[30] he supported Jewish religious practice within Judea;[31] and, most significant of all, he undertook a spectacular re-construction of the Jerusalem temple.[32] Despite these efforts, Herod was opposed to the very end by a significant proportion of his subjects: it seems he was never able to overcome the animosity aroused by his Roman allegiance, or to shake the illegitimacy of his Idumean blood. To be sure, Herod's infamous brutality probably did not help matters either, for the client king tolerated neither rivals nor rebels. He singlehandedly wiped out almost the entire Hasmonean royal house, including his own beloved wife, Mariamme I, and her sons;[33] and those who had the audacity to rebel were mercilessly put down.[34] It is not surprising, therefore, that when, towards the end of his reign, Herod heard messianic claims being made for a baby born in Bethlehem, he acted with characteristically ruthless efficiency to remove that threat also.[35]

---

[27] Josephus, *Ant.* 15.292-98, 331-41; 16.136-41; *J.W.* 1.407-16; Pliny, *Nat.* 5.14/69; Strabo, *Geogr.* 16.2.27. Herod could not build temples for the worship of Caesar in Judea proper due to the significant opposition there, but further afield, in Caesarea Philippi, Sebaste and elsewhere, the cultic worship of Caesar was well established (Josephus, *Ant.* 15.328-30; 363-64; *J.W.* 1.403-07).

[28] Josephus, *Ant.* 15.217, 342-48, 354-64; *J.W.* 1.398-400, 483; cf. Dio Cassius, *Hist.* 54.9.3.

[29] Josephus, *Ant.* 15.360-61; *J.W.* 1.399-400; cf. *Ant.* 12.125-28; 16.27-65, 160-78; but note the tensions that developed towards the end of Herod's reign (*Ant.* 16.271-85, 286-93, 335-55).

[30] Josephus, *J.W.* 1.432: Mariamme was the granddaughter of both Hyrcanus II and Aristobulus II.

[31] E.g. Herod refrained from depicting images of humans or animals on his coins (Meshorer, *Treasury*, pp. 61-77).

[32] This Herodian temple features prominently in the gospels (e.g. Mark 11:11; 13:1-2; John 2:20). Herod dedicated it (c. 18 BC) on the anniversary of his accession to the throne. In doing so, he claimed divine sanction for his rule, for in Jewish tradition only the true king, God's anointed, could build the temple (Josephus, *Ant.* 15.423; cf. 2 Sam. 7:1-17; 1 Kings 8; *Tg. Isa.* 53:5). In this context, Jesus statement recorded at John 2:19 ("Destroy this temple and in three days I will raise it up"; cf. Matt. 26:61; Mark 14:58) was full of explosive religio-political overtones. Cf. N. T. Wright, *The New Testament and the People of God* (Minneapolis: Fortress Press, 1992), pp. 160, 226, 308-09.

[33] Mariamme I: Josephus, *Ant.* 15.218-39; *J.W.* 1.438-44. Alexander III and Aristobulus IV (her sons): *Ant.* 16.66-85, 87-135, 188-270, 313-34, 356, 361-94; *J.W.* 1.445-48, 452-512, 526-29, 534-51.

[34] For example, the famous "golden eagle" incident: Josephus, *Ant.* 17.149-67 (cf. *J.W.* 1.647-55).

[35] Matt. 2:1-18. E. M. Smallwood, *The Jews Under Roman Rule from Pompey to Diocletian*

Nevertheless, the old one-sided portrait of Herod as unmitigated tyrant can no longer be sustained.[36] His economic policy was remarkably evenhanded.[37] His ambitious building projects created employment and provided much needed infrastructure. And, at times, Herod even showed himself a generous benefactor to all, especially to the Jews.[38] The first Roman client king of Palestine was an energetic and canny politician whose administration — though no doubt brutal and self-serving — brought considerable benefits to the inhabitants of the region. He died at Jericho in the spring of 4 BC,[39] and was buried with great pomp but little mourning at Herodium.[40] That many of his subjects requested direct Roman rule when he died shows both his remarkable success as a Roman client, and the ultimate failure of his attempts to win over an unsympathetic populace.

## (c) Herod's Kingdom Divided

Upon Herod's death, the simmering discontent spilled over into open rebellion across Palestine.[41] The various uprisings no doubt aimed at Jewish independence, or—as Luke puts it—"the redemption of Jerusalem" (Luke 2:38).[42] They were initially put down by Archelaus, the older of Herod's two sons by his fourth wife (Malthace the Samaritan), who had about 3,000 rebels slaughtered in and around the holy place during Passover. P. Quinctilius Varus, the Roman governor of Syria (7/6–4 BC), then finished the job: he crucified 2,000 of the worst offenders and sent others to Rome for trial.

In Rome, Augustus divided Herod's kingdom amongst his sons, who had sailed to the imperial capital to press their respective claims to the throne.[43] Archelaus, who had been named in Herod's final will as the successor, was appointed not as king but as ἐθνάρχης (ethnarch).[44] He was given

---

(Leiden: Brill, 1976), pp. 103-04 questions the historical reliability of the account, but cf. Schalit, *König Herodes*, p. 648, n. 11.

[36] The older portrait was largely drawn from an uncritical reading of Josephus (e.g. Josephus, *Ant*. 16.15-59). For the revision, see Richardson, *Herod*, pp. 11-13, 313-14.

[37] J. Pastor, "Herod, King of Jews and Gentiles: Economic Policy as a Measure of Evenhandedness," in M. Mor, A. Oppenheimer, J. Pastor and D. R. Schwartz, eds., *Jews and Gentiles in the Holy Land* (Jerusalem: Yad Ben-Zvi Press, 2003), pp. 152-64.

[38] Josephus, *Ant*. 15. 299-316, 365; 16.64.

[39] Josephus, *Ant*. 17.191, 196-99; *J.W.* 1.665, 670-73.

[40] Josephus, *Ant*. 17.168-79, 193; *J.W.* 1.656-60, 666 reports Herod's final barbarous plan—never carried out—to have "all the principal men of the entire Jewish nation" executed upon his death to ensure that the whole land would be in mourning at his passing.

[41] Josephus, *Ant*. 17.200-85, 286-98, 311-13; *J.W.* 1.670; 2.1-13, 39-88; *Ag. Ap.* 1.34; Tacitus, *Hist*. 5.9; and cf. P. Schäfer, *The History of the Jews in the Greco-Roman World* (London: Routledge, 2003), p. 101.

[42] Cf. Luke 1:50-55, 68-79; 2:25. Note also the striking similarity of this phrase with the inscriptions on the coins minted by rebels during the two Jewish wars with Rome (Meshorer, *Treasury*, pp. 115-66).

[43] Josephus, *Ant*. 17.219-227, 299-314 (cf. *J.W.* 2.14-22, 80-92); *Ant*. 317-23 (cf. *J.W.* 2.93-100). cf. Tacitus, *Hist*. 5.9; Luke 3:1.

[44] The title ἐθνάρχης implies rule (ἀρχή) over a particular ethnic group (ἔθνος), in this case the Jews, and designates that Archelaus enjoyed a status superior to that his brothers.

responsibility for Judea, Idumea and Samaria, about half of Herod's kingdom, and was promised the royal title if he could prove himself capable of the task. The other half of Herod's kingdom was itself divided in two: Antipas, Archelaus' younger brother, was made τετραάρχης (tetrarch)[45] of Galilee and Perea (on the eastern bank of the Jordan); and Philip, Herod's son by his fifth wife (Cleopatra of Jerusalem), was likewise made tetrarch, with responsibility for the regions to the north and east of the Sea of Galilee.[46]

Augustus' essentially tripartite division of the kingdom set the parameters for power relations in Palestine over the ensuing half-century (see *Table 2*). Archelaus, who ruled over Judea from 4 BC–AD 6,[47] and Philip, who ruled in the north until AD 33/34[48] are mentioned in the gospels only in passing, and must be passed over here. Antipas, however, features prominently, and it is his rule which provides the immediate political context for much of Jesus' ministry.

### (d) The Tetrarchy of Herod Antipas (4 BC–AD 39)

Herod Antipas[49] ruled as tetrarch of Galilee and Perea well into the first century.[50] He therefore held power of life and death over both John the Baptist and Jesus, who lived and worked in the areas over which he had jurisdiction.[51] The tetrarch's success may be attributed to the fact that he operated on the principles that had served his father so well: faithfulness to Rome above all, active hellenization where possible, and support for Jewish religious practice where expedient.

In many ways, Antipas was the perfect Roman client. He faithfully paid the required tribute and successfully kept his territory secure, leaving his Roman masters with little to worry about. This remarkable success in keeping

---

[45] The term τετραάρχης designates a minor ruler with less status and power than a king.

[46] Namely, Gaulanitis, Auranitis, Trachonitis, Batanea, Panias and probably also Iturea.

[47] Archelaus is mentioned explicitly only at Matt. 2:22, where his reputation as a cruel tyrant is given as the reason why Joseph relocated his young family from Bethlehem in Judea to Nazareth in Galilee. The events of his short rule probably also stand behind Luke 19:12-27 (cf. Josephus, *Ant.* 17.284, 339; *J.W.* 2.64, 111; N. T. Wright, *Jesus and the Victory of God* (Minneapolis: Fortress Press, 1996), pp. 632-39). He was deposed by Augustus, for ineptitude and brutality, in AD 6 (Josephus, *Ant.* 17.342-48; *J.W.* 2.111-13; Dio Cassius, *Hist.* 55.27.6; Strabo, *Geogr.* 16.2.46; cf. Hoehner, *Herod Antipas*, pp. 103-05).

[48] Philip is mentioned directly only at Luke 3:1, where his rule as tetrarch is used as a chronological marker for the beginning of Jesus' adult ministry. The reference to Caesarea Philippi at Mark 8:27/Matt. 16:13 is probably also significant: Jesus' messianic identity was first recognized in a city which bore the name of both the emperor and the Herodian tetrarch. The Philip, brother to Antipas, mentioned at Matt. 14:3/Mark 6:17/Luke 3:19 is not the tetrarch but the son of Herod's third wife, Mariamme II.

[49] The gospels refer to Antipas simply as "Herod," which is how he referred to himself (see the coins: Meshorer, *Treasury*, pp. 81-84). Here, however, for the sake of clarity, the tetrarch is referred to as "Herod Antipas" or simply "Antipas."

[50] The most comprehensive treatment of Herod Antipas is still Hoehner, *Herod Antipas*, but cf. now M. H. Jensen, *Herod Antipas in Galilee: The Literary and Archaeological Sources on the Reign of Herod Antipas and its Socio-Economic Impact on Galilee* (Tübingen: Mohr, 2006).

[51] E.g. Matt. 14:1-3, 10; Mark 6:14-16; Luke 3:1, 19-20; 9:9; 23:7.

the peace must be attributed at least in part to Antipas' judicious support for Jewish religious practice: he travelled regularly to Jerusalem for the Jewish feasts;[52] he refrained from using offensive images either of himself or his Roman master on his coins; and, when the opportunity arose, he delighted in presenting himself as the champion of the Jewish cause, even to the extent of petitioning the emperor on behalf of his subjects against the offensive actions of Pontius Pilate, the Roman governor of Judea.[53] These efforts no doubt won Antipas some favor amongst his predominantly Jewish subjects. And, while it is true that Antipas had an easier task than his father or his brother—Galilean Jews in this period were less conservative than their Judean brothers—the skill of Antipas' canny politicking should not be underestimated.[54]

The main aim of the tetrarch, however, like that of his father before him, was to strengthen his own position in power by gradually integrating his dominions with the wider Greco-Roman world. Antipas thus retained the hellenistic bureaucracy he had inherited from his father,[55] and continued with Greek as the language of his court, coins and inscriptions. Most importantly, Antipas advanced hellenistic forms of government and culture throughout his territory by establishing or renewing key urban settlements in Greco-Roman style: Sepphoris in Galilee and Betharamphtha in Perea (opposite Jericho) were Antipas' first such efforts; but Tiberias, his new capital, was the jewel in his crown, and took pride of place in Antipas' efforts to hellenize the region.[56]

All in all, then, Antipas must be counted a shrewd political operator. Like his father before him, he successfully negotiated the challenges of simultaneously being a friend of Rome and ruler of the Jews. Perhaps this is in part what Jesus intended when he referred to the tetrarch as "that fox" (Luke 13:32).

Antipas finally came undone, however, during the last years of his reign, as the result of a scandalous marriage and a change of emperors. The marriage—his second, to Herodias (the wife of his half-brother Herod Philip)—was the beginning of the end for Antipas: it outraged many of his

---

[52] Luke 23:7; Josephus, *Ant.* 18.122; Suetonius, *Vit.* 2. cf. Hoehner, *Herod Antipas*, pp. 175-76.

[53] Philo, *Legat.* 299-306.

[54] On the Jewish identity and sympathies of the population of Galilee in the first century, see esp. S. Freyne, *Galilee from Alexander the Great to Hadrian, 323 BCE to 135 CE: A Study of Second Temple Judaism* (Edinburgh: T. &T. Clark, 1980), pp. 71, 293-97; and M. A. Chancey, *The Myth of a Gentile Galilee* (New York: Cambridge University Press, 2002).

[55] Mark 6:21 mentions μεγιστᾶνες ("great ones"), πρῶτοι ("first ones"), χιλίαρχοι ("commanders of a thousand") as the key officers in Antipas' bureaucracy. See Hoehner, *Herod Antipas*, p. 102; cf. Freyne, *Galilee*, p. 69.

[56] Josephus, *Ant.* 18.36-38; *J.W.* 2.168, 618; 3.539; *Life* 37-39, 65-68, 92, 295, 331; cf. M. Avi-Yonah, "The Foundation of Tiberias," *Israel Exploration Journal* 1 (1950), pp. 160-69; Hoehner, *Herod Antipas*, pp. 91-100. The city was, however, built over an ancient cemetery and therefore unclean according to Jewish law (Josephus, *Ant.* 18.38; cf. Num. 19:11-16; *m. 'Ohal.* 17-18). Antipas was therefore forced to resort to "stick and carrot" measures to populate his new capital (Josephus, *Life* 277, 280, 293; *Ant.* 18.36-38). The episode neatly demonstrates both Antipas determination to hellenize, and the persistence of Jewish religious convictions in Galilee under his rule (cf. see esp. M. A. Chancey, *Greco-Roman Culture and the Galilee of Jesus* (New York: Continuum, 2006), pp. 71-99, 122-65, 193-220).

Jewish subjects, and raised the ire of the Nabatean king Aretas IV (father of Antipas' jilted first wife), who routed the tetrarch in a pitched battle in AD 36.[57] Antipas appealed to Tiberius for vengeance, but the Emperor died and was replaced by Gaius (Caligula) before his command to punish Aretas could be effected.[58] To make matters worse, the new emperor soon deposed Antipas—despite the tetrarch's efforts to win his favor—and established his friend, Agrippa I,[59] as βασιλεύς (king) in his place (AD 39–40). Antipas and Herodias were summarily, and almost certainly unjustly, accused of treachery. They were banished to southern Gaul, where they later died in exile.[60]

It was just prior to these last tumultuous years of Antipas reign that both John the Baptist and Jesus emerged in his territories as popular leaders of the Jewish people.[61] Both preachers proclaimed that "the kingdom of God" had "come near" (Matt. 3:2; 4:17),[62] a message which—with its unmistakable political overtones—was certainly not welcome at the palace in Tiberias.[63] It is no surprise, therefore, that when John criticized Antipas' adulterous marriage, he was soon arrested and imprisoned in the fortress of Machaerus on the Dead Sea;[64] that the Baptist later lost his head at Antipas' command is a gruesome but not unpredictable conclusion to the story (Matt. 14:6-11; Mark 6:21-28; Luke 9:9). What is surprising is that Jesus survived so long preaching his subversive message in Antipas' territory.[65] Like John before him, he also criticized Antipas' rule and adulterous marriage, albeit in a more subtle form,[66] and the gospels report that from the beginning Antipas recognized Jesus' work as a continuation of that of John (Matt. 14:1-2; Mark 6:14-16; Luke 9:7-9). To be sure, Antipas did at first try to see Jesus and then later

---

[57] Josephus, *Ant.* 18.109-119. The marriage is mentioned at Matt. 14:3/Mark 6:17/Luke 3:19.

[58] Josephus, *Ant.* 18.115, 120-26.

[59] Agrippa I was the son of Aristobulus IV and Berenice I and thus both Antipas' nephew and Herodias' brother (see *Figure 1*).

[60] Josephus, *Ant.* 18.240-55; *J.W.* 2.181-83.

[61] For the relative chronologies of John and Jesus, see Barnett, *Rise of Early Christianity*, pp. 19-22.

[62] Cf. Mark 1:15; Luke 3:3-6; 10:9-11. Josephus' account of John's preaching is recast in the categories of Greco-Roman thought (Josephus, *Ant.* 18.117-18). This *interpretatio hellenistica* was Josephus' habitual practice. The semitic categories employed in the gospels are much more likely to be authentic.

[63] Nevertheless, the gospels present Antipas as one who was drawn to both John and Jesus (Matt. 14:9; Mark 6:20, 26; Luke 9:9; 23:8; but cf. Matt. 14:5). Note also Luke 8:3: Joanna, the wife of Antipas' ἐπίτροπος (steward, a financial minister); and John 4:46-54: the βασιλικός (royal official) from Capernaum.

[64] Matt. 11:2; 14:3-5; Mark 1:14; 6:17-20; Luke 3:19-20; cf. Josephus, *Ant.* 18.118-19.

[65] Note, however, that Jesus does seem to have increasingly withdrawn from Antipas' territories. See Hoehner, *Herod Antipas*, pp. 197-202, 317-30; cf. now M. H. Jensen, "Herod Antipas in Galilee: Friend or Foe of the Historical Jesus?" *Journal for the Study of the Historical Jesus* 5 (2007), pp. 7-32.

[66] Antipas' rule: Matt. 11:7-8; Luke 7:24-25 (cf. Mark 8:15), where the "reed shaken by the wind" is most probably a veiled reference to Antipas who used the reed as his personal symbol on his coins (so G. Theissen, *The Gospels in Context* [Minneapolis: Fortress Press, 1991]), pp. 25-59). Antipas' marriage: Mark 10:11-12 where the reference to a woman divorcing her husband cannot but have evoked Herodias.

made plans to kill him (Luke 9:9; 13:31-32); that neither event transpired is probably due to the fact that Antipas could not run the risk of further agitating the crowds (Matt. 14:5). It was, therefore, not until after Jesus had been arrested in Jerusalem that Antipas and Jesus finally met, when Pilate sent Jesus to the tetrarch during the Passover feast (Luke 23:6-12).[67] On that occasion, however, Antipas was happy to leave the resolution of the difficult case to Pilate: it suited him just fine to have the troublesome preacher done away with while the Roman prefect dealt with the crowds.

## 3. Direct Roman Rule: The Roman Empire and the Province of Judea

The Herodian client kingdoms served their purpose in the advance of Roman domination in the East, but they were eventually replaced by direct Roman rule. This came first to the former territory of Archelaus (Judea proper, Samaria and Idumea) which the Roman emperor Augustus annexed in AD 6, forming the imperial province of Judea. Before we continue the narrative account of the period, it will be instructive to briefly outline the nature of the Roman Empire at the time of Jesus, with particular reference to the role of the emperor and the provinces within it.

### (a) Rome and Her Empire

#### (1) The Role of the Emperor

At the time of Jesus, the person of the Roman emperor dominated the Roman world. This had not always been the case. The old Roman Republic was an oligarchic political system, which carefully balanced the power of the small number of elites in the senatorial class with the increasing demands of the *equites* (knights) and the people. Its government had evolved to meet the needs of a city-state. But in the first century BC, following Rome's remarkable expansion over the preceding centuries, the old republican system proved inadequate to the task of administering a Mediterranean-wide empire. A series of generals used the power of the army to push the limits of republican order. Civil wars ensued. Finally, in September 31 BC, Octavian, the relatively unknown heir of Julius Caesar, defeated Antony at the battle of Actium and brought to an end the civil wars that had plagued Rome for decades. In the years that followed, Octavian became the architect of a new, and highly centralized, system of government for the Roman Empire.

Octavian's new order, now sometimes called "the principate," concentrated power in the hands of one man—the *princeps ciuitatis* or "first citizen"—while also granting honors and privileges to the senators, *equites* and people sufficient to placate any serious opposition. This new system undergirded the *pax Romana* (Roman peace) of the following centuries and secured stable government and prosperity for the Roman world. Thus, in 27

---

[67] Some scholars question the meeting, but cf. Hoehner, *Herod Antipas*, pp. 227-30.

BC, in recognition of his "services to the Republic," Octavian was granted an honorific title with quasi-divine overtones—Augustus (Revered One)—by which he was subsequently known. In the century that followed, his successors (Tiberius, Gaius, Claudius and Nero) quickly consolidated their position in Rome and established themselves as autocratic rulers of the empire.[68]

| | | |
|---|---|---|
| | Augustus | 27 BC–AD 14 |
| | Tiberius | 14–37 |
| Julio-Claudian Emperors | Gaius (Caligula) | 37–41 |
| | Claudius | 41–54 |
| | Nero | 54–68 |
| The "Year of the Four Emperors" | | 68–69 |
| | Vespasian | 69–79 |
| Flavian Emperors | Titus | 79–81 |
| | Domitian | 81–96 |

*Table 3. Julio-Claudian and Flavian emperors.*

These Roman emperors were not shy of making exalted claims for themselves in their imperial propaganda. In this, as in so much else, it was Augustus who set the precedent when he proclaimed his adopted father, Julius Caesar, a god (Suetonius, *Jul.* 88). This was not just a shrewd political move (who could argue with the son of a god?); it also prepared the ground for the posthumous divinization of Augustus himself, and then of those who followed him (Dio Cassius, *Hist.* 56.46). By the end of Augustus' life, imperial cults of ruler worship were well established across the empire; in the East, where the people were already accustomed to such things, the process was quicker still.[69] What's more, within this frame of reference, it was only natural—whensoever an emperor toured the empire—that the occasion of his arrival (ἡ παρουσία; Lat. *aduentus*) in a province should be duly celebrated, in a manner reminiscent of the honors accorded to the semi-divine hellenistic kings, with lavish pomp and ceremony.[70] How could the subject peoples do

---

[68] On the fall of the Republic and the origins of the principate, see esp. R. Syme, *The Roman Revolution* (Oxford: Oxford University Press, 1966). On the role of the emperor, F. Millar, *The Emperor in the Roman World: 31 BC to AD 337* (Ithaca: Cornell University Press, 1977). The principle literary sources for the period are collected in V. Ehrenberg and A. H. M. Jones, *Documents Illustrating the Reigns of Augustus and Tiberius* (Oxford: Clarendon Press, 1976).

[69] M. Beard, J. North and S. Price, *Religions of Rome, Vol. 1: A History* (New York: Cambridge University Press, 1998), pp. 313-63.

[70] G. A. Deissmann, *Light from the Ancient Near East* (London: Hodder & Stoughton, 1927), pp. 368-73.

anything less for the one who had brought salvation and peace to the known world?[71]

In this context, Jesus' announcement of the coming kingdom of Israel's God was no call to quietist spirituality. The acknowledgement of him in the gospels as Son of God and savior was, likewise, far from an innocuous "religious" doctrine.[72] And the early Christian expectation that he would soon make his "kingly arrival" (ἡ παρουσία) in royal glory as bright as lightening was much more than an individual hope or a private contemplation.[73] These things were political dynamite.[74]

## (2) The Roman Provincial System and the Province of Judea

If the emperor stood at the heart of the Roman world, then the provinces lay at the extremities. Once Augustus had established himself as *princeps*, he reorganized the old republican system for governing these regions with a characteristically keen eye on his own power and influence.[75] In particular, he made a distinction between two types of province. Those which were generally orderly and peaceful—often having been under Roman rule for a considerable period—were designated "senatorial" or "public" provinces; they generally obtained only a minimal force and fell to the Roman Senate. Those provinces, on the other hand, which required a significant armed force, or which were newly annexed to the empire, were (generally) designated "imperial"; they fell under the control of the *princeps*, who thereby retained direct command of the legions stationed in them.

The imperial provinces were further subdivided into three categories. Augustus entrusted those that required a significant deployment of troops to men of the senatorial class. Provinces that received more than one legion were staffed by a former consul (the highest Roman magistracy). Others received one legion only and were staffed by a former praetor (the next most senior magistracy).[76] A third class of imperial provinces—not deemed large or troublesome enough to warrant a significant deployment of troops—received no legion and were staffed by men of the less prestigious equestrian order.

---

[71] For this language, see e.g. the Priene inscription (*OGIS*, no. 458): Augustus is "a savior who put an end to war and established peace"; and "the birthday of the god (= Augustus) marked for the world the beginning of the good tidings through his coming."

[72] Son of God: Matt. 3.17/Mark 1:11/Luke 3:22; Matt. 17:5/Mark 9:7/Luke 9:35; John 1:34, 49; 3:18 etc. Savior: Matt. 1:21; Luke 1:69; 2:11; 19:10; John 4:42; 12:47.

[73] Note, in particular, Matthew's use of the technical term ἡ παρουσία to refer to the "coming" of Jesus (24:3, 27, 37, 39). This may have been intended to evoke the παρουσία of Titus at Antioch after the destruction of Jerusalem (Josephus, *J.W.* 7.100): from Matthew's point of view the "coming" of the general to the provincial capital was nothing more than a parody of the great "kingly arrival" of Jesus in the heavenly court.

[74] For a recent survey of the now considerable literature on this kind of "polemical parallelism," see D. G. Horrell, "Introduction: The Imperial Cult and the New Testament," *Journal for the Study of the New Testament* 27 (2005), pp. 251-55.

[75] Suetonius, *Aug.* 47; Strabo, *Geogr.* 17.3.25 (840); Dio Cassius, *Hist.* 53.12; cf. E. T. Salmon, *A History of the Roman World 30 BC to AD 138* (London: Methuen, 1968), pp. 74-82.

[76] In both cases, these men were styled *legatus Augusti pro praetore* (imperial legate).

From AD 6–73/4 Judea belonged to the third class of imperial provinces and was administered by equestrian governors. In the first half of this period, until 41, the governors were styled "prefects" (Lat: *praefectus*; Gk: ἔπαρχος) and ruled over the former territory of Archelaus (Judea, Samaria and Idumea).[77] After the brief interlude in 41–44 when the emperor Gaius (Caligula) installed Herod Agrippa I as king of all Palestine, the provincial regime was resumed, with two modifications: the governors were now styled "procurator" (Lat: *procurator*; Gk: ἐπίτροπος) and, more significantly, the territory they ruled was expanded to cover all of Agrippa's former kingdom.[78] The procuratorial system persisted until AD 73/74, just after the end of the First Jewish War (66–70), when Vespasian garrisoned Jerusalem with the tenth legion (*legio X Fretensis*) and thereby increased the status of Judea to that of an Imperial province staffed by a legate of praetorian (i.e. senatorial) rank (Josephus, *J.W.* 7.5, 17).

### (3) The Governors of Judea

The prefects/procurators of Judea were directly responsible to the Roman *princeps*. It is true that, in circumstances of emergency, the imperial legates of Syria were empowered to intervene in Judean affairs by virtue of their superior rank, but this was the exception rather than the rule. Under normal circumstances the governor of Judea was appointed by, and answered directly to, the emperor in Rome.

The powers entrusted to the Roman prefects/procurators of Judea included military command, judicial authority and financial responsibility for the province. To begin with, then, the Roman governors had command of a relatively small force of around 3,000 locally recruited auxiliary troops. The closest Roman legions (comprised of Roman citizens) were stationed in Syria under the command of the governor of that province, an imperial legate of proconsular (i.e. senatorial) rank.[79] The city of Jerusalem itself was garrisoned with only one cohort (600-1000 men) under the command of a Roman citizen officer, the χιλίαρχος (tribune), who was directly responsible to the governor. From its garrison in the Antonia fortress this cohort could keep the temple courts under constant surveillance, and during the great festivals armed guards were posted around the temple porticoes as an extra precautionary measure.[80]

---

[77] Josephus, *Ant.* 17.355; 18.2; *J.W.* 2.117. The title "prefect" emphasized the military role of the governor as commander of a small force of auxiliary troops. See A. H. M. Jones, *Studies in Roman Goverment and Law* (Oxford: Blackwell, 1960), pp. 115-25; and *AE* 1963, no. 104: a Latin dedicatory inscription discovered in the theater at Caesarea which designates Pilate *praefectus*.

[78] The change was in name only since the powers of the governors of Judea remained the same. Matthew and Luke employ the more general title ἡγεμών (governor): Matt. 27:2, 11, 14, 15, 21, 27; 28:14; Luke 3:1; 20:20. Mark and John avoid titles altogether, preferring instead to refer to Pilate simply by his name.

[79] Varus had three legions in 4 BC (Josephus, *Ant.* 17.286; *J.W.* 2.40, 66-67); by AD 14 this had increased to four (Tacitus, *Ann.* 4.5).

[80] For the tribune: John 18:12; Acts 21:31; cf. Josephus, *Ant.* 15.408; 18.93: φρούραρχος.

It is no surprise, therefore, that the auxiliary troops of the Roman army (and some of their commanders) feature prominently in the gospels. Indeed, although many modern readers are surprised to learn it, the Jesus of the gospels repeatedly predicted, in no uncertain terms, the coming destruction of the holy city at the hands of Roman legions.[81]

In addition to his military command, the Roman governor was ultimately responsible for the collection of taxes.[82] Taxes were levied directly on the person and on agricultural produce, as well as indirectly on trade and travel.[83] Direct taxes were collected for the prefect/procurator on an annual basis by local Jewish councils.[84] The indirect taxes were "farmed out" by auction: the highest bidder paid the agreed sum in advance out of his own resources, and then recuperated his expenditure (and collected a profit) in the course of gathering taxes in the region. The τελῶναι (tax-collectors) of the gospels belonged to this class of men.[85] Together, these taxes no doubt placed considerable pressure on the inhabitants of the region.[86] Just as significant, however, was the fact that they stamped Rome's mark of ownership on the land and the people of Palestine: for Jews who believed that the land and the people belonged to God alone, the taxation (like the census which served it) was an explosive religious and political issue.[87]

Finally, in addition to his military command and fiscal authority, the prefect/procurator was invested with supreme jurisdiction in all legal matters, including the authority to inflict capital punishment, if not on Roman citizens,

---

For the location of the garrison: Josephus, *J.W.* 5.238-47; cf. *Ant.* 20.106-07; Acts 21:31-40. For the strength of the cohort: S. R. Llewelyn, *New Documents Illustrating Early Christianity: A Review of the Greek Inscriptions and Papyri Published in 1980-81* (Sydney: Macquarie University, 1992), pp. 159-61.

[81] Matt. 24:2/Mark 13:2/Luke 21:6; Luke 19:41-44; 21:20-24; cf. Matt. 21:40-44/Mark 12:9-11/Luke 20:15-18; Matt. 22:7; Matt. 24:28/Luke 17:37.

[82] See esp. M. Rostovtzeff, *Geschichte der Staatspacht in der römischen Kaiserzeit* (Philologus supp. 9, 1904); F. Herrenbrück, *Jesus und die Zöllner: Historische und neutestamentlichexegetische Untersuchungen* (Tübingen: Mohr [Siebeck], 1990).

[83] Cf. Matt. 17:25: the indirect border tax (τέλος); and Matt. 22:19: the direct head tax (κῆνσος).

[84] Smallwood, *Jews Under Roman Rule*, p. 152; M. Stern, "The Herodian Dynasty and the Province of Judea at the End of the Period of the Second Temple," in M. Avi-Yonah, ed., *The World History of the Jewish People: The Herodian Period* (New Brunswick: Rutgers University Press, 1975), pp. 166-67.

[85] Interestingly, the only two τελῶναι mentioned by name in the Gospels, Matthew/Levi and Zacchaeus, worked at Galilee and Jericho respectively, and so most probably worked under Antipas rather than Rome (Matt. 9:9/Mark 2:14/Luke 5:27; 19:2).

[86] Indeed, in addition to these "foreign" taxes, Jews were liable to an annual half-shekel "temple tax" used for the maintenance of the Jerusalem temple and its cult (Matt. 17:24-27). Tacitus, *Ann.* 2.42 states that under Tiberius the provinces of Syria and Judea were "exhausted by their burdens"; cf. J. H. Kautsky, *The Politics of Aristocratic Empires* (Chapel Hill: University of North Carolina Press, 1982), pp. 73, 150: "to rule in aristocratic empires is, above all, to tax." Note, however, the salutary cautions of F. Udoh, *To Caesar What Is Caesar's: Tribute, Taxes, and Imperial Administration in Early Roman Palestine 63 B.C.E.–70 C.E.* (Providence: Brown Judaic Studies, 2005).

[87] E.g. Matt. 22:15-22/Mark 12:13-17/Luke 20:20-26.

then certainly on all others (Josephus, *J.W.* 2.117).[88] It is important to understand, however, that multiple legal systems operated within ancient empires and their provinces. In Judea during the first century, although supreme judicial authority rested with the Roman governor, the majority of the day-to-day judicial administration of the province was left in the hands of the Jerusalem Council (Sanhedrin) and the local Jewish courts.

### (4) Jewish Authorities: The High Priests and the Jerusalem Council

The Roman apparatus of government in the provinces was minimal and assumed the maintenance of existing administrative structures.[89] In Judea, the Roman governors resided in the former palace of Herod I at Caesarea and only visited Jerusalem during the great festivals or when there was otherwise need. They therefore granted the successive high priests, together with the Jerusalem council (Sanhedrin), legal autonomy to rule in relation to Jewish affairs in general, and over Jerusalem in particular. The council was permitted an independent police force empowered to arrest offenders,[90] and was granted authority to punish and imprison those convicted of crimes.[91] Nevertheless, the prefects/procurators reserved the right to intervene in Jewish affairs and/or overrule council decisions.[92] Moreover, it seems that while the Sanhedrin could pronounce a capital sentence (e.g. Acts 26:10), the Roman governors reserved the right of execution for themselves (John 18:31).[93] The one exception to this rule may have been cases of offence against the temple, in which it seems the Jewish council was granted authority to execute.[94] If so, then this would explain why the council sought to convict Jesus of blasphemy against the temple (Matt. 26:59-62/Mark 14:55-59), for such a conviction

---

[88] Jones, *Roman Goverment and Law*, pp. 51-65; A. N. Sherwin-White, *Roman Society and Roman Law in the New Testament* (Oxford: Clarendon Press, 1963), pp. 58-70.

[89] H. M. Cotton and W. Eck, "Roman Officials in Judaea and Arabia," in R. Katzoff and D. Schaps, eds., *Law in the Documents of the Judaean Desert* (Leiden: Brill, 2005), pp. 23-44; though note that the situation in Judea in the period 6-41 differed somewhat from that which is described here.

[90] Luke 22:4, 52; John 7:32, 45-46; 18:22; Acts 5:22, 26. Members of this body were probably at the core of the "crowd" sent by the Council to arrest Jesus: Matt. 26:47/Mark 14:43/Luke 22:52; and cf. John 18:2.12 where this group is carefully distinguished from the Roman soldiers who accompanied it.

[91] E.g. Acts 4:1-23; 5:17-40; 9:2; 22:4-5, 19-20, 30; 23:28-29; 26:10-11.

[92] E.g. Acts 22:30; 23:10, 12-24; 24:1-2, 22-23; 25:1-12.

[93] The reliability of this testimony has sometimes been questioned. For a convenient summary of the debate, with arguments for the traditional view, see B. Corley, "Trial of Jesus," in J. B. Green, S. McKnight and I. H. Marshall, eds., *Dictionary of Jesus and the Gospels* (Downers Grove: InterVarsity Press, 1992), pp. 841-54, esp. pp. 850-51.

[94] The evidence for the exception consists in: i. The warning inscription posted on Herod's temple, which threatened death to Gentiles who trespassed in the inner court (Josephus, *Ant.* 15.417; *J.W.* 5.194; cf. Philo, *Legat.* 212; 307; *m. Kelim.* 1.8, *CII* 1400: cf. Acts 21.27-29); ii. A speech attributed to the Roman general (later emperor) Titus by Josephus, which implies that the Romans had granted the Jews, by way of concession, the right to execute offenders of this kind (Josephus, *J.W.* 6.126); iii. The stoning of Stephen, which may fall into this category (Acts 6:13-14; 7:48-50, 57-58).

would have enabled them to put him to death without involving the governor. When they were unable to do this, they charged Jesus more directly with making a blasphemous messianic claim (Matt. 26:63-65/Mark 14:61-64/Luke 22:67-71), brought him before Pilate, and translated this very Jewish charge into one that would secure his condemnation under Roman law: sedition (Luke 23:2).[95]

The significant influence of the Jewish authorities is also seen in the important concessions they secured from the Roman governors: the copper coins minted by the governors carried only the name and not the customary portrait of the emperor;[96] the image-bearing standards of the Roman army were likewise kept out of Jerusalem (Josephus, *Ant.* 18.56, 121-22); daily sacrifices made at the temple on behalf of "Caesar and the Romans" were accepted in place of participation in the imperial ruler cults (Philo, *Legat.* 157, 317);[97] and Jews were granted exemption from appearing before a magistrate on holy days. In return for these privileges, the Jewish authorities were expected to keep the rebellious elements of the population in check: this proved to be a difficult task.

*(b) Judea Under the Prefects from Coponius to Marullus (AD 6–41)*

In AD 6, then, when Augustus first annexed Judea as a Roman province, he sent out an equestrian, Coponius, to take command as prefect. Following him, the first few governors, under Augustus, each ruled for a period of three years. Little more is known of them than their names: Coponius (6–9); Marcus Ambibulus (9–12); and Annius Rufus (12–15).[98] Tiberius subsequently extended the length of service[99] for Valerius Gratus (15–26); Pontius Pilate (26–36); Marcellus (36–37); and Marullus (37–41).[100]

---

[95] Cf. Luke 23:5; 23:14. The same charge of sedition is reflected in Pilate's question to Jesus at Matt. 27:11; Mark 15:2; Luke 23:3; John 18:33. It would be a mistake, however, to interpret this as the translation of a purely "religious" charge (blasphemy) into a "political" one (sedition), because the charges laid against Jesus in the Sanhedrin were already as much political as they were religious. Jewish tradition maintained a very close link between temple building and royal—or even messianic—authority (cf. n. 32 above). Thus, the initial Jewish charge against Jesus of blasphemy against the temple was closely related to the subsequent Jewish charge of claiming messiahship, and both of these Jewish charges—since they had to do with divinely appointed royal authority—constituted a challenge to the authority of the Roman emperor. The translation of the charge into Roman terms as sedition was thus a natural one.

[96] See Meshorer, *Treasury*, pp. 167-76. Though the larger silver *denarii* which bore the emperor's image were not minted in the province, they could not be kept out of circulation there (Matt. 22:20/Mark 12:16/Luke 20:24).

[97] Cf. Philo, *Legat.* 232; 356; Josephus, *J.W.* 2.197; 409-10; 412-17; *Ag. Ap.* 2.77.

[98] Josephus, *Ant.* 17.355; 18.2, 29-33; cf. *J.W.* 2.117.

[99] Josephus, *Ant.* 18.172-76 reports that Tiberius extended the length of tenure to curb the extortionist tendencies of Roman governors, stating that like flies on a wounded body their enthusiasm for illegitimate gain would wane with time in office. Cf. Tacitus, *Ann.* 1.80; 4.6; Suetonius, *Tib.* 32.

[100] Josephus, *Ant.* 18.33-35 (cf. *J.W.* 2.169; Tacitus, *Ann.* 15.44); Josephus, *Ant.* 18.89, 237. Note, however, the attractive hypothesis advanced by D. R. Schwartz, *Agrippa I: The Last King of Judaea* (Tübingen: Mohr [Siebeck], 1990), pp. 62-66, that there was no prefect in Judea

The relationship between the Roman governors and their subjects was marred from the very beginning for, at the same time as he appointed Coponius, Augustus also sent out Quirinius as the imperial legate of Syria to conduct a census of the people of Judea. From the Roman point of view this was a simple administrative measure: the tax liability of the new province needed to be assessed.[101] But for at least some of the Jews of Palestine in the period, it was nothing less than an attack on the sole prerogative of Israel's God to rule the holy land and its people. The Jewish high priest Joazar, the son of Boethus, convinced a portion of the population to acquiesce. But Judas "the Galilean" raised a revolt.[102] This initial uprising was put down, but from that point onwards a range of Jewish groups opposed to Gentile rule planned rebellion. Their zeal did not abate until it was finally crushed in the wars of 66–70 and 132–135.[103]

The situation was not helped by the frequently inept and occasionally brutal administration of the Roman governors. The prefecture of Pontius Pilate (26–36)[104] is of particular importance for our purposes, and it is striking that there were no less than <u>six controversial incidents</u> during Pilate's time in office, not counting the condemnation and crucifixion of Jesus.

1. To mark the beginning of his tenure, Pilate attempted to introduce Roman standards bearing images of the emperor into Jerusalem under the cover of night. He was forced to back down by a mass protest of the Jews (Josephus, *Ant.* 18.55-59; *J.W.* 2.169-74).
2. Pilate took funds from the temple treasury known as Korban to finance the construction of an aqueduct for Jerusalem, then brutally massacred a large number of those who protested (Josephus, *Ant.* 18.60-62; *J.W.* 2.175-77).[105]
3. On another occasion, presumably fearing a riot, Pilate sent troops to kill an unspecified number of Galileans who had come to Jerusalem to offer sacrifices at the temple (Luke 13:1).
4. Probably around 32, Pilate set up in Herod I's former palace in Jerusalem

---

between Pilate and Agrippa I.

[101] Josephus, *Ant.* 18.4-10, 23-25; *J.W.* 2.118, 433; 7.253; Luke 2:1-3; Acts 5:37. Since Luke appears to place Jesus' birth both during the reign of Herod I (d. c. 4 BC) and at the time of Quirinius' census (AD 6) scholars question the historical reliability of Luke's account at this point; cf. however, Barnett, *Rise of Early Christianity*, pp. 97-99.

[102] Josephus, *Ant.* 18.4-10, 23-25; *J.W.* 2.118, 433; 7.253; Acts 5:37. This Judas is almost certainly to be identified with the Judas son of Hezekiah who raised revolt in Galilee at the time of Herod's death (*J.W.* 2.56).

[103] Josephus, *Ant.* 18.23-25; cf. 18.4-10; *J.W.* 2.118. For Jewish revolutionary movements in this period, see Wright, *New Testament*, pp. 170-81.

[104] The principal literary sources for Pilate outside the gospels are: Josephus, *Ant.* 18.35, 55-64, 85-89; *J.W.* 2.169-77; Philo, *Legat.* 299-306; Tacitus, *Ann.* 15.44. For the coins, see Meshorer, *Treasury*, pp. 167-76. A single inscription discovered in 1961 at the theater at Caesarea also records Pilate's prefecture in Judea (*AE* 1963, no. 104). Cf. J.-P. Lémonon, *Pilate et le gouvernement de la Judée: textes et monuments* (Paris: Gabalda, 1981); H. Bond, *Pontius Pilate in History and Interpretation* (New York/Cambridge: Cambridge University Press, 1998).

[105] Cf. Eusebius, *Hist. eccl.* 2.6.6-7; Mark 7:11.

some gilded votive shields inscribed with his name and that of the emperor Tiberius. He was forced to remove them to the temple of Augustus at Caesarea when a delegation of leading Jews (including even Antipas and Philip the tetrarch) sent letters to the emperor (Philo, *Legat.* 299-306).[106]

5. A year later, Pilate captured and condemned the bandit Barabbas, who had led a bloody insurrection in Jerusalem, but later released him as a token of goodwill during the Passover (Mark 15:6-15/Matt. 27:15-23; Luke 23:18-25; John 18:39-40).[107]

6. Finally, Pilate brutally suppressed a popular prophetic movement in Samaria, killing many of the Samaritans involved at the foot of Mount Gerizim. The surviving Samaritans complained to Vitellius, the Roman legate of Syria, who removed Pilate from office and sent him to answer the accusations in Rome (Josephus, *Ant.* 18.85-89).

These events provide an illuminating context for the gospel accounts of the trial of Jesus before Pilate,[108] which took place during the Passover festival, probably in 33.[109] At this point in his rule Pilate found himself in a vulnerable position: the downfall in Rome, in October 31, of the influential L. Aelius Sejanus, to whom Pilate probably owed his position,[110] placed the prefect under suspicion in the capital; the incident of the votive shields (4 above) in which Tiberius was forced to intervene, cannot have helped; the combined effects of incidents 1, 2, 3 and 4 no doubt ensured that Pilate was unpopular with large sections of the Jewish populace; and incidents 3 and 4 had strained his relationship with Antipas as well (cf. Luke 23:12). Pilate could not afford to be seen to be unnecessarily provoking unrest again, and needed to take serious steps to appease those whom he had previously offended.

For these reasons, then, though Pilate seems to have enjoyed provoking the Jewish aristocracy,[111] the case of Jesus proved a difficult one for him. On learning that the prisoner was a Galilean, Pilate first sent him to Antipas, who was in Jerusalem for the festival (Luke 23:6-12). It seems he hoped both to share responsibility for the awkward case, and to win back Antipas' support after the recent tension between them. And indeed, the gesture was successful in regaining Antipas, and enabled Pilate to claim that the tetrarch too found

---

[106] Bond, *Pilate*, pp. 36-46.

[107] P. Winter, *On the Trial of Jesus* (New York: de Gruyter, 1974), p. 134 questions the historical reliability of the gospel accounts of a "passover privilege"; but cf. Corley, "Trial of Jesus," p. 849.

[108] Cf. Josephus, *J.W.* 2.301 for comparison with a trial held before Florus.

[109] H. W. Hoehner, *Chronological Aspects of the Life of Christ* (Grand Rapids: Zondervan, 1977), pp. 95-114. The only major alternative date is Passover AD 30 (so R. Riesner, *Paul's Early Period* [Grand Rapids: Eerdmans, 1998], pp. 57-58).

[110] Questioned by Lémonon, *Pilate*, pp. 275-76.

[111] Cf. Matt. 27:18/Mark 15:10; John 18:31; 19:14-15; and esp. John 19:22 (cf. Matt. 27:37; Mark 15:26; Luke 23:38). Pilate was also the first of the Roman governors to use Roman symbols on his coins (Meshorer, *Treasury*, pp. 167-73).

Jesus innocent (Luke 23:12-15).[112] Nevertheless, the chief priests were not persuaded, and they managed to turn the crowds against the captive. When it looked that a riot might break out (Matt. 27:24; Mark 15:15), and particularly when the chief priests threatened to report him to Caesar, Pilate relented to their demands and had Jesus crucified (John 19:12).[113] It was the only expedient option left.

### (c) Interlude: The Kingdom of Herod Agrippa I (AD 41–44)

The accession of the emperor Gaius (Caligula) in March 37 brought a change to imperial policy in Palestine: Herod Agrippa I, a friend of Gaius and a grandson of Herod I, was proclaimed king. In the years that followed, the various political units in the region were gradually re-united in his short-lived kingdom: in 37 he received the former tetrarchy of Philip; in 39/40 he acquired the former tetrarchy of Antipas; and from 41–44 he was granted control of the former province of Judea also. For a few short years, then, Agrippa I ruled over the whole of Palestine (see *Table 2*).[114]

Agrippa I pursued the characteristic Herodian policy of courting Roman favor above all, while also being careful not to unnecessarily offend his Jewish subjects. This conciliatory approach was much needed after the troubles of Pilate's prefecture, and especially after the crisis of 40. In that year the emperor Gaius had deliberately provoked the Jews by ordering that a statue of himself, in the form of the god Jupiter, be erected in the temple at Jerusalem. The consternation this caused amongst pious Jews cannot be overestimated. Similarly, amongst the early Christian communities the prospect of the emperor's statue being erected in the temple must have evoked powerful memories of Jesus' word about the "abomination of desolation" being set up in the holy place (Matt. 24:15/Mark 13:14). Almost certain war was averted only by the intervention of Agrippa, who managed to convince Gaius to retract his order, and then—after the command was reissued—by the timely assassination of the emperor in 41.[115]

The next emperor, Claudius (41–54), significantly revised Gaius' policy towards the Jews and sought to ease tensions in the region. It was perhaps because of Agrippa's proven track record of conciliating a notoriously difficult people that Claudius reconfirmed him as king and, in 41, added the province of Judea to his growing kingdom. Agrippa's untimely death in 44 (Acts 12:20-23; Josephus, *Ant.* 19.343-52), however, and the lack of a suitable

---

[112] Cf. Hoehner, *Herod Antipas*, p. 238.

[113] On the use of the title φίλος τοῦ Καίσαρος (friend of Caesar) under Tiberius, see Tacitus, *Ann.* 6.8; Philo, *Flacc.* 6.40 and the discussions in Millar, *Emperor*, pp. 110-22; G. H. R. Horsley, *New Documents Illustrating Early Christianity: A Review of the Greek Inscriptions and Papyri Published in 1978* (Sydney: Macquarie University, 1983), pp. 87-89. It seems quite probable that Pilate enjoyed official status as a φιλοκαίσαρ.

[114] Josephus, *Ant.* 18.237-39 (cf. *J.W.* 2.181-83); *Ant.* 19.274-75; 351-52 (cf. *J.W.* 2.214-16). The most important recent work on Herod Agrippa I is Schwartz, *Agrippa I*.

[115] Josephus, *Ant.* 18.261-309; *J.W.* 2.184-203; Philo, *Legat.* 184-348; Tacitus, *Hist.* 5.9; *Ann.* 12.54.1; cf. Schwartz, *Agrippa I*, pp. 77-89.

candidate to replace him as king (his son Agrippa II was too young), led to a reversion to the previous policy of administering Judea directly as a Roman province (Josephus, *Ant.* 19.360-63; *J.W.* 2.220).

### (d) The Road to War: Judea Under the Procurators From Fadus to Florus (AD 44–66)

In 44 Claudius extended the previous borders of the province of Judea so that it incorporated the majority of Palestine, and sent out procurators to administer the troublesome territory. According to Josephus, these governors, seven in all, went from bad to worse, and did much by their flagrant disregard for the ancestral traditions of the Jews to incite the people to revolt.[116]

The first two procurators seem to have been the best. According to Josephus, Cuspius Fadus (44–c. 46) and Tiberius Julius Alexander (46–48), "by abstaining from all interference with the customs of the country kept the nation at peace" (*J.W.* 2.220; cf. *Ant.* 19.363; 20.100); and yet even these procuratorships were not without disturbances.[117] The rule of Ventidius Cumanus (48–c. 52) was marked by more serious incidents, including the massacre of a large number of Jews (Josephus says 20,000) at the temple during the Passover after a Roman soldier incited riots when he insulted the assembled crowd.[118]

The situation worsened under Antonius Felix (c. 52–60) and Josephus says that from his term as procurator onwards Judea was in a state of constant turmoil: the notorious *sicarii* ("dagger-men") began their targeted political assassinations, and at their hands the high priest Jonathan met his death; various sign-prophets, most notably "the Egyptian", led large bands into the desert as a prelude to a religiously inspired attack on the Roman garrison in Jerusalem; bands of rebels targeted the wealthy; and violence erupted in Caesarea between Jews and Syrians. Everywhere, Felix met these disturbances with the sword, and innumerable rebels were crucified. He only barely held the province together by the force of arms and was eventually recalled by Nero.[119]

Porcius Festus (c. 60–62) was perhaps less brutal than Felix, but was

---

[116] See esp. D. M. Rhoads, *Israel in Revolution 6–74 CE* (Philadelphia: Fortress Press, 1976).

[117] These were: i. controversy over custody of the vestments of the high priest (Josephus, *Ant.* 20.6-14; cf. *Ant.* 15.403-08); ii. an uprising led by a would-be prophet named Theudas (*Ant.* 20.97-99 = Eusebius, *Hist. eccl.* 2.11; cf. Acts 5.36?); iii. the crucifixions of James and Simon, the sons of Judas the Galilean (*Ant.* 20.102).

[118] Josephus, *Ant.* 20.103-36; *J.W.* 2.223-46; cf. Tacitus, *Ann.* 12.54.3; Eusebius, *Hist. eccl.* 2.19.1.

[119] Josephus, *Ant.* 20.137, 141-43, 160-77, 180-82; *J.W.* 2.247, 252-70; Acts 21.38; 24.25; Suetonius, *Claud.* 28; Tacitus, *Ann.* 12.54; *Hist.* 5.9. On the *sicarii*, see further: Josephus, *Ant.* 20.186-87, 204-08; *J.W.* 2.433; 4.400-05, 516; 7.252-406; cf. R. A. Horsley and J. S. Hanson, *Bandits, Prophets and Messiahs: Popular Movements at the Time of Jesus* (Minneapolis: Winston, 1985), pp. 200-202. On "the Egyptian": P. W. Barnett, "The Jewish Sign Prophets— AD 40–70: Their Intentions and Origin," *New Testament Studies* 27 (1981), pp. 679-97.

nevertheless unable to make inroads into the turmoil in Judea. The *sicarii* continued their murderous activities. Another (unnamed) prophet led rebels into the desert and met his demise at the hands of Festus' troops. And in Rome, Nero's decision in favor of the Syrians in the dispute over Caesarea added fuel to the fire. When Festus died in office, Jerusalem descended into anarchy, and the high priest Annas II (son of the Annas of the gospels) used the opportunity to have his rivals, including James the brother of Jesus, stoned to death.[120]

In Albinus (62–64) and Gessius Florus (64–66) the Roman procurators of Judea plumbed new depths. Albinus primarily used his two years in office to garner wealth: he appropriated the private property of others, increased taxes, and took bribes from all sides in the developing conflicts. What is more, by releasing revolutionaries in exchange for Roman partisans whom they had captured, he "stimulated" the "audacity of the revolutionary party" (Josephus, *J.W.* 2.274; cf. *Ant.* 20.215). Florus, Josephus writes, was the worst of all: he made Albinus "appear by comparison a paragon of virtue" (*J.W.* 2.277). Though Josephus gives little specific detail, it seems that Florus continued the same downward trajectory: he did little to curb the activities of those inciting revolution, and brazenly plundered the wealth of the province.[121]

### 4. Roman Domination: The First Jewish War and its Aftermath

The tumultuous situation in Judea finally erupted into open revolt and warfare when, in April/May 66, Florus seized seventeen talents from the temple treasury in Jerusalem.[122] Mocking protests were put down by bloody force, and this incited further rebellion. Significantly, under the leadership of Eleazar, the son of Ananias the high priest, the rebels suspended the daily sacrifice for the emperor—an act tantamount to a declaration of war. Despite the efforts of Agrippa II, the chief priests, and other members of the aristocracy to control the rebels, Florus' troops were soon ousted from the city with great bloodshed. As news spread, further rebellions sprang up all over Palestine.[123]

The Roman response was slow to begin with, but ultimately effective. First, Cestius Gallus, the legate of Syria, marched on Jerusalem with over 10,000 men. He was quickly repulsed, however, and as news reached Rome, the emperor Nero dispatched Vespasian to suppress the revolt and regain control of Judea.[124] This general had more success, and by the end of 68 he had effectively pacified Galilee and Judea: of the major cities only Jerusalem

---

[120] Josephus, *Ant.* 20.182-97, 200; *J.W.* 2.271, 284; Acts 24.27-26.32; Eusebius, *Hist. eccl.* 2.23.1-24.

[121] Josephus, *Ant.* 20.197-210, 252-57; *J.W.* 2.272-79; Tacitus, *Hist.* 5.10.

[122] The best recent scholarly discussion of the First Jewish War is J. T. Price, *Jerusalem Under Siege: The Collapse of the Jewish State AD 66–70* (Leiden: Brill, 1992).

[123] Josephus, *J.W.* 2.293-308, 405-98.

[124] Josephus, *J.W.* 2.499-509, 517-22, 527-30, 533-55.

remained in rebel hands.[125]

Nero's death and the Roman civil wars that followed in 69 ("the Year of the Four Emperors") brought Roman operations in Judea to a halt. Vespasian was hailed as emperor by his troops and marched for Rome to claim power. He left his son, Titus, in Judea with four legions to prosecute the siege of Jerusalem. For three months in the summer of 70 Titus' troops surrounded the city and attacked its defences. Inside the Temple Mount, three rival revolutionary factions (one of which Josephus calls "the Zealots") fought with each other for control of the rebel cause.[126] The infighting hastened the city's downfall. Finally, on the ninth day of the fifth month—the anniversary of the destruction of Solomon's temple by the Babylonians—the Romans broke through and set fire to the temple. Roman standards were set up in the outer courts proclaiming Rome's domination of Jerusalem. Mass slaughter ensued. Within a month Titus commanded the whole city.[127] There is no doubt that many early Christians interpreted these events as the fulfillment of the prophetic words of Jesus concerning the downfall of the city.[128]

Some rebels held out for the next few years at the fortress strongholds of Herodium, Machaerus and Masada. Finally, however, in 73 (or possibly in 74), Masada fell to the tenth Roman legion when the revolutionaries chose suicide rather than surrender.[129] Judea was made a full Roman province under the command of an imperial legate of praetorian rank, and garrisoned with a full Roman legion. The Jerusalem Council was dissolved. The temple was destroyed, never to be rebuilt. And the failure of a further Jewish revolt in 132–135 ("the Bar Kokhba War") ensured that Roman domination in Palestine was complete.[130]

---

[125] Josephus, *J.W.* 3 & 4; cf. Eusebius, *Hist. eccl.* 3.5.3 according to whom certain Christians abandoned Jerusalem at this time and fled to Pella in the Decapolis (cf. Matt. 24:16/Mark 13:14/Luke 21:21).

[126] Contrary to an old consensus, it is now clear that during the first century there was no single, longstanding, organizationally unified and ideologically motivated movement of armed resistance against Rome known as "the Zealots." Amongst the considerable literature, see, esp. M. Hengel, *The Zealots: Investigations into the Jewish Freedom Movement in the Period from Herod I until 70 AD* (Edinburgh: T. & T. Clark, 1989); M. Smith, "Zealots and Sicarii, Their Origins and Relation," *Harvard Theological Review* 64 (1971), pp. 1-19; Horsley and Hanson, *Bandits, Prophets and Messiahs*; and T. L. Donaldson, "Rural Bandits, City Mobs and the Zealots," *Journal for the Study of Judaism* 21 (1990), pp. 19-40.

[127] Josephus, *J.W.* 5 & 6. Although it is often overlooked, the destruction of Jerusalem is a prominent theme in the gospels.

[128] E.g. Matt. 22:7; Matt. 24:1-2/Mark 13:1-2/Luke 21:5-6; Matt. 22; Luke 19:41-44; 21:20-22; cf. Josephus, J.W. 6.249-70. For discussion, see Wright, Jesus, pp. 333-68.

[129] Josephus, *J.W.* 7.252-388. For the archeological evidence, see E. Netzer, "Masada," in E. Stern, A. Lewinson-Gilboa and J. Aviram, eds., *The New Encyclopaedia of Archaeological Excavations in the Holy Land*, vol. 3 (New York: Simon & Schuster, 1993), pp. 973-85. For a critical treatment of Josephus' account of the siege, see S. J. D. Cohen, "Masada, Literary Tradition, Archaeological Remains, and the Credibility of Josephus," *Journal of Jewish Studies* 33 (1982), pp. 385-405.

[130] On the Bar Kokhba War, see now P. Schäfer, *The Bar Kokhba War Reconsidered: New Perspectives on the Second Jewish Revolt against Rome* (Tübingen: Mohr [Siebeck], 2003).

## C. Conclusion

This chapter has offered an outline of the political history of Palestine at the time of Jesus. If one theme has emerged from the survey, it is that the dichotomizing tendency of modern scholarship, which habitually separates the "religious" from the "political", is thoroughly alien to the world in which Jesus lived. In Jesus' world "religion" was thoroughly political, and "politics" deeply religious. The task of interpreting the gospels in their "political context", then, let alone that of applying them to the very different political situations which have arisen in the modern world, remains a challenging one. It must suffice to say here that Jesus' proclamation of the kingdom of God, along with his radical call for allegiance to himself, was pregnant not only with religious, but also with political significance. It cut across the demands of both the Roman emperors and the Jewish revolutionaries of his day. If Jesus was executed for sedition, then, he was (at least in one sense) guilty as charged.[131] His program was—and indeed remains—radically subversive, challenging all human ideologies and power structures in that day and this.

## Bibliography

Bond, Helen K. *Pontius Pilate in History and Interpretation*. New York/Cambridge: Cambridge University Press, 1998.

Goodman, Martin. *The Ruling Class of Judaea: The Origins of the Jewish Revolt Against Rome AD 66–70*. Cambridge/New York: Cambridge University Press, 1987.

Hoehner, Harold W. *Herod Antipas*. Grand Rapids: Zondervan, 1980.

Jensen, Morten Hoerning. *Herod Antipas in Galilee: The Literary and Archaeological Sources on the Reign of Herod Antipas and its Socio-Economic Impact on Galilee*. Tübingen: Mohr (Siebeck), 2006.

McLaren, James S. *Power and Politics in Palestine: The Jews and the Governing of their Land 100BC–AD70*. JSNTSS 63. Sheffield: JSOT Press, 1991.

Meshorer, Ya'akov. *A Treasury of Jewish Coins*. New York/Jerusalem: Amphora Books/Yad Ben-Zvi Press, 2001.

Millar, Fergus. *The Emperor in the Roman World: 31 BC to AD 337*. Ithaca: Cornell University Press, 1977.

Price, Jonathan T. *Jerusalem Under Siege: The Collapse of the Jewish State AD 66–70*. Leiden/New York: Brill, 1992.

Rhoads, David M. *Israel in Revolution 6–74 CE*. Philadelphia: Fortress Press, 1976.

Richardson, Peter. *Herod: King of the Jews and Friend of the Romans*. Columbia: Univesity of South Carolina Press, 1996.

Schäfer, Paul. *The History of the Jews in the Greco-Roman World*, rev. ed. London: Routledge, 2003.

Schürer, Emil. *The History of the Jewish People in the Age of Jesus Christ (175 BC–AD 135)*, rev. & ed. Geza Vermes, Fergus Millar & Matthew Black. 3 vols. Edinburgh: T. & T. Clark, 1973-1987.

Sherwin-White, Adrian Nicholas. *Roman Society and Roman Law in the New Testament*. Oxford: Clarendon Press, 1963.

Syme, Ronald. *The Roman Revolution*. Oxford: Oxford University Press, 1966.

Udoh, Fabian E. To Caesar What Is Caesar's: Tribute, Taxes, and Imperial Administration in Early Roman Palestine 63 BCE –70 CE. Providence: Brown Judaic Studies, 2005.

---

[131] I owe this expression to my brother, Byron Smith.

# 5. The Social Context

*James R. Harrison*

The Gospel of Luke is sensitive to what might be called Jesus' "social agenda." This is apparent in Jesus' famous address at the synagogue of Nazareth. In his Messianic declaration of the presence of the Isaianic age of salvation (Luke 4:16-21 [Isa. 61:1-2a; cf. 49:8-10; 58:6-7]),[1] Jesus prophetically announces that his Spirit-anointed ministry (Luke 3:22; 4:1, 14, 18 [cf. Isa. 61:1a]; Acts 4:27; 10:38) effects the Sabbatical cancellation of debts (Luke 4:18; cf. Deut. 15:1-2) and the Jubilee release of slaves (Luke 4:18; Lev. 25:8-17).[2] While the Sabbatical and Jubilee "release," as enunciated by Luke, embraces both spiritual and social dimensions,[3] Jesus envisages an upending of the social and economic relations of his day.[4] Other Lukan texts spell out a similar social agenda (Luke 7:22; 14:13, 21), including

---

[1] On Jesus' messianic consciousness and its relation to Qumran documents (4Q521 2 II, 1-14; 11QMelch II, 13-20) that understood particular Isaianic texts as referring to the Messiah (Isa. 35:5-6; 52:7; 61:1-2; cf. Luke 4:18-19; 7:22), see C. A. Evans, "Jesus and the Messianic Texts from Qumran: A Preliminary Assessment of the Recently Published Materials," in C. A. Evans, *Jesus and His Contemporaries: Comparative Studies* (New York: Brill, 1995), pp. 83-154, esp. pp. 118-124, 128-29. For abbreviations used throughout this article, see P. H. Alexander et. al., eds., *The SBL Handbook of Style for Ancient Near Eastern, Biblical, and Early Christian Studies* (Peabody: Hendrickson, 1999). The approach undertaken in this chapter differs from traditional New Testament introductions. Mostly they focus on the family, the household, schooling, marriage, the temple, the synagogue, and so on. However, I will concentrate on the *social values* animating Second Temple Judaism and investigate how they relate to Jesus' ministry as depicted in the gospels.

[2] The "release" imagery of Luke 4:18 alludes to the Jubilee (Lev. 25:8-17) and three Isaianic texts: "to proclaim release to the captives" (κηρύξαι αἰχμαλώτοις ἄφεσιν: cf. Isa. 52:7; 61:1); "to let the oppressed go free" [ἀποστεῖλαι τεθραυσμένους ἐν ἀφέσει: cf. Isa. 58:6; 61:1]). On Luke 4:18 and the Jubilee, see J. H. Yoder, *The Politics of Jesus* (Grand Rapids: Eerdmans, 1972), pp. 34-40, 64-77; A. Trocmé, *Jesus and the Nonviolent Revolution* (Scottdale: Herald Press, 1973); S. H. Ringe, *Jesus, Liberation, and the Biblical Jubilee: Images for Ethics and Christology* (Philadelphia: Fortress Press, 1985). *Contra*, D. P. Seccombe *Possessions and the Poor in Luke-Acts* (Linz: A. Fuchs, 1982), pp. 54-56 who argues that the Jubilee allusion is metaphorical rather than literal.

[3] On the "spiritual" dimensions of Luke 4:18, see I. H. Marshall, *The Gospel of Luke: A Commentary on the Greek Text* (Grand Rapids: Eerdmans, 1978), p. 184; Ringe, *Jubilee*, pp. 60, 65-80; C. F. Evans, *Saint Luke* (London: SCM, 1990), pp. 270-71; D. L. Bock, *Luke 1:1–9:50* (Grand Rapids: Eerdmans, 1994), pp. 408-10.

[4] J. H. Yoder observes regarding Luke 4:18 (*Politics*, p. 39): God will effect "a visible socio-political, economic restructuring of relations among the people of God, achieved by his intervention in the person of Jesus as the one anointed and endued with the Spirit."

the social elevation of the same marginalized groups mentioned in Luke 4:18.[5]

What is intriguing is that the list of people with physical disabilities ("the blind," "the lame," "lepers," "the deaf," "the maimed") who are included in the Messianic release (Luke 4:18; 7:22; 14:13, 21) are precisely those who are marginalized by the Jewish "holiness system," if the exclusions from the Aaronic priesthood (Lev. 21:17-23) and from the eschatological community of Qumran (1QSa 2.5-22; 1QM 7.4-6) are representative.[6] Moreover, the consistent mention of "the poor" in the Lukan texts also points to the inclusion of those who were normally marginalized by the Greco-Roman "reciprocity" system. Seemingly, Jesus was undermining the operation of two of the most fundamental social systems of his day in the Messianic community of the marginalized that he was establishing.

This intersection of the reciprocity and holiness systems provides us with a convenient aperture through which we can view the social context of Second Temple Judaism and evaluate its response to Jesus' ministry. In each case the system is described, its social underside articulated, and Jesus' response to its operations assessed.

## A. The Greco-Roman Benefaction System in First-Century Palestine: Its Social Implications

### 1. The Greco-Roman Benefaction System: Its Jewish Supporters and Critics

With Augustus' victory at Actium (31 BC), the Romans controlled the eastern and western Mediterranean basin, administering their empire by means of a bureaucracy of civil servants, garrisons, tax collectors, governors, prefects and client-kings. By the first-century BC, the Greco-Roman reciprocity system had deeply penetrated the society of Palestine and its conventions were familiar to the Judean elite, both in its Herodian and imperial expressions.[7]

---

[5] Ringe, *Jubilee*, p. 58.

[6] Ringe, *Jubilee*, pp. 58-59.

[7] A Phoenician honorific inscription from Greece (Piraeus: III BC or 96 BC)—rendered in Semitic apart from a concluding Greek reference to the Sidonian Council—confirms the presence of Hellenistic reciprocity rituals in the Semitic world. For a translation, see J. C. Gibson, *Syrian Semitic Inscriptions Volume III: Phoenician Inscriptions Including Inscriptions in the Mixed Dialect of Arslam Tash* (Oxford: Oxford University Press, 1980), §41, pp. 148-51. I am indebted to Dr. J. A. Davies for drawing my attention to this. On gift giving in ancient Israel and Second Temple Judaism, see T. Rajak, "Benefactors in the Greco-Jewish Diaspora," in H. Cancik et al. eds., *Geschichte—Tradition—Reflexion: Festschrift für Martin Hengel zum 70. Geburtstag Band I: Judentum* (Tübingen: Mohr Siebeck, 1996), pp. 305-19; G. Stansell, "The Gift in Ancient Israel," *Semeia* 87 (1999), pp. 65-104; V. H. Matthews, "The Unwanted Gift: Implications of Obligatory Gift Giving in Ancient Israel," *Semeia* 87 (1999), pp. 91-104; S. Joubert, *Paul as Benefactor: Reciprocity, Strategy and Theological Reflection in Paul's Collection* (Tübingen: Mohr [Siebeck], 2000), pp. 93-99; J. R. Harrison, *Paul's Language of Grace in Its Graeco-Roman Context* (Tübingen: Mohr Siebeck, 2003), pp. 97-166. For a convenient summary of the sociological literature on reciprocity in the gospels, see G. Stansell, "Gifts, Tributes, and Offerings," in W. Stegemann et al., ed., *The Social Setting of Jesus and the*

Herod the Great—a client of Augustus and an international benefactor himself[8]—established and maintained bonds of reciprocity throughout his reign.[9] Honorific inscriptions from the Athenian Acropolis (*OGIS* 414, 427) and the agora (*SEG* XII 150) praise Herod for his beneficence to the city (εὐεργεσία) and underscore his status as a friend of the Romans (Φιλορωμαῖος) and the Emperor (Φιλοκαίσαρ).[10] The Herodian dynasty created widespread networks of obligation and was rewarded with a return of favor from its clients, as the existence of a Herodian faction at the time of Jesus demonstrates (Matt. 22:16; Mark 3:6; 12:13).[11]

The Herods exploited the dynamics of the reciprocity system for their own purposes in their interactions with the imperial rulers.[12] Philo's rendering of Herod Agrippa's letter to Gaius Caligula regarding the erection of his statue in the temple is an example of Herodian astuteness in this regard. The letter illustrates how a dependent might invoke loyalty to his patron as tool of persuasion in order to pressure him to alter his policy.[13] The Roman Prefects were also dependent upon their imperial patrons and were vulnerable to threats of the withdrawal of Caesar's friendship, as was the case with Pilate (John 19:12; Josephus, *J.W.* 18.85-89; Philo, *Legat.* 299-305).[14]

How did the reciprocity system work in antiquity and what were its pitfalls?[15] A first century AD decree from Cardamylae best represents typical first-century belief and practice regarding reciprocity. For five centuries prior to the Christian era, acts of beneficence by heads of state, public officials and private individuals had been celebrated in the stereotyped language of generosity and gratitude on the inscriptions. The key word of the inscriptions summing up the ethos of reciprocity is χάρις. It refers to the generosity of the benefactor—thus its meaning of "favor, kindness, benefit." Conversely it

---

*Gospels* (Minneapolis: Fortress Press, 2002), pp. 349-64.

[8] Two inscriptions, one from Jerusalem (*Israel Exploration Journal* 20 [1970]: 97-98), the other from Ashdod (*Zeitschrift fürPapyrologie und Epigraphik* 105 [1995]: 81-84), refer to Herod the Great as respectively "Benefactor (εὐ[εργέτης])" and Friend of Caesar (φιλοκ[αίσαρος])" and "pious (εὐσέβειας) and Friend of Caesar (φιλοκαίσαρος)." For discussion, see P. Richardson, *Herod: King of the Jews and Friend of the Romans* (Columbia: University of South Carolina Press, 1996), p. 204.

[9] See Josephus, *Ant.* 15.18, 310-16; *J.W.* 1.457-58. On Herod the Great as benefactor see Richardson, *Herod*, pp. 93-94, 127, 174-77, 272-73.

[10] Richardson, *Herod*, pp. 207-8.

[11] Herod Antipas, like his father, cultivated and maintained client-patron relations with Greek cities overseas. Two inscriptions honor Herod Antipas as "guest and friend" (Cos: *OGIS* 416; cf. Luke 23:12) and praise him "on account of [his] piety and good" (Delos: *OGIS* 417). For discussion, see Richardson, *Herod*, pp. 208-9.

[12] On the imperial cult under the Herods, see M. Bernett, *Der Kaiserkult in Judäa unter den Herodiern und Römern: Untersuchungen zur religiösen und religiösen Geschichte Judäas von 30 v. bis 66 n. Chr.* (Tübingen: Mohr Siebeck, 2007).

[13] Philo, *Legat.* 276-329, esp. 285-89, 294-98, 323-26. Claudius' letter to the Alexandrians (10th November AD 41: *CPJ* 2.153) illustrates the boundaries that the imperial rulers occasionally erected between themselves and their overly enthusiastic Jewish clients.

[14] For Josephus' presentation of imperial reciprocity, see Harrison, *Grace*, pp. 138-40.

[15] The following material is drawn from Harrison, *Grace*, *passim*. For the pitfalls of the reciprocity system from a Greco-Roman viewpoint, see Harrison, *Grace*, Index of Subjects s.v. "Benefaction: critiques of the benefaction system."

could designate the response of the person who had received the benefit, and be translated as "gratitude, thankfulness," or the return of "favor" to the benefactor. Note how this important inscription illuminates the ethos of reciprocity at a civic level:

> . . . [I]t was resolved by the people and the city and the ephors to praise Poseidippos (the son) of Attalos on account of the aforesaid kindnesses and also to bring never-ending gratitude (ἀτελῆ χάριν) in recompense of (ἀμοιβῆς) (his bestowal) of benefits; and also to give to him both the front seats at the theater and the first place in a procession and (the privilege of) eating in the public festivals which are celebrated amongst us and to offer willingly (χαρ[ιζομέ]νους) all (the) honor (τειμήν) given to a good and fine man in return for (ἀντί) the many [kindnesses] which he provided, while giving a share of the lesser favor (ἐλάττονος χάριτος), (nevertheless) offering thankfulness (εὐχαριστίας) to the benefactors of ourselves as an incentive to the others, so that choosing the same favor (χάριν) some of them may win (the same) honors (τειμῶν). And (it was resolved) to set up this decree on a stone slab in the most conspicuous place in the gymnasium, while the ephors make the solemn procession to the building without hindrance, in order that those who confer benefits may receive favor (χάριν) in return for (ἀντι/) love of honor (φιλοτειμίας), and that those who have been benefited, returning honors (ἀποδιδόντας τειμίας), may have a reputation for thankfulness ([εὐ]χαριστίας) before all people, never coming too late for the sake of recompense (ἀμοιβήν) for those who wish to do kindly (acts).[16]

Here we see a careful tabulation of the reciprocal benefits for the benefactor (Poseidippos) and his beneficiaries (the citizens of Cardamylae). Poseidippos receives "favors" (public honors) in return for his "love of honor" (his civic benefactions). Cardamylae receives the coveted reputation of gratitude in its return of honor to Poseidippos. The grovelling reference to the "lesser favor" on the part of the city underscores how city-states ensured that no touch of hubris could cause affront and spoil the smooth operation of the reciprocity system. The ethos of reciprocity, as formulated in the Cardamylae decree, is striking for its calculation of the benefits to both parties. Furthermore, the decree is replete with the terminology of exchange. Apart from the obvious words "recompense" (ἀμοιβῆς) and "in return for" (ἀντί), χάρις shifts in its meaning as it moves its reference point from the beneficiary to the benefactor.

While many Jewish inscriptions from Diaspora synagogues retain distinctive features that differentiate them to some extent from their eastern Mediterranean counterparts, there are inscriptions that operate according to traditional Greek models of reciprocity. For example, in a third-century AD decree from Phocaea, Tation is accorded conventional honors in the standard eulogistic vocabulary:

---

[16] *SEG* XI 948.

Tation, daughter [or wife] of Straton, son of E(m)pedon, having erected the assembly hall and the enclosure of the open courtyard with her own funds (ἐκ τῶ[ν ἰδ]ίων), gave them as a gift (ἐχαρίσατο) to the Jews. The synagogue of the Jews honored (ἐ[τείμη]σεν) Tation, daughter [or wife] of Straton, son of E(m)pedon, with a golden crown (χρυσῷ στεφάνῳ) and the privilege of sitting in the seat of honor (προεδρίᾳ).[17]

What evidence is there for a critique of Greco-Roman reciprocity in our sources? The rarity of such critiques of the Greco-Roman benefaction system underlines how dominant reciprocity conventions were and their axiomatic status. Significantly, three of the most damning critiques come from the Jewish side.

First, Philo probes each side of the benefaction ritual, exposing (what he perceives to be) the mercenary nature of the relationship between benefactors and their beneficiaries:

> Look round you and you shall find that those who are said to bestow (χαρίζεσθαι) benefits sell rather than give (δωρουμένους), and those who seem to us to receive them (λαμβάνειν χάριτας) in truth buy. The givers are seeking praise (ἔπαινον) or honor (τιμήν) as their exchange (ἀμοιβήν) and look for the repayment (ἀντίδοσιν) of the benefit (χάριτος), and thus, under the specious name of gift (δωρεᾶς), they in real truth carry out a sale; for the seller's way is to take something for what he offers. The receivers of the gift (τὰς δωρεάς), too, study to make some return (ἀποδοῦναι), and do so (ἀποδιδόντες) as opportunity offers, and thus they act as buyers. For buyers know well that receiving and paying (ἀποδοῦναι) go hand in hand. But God is no salesman, hawking his goods in the market, but a free giver of all things, pouring forth fountains of free bounties (χαρίτων), and seeking no return (ἀμοιβῆς). For He has no needs Himself and no created being is able to repay His gift (ἀντιδοῦναι δωρεάν).[18]

In Philo's view, benefaction is at heart a financial transaction. Benefactors "sell" their benefits in exchange for praise and honor; conversely, the beneficiaries "buy" their benefits, with gratitude and public honors to the benefactor the currency of trade. The Cardamylae inscription, discussed above, bears a strong resemblance to Philo's portrait of the benefaction system and represents best the view that Philo is caricaturing. Last, while Philo highlights the spontaneous generosity of God, his theology is Stoic rather than Jewish.

---

[17] B. Lifshitz, *Donateurs et Foundateurs dans les Synagogues Juives* (Paris: J. Gabalda, 1967), §13. B. J. Brooten, *Women Leaders in the Ancient Synagogue* (Atlanta: Scholars Press, 1982), Appendix §3 pp. 143-44. For other examples, see Brooten, *Women Leaders*, §6. For two Samaritan inscriptions from Delos (150–50 BC) honoring benefactors with coronal awards, see S. R. Llewelyn, "An Association of Samaritans in Delos," in G. H. R. Horsley and S. R. Llewelyn, *New Documents Illustrating Early Christianity*, volume 8 (Sydney: Ancient History Documentary Centre, Macquarie University, (1998), pp. 148-51.

[18] Philo, *Cher.* 122-23.

Second, of particular interest is Ben Sirach's insightful exposé of the hostility implicit in benefaction rituals, engendered by the grudging hospitality of the benefactors, and by the ingratitude of their beneficiaries:

> The necessities of life are water, bread, and clothing, and also a house to assure privacy. Better is the life of the poor (βίος πτωχοῦ) under their own crude roof than sumptuous food in the house of others. Be content with little or much, and you will hear no reproach for being a guest. It is a miserable life to go from house to house; as a guest you should not open your mouth; you will play the host and provide drink without being thanked, and besides this you will hear rude words like these: "Come here, stranger, prepare the table; let me eat what you have there." "Be off, stranger, for an honoured guest is here; my brother has come for a visit, and I need the guest-room." It is hard for a sensible person to bear scolding about lodging and the insults of the moneylender (Sir. 29:21-28).

Ben Sirach's portrayal of the social humiliation implicit in the benefaction system stands in stark contrast to the positive inscriptional catalogues of honors that were rendered to benefactors in recompense of their munificence to their local communities. Clearly Jews other than Jesus were critical of the Greco-Roman reciprocity system, whether it be the civic munificence of the Hellenistic city-state and the imperial rulers or the hospitality of village households.[19]

Third, in the gospels Jesus is portrayed as one who criticized the rule of the Hellenistic and Roman benefactor-kings (Luke 22:25), along with their affluent Herodian clients in palaces (Matt 11:7-8; cf. Luke 13:32). He castigated the synagogue benefactors for seeking public honors in recompense of their acts of generosity (Matt. 6:2-4; *contra* Luke 7:4-8):

---

[19] Antigonos of Sokho rejects any expectation of reciprocation of one's service: "Be not like servants who serve the master for condition of receiving a reward, but [be] like servants who serve the master not on condition of receiving a reward" (*m. Abot* 1.3). After the Second Jewish Revolt, a rabbinic tradition (*b. Shabb.* 33[b]; cf. *'Abodah Zarah* 2[b]) cynically exposes the self-centered motives that animated the gift-giving rituals of imperial and local Roman benefactors: "'How splendid are the works of this people,' declared Rabbi Judah. 'They have built marketplaces, baths, and bridges.'. . . But Rabbi Simeon bar Yohai answered, 'Everything they have made they have made only for themselves—marketplaces, for whores; baths, to wallow in; bridges, to levy tolls.'" Cited in N. Elliott, "Paul and the Politics of Empire," in R. A. Horsley, ed., *Paul and Politics: Ekklesia, Israel, Imperium, Interpretation* (Harrisburg: Trinity Press International, 2000), p. 32. More generally, see N. R. M. de Lange, ed., "Jewish Attitudes to Roman Empire," in P. D. A. Garnsey and C. R. Whittaker, eds., *Imperialism in the Ancient World* (Cambridge: Cambridge University Press, 1978), pp. 255-81. *Sib. Or.* 8:52-55 (AD 185) criticizes Hadrian's beneficence thus: "there will be a grey-haired prince with the name of a nearby sea, inspecting the world with polluted foot, giving gifts. Having abundant gold, he will also gather more silver from his enemies, and strip and undo them." However, we must not assume that such negative attitudes to Roman benefactors, including the ruler, were universal in post-70 AD Judaism. One rabbinic commentator on Deut. 32:9 (*Midrash Ha-Gaddol* Deut. 32:9: see §1.3.10 in M. Maas, *Readings in Late Antiquity* [New York: Routledge, 2000]) speaks of the importance of choosing the imperial benefactor as a patron instead of his underlings because of the ruler's superior power.

So whenever you give alms, do not sound a trumpet before you, as the hypocrites do in the synagogues and in the streets, so that they may be praised by others. Truly I tell you, they have received their reward. But when you give alms, do not let your left hand know what your right hand is doing, so that your alms may be done in secret; and your Father who sees in secret will reward you (Matt. 6:2-4).

This (largely) negative attitude of Jesus towards the Jewish and Gentile representatives of the Greco-Roman benefaction system was extended to its underlying social dynamic. Jesus, as depicted in Luke 6:32-36, jettisoned the entire *modus operandi* of the reciprocity system, thereby setting himself against one of the most fundamental social conventions of antiquity.

Finally, as a radical social alternative to the status-riddled benefaction system, Jesus presents the vulnerable model of an impoverished widow as the true image of the "pious benefactor" (Mark 12:41-44). This paradoxically inverts the Jewish tradition of the affluent among the Jewish community caring for the poor (e.g. Ruth 2 [cf. Exod. 23:11; Lev. 19:10; 23:22]; Tob. 1:17; Sir. 34:21, 25). Moreover, Jesus establishes a counter-cultural community of "servant-benefactors" (Luke 22:26-27). These servant-benefactors are to invite those marginalized by the first-century benefaction and holiness system ("the poor, the crippled, the lame and the blind") to the eschatological banquet—unexpectedly prefigured in Jesus' new community (14:12-14; cf. Isa. 26:6; 35:5-6; *2 Bar.* 29.4; Mark 6:34-44; 8:1-10, 14-21)—precisely because such outcasts could not repay the favor (Luke 14:14).[20] The call to surrender one's possessions and to give alms is relentless in the Jesus tradition (Mark 10:17-22; Luke 5:11, 28; 14:3; 12:33; 16:1-13; 18:18-23; 19:1-10; 21:1-4; cf. Acts 2:41-47; 4:32-39; 4:36-5:11; 6:1-7; 11:12-30; 20:33-35; 24:17). Because Jesus is the broker of his Father's grace (Matt. 11:2-6; Mark 1:15; Luke 4:18-21, 32, 36) to the marginalized (Matt. 8:5-13; 11:19; Luke 7:34; 15:1-2), his dependents are also to act as patrons and brokers of divine grace in the dawning of the Kingdom (Matt. 5:42; 10:8; Mark 6:8, 11-12).[21] The honors of the benefaction system are now re-allocated to the lowly (Luke 14:7-11; cf. Prov. 25:6-7; Sir. 32.1-2; Mark 10:45) and its rewards postponed until the eschaton (Luke 14:14b).[22] This novel understanding of divine "grace" in action (Luke 6:27b, 35b-36, 37b-38; cf. χάρις: 6:32, 33,

---

[20] On feasts in the gospel tradition, see K. E. Corley, *Private Women, Public Meals: Social Conflict in the Synoptic Tradition* (Peabody: Hendrickson, 1993); G. F. Synder, *Inculturation of the Jesus Tradition: The Impact of Jesus on Jewish and Roman Cultures* (Harrisburg: Trinity Press International, 1999), pp. 129-74; D. E. Smith, *From Symposium to Eucharist: The Banquet in the Early Christian World* (Minneapolis: Fortress Press, 2003).

[21] On patronage and brokerage in Jesus' ministry, see B. J. Malina and R. L. Rohrbaugh, *Social Science Commentary on the Gospels* (Minneapolis: Fortress Press, 1992), pp. 75-76, 236-37, 328-29; Douglas E. Oakman, *Jesus and the Economic Questions of His Day* (Lewiston: Edwin Mellen Press, 1986), pp. 194-97.

[22] On the social reversal envisaged in Luke 14:7-11, see S. Scott Bartchy, "The Historical Jesus and Honor Reversal at the Table," in W. Stegemann et al., eds., *The Social Setting*, pp. 175-283.

34)—pressed down, shaken together, running over—would in time transform social relations in antiquity.

## 2. The Marginalized and the Greco-Roman Benefaction System

In the hierarchical structure of agrarian societies, the powerful and privileged—specifically, the governing class, merchants, retainers and priests—controlled the distribution of wealth to their dependents and φίλοι ("friends").[23] Those who were relegated to the margins of the Greco-Roman reciprocity system were placed in a vulnerable situation, economically and socially. These included the peasants, the artisans, the unclean and degraded, and the expendables.[24] The chilling truism of Jesus that "you always have the poor with you" (Matt. 26:11) underscored the terrible plight of those who had no access to a benefactor, both in the large cities and in the rural hinterlands. What economic and social challenges did they face?

The urban poor faced dangers from the rich and powerful. In Juvenal's *Third Satire* 282-301 a poor man, returning home with the light of a single candle, is despised, mocked, and beaten up by a rich thug and his retinue of attendants. The conclusion of the episode is ironic, mocking the rhetoric of the Cynics who vaunted their lifestyle of itinerant begging as one of "freedom" from the corruption of civilization: "This is a poor man's freedom: when he's been beaten and treated like a punchbag, he can beg and plead to be allowed to go home with a few teeth left" (Juvenal, *Sat.* 3.299-301).[25]

In Jesus' parables the plight of the urban poor is also powerfully underscored. A rich man, clothed in purple and fine linen, sumptuously feasts in his house while Lazarus, a πτωχός ("poor man"), daily begs at his gates and has his sores licked by the dogs (Luke 16:19-31; cf. Acts 3:2-3, 6, 10). Jesus himself came from a poor family, evidenced by Mary's offering of two doves for her purification (Luke 2:24; cf. Lev. 12:8) and by his own lower social strata occupation (Mark 6:3; Matt. 13:55).[26] Jesus' itinerant life of privation (Matt. 8:20; Luke 9:58; Mark 15:24), dependence upon the beneficence of others (Luke 8:1-3; 10:38-42; John 11:1; cf. Matt. 10:10; Luke 9:3; 10:4, 7-8) and inability to produce a coin when required (Matt. 17:24-27; Mark 12:13-17) underscores his personal poverty.[27]

---

[23] For a diagram of classes in agrarian societies, see G. Lenski, *Power and Privilege: A Theory of Social Stratification* (New York: McGraw-Hill, 1966), p. 284 fig. 1.

[24] Lenski, *Power and Privilege*, p. 284

[25] Cited in R. Saller, "Poverty, Honor and Obligation in Imperial Rome," *Criterion* 37/2 (1998), p. 19. On village violence, see Douglas E. Oakman, "The Countryside in Luke-Acts," in J. H. Neyrey, ed., *The Social World of Luke-Acts: Models for Interpretation* (Peabody: Hendrickson, 1991), pp. 163-64, 168.

[26] On the poverty of Joseph's family and Jesus himself as a τέκτων (Mark 6:3; cf. Matt. 13:55), see E. W. Stegemann and W. Stegemann, *The Jesus Movement: A Social History of Its First Century* (Minneapolis: Fortress Press, 1990), pp. 90, 199.

[27] On the poor in Jerusalem, see J. Jeremias, *Jerusalem in the Time of Jesus* (London: SCM Press, 1969), pp. 109-19. For rabbinic discussion of provision for beggars, see *m. Pe'ah* 4.1-9; 8.7 (D. Instone-Brewer, trans., *Traditions of the Rabbis from the Era of the New Testament.*

The rural poor in the eastern Mediterranean basin were also exposed to the harsh realities of violence (perpetrated by invaders, bandits and tax collectors), as well as harvest failures (cf. Acts 11:28) and other natural disasters. These might be offset by the reciprocal support networks provided through the family, village or town of the rural poor.[28] Villagers benefited from distributions of money (Dio Chrysostom, *Or.* 7.49) or from a benefactor's offer of grain either at reduced prices or *gratis* during times of famine (*CIL* XI 337, 339; *I.Priene* 108; *SIG³* 304, 366, 495, 976; *SEG* I 366; *IGRP* III 493).[29] Occasionally, some of the rural poor were able to effect through hard work a modest rise in their social location, as a moving inscription from the Roman province of Numidia in Africa testifies:

> I was born as a child of a poor family, of a father without property, who had neither wealth nor a house. From the day of my birth I lived and worked in the fields. Neither the fields nor I myself ever got any rest. If the year brought forth rich fruit, I was the first at the harvest. When the column of scythe-carrying men had harvested the field and then moved on to Cirta in Numidia . . . I was the first of all the reapers in the field and left behind me a thick row of sheaves. I have mowed twelve harvests under (the) burning sun, and then I went from country worker to leader of the column. For eleven years I was leader of the reaper column, and the fields of Numidia were mowed by us. This effort and a frugal life finally made me a master and gave me a house and estate.[30]

But the extremes of poverty that the rural poor faced should not be underestimated. Egyptian literary and iconographic evidence underscores this. A scribe writing in the Ramesside era (thirteenth and twelfth centuries BC)

---

*Volume 1: Prayer and Agriculture* [Grand Rapids: Eerdmans, 2004], pp. 138-39, 158-61). The gospel texts exclusively speak of the "destitute" (πτωχοί: 24 occurrences; πτωχεύω [2 Cor. 8:9]) as opposed to the "respectable poor" (πένητες). For the distinction, see C. R. Whittaker, "The Poor," in A. Giardina, ed., *The Romans* (Chicago: University of Chicago Press, 1993), pp. 279-80. The sole use of πένης ("poor man") in the New Testament derives from a LXX quotation (2 Cor. 9:9 [Ps. 112:9]). For other New Testament poverty terminology, see γυμνιτεύω, "to wear rags" (1 Cor. 4:11); πενιχρός, "poor, needy" (Luke 21:2); ἐνδεής, "poor, needy" (Acts 4:34). On the language of poverty, see G. H. Hamel, *Poverty and Charity in Roman Palestine, First Three Centuries C.E.* (Berkeley and Los Angeles: University of California Press, 1989), pp. 167-211. On the slipperiness of the definition of the "poor," in the Roman Empire, see Saller, "Poverty," pp. 13-16. For rabbinic discussion on who is "poor" enough for the poor tithe, see *m. Pe'ah* 8.8-9 (D. Instone-Brewer, trans., *Traditions*, pp. 161-66).

[28] See P. Garnsey and P. Woolf, "Patronage of the Rural Poor in the Roman World," in A. Wallace-Hadrill, *Patronage in Ancient Society* (New York: Routledge, 1990), pp. 153-70; more generally, C. R. Whittaker, "The Poor," pp. 272-99. Garnsey and Woolf ("Patronage," pp. 155-56) cite documentary and literary evidence for the survival strategies of the rural poor.

[29] For translations, see A. R. Hands, *Charities and Social Aid in Greece and Rome* (London and Southampton: Thames and Hudson, 1968), §D.2, §D.3, §D.4, §D.6, §D.14. On the resolution of food crises under the Principate, see P. Garnsey, *Famine and Food Supply in the Graeco-Roman World: Responses to Risk and Crisis* (Cambridge: Cambridge University Press, 1988), pp. 275-76.

[30] The inscription is cited by Stegemann and Stegemann, *Jesus Movement*, p. 94.

highlights the superiority of the profession of the scribe over against the field-hand:

> Do you not remember the condition of the field-hand in the face of the registration of the harvest-tax, the snake having taken away half of the grain and the hippopotamus having eaten the remainder? The mice are numerous in the field, the locust descends, and the cattle eat. The sparrows bring want to the field-hand. The remainder which is on the threshing floor is finished, and it is for the thieves. Its value in copper is lost, and the yoke of oxen is dead from threshing and ploughing. The scribe has moored at the river-bank. He reckons the tax, with the attendants bearing staffs and the Nubians rods of palm. They say: Give the grain! There is none! They beat [him] vigorously. He is bound and cast into the well. They beat him, drowning him head first, while his wife is bound in his presence. His children are manacled; his neighbours have abandoned them and fled. Their grain is gathered.[31]

An Egyptian relief confirms the harsh social conditions for the destitute, depicting starving nomads in a time of famine, their emaciated bodies revealing the outline of their rib cages. At the bottom lower left of the relief a woman picks vermin from her hair with her left hand and conveys the morsels to her mouth with her right hand.[32] It is little wonder, therefore, as Plutarch informs us (*Mor.* 497E), that the poor sometimes exposed or killed their children. The reason was that "since they consider poverty the worst of evils, they cannot endure to let their children share it with them, as though it were a kind of disease, serious and grievous."[33]

In cases where the reciprocity system did extend concern to the urban and rural poor, benefactors studied carefully the character and status of their beneficiaries and the projected return of honor that would accrue to them before they dispensed beneficence to impoverished citizens (e.g. Juvenal, *Sat.* 1.95-101; Seneca, *Ben.* 4.27.5; 4.34.2; Sir. 12.1-2; Lucian, *Tim.* 8).[34] In the case of Tiberius' subventions to impoverished senators (Tacitus, *Ann.* 2.148), the ruler distinguished between the *prodigi egentes* ("spend-thrift poor") and the *honesta paupertas innocentium* ("the honorable poverty of the innocent"),

---

[31] P.Salier I. 6.9-7.9. Provenance: Memphis. Tr. W. K. Simpson, *The Literature of Ancient Egypt: An Anthology of Stories, Instructions, and Poetry* (New Haven: Yale University Press, 1972), pp. 343-44. On the tendentiousness of this text, see H. Frankfort, *The Birth of Civilization in the Near East* (Bloomington: Indiana University Press, 1951), p. 88. Notwithstanding, see Eusebius' similarly graphic description (*Hist. eccl.* 9.8) of famine, plague and death in Palestine under Maximin (AD 312–313). On agricultural poverty in Roman Palestine, see G. H. Hamel, *Poverty and Charity*, pp. 94-141; *contra*, T. E. Schmidt, *Hostility to Wealth in the Synoptic Gospels* (Sheffield: JSOT Press, 1987), pp. 17-30. For a more complimentary comparison of the life of the scribe with agricultural workers, see Sir. 38.24-34. See also *t. Ber.* 6(7).2.14, *ll.* 24-30, cited Hamel, *Poverty and Charity*, pp. 111-12.

[32] O. Keel, *The Symbolism of the Biblical World: Ancient Near Eastern Iconography and the Book of Psalms* (London; SPCK, 1978), p. 76 n. 88. The limestone relief is found at Sakkarah on the causeway to the pyramid of Unis, 5th Dynasty (2052–1991 BC).

[33] Cited in Saller, "Poverty," p. 14. See also Stobaeus, *Ecl.* 75: "The poor man raises his sons, but daughters, if one is poor, we expose"; P.Oxy. IV 744.

[34] For discussion, see Hands, *Charities*, pp. 74-75.

giving money only to the latter.[35] Indeed, it is a point of comment in the inscriptions when a benefactor not only dispenses beneficence to his fellow citizens (cf. Pliny, *Ep.* 9.30.1) but also atypically includes outsiders in his purview. In a first century BC inscription of Pegae, we hear that Soteles "gave a dinner to all the citizens and residents and to the Romans residing with us and to the slaves of all these and their sons and the slaves' children."[36]

The social stigma of poverty meant the poor were not only seen as a threat to the social and political order but also to the divine order. A Pompeian graffito expresses the social contempt with which the poor were held: "I hate poor people. If anyone wants something for nothing he is a fool. He should pay for it" (*CIL* IV 9839b).[37] Seneca believed that a poor man's oath by the altars in Samothrace was fraudulent because, as a person with nothing to lose, the pauper held the gods' punishments in contempt (*Sat.* 3.145). Perhaps, in a Jewish context, Sirach's description of the πτωχός as an "abomination to the rich" captures best the social dishonor of the pauper.[38]

However, because of the legal, prophetic, and wisdom traditions regarding the mercy of the covenantal God towards the poor (Exod. 23:3, 6; Lev. 19:10, 15; Isa. 11:4; Zech. 7:10; Ps. 34:6; 68:10; Prov. 14:31; 19:17),[39] there was beneficence extended towards the destitute in Jewish society (e.g. Ps.-Phoc. 22-24; CD 14.12-17). In contrast to the classical world, the adjective φιλοπένης ("lover of the poor") appears as a laudatory epithet in Jewish epitaphs.[40] The Greek inscription of Theodotos, found on Mount Ophel in Jerusalem and (arguably) pre-dating the temple's destruction, illustrates the commitment of the synagogue community to beneficence:

> Theodotos, son of Vettenos, priest and head of the synagogue, son of a head of the synagogue, grandson of a head of the synagogue, built the synagogue for the reading of the Law and the teaching of the commandments, and the hostel and the side rooms and water facilities, as lodging for those from abroad who need (it). His fathers and the elders and Simonides founded (the synagogue).[41]

---

[35] R. Saller, "Poverty," p. 18.

[36] *IG.* VII. 190 (60 BC). Tr. A. R. Hands, *Charities*, §D.10. For additional examples, see Harrison, *Grace*, pp. 224-25 n. 47.

[37] Cited in R. Saller, "Poverty," p. 274.

[38] Sir. 13.20; cf. 40.28. For images of the "poor," in the Old Testament and in Second Temple Judaism, positive and negative, see W. E. Pilgrim, *Good News to the Poor: Wealth and Poverty in Luke-Acts* (Minneapolis: Fortress Press, 1981), pp. 19-38. On the place of the poor in Jesus' ministry, see Douglas E. Oakman, *Economic Questions*; L. Schottroff and W. Stegemann, *Jesus and the Hope of the Poor* (Maryknoll: Orbis, 1986).

[39] For the Near Eastern context, see H. C. Washington, *Wealth and Poverty in the Instruction of Amenemope and the Hebrew Proverbs* (Atlanta: Scholars Press, 1994).

[40] *CIJ* I 203 (two fragments of marble in a catacomb): "friend of the people, friend of the law, friend of the poor (φιλοπένης)." Both inscriptions are translated in P. W. van der Horst, *Ancient Jewish Epitaphs* (Kampen: Kok Pharos, 1991), p. 67. For Jewish inscriptions referring to the poor, see Hamel, *Poverty and Charity*, pp. 186-88.

[41] For discussion and translation, see Brooten, *Women Leaders*, pp. 24-26. *b. Pesah.* 101a mentions "strangers who ate, drank and slept in the synagogue."

What, then, was the place of the poor in early first-century Galilee, the main location of Jesus' ministry? Herod Antipas' foundation of Tiberias (c. AD 19), a strategic part of Roman-Herodian policy, and his rebuilding of Sepphoris (Josephus, *Ant.* 18:27) had a dramatic impact on the surrounding countryside. It destroyed the insulated smallholder autonomy of the past. Goods were now directed towards the city, with the result that the economy was reoriented towards urban consumption as opposed to traditional village agriculture. Day laborers were therefore often hired (Matt. 20:1-16; Tob. 5.15), land concentrated under tenants, and smallholdings lost in the new system. The economic gulf between the relatively wealthy and the rural peasantry dramatically widened.[42] Jesus' statement that the "meek will inherit the earth" (Matt. 5:5), his blessing of the poor (Luke 6:20-23) and his woes against the rich (Matt. 6:24; Mark 10:25; Luke 6:24-26 [cf. 1 *En.* 94:8; 96:8]; 8:14; 11:39, 42-44; 12:13-21; 16:19-31; 18:22-30; 20:47; 21:34) reflect the wide economic divide in Galilee, though Jesus also had contact with the rich (Mark 2:13-17; 10:17-22; Luke 8:3).[43]

The gap between rich and poor is illustrated by the problem of debt in Jesus' parable of the unforgiving servant (Matt. 18:23-35), with its chilling references to the violent treatment of the debtor (vv. 28, 34) and his family (v. 25). Debts were collected through the debtors being privately or publicly arrested (Matt. 5:25; 18:30; Luke 12:57-59; cf. Josephus, *J.W.* 2.273; *Ant.* 16:1-5).[44] The new economic system of first-century Galilee meant that numerous household and estate managers were scattered throughout the countryside and the large cities (Matt. 20:8; Luke 8:3; cf. Matt. 24:45; Luke. 12:44).

Finally, the economic situation was made more difficult by the multi-layered tax system in the province of Judea.[45] First, the imposition of the

---

[42] See J. L. Reed, *Archaeology and the Galilean Jesus: A Re-examination of the Evidence* (Harrisburg: Trinity Press International, 2000), pp. 96, 136-37; W. E. Arnal, *Jesus and the Village Scribes: Galilean Conflicts and the Setting of Q* (Minneapolis: Fortress Press, 2001), pp. 146-55.

[43] It is worth considering whether the "meek" (πραεῖς) of Matt. 5:5b refers to those who have no access to any benefactor at all other than God. The socio-economic base for such an argument is clear enough. Jesus partially quotes Ps. 37:11, 22, 29 in Matthew's beatitude. As W. Carter observes regarding the original context of Jesus' citation of Psalm 37, (*Matthew and the Margins: A Sociopolitical and Religious Reading* [New York: Orbis, 2001], p. 133), the "wicked" kill the "poor and needy" (vv. 14, 32), the group to which group the "meek" belong, and borrow without ever repaying their debts (v.21a). Without the intervention of a powerful benefactor on their behalf, the "meek" are continually abused and exploited by the rich and powerful. On the rhetoric of the charge that the Pharisees were "lovers of money" (φιλάργυροι: Luke 16:14), see H. Moxnes, *The Economy of the Kingdom: Social Conflict and Economic Relations in Luke's Gospel* (Philadelphia: Fortress Press, 1988), p. 147.

[44] For these references, see Stegemann and Stegemann, *Jesus Movement*, p. 136. On debts in Roman Palestine, see Hamel, *Poverty and Charity*, pp. 156-62. More generally, see W. R. Herzog II, *Parables as Subversive Speech: Jesus as Pedagogue of the Oppressed* (Louisville: John Knox, 1994); R. A. Horsley, *Sociology and the Jesus Movement* (New York: Continuum, 1994), pp. 88-90.

[45] See Stegemann and Stegemann, *Jesus Movement*, 114-23; Hamel, *Poverty and Charity*, p. 151.

Roman tribute of one denarius per head annually (Mark 12:13-17; cf. Tacitus, *Ann.* 2.42)—determined by regular census assessments of the population for land and head tax (Josephus, *Ant.* 18.1-2; Luke 2:1-3)—had led to insurrections against the census under Judas the Galilean in AD 6 (Josephus, *Ant.* 18.4-10, 23). The despised "tax-collectors" who brought in these taxes were all local Jews and considered rapacious quislings by their countrymen (Philo, *Legat.* 199-200; Luke 3:12-13), as well as "unclean" because of their contact with impure objects in assessing a person's wealth (*m. Tehar.* 7:6; cf. Mark 2:13-17; Luke 18:10-14; 19:1-10; Josephus, *J.W.* 2.287-92).[46] As a client of the Caesars, Herod Antipas had been granted the right, under Augustus' division of his father's Kingdom (4 BC), to collect annual taxes from subjects in Galilee and Perea equivalent to two hundred talents (Josephus, *Ant.* 17.317; cf. Luke 3:1). The mention of a customs and excise "booth" in Capernaum (Matt. 9:9) is part of the Herodian system of indirect taxes whereby traffic was monitored and customs duties paid in the sensitive border area between the tetrarchies of Antipas and his brother Philip.[47]

Second, the annual payment of the temple tax of a silver half shekel (Matt. 17:22-27; Philo, *Spec.* 1.178; cf. Exod. 30:13; Josephus, *Ant.* 3.196; 18.312; *J.W.* 7.218), equivalent to two denarii, lasted until the AD 70 destruction of the temple, only to be replaced by the humiliating *fiscus Judaicus*. This meant that the annual tax that formerly supported the temple at Jerusalem was now to be paid, by decree of Vespasian (Josephus, *J.W.* 7.218; Cassius Dio, *Hist.* 66.7.2), to the temple of Jupiter Capitolinus at Rome.

Third, the taxes for the priests (breads, first-fruits, tithes) were also levied on the population (Num. 18:21-32; Neh. 10:38; Josephus, *Life* 63, 80; Matt. 23:23; Luke 18:12). Significantly, whether Jesus is discussing the payment of the tribute or the temple tax (Mark 12:13-17; Matt. 17:22-27), he endorses its payment, but pointedly calls into question the ultimacy of the Caesars and their priestly collaborators (Mark 12:17b; Matt. 17:25-26 [cf. Matt. 12:6]).

Jesus, therefore, would have found eager listeners among the marginalized and must have discomforted the wealthy elites when he announced the Jubilee cancellation of debts for the poor (Luke 4:18-19). But, in contrast to the status-riddled distribution of wealth on the part of imperial and local benefactors to select groups of φίλοι ("friends"), Jesus encouraged believers to make "friends" for the Kingdom by divesting themselves sacrificially (Luke 16:9b: ἵνα ὅταν ἐκλίπῃ ["when it fails"]) of "unrighteous mammon" (Luke 16:9a; cf. 12:13-21; 16:13)—that is, "money" viewed from the perspective of its corrupting effects—in almsgiving to the needy (cf. 6:30-35, 38; 10:36-37; 12:33-35). These φίλοι, elevated to a new status in the

---

[46] *m. Tehar.* 7:6 ("If tax-gatherers enter a house, the house becomes unclean") is cited in Malina and Rohrbaugh, *Commentary*, p. 83; cf. S. R. Llewelyn, "Tax Collection and the τελῶναι of the New Testament," *New Docs* 8 (1998), pp. 47-76. On the "morality" of money, see Douglas E. Oakman, "Money in the Moral Universe of the New Testament," in Stegemann et al., eds., *The Social Setting*, pp. 335-48.

[47] C. S. Keener, *A Commentary on the Gospel of Matthew* (Grand Rapids: Eerdmans, 1999), p. 293.

Kingdom,[48] would welcome (δέξονται) their benefactors to their eternal dwelling (Luke 16:9b).

## B. The Jewish Holiness System in First-Century Palestine: Its Social Implications

### 1. The Jewish Holiness System: Its Structure and Operation

The contours of the Jewish "holiness" system are familiar and need not be canvassed in depth.[49] As a member of God's covenantal community, Jews understood that the holiness system—focused on individual uncleanness in daily activities (Leviticus 11–16) and sins of uncleanness at a national level (17–26)—was God's gift to Israel. It marked off Israel from the idolatrous practices of the surrounding nations and affirmed her unique relationship to God: "For I am the Lord your God. . . be holy as I am holy. . . I am the Lord who brought you out of the land of Egypt to be your God" (Lev. 11:44-45; 19:2; 20:7, 26; 21:28; cf. Matt. 5:48). Strict boundary markers isolated the nation's life from the contagion of ritual and moral impurity. Maps of purity distinguished between the clean and unclean and the holy and the common. People,[50] spaces,[51] times,[52] diet,[53] and bodies[54] were scrutinized under the

---

[48] H. Moxnes (*Economy*, pp. 142-43) agues that "friendship" (φιλία) relations in antiquity were based on equality, solidarity, and sharing. Therefore, "to "make friends" by "unrighteous mammon". . . was the opposite of enslaving people in need (Luke 16:9: ἑαυτοῖς ποίσατε φιλοὺς ἐκ τοῦ μαμωνᾶ τῆς ἀδικίας). Thus verse 9 indicates that the poor were liberated from economic threat and were placed on the same social footing as their benefactors (Matt. 23:5-12; Luke 22:24-27). On friendship, see D. Konstan, *Friendship in the Classical World* (Cambridge: Cambridge University Press, 1997). Contrary to the interpretation above, D. L. Bock (*Luke 9:51–24:53* [Grand Rapids: Eerdmans, 1996] p. 1334) suggests that δέξονται (Luke 16:9b) represents an impersonal use (cf. αἰτοῦσιν [12:20]) and is simply a circumlocution for "God" allocating the dwelling.

[49] M. J. Borg, *Conflict, Holiness, and Politics in the Teaching of Jesus* (Lewiston and Queenston: Edwin Mellen Press, 1984); J. H. Neyrey, "The Idea of Purity in Mark's Gospel," *Semeia* 35 (1986), pp. 91-128; J. H. Neyrey, "Symbolic Universe"; H. K. Harrington, *The Impurity Systems of Qumran and the Rabbis* (Atlanta: Scholars Press, 1993); D. A. de Silva, *Honor, Patronage, Kinship and Purity* (Downers Grove: InterVarsity Press, 2000), pp. 241-77; C. L. Blomberg, *Contagious Holiness: Jesus' Meals with Sinners* (Downers Grove: InterVarsity Press, 2005), pp. 32-96.

[50] Distinctions between people: Jew and Gentile (Lev. 18:24-30; cf. Acts 10:28; 21:28); the Levitical order (High Priest, priests and Levites: Lev. 21:1-15; cf. Josephus, *Ag. Ap.* 2.108; Luke 1:5-10, 21-23; Acts 4:36) over against ordinary Israelites; the physically defective over against the able bodied (eunuchs: Lev. 21:20; Deut. 23:1); those born outside of marriage and within marriage (Deut. 23:2; cf. 4QMMT 39); the prohibition of exogamous marriages (Neh. 13:23-28).

[51] Distinctions between spaces: the temple as a copy of the "holy tent" in the "holy heavens" (Wis. 9:8-10; cf. Acts 21:28; *m. Abot* 1.2: "On three things does the world stand: on the Torah, on the temple service, and on deeds of loving kindness"). Jesus criticized the scribal and Pharisaic ordering of temple space "in terms of progressive degrees of holiness" because, on the same criteria, they justified breaking their oaths (Matt. 23:16-22: J. H. Neyrey, "Symbolic Universe," p. 278). For ancient source references to Jerusalem and its temple as "holy", see C. S. Keener, *The Gospel of John: A Commentary*, vol. 1 (Peabody: Hendrickson, 2003), pp. 614-15 nn. 326-34.

[52] Distinctions between times: the Sabbath (Gen. 2:1-3; Exod. 20:8-11; 31:12-17; cf. Luke

holiness system, as well as ethical pollution.[55]

In Second Temple Judaism these maps of purity were transferred to social relations, with the result that certain groups were marginalized or categorized according to a hierarchical scale of purity. J. H. Neyrey cites two rabbinic texts that illustrate how the holiness system shaped social hierarchy within the Jewish community.[56] First, in *m. Kelim* 1:6-9, we see that the relentless progress of temple-centered holiness that effectively excludes the nations from worshipping in the Court of the Gentiles. The reason for their omission is easily discerned. The Gentile lands and their inhabitants, as the first degree of holiness implies, were unclean (cf. *Let. Aris.* 139; *Jub.* 22.16; Josephus, *Ant.* 12.120; 14:285; *m. Pesah.* 8.8; *m. Kelim* 1.8; cf. John 18:28; Acts 11:3):

> There are ten degrees of holiness:
> 1. The *land of Israel* is holier than any other land. . .
> 2. The *walled cities* (of the land of Israel) are still more holy. . .
> 3. Within *the walls (of Jerusalem)* is still more holy. . .
> 4. The *Temple Mount* is still more holy. . .
> 5. The *Rampart* is still more holy. . .
> 6. The *Court of the Women* is still more holy. . .
> 7. The *Court of the Israelites* is still more holy. . .
> 8. The *Court of the Priests* is still more holy. . .
> 9. Between *the Porch and the Altar* is still more holy. . .
> 10. The *Sanctuary* is still more holy. . .
> The *Holy of the Holies* is still more holy. . .

Second, in *t. Meg.* 2.7, the people allowed to be present for the reading of the scroll of Esther are ranked according to the priestly hierarchy of holiness, with bastards and people with physical anomalies relegated to the lowest purity echelons (Deut. 23:2; Lev. 21:18-20; Josephus, *J.W.* 1.270). The descending scale of purity was:

1. Priests.

---

6:1-5) and sacred days (Lev. 23:15-43) over against ordinary time. The Mishnah tractate, *Moed*, is devoted to the rules for observing special times.

[53] Distinctions regarding diet: animal blood as holy (Lev. 17:10-14; Deut. 12:16); clean foods over against unclean foods (Lev. 11:1-47; 20:22-26; Deut. 14:21; cf. Acts 10:14; 11:8).

[54] Distinctions between bodies: the physically unclean (e.g. lepers: Lev. 13:1-14:32; cf. Luke 5:12-16; 4QMMT 70-72) and times of bodily uncleanness (e.g. nocturnal emissions, sexual intercourse: Lev. 15:1-30; childbirth: 12:2-5; menstrual impurity: 18:19; 20:18; cf. Mark 5:24-34; 4Q274).

[55] On sexual purity, for example, see L. W. Countryman, *Dirt, Greed and Sex: Sexual Ethics in the New Testament and Their Implications for Today* (Philadelphia: Fortress Press, 1988), pp. 28-39.

[56] J. H. Neyrey, "The Symbolic Universe of Luke-Acts: 'They Turn the World Upside Down,'" in Neyrey, ed., *Social World*, pp. 278-79. Although Neyrey uses later rabbinic texts to establish the "holiness" ethos of Second Temple Judaism, we have sufficient evidence contemporary with the New Testament to be confident that the rabbinic purity maps were present in the first century.

2. Levites.
3. Israelites.
4. Converts.
5. Freed slaves.
6. Disqualified priests.
7. Netzins (temple slaves).
8. Mamzers (bastards).
9. Those with damaged testicles.
10. Those without a penis.

The qualifications for the hereditary Aaronic priesthood (Lev. 21:16-23)—which excluded physical anomalies (e.g. crushed testicles, 21:20; cf. 4QMMT 39-40)[57]—were extended to Israel's worshipping community, with prejudicial outcomes for the physically impaired in other social situations.[58] The rabbis theologically intensified this when they linked disability to divine retribution, attributing physical impairments to sexual impropriety or to God's foreknowledge of the person's earthly sins (cf. John 9:2; cf. 2 Sam. 12:15b-23; *Ruth Rab.* 6.4).[59]

Similar social outcomes occur in the priestly community of Qumran.[60] In 1QSa 2.5-11 (cf. 11QT 45.12-14; CD 15.15-18; 1QM 7.3-9), the divine presence, residing in the worshipping community, excludes people with deformities, though a blemished person could speak privately to the council:

---

[57] According to Josephus and Philo, the physical perfection required of the priests reflected the moral perfection of the order (Josephus, *Ant.* 3.278-79; Philo, *Spec.* 1.80, 117, 166, 260-61; *Ebr.* 135-36). I am indebted to the MTh (Hons) thesis of L. Gosbell ("The Inclusion of the Excluded: An Analysis of Luke's Portrait of Jesus and Disability in Its Jewish Context" [unpublished MTh(Hons) thesis: Sydney College of Divinity, 2006], p. 47 n. 105) for these references. Gosbell (*Inclusion*, pp. 47-48) observes that, in contrast to ancient Near Eastern religions, physical imperfection did not totally disqualify a person from becoming a priest. They were not allowed to approach the temple curtain and altar, but could perform other priestly functions and eat from the holy food of God (Lev. 21:22). On Judaism and disability, see A. Shemesh, "'The Holy Angels are in Their Council': The Exclusion of Deformed Persons from Holy Places in Qumranic and Rabbinic Literature," *DSD* 4 (1997), pp. 179-206; S. M. Olyan, "The Exegetical Dimensions of Restrictions on the Blind and the Lame in Texts from Qumran" *DSD* 2 (2001), pp. 38-50; T.C. Marx, *Disability in Jewish Law* (London: Routledge, 2002).

[58] L. Gosbell (*Inclusion*, p. 50) notes *m. Hag.* 1.1 which lists groups of people not obligated to make the annual pilgrimages: "All are bound to appear [at the temple] except for a deaf man, an imbecile and a minor, a person of unknown text, a hermaphrodite, women, unfreed slaves, the lame, the blind, the sick, the aged, and the one who is unable to go up on foot." However, E. P. Sanders (*Judaism: Practice and Belief 63 BCE–66 CE* [London: SCM, 1992], pp. 71, 76) argues that purity laws "affected daily life relatively little" and caused no social fear because contamination was so common.

[59] Citing the seven abominations hated by God (Prov. 6:16-17), "R. Yochanan said: 'All these are punished by leprosy'" (*Lev. Rab.* 16.1). Similarly, *b. Ber.* 58b: "if one sees a black, a very red or a very white person, a hunchback, a dwarf, or a dropsical person, he says: "Blessed be he who makes creatures different." But if he sees one with an amputated limb, or who is blind, or flatheaded, or lame, or smitten with boils, or pockmarked, he says: "Blessed be the true Judge.'" Cited by L. Gosbell, *Inclusion*, p. 44 n. 93, p. 56; also, T. C. Marx, *Disability*, p. 65.

[60] See L. Gosbell, *Inclusion*, pp. 51-54.

No man, defiled by any of the impurities of a man, shall enter the assembly of these. . . And everyone who is defiled in his flesh, paralyzed in his feet or in his hands, lame, blind, deaf, dumb, or defiled in his flesh with a blemish, or the tottering old man who cannot keep upright in the midst of the assembly, these shall not enter to take their place among the congregation of famous men, for the angels of holiness are among their congre[gation.] And if one of these has something to say to the holy council, they shall investigate it is private, but the man shall not enter in the midst of [the congregation,] because he is defiled.

(trans. Florentino García Martínez, *The Dead Sea Scrolls Translated: The Qumran Texts in English* [Leiden: Brill, 1994], p. 127)

One reason for the exclusion of the vision and hearing impaired was that the vision impaired could not see when they were mixing impure things and the hearing impaired could not hear "the regulations concerning purity. . . and the laws of Israel" (4MMT 52-54). Also, because the angels "cannot tolerate impurity or defect," physically impaired people such as the lame or tottering cannot participate in the eschatological battle (1QM 7.4-6) or the communal liturgies of the "seven-fold purified."[61]

Finally, people in antiquity discussed the relationship between the outer physical characteristics of people and their inner qualities (i.e. physiognomy). A number of Dead Sea Scrolls claim a correspondence between one's features and destiny and the configuration of the stars at one's birth (4Q186, 4Q534, 4Q561).[62]

Although the holiness system excluded various groups religiously and socially, a quest for holiness animated the various religious parties and splinter groups. The Sadducees defined holiness in terms of the perpetuation of the temple, its personnel and cult (cf. John 11:47-48),[63] but they were viewed as collaborators with Rome.[64] The Pharisees, a lay holiness

---

[61] H. K. Harrington, "Holiness and Law in the Dead Sea Scrolls," *DSD* 8/2 (2001), pp. 132-33. Harrington ("Holiness and Law," p. 133) cites M. Baillet, *Qumrân grotte 4.III (4 Q482–4Q520)* (Oxford: Oxford University Press, 1982), p. 237: "Among the seven-fold purified, God will sanctify unto himself a sanctuary of eternity and purity among those who are cleansed, and they shall be his priests, his righteous people, his hosts, and ministering (with) the angels of his glory."

[62] B. J. Malina and J. H. Neyrey, *Portraits of Paul: An Archaeology of Ancient Personality* (Louisville: John Knox, 1996), pp. 100-52; M. Popovic, "Physiognomic Knowledge in Qumran and Babylonia: Form, Interdisciplinarity, and Secrecy," *DSD* 13/2 (2006), pp. 150-76; M. C. Parson, *Body and Character in Luke and Acts: The Subversion of Physiognomy in Early Christianity* (Grand Rapids: Baker Academic, 2006).

[63] Since the Sadducean writings have not survived, our knowledge of Sadducean debates about priestly holiness is mediated through the polemical rabbinic sources. See L. Finklestein, *The Pharisees: The Sociological Background of Their Faith*, vol. 2 (Philadelphia: Jewish Publication Society of America, 1938), pp. 637-40; J. Le Moyne, *Les Sadducéens* (Paris: Gabalda, 1972), pp. 268-69, 279-80, 370-71. For rabbinic texts responding to Sadducean positions on holiness, see J. Bowker, *Jesus and the Pharisees* (Cambridge: Cambridge University Press, 1973), §4.11; §4.13; §4.19; §4.27; §4.37, §6.20.

[64] See *b. Pesah.* 57a; *t. Menah.* 13.21, cited by W. R. Herzog II, "Why Peasants Responded to Jesus," in R. A. Horsley, ed., *Christian Origins: A People's History of Christianity*, vol. 1 (Minneapolis: Fortress Press, 2005), p. 49.

movement, extended the quest for temple holiness to everyday life through their table "associations" (*havuroth*) and by their "zealous" application of the Mosaic and oral law to mundane purity concerns (*m. Abot* 3.14; cf. Mark 7:3-4; Matt. 23:23-26; Gal. 1:14; Phil. 3:5b-6).[65] Those outside their purity boundaries were dismissed as the *'am ha'arets* ("the people of the land"). The authors of the Dead Sea Scrolls understood temple holiness at Jerusalem to be hopelessly corrupt and facing divine wrath because of the compromised Hasmonean priesthood. The Qumran community ("the sons of light") was to withdraw from Jerusalem, establish a new temple community, and await vindication over the "sons of darkness" (those outside the community).[66] Previously the Samaritans had established their own temple at Mount Gerizim over against that at Jerusalem (Josephus, *Ant.* 11.310, 322-24). In the first century AD, the Samaritans continued to worship "open-air" at Mount Gerizim, notwithstanding their temple's destruction in 128 BC by John Hyrcanus (Josephus *Ant.* 13.254-6; 18:29-30; *J.W.* 1.62; cf. John 4:9, 20-21; Luke 9:52-56).[67] Josephus' "Fourth Philosophy"—a diverse grouping of sign prophets, brigands, *sicarii*, and zealots—pursued the removal of the polluting presence of the Romans from Judea through various strategies, some focused on prompting God's eschatological intervention, others focused on revolutionary action.[68] Last, ascetic wilderness figures such as John the Baptist (Mark 1:1-11; 6:14-29 and parr.) and Josephus' mentor, Bannus (*Life* 11), belonged to the Second Temple Judaism ablution movements,[69] though John's prophetic proclamation of judgment and restoration had wider religious, social and political implications.[70] Everyone, therefore, agreed on the centrality of holiness, but disagreed on the means of achieving it, with vastly differing social outcomes in each case.

## 2. Jesus' Alternative Quest for Holiness

Jesus' dismantling of the maps of purity based around times (Mark 2:23-3:6), places (5:1; 7:24, 31; 11:15-19; John 4:4-5) and diet (Mark 7:1-8, 14-23; Matt. 23:25-26) is well known and need not detain us here. Our focus is more on the social outworking of the Jewish holiness system. Jesus jettisoned the

---

[65] See S. Westerholm, *Jesus and Scribal Authority* (Lund: Gleerup, 1978); Borg, *Conflict*.

[66] On criticism of the temple, see C. A. Evans, "Opposition to the Temple: Jesus and the Dead Sea Scrolls," in J. H. Charlesworth, ed., *Jesus and the Dead Sea Scrolls* (New York: Doubleday, 1992), pp. 235-53. On Qumran and holiness, see E. Regev, "Abominated Temple and a Holy Community: The Formation of the Notions of Purity and Impurity in Qumran," *DSD* 10/2 (2003), pp. 243-78.

[67] See Keener, *John*, pp. 611-13.

[68] See R. A. Horsley, *Bandits, Prophets, and Messiahs: Popular Movements at the Time of Jesus* (San Francisco: HarperCollins, 1985); M. Hengel, *The Zealots: Investigations into the Jewish Freedom Movement in the Period from Herod I until 70 AD* (Edinburgh: T. & T. Clark, 1989).

[69] R. L. Webb, *John the Baptizer and Prophet: A Socio-Historical Study* (Sheffield: JSOT Press, 1991), pp. 95-162.

[70] Webb, *John the Baptizer and Prophet*; J. E. Taylor, *The Immerser: John the Baptist within Second Temple Judaism* (Grand Rapids: Eerdmans, 1997).

traditional maps of purity that ranked people hierarchically in Jewish society, charting instead a different set of social relations through the marginalized experiencing his Messianic grace. How did this new set of social relations challenge the holiness system of his day?

First, Jesus inaugurated the Messianic age (Isa. 35:5-6; 4Q521 frag. 2 col. 2) when he restored people with disabilities to wholeness of life (Mark 2:3-12; 3:1-57:31-37; 8:22-26; 10:46-52; Matt. 9:27-31; 9:32-33; Luke 13:11-13; John 5:1-9; 9:1-41) and incorporated them into his new covenantal community (Luke 14:12-14, 21-24; 22:20). He accepted and healed those who were considered "unclean" by the holiness system, whether physically (Mark 1:40-44; 5:25-29; Luke 8:43-48; 14:1-4; 11:11-19) or morally (Mark 2:9, 15-17; Luke 7:39; John 4:16-18; 8:4, 10-11).[71]

Second, over against the conventions of physiognomy of the Greco-Roman world and the Qumran community (n. 62 above), Jesus honored Zacchaeus, a tax collector of small stature, as "a son of Abraham" (Luke 19:2, 7). Moreover, Jesus, as his enemies observed, was intending to enjoy hospitality from Zacchaeus, a known "sinner," in violation of the purity laws (Luke 19:7: ἁμαρτωλῷ ἀνδρὶ εἰσῆλθεν καταλῦσαι).[72]

Third, Jesus elevated the social status of eunuchs in the kingdom of God (Matt. 19:12), notwithstanding the fact that they were excluded from the holiness system (*t. Meg.* 2.7; cf. Deut. 23:1; Lev. 21:20; 22:24) and sexually stereotyped as "effeminate" (Josephus, *Ant.* 4.290-1; Philo, *Spec.* 1.324-5).[73] Consequently, Jesus brought to Messianic fulfilment the post-exilic promises about the inclusion of the eunuch into God's eschatological household (Isa. 56:3-8; Wis. 3:13-14).[74]

Fourth, Jesus breached the purity divide between Jew and Gentile, even though his mission was focused upon the house of Israel (Matt. 15:24). Gentiles could approach Jesus and experience grace instead of condemnation (Mark 7:24-30; Luke 7:1-10; John 12:20-21). Provocatively, Jesus appealed to the Old Testament Gentile heroes of faith in order to undermine the opposition of his Jewish opponents (Luke 4:23-28) and cleansed the Court of the Gentiles of its traders to provide access for the Gentiles (Mark 11:15-19).[75]

Fifth, scholars have stereotyped the position of women in Second Temple Judaism as one of total marginalization and denigration in an oppressive

---

[71] See C. A. Evans, "'Who Touched Me?' Jesus and the Ritually Impure," in B. Chilton and C. A. Evans, eds., *Jesus in Context: Temple, Purity, and Restoration* (New York: Brill, 1997), pp. 353-76; S. L. Love, "Jesus Heals the Hemorrhaging Woman," in Stegemann et al., eds., *The Social Setting*, pp. 85-101; A. Weissenrieder, "The Plague of Uncleanness? The Ancient Illness Construct 'Issue of Blood' in Luke 8:43-48," in Stegeman et al, eds., *The Social Setting*, pp. 207-22.

[72] See M. C. Parsons, *Body*, pp. 97-108.

[73] F. Scott Spencer, *The Portrait of Philip in Acts: A Study of Roles and Relations* (Sheffield: JSOT Press, 1992), p. 169.

[74] Spencer, *Portrait of Philip*, p. 170.

[75] See C. A. Evans, "Jesus' Action in the Temple: Cleansing or Portent of Destruction?" in B. Chilton and C. A. Evans, eds., *Jesus in Context*, pp. 395-439.

patriarchal culture. It is undeniable that the Jewish literary evidence displays misogynist attitudes to women (e.g. Ben Sirach; Philo; Josephus; the later rabbinic evidence).[76] But this one-sided portrait not only overlooks the important position of Jewish women as synagogue leaders, benefactors (e.g. Luke 8:2-3) and royalty (e.g. Berenice: Acts 25:13-27), but also ignores the more positive portraits of women in the Jewish literature (e.g. Ruth, Prov. 31:10-31; Pseudo-Philo's *Biblical Antiquities, Joseph and Aseneth, Testament of Job*, Judith, 4 Maccabees) and in the funerary epitaphs.[77]

Either way, Jesus' actions did not sit easily with Jewish patriarchal culture that saw women as a continual threat to its canons of purity. It was a point of surprise to his disciples that Jesus spoke in public to a Samaritan woman, popularly regarded by the later rabbis as a menstruant from the cradle (John 4:27; cf. vv. 8-9; Lev. 18:19; 20:18).[78] Moreover, Jesus accepted the devotion of socially ostracized females (Luke 7:39), highlighted the role of women as "disciples" over against more traditional household roles (Luke 8:2-3; 10:38-42), healed their infirmities (Mark 1:3-31; 5:24-43; 7:24-30; Luke 8:2; 13:10-17), pointed to them as illustrations of piety (Matt. 26:6-13; Mark 11:41-44; Matt. 12:42) and of the kingdom (Luke 15:8-10),[79] and defended an adulteress against the demands of the Mosaic law (John 8:2-11).[80] Also, common to several of the episodes mentioned above is Jesus'

---

[76] W. C. Trenchard, *Ben Sira's View of Women: A Literary Analysis* (Chico: Scholars Press, 1982); B. Witherington III, *Women in the Ministry of Jesus* (Cambridge: Cambridge University Press, 1984).

[77] See Brooten, *Women Leaders*; C. A. Brown, *No Longer Be Silent: First Century Jewish Portraits of Biblical Women* (Louisville: Westminster/John Knox Press, 1992); P. W. van der Horst, "Women in Ancient Judaism," *Theology Digest* 40/3 (1993), pp. 211-16; A.-J. Levine, "Second Temple Judaism, Jesus, and Women: Yeast of Eden," *Biblical Interpretation* 2/1 (1994), pp. 8-33; M. H. Williams, *The Jews among the Greeks and Romans: A Diasporan Sourcebook* (London: Gerald Duckworth & Co Ltd, 1998) s.v. Index: "Women as benefactors (sole or leading)"; Harrison, *Grace*, pp. 149-50.

[78] For sources on Samaritan women as "menstruants," see Bowker, *Jesus and the Pharisees*, §3.17. See also Gosbell's excellent discussion (*Inclusion*, pp. 97-104) of Luke 8:42b-48. For discussion of rabbinic attitudes to impure menstruous women, see L. Swidler, *Women in Judaism: The Status of Women In Formative Judaism* (Metuchen: Scarecrow Press, 1976), pp. 130-39. For rabbinic discussion of the restrictions upon women in public spaces, see Swidler, *Women in Judaism*, pp. 118-21. While there were differences in practice between upper and lower classes and between villages in the country and towns and cities in this regard—seen in rural women having the freedom to draw water at the well (*m. Ketub.* 1.10; John 4:6-7)—Jewish women in first-century Alexandria in Egypt were to keep off the streets apart from going to the temple or the market at particular times (Philo, *Spec.* 3.171). *m. Ketub.* 7.6 sets out the grounds for divorce of a wife, focusing on specific violations relating to public space and public speech: "And what is the Jewish law? If (1) she goes out with her hair flowing loose, or (2) she spins in the marketplace, or (3) she talks with just anybody" (cf. John 4:9, 27). There were also rabbinic prohibitions on scholars speaking to women on the street, even including his wife, daughters, and female relatives (*b. 'Erub.* 53b; *m. 'Abot.* 1.5; *b. Ber.* 43b). See Swidler, *Women in Judaism*, pp. 118-21, 123-25.

[79] In the later rabbinic parable of the "lost coin," the hero is male (H. K. McArthur and R. M. Johnston, *They Also Taught in Parables: Rabbinic Parables from the First Centuries of the Christian Era* [Grand Rapids: Eerdmans, 1990], §115).

[80] The place of John 7:53–8:11 in the manuscript tradition is disputed. The pericope is present in medieval manuscripts, but it is absent from all early Greek manuscripts (with the sole

refusal to endorse the popular stereotype of women as sexual temptresses enticing men to sin (e.g. Sir. 23:22-26; 9.3-4, 6-7, 8-9; 19:2-3; 26:9; *T. Reu.* 5.1-7; *T. Jud.* 15.1-6).[81]

Sixth, equally radical was the attitude of Jesus towards children. He observed their play (Matt. 11:16-17), ensured their access to him (Mark 10:14-15), embraced them as illustrations of true discipleship (9:35-37) and healed them (Mark 5:36-43; 7:24-27; 9:14-28). This stands over against the Greco-Roman culture of infanticide (n. 33 above) and the unrestrained power assigned to the father in the Roman household (*patria potestas*).[82]

Perhaps Jesus' unconventional stance is best symbolized by the parable of the Leaven (Matt. 13:33; Luke 13:20-21) in which he chose (what was generally considered) an unclean substance as a metaphor for the unrelenting growth of the kingdom within the world.[83] Jesus subverted the purity canons of his day by celebrating the spectacular growth of the kingdom through the inclusion of the "unclean" in God's covenantal household. In so doing, he laid the path for the Gentile mission (cf. Acts 10:28; 11:9, 12) and for Paul's doctrine of justification of the ungodly by grace alone (cf. Matt. 20:1-16; Luke 15: 3-7, 11-32, esp. vv. 28 ff; 18:9-14).[84]

## Bibliography

Arnal, William E. *Jesus and the Village Scribes: Galilean Conflicts and the Setting of Q.* Minneapolis: Fortress Press, 2001.

Blomberg, Craig L. *Contagious Holiness: Jesus' Meals with Sinners.* Downers Grove: InterVarsity Press, 2005.

Borg, Marcus J. *Conflict, Holiness, and Politics in the Teaching of Jesus.* Lewiston and Queenston: Edwin Mellen Press, 1984.

---

exception of Western uncial D). The pericope is also missing from the Syrian and Coptic Gospels, along with the Old Latin, Old Georgian and Armenian translations. The early church fathers pass directly from 7:52 to 8:12 in their discussion of John's Gospel, making no reference to the pericope. Nor does the pericope fit harmoniously into its present Johannine context. Consequently, while most manuscripts place the text at 7:53–8:11, other manuscripts insert the pericope at Luke 21:38, John 7:44, 7:36 and 21:25. John 7:53–8:11, therefore, was originally a piece of independent floating oral tradition (cf. John 21:25), written down at some stage in the first century, but inserted by later editors into a variety of places in the manuscript tradition. The episode, however, is undoubtedly historically authentic, since it is consonant with what we know of Jesus' attitude towards "sinners" in the synoptic tradition (e.g. Luke 7:39) and reflects accurately the tactics of Jesus' opponents (Mark 12:13-17).

[81] For rabbinic references, see Swidler, *Women in Judaism*, pp. 126-30.

[82] On *patria postestas*, see J.-A. Shelton, *As the Romans Did: A Sourcebook in Roman History*, 2nd ed. (Oxford: Oxford University Press, 1998), §15; Cicero, *Sen.* 37. Generally, H.-R. Weber, *Jesus and the Children: Biblical Resources for Study and Preaching* (Geneva: World Council of Churches, 1979).

[83] On leaven, see H. F. Beck, "Leaven," in G. A. Buttrick et al., eds., *The Interpreter's Dictionary of the Bible K-Q* (Nashville: Abingdon, 1962) pp. 104-05; contra, A. J. Harland, *The Parables of Jesus: A Commentary* (Grand Rapids: Eerdmans, 2000) p. 406. For yeast used of the "evil inclination," see C. G. Montefiore and H. Loewe, eds., *A Rabbinic Anthology* (New York: Schocken Books, 1974) §777.

[84] Note G. Bornkamm (*Paul* [London: Hodder & Stoughton, 1971] p. 237): "Paul's gospel of justification by faith alone matches Jesus' turning to the godless and lost."

Corley, Kathleen E. *Private Women, Public Meals: Social Conflict in the Synoptic Tradition*. Peabody: Hendrickson, 1993.

deSilva, David A. *Honor, Patronage, Kinship and Purity*. Downers Grove: InterVarsity Press, 2000.

Evans, Craig A. "'Who Touched Me?' Jesus and the Ritually Impure." In *Jesus in Context: Temple, Purity, and Restoration*, edited by B. Chilton and C. A. Evans, pp. 353-76. Leiden/New York/Köln: Brill, 1997.

————. "Jesus' Action in the Temple: Cleansing or Portent of Destruction?" In *Jesus in Context: Temple, Purity, and Restoration*, edited by B. Chilton and C. A. Evans, pp. 395-439. Leiden/New York/Köln: Brill, 1997.

Hamel, Gildas H. *Poverty and Charity in Roman Palestine, First Three Centuries C.E.* Berkeley and Los Angeles: University of California Press, 1989.

Herzog II, William R. *Parables as Subversive Speech: Jesus as Pedagogue of the Oppressed*. Louisville: John Knox, 1994.

Horsley, Richard A. *Bandits, Prophets, and Messiahs: Popular Movements at the Time of Jesus*. San Francisco: HarrperCollins, 1985.

————. *Sociology and the Jesus Movement*. New York: Continuum, 1994.

Malina, Bruce J., and Richard L. Rohrbaugh. *Social Science Commentary on the Gospels*. Minneapolis: Fortress Press, 1992.

Neyrey, Jerome H. "The Idea of Purity in Mark's Gospel." *Semeia* 35 (1986): 91-128.

————. ed. *The Social World of Luke-Acts: Models for Interpretation*. Peabody: Hendrickson, 1991.

Oakman, Douglas E. *Jesus and the Economic Questions of His Day*. Lewiston: Edwin Mellen Press, 1986.

Reed, Jonathan L. *Archaeology and the Galilean Jesus: A Re-examination of the Evidence*. Harrisburg: Trinity Press International, 2000.

Ringe, Sharon H. *Jesus, Liberation, and the Biblical Jubilee: Images for Ethics and Christology*. Philadelphia: Fortress Press, 1985.

Schottroff, Luise, and Wolfgang Stegemann. *Jesus and the Hope of the Poor*. Maryknoll: Orbis, 1986.

Shemesh, Aharon "'The Holy Angels are in Their Council': The Exclusion of Deformed Persons from Holy Places in Qumranic and Rabbinic Literature." *Dead Sea Discoveries* 4 (1997): 179-206.

Stegemann, Ekkehard W., and Wolfgang Stegemann. *The Jesus Movement: A Social History of Its First Century*. Minneapolis: Fortress Press, 1990.

Stegemann, Wolfgang *et al.* eds. *The Social Setting of Jesus and the Gospels*. Minneapolis: Fortress Press, 2002.

Synder, Graydon F. *Inculturation of the Jesus Tradition: The Impact of Jesus on Jewish and Roman Cultures*. Harrisburg: Trinity Press International, 1999.

Whittaker, C. R. "The Poor." In *The Romans*, edited by A. Giardina, pp. 279-99. Chicago: University of Chicago Press, 1993.

Wallace-Hadrill, Andrew. *Patronage in Ancient Society*. London and New York: Routledge, 1990.

Westerholm, Stephen. *Jesus and Scribal Authority*. Lund: Gleerup, 1978.

Witherington III, Ben. *Women in the Ministry of Jesus*. Cambridge: Cambridge University Press, 1984.

# 6. The Gospels and Second Temple Judaism

*Mark Harding*

The number of Jews at the time of the Emperor Augustus (27 BC–AD 14) has been estimated at about 4.5 million, 500,000-750,000 of these living in Judea and Galilee.[1] The dispersal of Jews from their homeland was due to enforced exile, enslavement, and service as mercenaries. By the time of Jesus, Jews were to be found all around the Mediterranean, concentrated not only in towns and in the great cities of Rome, Antioch and Alexandria but also working subsistence farms in Palestine.

This chapter provides an overview of the history and religion of the Jews during the 600 year era in which a successor to the first temple, built by Solomon in the tenth century and destroyed by the Babylonians in 586 BC, stood in Jerusalem. This temple was extensively enlarged and beautified by Herod the Great, the work continuing up to the outbreak of the first Jewish War in AD 66. It became an increasingly important symbol of Jewish nationalism, and the goal of pilgrims from all over the Mediterranean as well as from Syria, Mesopotamia and North Africa. Its size can be appreciated by the 35 acre expanse of the enclosure on the Temple Mount and the scale of the remaining substantial remains, especially the Western Wall and blocks of stone weighing 400 tons used as a base for the platform on which Herod based his renovation. The immensity of the work, initiated in 18 BC, is described at length by the Jewish historian Josephus.[2] Its destruction in 70 deprived the world of a monument of impressive architectural achievement, its fame and beauty reported by Jewish and non-Jewish writers alike.

From its less than auspicious foundation in 539 BC until its destruction in

---

[1] Eduard Lohse, *The New Testament Environment* (Nashville: Abingdon, 1976), p. 122. Michael Avi-Yonah, *The Holy Land: A Historical Geography from the Persian to the Arab Conquest 536 B.C. to A.D. 640* (Jerusalem: Carta, 2002 [Hebrew original 1949]), pp. 219-21 puts the total Jewish population at close to 7 million, the number of Jews reported in the mid first-century census taken by the emperor Claudius according to the thirteenth-century Syrian bishop Gregory bar Hebraeus, almost 3 million of these living in Judea and Galilee. The spread of the Jews is attested by *Sib. Or.* 3.271 and Strabo (according to Josephus, *Ant.* 14.115). Note also the survey of centers of Jewish population in Emil Schürer, *The History of the Jewish People in the Age of Jesus Christ (175 B.C.–A.D. 135)*, a new English version, rev. and ed. by Geza Vermes and Fergus Millar, Volume III.1 (Edinburgh: T. & T. Clark, 1986), pp. 1-86.

[2] See *J.W.* 5.184-89. Note also the descriptions contained in Josephus, *Ag. Ap.* 2.103-9, Philo, *Spec.* 1.71-78, the quotation from Hecataeus in Josephus, *Ag. Ap.* 1.197-99, and Tacitus, *Hist.* 5.12.

AD 70, the second temple presided over turbulent times in which the Jews of the land enjoyed less than a century of independent rule, namely, the period from about 140 to 63 BC. At other times the ethnic and religious integrity of the people was compromised, at times severely. In his great work, the *Jewish War*, Josephus plumbs the depths of the tragedy in which the nation was overwhelmed, its population decimated and scattered, and its temple and many of its towns and villages destroyed.[3] The Jewish diaspora largely escaped harassment, though Josephus does report the slaughter of Jewish prisoners in the arena at Antioch (*J.W.* 7.23-24), a short-lived uprising in Cyrene that coincided with the end of the War, and the diverting of the two drachma temple tax to the support of the Temple of Jupiter Capitolinus in Rome. Violently suppressed Jewish uprisings in Cyrene, Egypt, Cyprus and Babylon in AD 114–117 testify to ongoing Jewish disquiet. In 132–135 there was a second revolt in Palestine which also ended in catastrophe. It was led by Bar Kokhba, who was proclaimed "messiah" by Rabbi Akiba.[4]

Wherever they lived the Jews sustained a distinctive culture, the essential characteristics of which will be outlined in Section C below. Jews maintained an uncompromising belief in one God—the creator and Lord of heaven and earth—who had expressly forbidden the making of images, revealed his moral will, and entered into a binding relationship with his people. In exile in Babylonia the people of the overthrown southern kingdom of Judah, which had been centered on Jerusalem, began to consolidate their epic tradition, legal deposit, prophetic oracles and other writings into what would become the Old Testament (OT). Apart from preserving the epic traditions of the Israelites, the Torah, consisting of the first five books of the OT (the Pentateuch), probably reached definitive form by the late fifth century BC. The Torah mandated the setting aside of the Sabbath as a day of rest and the observing of strictly delineated food and purity laws. Significantly, Jews believed that the performance of moral duty was integral to their religious commitment since the Torah required faithfulness to God in all aspects of life. In this the Jews were clearly distinguishable from the worshippers of the gods for whom cultic duty and propriety, not moral performance, took precedence in the religious sphere. Moreover, the Jewish religious commitment excluded other religious loyalties. It was thus well-nigh impossible for Jews to escape the attention of their non-Jewish neighbors. Observance of food laws meant that social contact with non-Jews was severely limited. Jewish beliefs and practices were the subject of much misinformation and prejudice.[5]

---

[3] See *J.W.* 1.1 for Josephus's summary of the extent of the human destruction. Note also the lament of *2 Baruch* 35.

[4] See *j. Ta'an.* 68d.

[5] See, for example, Tacitus, *Hist.* 5.5. It is for this reason that Jewish writers like Josephus and Philo are concerned to mount a defense of Judaism. See, for example, Josephus's comments on Abraham in *Ant.* 1.154-57, 166-68 and on the Solomonic Temple in *Ant.* 8.111-18. 3 Maccabees (first century BC) is particularly focused on apologetic concerns (see especially 3:1-7). Jews were not participants in civic cults or the mystery religions. It is likely that the destruction of the first temple in 586 BC and the experience of the exile had the effect of reinforcing Jewish commitment to aniconic monotheism.

Before we turn to a brief overview of Palestinian Jewish history, the following caveats should be registered. First, Second Temple Judaism was not ①
a monolithic religious and credal system. The period under review is one in which various currents of Jewish thought interact with and are influenced by historical events and contiguous cultures. The sources of our knowledge of the era demonstrate that we should properly speak of Second Temple *Judaisms*, and acknowledge that there is a plurality of ways in which a Jewish life-commitment comes to expression. The period is one in which there is ongoing reflection and debate about what it meant to be faithful to God and how one might express an authentic life-commitment to him.[6]

Second, some scholars speak of the era as "intertestamental." The term is ②
best avoided. It suggests that the period can only takes its identity from its relation to the OT (looking back) and the New Testament (NT) (looking forward). The church's canon supports this impression. The last OT historical book to be written was 1–2 Chronicles which covers the monarchy down to the exile and concludes with the edict of Cyrus in 539, thus ending the exile (for some, not all, Jews incidentally). Ezra and Nehemiah continue the story to the end of the fifth century and deal chiefly with the generation c. 460–430. There are other biblical works of this era. Haggai and Zechariah 1–8 emanate from the years 520–518 BC, Isaiah 56–66 from the sixth or fifth century BC, Joel from a slightly later period, and Malachi from the mid fifth century BC. Seow makes a good case for the view that the moneyed economy under the Persians provides the economic context in which the book of Ecclesiastes was written.[7] It is possible that Zechariah 9–14 was written in the first half of the fifth century BC. The majority of Isaiah 24–27 may have been written in the fifth century BC with later interpolations. Some of the Psalms clearly reflect the post-exilic situation.[8] The final form of Daniel emanates from the turbulent 160s BC, and reflects the emergency occasioned by the depredations of Antiochus IV Epiphanes in Jerusalem, his desecration of the temple and his proscription of a Jewish life-commitment. Chapters 7–12, written in response to the crisis, supplement the older collection of court tales of 1–6. Books of the OT canon thus continue to be written *de novo* or are supplemented and edited during the Second Temple era. In addition, as we shall see below, there was a vast amount of Jewish literature written in Judea and the diaspora that was produced in these "between times."

---

[6] This is exemplified by the teachings of the Pharisees Shammai and Hillel, contemporaries who flourished in the late first century BC. Rabbinic literature preserves the flavor of their debates, though consistently presenting Shammai as impatient and rigorous. Hillel is portrayed as more open to contemporizing biblical law. See further, Jacob Neusner, *The Rabbinic Tradition About the Pharisees Before 70: Part 1, The Masters* (Leiden: Brill, 1971), pp. 185-212 (Shammai traditions), 212-302 (Hillel traditions), and 303-40 (Shammai and Hillel). A good example of their contrasting styles and teachings can be found in *b. Shabb.* 30b-31a. Their contrasting positions on divorce are found in *m. Gitt.* 9.10.

[7] Choon Leong Seow, *Ecclesiastes* (New York: Doubleday, 1997), pp. 21-36. Seow dates the book to c. 450–350 BC.

[8] See, for example, Pss. 85 and 126. For discussion of the post-exilic dating of a number of the Psalms see Hans-Joachim Kraus, *Psalms 1-59* (Minneapolis: Augsburg, 1988), p. 65.

## A. Historical Overview

### 1. The Jews under the Persians (539–332 BC)

Cyrus, the Persian king who captured the city of Babylon in 539 BC, decreed that all people captured and displaced by the Babylonians were free to return to their homeland to re-establish their national and religious life (2 Chron. 36:22-23; Ezra 1:1-4). Judea was incorporated into the Persian Empire as a district of the satrapy "Beyond the River" (see Ezra 4:17; 5:3) with its administrative capital in Damascus. Judea was ruled by a governor stationed in Samaria. The Persians respected local cultures. However, when the temple was rebuilt in c. 520, there surfaced the hope of an independent monarchy focused on their leader Zerubbabel, a descendant of David.[9] It is possible that the Persians decisively dashed these hopes.

The books of Ezra and Nehemiah provide information about the period c. 460–430 BC. Despite local harassment, the fifth century proved to be a time of consolidation under a benevolent imperial hand. The walls of Jerusalem were rebuilt by Nehemiah with Persian (but not local, Samarian) approval. Ezra, who is described as "a scribe" and "a scholar of the text of the commandments of the Lord and his statutes and ordinances" (Ezra 7:11), was sent from Babylon to preside over the re-invigoration of Jewish religious and political affairs. His epic reading of the law of Moses, with explanations in Aramaic (the *lingua franca*) by the priests to the assembled people, is recorded in Nehemiah 8. Ezra's work amounted to a set of reforms that had the effect of mandating a rigorous distinction between Jews and non Jews, expressed most acutely in the forbidding of marriage outside the Jewish community (Ezra 9–10; cf. Neh. 13:23-31). Nehemiah enforced the Sabbath laws (Neh. 13:15-22). These laws and impositions are clearly reflected in the legal deposit of the Pentateuch, especially the so-called "holiness code" of Leviticus 17–26. The attitude in which the law of Moses is held in Nehemiah and Ezra is vital for understanding the Torah-centered ethos of Second Temple Judaism. Judea was incorporated into a monetized economy, which brought economic volatility and risk. Babylon, in which Jews continued to live after the edict of Cyrus, became a great Jewish center throughout the Second Temple period, and even more so after AD 135 and the extinction of all hopes for political autonomy.

### 2. The Jews under Greek Rule (332–175 BC)

We have meager information about the period from about 400 BC down to about 175 BC. Josephus can tell us little, and what he does relate verges on the legendary. There is fragmentary information about Judea in the Greek and Roman historians. The hill country was isolated from the great centers of trade

---

[9] See especially Hag. 2:1-9, 20-23.

for much of the period.[10] But these were turbulent times in the wider world. The Persian Empire was eclipsed by the campaigns of Alexander the Great, king of Macedonia from 336–323 BC. After the Battle of Issus in northern Syria (fought in October 333), Alexander pressed southwards along the coast. His general Parmenio captured Damascus. Alexander captured Sidon and began what was to be a long siege of Tyre. After reducing the city, he continued his march on his way to wrest Egypt from Persian control. After successfully besieging Gaza he resettled the town with his veterans.[11]

After Alexander's death Egypt was ruled by one of his generals, Ptolemy, who established a dynasty that ruled until the death of Cleopatra in 30 BC. Syria was ruled by the Seleucids, whose progenitor, Seleucus, was another of Alexander's generals.[12] Judea was first controlled by the Ptolemies.[13] The Seleucid Antiochus III wrested control of coastal Syria, including Judea after a series of campaigns that concluded in 198 BC. However, his military ambitions were severely checked by the Romans. Provoked by Antiochus's incursions into Greece, the Romans defeated him and his Greek allies at the battles of Thermopylae (191) and Magnesia (190), and imposed a huge indemnity by the Treaty of Apamea in 188 which remained an ongoing problem for his successors.[14]

The conquests of Alexander and the founding of a large number of cities based on Greek models both by Alexander and his successors created the conditions for the wide dissemination of Greek cultural values and institutions throughout the east. Both Alexandria in Egypt and Antioch in Syria, the largest of the cities of the east, became centers of Greek culture. Both had large Jewish populations. The Greek culture of the political masters of the Jews could not but impinge on them even in Judea, which was by no means a Jewish enclave as shown by the founding of Greek cities of Gaza and Samaria and later Sebaste and Caesarea.[15] In Egypt, Ptolemy II Philadelphus (285–246

---

[10] The so-called Samaria papyri written in c. 375–335 BC bear witness to life in the period. For texts, see Douglas Marvin Gropp, ed., *Wadi Daliyeh II: The Samaria Papyri for Wadi Daliyeh*, Discoveries in the Judaean Desert Volume XXVIII (Oxford: Clarendon, 2001).

[11] Josephus's account of Alexander's dealing with the Jews draws on traditions not paralleled in the extant Greek and Roman histories. He records the king's contact with the High Priest Jaddua in Jerusalem. Alexander had sought his help supplying his troops besieging Tyre and requested him to send the tribute the city customarily sent to Darius. After the king had reduced Gaza, Josephus, unlike the Greco-Roman historians who agree that the king now pressed on to Egypt, reports Alexander's respectful visit to Jerusalem, dutifully offering sacrifice in the temple under the High Priest's supervision (*Ant.* 11.336-37).

[12] See 1 Macc. 1:1-10 for a summary of the career of Alexander and the division of his vast empire ruled by his generals, known as the *diadochoi* (the "successors"), after his death.

[13] There are few Jewish sources for the period immediately after Alexander. Josephus himself is largely dependent on the *Letter of Aristeas* for his account of Judean Jewish relationships with the Ptolemies and Seleucids in *Ant.* 12.1-153.

[14] Antiochus III lost his life attempting to plunder the Temple of Baal at Susa in 187 BC. His son and successor, Seleucus IV (187-175 BC), sought to carry off the treasure of the Jerusalem temple through Heliodorus, who was prevented by the intervention of an angel (see 2 Maccabees 3; cf. Dan. 11:20). The bribes offered Antiochus IV, first by the high priest Jason and then his successor Menelaus, were sources of much needed revenue.

[15] In *Ant.* 12.160-227 Josephus recounts the story of the Tobiads that reveals a Jewish

BC) sponsored the translation of the Pentateuch into Greek by scholars from Jerusalem since his library did not contain a copy of the Hebrew (let alone a Greek translation) and Alexandrian Jews could not read Hebrew to undertake the task.[16] The influence of Greek culture in Jerusalem becomes quite apparent in the second century BC. From 1 Macc. 1:11 it is clear that there was Jewish ("renegade") support for a program of hellenization designed to redress economic and cultural marginalization.

## 3. Antiochus IV and the Maccabean Revolt

The reign of Seleucus IV (187–175 BC), son of Antiochus III, witnessed a power struggle between rival priestly families, the Oniads—the high priestly dynasty descended from Zadok, who had been elevated to the role of sole high priest by Solomon—and the Tobiads, whose rise to prominence is chronicled by Josephus in *Ant.* 12.160-227. Simon, the Captain of the Temple and grandson of Tobias, reported to the Syrian governor of the region that the temple treasury contained a previously unreported vast amount of wealth. When the king was informed he made plans to appropriate it through his agent Heliodorus. His failure to plunder the treasury (see 2 Maccabees 3) provided further pretext for Simon to undermine the high priest Onias III.

During Onias' sojourn in Antioch in the attempt to counter Simon's influence there, Seleucus died and was succeeded by Antiochus IV. Onias's brother Jason offered Antiochus a bribe in exchange for support for a bid for the high priesthood, and in addition promised another sum of money if permission was granted to establish a gymnasium, that most distinctive of Greek civic institutions.[17] Jason also promised to draw up of a list of Antiochene citizens in Jerusalem (2 Macc. 4:7-9). This is consistent with Antiochus's aspirations to mount a defense of his realm against Roman imperial design by encouraging the extension of Antiochene citizenship to an

---

aristocratic family based in Jerusalem under definite Greek influence.

[16] This translation, the first instalment of what is now called the Septuagint, the Greek OT, provided an important medium for the dissemination of Jewish religious values. The name "Septuagint" derives from the Greek word for "seventy," there being 72 translators (six from each of the 12 tribes) at work. Though operating independently each produced an identical translation after a 72 day period. The story of the translation is found in the *Letter of Aristeas*, a work that dates from any time between the middle of the third century BC and AD 100. Josephus (d. c. AD 100) knows this work (see *Ant.* 12.12-118). See Abraham and David J. Wasserstein, *The Legend of the Septuagint* (Cambridge: Cambridge University Press, 2006), esp. pp. 19-26.

[17] This shows that there were Jews in Jerusalem who advocated its becoming a city after the Greek model with the expected cultural and civic institutions long associated with Greek towns and cities. The writer of 2 Maccabees asserts not only that Jason the High Priest was responsible for the establishment of the gymnasium, with the full support of Antiochus IV, but also that it was frequented by priests (see 2 Macc. 4:13-15, cf. 1 Macc. 1:14-15). It should be noted that it was the custom for athletes to exercise nude. The writer of 1 Maccabees remarks that the Jewish athletes, embarrassed by their circumcision, underwent surgical procedure to disguise it (1 Macc. 1:15). *Jubilees*, a work that emanates from the mid second century BC, condemns nudity, a reaction, possibly, against the Jerusalem gymnasium (see 3:30-31).

array of cities, not just Jerusalem, on the analogy of the Roman practice of granting citizenship to her Italian allies thus solidifying her hegemony over Italy. Antiochus had been held hostage in Rome by the terms of the Treaty of Apamea and, it is surmised, witnessed the manner in which Rome was in the process of consolidating her power over her disparate and potentially troublesome neighbors.[18] Onias was imprisoned in Antioch. But Jason was himself deposed a few years later by Menelaus, the brother of Simon (2 Macc. 4:23-26). Menelaus organized the murder of Onias. Jason fled the city.

In time violent demonstrations broke out in Jerusalem against the new high priestly regime. These coincided with Antiochus's second invasion of Egypt in 169. Acting on a rumor that Antiochus has died, Jason mounted a bloody but unsuccessful attack on the city (2 Macc. 5:6). In Egypt, meanwhile, Antiochus was rebuffed by Roman intervention (1 Macc. 1:20; Dan. 11:29-30). Believing that all Judea was in revolt, Antiochus stormed Jerusalem and plundered the treasury (1 Macc. 1:20-28; 2 Macc. 5:11-20). Two years later, in 167, Antiochus issued a kingdom-wide decree to the effect that all religious customs that diverged from the king's were outlawed (1 Macc. 1:41). The effect of the decree is graphically described in 1 Macc. 1:41-64. Many Jews, it should be noted, adopted the "king's religion" (1 Macc. 1:43, 52). The Akra was built in the city of David (the Ophel) to protect the Jewish colony of Antiochene citizens.[19] A garrison of Macedonian soldier-colonists was also supplied (*Ant.* 12.252). Antiochus's agents imposed a cult in Jerusalem and throughout Judea which struck at the sanctity of the temple and its priests, outlawed circumcision, profaned the Sabbath, and established altars for the sacrifice of swine and other unclean animals. The proscription of Judaism culminated in the erection of a "desolating sacrilege" on the altar of burnt offering (1 Macc. 1:54; Dan. 11:31; 12:11; *Ant.* 12.253; cf. Matt. 24:17) and the offering of a sacrifice on the altar extension (1 Macc. 1:57).[20] The temple was appropriated to the worship of Olympian Zeus, a Greek equivalent to the conception of the God of the Jews as the Lord of Heaven (2 Macc. 6:2).

It is not clear from the biblical sources why Antiochus acted so provocatively. The author of Daniel 7–12 was convinced that Antiochus was a megalomaniac (see Dan. 11:36-39).[21] In the face of a Roman threat to his

---

[18] This is argued at length by Jonathan A. Goldstein, *1 Maccabees* (Garden City: Doubleday, 1976), pp. 111-17.

[19] See Goldstein, *1 Maccabees*, p. 218. For the location of the Akra, see Herbert G. May, ed., *Oxford Bible Atlas* (London/New York: Oxford University Press, 1974), p. 80. May refers to the Akra as a "citadel."

[20] It is not clear what the "desolating sacrilege" was. It has been supposed that it was an image. However, this is highly unlikely since the "sacrilege" was placed over the altar of burnt offering. There is no mention of an image, and if one had been erected it would have stood, as was the custom in Syrian and Phoenican temples, in the Most Holy Place or Holy of Holies. See Elias Bickerman, *The God of the Maccabees* (Leiden: Brill, 1979), pp. 65-71. When the temple was finally cleansed, the stones that formed the altar erected over the altar of burnt offering were torn down and deposited in "an unclean place" (1 Macc. 4:43). Bickerman, *God of the Maccabees*, pp. 70-71 argues that the abomination was a cult stone that represented the divinity after the custom of Syrian and Phoenician cults. See also Goldstein, *1 Maccabees*, pp. 141-57.

[21] Antiochus took the epithet "Epiphanes," claiming thereby to be a god "manifest" on

empire Antiochus might well have surmised that there could be no place for Jewish religious autonomy if it fomented revolt. He was soon faced by armed and determined resistance.

In 167 BC, at the Judean village of Modein, Mattathias, a member of a priestly family, refused to sacrifice when ordered to do so. He killed the Jew who ran forward to do it, and then the overseeing Syrian officer. Mattathias and his sons escaped to the wilderness from where, under the leadership of Judas "Maccabeus" (the "Hammer"), they conducted a guerrilla war against the Syrians and their Jewish collaborators. The Hasidim, the "pious ones," who made common cause with the rebels at the outbreak of the revolt (1 Macc. 2:42), are best understood as resisting the threat posed by Greek cultural values with overt Syrian backing. The Hasidim might be regarded as the spiritual ancestors of the Pharisees. Incidentally, Mattathias' grandfather was named Asmoneus—hence the name "Hasmonean" for the family which was to exercise authority for the next 130 years in Judea.

By 164 Antiochus was dead. Despite suffering a number of defeats, the Syrians continued to wield considerable power over Judean affairs for several more decades. The temple was cleansed, an action celebrated today in the festival of Hanukkah, the festival of lights (1 Macc. 4:36-61). Jerusalem was re-fortified and the struggle for independence continued. After the death of Judas Maccabeus in 160, his brothers, first Jonathan and then Simon, sought to broker a modicum of Jewish autonomy. In 152 Alexander Balas, son of Antiochus IV, appointed Jonathan High Priest, the first Hasmonean to hold this office. Jonathan supported Alexander in his struggle to consolidate the Seleucid throne. However, in 143 Jonathan was murdered by Syrian agents, having switched his allegiance to a new Syrian patron, Demetrius, who guaranteed autonomy for Jerusalem. Demetrius's claim to the Seleucid throne was backed by the Romans.

## 4. Jewish Independence (143–63 BC)

Simon, the younger brother of Judas Maccabeus and Jonathan, succeeded to the high priesthood on Jonathan's death and was formally acclaimed high priest by the populace. Aware no doubt that a Hasmonean high priesthood stood outside biblical precedent that required a Zadokite to assume the high priestly role, the people formerly declared that "Simon should be their leader and high priest forever, until a trustworthy prophet should arise" (1 Macc. 14:41).[22] Simon's elevation was confirmed by his Seleucid patron Demetrius.

---

earth. Polybius (26.1a.1) reports that Antiochus was also called "Epimanes," "mad." Diodorus Siculus (29.32; 32.16) and Livy (*Hist.* 41.20) also comment on the eccentricity of Antiochus.

[22] The last Hasmonean to officiate was Aristobulus III, Herod the Great's young brother-in-law. Herod's first High Priest, the undistinguished Hananel (*Ant.* 15.22), had been summoned from Babylon. However, it became expedient for Herod to depose him quickly in favor of Aristobulus. His popularity alarmed Herod, who had him drowned after he had officiated at Passover in 36 BC (*Ant.* 15.55). Hasmonean tenure of the high priesthood is a likely cause of the schism between the dissident priestly group that formed the nucleus of the Qumran community

The expulsion of the defenders of the Akra (1 Macc. 13:49-52) ushered in an era of Jewish independence.

Simon was succeeded by his son John Hyrcanus (134–104). Taking opportunity of a power vacuum in Syria he set about extending his control over Palestine, destroying the Samaritan temple in 128 and forcibly converting Galilee and Idumea. During his high priesthood Josephus first mentions the Sadducees and Pharisees by name. Alexander Jannaeus (103–76) ruled an extensive territory whose borders approximated to the kingdom ruled by Solomon. He conducted a fierce campaign against the Pharisees, crucifying 800 of them.[23] Jannaeus appointed the Idumean, Antipater, father of Herod the Great, governor of Idumea. Antipater and his sons Herod and Phasael were to take a significant part in the later administration of Palestine as Roman clients.

A number of factors explain the decisive military intervention of the Romans in Jerusalem in 63 BC. Seleucid hegemony had effectively crumbled. The Parthians, a confederacy of peoples living in modern day Iran, began incursions into the eastern Mediterranean. The supporters of Alexander Jannaeus' rival sons, Hyrcanus II (high priest 76–67) and Aristobulus II (high priest 67–63), threatened to destabilize Palestine. The Roman general Pompey, who in 64 had been given a wide-ranging command in the east to deal with the threat of pirates, found himself drawn into Syrian and Judean affairs. He created a new Roman province of Syria with its administrative capital in Antioch and chose to support the claims of Hyrcanus against Aristobulus, who refused to comply with this decision. Subsequently Pompey marched on Jerusalem. The gates of the city were opened to him by the supporters of Hyrcanus while the supporters of Aristobulus barricaded themselves in the temple, which Pompey now subjected to a siege that lasted four months.[24] At its successful conclusion the curious Pompey, much to Jewish outrage, penetrated the Most Holy Place.[25] Aristobulus was taken captive to Rome with thousands of his supporters, thus swelling the Jewish population there. Judea was incorporated into the province of Syria and tribute was imposed. Hyrcanus, now a client of Rome, was re-established as High Priest, serving until 40 BC.

There had been some contact between the Jews and Rome before the time of Pompey. In 161 BC, Judas Maccabeus concluded a pact of friendship with Rome (1 Maccabees 8) which was renewed under Simon (see 1 Macc. 14:25-49).[26] The Romans proclaimed protection of Jewish populations in twenty

---

and which supported the "Righteous Teacher" in his struggle with the so-called "Wicked Priest," possibly Simon or Jonathan. See Geza Vermes, *The Complete Dead Sea Scrolls in English* (New York: Allen Lane/Penguin, 1997), pp. 60-62.

[23] See Josephus, *Ant.* 13.379-81; *J.W.* 1.96-98. It is likely that column 1 of the *Nahum Pesher* found at Qumran (4QpNahum) refers to this incident.

[24] Josephus, *Ant.* 14.58-59.

[25] Pompey's sacrilege rankled with the author of the *Psalms of Solomon*. His ignominious assassination in Egypt in 48 BC (15 years after the event) is seen as just punishment. See *Pss. Sol.* 2:1-10.

[26] The treaty was supposedly based on a precedent going back to the embassy of John the father of Eupolemus (2 Macc. 4:11) before the Maccabean Revolt.

Greek cities of the Empire. Hyrcanus II also elicited significant protection for diaspora Jews, including exemption from serving in the army, which would have involved marching on the Sabbath and the worship of military standards.[27] In 44, just before his assassination, Caesar allowed the rebuilding the walls of Jerusalem still in a state of disrepair following Pompey's leveling of them in 63 BC (*Ant.* 14.144).

Antipater was poisoned in 43.[28] Both his sons were ousted by invading Parthians in 40, Phasael losing his life in the struggle. Herod escaped to Rome where the Senate proclaimed him King of the Jews. The invaders restored Aristobulus II to the high priesthood.

## 5. Herod the Great (37–4 BC)

Herod returned to Palestine. By 37 BC he had established his power as king. For most of his rule he enjoyed the considerable trust of the emperor Augustus. Increasingly fearful for the security of his throne, his rule degenerated into megalomania in which his brother-in-law (the High Priest Aristobulus III), his father-in-law (Hyrcanus II), his wife Mariamme, and three of his sons (Alexander and Aristobulus by his wife Mariamme, and Antipater) were murdered at his command. Herod was a great builder. The port city of Caesarea, the three fortresses of Machaerus, Herodium and Masada, Sebaste (on the site of Samaria) and the temple were all built or extensively renovated by him. He bestowed considerable benefactions on those cities in which there were sizable Jewish minorities.[29] However, he never enjoyed the trust of the Jews to whom he was religiously suspect as an Idumean and a minimally observant Jew.

When Herod died the Romans debated whether to impose direct rule. It was decided to permit one of his sons, Archelaus, to rule as their client in Judea. He was deposed and exiled in AD 6. Antipas, another of Herod's sons, ruled in Galilee until he too was deposed in 37.

---

[27] See, e.g., *Ant.* 14.213-16 for Julius Gaius' (Augustus?) letter to the people of Parium upholding the right of Jews to meet unhindered in their synagogue and to conduct themselves as they do even in Rome. Josephus also records decrees of the Romans guaranteeing Jewish freedom to practice their laws, to remit the temple tax, and to meet in synagogues. These freedoms continued to be upheld after the Jewish War, with the exception of the temple tax which was diverted to support the cult of Jupiter Capitolinus in Rome.

[28] See *Ant.* 14.277-84; *J.W.* 1.229-35. Note E. Mary Smallwood's assessment of Antipater: "So died the statesman who had grasped the fact that, once Rome had the east under her heel, voluntary cooperation was the only practical course for the Jews" (*The Jews under Roman Rule* [Leiden: Brill, 1981], p. 47).

[29] Herod intentionally did not favor Alexandria, the city of Cleopatra, who sought to extend Ptolemaic influence over Palestine. He also sponsored the Olympic Games in 9 BC (Josephus, *J.W.* 1.426-27).

## 6. Direct Roman Rule (AD 6–70)

In AD 6 the Romans imposed direct rule over Judea as a procuratorial province, entrusting its administration to "prefects" (termed "procurators" after AD 44) of the Equestrian order. Little is known about the first four office holders. However, they were followed by Pontius Pilate (AD 26–37) about whom Josephus reports comparatively much.[30] In 41 Rome allowed the province to revert to Jewish control. From 37 Herod's grandson, Agrippa I, a companion of the Emperor Caligula, had been ruling pockets of territory previously governed by Herod the Great. Agrippa's death in 44 was a tragedy for Jewish interests.[31] The Romans re-imposed direct rule over Judea, and for the first time incorporated Galilee into the province.

In Book Two of the *Jewish War* Josephus concisely narrates the breakdown of law and order from 44. It is a period marked by famine, Jewish banditry, violent suppressions of anti-Roman sentiment, misrule by most of the procurators, and the emergence of religious extremism by so-called sign prophets and the *sicarii*, the "dagger-men," who murdered prominent Jewish collaborators with Rome. The Romans proved unable to prevent the descent of the province into rebellion which broke out in 66. The Jewish war effort was initially led by the high priestly elements in Jewish society, such as Josephus who was given the command of Galilee. By 68 priestly leadership had been superseded by groups, led by those whom Josephus regards as little more than bandit chiefs, who had flooded into the city as the Roman troops overran first Galilee and then the Judean countryside. In 68 Vespasian took charge of the Roman campaign. However, he was proclaimed emperor by his troops in mid 69 leaving his son Titus (emperor from 79 to 81) to prosecute the siege of Jerusalem.

The War culminated in 70 with the destruction of the city and the temple, and was finally concluded by the epic capture of the fortress of Masada in 73 (or 74) under the control of the *sicarii*. Realistic hopes that the Jews would be able to maintain a homeland disappeared in 70. Jerusalem became a Gentile city.

## B. Sources

### 1. Apocrypha and Pseudepigrapha

The Second Temple period bears witness to a diverse array of Jewish writings. These emanate from Jewish communities in the eastern Mediterranean, especially the major centers of Antioch, Alexandria and Judea. Apart from the

---

[30] Josephus recounts, for example, an incident involving Pilate's secretive bringing of iconic military standards into Jerusalem, a matter grossly offensive to the Jews, (*J.W.* 2.169-74) and another relating to the violent quelling of a Jewish demonstration occasioned by his raiding of the temple treasury to pay for the extension of an aqueduct into the city (*J.W.* 2.175-77).

[31] Acts 12:20-23 and Josephus, *Ant.* 19.343-50 both narrate the events leading up to his death.

books of the OT that were written at this time, the best known are found in the collection of books and additions to OT books (Esther, Daniel) comprising the OT Apocrypha. These books were accepted as authoritative in the early church but not by the rabbis.[32] Slightly different collections have been accorded deutero-canonical status in the Orthodox and Roman Catholic Churches.

Much of the corpus of Jewish literature that is not found in the OT or the Apocrypha has been gathered up into an artificial collection known as the "OT Pseudepigrapha," a term which implies that the books comprising the collection were written under assumed names. Strictly speaking, however, only the apocalypses of this collection, such as *4 Ezra*, *2 Baruch* and the *Apocalypse of Abraham*, are pseudepigrapha. The books of the Pseudepigrapha, like the works of Philo and Josephus, were preserved in Christian churches, and are extant only in the languages of those churches— Latin, Greek, Syriac, Slavonic, Georgian, Armenian and Ethiopic—though most were originally composed in Hebrew or Aramaic.[33] There is evidence of Christian interpolation and addition in a number of them.[34]

Apocalypses are well represented in the collection. The term "apocalypse" derives from the Greek word ἀποκάλυψις which means an unveiling or a revelation. The distinguishing mark of this genre is that the secrets of this world or the world to come are revealed to the seer through angelic mediation.[35] The seer writes in the name of a venerable figure from the past, thus enhancing the authority of the writing. A number of apocalypses reveal how God will intervene decisively in human affairs to correct all that is out of step with his will. God will bring the rule of those who oppress the faithful to a catastrophic end and will vindicate the beleaguered and persevering. This theme can be found among the latest written sections of the OT, chiefly Zechariah 12–14, Isaiah 24–27 and 56–66, Joel, and Daniel 7–12. The eschatological worldview of much of the NT is clearly indebted to the apocalypses.[36] The genre of the testament, or the farewell discourse, is also

---

[32] See David A. deSilva, *Introducing the Apocrypha: Message, Context, and Significance* (Grand Rapids: Baker Academic, 2002), pp. 15-41. The early codices, Alexandrinus, Vaticanus, and Sinaiticus, all include books of the Apocrypha among the books of the OT.

[33] Some Hebrew and Aramaic fragments of Tobit, *1 Enoch* and *Jubilees* have been discovered among the Dead Sea corpus. Hebrew fragments of Sirach and *Jubilees* have been found among the texts excavated at Masada.

[34] There are interpolations in the *Testaments of the Twelve Patriarchs* and *Sibylline Oracles* 1, 2 and 8. There are Christian additions to the *Martyrdom and Ascension of Isaiah* (3:13–4:22; 6–11), *Sibylline Oracles* (Oracles 6 and 7), and *4 Ezra* (chapters 1–2 [note 2:42-48], 15–16). The Pseudepigrapha can be conveniently accessed in the two volume collection entitled *Old Testament Pseudepigrapha* edited by James H. Charlesworth (Garden City: Doubleday, 1983, 1985).

[35] For this definition see John J. Collins, *Apocalypse, Morphology of a Genre*, Semeia 14 (1979), pp. 1-20. Some scholars argue that the genre arose as a protest against the conventional wisdom of the oppressive establishment exercised either by apostate Jews (from the perspective of the seers) or Gentile imperial overlords (in the case of Antiochus IV Epiphanes or the Romans). See Paul D. Hanson, *The Dawn of Apocalyptic* (Philadelphia: Fortress, 1979).

[36] In the NT the non-pseudonymous book of Revelation is the one example of the genre. However, there are examples of apocalyptic eschatological speculation in the gospels (Mark 13;

frequently encountered in the Pseudepigrapha, sometimes replete with eschatological speculation.[37] The *Testaments of the Twelve Patriarchs* is the best-known example of the genre. In the NT, 2 Peter and 2 Timothy, though formally letters, have much in common with the Jewish testament.

Considerable literary energy was invested in applying and contemporizing the narrative traditions of the OT through interpretation and expansion to meet new challenges and crises. The book of *Jubilees*, a re-telling of the biblical traditions found in Genesis down to Exodus 12, most likely emanating from Judea, and *Joseph and Aseneth*, a book originating in Egypt and based on the record of Joseph's marriage to Aseneth daughter of the Priest of On (Gen. 41:45), are well known examples of this literary enterprise. The wisdom literature of Second Temple Judaism owes much to the wisdom tradition of the Ancient Near East and more particularly to the OT. This continuity is exemplified in Sirach, in which the law is equated with wisdom (Sirach 24), and the Wisdom of Solomon. The Thanksgiving Hymns (the *Hodayot*) found among the Qumran scrolls and the *Psalms of Solomon* are substantial collections of hymns and prayers that were written in the period. A third collection, known as the *Odes of Solomon*, emanates from the end of the first or early second century AD.[38]

## 2. Jewish Historiography

Fragments of Jewish histories, from what must have been a considerable corpus, have been preserved by Eusebius (c. AD 260–340). The Apocrypha contains two major Jewish histories, 1 and 2 Maccabees, which focus on the crisis occasioned by Antiochus Epiphanes. The first book opens with an account of the struggles of the priestly Hasmonean family against Antiochus, records the major events of the revolt, narrates the concluding of a treaty with Rome and the death of Judas in 160, and recounts the high priesthood of Judas's younger brothers Jonathan and Simon. The book seeks to legitimate the Hasmonean dynasty and lauds its representatives as Jewish nationalists. The second book, a summary of a five volume work by Jason of Cyrene, was produced before the capture of Jerusalem in 63 BC. It focuses on the career of the saintly Onias III, the last legitimate Zadokite High Priest, and the conduct of the revolt against Antiochus IV. The book contests the legitimacy of the Hasmonean dynasty.

---

Matthew 24). Moreover, the undisputed letters of Paul bear the imprint of an apocalyptic worldview. Like the apocalyptic seers, Paul believes in the imminent triumph of God, and, like some of them, believes that God's triumph will be marked by the interposing of a divinely appointed agent, the resurrection of the dead, and the revealing of a new creation.

[37] In the OT, Genesis 49 and Deuteronomy (see esp. chapters 31–34) purport to be the farewell discourses of Jacob and Moses respectively.

[38] With the exception of the *Psalms of Solomon*, which is present in the fifth-century AD Codex Alexandrinus, the *Hodayot* and the *Odes* were only brought to light in the modern era in the twentieth century.

## 3. *The Dead Sea Scrolls*

From the time of their discovery the Scrolls have been associated with a Jewish group knows as Essenes. The initial conjecture linking the scrolls, found in 11 caves between 1947 and 1956, with the settlement known as Qumran that was destroyed by the Romans in AD 68 has now been more fully confirmed.[39] Three broad categories of documents have been discovered. These are (1) copies of books of the OT, notably two scrolls of Isaiah, one complete;[40] (2) copies of certain books now collected in the Pseudepigrapha, namely, fragments of *1 Enoch* (though not the section known as the *Similitudes*, chapters 37–71) and *Jubilees*, as well as the deutero-canonical Tobit; and (3) documents presumably composed by Qumran Essenes such as the Thanksgiving Hymns (the *Hodayot*) (1QH), the Rule of the Community (1QS), the War Scroll (1QM), and the Pesharim (commentaries on biblical books). This third category can be further divided into regulations, prayers and hymns, and apocalyptic scenarios. These documents express the distinctive theology of the Qumran Essenes.[41] It is commonly agreed that the community functioned as the center of a Jewish sect that was established some time after the middle of the second century BC as a result of conflict between its founder, the Righteous Teacher, and his followers and the Hasmonean priestly establishment.

## 4. *Philo*

The Alexandrian Jewish philosopher Philo (c. 30 BC–AD 45) forged a synthesis of Platonic, Stoic and Jewish thought.[42] His work might be divided

---

[39] Caves 1, 2, 3 and 11 are up to 2 and 3 kilometers from the ruins of Qumran. Caves 4–10 are grouped near the ruins. See Vermes, *Complete Dead Sea Scrolls*, p. xvi (map 2). Texts from Qumran are identified according to the number of the cave in which the scrolls were found. The Romans seem to have used Qumran as a camp because Roman coins of the period have been found above the layer of destruction. According to Josephus, Vespasian campaigned in Jericho (*J.W.* 4.451) and visited the shores of the Dead Sea in AD 68 (*J.W.* 4.477). The hypothesis linking the scrolls to the ruins at Qumran has been contested and alternative explanations of the purpose of Qumran have been proposed, such as the ruins are those of a villa, but without persuading the majority of scholars. See Jodi Magness, "A Villa at Qumran?" *Revue de Qumran* 16 (1994), pp. 397-419, and "Archaeology," in Peter W. Flint and James C. VanderKam (eds.), *The Dead Sea Scrolls after Fifty Years: A Comprehensive Assessment, Volume 1* (Leiden: Brill, 1998), pp. 46-75. The recent discovery of first-century AD inscribed ostraca in the cemetery wall adjacent to the ruins establishes an even more probable connection between the community of the scrolls and Qumran. See Frank Moore Cross Jr. and Esther Eshel, "Ostraca from Khirbet Qumran," *Israel Exploration Journal* 47 (1997), pp. 17-28; Vermes, *Complete Dead Sea Scrolls*, pp. 21, 596-97.

[40] These Hebrew manuscripts extend knowledge of the biblical text 1,000 years earlier than previously existing Hebrew manuscripts. All books of the OT, except Esther, are represented among the Dead Sea texts.

[41] With the exception of the so-called Damascus Document (CD) found in the Cairo Synagogue Genizah (store-room) at the end of the nineteenth century, fragmentary copies of which have been found in certain Qumran caves, none of these documents were known before 1947.

[42] An earlier (possibly second century BC) Jewish philosopher, Aristobulus, had also

into midrash (or contemporizing commentary on Scripture), treatises on various topics, and works with an apologetic intent. In his commentaries, which were influential in the early church, he emphasized the superiority of the Jewish law over the constitutions of other peoples, especially the Greeks and Romans, and the surpassing excellence of Israelite heroes, such as Abraham and Moses, over their Roman and Greek counterparts. In his apologetic works Philo mounts a bold defense of Jewish rights against virulent anti-Jewish elements in Alexandria, writing *Against Flaccus* and *On the Embassy to Gaius* to further the Jewish cause.[43] Incidentally, Philo's nephew, Tiberius Alexander, an apostate Jew, served as procurator of Judea in 46–48 and was Prefect of Egypt at the time of the outbreak of the Jewish War in 66.[44]

## 5. *Flavius Josephus*

It is no exaggeration to claim that, outside of the Apocrypha and Pseudepigrapha, the work of Josephus constitutes the most significant literary corpus for understanding Second Temple Judaism. He was born into an aristocratic priestly family, with links to the Hasmoneans, in c. AD 36. As an adult he chose to live as a Pharisee (*Life* 12). He died in Rome in c. 100 having enjoyed the patronage of the Flavian emperors Vespasian (69–79), Titus (79–81) and Domitian (81–96). He wrote four works: *The Jewish War*, *The Jewish Antiquities*, the *Life*, and *Against Apion*.[45] At the outbreak of the War in 66, Josephus was appointed the general in charge of preparing Galilee to resist the Roman campaign that began in 68 under Vespasian (*J.W.* 2.566-71). He quickly captured the fortified cities of the region and besieged Josephus in Jotapata. Josephus survived a suicide pact among his commanders, claiming that God had revealed to him that the Jewish cause was lost and the Roman emperors were destined to rule the world. When brought before Vespasian, he tells his audience that speaking by the Holy Spirit he pronounced the Roman general and his son, Titus, future emperors. By 69 Vespasian was indeed emperor; Titus succeeding him in 79. Josephus passed the remainder of the War as their adviser and as a witness of the catastrophe that enveloped his nation. He was the target of malicious attacks immediately after the War (see *J.W.* 7.448-50; *Life* 424-25), but was steadfastly protected by his Flavian patrons. He made use of the 144 book history of Nicolaus of

---

attempted this. Five fragments of his writings, all preserved in Eusebius, can be accessed in Charlesworth (ed.), *Old Testament Pseudepigrapha*, volume 2, pp. 837-42.

[43] See *Embassy to Gaius* 298-305.

[44] Tiberius Alexander was an early supporter of Vespasian's quest for the principate. As far as is known, he is the only governor of Judea who, subsequent to holding that position, had a career of substance.

[45] The *Jewish War* (seven books) was written to persuade Jews not to rebel against Rome again. The later *Antiquities of the Jews* (20 books) is a re-telling of the history of the Jews from the time of Abraham down to the outbreak of the War. *Against Apion* is a two book apologetic work written to counter the anti-Jewish polemic of his older contemporary Apion of Alexandria. The *Life* is a defence of the outcome of his military career against Jewish detractors.

Damascus (c. 64 BC– after 4 BC), whose work has survived in fragments only, as well as the work of many Greco-Roman writers such as Strabo and Hecataeus of Abdera.

## C. Jewish Institutions

My focus now turns to the major distinctive Jewish institutions—the temple, the synagogue and the Mosaic law.

### 1. Temple

As noted above, Herod substantially renovated and enlarged the modest post-exilic structure.[46] No other shrine was tolerated in accordance with the reforms of Josiah (640–609 BC), which were subsequently mandated in the book of Deuteronomy.[47] In the Second Temple period, when large numbers of Jews lived outside Judea, it was only convenient for them to be present (if at all) for a major festival. Consequently diaspora Jews undertook pilgrimages to the city, especially at Passover.[48] To support the cult an annual tax of two drachmas was levied on all Jewish males.

The integrity of the temple was jealously guarded by the Jews, and especially by the priestly caste, for which it was a potent symbol of nationalistic aspiration. Its sanctity was violated at risk of death: no Gentile could proceed beyond the outer court; no woman could proceed beyond the Court of Women; no Jewish layman could proceed beyond the Court of Israel; only priests could enter the Holy Place; and only the High Priest into the Most Holy Place (or the Holy of Holies). The desecration of the temple by order of Antiochus Epiphanes understandably heightened Jewish anxieties of the risk of further violations of its sanctity and helps to explain the vehement protest which followed Pompey's incursion in 63 BC. The period of direct Roman rule witnessed several regrettable incidents that compromised Jewish oversight of the temple and which only served to inflame Jewish hostility. Indeed the rebellion that erupted in AD 66 was prompted by the action of the procurator, Gessius Florus, who took 17 talents from the treasury to pay his staff (*J.W.* 2.305-8).

---

[46] Note Jesus' disciples' wonder at the immensity of Herod's temple (Mark 13:1). With justification Tacitus notes that the Jerusalem temple was built "like a citadel" (*in modum arcis*; *Hist.* 5.12).

[47] Note the concern that sacrifice be offered in "the place the Lord your God will choose out of all your tribes as his habitation to put his name there" (see Deut. 12:5). Despite the Deuteronomic prescription there was a Jewish temple in Egypt at Elephantine in c. 400 BC and at Leontopolis, also in Egypt, from the second century BC. This temple was served by descendants of the Zadokite high priestly family in exile. The Romans destroyed this temple soon after the destruction of the temple in Jerusalem (see Josephus, *J.W.* 7.421).

[48] See Luke 2:41-44; Acts 2:5-11; *J.W.* 6.420. Deut 16:16 obliges all Jewish males to present themselves three times per annum for the feasts of Passover, Weeks (Pentecost) and Tabernacles.

## 2. Synagogue

While its origins are obscure, some scholars contend that the synagogue can be traced to the exilic period when Jews met for encouragement and edification. The meetings recorded in Ezek. 8:1; 14:1 and 20:1, where the elders of Israel gather at the prophet's house, are said to be its forerunners.[49] Not a priestly preserve like the temple, any adult Jewish male could take a leading part in the service of which there were three main parts, namely, the reading of Scripture, the prayers, and the homily based on the lectionary (see Luke 4:16-30; Acts 13:15).[50]

For the majority of Jews the synagogue was a far more accessible institution than the temple could ever be. All around the Mediterranean, and in Palestine and Syria, the synagogue was paramount for the expression of Jewish piety and identity. It was also the locus of the public rehearsing of Jewish salvation-historical traditions and the center of Jewish learning. Because synagogues were built in Greek and Roman cities, non-Jews could access the services. It is clear that Judaism exercised an attraction for those who identified with the high ethics and monotheism of Judaism. Josephus and the author of Acts attest a class of Gentile adherents to Judaism called "God-worshippers" (σεβόμενοι τὸν θεόν) or "God-fearers" (φοβούμενοι τὸν θεόν). Josephus informs his readers that Gentile God-fearers contributed to the wealth of the temple. According to Acts these people were Paul's links between the Jewish community and the wider Gentile world to which he directed his mission. Indeed Acts is a major literary source for our understanding of the synagogue in Second Temple times. The author reports that there are synagogues in which Moses is read "in every city" Sabbath by Sabbath.[51] As noted above (see n. 27) the Romans upheld the right of Jews to meet in their synagogues.

## 3. The Law

We have already had cause to note the centrality of the Mosaic law to the Jewish life-commitment. The rite of circumcision, the keeping of the food laws, and observing of the Sabbath are the chief distinguishing boundary markers of Jewish identity. The rite of circumcision marked incorporation into the people of God and into the covenant God made with Abraham. Submitting

---

[49] See George Foot Moore, *Judaism in the First Centuries of the Christian Era,* Volume 1 (Cambridge, MA: Harvard University Press, 1932), p. 283. Note also Lee I. Levine, *The Ancient Synagogue* (New Haven/London: Yale University, 2000). Levine argues that the synagogue arose as a focus of Jewish communal identity as a substitute for meetings at the city gate in the towns of Judea. In alien environments such meetings could not be held in a public thoroughfare.

[50] The earliest synagogue that has been excavated is on the Aegean island of Delos (first century BC). Synagogues have also been excavated at 55 sites in Judea and Galilee, including the fortresses of Herodium and Masada. See David Noel Freedman, ed., *Anchor Bible Dictionary*, Volume Six (New York: Doubleday, 1992), p. 254.

[51] See Acts 6:9; 13:5, 14; 14:1; 15:21. Note also Philo, *Mos.* 2.216; Josephus, *Ag. Ap.* 2.175.

to the rite was a decisive undertaking for Jewish converts. While the Jews were not the only group in the ancient world that practiced circumcision, it was routinely regarded by Greco-Roman writers as a barbaric mutilation. That some believers argued that Gentile converts ought to be circumcised was roundly rejected by Paul (Gal 5:2-6; 6:12). The keeping of the food laws (based on Leviticus 11) created a decisive social demarcation between Jews and non-Jews such that social interaction was rendered problematic. Accordingly, Greek and Roman writers consider the Jews inhospitable and misanthropic. The keeping of the Sabbath is also well-known among contemporary writers. For some of them it is a mark of Jewish indolence.[52] Like the food laws and circumcision, Sabbath-keeping underscored the separateness of the Jews in mixed ethnic contexts and, as noted above, made it impossible for observant Jews to serve in the Roman army.[53] In conflict with the Pharisees on this issue, Jesus argues that human need must be satisfied over observing the day, arguing, for example, that healing a person (the work of a doctor) or plucking grain on the Sabbath (the work of a harvester) to satisfy hunger took precedence over the obligation to keep the day work-free (see Mark 2:23–3:6). His principle is that the Sabbath was made for humankind not humankind for the Sabbath (Mark 2:27).[54] The Pharisees of the NT appear rigorous enough in their interpretation of the law of the Sabbath, but the Dead Sea sect went well beyond them in its observance.[55]

## D. Major Jewish Groups

A cursory reading of the NT shows that there were a number of Jewish groups at the time of Jesus. The most prominent of these were the Pharisees and Sadducees who appear in the Gospels and Acts. Other sources fill out the picture. In his *Life*, Josephus writes that as a youth he made a thorough examination of the three major groups within Judaism, learning as much as he could about the Pharisees, the Sadducees, and the Essenes. In the *Jewish War* and the *Antiquities* he outlines their beliefs under the guise of "philosophies,"

---

[52] See Tacitus, *Hist.* 5.4, 8-10; Juvenal, *Sat.* 14.96-106.

[53] The issue of whether Jews should fight on the Sabbath or not had been keenly debated (see 1 Macc. 2:29-41). The Dead Sea sect took a resolutely stringent position on observing the day. See CD 10.20-21; 11.14-15. Such regulations, if practiced, would render fighting on the Sabbath impossible.

[54] With regard to Jesus' mode of arguing with his Jewish interlocutors, see Herbert Basser, "The Gospels and Rabbinic Halakah," in Bruce Chilton, Craig Evans and Jacob Neusner, eds., *The Missing Jesus* (Boston/Leiden: Brill, 2002), pp. 77-99. Basser argues that by way of justifying his teaching Jesus uses the techniques of the Pharisees and the principles of disputation they themselves used.

[55] See CD 10.14–12.2 and contrast Matt. 12:9-14. The Jewish-Christian group known as Ebionites continued to observe the Sabbath as well as Sunday (see Eusebius, *Hist. eccl.* 3.27.5). While the book of Acts shows that meetings of early Christian communities took place on the Sabbath (though see Acts 20:7 [cf. 1 Cor. 16:2]), by the beginning of the second century, Gentile Christians appear to be losing any sense of obligation to keep the day separate as Christian writers seek to draw distinctions between the church and Judaism. See Ignatius, *Magn.* 9.1; *Did.* 14.1 (cf. 8.1-3); cf. Pliny, *Ep.* 10.97. Note also Justin, *Apol.* 1.67 (mid second century).

a term he uses for the benefit of his sophisticated Greek-speaking audience.

## 1. Pharisees

It is possible that the Pharisees originated in the struggle for Jewish identity during the establishment of the gymnasium in Jerusalem and the imposition of a foreign cult by Antiochus Epiphanes that precipitated the Maccabean revolt.[56] The Hasidim are their possible forbears.[57] The first mention of the Pharisees occurs in Josephus's account of the high priesthood of John Hyrcanus (*Ant.* 13.288-92). Here they assume a highly politicized role by questioning his legitimacy. Under Alexander Jannaeus they were vigorously persecuted, but were restored to favor by his widow, Salome. As Herod lay dying, out of zeal for the law, two Pharisees hacked down the golden eagle he had erected over the gates of the temple.[58] Another Pharisee, Saddok, was responsible for the ideology that inspired the movement Josephus terms the "Fourth Philosophy" which advocated direct action against the Romans.[59] But by Jesus' day Pharisaism does not appear as politically active as it had been in the previous century. However, we should not doubt the movement's commitment to promoting a national ideal based on adherence to the law applied to all aspects of life.

According to Josephus, the Pharisees believed in divine providence and predestination, the resurrection of the body, angels and demons (cf. Acts 23:8), and the linkage of Scripture with the body of interpretive tradition, the "tradition of the elders" (see Josephus, *Ant.* 13.297-98; Mark 7:3), which sanctioned the contemporizing of the scriptural deposit. The Sadducees denied these tenets, preferring to restrict their beliefs and action to what was explicit or reasonably implied in the Pentateuch alone. Josephus draws attention to the urban focus of the Pharisees (*Ant.* 18.15). He reports that they were friendlier to strangers than the Sadducees (*J.W.* 2.166) and interpreted the law "more freely" than they did (*Ant.* 18.12), and that they were esteemed by the populace (*Ant.* 13.298). After the fall of Jerusalem and the destruction of the temple in AD 70, Pharisaic Judaism, alone of the Jewish groups, was able to regroup and to maintain and propagate a distinctive Jewish witness.

---

[56] The term "Pharisee" seems to derive from the Hebrew *parash*, a root that means to separate. The Pharisees, it is argued, were given this name because they were separatists, eager to maintain the laws of Levitical purity. Note the survey in Joachim Jeremias, *Jerusalem in the Time of Jesus* (Philadelphia: Fortress, 1969), pp. 246-67.

[57] This hypothesis has its complexities. See John Kampen, *The Hasideans and Origins of Pharisaism: A Study in 1 and 2 Maccabees* (Atlanta: Scholars Press, 1988). Kampen argues that the Hasidim were originally scribes, and that the Pharisees derived from them.

[58] Judas and Mathias took this action on the grounds that the eagle compromised the ban on the making of idols (Josephus, *Ant.* 17.149-67; cf. *Life* 65; Exod. 20:4; Deut. 5:8-9). Both men are described as scholars who were "unrivalled interpreters of the ancestral laws," and educators of the youth (*Ant.* 17.149). They appealed to the need to uphold the ancestral laws of the people.

[59] See *Ant.* 18.4-10. Saddok aided Judas the Gaulanite in his rebellion against the Romans in AD 6. Judas was the instigator of the Fourth Philosophy, and is referred to by Josephus as Judas the Galilean in *Ant.* 18.23 and *J.W.* 2.118 (see also Acts 5:37).

In the NT the Pharisees appear as scrupulous observers of regulations concerning ritual purity, tithing, Sabbath-keeping, and the application of the "tradition of the elders" throughout Judea and Galilee. They formed themselves into local associations. They were represented in the Jewish Council, the Sanhedrin (John 3:1; Acts 5:34; 23:6). Josephus estimates there were 6,000 of them in Herodian times (*Ant.* 17.42). They held themselves rigorously separate from the non-observant. The Fourth Gospel depicts the Pharisees dismissing the "crowd" as "accursed" (John 7:49). They applied the priestly purity rules to themselves thus establishing a living bond between the people and the ritual purity of the temple and its priestly establishment. Their performance of these regulations was most visible at the table. They exercised strict control of what they ate (in strict accordance with the food laws of Scripture), how they ate it (with washed hands), and with whom they ate (not with Gentiles and non-observant Jews).

## 2. Sadducees

The Sadducees are also first mentioned during the high priesthood of John Hyrcanus.[60] But whereas the Pharisees disputed his legitimacy, the Sadducees defended the dynasty. Unlike the Pharisees, who gave weight to Scripture and the interpretive tradition, the Sadducees gave authority to the written word alone (see Josephus, *Ant.* 13.297-98). Josephus presents their beliefs largely as negations of the doctrines of the Pharisees and Essenes. The Sadducees denied the doctrine of the resurrection as unscriptural (see Mark 12:18-27 and parr.; Acts 23:8).[61]

The sources reveal that the Sadducees were small in number and confined to the leading families with overlapping ties to the temple establishment.[62] From 63 BC the ascendancy of the Romans and their clients required a close working relationship if the power and prestige of the priestly and lay aristocracy were to be maintained. This came to an end in AD 66. The priestly leadership found that it could not sustain its prestige among the people in the face of outrages committed by the procurator Gessius Florus, including the crucifixion of high status Jews, unless it took the step of rebelling against the Romans. Eleazar, the Captain of the Temple (and son of Ananias, the High Priest who appears in Acts 23:1), persuaded the priests not to offer sacrifices for the emperor, thus precipitating the Revolt.

---

[60] See Josephus, *Ant.* 13.293-6. The term "Sadducee," it has been argued, may be traced to Zadok, High Priest under Solomon (according to 1 Kgs. 2:35; and in the idealized temple, Ezek. 40:46; 43:19; 44:15; 48:11), and whose family provided the high priests down to the advent of Antiochus Epiphanes. See Moore, *Judaism*, volume 1, pp. 68-69.

[61] There are passages in the Prophets, and more especially the Writings (Job 19:25; Dan. 12:1-3), that support the doctrine. Jesus' bases his reply to his Sadducean interlocutors about the resurrection on passages from the Pentateuch.

[62] E. P. Sanders, *Judaism: Practice and Belief, 63 BCE–66 CE* (Philadelphia: Trinity Press International, 1992), pp. 317-40. While the Sadducees were not wholly identified with the families of the priestly establishment, their political aspirations would have been identical, namely the preservation of their ascendancy in Judean Jewish society.

The NT also mentions a group called "chief priests."[63] These were members of the families of the leading priestly families who provided the high priests, of which there were 28 from 4 BC to AD 70. Two were contemporaries of Jesus, namely, Annas (Luke 3:2), appointed in AD 6, and his son-in-law Caiaphas whose tenure lasted from AD 18 to 36. The gospels show that Annas still wielded considerable power (see Luke 3:2; John 18:3).[64]

## 3. Scribes

Scribes constituted a professional scholarly body drawn from Judea and Galilee (see Luke 5:17).[65] Their opinions were incorporated into the evolving "tradition of the elders." Their role as teachers can be seen in Mark 1:22 (and parr.) where it is acknowledged that Jesus taught with authority and "not as the scribes."[66] Many scribes belonged to the movement of the Pharisees, and the two are often mentioned together in the gospels.[67] Gamaliel, for example, was both a scribe and a Pharisee, and a member of the Sanhedrin (Acts 5:34). Whereas Pharisees were popular expounders of Scripture and the oral tradition, scribes spent their time in study thus providing the scholarly authority for the movement of the Pharisees.

## 4. Essenes

The Essenes receive considerable attention from Josephus, Philo, and Pliny the Elder.[68] Both Josephus and Philo agree that there were about 4,000 throughout Palestine.[69] According to Josephus, the Essenes, together with the Pharisees and Sadducees, had been in existence since "ancient times."[70] However, scholars argue that the Essenes, like the Pharisees, probably

---

[63] See, for example, Matt. 16:21; 26:47; 27:12; Mark 15:3; Luke 22:2; John 7:32; Acts 9:14.

[64] Five of his sons and a grandson, Annas II, became High Priest. Annas II was responsible for the judicial murder of James the "Lord's brother" in AD 62.

[65] For the esteem with which the scribe was held, see Sirach 38:24–39:11. Note also the survey in Jeremias, *Jerusalem*, pp. 233-45.

[66] In Matt. 22:25 Jesus is questioned regarding a point of law (the identity of the greatest commandment) by a *nomikos* (i.e., lawyer/scribe). See too Luke 10:25 where a lawyer asks Jesus, "Who is my neighbor?" after "testing" Jesus with the question, "How shall I inherit eternal life?" See Luke 5:17 and Acts 5:34 for the phrase "teacher of the law."

[67] Matt. 23:13; Mark 2:16; Luke 5:17; 15:2. Josephus reports that there were scribes of the Pharisees and scribes of the Sadducees (*J.W.* 6.291).

[68] The references are brought together in Geza Vermes and Martin D. Goodman, *The Essenes According to the Classical Sources* (Sheffield: JSOT Press, 1989). The major writers on the Essenes are Josephus and Philo.

[69] See Josephus, *Ant.* 18.20; Philo, *Every Good Man is Free* 75. In *On the Contemplative Life*, Philo describes a group of Jewish ascetics in Egypt whom he calls "healers" (*therapeutae*). See *Contempl.* 1-2, 11-40, 63-90. The Therapeutae bear considerable affinity with the Essenes of Palestine.

[70] Josephus, *Ant.* 18.11. Cf. Pliny the Elder (*Nat.* 5.73). Pliny writes that the Essenes have been conducting their ascetic and celibate lifestyle yet perpetuating their numbers "through thousands of ages."

147

originated in the movement of the Hasidim, who opposed the measures taken by Antiochus Epiphanes (see 1 Macc. 2:42).[71]

Josephus describes Essenes who were celibate.[72] Celibacy was unusual in Second Temple Judaism and may indicate an acute anxiety by those who practiced it about the ritual defilement occasioned by sexual intimacy (cf. Lev. 15:16-18; 18:19). Essenes, he writes, lived in communities in which possessions were shared. They observed ascetic discipline and avoided unnecessary contact even with other Jews. He also attests strict rules for admission to an Essene community. One such community, it would appear, was Qumran, whose ruins were excavated by Roland de Vaux in the 1950s.[73]

There is keen debate about the origins of the Qumran community. The present consensus is that the community was founded in the middle of the second century BC as the result of a bitter dispute within priestly circles in Jerusalem concerning the integrity of the priestly establishment that was no longer the preserve of the Zadokites.[74] According to the Cairo Damascus document (CD) the community had earlier experienced a 20 year period of "wandering" during a time of "wrath" when God delivered up his people to the sword and forsook his sanctuary. This period seems to describe the years 175–164 BC which witnessed the implementation of a program of Hellenization sponsored by the High Priest Jason and the crisis occasioned by the desecration of the temple and the proscription of Judaism by Antiochus Epiphanes. During this time, CD says that God kept his faithful ones safe, though leaderless. After 20 years, God raised up for this "remnant" a "Righteous Teacher." However, he was opposed by a "Wicked Priest" (see the Habbakuk pesher, 1QpHab 8.8), an otherwise unknown person who was probably the reigning High Priest. The Righteous Teacher led his people to "Damascus" (CD 6.5; 7.13-21) where they entered into a "new covenant" (CD

---

[71] The etymology of the terms "Essene" and "Hasidim" are similar. See Hartmut Stegemann, *The Library of Qumran* (Grand Rapids: Eerdmans, 1998), pp. 150-51; Vermes, *Complete Dead Sea Scrolls*, p. 18. However, for a critique of this position, see Florentino Garcia Martínez, "The Origins of the Essene Movement and of the Qumran Sect," in Florentino García Martínez and Julio Trebolle Barrera, *The People of the Dead Sea Scrolls* (Leiden/New York: Brill, 1995), pp. 77-96 (especially pp. 86-91). Martínez argues that the sect had its origins in apocalypticism, and that the writer of the *Book of Dreams* (*1 Enoch* 83–90) recounts the origins of the group (to which he belongs) in *1 Enoch* 90.

[72] *J.W.* 2.120; cf. Hippolytus, *Refutation of all Heresies* 9.18; Philo, *Apol.* 14 (according to Eusebius, *Praep. ev.* 8.6-7). *J.W.* 2.160-61 also describes married Essenes.

[73] See Roland de Vaux, *Archaeology and the Dead Sea Scrolls* (London: Oxford University Press, 1973). The ruins suggest that the community could have supported no more than about 300 people at any one time. Some graves in the main cemetery have been excavated, revealing male remains in every case, the bodies buried on a north-south axis. Graves in an extension nearby have brought to light the remains of some women and children. It is reported that the bodies in the extension, unlike the men in the main cemetery, postdate the burials in the main cemetery, and have been buried in Moslem fashion on an east-west axis. See Joseph Zias, "The Cemeteries of Qumran and Celibacy: The Confusion Laid to Rest?" *Dead Sea Discoveries* 7 (2000), pp. 220-53.

[74] For a proposed four-stage history of the community, see James H. Charlesworth, "The Origin and Subsequent History of the Authors of the Dead Sea Scrolls: Four Transitional Phases among the Qumran Essenes," *Revue de Qumran* 10 (1981), pp. 213-33.

6.19; 8.21). The cause of the exile seems to have centered on the flouting of the Levitical Holiness Code by the priests not associated with the Teacher and the maintenance of the lunar calendar by the priestly establishment. The Qumran sect adopted a solar calendar. The members replaced animal sacrifice with the sacrifice of praise and thanksgiving, and perceived themselves to have been joined to the congregation of the angels.[75] The Community Rule (1QS 5–6) describes in detail the procedure by which one became a member of the community.

## 5. *The "Fourth Philosophy"*

In his account of the Jewish "philosophies," Josephus lists the Pharisees as the first philosophy, the Sadducees as the second, and the Essenes as the third. The "fourth philosophy" arose when the province of Judea was fully incorporated into the Roman imperial system after Archelaus was deposed in AD 6. Its originator is said to be Judas the Galilean who enlisted the support of the Pharisee Saddok (see *Ant.* 18.4-10) and conducted a short-lived rebellion against the Romans that is referred to by Gamaliel in Acts 5:37. It was not lawful, Judas and Saddok taught, to pay tribute to Rome and to tolerate "mortal masters" after having God as their lord (*J.W.* 2.118; *Ant.* 18.23). According to Josephus, the adherents of this philosophy, whom he blames above all other groups for the War, adopted policies of direct action against the Romans and their Jewish collaborators, and were for that reason to be sharply distinguished from the other Jewish groups. The "philosophy" was to assume various guises in the first century.

Any discussion of this "philosophy" must also take account of the problem posed to Roman rule by bandits, who were also prepared to take direct action. Josephus draws family links between earlier bandit leaders of the mid first century BC and Judas the Galilean, who, in turn, is the forebear of the bandits leaders and the *sicarii* who appear in the mid first century AD. There were outbreaks of banditry in 4 BC led by Judas, the son of the Hezekiah executed during Herod's campaign against the bandits in the 40's BC.[76] Disturbances were in evidence again in AD 6.[77] Bandit uprisings continued to feed on harsh economic conditions. There was a severe famine in 46–48 (see Acts 11:27). Outbreaks of banditry infested the country during the procuratorship of Felix (52–59) (*J.W.* 2:238). The situation has rightly been described as a wholesale peasant rebellion against the Romans, the bandits able to find support, sympathy, and protection at will.[78] After the outbreak of the War, the bandits, easily defeated in the countryside by well-armed

---

[75] See, for example, 1QS 11.7-8; 1QH 11.19-22; 1QH 14.12-13; 19.10-13.

[76] See Josephus, *J.W.* 1.204-7; *Ant.* 14.420-30.

[77] Bandits were crucified with Jesus. The Fourth Gospel terms Barabbas a bandit (John 18:40). He had committed murder in an insurrection (Mark 15:7; Luke 23:19), and was clearly popular with the mob, as each of the gospels record.

[78] See Richard A. Horsley with John S. Hanson, *Bandits, Prophets, and Messiahs: Popular Movements at the Time of Jesus* (San Francisco: Harper and Row, 1988), pp. 48-87.

Romans troops, streamed into Jerusalem and wrested the leadership from the aristocratic establishment, much to the outrage of Josephus.

Josephus reserves some of his most bitter invective for the *sicarii*. This group arose during Felix's procuratorship. The name is derived from the Latin *sica*, dagger. Their practice was to mingle with the crowd and assassinate Roman collaborators. Their first victim was the former High Priest, Jonathan, who had brokered the appointment of Felix. The activity of the *sicarii* instilled a sense of terror in Jerusalem. They made a bid for leadership in Jerusalem in the early days of the War. Their leader, Menahem, a son (or grandson) of Judas the Galilean (*J.W.* 2.433) appeared in the city wearing purple (*J.W.* 2.444), but he was killed and his followers were ousted. Thereupon the *sicarii* retreated to Masada, which they held until AD 73 (or 74).

## E. Jesus the Jew

Earliest Christianity took root in the countryside and small towns of Galilee. Jesus moves among the non-observant Jewish population, the "people of the land." Contact with Gentiles is exceptional. Especially in Syria and Palestine, the movement was marked by the activity of wandering teachers and charismatic healers, Jesus himself being the chief exemplar.[79] Josephus records valuable corroborative information about Jesus, namely that he was a worker of miracles and that he met his death by the order of Pontius Pilate.[80]

Jesus preached the imminence of the inbreaking of the kingdom (or rule) of God. His miracles should be seen as signs confirming the inauguration of the kingdom because they are integrally linked to his message (Matt. 10:7-8; 11:2-6). The effect of the work of Jesus is to undermine commonly accepted social hierarchies. Women are numbered among his followers and his closest associates (see Luke 8:2-3).[81] The kingdom of God, he taught, is to be entered as a child (see Mark 10:15 and parr.).[82] Jesus appointed 12 men as his inner circle, symbolically foundational of a new Israel and drawn from the non-elites, to witness to the expectation that the rule of God was about to irrupt into the conflicted political and social context. Jesus presided over a movement that modeled inclusivity and porous social boundaries among Jews.

---

[79] Matt. 10:5-15, 23; Mark 6:7-13; 10:28; 2 John 10; 3 John 5-8; *Did.* 11:4-6. Jesus' activity has been compared to a number of Jewish contemporaries, Hanina ben Dosa and Honi the Circle Drawer being the best known. See Geza Vermes, *Jesus the Jew* (London: Collins, 1973), pp. 58-85.

[80] See *Ant.* 18.63-64. It is likely that there are Christian interpolations in this section, chiefly the claims that Jesus was divine, that he was the Messiah and that he appeared to his disciples after his death. See John P. Meier, *A Marginal Jew: Rethinking the Historical Jesus*, Volume One (New York: Doubleday, 1991), pp. 56-88.

[81] See Richard Bauckham, *Gospel Women* (London and New York: T. & T. Clarke, 2002), chs. 5-6.

[82] The word for child (*pais*) was also used of servants and slaves. In Mark 3:31-35 and 10:28-30 there is no mention of converts acquiring "fathers," though they will gain brothers, sisters and mothers (see also Matt. 23:9). See John E. Stambaugh and John L. Balch, *The New Testament in Its Social Environment* (Philadelphia: Westminster, 1986), p. 106.

This is seen most acutely in his practice of an open table. The Pharisees, as we have seen, drew precise distinctions between observant and non-observant Jews, relentlessly exercising these distinctions in the observing of the laws of purity applied to meals. Not surprisingly the gospels frequently depict Jesus in hostile debate with the Pharisees. Their sense of outrage that he ate with sinners, encountered in passages like Mark 2:16 (parr.) and Luke 15:2, and that he did so with defiled hands (Mark 7:1-5 and parr.), can only be understood from the perspective that he was perceived to be challenging their observance of the laws of purity and therefore their appeal to Jewish ethnic and national integrity in the face of threats posed by Greeks and Romans. For Jesus, on the other hand, the laws of purity practiced by the Pharisees were irrelevant in the era of the dawning of the kingdom and the formation of a new community of expectation gathered around him.[83]

But there are other, ultimately more serious issues, on which the Pharisees clashed with Jesus which have to do with his assumption of roles which they considered God reserved for himself. For example, in Mark 2:1-12 (and parr.) the scribes dispute his implicit claim to equality with God when he forgives the sins of the man he heals. In Mark 3:1-6 (and parr.) the Pharisees attack Jesus' presumption in healing a man (the work of a doctor) on the Sabbath. It is enough for them to take counsel—in Mark they do so with the Herodians— to destroy him (Mark 3:6 and parr.). Nevertheless, it would be a misconception to conclude that the Pharisees were implacably opposed to Jesus on all points. His reply to the Sadducees in Mark 12:18-27 (and parr.) would have resonated with them (cf. Acts 23:6-10). The successfully argued counsel of the Pharisee Gamaliel (Acts 5:33-39) probably represents the view of many within the movement.

In speaking of himself as "temple" (Mark 14:48; Matt. 26:61; John 2:19, 21), Jesus challenged traditional perceptions of its place as the focus of Jewish nationalist aspirations. Moreover, his casting out of the money changers and the upsetting of their tables may have been crucial in the high priestly resolve to act decisively against Jesus since he threw down a challenge to high priestly control of the holy place and may have been understood to be acting out its destruction.[84] Thus his words and deeds posed a challenge to religious authority exercised by Pharisees and the high priestly establishment alike. Ultimately, a lonely and isolated Jesus is arrested by retainers of the chief

---

[83] For consideration of Jesus' movement offering a contrast to the reform program of the Pharisees, see Anthony J. Saldarini, *Pharisees, Scribes and Sadducees in Palestinian Society: A Sociological Approach* (Wilmington: Michael Glazier, 1988), pp. 150-51. E. P. Sanders argues that Jesus incurred the anger of the religiously conventional because he offered "sinners" a place in the kingdom and associated with them "even though they did not make restitution, sacrifice, and turn to obedience to the law" (*Jesus and Judaism* [Philadelphia: Fortress, 1985], p. 207).

[84] See E. P. Sanders, *Jesus and Judaism*, esp. pp. 296-306. He argues that a charge of blasphemy was sustained against Jesus on the basis of his pronouncements against the temple combined with his action against it. Sanders underscores Jewish sensitivity on this score by appealing to the lone anti-temple protester who from 62 until his death in the Roman siege of the city maintained a message of doom. He was denounced to the Romans and scourged (see *J.W.* 6.301-9).

priests having been betrayed into their hands by one of his own (Mark 14:10-11 and parr.).[85] It is the High Priest, Caiaphas, and in John's Gospel his father-in-law Annas, who first interrogate him. He next appears before the Sanhedrin where the charges against him relate to an implied threat to the temple. He is handed over to Pilate. The Jerusalem mob seals his fate.[86]

Paul spent the first half of his life as a Pharisee (Acts 26:4-5; Phil. 3:5). He took the message of Jesus and translated it into the urban centers of the Mediterranean. Like the community gathered around Jesus, the Pauline churches were communities that testify to an undermining of prevailing social and hierarchical structures whether Jewish or Greco-Roman (Gal. 3:28). Although Paul did not surrender his Jewish identity he did challenge the relentlessly discriminating ideals of observant Jews. When arrested in the temple he was immediately accused of subverting Jewish ethnic integrity and national aspirations. Everywhere, his accusers claimed, he was preaching "against our people, our law, and this place," and, what is more (and here we remember the anxieties of Jews on this score from their experience of Antiochus Epiphanes and Pompey), he had "brought Greeks into the temple and defiled this holy place" (Acts 21:28).

Paul rejected the proposition that in the light of the Christ-event the followers of Jesus were required to accept (if Gentile) and maintain (if Jewish) a specific Jewish identity marked by observing the law that began with circumcision. By contrast Paul proclaimed the sufficiency of a faith response to the saving work of God in Christ, perceived to be the pre-eminent redemptive event. He decisively rejected the law with its demands for ethnic distinctiveness in the face of dawning eschatological realities that were now encompassing Jew and Gentile. Consequently, the "works of the law," as Paul terms these requirements which mark out a distinctive Jewish life style, were no longer mandatory because they re-imposed ethnic boundary markers and compromised the full inclusion of non-observant Gentiles into the people of God.[87]

The seeds of a more radical disjunction with Judaism can be seen in the NT. The authors of Luke-Acts and the letter to the Hebrews imply that Christianity supersedes Judaism and that it is the heir of all the promises made to Moses and the Prophets.[88] Greek-speaking Jews from Cyprus and Cyrene took the message about Christ directly to Gentiles in Antioch, outside the

---

[85] The gospels are not agreed as to the precise identity of those who arrest Jesus. Matthew (26:47-48) and Mark (14:43) agree that there was a crowd from the chief priests and the scribes and the elders. Luke (22:47) only refers to a crowd. John (18:3) refers to a band of soldiers and officers from the chief priests and the Pharisees.

[86] It is important to note that there is ample evidence for violent, even deadly, religious conflict in late Second Temple Judaism, and that it is easy to conceive how offensive Jesus' teaching, not least his call to repentance, might have proven. So Raymond E. Brown, *The Death of the Messiah*, Volume One (New York: Doubleday, 1994), pp. 391-97.

[87] The phrase "works of the law," with a meaning consistent with that noted above, is encountered in the Qumran text 4QMMT.

[88] This is a view not shared in the undisputed Pauline letters. See J. Christiaan Beker, *Paul the Apostle* (Philadelphia: Fortress, 1980), pp. 328-47.

Jewish contexts in which it had hitherto been articulated, and thereby created a Gentile church.[89] On the other hand there were other believers who remained observant Jews, such as the members of the community around James the Lord's brother.[90]

Despite the diverse ethnic and cultural heritages represented among the earliest Christian communities, the believers were united in their confidence that Jesus was the anointed one—the Christ, the Messiah—of Jewish expectation, and that, although crucified in weakness and shame, he had been vindicated by God and raised to life.

## Bibliography

Bickerman, Elias. *The God of the Maccabees.* Leiden: Brill, 1979.

Charlesworth, James H., ed. *Old Testament Pseudepigrapha.* 2 vols. Garden City: Doubleday, 1983, 1985.

Cohen, Shaye J. D. *From the Maccabees to the Mishnah.* Louisville: Westminster John Knox Press, 2006.

Goodblatt, David M. *Elements of Ancient Jewish Nationalism.* New York/Cambridge: Cambridge University Press, 2006.

Goodman, Martin D. *The Ruling Class of Judaea: The Origins of the Jewish Revolt against Rome, A.D. 66–70.* New York/Cambridge: Cambridge University Press, 1987.

Harding, Mark. *Early Christian Life and Thought in Social Context.* London/New York: T. & T. Clark International, 2003.

Hengel, Martin. *Judaism and Hellenism: Studies in their Encounter in Palestine during the Early Hellenistic Period.* London: SCM, 1974.

Mendels, Doron. *The Rise and Fall of Jewish Nationalism: Jewish and Christian Ethnicity in Ancient Palestine.* Grand Rapids/Cambridge: Eerdmans, 1992.

Murphy, Frederick J. *The Religious World of Jesus: An Introduction to Second Temple Judaism.* Nashville: Abingdon, 1991.

————. *Early Judaism: The Exile to the Time of Jesus.* Peabody: Hendrickson, 2002.

Neusner, Jacob. *The Rabbinic Tradition About the Pharisees Before 70: Part 1, The Masters.* Leiden: Brill, 1971.

Newsome, James D. *Greeks, Romans, Jews: Currents of Culture and Belief in the New Testament World.* Philadelphia: Trinity Press International, 1992.

Nickelsburg, G. W. E. *Jewish Literature between the Bible and the Mishnah.* Second Edition. Minneapolis: Fortress, 2005.

Rajak, T. *Josephus.* Second Edition. London: Duckworth, 2002.

Sanders, E. P. *Judaism: Practice and Belief, 63 BCE–66 CE.* Philadelphia: Trinity Press

---

[89] See Acts 11:19-21; Sean Freyne, *The World of the New Testament* (Wilmington: Michael Glazier, 1980), p. 171. It would appear that those who preached the gospel in Antioch were Greek speaking Jews "from Cyprus and Cyrene." It was they who, on arriving in Antioch, preached to the "Hellenists" (NRSV). Elsewhere this term is usually taken to mean Jews who spoke Greek and not a semitic language, though the implication of the passage is that these "Hellenists" were not Jews (see v. 19). Not surprisingly the Greek manuscript tradition also strongly attests "Greeks" at this juncture. For an extensive discussion, see Bruce M. Metzger, *A Textual Commentary on the Greek New Testament* (Stuttgart: United Bible Societies, 1975), pp. 386-89. There is no doubt that, according to Luke, the action of the preachers in Antioch marked a new strategy in the early Christian mission.

[90] See Richard J. Bauckham, *James: Wisdom of James, disciple of Jesus the sage* (London/New York: Routledge, 1999). Note Josephus's respect for James in *Ant.* 20.200-201.

International, 1992.

Smallwood, E. Mary. *The Jews under Roman Rule*. Leiden: Brill, 1981.

Stambaugh, John E., and John L. Balch. *The New Testament in Its Social Environment*. Philadelphia: Westminster, 1986.

Vermes, Geza. *The Complete Dead Sea Scrolls in English*. New York: Allen Lane/Penguin, 1997.

Vermes, Geza, and Martin D. Goodman. *The Essenes According to the Classical Sources*. Sheffield: JSOT Press, 1989.

# 7. The Gospels and the Old Testament

*Theresa Yu Chui Siang Lau*

The writing and reading of any text involves much more than that text alone. When a document is produced and read:

> [T]he writer assigns meaning to his own context and in interaction with other texts. . . shapes and forms a text. The reader, in much the same way, assigns meaning to the generated text in interaction with other texts he knows.[1]

This observation by Ellen van Wolde reveals the importance of studying a document's inter-textual matrix in the attempt to gather meaning from the document at hand. A simple glance at the four gospels gives the impression that they frequently refer, either explicitly or implicitly, to the Hebrew Scriptures/Old Testament (OT). It is evident that there are interactions with other textual sources, especially Second Temple Jewish works,[2] and even other early Christian writing.[3] However, the majority of the quotations and allusions in the gospels are to the OT. Matthew begins his gospel with a reference to Jesus as "the son of David, the son of Abraham" (Matt. 1:1). Mark commences by appealing explicitly to Isaianic prophecy (Mark 1:2-3).[4] The introductory chapters of both Luke and John are saturated with scriptural echoes and allusions. The literary and theological influence of the OT upon the gospels is profound and pervasive. It may be possible to say, as Barrett has about Luke and Acts, that there is no major concept in the four gospels that does not to some extent reflect the beliefs and theological vocabulary of Hebrew Scripture.[5] Hence, a study of the unique relation of the gospels and

---

[1] Ellen van Wolde, "Trendy Intertextuality?" in Sipke Draisma, ed., *Intertextuality in Biblical Writings* (Kampen: Kok, 1989), p. 47.

[2] For examples, 1 Esd. 1:32 in Matt. 1:11, Jdt. 11:19 in Mark 6:34, *1 En.* 51:2 in Luke 21:28, *Pss. Sol.* 7:6 in John 1:14. Other examples are listed in Barbara Aland, Kurt Aland, et al. eds., *The Greek New Testament*, 4th rev. ed. (Stuttgart: Deutsche Bibelgesellschaft/United Bible Societies, 1993), pp. 900-901. It has been argued that the gospels, especially Luke, were written following "the prototypes of the early Greek histories of Herodotus and Thucydides" or various other biographical writings. See for example, Joel B. Green, *The Gospel of Luke* (Grand Rapids: Eerdmans, 1997), pp. 2-6. Refer also to Carl Clemen, *Primitive Christianity and its Non-Jewish Sources* (Edinburgh: T. & T. Clark, 1912), pp. 267-73.

[3] A familiar example is the use of Mark's Gospel in Matthew and Luke.

[4] Mark, however, proceeds to cite more OT passages than just Isaiah. See discussion below.

[5] C. K. Barrett, "Luke/Acts," in D. A. Carson and H. G. M. Williamson, eds., *It is Written:*

the OT is of considerable value to every student of the Bible.

In this area of contemporary gospel research, there exist a number of persistent difficulties or confusions over terminology and definition. Some of the confusion is inherent in the terms themselves. The rest may be rectified through further clarification and more nuanced investigation.[6] Each dimension of this investigation raises a number of questions for which satisfactory answers may not be available, at least not yet. They call for caution and warn against any simplistic discussion of the use of the OT by the gospel writers.

## A. The Question/Problem in the Terminology and Canonicity of the Old Testament

The first difficulty we encounter is our reference to the "Old Testament" or "Hebrew Scripture." The terms are anachronistic and can mislead. Although the use of this shorthand is necessary, it has masked complex issues related to a tenuous history of the canon of the two testaments.[7] First of all, the canon of what we know as the OT was not officially closed at the time of the writing of the gospels; the use of the term "Old Testament" is thus misleading to the extent that it may indicate to the uninformed that there was an established canon called the "Old Testament" by the first century. Although one might presume that by the first century the extent of authoritative writings was fixed *de facto*,[8] the actual and complete delimitation of the canon, especially the Hagiographa (the "Writings"), was still uncertain.[9] Second, before the formation of the New Testament (NT) there could not have been a corpus of

---

*Scripture Citing Scripture* (New York: Cambridge University Press, 1988), p. 231.

[6] Stanley E. Porter, "The Use of the Old Testament in the New Testament: A Brief Comment on Method and Terminology," in Craig A. Evans and James A. Sanders, eds., *The Early Christian Interpretation of the Scriptures of Israel: Investigations and Proposals* (Sheffield: Sheffield Academic Press, 1997), pp. 79-96.

[7] Richard B. Hays and Joel B. Green, "The Use of the Old Testament by New Testament Writers," in Joel B. Green, ed., *Hearing the New Testament: Strategies for Interpretation* (Grand Rapids: Eerdmans, 1995), p. 223.

[8] Luke refers to the Law, the Prophets and the Psalms (Luke 24:44). Philo, Josephus and the New Testament usage generally confirm the existence of a threefold classification by this time. The prologue of the Wisdom of Jesus Ben Sirach, written by Ben Sirach's grandson when translating his grandfather's book from Hebrew into Greek, written almost two centuries before any New Testament book, makes three references to the three parts: "the study of the Law, the Prophets, and the other books." See Patrick W. Skehan, *The Wisdom of Ben Sira* (New York: Doubleday, 1987), p. 131 (vv. 1, 3, 7; Skehan's own numbering based on his translation).

[9] See "Canon," in *ABD*, vol. 1, pp. 852-61. Note the discussion in D. Moody Smith, "The Use of the Old Testament in the New," in James M. Efird, ed., *The Use of the Old Testament in the New and Other Essays* (Durham: Duke University Press, 1972), pp. 4-8; Schnayer Z. Leiman, *The Canonization of Hebrew Scripture: the Talmudic and Midrashic Evidence* (Hamden: Archon, 1976); Roger Beckwith, *The Old Testament Canon of the New Testament Church and Its Background in Earliest Judaism* (Grand Rapids: Eerdmans, 1985); F. F. Bruce, *The Canon of Scripture* (Downers Grove: InterVarsity Press, 1988), pp. 25-114; Lee McDonald, *The Formation of the Christian Biblical Canon* (Peabody: Hendrickson, 1995); E. Earle Ellis, "The Old Testament Canon in the Early Church," in Martin Jan Mulder, ed., *Mikra: Text, Translation, Reading and Interpretation of the Hebrew Bible in Ancient Judaism and Early Christianity* (Philadelphia: Fortress Press, 1988), pp. 653-90.

writings called the "Old Testament." The evangelists would not have adopted a two-testament view of Scripture.[10]

Although the problem of canonicity is real and should not be bypassed, the status and authority of the OT text is not to be doubted. The fact that the writers of the NT refer to the OT books as "Scripture(s)" (γραφή; cf. e.g. Matt. 21:42; Luke 4:21; John 13:18; Rom. 4:3; James 2:23; 1 Pet. 2:6; and 2 Tim. 3:16[11]), suggests that the authority of these books was established even if the extent of the canon might not be. Therefore, a qualified usage of the term "Old Testament" or "Hebrew Scriptures" in relation to the gospels is justifiable. The terms are used here to refer to a body of canonical Scriptures whose existence, even if its exact delimitation was still not fixed, was scarcely in doubt.

## B. The Question of Definition: Quotations, Allusions or Echoes?

The criteria and categories used by scholars in this area to determine and describe the use of OT in the gospels are rather confusing. Many simply do not define their terms, and those who attempt to do so often fail to agree with one another. Stanley Porter has pointed out that:

> [T]he range of terminology used to speak of the way that a New Testament writer may use the Old Testament or a related text is simply astounding. Without attempting to be comprehensive, at least the following terms have been used with some regularity or in important works on the topic: citation, direct quotation, formal quotation, indirect quotation, allusive quotation, allusion (whether conscious or unconscious), paraphrase, exegesis (such as inner biblical exegesis), midrash, typology, reminiscence, echo (whether conscious or unconscious), intertextuality, influence (either direct or indirect), and even tradition, among other terms. Sometimes all instances that are not direct quotation are subsumed under one of the above (or another) terms. Other times fine distinctions in meaning are made between many of the above terms. It is this situation that needs to be addressed.[12]

It is not surprising that the estimates of the number of references to the OT in a given gospel vary greatly among scholars. For example, Lindsay lists twenty-three references to the OT in Mark; Scroggie, sixty-three; Swete,

---

[10] It may be argued that the evangelists already reflect a view of the authority of Jesus' words as being equally important as Scripture. Paul had already spoken of the Jews reading the "Old Covenant" (2 Cor. 3:14), by which he certainly means part, if not all, of the OT, and thus prepares the way for the adoption of the term "Old Testament." See Smith, *Uses*, p. 4. The twofold demarcation of the Scripture only comes into existence in the late second century AD. Melito of Sardis (c. AD 180) was the first to name a list of the Hebrew Scriptures as ἡ παλαιὰ διαθήκη (Eusebius, *Hist. eccl.* 4.26.14). Later, an anti-Montanist writing (c. AD 192) used the designation ὁ τῆς τοῦ εὐαγγελίου καινῆς διαθήκης λόγος to refer to a group of authoritative writings (Eusebius, *Hist. eccl.* 5.16.3).

[11] In 2 Tim. 3:16 it is the OT "Scriptures" that are being referred to as "God-breathed" and "profitable" for Christians.

[12] Porter, "Uses," p. 80.

sixty-eight; Kee, more than 217![13]

Therefore, it is not unfair to say that, in most cases, the estimates of scholars are subjective and depend very much on their individual definitions of what constitutes a quotation or an allusion. The variegated text forms of the OT coupled with the fact that manuscripts of the NT did not use modern conventional markers (such as our quotation marks) to indicate quoted material make the problem of definition a perennial one and our final judgment an artificial one. Furthermore, discussion regarding some of the above definitions has reached a state of a stalemate. Yet, clearer and workable definitions and criteria are necessary to avoid the symptom of "parallelomania."[14]

Short of a common language, the way forward is to continue the debate, perhaps in a more innovative way, until common ground can be found. However, as Porter has stated, this might be an unreasonable expectation. Therefore, interpreters who wish to perform in-depth studies will need to be clear in their terminology and application of their terms. This would at least allow categories of usages to be compared and discussed.[15]

Our aim here is not to continue this debate—neither to provide a definitive set of statistics or criteria for such a search nor to provide a comprehensive discussion of every usage of the OT in the gospels. Instead, we will attempt to give a brief survey of each evangelist's general usage, highlighting their distinctive or more obvious styles of emphasis, whether by explicit quotation or implicit echo. Though our assessment will inevitably share the subjectivity of others, it is consistent with widely accepted observation. Our definition of terms will also reflect this general purpose. Accordingly, "quotation" is used here to refer to passages which contain an explicit indication of a citation, usually with a formula such as "it is written" (Mark 1:2) or "this was to fulfill" (Matt. 2:15). "Allusion" is used to refer to passages with clear reference to Scripture but woven into the new text rather than merely "quoted," such as the OT allusions present in Jesus' answer to the Baptist's question in Luke 7:22. "Echo" indicates a faint reference to Scripture, conscious or unconscious. An example of echo can be seen in John 11:41 (cf. Ps. 118:21). It must be stated that most, if not all, of the evangelists are so immersed in Scripture that they naturally used many of its idioms and expressions as their own. Hence, many of the echoes can be quite unconscious and emerge from minds soaked in the scriptural heritage of Israel.

---

[13] Kee does not give an exact figure for the whole Gospel; he only lists fifty-seven quotations and about 160 allusions (not counting passages which had possibly "influenced" Mark) in chapters 11–16 alone. Thus, on average more than fourteen "quotations and allusions" can be found in each chapter of Mark. H. C. Kee, "The Function of Scriptural Quotations and Allusions in Mark 11-16," in E. Grässer and E. E. Ellis, eds., *Festschrift für Werner Georg Kümmel* (Göttingen: Vandenhoeck & Ruprecht, 1975), pp. 165-88. W. Graham Scroggie, *A Guide to the Gospels* (Grand Rapids: Kregel, 1995), p. 190. Lindsay's and Swete's statistics are cited in Scroggie.

[14] Or the excessive identification of parallels and similarities between texts. Porter, "Uses," p. 87.

[15] Porter, "Uses," p. 95.

Before moving on to discuss the specific quotations, allusions and echoes of the Hebrew Scripture found within each gospel text, it is important to consider the comparative value of these categories. The labels seem to have some heuristic value. They often lead people to an intuitive assumption that the explicit quotation is more important than the implicit allusion, which in turn is more important than the echo. Therefore, many studies on the use of the OT, perhaps daunted by the potential amount of data to process, or overwhelmed by the debate on "definition," or threatened by the danger of parallelomania, choose to limit themselves to discussion of the passages that contain an explicit quotation. These passages are generally regarded as less controversial, most relevant, and the number of occurrences most representative of the relative importance of the Hebrew Scripture in the particular document.[16]

This limitation, however, is only legitimate if the study is specifically established to explore the explicit quotations of the OT in a given text. Such an investigation would be a highly inadequate and unjustifiably narrow one. The explicit quotation, though important, is certainly not the most important, nor the most representative of the relationship between a given text and the OT. For instance, in the *Greek New Testament* (United Bible Society) the numbers of quotations listed for Matthew, Mark, Luke and John are fifty-four, twenty-seven, twenty-five and fourteen respectively.[17] These numbers can easily give an impression that among the four gospels, John is least strongly linked to the OT because it does not quote the OT as frequently as others. Yet, this conclusion cannot be further from the truth. As we shall see below, John's Gospel in many ways surpasses the other gospels in its usage of the OT.

Richard Hays has aptly observed that "the most significant elements of intertextual correspondence between old context and new can be implicit rather than voiced, perceptible only within the silent space framed by the juncture of two texts."[18] Allusions can imply texts that are well known, whereas explicit quotations show the need to highlight them; and echoes can be quite loud if they reverberate in an echo chamber.[19] Thus, to neglect the implicit allusion and echo might turn out to be neglecting the most obvious evidence.

Steve Moyise provides this helpful illustration:

A particular allusion or echo can sometimes be more important than its "volume" might suggest. . . [I]t is not just the loudest instruments in the orchestra that give a piece its particular character. Sometimes, subtle allusions or echoes, especially if they are frequent and pervasive, can be more

---

[16] Porter, "Uses," p. 91.

[17] Compare with the Westcott-Hort list of 124, 70, 109 and 27 for Matthew, Mark, Luke and John respectively; another example of varying estimations.

[18] Richard B. Hays, *Echoes of Scripture in the Letters of Paul* (New Haven: Yale University Press, 1989), p. 155.

[19] Steve Moyise, "Intertextuality and the Study of the Old Testament in the New Testament," in Steve Moyise, ed., *The Old Testament in the New Testament: Essays in Honor of J. L. North* (Sheffield: Sheffield Academic Press, 2000), pp. 18-19.

influential than explicit quotations.[20]

Furthermore, distinctive styles of different writers should be taken into consideration. Appearances can be deceptive. Two writers with the same regard and knowledge of the OT may choose to express this in two totally different ways. One writer may prefer explicit quotation with distinctive formula; the other may prefer to subtly woo the reader into the OT world by providing a skillfully crafted narrative that echoes Hebrew Scripture. This awareness is especially important as we begin the discussion of the specific usages of the OT in the four gospels.

## C. Mark

Among the four canonical gospels, Mark provides the least number of editorial quotations[21] of the OT. He has only one explicit editorial quotation, in the prologue (1:2-3). All the other references to the OT are found on the lips of Jesus or those who conversed with him. Yet, the singularly significant position and format of this one and only editorial quotation may have been consciously designed to act as a key for the understanding of the whole narrative, as Hooker claims, "[Mark's] story is good news precisely because it is the fulfillment of scripture."[22]

Unlike the other gospels which provide a set of explicit editorial quotations as a sort of running commentary on the narrative story, Mark begins with such a quotation and thereafter chooses to enfold into the narrative a web of extensive quotations, allusions and echoes of the OT until what is "written" of the Son of Man (9:12-13; 12:10-11; 14:21) is finally fulfilled.

Other quotations on the lips of the actors of the story (mainly Jesus) include the reference to the hypocrisy of the Pharisees in 7:6-7; interpretation of the law in 7:10, 10:5-9, 10:19, 12:26, 12:28-31; purpose of the temple in 11:17; rejection of Jesus in 12:10-11; the Sadducees' question about the resurrection in 12:19; puzzle of the identity of David's Lord in 12:36; striking the shepherd in 14:27. Some obvious allusions include the purpose of the parables in 4:12, Jesus' entry into Jerusalem in 11:9-10, apocalyptic sayings in 13:24-26 and 14:62, and words from the cross in 15:34.

A particular striking feature of Mark's use of the OT is its concentration on the passion of Jesus.[23] Joel Marcus has listed 14 references to the Book of

---

[20] Moyise, "Intertextuality," p. 17.

[21] This phrase is used here to refer to the narrator or implied author's quotation of Scripture in contrast to a quotation that has been found in the mouth of a character of the story.

[22] Morna D. Hooker, "Mark," in Carson and Williamson, eds., *It is Written*, p. 220; Joel Marcus, *The Way of the Lord: Christological Exegesis of the Old Testament in the Gospel of Mark* (Edinburgh: T. & T. Clark, 1992). The oddity of Mark's citation here will be discussed later, suffice now to say that the quotation shows Mark's interest in emphasizing Isaiah's restoration promise as being fulfilled by the gospel.

[23] For a detailed estimation and discussion, refer to Rikk E. Watts, "Mark," in G. K. Beale and D. A. Carson, *Commentary on the New Testament Use of the Old Testament* (Grand Rapids:

Psalms alone in Mark 14-15.[24] Moyise has aptly commented:

> [Mark] has told the story of Jesus' passion in such a way that it evokes the righteous sufferer of the psalms and probably also the suffering servant of Isaiah and the smitten shepherd of Zechariah. He does not try to prove that Jesus is any of these figures. He simply uses them as his "palette" as he constructs his portrait of Jesus.[25]

## D. Matthew

Matthew is well known as the Gospel which contains the highest number of explicit quotations of Hebrew Scripture. Besides incorporating all of Mark's quotations, Matthew has added into his narrative many more quotations, allusions and echoes of the OT. The most striking feature of Matthew's usage of Scripture is the distinctive series of ten explicit editorial quotations interspersed throughout the narrative acting as commentaries to the story of Jesus (1:22-3; 2:15; 2:17-18; 2:23; 4:14-16; 8:17; 12:17-21; 13:35; 21:4-5; 27:9).[26] They are all introduced by a typical fulfillment formula, "to fulfill what had been spoken . . . through the prophet" (with variations to suit each context). The fulfillment theme appears also in other quotations which imply that Scripture is being fulfilled but the passages quoted are not introduced by Matthew's typical fulfillment formula (e.g. 3:3; 11:10). There are other quotations, allusions and echoes which emphasize fulfillment but are spoken by Jesus or others in the story (e.g. 2:6; 15:8-9; 9:13; 12:7). Some of Mark's quotations and allusions have also been injected with the hope of fulfillment which is not explicitly spelled out in Mark (e.g., 13:13-15, cf. Mark 4:12). The cumulative effect of these quotations and allusions of fulfillment is noteworthy. For this reason, if for no other, the Gospel of Matthew rightly occupies the first place in canonical lists of the NT, bridging it thematically and intimately with the OT.

Four of Matthew's formula quotations are introduced with an explicit reference to Isaiah and two to Jeremiah. Scholars have pointed to Matthew's special interest in these two books, the "rejected" prophets who were preoccupied with the salvation of Israel.[27] Most of the formula quotations are

---

Baker Academic, 2007), pp. 111-249.

[24] 14:1//Ps. 10:7-8; 14:18//Ps. 41:9; 14:34//Ps. 42:5, 11; 43:5; 14:41//Ps. 140:8; 14:55//Ps. 37:32; 14:57//Ps. 27:12; 35:11; 14:61//Ps. 35:13-15; 15:24//Ps. 22:18; 15:29//Ps. 22:7; 15:30-31//Ps. 22:8; 15:32//Ps. 22:6; 15:34//Ps. 22:1; 15:36//Ps. 69:21; 15:40//Ps. 38:11. See Marcus, *The Way of the Lord*, pp. 174-75. For the importance of Psalm 22 in the passion narratives see Raymond Brown, *The Death of the Messiah*, vol. 2 (New York: Doubleday, 1994), pp. 1455-65.

[25] Steve Moyise, *The Old Testament in the New: An Introduction* (New York: Continuum, 2001), p. 32.

[26] The quotation Zech. 9:9 found in Matt. 21:4-5 is the only one within this group of scriptural quotation that is cited elsewhere in the New Testament (John 12:14-15). However, the form of the two quotations differs so markedly that a direct link is most unlikely. For this reason it is also regarded as distinctive to Matthew. See Graham Stanton, "Matthew," in Carson and Williamson, eds., *It is Written*, p. 217.

[27] Michael Knowles, *Jeremiah in Matthew's Gospel: the Rejected Prophet Motif in*

located in the first half of the Gospel (1:1–13:40), in fact, nearly half of them are in the nativity narrative. From 13:41 onwards Matthew begins to follow Mark rather closely, therefore it is not surprising that most of the distinctive Matthean quotations, allusions and echoes are found in the first half of the Gospel, whereas most of the quotations, allusions and echoes which Matthew takes over from Mark occur in the latter half of the Gospel. It has been suggested that whereas Mark had already set the passion narratives against the backdrop of Hebrew Scripture, traditions concerning the birth and infancy of Jesus had not been interpreted in this way, Matthew thus supplemented the narrative of Mark by emphasizing the fulfillment of Scripture in the nativity narratives.[28]

Since Matthew usually follows his sources closely, it is no surprise to find that he takes over with little modification many of the OT citations found in Mark. He retains their language and their Greek (Septuagintal) form. But in numerous passages Matthew also makes abbreviations, expansions and modifications in line with his own stylistic and theological concerns. He usually treats the OT quotations the same way as he treats the Marcan and other source material.[29]

## E. Luke

Compared to Matthew, Luke provides less editorial commentary on the fulfillment of OT prophecy in the story of Jesus. Nevertheless, Luke is very far from neglecting the issues of fulfillment or being less influenced by the OT. Besides carrying over all but four of Mark's quotations, thus inheriting a Scripture-imbued narrative, Luke has further added to his narrative some idiosyncratic and important references to the OT.[30] Though not as many and not as abrupt as Matthew (since all of the quotations have been skillfully knitted into the narrative of the Gospel), all of the passages peculiar to Luke speak distinctly about the fulfillment of the prophecy. Although there is much to discuss about Luke's inherited quotations, we shall only pay attention to the four distinctive Lukan additions.

First, like Matthew, Luke's nativity account is freighted with OT imagery and correspondence. The quotations that appear in 2:22-24, coupled with numerous allusions and echoes of the OT language in the nativity account, communicate to the readers that here is the fulfillment of all hopes for salvation; hopes such as those of Simeon and Anna who "were looking for the redemption of Israel." Mary's song, the Magnificat (1:46-55), echoes the song of Hannah (1 Sam. 2:1-10), revealing God's great act of fulfilling his

---

*Matthean Redaction* (Sheffield: JSOT Press, 1993).

[28] Stanton, "Matthew," pp. 214-15.

[29] Stanton, "Matthew," p. 213.

[30] Barrett lists three categories of quotation: (a) Marcan-based passages: 3:4; 3:5-6; 10:27; 18:20; 19:31; 19:38; 19:46; 20:17; 20:28; 20:37; 20:42, 43; (b) passages shared with Matthew only: 4:1-13; 7:27; (c) material peculiar to Luke: 2:22-24; 4:18-19; 22:37. See Barrett, "Luke/Acts," pp. 232-37.

promises to the Hebrew patriarchs. Zechariah's song, the Benedictus (1:67-79), alludes to God's promises "as he spoke through the mouth of his holy prophets from of old," that he will raise up "a mighty savior . . . in the house of his servant David."[31]

Second, in the programmatic passage of 4:18-21, through the words of Jesus, Luke brings the note of fulfillment to the surface, announcing in advance that Jesus' person, work and destiny were fulfillments of Scripture. Third, after the words of institution of the Lord's Supper, Luke portrays Jesus quoting Isa. 53:12 and announcing that "this scripture must be fulfilled in me." Finally, in the summarizing passage of 24:13-49, Luke reveals that the OT as a whole can be explained christologically: "beginning with Moses and all the prophets, he [Jesus] interpreted to them the things about himself in all the scriptures" (v. 27). This statement reveals the hermeneutical maxim of the early church which governs how the OT was read, as far as it has been reflected through the NT writings.

In fact, the placing of the two important and extended narratives of Scripture fulfillment, one at the beginning (4:18-21), the other at the end of Jesus' earthly ministry (24:13-49), is rather intriguing. Thus, it is possible to perceive the two passages as a frame which acts to highlight the meaning of the content of the gospel: the gospel is the fulfillment of the OT in the life of Jesus. To be sure, the OT has permeated not only the presentation of the gospel message, but also the language of this Gospel. Scholars have pointed to what Tasker calls "Luke's quite amazing power of writing Greek so that it evokes the memory of the Greek OT."[32] The structure, plus the deliberate use of Septuagintal language (in spite of the fact that Luke is also capable of a Greek style less dependent on Septuagintal style), places the Gospel in an echo chamber of the OT. Hence, it is no surprise to encounter Barrett stating that the influence of the OT upon the Lukan writings "is profound and pervasive. It is safe to say that there is no major concept in the. . . [book] that does not to some extent reflect the beliefs and theological vocabulary of the OT."[33]

## F. John

Compared with the Synoptic Gospels, John has a relatively small number of explicit quotations. However, this does not mean that he is less influenced by Hebrew Scripture, as we have stated earlier. Rather, the opposite is the case. A. T. Hanson argues that the influence of Hebrew Scripture was so pervasive in John that it is possible to see it as a source for John's narrative as much as the Jesus tradition. It has permeated the very words he used and the concepts

---

[31] R. V. G. Tasker, *The Old Testament in the New Testament* (London: SCM Press, 1954), p. 48.

[32] Tasker, *The Old Testament*, p. 53. This is especially distinctive in the nativity account. See David W. Pao and Eckhard J. Schnabel, "Luke," in Beale and Carson, *Commentary on the New Testament*, pp. 253-54.

[33] Barrett, "Luke/Acts," p. 231.

he adopted.[34]

Readers are bombarded with rich scriptural imagery, commencing with the prologue (1:1-18). This remarkable introduction contains echoes from all three sections of the OT canon, right from the evocation of Gen. 1:1 in the opening words of the Gospel, "In the beginning . . . ." Throughout the successive narratives the incarnate Word is related to a number of concepts encountered in the OT. He is the Lamb of God (1:29), the Messiah (1:41), the one written of by Moses in the Law and by the Prophets (1:45, 5:46), the temple (2:18-22), the serpent in the wilderness (3:14), the living water (4:7-15), the bread and manna (6:48-51), the vine and the branches (15:1-6), the good shepherd (10:11), and the Pool of Siloam (9:7).[35] He is true focus of the various Jewish festivals—the true and final fulfillment of all that was prefigured and commemorated in those great redemptive acts. Added to these important images, it has been observed that John also employs many other less christologically loaded images within the narrative, such as the murmuring of the Jews that echoes the Israelite's murmuring (6:41-43; cf. Exod. 16:2), to reflect the idea that the gospel story is "played on the template of that scripture."[36] Concerning this plethora of images, Carson has rightly commented that, "the precise line of connection with the OT is sometimes difficult to determine, not because of a want of OT evidence, but because of an overabundance."[37]

Thus, in reading through the Gospel, a reader nurtured by the OT might, without consciously marking the allusion, experience various moments of familiarity. Those momentary ripples of elevated diction help to heighten the dramatic effect of the story. Furthermore, the reader whose ear is able not only to discern the echo but also to locate the source of the original voice will experience a number of resonances. Such resonances find their explanations from time to time in the narrative through the direct quotation of the OT.

John's quotations of the OT text are quite evenly spread throughout the book, though not great in number. Even though the introductory formulae he uses are less formal than Matthew, they can be divided into two categories, following the common division of the book into two halves. In the first half of the book (the Book of Signs: chapters 1–12), John seems to prefer the phrase "it is/was written" (2:17; 6:31; 6:45, 8:17; 10:34; 12:14). In the second half of the book (the Book of Glory: chapters 13–20), John frequently introduces

---

[34] A. T. Hanson, "John's Use of Scripture," in *The Gospels and the Scriptures of Israel* (Sheffield: Sheffield Academic Press, 1994), pp. 358-79. See also his *The Prophetic Gospel: A Study of John and the Old Testament* (Edinburgh: T. & T. Clark, 1991) and *The New Testament Interpretation of Scripture* (London: SPCK, 1980).

[35] Davies has pointed out how John 9:7 intentionally mentions that Siloam means "sent" as though to invite comparison with Jesus the Sent One *par excellence*. For more discussion of how Jesus replaces various forms of holy space, see W. D. Davies, *The Gospel and the Land* (Berkeley: University of California Press, 1974), p. 288.

[36] Judith Lieu, "Narrative Analysis and Scripture in John," in Steve Moyise, ed., *The Old Testament in the New Testament* (Sheffield: Sheffield Academic Press, 2000), pp. 147-48.

[37] D. A. Carson, "John and the Johannine Epistles," in Carson and Williamson, eds., *It is Written*, p. 253.

quotation with the word "fulfill" (12:38; 13:18; 15:25; 17:12; 19:24, 19:28). While nearly half of Matthew's fulfillment-formula quotations are found at the nativity account, John's fulfillment-formula quotations only occur in the passion narrative. There are seven of these: four of them point to Jesus' rejection and three relate to the details of his crucifixion.[38] Though not completely comparable, Matthean fulfillment quotations seek to authenticate the birth and life of Jesus whereas Johannine fulfillment quotations seek to authenticate the fate of Jesus.[39] As Craig Evans has stated in his explanation of the interesting division of formulae within the two halves of John:

> Whereas Jesus' ministry of signs was in keeping with scriptural requirements and expectations, his rejection (first formally acknowledged at 12:37 in reference to his ministry of signs) was in fulfillment of scriptural prophecy. Herein lies the Fourth Evangelist's apologetics: Rejection and crucifixion did not disprove Jesus' claim to messiahship (a position likely held in the late first-century synagogue); on the contrary, they proved it, as seen in the numerous fulfillments of scripture. Consequently, we should not be surprised that the fundamental function of the OT in the Fourth Gospel is christological.[40]

As Carson has noted, the most striking thing about John and its relation to the OT is the large number of passages in which it is either presupposed or argued that the Hebrew Scriptures "speak of Christ, and therefore *ought* to be interpreted christologically (1:45; 2:22; 3:10; 5:39, 45f; 20:9)."[41] As we have seen, Luke only spells out this Christian hermeneutical maxim in the concluding chapter of his Gospel, but John has applied this maxim throughout.

Since the Fourth Gospel is saturated with the language, concepts and imagery of Hebrew Scripture, it is appropriate to conclude with this verdict of Judith Lieu:

> More than in any of the other gospels, scripture provides the indispensable reference point and scaffolding for the argument and the thought of John. From apparently inconsequential allusions through to John's distinctive Christology, it is scripture that makes the gospel "work."[42]

The above discussion represents some of the basic observations concerning the available data. Much remains to be discussed, especially in relation to the origin and interpretation of the scriptural quotation in the gospels. Do they originate from Jesus or from the Evangelist himself?[43] Or are

---

[38] Only half of these quotations are comments of the evangelist.

[39] Stanton, "Matthew," p. 217.

[40] C. A. Evans, "Old Testament in the Gospels," in Joel B. Green and Scot McKnight, eds., *Dictionary of Jesus and the Gospels* (Downers Grove: InterVarsity Press, 1992), p. 587.

[41] Carson, "John and the Johannine Epistles," p. 252.

[42] Lieu, "Narrative Analysis," p. 144.

[43] Space does not allow a detailed discussion here. However, it should be mentioned that it

they taken from some source, perhaps from an early Christian collection of OT passages—a book of testimonies? What theological purposes do they serve? Answers to these questions have been used to support widely differing views of the origin and purpose of each gospel. We will not venture there. However, these questions of text form and interpretation must be mentioned in brief.

## G. The Question of the Text Form

Investigation of the text form is basic to any study of the use of the OT in the New, yet the plurality and fluidity of OT text forms at the beginning of the Christian era have complicated any straightforward investigation of their usage and influence in the gospels. There were Hebrew, Greek and Aramaic text forms, each with its own variegated versions, recensions or revisions.[44] We will introduce the different text forms briefly here before entering into the discussion of their usages.

### 1. Hebrew Masoretic Text (MT)

The OT text of our modern English Bible is based mainly on the Hebrew Masoretic Text. Yet, our knowledge of the Hebrew text(s) available in the early Christian era is highly limited. This relatively late text[45] was the only existing representation of the OT in Hebrew before the discovery of the Dead Sea Scrolls. However, evidence indicates that there were different versions of the Hebrew text in the first century,[46] in particular, the Dead Sea Scrolls raise the question to what degree we can assume a fixed text form during the period of earliest Christianity.[47] That is, we have no absolute confidence in assuming that the version of the Hebrew Bible that we have today is the very version which the early church used.

### 2. Greek Septuagint (LXX)

The complexity remains, if not increases, when we turn to consider the text forms of the Greek translation of the OT—the Septuagint. The state of the Septuagintal text in early Christian eras is itself a highly complex and

---

is generally believed that much of the usage must have originated with Jesus himself. See, e.g., B. D. Chilton, *A Galilean Rabbi and His Bible* (Wilmington: Glazier, 1984) and R. T. France, *Jesus and the Old Testament* (London: Tyndale, 1971).

[44] An excellent introduction can be found in Emanuel Tov, *Textual Criticism of the Hebrew Bible* (Minneapolis: Fortress Press, 2001).

[45] The oldest fragments we have date from the ninth century AD, the oldest complete texts comes from as late as the tenth or eleventh centuries AD.

[46] Evidences from the Dead Sea Scroll, the Septuagint, Philo and Josephus are often used to point to Hebrew texts that differ from MT. Even at Qumran, there were differing Hebrew versions. See Tov, *Textual Criticism*, pp. 111-17.

[47] Hays, Green, "Use," p. 224.

extensive question.[48] To say the least, there are different later versions or recensions of the LXX[49] which begs the question as to what Greek text or texts were being used by Jews and Christians in the first century.

It is helpful to note also that the style of translation varies across the books of the OT. In some books, the translations are literal and wooden (e.g., Pentateuch and Ecclesiastes). In others, they are more free and periphrastic (e.g., Proverbs). Some are much longer in the LXX than the MT (e.g., Job,[50] Esther[51] and Daniel[52]), while others are shorter (e.g., Jeremiah[53]) or different to the MT in many places because of omission or addition of material, thus resulting in different order of verses and chapters (especially in Exodus, Jeremiah and Ezekiel).

The majority of the scriptural quotations in the NT can be linked to the Septuagint. Thus, it may not be too much to claim that the Septuagint was the Bible of the early Christian community and of the gospel writers. Even so, it is difficult to know with certainty which form of the Septuagint might have been employed by each writer.[54]

---

[48] A good introduction can be found in N. Fernandez Marcos, *The Septuagint in Context: Introduction to the Greek Versions of the Bible* (Leiden: Brill, 2000) or Karen H. Jobes and Moisés Silva, *Invitation to the Septuagint* (Grand Rapids: Baker Academic, 2000).

[49] For example, some of the Greek translations underwent revision in order to bring them closer to a particular Hebrew text. NT quotations from the book of Daniel, for instance, tend to agree with the later version known as Theodotion, the so-called "standard" LXX rather than the Old Greek version in the so-called "original" LXX. In editions of the LXX, both texts are usually printed. However, most early Christians were not aware of or being bothered by the different versions. As far as most early Christians were concerned, any Greek translations of the OT read in church were called "the Greek," i.e., their designation for the Septuagint.

[50] LXX Job is about one sixth shorter than MT Job, and includes an ending not extant in the Hebrew.

[51] LXX Esther is twice as long as MT Esther. Almost half of the verses in LXX Esther are not found in MT Esther.

[52] LXX Daniel contains two extra concluding chapters and some additional verses near the beginning of the book that are not found in MT Daniel.

[53] LXX Jeremiah is shorter than MT Jeremiah by roughly one eighth. The order of the chapters of the latter half of the book is quite different.

[54] For example, Maarten Menken has recently argued that the fulfillment quotation in Matthew was taken from a revised version of LXX. See Maarten J. J. Menken, "Messianic Interpretation of Greek Old Testament Passages in Matthew's Fulfilment Quotations," in Michael A Knibb, ed., *The Septuagint & Messianism* (Leuven: Peeters, 2006), pp. 460-62. Compare the similar view in R. Beaton, *Isaiah's Christ in Matthew's Gospel* (New York: Cambridge University Press, 2002), pp. 86-172. Note the different opinion of Krister Stendahl, *The School of St. Matthew and its Use of the Old Testament* (Philadelphia: Fortress Press, 1968), who argues that, in contrast to other Old Testament citations in the gospels, fulfillment quotations in Matthew follow no one textual tradition but represent a selective targumizing procedure in which the interpretation is woven into the text itself. The rendering is not the result of a free paraphrase or looseness but raises out of a scholarly, detailed study and interpretation of the texts themselves. This approach parallels the midrash pesher method of the Qumran sect which will be discussed below. Cf. also Robert H. Gundry, *The Use of the Old Testament in St. Matthew's Gospel* (Leiden: Brill, 1967).

### 3. Aramaic Targum

Targum (Targums/Targumim for plural) refers to Aramaic interpretative translations or paraphrases of the OT. When Aramaic replaced Hebrew among the Jews during the Second Temple period, public reading of the Scriptures was often accompanied by oral translation (or paraphrase) into Aramaic.[55] These oral Aramaic interpretive paraphrases were, in the course of time, fixed and preserved in literary form under the name Targum ("translation, interpretation"). The translation in the Targumim can be so loose that it is not infrequent to find the original meaning modified or significantly altered. Hence, it is commonly regarded as a type of implicit midrash, a term which will be discussed later.

A number of different Targumim survive but unfortunately they are mostly found in late manuscripts. The Cairo Genizah yielded seven manuscripts of the seventh to the ninth century AD. Although their significance for our study here is debated, the existence of Targumim in the early Christian era is not in doubt.[56] Targum fragments found among the corpus of the Dead Sea Scrolls point to their existence in pre-Christian times. In particular, two targumim which were found at Qumran (Leviticus and Job) have been dated by scholars to the second century BC. Furthermore, many Targumim of the Cairo Genizah collection are believed to contain early interpretative traditions.[57]

Even though the precise form(s) of targumic material that might have been available to the evangelists remains debated, more and more evidence points to the use of targumic traditions in the gospels. Scholars have long noted that most of the gospel quotations do not follow the Masoretic text. Often the quotations follow the Septuagint closely. However at other times the citations are of mixed type, falling somewhere between the Septuagint and the Masoretic text. Many scholars are now reassessing these quotations in light of the older Targumim and finding some close parallels. For example, the scriptural citation in Luke 6:36—"Be merciful, just as your Father is merciful"—reflects more closely Targum Yerushalmi I[58] on Lev. 22:28, "My people, children of Israel, since our Father is merciful in heaven, so should you be merciful on the earth," than either the Hebrew or Greek texts.[59]

### 4. Private or semi-Private Translation and Memory

To add to the above complication, it has been argued that the early Christians might have made their own collections or translations of important OT verses so as to facilitate teaching or debate. A florilegium (lit. "flower-culling") of

---

[55] The event recorded in Neh. 8:8 may mark its beginning.

[56] See the excellent introduction by M. McNamara, *Targum and Testament* (Grand Rapids: Eerdmans, 1972).

[57] Moyise, *The Old Testament*, pp. 16-17.

[58] Also known as *Targum Pseudo-Jonathan*.

[59] Hays, Green, "Use," p. 224.

OT verses with similar theme such as the fulfillment of prophecy in Jesus may have been made privately or copied within a community and passed down. The parallel materials found at Qumran[60] and the fact that NT quotations sometimes agree in wording against all known versions of the OT are evidence of the existence of such florilegia or testimonia.[61] It has also been used to explain why texts are often quoted out of context, at least this is how it looks on the surface.[62]

Given the rarity of individual possession of many of the scriptural scrolls,[63] let alone the physical difficulty of finding a particular passage in a long scroll, it is unlikely that any of our evangelists quoted texts in the modern sense of locating physically the actual passage and copying it. They must surely have used notes and florilegia of some kind such that it is probable that at least some of the gospel quotations were taken from these rather than directly from an ancient scroll. Furthermore, operating within a largely oral milieu, though literate, the evangelists must have known a good many scriptural texts through recited, confessed and heard tradition. Hence, a citation may differ from a known text form simply because of a lapse of memory. However, scholars have been able to show that such an explanation is often less probable than has been supposed in the past. More frequently, citations were altered deliberately either by *ad hoc* translation and interpretation or by the selection of a variant reading, or by the conflation of similar texts, so that the purpose of the author might be served. The variations, then, become an important clue to discover not only the author's interpretation of the individual OT passage but also his perspective on the Hebrew Scripture as a whole.[64] Lindars comments in this regard: "There was nothing morally reprehensible about such treatment of the text, because it was felt that the real meaning of the Scripture was being clarified by it."[65] It is a kind of implicit midrash, a common exegetical practice of that time to adapt the text more clearly to its present application.

In summary, when encountering an OT quotation in the gospels, we have to bear in mind that it could come from one or more of the following text forms: (1) a Hebrew text similar to the Masoretic Text of the tenth century AD; (2) a different type of Hebrew text; (3) a Greek text similar to that found

---

[60] For examples, 4Q174 and 4Q177.

[61] On the use of testimonia in the early Christian preaching see F. F. Bruce, *The Book of Acts* (Grand Rapids: Eerdmans, 1988), pp. 34-40.

[62] It must be noted, as Judith Lieu has, that the majority of the reader's, if not the author's, knowledge of Scripture would more likely be the result of oral recitation, confession and exposition. Hence, the importance of the context for the first reader or even the author is debated. The identification of context may be more obvious and important for the modern reader for whom literary work is the primary point of access than for the first reader. See Lieu, "Narrative Analysis," p. 148. Even so, it is not uncommon to find in New Testament where a single quote has been used as a pointer or reminder of the larger passage. See C. H. Dodd, *According to the Scriptures* (London: Nisbet, 1952), pp. 61-110.

[63] Even synagogues would be unlikely to possess a set of scrolls comprising the complete Scriptures.

[64] E. Earle Ellis, *Prophecy & Hermeneutic* (Tübingen: Mohr [Siebeck], 1978), pp. 147-48.

[65] Barnabas Lindars, *New Testament Apologetic* (London: SCM Press, 1961), p. 27.

in the major fourth and fifth century codices, such as Alexandrinus, Vaticanus and Sinaiticus; (4) a different or revised form of the Greek text; (5) an Aramaic translation/paraphrase of a Hebrew text; (6) a Christian collection, or translation, or interpretive rendering; (7) quotation from the evangelist's own memory.[66]

These variegated text forms have certainly added difficulty to our analysis of the gospels' usage of the OT. The gospels reveal that the early Christians were little disturbed by the existence of competing textual traditions; in fact, they made the most of them.[67] Therefore, there is no need to assume that the one NT writer will have always used the same OT textual tradition in his work(s). In the case of Matthew and Luke this is clearly not so. As Richard Hays and Joel Green have observed:

> They quote texts in various ways, which show eclectic freedom to select from among various available text forms the readings most suitable for the purpose at hand; in this way, they provide historical precursors for modern-day preachers and teachers who select from among various English translations of the Bible the rendering of a passage that most lends itself to their homiletical and pedagogical aims. One must also allow for the possibility that NT authors worked from memory in citing some texts. Moreover, as we shall see, NT writers shaped their quotations of OT texts—even amending the language of the OT—so as to work at the interpretive task already in the way the text is cited.[68]

This leads naturally to the issue of the interpretation of the OT.

## H. The Question of Interpretation

Probably the most difficult question encountered in the study of the gospels and the OT is the question of interpretation: How does the writer use and interpret a scriptural text? Which type of interpretative method is employed? Does it reflect the common practice of the evangelists' times? Does the interpretation respect the original context of the quotations? Is the interpretation legitimate?

Most NT citations are faithful to the original context. Yet, there are a few oddities. Passages such as Matt. 2:6 have often been quoted in support of the view that the evangelist has changed the meaning of the OT text in order to make his point. Here, Matthew quotes Mic. 5:2 and inserts the Greek word οὐδαμῶς ("by no means") thus changing the original expression that "Bethlehem *is* the least among the tribes of Judah" to that "Bethlehem *is by no means* the least." This type of usage is highly illegitimate to us who live in a world abounding with the means of precise referencing and a mindset preoccupied with copyright and intellectual property. However, one must

---

[66] List adapted from Moyise, *The Old Testament in the New*, p. 18.
[67] Cf. Stendahl, *School*, pp. 183-90.
[68] Hays and Green, "Use," pp. 225.

remember that the evangelists lived in a world different from ours. Literary texts were relatively rare and were often regarded as *living* traditions, regularly updated to be applied to new situations. The task of the interpreter, then, was not just to discern primarily what the text meant in the past but primarily what it meant for their age.[69] The Targumim and some sections of the Septuagint demonstrate that extensive paraphrasing and interpretation are legitimately called forth even in the act of translation. Such re-adaptation should not be a surprise when the writer was obviously involved in the reinterpretation of the past in view of the new.

Furthermore, postmodern intertextual studies have shown that there is never only one way of configuring meaning. The fact that a text always points to other texts and a reader always bring texts they know to every reading (in the case of biblical studies, quite often a whole history of interpretation)[70] reminds us of how the process of reading and interpreting is inherently unstable and the issue of context is broader than the original text itself. Hence, there is never just one way of interpreting a text and configuring the interaction between text and subtexts.[71]

This, however, does not mean that the evangelists are justified in making a text mean whatever they like or that there is no control over the meaning of a text. If we use Moyise's example to illustrate the usage of the OT in the gospels, it is obvious that:

> [E]very performance of a musical symphony is different. The conductor will never conduct in exactly the same way. Each of the violinists will differ depending on how they feel that day. The horns will differ. Sickness might mean that one or two players are making their debut. All of which means that there are literally thousands of interacting factors which determine the final performance. Nevertheless, there will be no doubt that one is hearing Beethoven's fifth symphony and not his sixth (for example).[72]

Every time the OT is used in a gospel, the emphasis, nuance of expression and point of reference may vary, but it is undoubtedly the OT that we are hearing. As can be observed in a series of musical performances, the differences in each performance are real and worthy of study. Yet, instead of entering into the cul-de-sac of a debate about the legitimacy of the "improvisation," one will gain more to be acquainted with the circumstances which created it.

Therefore, in order to appropriately appreciate the evangelists' approach to the OT, a student needs to be acquainted first with the various interpretive techniques of the first century. Jewish exegetical tradition is rooted in the

---

[69] Moyise, *The Old Testament*, p. 4

[70] For example, see Moyise, *Intertextuality*, p. 37: "protestant scholars have only recently acknowledged the fact that their reading of Paul owed a great deal to significant 'intertexts', such as the writings of Luther and Calvin."

[71] Moyise, *Intertextuality*, p. 37.

[72] Moyise, *Intertextuality*, p. 40.

reinterpretation, extension and explanation of the sacred tradition.[73] This is clearly seen in most of the exegetical methods to be discussed below. While some categorization is inevitable, we must bear in mind, as Richard Longenecker aptly remarks, that "the evidence relating to first-century Jewish and Christian exegetical procedures is both voluminous and partial, requiring on the one hand a mastery of subject matter such as no one person can accomplish fully, and on the other, a realization that further evidence (as the discovery of the Dead Sea texts illustrates) will undoubtedly be forthcoming."[74]

## I. Rabbinic Midrash[75]

"Midrash" is frequently used to explain the imaginative and creative usage of the OT in the gospels (e.g., Matt. 2:23, John 1:14-18).[76] This Hebrew term simply means "interpretation" and is used in pre-Christian Judaism to refer to the act of interpreting Scripture or the commentary produced on Scripture. As an interpretive activity the midrashic procedure is a contemporization of Scripture in order to apply or render it relevant for the current situation. It can be seen implicitly (1) as a process of rewriting that occurs within the Hebrew OT itself,[77] (2) in interpretive renderings of the Hebrew text in translations (e.g. the Greek Septuagint and the Aramaic Targumim), and (3) in interpretive emendations within OT quotations.[78] Explicitly, midrash occurs in a more

---

[73] See Geza Vermes, "Bible and Midrash: Early Old Testament Exegesis," in P. R. Ackroyd and C. F. Evans, eds., *The Cambridge History of the Bible, Vol. 1, From the Beginnings to Jerome* (New York: Cambridge University Press, 1970), pp. 199-231.

[74] Richard N. Longenecker, *Biblical Exegesis in the Apostolic Period* (Grand Rapids: Eerdmans, 1975), p. 14.

[75] Midrash is a loosely defined term. It can be used to refer to a specific group of rabbinic works or just the general act of "interpretation." The *Encyclopedia Judaica* vol. 1 (Jerusalem: Keter, 1971), p. vii, defines "midrash" as "a method of interpreting Scripture to elucidate legal points (Midrash Halakhah) or to bring out lessons by stories or homiletics (Midrash Aggadah). Also, the name for a collection of such rabbinic interpretations." This term is used here in a most general way, though in this particular section it carries also the specific meaning. However, in the later sections the general sense will be stressed. For a discussion on the definition of midrash, see Gary Porton, "Defining Midrash," in Jacob Neusner, ed., *The Study of Ancient Judaism*, vol. 1 (New York: Ktav, 1981), pp. 55-92.

[76] Matt. 2:23 is often being treated as midrash on texts such as Isa. 11:1 or 49:6. John 1:14-18 is viewed as a midrash on Exodus 34.

[77] As Earle Ellis has demonstrated, implicit midrash "involved the transposition of a biblical text to a different application. For example, the prophecy in Isa. 19:19-22 transposes the words and motif of Israel's redemption from Egypt (Exodus 1–12) to God's future redemption of Egypt." See his "Biblical Interpretation in the New Testament Church," in Martin Jan Mulder, ed., *Mikra,* p. 703.

[78] These may involve either elaborate alterations of the Old Testament text or the simple but significant change of one or two words, as observed in various Qumran writings and the New Testament. Ellis has listed some examples: "*Word-play* in Matt. 2:23 connects Jesus' residence in Nazareth to an OT messianic text such as Isa. 11:1 (*netser,* "branch") or Is. 49:6 (*nêtsire,* "preserved"?, "branch"?, "Nazorean"?). Luke 1–2 offers examples of the *transposition* of the OT texts. The prophecy of Gabriel (Luke 1:30-35) is given literary expression via allusion to 2 Samuel 7, Isaiah 7 and other passages," Ellis, "Biblical Interpretation," p. 704. Ellis includes

formal "text + exposition" patterns as seen in the later collection of rabbinic commentaries.[79]

When we study the Jewish midrashic collection, it is apparent that the form of exegesis varies greatly, ranging from that of a brief lexicography to such techniques as typology, allegory, catch-word links, reading the text in an unorthodox or surprising manner and that of a creative elaboration, usually via wordplay, where a biblical word or verse has been modeled into a fictional story.[80] For example, in trying to answer the question whether future punishment will be limited to the spirit or to the body, or to both, Rabbi Ishmael (c. AD 100)[81] tells this story:

> This may be compared to the case of a king who had an orchard containing excellent early figs, and he placed there two watchmen, one lame and the other blind. He said to them: "Be careful with these fine early figs." After some days the lame man said to the blind one: "I see fine early figs in the orchard." Said the blind man to him: "Come let us eat them." "Am I then able to walk?" said the lame man. "Can I then see?" retorted the blind man. The lame man got astride the blind man, and thus they ate the early figs and sat down again each in his place. After some days the king came into the vineyard, and said to them: "Where are the fine early figs?" The blind man replied: "My lord the king, can I then see?" The lame man replied: "My lord, the king, can I then walk?" What did the king, who was a man of insight, do with them? He placed the lame man astride the blind man, and they began to move about. Said the king to them: "Thus have you done, and eaten the early figs." Even so with the Holy One, blessed be He, in the time to come, say to the soul: "Why hast thou sinned before Me?" and the soul will answer: "O Master of the Universe, it is not I that sinned, but the body it is that sinned. Why, since leaving it, I am like a clean bird flying through the air. As for me, how have I sinned?" God will also say to the body: "Why hast thou sinned before Me?" and the body will reply: "O Master of the Universe, not I have sinned, the soul it is that has sinned. Why, since it left me, I am cast about like a stone thrown upon the ground. Have I then sinned before Thee?" What

---

more examples in the following paragraphs and in *Prophecy & Hermeneutic*, pp. 152-54.

[79] Ellis, "Biblical Interpretation," pp. 702-9. Though some scholars prefer to restrict the use of the term midrash to explicit interpretation, it is more helpful to note that midrashic procedure can be and has been applied implicitly. See also Earle Ellis, "Biblical Interpretation," pp. 691-709 for a detailed explanation of the "proem midrash," the "yelammendenu rabbenu midrash" and the seven exegetical middoth (rules) of Hillel which have been used rather commonly in the NT.

[80] J. D. G. Dunn has distinguished five categories of Jewish exegesis: targum, midrash, pesher, typology and allegory. See his *Unity and Diversity in the New Testament* (London: SCM Press, 1990), pp. 81-102. However, this categorization is rather arbitrary and misleading. Recent scholarship tends to view all the other four categories as types of midrash. Cf. Boyarin, *Intertextuality and the Reading of Midrash* (Indiana: Indiana University Press, 1990), pp. 1-92. Cf. Rivka Ulmer, "The Boundaries of the Rabbinic Genre Midrash," *Colloquium* 38 (2006), pp. 59-73.

[81] Rabbi Ishmael was the founder of one of the two prominent schools of halakhic midrash. He is famous for the extension of the seven hermeneutic rules of Hillel to a set of thirteen and laid the foundation for the halakhic midrash on the Pentateuch.

will the Holy One, blessed be He, do to them? He will bring the soul and force it into the body, and judge both as one, as it is said, *He will call to the heaven above*, etc. (Ps. 50:4). *"He will call to the heavens above,"* to bring the soul, *And to the earth* to bring the body, *For judgment before Him.*[82]

It is hard not to recall some of Jesus' parables when reading the above midrash.[83] Though dated later than Jesus, it is hardly borrowed from the Christians. Rather, it demonstrates that Jesus and his followers' interpretation of Scripture was shared with the larger community of religious Judaism. Since Jewish midrashic material takes various forms, one example may not suffice. Another example of midrash is worth quoting here:

When Moses said to the people, "After the Lord your God shall ye walk" (Deut. 13), they took alarm at the formidable, or rather impossible, task imposed upon them. "How," said they, "is it possible for man to walk after God, who hath his way in the storm and in the whirlwind, and the clouds are the dust of his feet" (Nah. 1), "whose way is in the sea and his path in the great waters" (Ps. 77). Moses explained to them that to walk after God meant to imitate humbly his attributes of mercy and compassion by clothing the naked, visiting the sick, and comforting the mourner.[84]

The above sample reflects a rather common feature in Jewish midrash where a cluster of scriptural texts are linked to explain a particular theme and the words of one are often put or find their application in the mouth of another.

Daniel Boyarin has pointed out that the purpose of midrash, was not to expose the true meaning of a text once and for all and thereby end all discussion. Rather, the intent is the "laying bare of an intertextual connection between two signifiers which mutually 'read' each other. It is not, nor can it be, decided which signifier is the interpreter and which the interpreted."[85] In this way, rabbinic midrash reveals an assumption about the biblical text:

The biblical narrative is gapped and dialogical. . . the role of the midrash is to

---

[82] *Leviticus Rabbah*, iv.5. Translated by H. Freedman and M. Simon, *Midrash Rabbah* (London: Soncino, 1961), pp. 53-54.

[83] Note Earle Ellis' statement in *Prophecy and Hermeneutic*, p. 162: "Rabbinic parables often are found in midrashim as commentary on the Old Testament texts. Christ's parables also occur within an exegetical context, e.g. in Matt. 21:33-44, Luke 10:25-37 and elsewhere, when they appear independently or in thematic clusters, they sometimes allude to Old Testament passages (e.g. Mark 4:1-22 [on Jer. 4:3]; Luke 15:3-6 [on Ezek. 34:11]). Probably such independent and clustered parables originated within an expository context from which they were later detached. If so, their present context represents a stage in the formation of the Gospel traditions secondary to their use within an explicit commentary format."

[84] Gen. 35:9 in W. Wynn Westcott et. al., *Midrash Tanhuma* (London: Parke, Austin and Lipscomb, 1917), p. 19. This is also available on the internet at:
http://sacred-texts.com/jud/mh1/mh104.htm (accessed 1 May 2008).

[85] Daniel Boyarin, "The Song of Songs: Lock or Key? Intertextuality, Allegory and Midrash," in Regina M. Schwartz, ed., *The Book and the Text: the Bible and Literary Theory* (Cambridge: Blackwell, 1990), p. 223.

fill in the gaps. . . This story of midrash quite reverses the narrative of hermeneutic that is presupposed by the historical school. . . . [Its] assumption is that the text is clear and transparent at the moment of its original creation, because it speaks to a particular historical situation, and it becomes unclear, owing to the passing of time and that situation. In contrast to this, our conception of midrash is one in which the text makes its meaning in history. We find this insight adumbrated in a crucially important text in the midrash on Genesis, *Bereshit Rabbah*:

*Rabbi Yehuda the son of Simon opened: "And He revealed deep and hidden things" (Dan. 2:22). In the beginning of the creation of the World, "He revealed deep things, etc." For it says, "In the beginning God created the heavens," and He did not interpret. Where did He interpret it? Later on, "He spreads out the heaven like gossamer" (Isa. 40:22). "And the earth," and He did not interpret. Where did He interpret it? Later on, "To the snow He said, be earth" (Job 37:6). "And God said, let there be light," and He did not interpret. Where did He interpret it? Later on, "He wraps Himself in light like a cloak." (Ps. 104:2).*[86]

This understanding of the Scripture carries with it an <u>assumption</u> of the <u>progressive nature of God's revelation in history and in the scriptural deposit.</u> What was spoken earlier would need to be clarified by what will be proclaimed later. This assumption concerning the nature of Scripture explains not only rabbinic midrash but also the Qumran and Christian midrashim, both of which will be discussed below. Such an understanding also helps to explain many of the peculiar quotations of the OT found in the gospels. The better we are acquainted with the rabbinic midrashim the easier it is for us to appreciate the colorful and creative usage of the OT found in the gospels. Instead of questioning the validity of usage, we will achieve more if we ask whether the particular usage gives us a glimpse into the understanding of Scripture in the first century.

For example, Morna Hooker states that "Mark includes only one explicit editorial quotation, in 1:2f., and gives that a wrong attribution."[87] Mark introduces the citation as "it is written in Isaiah the prophet," yet the quotation that follows is a conflation of Exod. 23:20; Mal. 3:1 and Isa. 40:3. The "wrong" attribution may not be an error if we take into consideration the midrashic phenomenon observed above where a cluster of Hebrew Scriptures was linked. Often the words of one scriptural author were put in the mouth of another for the purpose of clarification and application. In fact, in the rabbinic midrash, Exod. 23:20 and Mal. 3:1 had already been combined.[88]

Furthermore, instead of focusing on the "accuracy" of the citation, and asking the question of "legitimacy" of the interpretation, which answer is

---

[86] Boyarin, *Intertextuality*, p. 17.

[87] Hooker, "Mark," p. 220.

[88] Cf. *Exodus Rabbah* 23:20. The identical phrase, "Behold I send my messenger," provides the link between Exod 23:20 and Mal. 3:1. See William Lane, *The Gospel of Mark* (Grand Rapids: Eerdmans, 1974), pp. 45-46.

already predetermined by our modern historio-grammatical presuppositions, it might be more helpful to be asking other substantive questions about the perspective and presuppositions with which the interpreter approaches the text. What makes these imaginative connections possible? What effects are produced in the writer's usage and interpretation? For example, the oddity of the citation in Mark 1:2-3 is illuminated by what is seen as a characteristic throughout Mark of organizing narratives in "sandwich" form, a style noted by F. Neirynck and others.[89] A sandwiching style may be observed here where the prophet Isaiah was mentioned first, then the midrashic conflation of Exodus and Malachi, then the passage from Isaiah. In this way various Hebrew scriptural texts were made to reinforce one another at a strategic point of the Gospel while the fulfillment of Isaiah prophecy was being stressed. It demonstrates Mark's literary consistency and provides a possible explanation for the imaginative connection. Of course, such a design does not rule out altogether the possibility of the three texts being combined in pre-existing midrashim or testimonia.

It is debatable whether the extant rabbinic midrashim can be viewed as the direct source of the citations in the gospels. Nevertheless they represent the kind of matrix within which the evangelists had been operating and the template from which the OT usage appears to be derived. Rather than discrediting the evangelists or their sources, those creative and peculiar usages of the OT found in the gospels show, as Ellis observes, that "the prophets and teachers in the early church were not content merely to cite proof texts but were concerned to establish by exegetical procedures the Christian understanding of the OT."[90] Though odd to our modern historical-critical sensibilities, their method and approach represent a serious and consistent effort to expound the texts.

## J. "Pesher" Midrash[91]

While the gospels provide numerous examples of Jesus' and the evangelists' use of the rabbinic type of midrash, their most characteristic employment of Scripture is portrayed as being a pesher type of midrash. It receives its name from the Hebrew word used in the introductory formula, "the interpretation

---

[89] The sandwiched episodes which Neirynck listed have been called the six classical examples: 3:20-21 (22-30) 31-35; 5:21-24 (25-43); 6:7-13 (14-29) 30-31; 11:12-14 (15-19) 20-25; 14:1-2 (3-9) 10-11; 14:53 (54), 55-65 (66-72). F. Neirynck, *Duality in Mark: Contributions to the Study of Markan Redaction* (Leuven: Leuven University Press, 1972). Cf. James Edwards, "Markan Sandwiches: The Significance of Interpolations in Markan Narratives," *Novum Testamentum* 31 (1989), pp. 193-216; Tom Shepherd, "The Narrative Function of Markan Intercalation," *New Testament Studies* 41 (1995), pp. 522-40; David Rhoads, Joanna Dewey, and Donald Michie, *Mark as Story* (Minneapolis: Fortress Press, 1999), pp. 51-55.

[90] Ellis, *Prophecy and Hermeneutic*, p. 162.

[91] "Pesher" and "Midrash" are sometimes used in contrast to one another. Scholars are divided as to whether the pesher can be viewed as a distinct genre. However, it has been proposed that since pesher is strictly a type of midrash, and midrash is a very general term, it is better not to make such a distinction unless it is necessary.

(*pesher*) is" (and sometimes occurs as the equivalent of "this is").

Since the discovery of the Dead Sea Scrolls in 1947 this specific type of exposition has been subjected to extensive research and has subsequently revolutionized the study of the use of the OT in the New. Research has been carried out to compare scriptural interpretation in the Qumran scrolls and in the NT. Since then, "pesher" midrash has been defined in several ways. By some it is understood to refer only to the peculiarities of Qumran hermeneutics and theology, and is thus, by definition, not to be found in the NT. However, as Jacob Neusner has stated, it is more appropriate to define pesher in a general way as prophetic midrash which is characterized by fulfillment hermeneutics.[92] It reflects a state in which a charismatic exegete gives the OT text an interpretive shaping so that contemporary events may be more clearly presented as the "eschatological" fulfillment of the OT Scriptures. Unlike the rabbis, the Qumran sectaries responsible for the pesharim and the NT writers have a similar eschatological perspective in which the end of the age is impending and their own time is "the end time" to which the biblical prophecies referred.[93] It is clear that both communities employed pesher exegesis to claim the fulfillment of Scripture in the events in which they were participating. The "this is that" fulfillment motif, which is distinctive to pesher exegesis, repeatedly comes to the fore in the words of Jesus and the evangelists as we have discussed above.

## K. Christological Midrash[94]—Inherited from Jesus

To acknowledge the evangelists' debt to Jewish exegesis does not mean we should see it as an adequate explanation for the use of the OT in the New. The exegetical techniques in the gospels may be similar to those found in contemporary Judaism(s), but the underlying hermeneutical axioms are distinctively different.

Many scholars agree that both the relevant Qumran scrolls and the NT adopt the same appropriation techniques, but with different presuppositions. The NT authors viewed the Scriptures through the lens of the Christ-event and the establishment of the church. The Qumran authors viewed them through the lens of the Teacher of Righteousness and the establishment of their own community.[95] Furthermore, as Carson insightfully argued:

[The differences between contemporary Judaism and Christian usage of the OT] relate not only to christology and the way the Old Testament is read as a

---

[92] J. Neusner, *What is Midrash?* (Philadelphia: Fortress Press, 1987), pp. 7-8, 31-40.

[93] Ellis, *The Old Testament*, pp. 68-70.

[94] This term, including the three categories of interpretative technique, is selected based on the observation of Geza Vermes that the Pharisees, the Qumran sectaries and the Judeo-Christians represent "the three cognate schools of exegesis" which existed side by side, and which must be understood in the light of one another. See G. Vermes, "The Qumran Interpretation of Scripture in its Historical Setting," *The Annual of Leeds University Oriental Society* 6 (1966–68), p. 95.

[95] Moyise, *The Old Testament*, pp. 131-32.

prefiguration of Jesus Christ, but even to the eschatological stance of the evangelist. . . Thus, Black. . . writes: "Like the primitive church, the Qumrân Essenes believed they were living in the End-Time, so that many pesharim or pesherised texts are apocalyptic and eschatological." But the understanding of "End-Time" in the two corpora is quite different. . . [T]he Qumran sectarians believed they were in the end times such that they emphasized the coming fulfillment of the OT scriptures. The New Testament writers. . . hold they are in the end times such that they emphasize the fulfillment of the OT scriptures that has already taken place-even if their perception of the tension between the "already" and the "not yet" also leaves them anticipating the future.[96]

Moreover, Earle Ellis has pointed to the difference between narrative midrash found in the gospels and some rabbinic midrash which elaborate on a verse or word of Scripture. In general, while the OT text is primary for the rabbinic midrash, the NT midrash gives primacy to the events of Jesus and only uses the texts to explain or illuminate.

> While they may describe the events in biblical language and may on occasion allude to a prior fictional midrash. . . they never seem to reverse their priorities so as to make the OT text the locus for creating stories about Jesus. This holds true also for the Infancy Narratives where. . . the wide-ranging mélange of citations and allusions could only have coalesced around preexisting traditions and, in any case, could not have produced the stories in the gospels. For example, only because Matthew (2:6; 23; 4:15) had a tradition that Jesus was born in Bethlehem and raised in Galilee does he use Mic. 5:2 of Jesus' birth and Jer. 23:5; Isa. 11:1; 9:2f (8:23f) of his youth and ministry and not vice versa. The texts themselves could be applied to either eventuality.[97]

Here, we see a shift in the focus of primary revelation from the text to the person. Jesus Christ functions as the central organizing principle for the interpretation of the OT. Here lies the uniqueness of the NT's appropriation of the OT. Thus, it is not inappropriate to call most of the NT's use of the OT "christological midrash."[98]

Owing to such intertextuality, the gospels display both continuity and discontinuity with the OT. The OT and its interpretative traditions provide the matrix out of which the kerygma sprang. Yet, the message the evangelists present does not simply interpret the OT, or simply utilize its language to explain Jesus and his gospel, but also becomes the vehicle by which Jesus and his gospel effectively replace and redefine the OT. Carson aptly observes,

---

[96] Carson, "John and the Johannine Epistles," p. 257. The reference cited in Carson is M. Black, "The Theological Appropriation of the Old Testament by the New Testament," *Scottish Journal of Theology* 39 (1986), pp. 1-17.

[97] Ellis, "Biblical Interpretation," pp. 704-5.

[98] Apart from this christological focus, the NT usage of Scripture appears to be influenced by other Christian perspectives also. Earle Ellis lists four: "a particular understanding of history, of man, of Israel and of Scripture." See Ellis, *Prophecy and Hermeneutic*, pp. 163-97.

"This does not mean, for the Evangelist, that they are discarded so much as fulfilled: they find their true significance and real continuity in him who is the true vine, the true light, the true temple, the one of whom Moses wrote."[99] This continuity and discontinuity must be held in tension. To emphasize one against another is not being true to the gospel, as Jesus has proclaimed: "Therefore every scribe who has been trained for the kingdom of heaven is like the master of a household who brings out of his treasure what is new and what is old" (Matt. 13:52).

Thus, it has often been observed that a knowledge of the OT is essential for an understanding of the NT. However, in knowing the OT one must be prepared to see it in a new light. Perhaps, Greg Beale's analogy is helpful here:

> [W]e can compare an author's original, unchanging meaning to an apple in its original context of an apple tree. When someone removes the apple and puts it into another setting (say, in a basket of various fruits in a dining room for decorative purposes), the apple does not lose its original identity as an apple, the fruit of a particular kind of tree, but the apple must now be understood not in and of itself but in relation to the new context in which it has been placed. . . The new context does not annihilate the original identity of the apple, but now the apple must be understood in its relation to its new setting.[100]

The point of the analogy is that the apple, though different now, will never become a pear even though it may be mixed with pieces of pear in a bowl of fruit salad. Therefore when trying to study the OT in the New, the original context (both literary and exegetical) is important but the new context is essential.

## L. Conclusion

Much remains to be discussed. Yet, our brief survey has been able to show that the gospel was being repeatedly defined by the four evangelists utilizing various terms and concepts found in the OT. Though their expression varies, the key message is consistent: the gospel is primarily about Jesus, how he lived, died and rose again *according to the Scriptures*. In other words, "Christianity did not spring out of a vacuum but is in direct continuity with the religion enshrined in what Christians now call the OT."[101] In short, the diversity of the earliest Christian use of the OT reflects the diversity within Judaism of that time. Yet, their use of the OT is at the same time the unifying point within first-century Christianity. As Dunn aptly observes: "the OT provided a bond of unity within first-century Christianity—but not the OT as

---

[99] Carson, "John and the Johannine Epistles," pp. 255-56.

[100] G. K. Beale, *John's Use of the Old Testament in Revelation* (Sheffield: Sheffield Academic Press, 1998), pp. 51-52. Note the response of Steve Moyise, "The Old Testament in the New: A Reply to Greg Beale," *Irish Biblical Studies* 21 (1999), pp. 54-58.

[101] Moyise, *The Old Testament*, p. 1.

such, not the OT in itself, rather the OT *interpreted . . . in the light of the revelation of Jesus.*"[102]

## Bibliography

Beale, G. K. *John's Use of the Old Testament in Revelation*. Sheffield: Sheffield Academic Press, 1998.

Beale, C. K., and D. A. Carson, eds. *Commentary on the New Testament Use of the Old Testament*. Grand Rapids: Baker Academic, 2007.

Boyarin, Daniel. *Intertextuality and the Reading of Midrash*. Bloomington: Indiana University Press, 1990.

Buren, Paul M. *According to the Scriptures: The Origins of the Gospel and of the Church's Old Testament*. Grand Rapids: Eerdmans, 1998.

Carson, D. A., and H. G. M. Williamson, eds. *It is Written: Scripture Citing Scripture*. New York: Cambridge University Press, 1988.

Chilton, Bruce D. *A Galilean Rabbi and His Bible: Jesus' Use of the Interpreted Scripture of His Time*. Wilmington: Michael Glazier, 1984.

Dodd, Charles Harold. *According to the Scriptures*. London: Nisbet, 1952.

Draisma, Sipke, ed. *Intertextuality in Biblical Writing: Essays in Honour of Bas Van Iersel*. Kampen: Kok, 1989.

Evans, Craig A., and James A. Sanders, eds. *The Early Christian Interpretation of the Scriptures of Israel: Investigations and Proposals*. Sheffield: Sheffield Academic Press, 1997.

Evans, Craig A., and W. Richard Stegner. *The Gospels and the Scriptures of Israel*. Sheffield: Sheffield Academic Press, 1994.

Hanson, Anthony T. *The New Testament Interpretation of Scripture*. London: SPCK, 1980.

Holmgren, Fredrick C. *The Old Testament and the Significance of Jesus*. Grand Rapids: Eerdmans, 1999.

Longenecker, Richard N. *Biblical Exegesis in the Apostolic Period*. Grand Rapids: Eerdmans, 1999.

Knowles, Michael. *Jeremiah in Matthew's Gospel: The Rejected Prophet Motif in Matthean Redaction*. Sheffield: JSOT Press, 1993.

Moyise. Steve, ed. *The Old Testament in the New Testament: Essays in Honor of J. L. North*. Sheffield: Sheffield Academic Press, 2000.

————. *The Old Testament in the New: An Introduction*. New York/London: Continuum, 2001.

Mulder, Martin Jan, ed. *Mikra: Text, Translation, Reading and Interpretation of the Hebrew Bible in Ancient Judaism and Early Christianity*. Peabody: Hendrickson, 2004.

Porter, Stanley E, ed. *Hearing the Old Testament in the New Testament*. Grand Rapids: Eerdmans, 2006.

Swartley, Willard M. *Israel's Scripture Traditions and the Synoptic Gospels*. Peabody: Hendrickson, 1994.

---

[102] Dunn, *Unity and Diversity*, p. 101 (his italics).

# 8. The Gospels in Early Christian Literature

*Murray J. Smith*

This chapter examines the important—but complicated—role played by gospel traditions in early Christian literature down to the beginning of the third century. Section A offers a survey of the historical processes by which gospel traditions were transmitted in the early church, and thereby delineates the *forms* in which "the gospel" was known to early Christian writers. Section B then explores some of the ways in which early Christian authors *used* the gospel materials available to them, and offers a case study in the Apostolic Fathers.[1]

## A. The One, the Four and the Many: Forms of Gospel Tradition in Early Christianity

The Greek word εὐαγγέλιον (gospel) is used in a variety of ways in the early Christian literature. It can mean:

1. The original message of "good news" preached by, or about, Jesus;
2. Oral traditions which preserve the words and/or deeds of Jesus; or
3. Written texts of various kinds, including the four canonical gospels, which narrate the story of Jesus or preserve sayings attributed to him.

These different shades of meaning reflect the various forms in which early Christian writers knew "the gospel," and highlight the complexity of the processes by which gospel traditions were transmitted in early Christianity. In what follows we trace, first, the way in which the very earliest Christian

---

[1] A full history of the reception of each of the four canonical gospels in the early Christian literature is the beyond the scope of this short chapter. For that the reader is referred to more detailed studies. On Matthew: E. Massaux, *The Influence of the Gospel of Saint Matthew on Christian Literature before Saint Irenaeus Vol. 1: The First Ecclesiastical Writers* (Leuven: Peeters, 1990); M. Simonetti, *Matthew* (Downers Grove: InterVarsity Press, 2001–2002). On Mark: C. C. Black, *Mark: Images of an Apostolic Interpreter* (Edinburgh: T. &T. Clark, 1994); T. C. Oden, C. A. Hall, *Mark* (Downers Grove: InterVarsity Press, 1998). On Luke: A. Gregory, *The Reception of Luke and Acts in the Period Before Irenaeus* (Tübingen: Mohr Siebeck, 2003); A. A. Just, *Luke* (Downers Grove: InterVarsity Press, 2003). On John: T. Nagel, *Die Rezeption des Johannesevangeliums im 2. Jahrhundert* (Leipzig: Evangelische Verlagsanstalt, 2000); C. E. Hill, *The Johannine Corpus in the Early Church* (New York: Oxford University Press, 2004).

gospel—the apostolic proclamation that Jesus Christ is Lord—was augmented by a plurality of written gospel texts (sections A.1 and A.2). Next (in section A.3), we demonstrate how, despite the multiplication of written gospel sources during the second century, the four most ancient written gospels had emerged by the end of the century as the definitive fourfold gospel we know from the New Testament (NT).

## 1. The One: The Gospel of Apostolic Proclamation

To begin with, it is important to note that in earliest Christianity, there was only *one* gospel (εὐαγγέλιον): the grand announcement made by Jesus that the kingdom of God had arrived;[2] the good news preached by the apostles that God had established his rule by exalting his Son, Jesus the Christ, as Lord.[3] Though this gospel was proclaimed in different ways by a variety of preachers to a range of audiences, the earliest Christians recognized that together they preached only one gospel—that of the crucified and risen Lord Jesus.[4]

This earliest Christian use of the term εὐαγγέλιον drew heavily on both the classical and biblical traditions, but was also remarkably distinctive.[5] In classical Greek usage, εὐαγγέλιον originally denoted "that which is proper to the εὐαγγέλος," that is, to the messenger bringing news of victory from the battlefield. The term thus connoted both the reward received by the messenger, and the victory message itself. Later, εὐαγγέλιον came to be used of a range of other "news" announcements, and in the imperial propaganda of the early Roman Empire, the plural εὐαγγέλια was used to refer to the series of "good news" announcements which followed from the fact that that the divine Augustus had established his rule, bringing salvation and peace to the known world.[6] Similarly, in the biblical tradition, the Hebrew verb *basar* (to

---

[2] E.g. Matt. 4:23; 9:35; 24:14; Mark. 1:14-15; Luke 4:43; 8:1; 16:16.

[3] E.g. Acts 8:12; 10:36; 13:32-33; 17:18; Rom. 1:1-4; 1 Cor. 15:1-8; 2 Cor. 4:1-6; 2 Tim. 2:8.

[4] On the impossibility of there being "another gospel," i.e. a gospel other than the one originally proclaimed, see Gal. 1.6-9; cf. 1 Cor. 15.1-3, 11; 2 Cor. 11.4. For recent and illuminating discussions of the lines of continuity and discontinuity between the gospel preached *by* Jesus, and that preached *about* him, see G. Stanton, *Jesus and Gospel* (New York: Cambridge University Press, 2004), pp. 9-62; and N. T. Wright, *Paul: In Fresh Perspective* (Minneapolis: Fortress Press, 2005), pp. 154-61.

[5] On the origins and use of the of the term εὐαγγέλιον in antiquity see G. Friedrich, "εὐαγγελίζομαι, εὐαγγέλιον, εὐαγγελιστής, προευαγγελίζομαι," in G. Kittel, ed., *TDNT* vol. II (Grand Rapids: Eerdmans, 1964), pp. 707-37; cf. D. Dormeyer and H. Frankemölle, "Evangelium als literarischer Gattung und als theologischer Begriff," *ANRW* 2.25.2 (1984), pp. 1543-1704.

[6] For example, the inscription from Priene (9 BC), in the Roman province of Asia, claims that "the birthday of the god (Augustus) was the beginning for the world of the glad tidings (εὐαγγέλια) that have come to men through him." For the full text, see *OGIS* 2.458. For further examples, see A. Deissmann, *Light from the Ancient East* (Grand Rapids: Baker, 1978), pp. 366-67; V. Ehrenberg and A. H. M. Jones, *Documents Illustrating the Reigns of Augustus and Tiberius* (Oxford: Clarendon, 1976), nos. 14, 38, 41, 98, 99. A more detailed study of the use of εὐαγγέλιον and its cognates in the immediate historical context of earliest Christianity is offered by W. Horbury, "'Gospel' in Herodian Judaea," in M. Bockmuehl, D. A. Hagner, eds., *The*

announce) was, in the Greek Septuagint, regularly translated by εὐαγγελίζομαι (or sometimes εὐαγγελίζω),[7] and at several points this verb refers to the announcement of God's victory over his enemies, or to the proclamation of the coming kingdom of YHWH.[8] Thus, in both the classical and biblical traditions, a εὐαγγέλιον was an announcement of "news," a proclamation of an important message.[9]

In this context it is easy to see why the earliest Christians employed a term so filled with theological and political significance to express what they believed God had achieved in Christ.[10] It is striking, however, that although the εὐαγγελ- root appears more than one hundred times in the NT, the plural εὐαγγέλια is entirely absent: in the earliest Christian understanding there was—and indeed could only ever be—one gospel that really mattered, the gospel of what God had achieved by his Son.[11]

Moreover, it is significant that this most ancient Christian gospel was neither Mark, nor "Q," nor *Thomas*, nor, indeed, any written text. This most ancient Christian gospel was an *oral* proclamation, an *announcement* of good news. Thus, in the NT, the noun εὐαγγέλιον is consistently coupled with verbs such as κηρύσσω (proclaim),[12] καταγγέλλω (announce),[13] ἀναγγέλλω (report),[14] διαμαρτύρομαι (testify),[15] λαλέω (speak),[16] and ἀκούω (hear),[17] so that in each case it is clear that verbal proclamation is on view. And similarly, the verb εὐαγγελίζω (to bring/proclaim good news), which customarily denotes oral annunciation,[18] appears fifty-two times in the NT in connection with the Christian message.[19] In the very earliest period, then, there was only one Christian εὐαγγέλιον; and it was not a written text but an announcement of good news, a spoken message which was "proclaimed" and "heard" rather than written and read.

---

*Written Gospel* (New York: Cambridge University Press, 2005), pp. 7-30.

[7] E.g. 1 Kgs. 1:42; Jer. 20:15; cf. 2 Sam. 4:10; 2 Kgs. 7:9; 2 Sam. 18:19-33.

[8] Ps. 40:9; 68:11; 96:2; Isa. 40:9; 27; 52:7 (cf. Nah. 2:1 = Eng. 1:15); 61:1.

[9] cf. J. P. Dickson, "Gospel as News: εὐαγγελ- from Aristophanes to the Apostle Paul," *New Testament Studies* 51 (2005), pp. 212-30.

[10] On the earliest Christian use of εὐαγγέλιον, see especially Stanton, *Jesus and Gospel*, pp. 9-62.

[11] For this language, see Rom. 1:1; 15:16; 1 Thess. 2:2, 8, 9; 1 Pet. 4:17.

[12] Matt. 4:23, 9:35, 24:14, 26:13; Mark 1:14, 13:10, 14:9, 16:15; 2 Cor. 11:4; Gal. 2:2; 1 Thess. 2:9; cf. the noun κήρυγμα (preaching/proclamation) at Rom. 16:25.

[13] 1 Cor. 9:14.

[14] 1 Pet. 1:12.

[15] Acts 20:24.

[16] 1 Thess. 2:2, 4.

[17] Acts 15:7; Eph. 1:13 (cf. Col. 1:5); Col. 1:23.

[18] *BDAG*, p. 401.

[19] See Matt. 11:5; Luke 1:19; 2:10; 3:18; 4:18, 43; 7:22; 8:1; 9:6; 16:16; 20:1; Acts 5:42; 8:4, 12, 25, 35, 40; 10:36; 11:20; 13:32; 14:7, 15, 21; 15:35; 16:10; 17:18; Rom. 1:15; 10:15; 15:20; 1 Cor. 1:17; 9:16; 9:18; 1 Cor. 15:1; 2 Cor. 10:16; 11:7; Gal. 1:8-9, 11, 16, 23; 4:13; Eph. 2:17; 3:8; Heb. 4:2, 6; 1 Pet. 1:12, 25; 4:6; Rev. 14:6.

## 2. The Many: A Plurality of Written Gospels

Remarkably quickly, however, the oral proclamation of the one gospel came to be supplemented by a plurality of written "Jesus narratives," which in turn developed into what we know as the four canonical gospels. Luke, for example, writing his Gospel probably somewhere between AD 60 and 85, could already refer to the plurality of written gospel sources available to him:

> Since many (πολλοί) have undertaken to set down an orderly account (ἀνατάξασθαι διήγησιν) of the events that have been fulfilled among us, just as they were handed on (παρέδοσαν) to us by those who from the beginning were eyewitnesses and servants (αὐτόπται καὶ ὑπηρέται) of the word, I too decided, after investigating everything carefully from the very first, to write an orderly account for you, most excellent Theophilus, so that you may know the truth concerning the things about which you have been instructed.[20]

Luke's introduction hints at two distinct but complementary processes by which memories of Jesus were preserved in the earliest period: it seems that he had access not only to "many" written accounts but also to the oral testimony of surviving eyewitnesses.[21] It is beyond the scope of this chapter to examine the complex inter-relationship between the oral proclamation of the gospel and the crafting of written accounts to augment its propagation. It is enough to note here that the evolution of written gospels probably proceeded in four overlapping phases:[22]

1. Initial Oral Phase (AD 33–90)—eyewitness testimony about Jesus was preserved in oral form amongst the earliest Christian communities, probably under the names of specified individuals who guaranteed its authenticity.[23]
2. Written Gospel Sources (AD 40–70)—oral eyewitness testimony about Jesus was committed to writing in works that became the first Christian gospel sources. This quite probably occurred under the supervision of the apostles themselves, the gospel sources being designed for use in the four apostolic missions of James, John, Paul, and Peter (see further section A.3.d below). Probably the Gospel of Mark (at least in its earliest form), and perhaps the hypothetical sources "Q," "proto-Matthew" and "proto-Luke" belong to this phase.
3. Canonical Gospels (AD 60–100)—the evangelists (at least Matthew,

---

[20] Luke 1:1-4.

[21] For discussion of this point, see R. Bauckham, *Jesus and the Eyewitnesses: the Gospels as Eyewitness Testimony* (Grand Rapids: Eerdmans, 2006), pp. 21-38, 116-24.

[22] The scheme presented here reflects a broad scholarly consensus about the origins and evolution of the written gospels, which has been widely accepted since the nineteenth century. For more detailed discussion, see D. A. Carson and D. J. Moo, *An Introduction to the New Testament* (Grand Rapids: Zondervan, 2005), pp. 77-133.

[23] See Bauckham, *Jesus and the Eyewitnesses*, who argues persuasively that the four canonical gospels "embody the testimony of the eyewitnesses" of Jesus' life (p. 6).

Luke and John) used these earlier written sources (as well as oral sources) to construct their own gospels in narrative-biographical form[24]—the gospels we know from the NT.[25]

4. "Apocryphal" Gospels (after AD 100)—various other authors later used the range of written and oral sources available to them to compose additional gospels, which vary significantly in style and content (see further A.3.a).[26]

For our purposes, the key point to note is that this augmentation of the oral gospel, first by written gospel sources of various kinds ("Q"?, "proto-Luke"? and "proto-Matthew"?), and then by the canonical and apocryphal gospels, constituted a two-fold development in the early Christian understanding of the gospel. On the one hand, εὐαγγέλιον came to refer not only to oral proclamation but also to certain written texts; on the other hand, it came to be used not only in connection with the singular apostolic gospel but also as a title for a plurality of gospel sources.

### (a) From Oral to Written

First, then, in early Christian usage the term εὐαγγέλιον came, relatively quickly, to refer not only to oral proclamation, but also to certain written texts used to augment the activity of "gospelling." This new usage of εὐαγγέλιον probably took its lead from Mark 1.1, which refers to "the beginning of the gospel of Jesus Christ" (Ἀρχὴ τοῦ εὐαγγελίου Ἰησοῦ Χριστοῦ). Although in Mark the phrase functions as a kind of heading for the prologue (or even for the Gospel as a whole), εὐαγγέλιον still most probably refers to the "content rather than the (literary) form of the book."[27] Nevertheless, Mark's use of εὐαγγέλιον in this context seems to have provided the model and impetus for the identification of other written works as "gospels." Indeed, as Martin

---

[24] Despite the tendency of older scholarship to classify the canonical gospels as a *sui generis*, a new and unique kind of literature, more recent studies have demonstrated that the gospels are best understood as a sub-genre of ancient Hellenistic biography (βίος). See especially, R. A. Burridge, *What are the Gospels? A Comparison with Graeco-Roman Biography* (Grand Rapids: Eerdmans, 2004).

[25] The dates of composition of the four canonical gospels are debated. The range assigned here reflects that accepted by most scholars. It is quite possible however, that the four canonical gospels should all be dated to the beginning of this period (i.e. before AD 70). For the arguments, see especially J. A. T. Robinson, *Redating the New Testament* (London: SCM Press, 1976), pp. 86-117, 254-312; cf. the early dates assigned to the Synoptic Gospels by J. W. Wenham, *Redating Matthew, Mark and Luke: A Fresh Assault on the Synoptic Problem* (London: Hodder & Stoughton, 1991), p. 238-44, (Matthew c. AD 42; Mark c. AD 45; Luke c. AD 50–55).

[26] Some argue that certain apocryphal gospels (the *Gospel of Thomas*, and the *Gospel of Peter*), or sources underlying apocryphal gospels (the so-called "Cross Gospel"), predate the canonical gospels. See e.g. J. D. Crossan, *Four Other Gospels: Shadows on the Contours of Canon* (San Francisco: Harper & Row, 1985), pp. 132-33, 90-121. These arguments are, however, not widely accepted. See, for example, the critique in H. Koester, *Ancient Christian Gospels: Their History and Development* (Philadelphia: Trinity, 1990), pp. 218-20.

[27] See R. T. France, *The Gospel of Mark* (Grand Rapids: Eerdmans, 2002), pp. 52-53.

Hengel has argued, some form of "title" for the gospels would have been necessary as soon as two or more separate gospel manuscripts were collected together, in order to distinguish them from each other.[28] Since we have good evidence of collections of at least two gospels from the latter part of the first century (see section A.3.c below), it is quite likely that these works were being identified by the title "Gospel according to . . ." (εὐαγγέλιον κατά. . .) as early as that.[29]

Certainly, from beginning of the second century, the term εὐαγγέλιον appears in early Christian writings with a new double valency.[30] On the one hand, εὐαγγέλιον can still be used to refer to the oral gospel message.[31] On the other hand, however, the term is also used—with steadily increasing frequency—to refer to written gospel texts. At least two authors from the first half of the second century employ the term in this way.[32]

1. The *Didache* (c. AD 100) refers at several points to "the gospel" or "the Lord's Gospel" in close association with material from a source similar to, if not identical with, our Matthew. In particular, at 8.2 the Didachist introduces a version of the Lord's Prayer very similar to that found in Matt. 6:9-13 with the words: "pray like this, just as the Lord commanded in his Gospel." The verbal similarities leave little room for doubt that the author had the Gospel of Matthew in mind.[33]

2. Ignatius of Antioch (c. AD 110), in his letter to the Smyrneans (5.1), juxtaposes τὸ εὐαγγέλιον with "the prophecies" and "the law of Moses." The parallel thus drawn between "the gospel" and other written Scriptures strongly suggests that Ignatius intends a reference to the gospel in written form. Indeed, this reading is confirmed by the observation that in the

---

[28] M. Hengel, "The Titles of the Gospels and the Gospel of Mark," in M. Hengel, ed., *Studies in the Gospel of Mark* (London: SCM Press, 1985), pp. 64-84; M. Hengel, *The Four Gospels and the One Gospel of Jesus Christ: An Investigation of the Collection and Origin of the Canonical Gospels* (Harrisburg: Trinity, 2000), pp. 48-56.

[29] It is true that the earliest extant examples of the use of titles in this way date from the beginning of the third century: $\mathfrak{P}^{66}$ (c. AD 200) bears the clear *inscriptio* εὐαγγέλιον κατὰ ᾿Ιωάννην; and $\mathfrak{P}^{75}$ (c. AD 220) has a *subscriptio* to Luke and an *inscriptio* to John on the same page. Hengel's arguments, which rely on a detailed study of the practice of book distribution in the ancient world, nevertheless stand, since only a few manuscripts predate these examples, and the opening and closing leaves of papyri codices are, at any rate, often missing.

[30] For more detailed discussion of the alternative views on this question, see R. H. Gundry, "EUAΓΓEΛION: How Soon a Book?" *Journal of Biblical Literature* 115 (1996), pp. 321-25; and J. A. Kelhoffer, "'How Soon a Book' Revisited: EUAΓΓEΛION as a Reference to 'Gospel' Materials in the First Half of the Second Century," *Zeitschrift für die neutestamentliche Wissenschaft* 95 (2004), pp. 1-34.

[31] *1 Clement*, for example, probably written from Rome in the mid-90s AD, refers (at 47:2) to the earliest days of Christianity—in terms reminiscent of Mark 1:1 or Phil. 4:15—as "the beginning of the gospel." And, similarly, a generation later, the *Epistle of Barnabas* (probably c. AD 130) speaks of the "apostles who were destined to preach the gospel" (5:9, cf. 8:3).

[32] On the possible, but less convincing case of *2 Clem.* 8:5, see section B.1 below.

[33] See *Did.* 11:3; 15:3-4. For detailed discussion, see C. M. Tuckett, "Synoptic Tradition in the Didache," in J.-M. Sevrin, ed., *The New Testament in Early Christianity: La réception des écrits néotestamentaires dans le Christianisme primitif* (Leuven: Peeters, 1989), pp. 197-230.

creed-like opening of the letter (at 1.1) Ignatius says that Jesus was baptized by John "so that all righteousness might be fulfilled in him" (ἵνα πληρωθῇ πᾶσα δικαιοσύνη ὑπ᾽ αὐτοῦ). Again, the verbal similarity with Matt. 3:15, a verse unique to the First Gospel, makes it highly likely that Ignatius is quoting from that work.[34]

From the second half of the second century onwards, use of the term εὐαγγέλιον with this newly expanded semantic range became more common. Justin Martyr, for example, addressing the Emperor in his *First Apology* (c. 155–161), appeals to the authority of the "memoirs of the apostles. . . called gospels" and thus clearly has written works on view.[35] Likewise, Irenaeus, the Bishop of Lyons, writing towards the end of second century, employs the term εὐαγγέλιον no less than seventy-five times in the third book of his influential *Adversus haereses* (c. 180–192), and uses it there to refer both to the original apostolic proclamation and to written accounts of Jesus' life.[36] Irenaeus is, indeed, the first to make the distinction between the oral gospel and written gospels explicit, when he writes that the apostles at first "proclaimed the gospel in public" and "later, by the will of God, handed it down to us in the scriptures."[37]

Clearly, then, the use of εὐαγγέλιον in the Christian literature of the second century, bears witness to the increasing significance of written gospel accounts in that period. This, of course, is not to say that oral gospel sources were immediately abandoned as soon as the written gospels began to circulate, and it is most likely that oral traditions concerning Jesus persisted well into the second century. Nevertheless, as Bauckham has now shown, the early Christians valued, above all, access to those who had been eyewitnesses of Jesus. From the death of the primary witnesses of the first generation onwards, therefore, it was increasingly recognized that first-hand testimony about Jesus was best preserved in the written accounts they had left behind.[38]

---

[34] Following Stanton, *Jesus and Gospel*, pp. 54-55. cf. also Ignatius, *Smyrn.* 7.2, and the less certain examples at *Phld.* 5.1-2; 8.2; 9.2. Note, however, W. R. Schoedel, *Ignatius of Antioch: A Commentary on the Letters of Ignatius of Antioch* (Philadelphia: Fortress Press, 1985), *loc. cit.*; and C. T. Brown, *The Gospel and Ignatius of Antioch* (New York: Peter Lang, 2000), pp. 1-6, 15-23, both of whom conclude that oral proclamation is on view.

[35] Justin, *1 Apol.* 66.3.3. It seems, however, that Justin preferred the designation "Memoirs of the Apostles" (ἀπομνημονεύματα τῶν ἀποστόλων) for these works: he refers to them as such fifteen times, but only labels them "gospels" thrice. "Memoirs of the Apostles": *1 Apol.* 66.3; 67.3; *Dial.* 100.4; 101.3; 102.5; 103.6; 104.1; 105.6; 106.1.4. "Gospel": *1 Apol.* 66.3; *Dial.* 10.2 (where Trypho the Jew confesses that he has read "the gospel"); and *Dial.* 100.1, (where Justin introduces a quotation from Matt. 11:27 with the formula "in the gospel it is written" = γέγραπται).

[36] For further discussion, see Hengel, *The Four Gospels*, pp. 10-11.

[37] Irenaeus, *Haer.* 3.1.1. Interestingly, at *Haer.* 2.27.2 Irenaeus divides the whole of Scripture into the "Prophets" (presumably the Old Testament) and the "Gospels" (presumably the NT): *universae Scripturae et Prophetiae et Evangelica.* It seems, then, that at least for Irenaeus "Gospels" could refer not only to narrative accounts of Jesus' life, but to other literary works, such as the epistles, which contained the gospel message.

[38] Bauckham, *Jesus and the Eyewitnesses*, pp. 21-38. The example of Papias, the Bishop of Hierapolis, is instructive. As Bauckham demonstrates, Papias' stated preference for "a living and

The original and continuing oral proclamation of the gospel was, therefore, remarkably quickly augmented by a range of written gospel accounts, and these written accounts took on increased significance as authoritative witnesses when there were no longer any people left who could authoritatively speak of their first-hand experience of Jesus.

### (b) From Singular to Plural

The second transformation in the early Christian understanding of "the gospel" may be dealt with quite briefly. The striking point here is that, even though written gospel sources multiplied from the second half of the first century onwards, and even though the plural term εὐαγγέλια ("glad tidings" or "gospels") appears with relative frequency in the pagan context of early Christianity, Christian writings right up to the end of the second century—almost without exception—employ εὐαγγέλιον in the singular. As noted previously, the plural εὐαγγέλια is entirely absent from the NT. And indeed, prior to Irenaeus, εὐαγγέλια appears only twice in the extant literature: first, and with some reticence, in Justin's *First Apology* 66.3; and then, in a fragment of Apollinaris, the Bishop of Hierapolis, who wrote at the time of Marcus Aurelius (c. 170s AD).[39] Even Irenaeus markedly prefers the singular to the plural, and of the seventy-five occurrence of εὐαγγέλιον in Book 3 of his *Adversus haereses* only five are plural. Clement of Alexandria, likewise, tends to retain the singular εὐαγγέλιον for the Christian message, using the plural only rarely.[40] Therefore, even though a plurality of written gospel sources were in circulation from the apostolic era onwards, it was not until the third century that Christian writers began to refer to "the gospels," plural, with any frequency. Even Augustine, writing early in the fifth century, was keen to clarify, when he referred to the "four gospels," that it was better to say "in the four books of the one gospel."[41]

The best explanation for this phenomenon was first mooted by Oscar Cullman, who argued persuasively that Christian writers preferred to use the singular εὐαγγέλιον because they understood the idea of a plural "gospel" as a "theological impossibility": God had announced only one gospel, that of his Son, and none other was either necessary or conceivable.[42] Thus, although a plurality of written gospel texts were recognized and accepted as authoritative from quite an early date (see A.3.c-d below), early Christian writers

---

surviving voice" over "information from books" (*apud* Eusebius, *Hist. eccl.* 3.39.4) stemmed not from a general preference for orality over textuality, but for a desire for access to first-hand information which, in the period to which he refers (c. 80s AD), was still available from living eye-witnesses.

[39] The fragment of Apollinaris' Περὶ τοῦ Πάσχα (On the Passover) is preserved in the Preface to the *Chronicon Paschale*. See M. J. Routh, *Reliquiae Sacrae*, vol. 1 (Oxford: Oxford University Press, 1846), p. 160.

[40] Hengel, *The Four Gospels*, p. 10.

[41] *Tract. ep. Jo.* 36:1.

[42] O. Cullmann, "Die Pluralität der Evangelien als theologisches Problem im Altertum," *Theologische Zeitschrift* 1 (1945), pp. 23-42; cf. Hengel, *The Four Gospels*, p. 4.

throughout the first few centuries preferred to emphasize that there was only one gospel of Jesus Christ, even if it was promulgated in a variety of written texts.[43]

## 3. The Four: Apocryphal Gospels, Gospel Harmonies & the Emergence of the Fourfold Gospel Canon

The emergence of a plurality of written gospel sources during the second part of the first century gave way during the second century to two competing tendencies: the tendency towards multiplication, and the tendency towards harmonization. It was in the context of these competing tendencies that the four NT gospels, individually recognized as uniquely authoritative from the very earliest period, emerged as the fourfold gospel canon.

### (a) The Tendency Towards Multiplication: Apocryphal Gospels

On the one hand, there was a strong tendency to extend and augment the existing plurality of gospel sources with a range of alternative gospel authorities. In addition to the strong oral traditions about Jesus that persisted alongside the earliest written gospels, the second century saw the emergence of a new range of written gospels—the so-called "apocryphal gospels"— which soon began to gain some currency.[44]

The apocryphal gospels differ from each other as much in their origins and style as they do in theology and substance (*Table 1*). The *Gospel of Thomas*, for example, probably written around the first half of the second century, is a collection of one hundred and fourteen *logia* or sayings of Jesus with distinctly Gnostic flavor, and lacks the extended narrative so characteristic of the canonical gospels. In contrast, the "Jewish-Christian gospels" of the *Nazarenes* and *Ebionites*, written around the same time, were similar in genre to the canonical gospels, sharing with them a similar structure and a number of narratives.[45]

---

[43] This same theological conviction probably also explains the form of the titles attached to the gospels from early in the second century: "Gospel according to..." (εὐαγγέλιον κατά . . . ). So Hengel, *The Four Gospels*, pp. 48-56.

[44] For introduction and commentary on the apocryphal gospels, see W. Schneemelcher, *New Testament Apocrypha, Vol. 1: Gospels and Related Writings* (Louisville: Westminster John Knox, 1991). See also chapter nine of this volume.

[45] For detailed discussion, see S. Gero, "Apocryphal Gospels: A Survey of Literary and Textual Problems," *ANRW* 2.25.5 (1988), pp. 3969-96; A. F. J. Klijn, "Das Hebräer- und das Nazoräerevangelium," *ANRW* 2.25.5 (1988), pp. 3997-4033; G. Howard, "The Gospel of the Ebionites," *ANRW* 2.25.5 (1988), pp. 4034-53.

| Name | Original Language | Date | Provenance |
|---|---|---|---|
| *Thomas* | Greek (extant Coptic) | c. 100–150? | Syria |
| *Peter* | Greek | c. 150 | Syria? |
| *Hebrews* | Greek | c. 100–150 | Egypt |
| *Nazarenes* | Aramaic/Syriac | c. 100–150 | Syria |
| *Ebionites* | Greek | c. 100–150 | Trans-Jordan? |
| *Egyptians* | Greek | c. 100–150? | Egypt |
| *Secret Mark* | Greek | ? | Egypt |
| *Protoevang. of James* | Greek | c. 150–200 | Syria |
| *Judas* | Greek (extant Coptic) | Late second century? | Egypt |
| *Infan. G. Thom.* | Greek | Late second century | ? |
| *Phillip* | Greek (extant Coptic) | c. 200–250? | Syria? |

*Table 1. Apocryphal Gospels.*[46]

The relationship of these works to the canonical gospels also varies enormously. Some, like the *Protoevangelium of James*, the *Gospel of the Nazarenes*, and the *Gospel of the Ebionites*, are clearly dependent on the canonical gospels. Others, like the *Gospel of the Hebrews* show no sign of such dependence. And yet others, like the *Gospel of Peter* and the *Gospel of Thomas*, stand in an unclear relationship to the earlier gospels. For our purposes, a range of written gospels became available from the second century onwards, and these appear in various ways in the other early Christian literature (see further section B and chapter 9 of this volume).[47]

### (b) The Tendency towards Harmonization: Marcion and Tatian

On the other hand, in some quarters there was an equally strong tendency to harmonize the plurality of gospels sources in an effort to produce one single authoritative written gospel. This tendency took various forms, and could be motivated by significantly different factors, as the two most important examples from the second century demonstrate.

In 144, Marcion of Sinope in Pontus was expelled from the church of Rome for heretical opinions, which included, among other things, the

---

[46] Based on Schneemelcher, *NT Apocrypha 1*. For the *Secret Gospel of Mark*, see M. Smith, *The Secret Gospel: The Discovery and Interpretation of the Secret Gospel According to Mark* (New York: Harper & Row, 1973); but note the critique of S. C. Carlson, *The Gospel Hoax: Morton Smith's Invention of Secret Mark* (Waco: Baylor University Press, 2005). For the *Gospel of Judas* see, most recently, S. Gathercole, *The Gospel of Judas: Rewriting Early Christianity* (Oxford: Oxford University Press, 2007).

[47] For a recent introductory survey of the apocryphal gospels, see C. Tuckett, "Forty Other Gospels," in M. Bockmuehl, D. A. Hagner, eds., *The Written Gospel*, pp. 238-53.

rejection of all gospels except Luke (which was itself excised of those sections Marcion considered too "Jewish").[48] Marcion's radical redaction of the gospel traditions later drew from Tertullian, with characteristically colorful invective, the accusation that Marcion was "the Pontic Mouse. . . who gnawed the Gospels to pieces."[49] Although our only access to Marcion is through the words of his detractors, it seems he distinguished the merciful supreme God (the Father of Jesus) from the vengeful creator of the Hebrew Scriptures, and offered a semi-gnostic theology mixed with a strict asceticism. Marcion rejected all the gospels but Luke (and much else besides) because they contradicted his radical vision of God. His attempt to limit the number of written gospels was thus driven by a profoundly theological motivation.[50]

In contrast, Tatian, who composed his *Diatessaron* in Rome (or perhaps Syria) sometime before 170, was the thoroughly "orthodox" student of Justin Martyr. His work was an attempt to harmonize the four NT gospels while retaining the entire text of all four.[51] To achieve this, it seems that Tatian set three of the gospels in the framework of the fourth (either Matthew or John).[52] His aim seems to have been to create one authoritative gospel to replace the others, and thus simultaneously provide a sure foundation for the church and a united answer to its critics.[53] His motivation was more pragmatic than theological, as he aimed to serve the pastoral and apologetic needs of the church.

What the examples of Marcion and Tatian show is that, in addition to the proliferation of written gospels which characterized the second century, there were also attempts made in some quarters to excise or harmonize the written gospel traditions to create a single authoritative text. It was in the context of these competing tendencies that the fourfold gospel canon emerged.

---

[48] Irenaeus, *Haer*. 1.27.2; 3.11.7-9; 3.12.12; 3.14.3.

[49] Tertullian, *Marc*. 1.1; cf. 1.19.

[50] The classic work on Marcion is still A. Harnack, *Marcion: Das Evangelium vom fremden Gott. Ein Monographie zur Geschichte der Grundlegung der katholischen Kirche* (Leipzig: Hinrichs, 1924). Of the more recent works, see esp. P. M. Head, "The Foreign God and the Sudden Christ: Theology and Christology in Marcion's Gospel Redaction," *Tyndale Bulletin* (1993), pp. 307-21; G. May, K. Greschat and M. Meiser, *Marcion und seine kirchengeschichtliche Wirkung—Marcion and His Impact on Church History* (New York: de Gruyter, 2002).

[51] The same tendency towards harmonization is evident in the *Gospel of the Ebionites* which harmonizes the three Synoptic Gospels around a Matthean framework. See Schneemelcher, *NT Apocrypha 1*, pp. 166-71.

[52] Eusebius, *Hist. eccl.* 4.29.6. Hengel, *The Four Gospels*, p. 137 believes that the *Diatessaron* was structured around John. Note, however, W. L. Petersen, "Tatian's Diatessaron," in H. Koester, ed., *Ancient Christian Gospels: Their History and Development* (Philadelphia: Trinity, 1990), pp. 403-30, who believes that Matthew was used to structure the work (p. 430). For further discussion, see esp. W. L. Petersen, *Tatian's Diatessaron: Its Creation, Dissemination, Significance and History of Scholarship* (Leiden: Brill, 1994).

[53] T. Baarda, "ΔΙΑΦΩΝΙΑ-ΣΥΜΦΩΝΙΑ: Factors in the Harmonisation of the Gospels, Especially in the Diatessaron of Tatian," in W. L. Petersen, ed., *Gospel Traditions in the Second Century: Origins, Recensions, Text and Transmission* (Notre Dame: University of Notre Dame Press, 1989), pp. 133-54.

## (c) The Fourfold Gospel Collection

It is difficult to identify a single point at which individual gospel manuscripts were first collected together; the absolute origins of the fourfold gospel collection we know from the NT are likewise elusive. Nevertheless, it is possible to discern some key points in the process by which the four gospels were collected together—and recognized as an authoritative unit—during the course of the second century.

The earliest reference to a collection of written gospel sources comes from Luke (c. AD 60–85), who testifies (as noted previously) that even as early as his time "many (had) undertaken to set down an orderly account" of the events of Jesus life (Luke 1:1-4). Most probably, Luke had at least some of these accounts in front of him as he wrote. Indeed, on the basis of the verbal similarities between large sections of the three Synoptic Gospels, it is widely accepted that not only Luke but also Matthew had access at least to the Gospel of Mark, and probably also to other (no longer extant) written gospel sources ("Q," "proto-Luke," "proto-Matthew"). It seems reasonable to suggest, therefore, that already by the last quarter of the first century, collections of individual gospel manuscripts had begun to be assembled at major Christian centers such as Caesarea (Luke?) and Antioch (Matthew?).[54]

It is therefore not unlikely that John, writing from Ephesus towards the end of the century,[55] had access to a collection of gospel manuscripts which included Matthew, Mark and Luke. This, at least, is the testimony of a widespread early tradition, which avers that the Fourth Evangelist knew the three Synoptics and consciously wrote his gospel as a supplement to them.[56] It may be, then, that the four gospels were first collected together in Ephesus at the end of the first century.

This does not mean, of course, that such a collection was universally available at that time. Nevertheless, evidence from the first half of the second century demonstrates that collections of individual gospel manuscripts, and particularly of the four NT gospels, continued to be made, and took on

---

[54] For the argument that Luke accessed a collection of written gospel sources at Caesarea, see E. E. Ellis, "New Directions in the History of Early Christianity," in T. W. Hilllard, R. A. Kearsley, C. E. V. Nixon, A. M. Nobbs, eds., *Ancient History in a Modern University, Vol. 2: Early Christianity, Late Antiquity and Beyond* (Grand Rapids: Eerdmans, 1998), pp. 71-92. In relation to Matthew, the majority view is that the First Gospel was composed in Antioch, but the precise location is immaterial to our argument here: wherever Matthew was located when he wrote, he seems to have had access to earlier written gospel sources.

[55] For a concise and balanced discussion of the provenance of John, favoring Ephesus c. AD 80-85, see Carson and Moo, *New Testament*, pp. 229-67.

[56] Eusebius records the earlier testimony of Clement of Alexandria (*Hist. eccl.* 6.14.7), and lends his own weight to the tradition at 3.24.1-13. Cf. the less direct accounts of Irenaeus (*Haer.* 3.1.1; cf. Eusebius, *Hist. eccl.* 5.8.2-4) and Papias (*apud* Eusebius, *Hist. eccl.* 3.39.1-16); and the later evidence of the fourth century *Acta S. Timothei* (Greek text in R. A. Lipsius, *Die Apokryphen Apostelgeschichten und Apostellegenden*, vol. 2 (Braunschweig: C. A. Schwetschke und Sohn: 1884), pp. 372-400). For a full account of the parallel evidence for the tradition, see T. Zahn, *Geschichte des neutestamentlichen Kanons*, vol. 2 (Erlangen/Leipzig: Deichert, 1890–92), p. 37, n. 1.

increasing significance. At the beginning of the century Papias, Bishop of Hierapolis in Asia, "the hearer of John" and "companion of Polycarp,"[57] knew at least Matthew and Mark, and possibly also John.[58] More significantly, both the Longer Ending of Mark (Mark 16:9-20) and the *Epistula Apostolorum* (both best dated pre-150)[59] make use of all four gospels later accepted in the canon.[60] These texts testify, therefore, that a fourfold collection was becoming established in the churches by the middle of the second century.[61] Moreover, to this literary evidence must be added that of the gospel manuscripts themselves. Although it is true that the earliest four gospel codices date from the end of the second century,[62] the nature of these manuscripts makes it quite likely that they reflect earlier editions dating back at least to the middle of the century.[63]

Taken cumulatively, then, this evidence suggests that the fourfold gospel collection had been adopted—at least in some of the churches—by around the year 150. As such, although it is often asserted that the development of the fourfold gospel was a reaction of the early church to Marcion, it is more likely that Marcion's radical excision of the gospels only served to consolidate a process that was already well underway.[64]

Certainly, from the second half of the second century onwards, a growing chorus of voices begins to attest to the unique status of the four most ancient gospels. First, Justin Martyr, who wrote from Rome in the 150s AD, is

---

[57] Irenaeus *apud* Eusebius, *Hist. eccl.* 3.39.1. For detailed discussion and arguments in favor of an early date (c. AD 110), see U. H. J. Körtner, *Papias von Hierapolis: ein Beitrag zur Geschichte des frühen Christentums* (Göttingen: Vandenhoeck & Ruprecht, 1983), pp. 89-94, 167-72, 225-26.

[58] For Papias on Matthew and Mark, see Eusebius, *Hist. eccl.* 3.39.15-16. Stanton, *Jesus and Gospel*, p. 79 suggests that Papias' listing of the disciples in the order Andrew, Peter, Philip and Thomas—an order found in Fourth Gospel and no where else—is a telltale sign of Papias' knowledge of John.

[59] For the Longer Ending of Mark see Kelhoffer, "How Soon a Book?" p. 10. For the *Epistula Apostolorum* see C. E. Hill, "The *Epistula Apostolorum*: An Asian Tract from the Time of Polycarp," *Journal of Early Christian Studies* 7 (1999), pp. 1-53.

[60] Hengel, "The Titles of the Gospels and the Gospel of Mark," p. 72 concludes that Mark 16.9-20 and the *Epistula Apostolorum* are "probably the earliest Christian texts to presuppose all the gospels and Acts." For detailed analysis of the use of the four gospels in the longer ending of Mark, see J. A. Kelhoffer, *Miracle and Mission: The Authentication of Missionaries and Their Message in the Longer Ending of Mark* (Tübingen: Mohr Siebeck, 2000), pp. 48-156.

[61] Cf. Stanton, *Jesus and Gospel*, pp. 63-91.

[62] Three separate papyri (i. $\mathfrak{P}^{45}$; ii. $\mathfrak{P}^{75}$; and iii. $\mathfrak{P}^{4}$, $\mathfrak{P}^{64}$, $\mathfrak{P}^{67}$ understood as a single codex) vie for the honor of the earliest extant four gospel codex. For the debate, see T. C. Skeat, "The Oldest Manuscript of the Four Gospels?" *New Testament Studies* 43 (1997), pp. 1-34; G. N. Stanton, "The Fourfold Gospel," *New Testament Studies* 43 (1997), pp. 317-46; and P. M. Head, "Is P4, P64 and P67 the Oldest Manuscript of the Four Gospels? A Response to T. C. Skeat," *New Testament Studies* 51 (2005), pp. 450-57.

[63] Stanton, *Jesus and Gospel*, pp. 71-75.

[64] For similar conclusions, see B. M. Metzger, *The Canon of the New Testament: Its Origin, Development, and Significance* (Oxford: Clarendon, 1987), pp. 90-99; cf. Stanton, *Jesus and Gospel*, p. 81. For a recent discussion of the influence of Marcion on the development of the fourfold gospel canon, see U. Schmid, "Marcions Evangelium und die neutestamentlichen Evangelien: Rückfragen zur Geschichte und Kanonisierung der Evangelienüberlieferung," in May, Greschat and Meiser, eds., *Marcion*, pp. 67-77.

particularly important as the first Christian writer for whom we have a significant corpus. There is no doubt that Justin knew the Gospels of Matthew and Luke, since he cites them regularly. He most probably also knew Mark, since at one point he refers to the name Boanerges—which Jesus gave to the sons of Zebedee—and cites the "Memoirs of Peter" (= Mark) as his source.[65] Justin's knowledge of the Fourth Gospel cannot be so easily demonstrated, but it is quite possible that *1 Apol.* 61.4 reflects John 3:3-5 and *Dial.* 88.7 relies on John 1:19-20.[66] Be that as it may, it is significant that Justin does not cite any non-canonical gospel source, despite the fact that at least some of the apocryphal gospels had been written by his time (see A.3.a above).[67] Justin therefore provides good evidence that, at least in Rome around the middle of the second century, a gospel collection consisting of at least Matthew, Mark and Luke, and quite possibly also John—but not any other gospel—was in use.[68]

Second, the likelihood that Justin knew a collection of all four gospels is strengthened by the fact that his student, Tatian, certainly did. For Tatian's *Diatessaron*, composed c. 170, presupposes both that its author had access to the four canonical gospels, and that he considered them authoritative in some way, even if his work sought to surpass the four gospels by resolving their differences.

Third, towards the end of the century Irenaeus, Bishop of Lyons, became the first early Christian author to explicitly outline the fourfold gospel (c. 180s AD). In book three of his *Adversus haereses*, Irenaeus argues that "it is not possible that the gospels can be either more or fewer in number than they are" since "he who was manifested to men has given us the gospel under four aspects but bound together by one Spirit."[69] This argument was novel. As we have seen, however, Irenaeus' basic assertion of an irreducible fourfold gospel was no innovation. Indeed, the Bishop's arguments at *Haer.* 3.11.9 are clearly framed with at least two sets of opponents in mind, and thus reveal that he was motivated by recent attacks on the (heretofore widely accepted) concept

---

[65] *Dial.* 106.3. The designation Boanerges is unique amongst the four gospels to Mark 3:17, and it is therefore most likely that Mark was Justin's source. See C.-J. Thornton, "Justin und das Markusevangelium," *Zeitschrift für die neutestamentliche Wissenschaft* 84 (1993), pp. 93-100.

[66] Stanton, *Jesus and Gospel*, pp. 76, 101-2.

[67] The most comprehensive discussion of Justin's use of the gospels is still Zahn, *Geschichte des neutestamentlichen Kanons*, vol. 1 (Erlangen/Leipzig: Deichert, 1888-89), pp. 463-560. For a considered rejection of the suggestion that Justin used apocryphal gospels see A. J. Bellinzoni, *The Sayings of Jesus in the Writings of Justin Martyr* (Leiden: Brill, 1967), p. 139; cf. T. K. Heckel, *Vom Evangelium des Markus zum viergestaltigen Evangelium* (Tübingen: Mohr, 1999), pp. 310-29.

[68] Justin's statement in *Dial.* 103.8 may also be significant in this connection. He states there that the gospels "were composed by the apostles and their successors." Stanton, *Jesus and Gospel*, p. 76 plausibly suggests that the double plural here ("apostles" and "successors") indicates that Justin knew at least four gospels: perhaps, under the title "apostles" Justin thought of Matthew and John, while the designation "successors" was his way of referring to Mark and Luke.

[69] For discussion, see E. Osborn, *Irenaeus of Lyons* (New York: Cambridge University Press, 2001), pp. 175-77.

of the fourfold gospel.[70] On the one hand, Irenaeus' insistence that the one spirit had inspired a diversity in the apostolic witness to Christ is a defence against the likes of Marcion and Tatian who, in very different ways, had attempted to limit the written gospel to a single volume. On the other hand, his limitation of this diversity to *four* recognized gospels is designed to undercut gnostic claims that the risen Christ had revealed himself secretly to a plethora of authorized witnesses. The Bishop of Lyons was, then, the first to articulate the concept of the fourfold gospel, but his arguments imply that the concept had previously been, in many quarters, simply assumed.

Finally, then, the Muratorian Fragment,[71] which is probably best dated to the end of the second century,[72] is the first Christian text to contain a kind of "canon list." Although the initial part of the fragment is missing, it commences with what must be a description of Mark, and goes on to list Luke and John as the "Third" and "Fourth" Gospels respectively. The Muratorian Fragment, therefore comports well with the evidence from the papyri, and from Justin, Tatian and Irenaeus, and confirms that by the end of the second century the fourfold gospel had become widely established amongst the churches from Rome to Alexandria.[73]

This consensus was, of course, not unchallenged. Gaius, an otherwise "orthodox" Roman presbyter, rejected the Gospel of John because of its perceived affinity with Montanism.[74] Clement of Alexandria, likewise, while accepting the superior authority of "the four gospels that have been handed down to us,"[75] still regularly quotes from apocryphal gospels and seems to have to recognized some sort of authority in them also.[76] And Serapion, the Bishop of Antioch, happily permitted the church in Rhossos in Syria to read

---

[70] See further H. von Campenhausen, *The Formation of the Christian Bible* (Philadelphia: Fortress Press, 1972), pp. 155-209; Stanton, "The Fourfold Gospel," here: pp. 319-22; Hengel, *The Four Gospels*, pp. 10-12.

[71] An English translation of the Fragment may be conveniently accessed in H. Bettenson, *Documents of the Christian Church* (New York: Oxford University Press, 1967), pp. 28-29.

[72] A. C. Sundberg, "Canon Muratori: a Fourth Century List," *Harvard Theological Review* 66 (1973), pp. 1-41 questioned the traditional date, assigning the list the fourth century. Cf. now G. M. Hahneman, *The Muratorian Frgament and the Development of the Canon* (Oxford: Clarendon, 1992), esp. 215-18. The traditional dating has, however, been convincingly defended by E. Ferguson, "Canon Muratori: Date and Provenance," *Studia Patristica* 17 (1982), pp. 677-83; C. E. Hill, "The Debate Over the Muratorian Fragment and the Development of the Canon," *Westminster Theological Journal* 57 (1995), pp. 437-52; cf. Heckel, *Evangelium*, pp. 340-42. For our purposes it is important to note that even if the Muratorian Fragment does belong to the fourth century, this hardly undermines the argument outlined above.

[73] Cf. the similar conclusion reached by R. A. Piper, "The One, the Four and the Many," in M. Bockmuehl and D. A. Hagner, eds., *The Written Gospel* (New York: Cambridge University Press, 2005), pp. 254-73.

[74] Eusebius, *Hist. eccl.* 2.25.6-7; 3.28; 6.20.3; cf. Irenaeus, *Haer.* 1.26.1; 3.11.9.

[75] Clement of Alexandria, *Strom.* 3.92; 3.93.1: "We do not have this saying [the saying in dispute] in the four gospels that have been handed down to us, but in that according to the Egyptians." Cf. Clement of Alexandria, *Hypotyposes* Book 6, *apud* Eusebius, *Hist. eccl.* 6.14.5-7.

[76] *Gospel of the Egyptians*: Clement of Alexandria, *Strom.* 3.45.4; 3.63.1; *Gospel of the Hebrews*: Clement of Alexandria, *Strom.* 2.45.4 f.; cf. 5.96.2-4; an otherwise unknown gospel: Clement of Alexandria, *Strom.* 5.63.7.

the *Gospel of Peter* in worship, before later retracting this permission in objection to the docetic tendencies of the work.[77] These examples attest to a continuing fluidity around the edges of the fourfold gospel collection at the turn of the third century. Nevertheless, such challenges seem to have presupposed the authority of an existing collection, and this in itself provides further evidence for the unique position that the "quadriform gospel" had achieved by the end of the second century.

### (d) The Four Gospels as Canonical Scripture

A brief note must be added here on the vexed question of canonicity, which is essentially a question about the authority and status of the gospels (or other works) within the early church.[78] At this point, definitions are crucial, for as Metzger notes, much confusion has resulted from the failure to distinguish the "fundamental idea of canonicity from the actual drawing up of a list of canonical books."[79] This "fundamental idea of canonicity" is the recognition that a limited number of works bear a unique authority as Scripture. Thus, although we have no record of NT canon lists being drawn up until the end of the second century,[80] and the canon was not officially closed until the end of the fourth century,[81] this does not preclude the possibility that many of the books of the NT (including the four gospels) were nevertheless recognized as uniquely authoritative Scripture, and therefore in principle as "canonical," at a much earlier date.[82]

Indeed, there is little doubt that the four NT gospels were, individually, recognized as uniquely authoritative already in the first century. As E. E. Ellis has demonstrated, each of the four gospels was most probably associated with a distinct apostolic mission, and was thus recognized from the beginning as bearing the authority of the apostle with whom it was associated (James/Matthew, Peter/Mark, Paul/Luke, John/John).[83] Since apostolic

---

[77] Eusebius, *Hist. eccl.* 6.12; cf. 5.19.

[78] On the question of the gospels in the NT canon see now: L. M. McDonald and J. A. Sanders, *The Canon Debate* (Peabody: Hendrickson, 2002), esp. pp. 295-320, 372-86, 416-39; and L. M. McDonald, *The Biblical Canon: Its Origin, Transmission and Authority* (Peabody: Hendrickson, 2007), pp. 250-64.

[79] Metzger, *Canon*, pp. 98-99.

[80] The earliest is probably the Muratorian Fragment from the end of the second century, on which see section A.3.c above.

[81] Athanasius of Alexandria's *Festal Letter 39* for AD 367 is first ancient list to match our twenty-seven book NT canon exactly, and the same list was first ratified—on Augustine's recommendation—by the Councils of Hippo (393) and Carthage (397).

[82] See further the helpful discussion in E. Ferguson, *Church History Volume 1—From Christ to Pre-Reformation: The Rise and Growth of the Church in Its Cultural, Intellectual, and Political Context* (Grand Rapids: Zondervan, 2005), pp. 114-19.

[83] The argument turns on three distinct sets of evidence: i. a number of key NT texts suggest distinct but co-ordinated apostolic missions (Gal. 2:9; 1 Cor. 15:3-8; Acts 3:1; 4:13; 8:14; 12:17; 15:7, 12-21; 21:17-26); ii. analysis of the NT literature reveals several important parallels between the four gospels and epistles associated with the four key apostles (James/Matthew, Paul/Luke-Acts, Peter/Mark, John's letters /John); and iii. the unusual, and therefore probably significant, reference in Clement of Alexandria's *Stromata* 1.1.11, to the

authority was associated from the beginning with the authority of Jesus himself, and Jesus' authority in turn with divine authority, the groundwork for the recognition of the apostolic testimony to Jesus as Scripture was laid at a very early date.[84]

It is therefore no surprise to find that, already in the first half of the second century, *Barnabas* 4.14 could introduce Matt. 22:14 with the formula "as it is written" (ὡς γέγραπται)—a formula that was customarily used to introduce scriptural quotations. Similarly, *2 Clement* 2.4 could straightforwardly refer to Matt. 9:13/Mark 2:17 as "another scripture" (ἑτέρα γραφή). In the second half of the century, likewise, Justin in his *Dialogue with Trypho* (100.2) could introduce a quotation from Matt. 11:27/Luke 10:22 with the formula "in the gospel it is written" (= γέγραπται). And towards the end of the century Irenaeus could refer to the gospels as Scripture, arguing at one point that "the entire Scriptures, the Prophets, and the Gospels [*cum itaque universae scripturae, et prophetiae et Euangelii. . .*] can be clearly, unambiguously, and harmoniously understood by all."[85] Clearly, then, although second century Christian authors primarily employed the designation "Scripture" to refer to the texts of the Old Testament (OT), there is ample evidence that the gospels began to enjoy a similar status as Scripture from at least as early as the first half of that century.[86]

Furthermore, it seems most probable that an important part of the original purpose of constructing written gospel sources was for them to be read in the early Christian assemblies, whether the messianic "synagogues" of Judea, Galilee and Samaria, or the Christian assemblies of Asia Minor, Greece and Rome.[87] Since the practice of Jewish synagogues in the first and second centuries was that only canonical Scriptures may be read in the assembly, it is

---

"tradition . . . from Peter, James, John and Paul." See E. E. Ellis, "Gospels Criticism: A Perspective on the State of the Art," in P. Stuhlmacher, ed., *The Gospel and the Gospels* (Grand Rapids: Eerdmans, 1991), pp. 45-54; Ellis, "New Directions"; cf. P. W. Barnett, *Jesus and the Rise of Early Christianity: A History of New Testament Times* (Downers Grove: InterVarsity Press, 1999), pp. 376-94. It is important to note that this argument does not necessarily imply that all four gospels had reached their final form by the end of the apostolic era, only that the key written gospel sources (Mark, "Q," "proto-Matthew," "proto-Luke"), which later formed the core of the canonical gospels in their final form, were composed by, or under the supervision of, the apostles.

[84] E.g. Matt. 10:1-5/Mark 3:14-16/Luke 6:13; 9:1-2; Matt. 10:40-42/Mark 9:41/Luke 10:16; Matt. 28:18-20; John 17:18; 20:21-23; 1 Thess. 2:13; 2 Pet. 3:15-16.

[85] *Haer.* 2.27.2; cf. also *Haer.* 4.41.1 which introduces a tradition similar to Matt. 13:18 with "Scripture says," and *Haer.* 2.22.3; 4.20.6 both of which introduce a citation from the gospels with the formular "it is written." On the status of Jesus traditions and the gospels in Justin and Irenaeus, see now especially Stanton, *Jesus and Gospel*, pp. 92-109 (= G. Stanton, "Jesus Traditions and Gospels in Justin Martyr and Irenaeus," in J.-M. Auwers and H. J. De Jonge, eds., *The Biblical Canons* [Leuven: Peeters, 2003], pp. 353-70).

[86] It is true that certain non-canonical Jesus traditions are occasionally identified as "Scripture" in the early Christian literature (e.g. *1 Clem.* 23.3). These are, however, the exception rather than the rule.

[87] See esp. Mark 13:14/Matt. 24:15 where the instruction to the reader ("let the reader understand") is most probably intended for the one who was to read the gospel in the public assembly.

likely that the fourfold gospel, or the sources that underlie them, were accorded something akin to the status of Scripture from the start.[88] Certainly, by the middle of the second century in Rome, Justin could attest to the Christian practice of reading "the memoirs of the apostles or the writings of the prophets" for "as long as time permits" in the regular Sunday gatherings of the Christian communities (*1 Apol.* 67.3). There are no hints in Justin's account that the practice was a recent innovation; it may well have been characteristic practice amongst the churches for many decades. Significantly, the fact that the "Memoirs of the Apostles" (= gospels) were being read in worship, in concert with the prophetic literature, speaks volumes for the status accorded to the gospels, at least in the Christian communities known to Justin.

It is clear, then, that the "fundamental idea of canonicity" was attached to the four gospels from at least the first half of the second century, if not even earlier.[89] To be sure, the challenges posed by Marcion and others (Gnosticism, Montanism) during the second century provided an important impetus to the closing of the canon.[90] As noted previously, it was in part these challenges which drew from Irenaeus the explicit defence of the *four* gospels. Nevertheless, the process of recognizing the gospels as Scripture, and therefore in principle as canonical, had begun much earlier.

## 4. Conclusion

The transmission of gospel traditions in the early church took place through a range of overlapping processes. The earliest oral proclamation of the gospel was augmented, remarkably quickly, first by a range of written gospel sources, then by what became the four canonical gospels, and finally, from the second century onwards, by a thicket of other gospels which began to grow up alongside the earlier traditions. The result of this complex set of processes was that, at least from latter part of the first century to the beginning of the third, gospel traditions were available from a range of sources and in a variety of forms. In what follows we shall address the remaining question: how did the earliest Christian authors outside the NT put these gospel traditions to use?

---

[88] E. E. Ellis, "The Making of Narratives in the Synoptic Gospels," in H. Wansbrough, ed., *Jesus and the Oral Tradition* (Sheffield: Sheffield Academic Press, 1991), pp. 310-33: here p. 331; Ellis, "New Directions." pp. 89-92. cf. John 2:22 where the words of Jesus are already set in parallel with the Hebrew Scriptures.

[89] For a very different view, see H. Koester, "The Text of the Synoptic Gospels in the Second Century," in W. E. Petersen, ed., *Gospel Traditions in the Second Century* (Notre Dame: University of Notre Dame Press, 1989), pp. 19-37, who argues that it was only after the year 200 that the gospels were "considered holy scripture" and "no such respect was accorded them in the earliest period" (p. 19).

[90] Cf. E. Ferguson, "Factors Leading to the Selection and Closure of the New Testament Canon: A Survey of Some Recent Studies," in L. M. McDonald and J. A. Sanders, eds., *The Canon Debate*, pp. 295-320.

## B. The Use of Gospel Materials in Early Christianity: Case Studies in the Apostolic Fathers

The task of analyzing the use of gospel materials in the collection of works known as the Apostolic Fathers is a vexed one.[91] The collection itself is a modern construction with somewhat blurred boundaries dating to the seventeenth century. It contains a diverse body of works. They range in provenance from Rome (e.g., *1 Clement*) and Athens (Quadratus) to Antioch (e.g. the *Didache*?) and Alexandria (*Barnabas*). They encompass a variety of genres including letters (*1 Clement*, Polycarp, Ignatius) and an apocalypse (of sorts: the *Shepherd*), a church manual (the *Didache*) and a martyrology (*Martydom of Polycarp*). And they date from anywhere between the mid 90s AD (*1 Clement*) to perhaps the 170s (*Martyrdom of Polycarp*).[92] The unity of such a diverse collection is found in the fact that these texts together represent the earliest proto-orthodox non-canonical writings outside the NT.

The Apostolic Fathers are thus located at a pivotal point in the development of the gospel traditions. To begin with, oral traditions about Jesus were still alive and well amongst the churches as the Apostolic Fathers began to write. Moreover, the first stages in the composition of their works overlapped with the final stages in the composition of the four canonical gospels. Not long afterwards, the first apocryphal gospels began to appear. And at the same time the fourfold gospel collection had begun to take shape, even if it was definitely still in its infancy.

In what follows we shall first address the problem of identifying the sources of gospel materials in the Apostolic Fathers, before outlining some patterns and tendencies in the way these authors used the gospel traditions.

### 1. The Problem of Identifying the Sources of Gospel Materials in the Apostolic Fathers: 1 & 2 Clement

Older scholarship tended to assume that citations (whether direct quotations or allusions) of gospel materials in the Apostolic Fathers must have been drawn from the four canonical gospels. From the late 1950s onwards, however, a steady stream of scholars successfully questioned this traditional assumption by showing that, in many cases, gospel materials which appear in the

---

[91] The Apostolic Fathers may be conveniently accessed in the recent translations of: B. D. Ehrman, *The Apostolic Fathers*, vols. 1 & 2 (Cambridge, Harvard University Press, 2003); and M. Holmes, *Apostolic Fathers: Greek Texts and English Translations* (Grand Rapids: Baker, 1999). Most recent collections contain the following works: *1 Clement, 2 Clement*, seven letters of Ignatius, Polycarp's letter to the Philppians, the *Didache*, the *Epistle of Barnabas*, fragments of Papias (and Quadratus), the *Epistle to Diognetus*, and the *Shepherd of Hermas*.

[92] The other contender for the honor of the earliest work in the collection is the *Didache*, which most would date to around AD 100, but almost certainly contains much earlier material. At the other end of the spectrum, it is quite possible that the *Epistle to Diognetus* postdates the *Martydom of Polycarp*. That work was most probably written sometime during the second half of the second century, but the evidence is inconclusive. For discussion see the introduction to each work in Ehrman, *Apostolic Fathers*, and the bibliographies there.

Apostolic Fathers are just as likely to have been drawn from oral tradition as from the canonical gospels.[93] The problem, of course, is that the four canonical gospels overlap significantly with each another, with other written gospels, and with the oral traditions about Jesus that persisted well into the second century. Moreover, the situation is further complicated by the tendency of some authors to quote rather freely from their sources. The result is that it is difficult to determine which gospels, if any, were known to any given early Christian author in the first part of the second century.

Nevertheless, some more recent studies have again begun to argue, in response to the excesses of the minimalist position, that at least some of the gospel citations in the Apostolic Fathers are drawn from the four NT gospels.[94] Demonstrating direct literary dependence is, however, often difficult, and it is increasingly recognized that the use of gospel *materials* in the Apostolic Fathers must be carefully distinguished from the use of the canonical gospels. Judgments about the source of gospel materials must be made on a case by case basis.[95]

The point may be illustrated by reference to the use of gospel materials in *1 Clement* and *2 Clement*. Despite the common name, and the association of these two texts in the manuscript tradition,[96] they are essentially unrelated. *1 Clement* is a letter written c. AD 95–96 by Clement of Rome (whether "bishop" or not is debated) to the church in Corinth.[97] It has the distinction of being the first extant, and securely dateable, early Christian writing outside the canon of the NT, and was widely known in antiquity. In contrast, *2 Clement* was not well known. It is an early Christian homily (probably the earliest extant homily outside the NT), written by a different hand somewhere around the middle of the second century.[98] In both texts the difficulty of identifying the sources of the gospel materials cited is manifest.

To begin with *1 Clement*, then, it is clear that the "bishop" of Rome was at least aware of the synoptic tradition which stood "behind or parallel with" the Synoptic Gospels.[99] At 13.2 (cf. Matt. 5:7; 6:14; 7:1-2; Luke 6:31, 36-38) and 46.8 (cf. Matt. 26:24; Luke 17:1-2) Clement quotes "the words of the

---

[93] The seminal work was H. Koester, *Synoptische Überlieferung bei den apostolischen Vätern* (Berlin: Akademie, 1957), anticipated in some ways by J. V. Bartlett, K. Lake, A. J. Carlyle, W. R. Inge, P. V. M. Benecke, J. Drummond, *The New Testament in the Apostolic Fathers* (Oxford: Clarendon, 1905). For a bibliography of works in this stream, see Kelhoffer, "How Soon a Book?," p. 2, n. 2.

[94] See here: Tuckett, "Synoptic Tradition in the Didache"; C. N. Jefford, *The Sayings of Jesus in the Teaching of the Twelve Apostles* (Leiden: Brill, 1989); Brown, *Gospel*.

[95] Kelhoffer "How Soon a Book?," pp. 9-10. A full compendium of more recent research, with extensive bibliographies, may be found in C. Kannengiesser, *Handbook of Patristic Exegesis: the Bible in Ancient Christianity* (Leiden/Boston: Brill, 2004), pp. 404-28.

[96] *2 Clement* appears after *1 Clement* in both the two Greek Codices (Alexandrinus, fifth century AD; Hierosolymitanus AD 1056) and the Syriac manuscript (dated AD 1169) which preserve the first letter. See Ehrman, *Apostolic Fathers*, pp. 1:161-62.

[97] Ehrman, *Apostolic Fathers*, vol. 1, pp. 18-31.

[98] On the date of *2 Clement* see Ehrman, *Apostolic Fathers*, vol. 1, pp. 159-60.

[99] D. A. Hagner, *The Use of the Old and New Testaments in Clement of Rome* (Leiden: Brill, 1973), p. 135.

Lord Jesus" in terms which clearly evoke traditions preserved in the Synoptic Gospels. Likewise, at 24.5 there is an unmistakable allusion to the parable of the Sower (cf. Mark 4:3 and par.). In none of these cases, however, does Clement preserve the words of the Synoptic Gospels verbatim, and the order in which he cites Jesus' maxims is also idiosyncratic. Given that Clement often seems to have quoted loosely from his sources, it is quite possible that he had before him one or more of the Synoptic Gospels.[100] For the reasons just cited it is, however, perhaps just as likely that his source was oral gospel tradition.[101]

Similarly, in regards to John, Clement again seems to reflect some knowledge of the gospel and its thought at various points in his letter.[102] Nevertheless, verbal identity is lacking in every instance, and in several cases the apparent similarity to the Fourth Gospel can be explained by reference to other passages in the Jewish and Christian literary corpus. It is therefore unlikely that Clement knew the Gospel of John.[103]

In contrast, it seems quite likely that the author of *2 Clement*, writing a full generation later, had access to written gospel traditions very similar to (if not identical with) the canonical gospels, and that he held them in very high esteem. For example, *2 Clem.* 2.4 reads: "And another scripture says, 'I have not come to call the righteous, but sinners'" (καὶ ἑτέρα δὲ γραφὴ λέγει ὅτι Οὐκ ἦλθον καλέσαι δικαίου, ἀλλὰ ἁμαρτωλούς). The use of γραφή (writing, or Scripture) here, together with the fact that the quote is set in parallel with an earlier quote from Isa. 54.1 (*2 Clem.* 2.1-3), demands that a written source is on view. In addition, the Greek is verbally identical to Mark 2:17/Matt. 9:13 (cf. Luke 5:32), which makes it highly probable that *2 Clement* is here directly dependent on one of those two Gospels. If this conclusion is correct, then *2 Clem.* 2.4 is most probably the first instance of a NT passage being cited as "Scripture."[104]

It does not follow, of course, that any and every allusion or semi-quotation of a gospel tradition in *2 Clement* should be ascribed to the author's dependence on a canonical gospel. Nowhere near the same degree of certainty is possible, for example, with a reference like that of *2 Clem.* 9.5 which speaks of Christ who "became flesh." Although the statement seems to reflect John 1:14, it is so short that nothing approaching certainty is possible, and, indeed, it could just as easily have been drawn from the general stock of

---

[100] So J. B. Lightfoot, *The Apostolic Fathers*, vol. 1.2 (London: Macmillan, 1889–90), p. 52.

[101] For detailed discussion see Hagner, *Clement of Rome*, pp. 135-78.

[102] *1 Clem.* 42.1 cf. John 17:18; 20:21; *1 Clem.* 43.6 & 59.3 cf. John 17:3; *1 Clem.* 48.4 cf. John 10:9; *1 Clem.* 49.1 cf. John 14:15; 15:10; *1 Clem.* 49.6 cf. John 6:51; *1 Clem.* 54.2 cf. John 10:2-16, 26-28; 21:16-17; *1 Clem.* 60.2 cf. John 17:17.

[103] Hagner, *Clement of Rome*, pp. 264-68. This conclusion is made all the more probable by the observation that many would date the Fourth Gospel as late as AD 90-95 which, if correct, scarcely leaves time for Clement to obtain a copy and assimilate its contents.

[104] cf. *2 Clem.* 3.2 which bears some redactional features of Matt. 10:32 and is therefore probably dependent on the Gospel of Matthew.

Christian oral traditions as from a written gospel.[105] Similarly, at *2 Clem.* 8.5, the author invokes the formula "For the Lord says in the gospel" (λέγει γὰρ ὁ κύριος ἐν τῷ εὐαγγελίῳ) to introduce a saying of Jesus. The quote is similar to, but not identical with, the canonical tradition at Luke 16:10-12, so it is quite probable that what we have here is simply a loose rendition of the Third Gospel.[106] It is, however, also possible that *2 Clement* is relying on oral tradition, a non-canonical text he knew as "the gospel," or some combination of all of these. Certainty is not attainable.

Moreover, the author of *2 Clement* does seem to have had access to a range of extra-canonical gospel materials which he regarded as having an authority similar to that of the written gospel source cited at *2 Clem.* 2.4. At *2 Clem.* 4.5 and 12.2, for example, the author introduces sayings of Jesus, paralleled in the *Gospel of Thomas* and the *Gospel of the Egyptians*, with the formula "the Lord said" (εἶπεν ὁ κύριος).[107] And similarly, at *2 Clem.* 11.2 a "prophetic word" not known from the NT canon is cited with authority.[108] In both of these cases, it is difficult to determine whether the author had access to the apocryphal gospels as written texts, or alternatively to a common oral tradition.

Clearly, distinguishing between oral gospel traditions and various kinds of gospel texts as they appear in *1 Clement* and *2 Clement* is no easy task. It is, indeed, made all the more difficult by the fact that neither of these texts, nor any of the Apostolic Fathers for that matter, ever cite a gospel source by name. The problems we have noted with regard to *1 Clement* and *2 Clement* are, therefore, repeated in numerous instances across the Apostolic Fathers, and this fact testifies to the complexity of the situation during the second century.

## 2. The Use of Gospels Materials in the Apostolic Fathers: Some Patterns and Tendencies

The various Apostolic Fathers used gospel materials in different ways and to varying extents. This is abundantly evident, for example, in the contrast between the *Didache*, which is rich with citations from, and allusions to, certain strands of gospel tradition, and the *Shepherd of Hermas*, which makes only limited use of gospel materials.

Nevertheless, it is possible to make some generalizations about the use of

---

[105] cf. *2 Clem.* 9.6 which may be indebted to John 13:34.

[106] *2 Clem.* 8.5: "For the Lord says in the gospel, 'If you do not keep what is small, who will give you what is great? For I say to you that the one who is faithful in very little is faithful also in much.'" The second sentence in the quote is identical to Luke 16:10, but the first sentence does not resemble any known source.

[107] A shorter version of the saying at *2 Clem.* 12.2 is found in Clement of Alexandria's *Stromata* 3.13.92, where it is attributed to the *Gospel of the Egyptians*. A longer form of the saying is found at *Gospel of Thomas* 22. The source of the saying at *2 Clem.* 4.5 is unknown. For discussion, see T. Baarda, "2 Clement and the Sayings of Jesus," in J. Delobel, ed., *Logia: Les Paroles de Jésus—The Sayings of Jesus* (Leuven: Peeters, 1982), pp. 529-56.

[108] Cf. the same word, referred to as "this scripture" (ἡ γραφὴ αὕτη), at *1 Clem.* 23.3.

gospel materials in these texts. At the most basic level, it is clear that none of the Apostolic Fathers offers anything like a detailed commentary on a whole gospel.[109] They likewise provide no developed hermeneutical theory and, indeed, engage only little in any kind of explicit interpretation of the gospel traditions. This is not to say, however, that gospel materials were unimportant to the Apostolic Fathers. Rather, the tendency of these authors was to weave gospel traditions into the fabric of their works—often without even acknowledging the source—and to use them, as Joseph Trigg notes, as a kind of "specifically Christian language."[110]

What were the patterns in the Apostolic Fathers' use of this language? At least three tendencies may be identified, and briefly outlined, as follows.

## (a) Synoptic more than Johannine Traditions

First, as *Table 2* clearly demonstrates, the gospel materials present in the Apostolic Fathers consistently reflect synoptic more than Johannine traditions.

| Text | Instances of traditions similar to. . . | | | |
|---|---|---|---|---|
| | Matthew | Mark | Luke | John |
| *1 Clem.* | 4 | 3 | 4 | 0 |
| *2 Clem.* | 10 | 8 | 8 | 1 |
| *Ignatius* | 8 | 1 | 2 | 5 |
| *Polycarp* | 5 | 2 | 5 | 0 |
| *Mart. Pol.* | 2 | 2 | 2 | 0 |
| *Didache* | 20 | 4 | 10 | 0 |
| *Barnabas* | 3 | 2 | 1 | 1 |
| *Hermas* | 0 | 0 | 0 | 0 |
| *Diognetus* | 1 | 0 | 0 | 0 |
| *Papias* | 0 | 0 | 1 | 1 |
| Total | 53 | 22 | 33 | 8 |

*Table 2: Gospel materials in the Apostolic Fathers.[111]*

---

[109] The first Christian commentary on a gospel was written by the Gnostic Heracleon (on the Gospel of John) in the middle of the second century. Irenaeus certainly showed interest in the individual characteristics of each of the four gospels, but it was not really until Origen (c. AD 185–254) wrote his commentary on Matthew that gospel commentaries began to emerge as a recognizable genre of Christian literature. See M. Bockmuehl, "The Making of Gospel Commentaries," in M. Bockmuehl and D. A. Hagner, eds., *The Written Gospel* (New York: Cambridge University Press, 2005), pp. 274-95.

[110] J. W. Trigg, "The Apostolic Fathers and the Apologists," in A. J. Hauser, D. F. Watson, eds., *A History of Biblical Interpretation: Volume 1—The Ancient Period* (Grand Rapids: Eerdmans, 2003), pp. 304-33: here, p. 305.

[111] The table reflects references to gospels materials in the Apostolic Fathers identified in the footnotes of Holmes, *Apostolic Fathers*. It provides only a rough measure, and two important limitations must be noted. i. Holmes' footnotes identify instances where traditions similar to

Out of a possible 116 references to gospel materials in the Apostolic Fathers, only eight involve traditions known to us from the Gospel of John. Thus, despite the tendency of later patristic authors to privilege the Gospels of Matthew and John as those written by apostles of Jesus,[112] the earlier use of gospel traditions in the Apostolic Fathers exhibits no such emphasis on Johannine material.

The one exception to this rule is Ignatius of Antioch who seems to use Johannine language at a number of points. He speaks of "the bread of God,"[113] of "God in man" or perhaps—as in some manuscripts—"God come in flesh,"[114] of "water living and speaking in me,"[115] of God's Spirit which "knows from where it comes and where it is going,"[116] and of the "High Priest" (= Jesus) who is "the door of the Father."[117] While none of these allusions is strong enough to demonstrate direct literary dependence on the Fourth Gospel, it does seem likely that Ignatius had been influenced by Johannine traditions in some form.[118] Nevertheless, even Ignatius makes more use of synoptic than Johannine traditions.

It seems, then, that the synoptic traditions about Jesus (whether in written or oral form) were more widely known to the Apostolic Fathers than their Johannine counterparts. Indeed, outside of Ignatius, none of the remaining possible allusions to Johannine tradition is unambiguous.[119]

### (b) Words of Jesus more than His Deeds

Second, the vast majority of references to gospel materials in the Apostolic Fathers take the form of quotations of, or allusions to, the *words* of Jesus. Apart from references to Jesus' death and resurrection, remarkably little mention is made of the gospel story as a whole. Likewise, individual narratives of Jesus' deeds—whether his symbolic acts or his mighty works of healing and exorcism—receive little attention. Gospel traditions about the

---

those in the four canonical gospels seem to be reflected in the texts of the Apostolic Fathers. The table therefore reflects a whole range of possible relationships (from verbatim quotation to probable allusion) between the existing gospel traditions in their various forms (whether oral or written) and the texts of the Apostolic Fathers. It is not a count of citations from the canonical gospels. ii. It is often the case that the gospel materials incorporated by any given author reflect the tradition as it is preserved in two or more gospels. Where this is the case, the reference has been counted once under each possible gospel, thus distorting the numbers somewhat. Despite these limitations, however, the table is included here as rough indication of the frequency with which gospel materials we know from the canonical gospels were cited by the Apostolic Fathers.

[112] See S. R. Llewelyn, *New Documents Illustrating Early Christianity: A Review of the Greek Inscriptions and Papyri Published in 1982–83*, vol. 7 (Sydney: Macquarie University, 1994), Appendix B, pp. 260-62.

[113] Ignatius, *Eph*. 5.2 cf. John 6:33.

[114] Ignatius, *Eph*. 7.2 cf. John 1:14.

[115] Ignatius, *Rom*. 7.2 cf. John 4:10, 14.

[116] Ignatius, *Phld*. 7.1 cf. John 3:8.

[117] Ignatius, *Phld*. 9.1 cf. John 10:9.

[118] Schoedel, *Ignatius*, p. 206.

[119] *2 Clem*. 17.5 (cf. John 8:24, 28; 13:19); *Barn*. 12.7 (cf. John 3:14-15); Papias *apud* Eusebius, *Hist. eccl*. 3:39 (cf. John 7:53–8:11).

words of Jesus, however, are often woven into the texts of the Apostolic Fathers. And, what is more, while certain extended parables of Jesus are referred to at some points,[120] it is the aphoristic sayings of Jesus which dominate the landscape of these texts.

Three examples must suffice to illustrate the point. To begin with the Didachist underlines his call to humility with a word of Jesus also reflected in Matt. 5:5: "My child, do not be a grumbler, since it leads to blasphemy. Do not be arrogant or evil minded, for all these things breed blasphemies. Instead, be humble, for "the humble [οἱ πραεῖς] shall inherit the earth."[121]

Similarly, Ignatius of Antioch uses a pithy saying from the gospel tradition to address the problem of false teachers in the Ephesian church of his day: "No one professing faith sins, nor does anyone possessing love hate. 'The tree is known by its fruit' thus those who profess to be Christ's will be recognized by their actions."[122]

And, in the same way, Polycarp of Smyrna exhorts the Philippian church in words drawn from the "sayings of the Lord":

[T]he Lord said as he taught: "Do not judge, that you may not be judged; forgive, and you will be forgiven; show mercy, that you may be shown mercy; with the measure you use, it will be measured back to you"; and, "blessed are the poor and those who are persecuted for righteousness' sake, for theirs is the kingdom of God."[123]

Examples of this kind of reference to the aphoristic words of Jesus abound in the Apostolic Fathers.[124]

This is not to say that the Apostolic Fathers contain no references to the narrative elements of the gospel tradition. Ignatius makes much of the significance of the star of Bethlehem as a sign of the dawning of a new age.[125] He offers a brief allegorical interpretation of the anointing of Jesus at Bethany.[126] And he makes mention, in a semi-credal statement, of Jesus' virgin birth, baptism by John, crucifixion under Pilate and Herod, and bodily appearances after the resurrection.[127] Likewise, the account of the *Martyrdom of Polycarp* seems to have been deliberately modeled on the gospel accounts of Jesus' passion, and delights in depicting parallels between the deaths of

---

[120] E.g. *1 Clem.* 24.5 alludes to the parable of the Sower found at Matt. 13:3-8/Mark 4:3-8/Luke 8:5-8.

[121] *Did.* 3.6-7.

[122] Ignatius, *Eph.* 14.2 (cf. Matt. 12:33/Luke 6:44).

[123] Polycarp, *Phil.* 2.2-3 (cf. Matt. 7:1-2/Luke 6:36-38 and Matt. 5:3, 10/Luke 6:20). A tradition similar to Matt. 7:1-2 is also referred to at *1 Clem.* 13.2. Further discussion in B. Dehandschutter, "Polycarp's Epistle to the Philippians: An Early Example of 'Reception,'" in J.-M. Sevrin, ed., *The New Testament in Early Christianity* (Leuven: Peeters, 1989), pp. 275-91.

[124] Further examples may be found at: *1 Clem.* 13.2; 46.8; *2 Clem.* 3.2; 4.2; 5.4; 6.1; 7.6; 9.11; 13.4; Ignatius, *Smyrn.* 6.1; *Trall.* 11.1; *Poly.* 2.2; Polycarp, *Phil.* 2.2-3; 5.2; 7.2; 12.3; *Did.* 1.2-5; 3.7; 7.1; 8.2; 9.5; 11.7; 13.2; 16.1, 4-6, 8; *Barn.* 4.14; 5.12; 12.7; *Diogn.* 9.6.

[125] Ignatius, *Eph.* 19.2-3 (cf. Matt. 2:2, 7, 9-10).

[126] Ignatius, *Eph.* 17.1 (cf. Matt. 26:7; Mark 14:3).

[127] Ignatius, *Smyrn.* 1.1-3.3 (cf. Matt. 3:15; Luke 24:39).

Polycarp and Jesus.[128]

Nevertheless, such allusions to narrative elements in the gospel tradition are the exception rather than the rule in the Apostolic Fathers, and it is the sayings of Jesus which most frequently provide the "specifically Christian language" as it appears in these texts.

### (c) Practical Instruction more than Theological Reflection

A final tendency evident in the Apostolic Fathers is that gospel materials are employed to the end of practical instruction more than they are used as a basis for theological reflection.

To begin with, gospel traditions are used by the Apostolic Fathers as a legitimating source of authority for church practices. The *Didache*, for example: provides instruction for prayer in line with what "the Lord commanded in his gospel" (*Did.* 8.2, cf. Matt. 6:9-13); links teaching about baptism to a trinitarian formula the same as that recorded in Matt. 28:19 (*Did.* 7.1); asserts that "every genuine teacher is. . . worthy of his food" in a manner reminiscent of Matt. 10:10 (*Did.* 13.2); and warns against allowing unbaptized persons to participate in the Eucharist on the basis of what "the Lord has also spoken concerning this: 'Do not give what is holy to dogs'" (*Did.* 9.5, cf. Matt. 7:6).

In addition, the Apostolic Fathers regularly use gospel materials as the authoritative ground for moral exhortation. Clement, for example, warns his Corinthian correspondants against schism on the basis of "words of Jesus our Lord" like those in Matt. 18:6; 26.24 and parallels (*1 Clem.* 46.8). Polycarp, likewise, takes up the language of Jesus at Matt. 5:44/Luke 6:27 in encouraging the Philippian Christians to pray "for those who persecute and hate you." And the *Didache*, in the most striking example of all, creates a rich collage of gospel traditions in order to contrast—in almost exclusively ethical terms—the "way of life" with the "way of death" (*Did.* 1.1-6).

Certainly, the Apostolic Fathers were capable, on occasion, of using gospel traditions as the ground for theological reflection. In one remarkable passage, for example, Clement creatively combines the Pauline "first fruits" imagery with the parable of the Sower to reflect on the nature of the future resurrection (*1 Clem.* 24.1-5). And *Barnabas*, similarly, takes Zechariah's (Zech. 13.7) image of the shepherd being struck and the sheep scattered—which appears in the canonical gospels as a prophecy of the desertion of the disciples—and incorporates it into a reflection on the salvific significance of Jesus' death.[129] These are, however, rare examples of theological reflection around gospel traditions. Much more characteristic in the Apostolic Fathers is the use of gospel materials to buttress ecclesiastical practices and moral

---

[128] Like Jesus, Polycarp: waited to be betrayed (*Mart. Pol.* 1.2); predicted his death (5.2); prayed earnestly before his arrest (7.2-3); asked that God's will be done (7.1); was arrested as though he were an armed rebel (7.1); was executed under an official named Herod (6.2); rode into town on a donkey (8.3), and so on.

[129] *Barn.* 5.12 (cf. Matt. 26:31/Mark 14:27).

injunctions.

## 3. Summary: Gospel Traditions in the Apostolic Fathers

The Apostolic Fathers stand at a pivotal point in the development of gospel traditions in the early church. It seems that most of these authors had access to gospel materials in a range of forms (oral and written, canonical and extra-canonical) and made use of the material at their disposal to serve the practical needs of the churches to whom and for whom they wrote. If an explanation is sought, then, for the patterns and tendencies just outlined, it is not necessary to look beyond the occasional nature of these works and the multiplicity of forms in which gospel materials were available in the first half of the second century.

## C. Conclusion

Gospel traditions occupy an important place in the early Christian literature. Memories of the words and deeds of Jesus were preserved and transmitted in the early churches by a range of historical processes which produced a variety of "gospel" forms. During the course of the second century, the four most ancient written gospels, which had been accorded a unique authority from the beginning, emerged at the center of these gospel traditions as the authoritative fourfold gospel we know from the NT. At the same time, early Christian authors wove strands of gospel material into the fabric of their own works, and thereby further contributed to the rich vibrancy of the gospel tapestry. The breadth and strength of the gospel traditions in this period are testimony to the remarkable impact Jesus of Nazareth had on the generations who followed him.

## Bibliography

Bartlett, J. V., Lake, K., Carlyle, A. J., Inge, W. R., Benecke, P. V. M. and Drummond, J. *The New Testament in the Apostolic Fathers*. Oxford: Clarendon Press, 1905.

Bauckham, Richard. *Jesus and the Eyewitnesses: the Gospels as Eyewitness Testimony*. Grand Rapids: Eerdmans, 2006.

Bellinzoni, Arthur J. *The Sayings of Jesus in the Writings of Justin Martyr*. Leiden: Brill, 1967.

Brown, Charles Thomas. *The Gospel and Ignatius of Antioch*. New York: Peter Lang, 2000.

von Campenhausen, Hans. *The Formation of the Christian Bible*. Philadelphia: Fortress Press, 1972.

Ellis, E. Earle. "New Directions in the History of Early Christianity." In *Ancient History in a Modern University, Vol. 2: Early Christianity, Late Antiquity and Beyond*, edited by T. W. Hillard, R. A. Kearsley, C. E. V. Nixon and A. M. Nobbs, pp. 71-92. Grand Rapid: Eerdmans, 1998.

Gero, S. "Apocryphal Gospels: A Survey of Literary and Textual Problems." *ANRW* 2.25.5 (1988): 3969-96.

Gregory, Andrew F. *The Reception of Luke and Acts in the Period Before Irenaeus*.

Tübingen: Mohr (Siebeck), 2003.

Hagner, Donald Alfred. *The Use of the Old and New Testaments in Clement of Rome*. Leiden: Brill, 1973.

Hengel, Martin. *The Four Gospels and the One Gospel of Jesus Christ: An Investigation of the Collection and Origin of the Canonical Gospels*. Harrisburg: Trinity Press International, 2000.

Hill, Charles E. *The Johannine Corpus in the Early Church*. Oxford/New York: Oxford University Press, 2004.

Jefford, Clayton N., *The Sayings of Jesus in the Teaching of the Twelve Apostles*. Leiden/New York: Brill, 1989.

Kannengiesser, Charles. *Handbook of Patristic Exegesis: the Bible in Ancient Christianity*. Leiden/Boston: Brill, 2004.

Koester, Helmut. *Ancient Christian Gospels: Their History and Development*. Philadelphia: Trinity Press International, 1990.

Massaux, Edouard. *The Influence of the Gospel of Saint Matthew on Christian Literature before Saint Irenaeus*. Leuven: Peeters, 1990.

Metzger, Bruce Manning. *The Canon of the New Testament: Its Origin, Development, and Significance*. Oxford: Clarendon Press, 1987.

Stanton, Graham N. *Jesus and Gospel*. Cambridge/New York: Cambridge University Press, 2004.

Tuckett, Christopher M. "Synoptic Tradition in the Didache." In *The New Testament in Early Christianity: La réception des écrits néotestamentaires dans le Christianisme primitif*, edited by J.-M. Sevrin, pp. 197–230. Leuven: Leuven University Press, 1989.

Zahn, Theodor. *Geschichte des neutestamentlichen Kanons*. 2 vols. Erlangen/Leipzig: Deichert, 1888–92.

# 9. The Non-Canonical Gospels

*Johan Ferreira*

## A. Why Study the Other Gospels?

Besides the four canonical gospels there are many other documents about Jesus, dating from the early centuries of the Christian era, that relate aspects of his life and teachings. They are often referred to as the apocryphal or non-canonical gospels and are included under the general category of New Testament Pseudepigrapha. In general, as far as research into the historical Jesus is concerned, despite claims to the contrary, they are not of much value as source material, in my opinion. Instead, they were written by and large to support, to supplement, or to supplant the canonical gospels. However, global statements with respect to these gospels can be very problematic. The *Gospel of Thomas*, for example, contains very early traditions, which provide a window not only into the history of gospel literature but also into the teachings and self-understanding of the historical Jesus. But this is the exception rather than the rule. Nevertheless, it is important for the student of the New Testament to be aware of these other gospels and to understand something about their context and content.[1]

There are several reasons why an acquaintance with the non-canonical gospels is significant for the study of the New Testament. First, it enhances our understanding of the *historical* development of early Christianity. The New Testament contains only a small sample of the history and literature of early Christianity. Reading the other gospels widens our horizons. The history and theology of the early followers of Jesus were not homogeneous but diverse. The idea that there was a pure, monolithic, and unified church in the first century—an ideal Christian age—is a myth. The history of Christianity has never seen such an ideal period devoid of diversity and internal conflict. Peter and Paul were not the only important Christian missionaries in the first century AD, and Christianity did not only spread to Asia Minor and Europe. There were many itinerant missionaries going to other parts of the world,

---

[1] The study of the other gospels is also justifiable in its own right. As historical artifacts from antiquity they preserve a part of the human experience and as such enrich our understanding of what it means to be human. In particular, they are indispensable for the study of religions in the Greco-Roman world.

including Syria (and from there probably into central Asia and even India) and Egypt (and from there probably into central Africa). Consequently, it is a distortion to represent the history of earliest Christianity by means of a singular timeline focusing only on one geographical area, usually Asia Minor and Europe. Jesus traditions developed simultaneously and, in some measure, independently in different parts of the world.[2] The New Testament itself contains the seeds and provides evidence of this expansive diversity. Therefore, knowledge of the other gospels will enable us to have a more comprehensive and refined understanding of early Christianity.

Second, studying the other gospels also challenges us *theologically*. The other gospels raise many theological questions. Reading these works we soon discover that many represent different understandings of the life and significance of Jesus and, consequently, espouse different ideas about the world, the church, and the religious life. As such, the other gospels compel us to grapple with our definition of Christianity and our understanding of the gospel. How did these gospels come to be written? Why were they excluded from the New Testament canon? Why were some later branded as "heretical"? In addition to these particular issues, the other gospels raise more fundamental theological questions. What is the basis of religious or spiritual authority? What are the contours of divine revelation, or what is the legitimacy of the New Testament canon? To what extent should society determine the shape of Christianity? Studying the other gospels forces us to formulate our own position regarding these questions in an increasingly pluralistic environment, an environment not unlike that of the early centuries of the Christian era. The student of the New Testament, in order to give full justice to the subject matter, cannot only focus on historical problems, but must also honestly and openly deal with the ensuing theological issues.

Therefore, on the one hand, studying the other gospels should lead us to affirm and celebrate the *diversity* of Christianity and the church.[3] The New Testament and early Christianity affirm the multiplicity of views and practices, which not only allows for freedom or individuality in the expression of faith but also positively encourages or even demands it. This particularity in fact stands at the heart of the gospel message itself—God accommodated

---

[2] Walter Bauer's influential work *Rechtgläubigkeit und Ketzerei im ältesten Christentum*, first published in 1934, (*Orthodoxy and Heresy in Earliest Christianity* [Philadelphia: Fortress Press, 1971]), argued that in some geographical regions, especially Edessa and Egypt, alternative forms of Christianity—later described as "heresy"—were not only more prominent than what we refer to as "orthodoxy" but also prior to the arrival of "orthodoxy." The observation that early Christianity was very diverse and developed simultaneously in different geographical regions is valid. However, the assertion that this diversity was dominated by what later came to be referred to as "heresy" is problematic. Consequently, Bauer's work has received extensive criticism due to selective use of evidence and arguments from silence. The evidence simply cannot support the weight of Bauer's elaborate edifice.

[3] See David Rhoads, *The Challenge of Diversity: The Witness of Paul and the Gospels* (Minneapolis: Fortress Press, 1996), p. 1: "A multiplicity of Christian visions, beliefs, practices, and community formations is at the heart of the Christian faith in its origins. The early Christian movement reached out for the very purpose of creating and encompassing incredible diversity within the larger reach of God's reconciling unity."

himself to the individuality or uniqueness of the human situation by becoming flesh—and flies in the face of the globalizing trends of local economies, societies, and lifestyles.

However, on the other hand, studying the other gospels should also lead us to affirm and celebrate the *unity* of Christianity and the church.[4] One should not overstate diversity at the expense of the commonalities that characterized early Christianity. This tendency toward overstatement is especially prominent in North American scholarship.[5] Although early Christianity was a multifaceted movement it was in most instances still clearly identifiably Christian. The New Testament and, for the most part, early Christianity anchored the beliefs and practices of Christians in the life, death, and resurrection of the historical figure, Jesus Christ. If the connection between the earthly Jesus of history—the meaning of his life and death—and the life of the post-Easter community is broken then there is a recognizable departure from the tradition based on the legacy of Jesus and his apostles.[6] Therefore, although there are many gospels dating from the era of nascent Christianity, for most Christians and certainly for the New Testament, there can be no "other gospel" (Gal. 1:7). Otherwise, we will not only remove Christianity from its historical actuality, but also circumvent the challenge of the cross, constructing a Christianity that is both irrelevant and meaningless.

## B. What were the Other Gospels all about?

As we have already intimated, early Christianity developed into divergent traditions, reflecting the environments in which it grew. At the risk of oversimplification, we may identify three basic trajectories within the early Christian movement. The early Jesus movement, located within Second Temple Judaism, issued in Jewish Christianity. The second group, which became the most dominant, was Gentile Christianity. Paul was a

---

[4] See Arland J. Hultgren, *The Rise of Normative Christianity* (Minneapolis: Fortress Press, 1994), p. 4: "In spite of the diversity of early Christianity, an expression of Christian faith arose in the first three centuries that claimed continuity with the faith of the apostles and is exhibited in the classic texts that came to make up the New Testament. Alternative expressions of faith, such as Marcionism, Montanism, Ebionitism, and Gnosticism, arose and made—to one degree or another—the same or similar claims. But there were factors within them—confessional and communal—that made those claims difficult to sustain. James Dunn sees the unifying strand of earliest Christianity, despite all its diversity, as Jesus and faith in him. See his *Unity and Diversity in the New Testament: An Inquiry into the Character of Earliest Christianity* (London: SCM Press, 1990).

[5] For example, H. Koester, *Ancient Christian Gospels: Their History and Development* (Philadelphia: Trinity Press International, 1990); John Dominic Crossan, *Four Other Gospels: Shadows on the Contours of Canon* (San Francisco: Harper & Row, 1985); and especially Elaine Pagels, *The Gnostic Gospels* (New York: Random House, 1979).

[6] Hultgren identified six commonalities or shared factors within what he calls "normative Christianity." These are: i. a positive view of the Old Testament; ii. Jesus is the revealer of God and the savior of humanity; iii. the way to salvation is by trust in God's redemptive work in Christ; iv. the Christian is to love and care for others; v. Christians are to live as disciples in a community of believers; and vi. the Christian community is part of a larger worldwide fellowship of believers. See *The Rise of Normative Christianity*, p. 86.

representative of this development, but his circle of churches was one only wing of Gentile Christianity. The last group can be associated with Gnosticism. However, sometimes it is difficult to distinguish clearly between these trajectories, as there was often cross-fertilization and a blurring of the boundaries. We may therefore represent these trajectories by means of three overlapping circles. The non-canonical gospels in general reflect these developing traditions of the first three centuries of the Christian era. However, the real situation was much more complex as these trajectories changed shape through time. The three overlapping circles highlight the fluidity of traditions through time and the difficulty of classification.

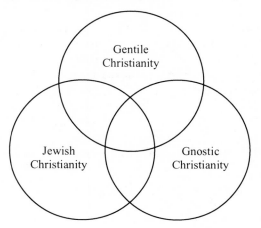

## C. Jewish Christianity

The expression "Jewish Christianity" needs clarification. It goes without saying that Christianity owes its existence and shape to Jewish history and experience. Christianity cannot, and should not, be divorced from its Jewish heritage. Paul described Gentile Christianity as a wild branch that has been grafted into the olive tree, and cautions his Gentile readers not to be haughty but to remember their debt to the Jews (Rom. 11:17-24). Christianity belongs both historically and theologically to the Jewish tradition. Jesus, all the apostles, and most followers of the Way in the first half of the first century were Jews. In other words, strictly speaking there cannot be a non-Jewish Christianity. Therefore, when scholars talk about Jewish Christianity it is to emphasize that this branch of Christianity maintained much more of the Jewish heritage than others. It not only maintained more elements of Judaism but also insisted, to varying degrees, that Jewish customs must be maintained in order to remain faithful to God's covenant requirements. This point of view is reflected in some of the New Testament documents. The Gospel of Matthew, for example, states that although its readers must not follow the hypocritical practices of the teachers of the law and the Pharisees, they must still obey everything they teach them (Matt. 23:3). The Jewish Christian

Gospels follow the same traditions.

Several Jewish Christian groups have been identified. The most well known were the Ebionites (from the Hebrew *ebyonim*, "the poor"). They are not to be confused with Aramaic speaking Christians or the early Jewish followers of Jesus. Our knowledge of them derives from a few church fathers and a small number of texts stemming from them.[7] They were a group of Jews who regarded Jesus as the great prophet promised by Moses, but they did not believe that Jesus was the Son of God. Therefore, they did not accept the pre-existence and the divinity of Christ. They looked upon Jesus as a teacher, not as a Savior. They continued to obey the Mosaic law, practiced circumcision, and kept the Sabbath. Similarly to the Essenes, they maintained ritual baths and espoused an ascetic way of life. They regarded Paul as an impostor and adhered only to the Gospel of Matthew. The group was especially prevalent in Syria and appears to have influenced the second century Encratites.[8] In addition to the Ebionites there were other less prominent Jewish Christian sects, which shared many of the characteristics of the Ebionites. The Nazarenes were a Syrian Judeo-Christian group of the fourth century. Their origins and relationship with the Ebionites are unclear. Unlike the Ebionites, they accepted Christ as divine. Gnosticism also influenced a number of these groups. For example, Elkasai and his disciples, in addition to being ardent adherents of Jewish customs, emphasized a special revelation that Elkasai received. Other Jewish gnostic groups, especially prevalent in Egypt, were the Dositheans, Simonians, Sethians, and Ophites. Finally, we may refer to James the Just, the leader of the Jerusalem church (cf. Acts 12:17; 15:13; 21:18; Gal. 1:19; 2:9, 12; Josephus, *Ant.* 20.200). Although details are vague, some scholars have argued that James represented a Torah-oriented and nationalist Jewish group within early Christianity.[9]

## D. Gentile Christianity

The expression "Gentile Christianity" is used by scholars to refer to groups who confessed that Jesus is Lord, but who did not adhere to any strict observance of the Mosaic law or Jewish customs. The most prominent representative of this branch of Christianity is Paul who maintained that "a man is not justified by observing the law, but by faith in Jesus Christ" (Gal. 2:16). However, there were other branches of Gentile Christianity in addition to Pauline Christianity, most notably in Syria and to a lesser extent in Africa. The Gospel of Mark, First Peter, The Epistle to the Hebrews and, perhaps in some respects, the Gospel of John represent non-Pauline Gentile Christianities in the New Testament. The distinction between "Jewish Christianity" and

---

[7] Especially, Irenaeus and Origen. The most important texts that have been identified as belonging to the Ebionites are the *Pseudo-Clementine Homilies* and the *Recognitions*.

[8] The Encratites were a group with ascetic tendencies. They abstained from alcohol, eating meat and marriage. Tatian (fl. AD 180) was their most prominent member.

[9] For an overview of the documents, see John Painter, *Just James: The Brother of Jesus in History and Tradition*, 2nd ed. (Columbia: University of South Carolina Press, 2004).

"Gentile Christianity" therefore is not so much a differentiation in terms of ethnicity but rather indicates a difference of theological standpoint. Accordingly, Gentile Christian documents emphasize the importance of faith in Jesus and downplay Jesus' Jewishness or the need for believers to adhere to the Mosaic law and to follow Jewish customs. Due to the intense missionary zeal of the early followers of Jesus and the phenomenal spread of Christianity in the Gentile world it was inevitable that these traditions would become the most influential form of Christianity.

## E. Gnostic Christianity

The expression "Gnostic Christianity" is much more problematic. Many of the non-canonical gospels can be associated with Gnosticism. The origins and definition of Gnosticism, however, have been intensely debated in the history of scholarship. The church fathers, and consequently Christian tradition, regarded Gnosticism as a Christian heresy. However, most recent research has questioned this view.[10] The evidence suggests that Gnosticism should not be regarded as an aberration of Christianity but rather as a distinct religious tradition and one that did not originate with the early Jesus movement. Some scholars, especially Bultmann, have even tried to argue that Gnosticism predates Christianity. However, few scholars have been convinced. It appears rather that Gnosticism developed simultaneously with Christianity and later, especially in the second century AD, borrowed much of its language and imagery from Christianity. Be that as it may, many groups in the second and third centuries who were Gnostics called themselves Christians.

Gnosticism, a complex phenomenon, was the foremost result of the syncretistic tendencies at work in the Greco-Roman world.[11] It contained a fusion of Greek (e.g. philosophical speculation, emphasis on knowledge, secrecy motifs associated with mystery religions, dualism) and oriental thought (e.g. Zoroastrianism, Judaism, Christianity). Gnosticism also comprised various sects and movements, the most influential being Manicheism.[12] According to the gnostic myth, the creation of the world was one of the unfortunate results of the battle between the forces of Light and Darkness (dualism). Therefore, the material creation is evil. The human being, or more accurately the gnostic, has become entrapped within this conflict. The Father of Light, however, sent a Redeemer to call those belonging to the Light to return to their true home. Through the call they awake from their sleep

---

[10] See Hans Jonas, *The Gnostic Religion: The Message of the Alien God and the Beginnings of Christianity* (Boston: Beacon Press, 1963); and Kurt Rudolph, *Gnosis: The Nature and History of an Ancient Religion* (Edinburgh: T. & T. Clark, 1983).

[11] British scholars have generally preferred a narrow definition of Gnosticism, applying the term to the elaborate second-century religious systems of the several sects of Gnosticism. German scholars, on the other hand, have used the term much more loosely, describing many documents or communities that emphasize *gnosis* as gnostic.

[12] The Manichean canon consisted of several books stemming from Mani himself. These include the *Great Gospel*, the *Treasure of Life*, the *Pragmateia* or *Treatise*, the *Secrets*, the *Book of the Giants*, the *Epistles*, and *Psalms and Prayers*, and the *Kephalaia*.

(ignorance), recognize who they really are, and then proceed to return to the Realm of Light. Salvation in Gnosticism, therefore, consists in the emancipation of the soul from the body and the fallen world that results in the return of the captured light element to its original home in the Realm of Light. The divine messenger who issues this call takes on many forms. For example, it may be Simon Magus, Jesus, or Mani. There were many different varieties and elaborations of this basic Gnostic myth, which can be quite complex, within Gnosticism (e.g. Marcionites, Valentinians, Carpocratians). The common denominator of these movements was the stress on the necessity of a special kind of *gnosis* (knowledge) for salvation.

The Gnostic Gospels, as one would expect, do not emphasize the death and resurrection of Christ, but rather his teaching or revelation, often in secret, to a select group of disciples. The dialogues of these gospels, in addition to articulating the basic gnostic soteriological myth, often reveal a *Sitz im Leben* of in-house theological conflict with respect to the historicity of the cross and resurrection, the identity of the true church, and the nature of knowledge or salvation. The development of Western Christianity was in large measure shaped by the need to deal with the rise of Gnosticism. The "orthodox" church had to identify its authoritative Scripture, which led to the formation of the New Testament canon; it had to implement a structure of church government to control the activities of conflicting religious teachers, which led to the elaborate hierarchical organization of the medieval church; and it had to develop a system of doctrine to refute conflicting theologies, which issued in the theological formulations of the ecumenical councils.

## F. Which are the Other Gospels?

A large number of ancient documents contain the word "gospel" in their title. We may list more than fifty extant documents, apart from the canonical gospels, under this general heading.[13] However, these documents differ

---

[13] It is very difficult to provide a definitive list of all the extant non-canonical gospels as the authenticity (e.g. *Secret Gospel of Mark*) and identification (e.g. various fragments) of a number of texts are in dispute. The list is also expanding with new discoveries (e.g. *Gospel of Judas*). With these difficulties in mind, we may offer the following classification: i. Fragments of Gospels: Papyrus Egerton 2, Papyrus Oxyrhynchus 840, Papyrus Berolinensis 11710, The Fayyum Fragment, The Strasbourg Coptic Papyrus, *The Unknown Berlin Gospel*, *The Secret Gospel of Mark*, *The Gospel of the Hebrews*, *The Gospel of the Nazarenes*, *The Gospel of the Ebionites*; various Agrapha; ii. Infancy Gospels: *The Protevangelium of James*; *The Infancy Gospel of Thomas*; *The Gospel of Pseudo-Matthew*; *The Arabic Infancy Gospel*; Arundel 404; *The History of Joseph the Carpenter*; iii. Passion Gospels: *The Gospel of Peter*; *The Gospel of Nicodemus (Acts of Pilate)*; *The Gospel of Bartholomew*; *The Gospel of Gamaliel*; iv. Sayings and Extended Dialogues: *The Gospel of Thomas*; *"John's Preaching of the Gospel,"* *(The Acts of John 87–105)*; *The Gospel of Philip*; *The Gospel of Truth*; *The Greek Gospel of the Egyptians*; *The Gospel of the Egyptians (Nag Hammadi)*; Papyrus Oxyrhynchus 1081; *The Sophia of Jesus Christ*; *The Gospel of Mary*; *The Apocryphon of John*; *The Epistle of the Apostles (Epistula Apostolorum)*; *The Book of Thomas*; *The Dialogue of the Savior*; *The Abgar Correspondence; The Preaching of Peter (Kerygma Petrou)*; *The Gospel of James*; *The Gospel of the Nativity of Mary*; *The Gospel of Mary (Magdalene)*; *The Apocryphon of James*; *The Gospel of the Lord (by*

widely in terms of style, design, contents, and scope. In other words, when we discuss the non-canonical gospels we inevitably come up against the problem of genre. How are we to define a "gospel"? This is a historical as well as a literary and theological question. Our understanding of what a gospel is has by and large been determined by the use of this term as a title attached to the four tractates on Jesus in the New Testament. However, in the New Testament itself, the term "gospel" (*euaggelion*) is nowhere used to designate a literary document.[14] Rather, the title "gospel" was attached to the four evangelists' works sometime in the second century AD and has subsequently been used to classify these accounts about Jesus and more recently their literary style.

Scholars have made a distinction between different types of gospels according to their content. There are sayings gospels, like the so-called Q used by Matthew and Luke; miracle gospels, like the signs source used by the Gospel of John; infancy gospels, which highlight the birth and childhood of Jesus; and passion gospels, like the *Gospel of Peter*, which contains only a passion and resurrection narrative. However, questions remain. According to most scholars Q did not contain a passion narrative. Can it then still be considered a "gospel," or is it simply a collection of Jesus' teachings? Also, should a "gospel" be defined solely in terms of its content or does literary genre come into play as well? These are questions that we cannot address here. Suffice it to say that we have incorporated a wide range of materials under the category of non-canonical gospels. We have included examples of documents relating aspects of the life and teachings of Jesus, with emphasis on the former. The sample here is by no means comprehensive, but serves as a brief overview in order to illustrate the basic types of non-canonical gospels. Our choices were governed by the antiquity of the texts and their significance for the study of the New Testament. We have classified the material under three headings: Jewish Gospels, Gentile Gospels, and Gnostic Gospels, but with the awareness that these categories often overlap. We have indicated the most probable date for the composition of the document at the beginning of each section.

## G. Jewish Gospels

The following Jewish-Christian Gospels, except for *The Protevangelium of James*, all demonstrate a gospel-narrative framework. Several patristic writers referred to these gospels (Clement of Alexandria, Origen, Eusebius, Epiphanius, and Jerome) and quoted a few short segments from them. From these segments it is highly likely that these gospels would have looked very similar to the Synoptic Gospels in content and length. However, interestingly, many of the quotations have a Johannine flavor, leading us to conclude that these distinct traditions must have crossed paths at a very early date.

---

*Marcion); The Gospel of Judas.* In addition to this list, the church fathers and early councils refer to numerous other non-canonical gospels that are not extant today.

[14]Although Mark 1:1 uses the term "gospel" (*euaggelion*) to introduce the story about Jesus, the term was not used to refer to a literary genre at the time.

However, the identification of these gospels is precarious. There often appears to be confusion between the titles of these gospels in the Fathers. Therefore, we cannot be totally sure that all quotations have been correctly identified.

## 1. The Gospel of the Hebrews (c. AD 100–150)

Of great interest among these Jewish-Christian Gospels is *The Gospel of the Hebrews*. The title appears to have been a general designation for several Jewish Gospels. It is sometimes confused with the *Gospel of the Nazarenes*, the *Gospel of the Ebionites*, and even with the Gospel of Matthew. It was probably written in Aramaic. Unfortunately, however, no Aramaic text is extant. Eusebius regarded it positively, although he did not deem it canonical, and mentions that it was the only gospel accepted by the Ebionites (*Hist. eccl.* 3.25, 27, 39; 4.22). Epiphanius informs us that it did not contain a genealogy of Jesus or a birth narrative (*Haer.* 30.14.3). Though there is some measure of debate, at least seven fragments of the *Gospel of the Hebrews* have been preserved. Below are two quotations found in the writings of Jerome. Both reveal a Jewish outlook.

> The Gospel also entitled "according to the Hebrews" which I lately translated into Greek and Latin, and which Origen often quotes, contains the following narrative after the Resurrection: "Now the Lord, when he had given the cloth to the servant of the priest, went to James and appeared to him." For James had taken an oath that he would not eat bread from that hour on which he had drunk the cup of the Lord till he saw him risen from the dead. Again a little later the Lord said, "Bring a table and bread", and forthwith it is added: "He took bread and blessed and broke it and gave it to James the Just and said to him, 'My brother, eat your bread, for the Son of man is risen from those who sleep.'"
> (Jerome, *Vir. ill.* 2; trans. James K. Elliott, *The Apocryphal New Testament: A Collection of Apocryphal Christian Literature in an English Translation* [New York: Oxford University Press, 1993], pp. 9-10).

> But in the Gospel which is written in Hebrew and which the Nazarenes read, "the whole fountain of the Holy Spirit shall descend upon him." And the Lord is spirit, and where the Spirit of the Lord is, there is liberty. And in the Gospel referred to above I find this written: "And it came to pass, as the Lord came up out of the water, the whole fountain of the Holy Spirit descended upon him and rested on him and said to him, 'My Son, in all the prophets I expected that you might come and that I might rest upon you. You are my rest, you are my firstborn Son, who reigns in eternity.'"
> (Jerome, *Comm. Isa.* 11.2; trans. Elliott, *The Apocryphal New Testament*, p. 10).

## 2. The Gospel of the Nazarenes (c. AD 150)

*The Gospel of the Nazarenes*, again probably written in Aramaic, appears to be a version of the Gospel of Matthew that has undergone a few redactional changes.[15] It is referred to by Clement of Alexandria, Hegesippus, Origen, Epiphanius, and Jerome. The Nazarenes, as indicated above, were a group of Jewish Christians in Western Syria. The following quotations are from Jerome. There is nothing unorthodox in these quotations.

> In the Gospel that the Nazarenes and the Ebionites use, which I recently translated from the Hebrew into Greek, and which most people designate as the authentic text of Matthew, we read that the man with the withered hand was a mason, who asked for help with these words: "I was a mason, working for my bread with my hands. I pray to you, Jesus, restore me to health so that I do not eat my bread in disgrace."
> (Jerome, *Comm. Matt.* 12.13; trans. Elliott, *The Apocryphal New Testament*, p. 12).

> In the Gospel of the Hebrews which is written in the Syro-Chaldaic tongue but in Hebrew characters, which the Nazarenes make use of at this day, and which is also called the "Gospel of the Apostles," or as many think, "that of Matthew," and which is in the library of Caesarea, the following narrative is given: "Behold, the mother of the Lord and his brothers said to him, 'John the Baptist baptizes for the remission of sins; let us go and be baptized by him.' But he said, 'What have I committed, that I should be baptized of him, unless it be that in saying this I am in ignorance?'" In the same volume [i.e. in the *Gospel of the Hebrews*] we read, "If your brother has sinned in word against you and has made satisfaction, forgive him up to seven times a day." Simon, his disciple, said to him, "seven times?" The Lord answered saying, "Verily I say to you: until seventy times seven! For even in the prophets the word of sin is found after they have been anointed with the Holy Spirit."
> (Jerome, *Dialogi contra Pelagianos* 3.2; trans. Elliott, *The Apocryphal New Testament,* p. 13).

## 3. The Gospel of the Ebionites (c. AD 100–150)

A few segments of the *Gospel of the Ebionites* are preserved in the works of Epiphanius, and possibly also in Origen, Ambrose, and Jerome. Epiphanius does not use any title to refer to the Gospel but simply says that it was the gospel used by the Ebionites. Again, like the *Gospel of the Nazarenes*, it

---

[15] The term Nazarene is probably derived from the designation of Jesus as a "Nazorean" (Matt. 2:23), which may refer either to his hometown of Nazareth or to the Hebrew term meaning "consecrated." The early followers of Jesus were called Nazarenes (Acts 24:5), but later the term was applied to a sect of Jewish Christians. Although the term does not appear in the source material, scholars refer to the gospel this sect used as the *Gospel of the Nazarenes* [or sometimes *Gospel of the Nazaraeans*]. See H.-J. Klauck, *Apocryphal Gospels: An Introduction* (London/New York: T. & T. Clark, 2003), p. 43.

appears to have been a version of the Gospel of Matthew. Some scholars have suggested that the text is a harmony of the Synoptic Gospels. Jerome confused it with the *Gospel of the Hebrews*. The theology of the Ebionites is clearly reflected in the text. There is no birth narrative (according to Epiphanius), Jesus is a vegetarian, and there is a denunciation of the temple sacrifices.

> They say that he is not begotten by God the Father but created like one of the archangels, being greater than they. He rules over the angels and the beings created by God and he came and declared, as the gospel used by them records: "I have come to abolish the sacrifices: if you do not cease from sacrificing, the wrath [of God] will not cease from weighing upon you."
> (Epiphanius, *Haer.* 30.16; trans. Elliott, *The Apocryphal New Testament*, p. 15).

> Those who reject meat have inconsiderately fallen into error and said, "I have no desire to eat the flesh of this Paschal Lamb with you." They leave the true order of words and distort the word which is clear to all from the connection of the words and make the disciples say: "Where do you want us to prepare for you to eat the Passover?" To which he replied, "I have no desire to eat the flesh of this Paschal Lamb with you."
> (Epiphanius, *Haer.* 30.22; trans. Elliott, *The Apocryphal New Testament*, pp. 15-16).

## 4. The Protevangelium of James (c. AD 150)

*The Protevangelium of James*, also called the *Infancy Narrative Gospel of James*, focuses on the births of Mary and Jesus. The fact that it is preserved in over 140 manuscripts shows that it was very popular during the Middle Ages.[16] However, it is certainly much older because Origen refers to it. It is a composite of the birth narratives of Matthew and Luke, the Old Testament, and extracanonical traditions. The following excerpt explains how Mary and Joseph were vindicated after the discovery of Mary's pregnancy.

> 15. 1. And Annas the scribe came to him and said to him, "Joseph, why have you not appeared in our assembly?" And Joseph said to him, "Because I was weary from the journey and I rested the first day." And Annas turned and saw that Mary was pregnant. 2. And he went running to the priest and said to him, "Joseph, for whom you are a witness, has grievously transgressed." And the high priest said, "In what way?" And he said, "The virgin, whom he received from the temple of the Lord, he has defiled, and has secretly consummated his marriage with her, and has not disclosed it to the children of Israel." And the priest said to him, "Has Joseph done this?" And Annas said to him, "Send officers, and you will find the virgin pregnant." And the officers went and found as he had said, and brought her and Joseph to the court. And the priest said, "Mary, why have you done this? Why have you humiliated your soul

---

[16] They all date from the tenth century.

and forgotten the Lord your God, you who were brought up in the Holy of Holies and received food from the hand of an angel, and heard hymns, and danced before him? Why have you done this?" But she wept bitterly saying, "As the Lord my God lives, I am pure before him and I know not a man." And the priest said to Joseph, "Why have you done this?" And Joseph said, "As the Lord my God lives, I am pure concerning her." And the priest said, "Do not give false witness, but speak the truth. You have consummated your marriage in secret, and have not disclosed it to the children of Israel, and have not bowed your head under the mighty hand in order that your seed might be blessed." And Joseph was silent.

16. 1. And the priest said, "Give back the virgin whom you have received from the temple of the Lord." And Joseph began to weep. And the priest said, "I will give you both to drink of the water of the conviction[17] of the Lord, and it will make your sins manifest in your eyes." 2. And the priest took it and gave it to Joseph to drink and sent him into the hill-country, and he returned whole. And he made Mary drink also, and sent her into the hill-country, and she returned whole. And all the people marveled, because sin did not appear in them. And the priest said, "If the Lord God has not revealed your sins, neither do I judge you." And he released them. And Joseph took Mary and departed to his house, rejoicing and glorifying the God of Israel.
(*Protevangelium of James*; trans. Elliott, *The Apocryphal New Testament*, pp. 62-63).

## H. Gentile Gospels

The Gentile Gospels have much more in common with the canonical gospels. Their primary concern is to portray Jesus as the divine Son of God bringing healing and salvation to the world. They often attempt to provide further details of Jesus' life and ministry. The main purpose of these extrapolations is to encourage faith in Jesus' divine power. At times one can also detect a polemic against Jewish practices, showing that they were written during a time when Christianity was still closely associated with its Jewish heritage. It appears that these gospels were more concerned to deal with pressure from Judaism than with the challenge of Gnosticism.

### 1. Papyrus Oxyrhynchus 840 (c. AD 100–150)

Oxyrhynchus is one of the most significant archaeological sites in Egypt. Over the last century, thousands of papyrus texts have been excavated at the site. Papyrus Oxyrhynchus 840 is one of these texts. It is also known as a "Fragment of an Uncanonical Gospel." The manuscript itself dates from the fourth century, but the text was probably composed in the first half of the second century. It contains two stories that are not found in the New Testament Gospels. The major part of the extant text contains a controversy

---

[17] Cf. Num. 5:11-37.

story, containing a veiled polemic against Judaism (cf. Mark 7:1-23).

> ... before he does wrong he makes all kinds of ingenious excuses. "But take care lest you also suffer the same things as they did, for those who do evil not only receive their chastisement from men but they await punishment and great torment." Then he took them with him and brought them into the place of purification itself, and was walking in the temple. A Pharisee, a chief priest named Levi, met them and said to the Savior, "Who gave you permission to walk in this place of purification and look upon these holy vessels when you have not bathed and your disciples have not washed their feet? But you have walked in this temple in a state of defilement, whereas no one else comes in or dares to view these holy vessels without having bathed and changed his clothes." Thereupon the Savior stood with his disciples and answered him. "Are you then clean, here in the temple as you are?" He said, "I am clean, for I have bathed in the pool of David and have gone down by one staircase and come up by the other, and I have put on clean white clothes. Then I came and viewed the holy vessels." "Alas," said the Savior, "you blind men who cannot see! You have washed in this running water, in which dogs and pigs have wallowed night and day, and you have washed and scrubbed your outer skin, which harlots and flute-girls also anoint and wash and scrub, beautifying themselves for the lusts of men while inwardly they are filled with scorpions and unrighteousness of every kind. But my disciples and I, whom you charge with not having bathed, have bathed ourselves in the living water which comes down from heaven. But woe to those who. . ."

(trans. Elliott, *The Apocryphal New Testament*, pp. 33-34).

## 2. Papyrus Egerton 2 (c. AD 100)

Papyrus Egerton 2, sometimes also referred to as the "Egerton Gospel," consists of three papyrus leaves from a Greek codex that dates to c. AD 200.[18] It was discovered in Egypt and first published in 1935. It is the earliest text from a non-canonical gospel. The fragments contain two controversy and two miracle stories. One of the miracle stories is unknown from any other source and provides evidence for the existence of larger collections of miracle stories (oral traditions). Its relationship with the canonical gospels is disputed. We include two stories here.

Fragment 1 Verso

[And Jesus said] to the lawyers: "[Punish] every wrongdoer and transgressor, and not me. . . what he does, as he does it." Then, turning to the rulers of the people, he spoke this word, "Search the scriptures, in which you think you have life; it is they which bear witness to me. Do not think that I have come to accuse you to my Father; your accuser is Moses, on whom you have set your hope." When they said, "We know well that God spoke to Moses; but as

---

[18] See Klauck, *Apocryphal Gospels*, p. 23.

for you, we do not know where you come from." Jesus said in reply, "Now your unbelief is exposed to the one who was witnessed to by him. If you had believed [in Moses] you would have believed me, because he wrote to your fathers about me . . ."

Fragment 2 Verso

. . . enclosed in its place, . . . placed below invisibly, . . . its weight immeasurable. . . And when they were perplexed at his strange question, Jesus, as he walked, stood on the bank of the Jordan and, stretching out his right hand, filled it [with seed] . . . and sowed on the river. Then . . . the water which had been sown [with seed] . . . in their presence and it produced much fruit . . . to their joy. . .
(trans. Elliott, *The Apocryphal New Testament*, pp. 39-40).

## 3. The Gospel of Peter (c. AD 80–150)

*The Gospel of Peter* is a passion and resurrection narrative that relates how the Jews were responsible for Jesus' crucifixion and how they tried to conceal their guilt even after they recognized their mistake. Its relationship with the canonical gospels is debated. Although it may contain some independent traditions, many scholars consider that it drew on materials within the canonical gospels and place it sometime in the second century.[19] Others, however, argue that it dates from the second half of the first century and provides evidence of an independent passion narrative tradition.[20] It is the only gospel that describes the resurrection itself.

8. 28. But the scribes and Pharisees and elders, being assembled and hearing that the people were murmuring and beating their breasts, said, "If at his death these exceeding great signs happened, behold how righteous he was!" 29. They were afraid and came to Pilate, entreating him and saying, 30. "Give us soldiers that we may guard his sepulcher for three days, lest his disciples come and steal him away and the people suppose that he is risen from the dead, and do us harm." 31. And Pilate gave them Petronius the centurion with soldiers to guard the sepulcher. And with them there came elders and scribes to the sepulcher, and all who were there together rolled a large stone 32. and laid it against the door to the sepulcher to exclude the centurion and the soldiers, and they 33. put on it seven seals, pitched a tent there and kept watch.

---

[19] According to the account of Serapion preserved in Eusebius, Christians at Rhossus (in Syria) used the Gospel in the second half of the second century (*Hist. eccl.* 6.12).

[20] Crossan, Koester and Cameron consider the *Gospel of Peter* to be independent of the canonical gospels. Others, like Raymond Brown, argue that the Gospel is dependent on the canonical gospels. For Crossan's argument, see *The Cross that Spoke: The Origins of the Passion Narrative* (San Francisco: Harper & Row, 1988), pp. 16-30. For Raymond Brown's counter-argument, see *The Death of the Messiah*, Volume 2 (New York: Doubleday, 1994), 1,317-49.

9. 34. Early in the morning, when the Sabbath dawned, there came a crowd from Jerusalem and the country round about to see the sealed sepulcher. 35. Now in the night in which the Lord's day dawned, when the soldiers were keeping guard, two by two in each watch, there was a loud voice in heaven, 36. and they saw the heavens open and two men come down from there in a great brightness and draw near to the sepulcher. 37. That stone which had been laid against the entrance to the sepulcher started of itself to roll and move sidewards, and the sepulcher was opened and both young men entered. 10. 38. When those soldiers saw this, they awakened the centurion and the elders, for they also were there to mount guard. 39. And while they were narrating what they had seen, they saw three men come out from the sepulcher, two of them supporting the other and a cross following them 40. and the heads of the two reaching to heaven, but that of him who was being led reached beyond the heavens. 41. And they heard a voice out of the heavens crying, "Have you preached to those who sleep?," 42. and from the cross there was heard the answer, "Yes."
(trans. Elliott, *The Apocryphal New Testament*, pp. 156-57).

## 4. The Infancy Gospel of Thomas (c. AD 150–200)

The *Infancy Gospel of Thomas* is part of a popular tradition of miracle stories supposedly performed by Jesus during his childhood.[21] Several factors contributed to the development of these fantastic stories: the hunger to satisfy curiosity concerning Jesus' childhood, to encourage the faithful and to warn the impious, and possibly just to provide entertainment. However, the modern reader may not find the stories edifying. Jesus is not just a *Wunderkind* but much more the *enfant terrible*. These kinds of stories became very popular during the Middle Ages, inspired religious art, and one story even found its way into the Qur'an.[22] The attribution of the Gospel to Thomas suggests a Syriac provenance. The original language could have been either Syriac or Greek.

1. I, Thomas the Israelite, announce and make known to you all, brothers from among the Gentiles, the mighty childhood deeds of our Lord Jesus Christ, which he did when he was born in our land. The beginning is as follows.

2. 1. When this boy Jesus was five years old he was playing at the crossing of a stream, and he gathered together into pools the running water, and instantly made it clean, and gave his command with a single word. 2. Having made soft clay he molded from it twelve sparrows. And it was the sabbath when he did these things. And there were also many other children playing with him. 3. When a certain Jew saw what Jesus was doing while playing on the sabbath, he at once went and told his father Joseph, "See, your child is at the

---

[21] The Greek manuscripts date from the thirteenth century. There is an abbreviated Syriac manuscript dating from the sixth century, and a Latin manuscript dating from the fifth century.

[22] The story about Jesus modeling birds is found in the Qur'an 3.49.

223

stream, and he took clay and molded twelve birds and has profaned the sabbath." 4. And when Joseph came to the place and looked, he cried out to him, saying, "Why do you do on the sabbath things which it is not lawful to do?" But Jesus clapped his hands and cried out to the sparrows and said to them, "Be gone!" And the sparrows took flight and went away chirping. 5. The Jews were amazed when they saw this, and went away and told their leaders what they had seen Jesus do.

3. 1. Now the son of Annas the scribe was standing there with Joseph; and he took a branch of a willow and with it dispersed the water which Jesus had collected. 2. When Jesus saw what he had done he was angry and said to him, "You insolent, godless ignoramus, what harm did the pools and the water do to you? Behold, now you also shall wither like a tree and shall bear neither leaves nor root nor fruit." 3. And immediately that child withered up completely; and Jesus departed and went into Joseph's house. But the parents of the boy who was withered carried him away, bemoaning his lost youth, and brought him to Joseph and reproached him. "What kind of child do you have, who does such things?"
(trans. Elliott, *The Apocryphal New Testament*, pp. 75-76).

## I. Gnostic Gospels

The Nag Hammadi Library, discovered in the sands of Egypt in 1945, is our greatest and most important collection of gnostic gospels. The library was hidden sometime during the fourth century. It contains thirteen codices incorporating fifty-two separate tractates, most relating to Gnosticism. The substance of the gnostic gospels is very different from the other gospels. In the main they contain philosophical discussions about the nature of existence and about cosmology, enlightenment, and self-knowledge. The transparency of the gnostic myth varies from document to document. It is also clear that the communities, which produced the texts, felt themselves to be in the minority and under pressure from the "orthodox" church. Their method of defense was not to appeal to apostolic tradition but rather to refer to new revelation, often secret and exclusive, that the community had received.

## 1. The Gospel of Thomas (c. AD 80–150)

Perhaps the most well known of all the non-canonical gospels is the Coptic *Gospel of Thomas*. The *Gospel of Thomas* is fully preserved in the Nag Hammadi Library. A few Greek fragments, which date from c. AD 200, have also been unearthed. It is a sayings gospel, containing 114 logia of Jesus, and has been associated with the hypothetical Q. Many scholars regard the *Gospel of Thomas* as a translation of the Greek text, which originated in the first century AD, most probably in Syria. The majority of scholars however prefer a second-century dating for the Gospel in its final form.[23] Although the

---

[23] Klauck, *Apocryphal Gospels*, pp. 107-22.

Gospel contains very early non-gnostic traditions, which are also independent of the Synoptic Gospels, its general tendency is gnostic.[24]

> These are the secret sayings which the living Jesus spoke and which Didymos Judas Thomas wrote down.

> (1) And he said, "Whoever finds the interpretation of these sayings will not experience death."

> (3) Jesus said, "If those who lead you say to you, 'See, the kingdom is in the sky,' then the birds of the sky will precede you. If they say to you, 'It is in the sea,' then the fish will precede you. Rather, the kingdom is inside of you, and it is outside of you. When you come to know yourselves, then you will become known, and you will realize that it is you who are the sons of the living father. But if you will not know yourselves, you dwell in poverty and it is you who are that poverty."

> (8) And he said, "The man is like a wise fisherman who cast his net into the sea and drew it up from the sea full of small fish. Among them the wise fisherman found a fine large fish. He threw all the small fish back into the sea and chose the large fish without difficulty. Whoever has ears to hear, let him hear."

> (9) Jesus said, "Now the sower went out, took a handful (of seeds), and scattered them. Some fell on the road; the birds came and gathered them up. Others fell on the rock, did not take root in the soil, and did not produce ears. And others fell on thorns; they choked the seed(s) and worms ate them. And others fell on the good soil and it produced good fruit: it bore sixty per measure and a hundred and twenty per measure."

> (13) Jesus said to his disciples, "Compare me to someone and tell me whom I am like." Simon Peter said to him, "You are like a righteous angel." Matthew said to him, "You are like a wise philosopher." Thomas said to him, "Master, my mouth is wholly incapable of saying whom you are like." Jesus said, "I am not your master. Because you have drunk, you have become intoxicated from the bubbling spring which I have measured out." And he took him and withdrew and told him three things. When Thomas returned to his companions, they asked him, "What did Jesus say to you?" Thomas said to them, "If I tell you one of the things which he told me, you will pick up stones and throw them at me; a fire will come out of the stones and burn you up."

> (55) Jesus said, "Whoever does not hate his father and his mother cannot become a disciple to me. And whoever does not hate his brothers and sisters and take up his cross in my way will not be worthy of me."

---

[24] About half of the sayings (logia) in the Gospel have no parallels in the New Testament. Again, about half of the sayings are non-gnostic whereas the other half are gnostic.

(56) Jesus said, "Whoever has come to understand the world has found (only) a corpse, and whoever has found a corpse is superior to the world."

(63) Jesus said, "There was a rich man who had much money. He said, 'I shall put my money to use so that I may sow, reap, plant, and fill my storehouse with produce, with the result that I shall lack nothing.' Such were his intentions, but that same night he died. Let him who has ears hear."

(82) Jesus said, "He who is near me is near the fire, and he who is far from me is far from the kingdom."

(107) Jesus said, "The kingdom is like a shepherd who had a hundred sheep. One of them, the largest, went astray. He left the ninety-nine sheep and looked for that one until he found it. When he had gone to such trouble, he said to the sheep, 'I care for you more than the ninety-nine.'"

(108) Jesus said, "He who will drink from my mouth will become like me. I myself shall become he, and the things that are hidden will be revealed to him."

(114) Simon Peter said to him, "Let Mary leave us, for women are not worthy of life." Jesus said, "I myself shall lead her in order to make her male, so that she too may become a living spirit resembling you males. For every woman who will make herself male will enter the kingdom of heaven."
(trans. Thomas O. Lambdin, in James M. Robinson, ed., *The Nag Hammadi Library in English*. 3rd revised ed. [San Francisco: Harper & Row, 1990], pp. 126-38).

## 2. The Sophia of Jesus Christ (c. AD 150)

*The Sophia of Jesus Christ* is a gnostic work that is based on the tractate the *Epistle of Eugnostos*. *Eugnostos* is a first-century document that provides important evidence for a non-Christian Gnosticism. The main text of the *Sophia* is the Coptic text found in the Nag Hammadi codices. A few Greek fragments of the text have been found dating from the third century. In the following extract Jesus begins to reveal to his disciples the underlying reality of the universe and the futility of previous efforts to seek God.

The Sophia (Wisdom) of Jesus Christ.
After he rose from the dead, his twelve disciples and seven women continued to be his followers, and went to Galilee onto the mountain called "Divination and Joy." When they gathered together and were perplexed about the underlying reality of the universe and the plan, and the holy providence, and the power of the authorities, and about everything the Savior is doing with them in the secret of the holy plan, the Savior appeared—not in his previous form, but in the invisible spirit. And his likeness resembles a great angel of light. But his resemblance I must not describe. No mortal flesh could endure

it, but only pure, perfect flesh, like that which he taught us about on the mountain called "Of the Olives" in Galilee. And he said: "Peace be to you, My peace I give you!" And they all marveled and were afraid.

The Savior laughed and said to them: "What are you thinking about? Are you perplexed? What are you searching for?" Philip said: "For the underlying reality of the universe and the plan."

The Savior said to them: "I want you to know that all men are born on earth from the foundation of the world until now, being dust, while they have inquired about God, who he is and what he is like, have not found him. Now the wisest among them have speculated from the ordering of the world and (its) movement. But their speculation has not reached the truth. For it is said that the ordering is directed in three ways, by all the philosophers, (and) hence they do not agree. For some of them say about the world that it is directed by itself. Others, that it is providence (that directs it). Others, that it is fate. But it is none of these. Again, of the three voices I have just mentioned, none is close to the truth, and (they are) from man. But I, who came from Infinite Light, I am here—for I know him (Light)—that I might speak to you about the precise nature of the truth. For whatever is from itself is a polluted life; it is self-made. Providence has no wisdom in it. And fate does not discern.

But to you it is given to know; and whoever is worthy of knowledge will receive (it), whoever has not been begotten by the sowing of unclean rubbing but by First Who Was Sent, for he is an immortal in the midst of mortal men."

(trans. Douglas M. Parrott, in Robinson, ed., *The Nag Hammadi Library in English*, pp. 222-24).

### 3. Apocryphon of James (c. AD 100–150)

*The Apocryphon of James*, also from the Nag Hammadi Library and sometimes referred to as the *Secret Book of James*, is cast in the frame of a letter that relates a dialogue between Jesus and two of his disciples, Peter and James, after the resurrection.[25] It contains a diverse range of literary material, including sayings, prophecies, parables, and rules for the community. Although there are gnostic influences, the content bears closer relationship with the New Testament Gospels than second-century Valentinianism or the *Gospel of Philip*. Interestingly, the text also contains some Johannine traditions, which appear to be more primitive than the Gospel of John. The document is not dependent on either the synoptic or Johannine tradition. In other words, the *Apocryphon of James* provides evidence of a very early convergence between synoptic and Johannine traditions. The prominence of James and Peter pushes the dating of the text to the first half of the second century as other disciples subsequently become more prominent in gnostic circles.

---

[25] The text is contained in the first of the thirteen codices of the Nag Hammadi library, also known as the Jung Codex.

. . . the twelve disciples were all sitting together and recalling what the Savior had said to each one of them, whether in secret or openly, and putting it in books— [But I] was writing that which was in [my book]—lo, the Savior appeared, after departing from us while we gazed after him. And five hundred and fifty days since he had risen from the dead, we said to him, "Have you departed and removed yourself from us?"

But Jesus said, "No, but I shall go to the place from whence I came. If you wish to come with me, come!" They all answered and said, "If you bid us, we come."

He said, "Verily I say unto you, no one will ever enter the kingdom of heaven at my bidding, but (only) because you yourselves are full. Leave James and Peter to me, that I may fill them." And having called these two, he drew them aside and bade the rest occupy themselves with that which they were about.

The Savior said, "You have received mercy. . . Do you not, then, desire to be filled? And your heart is drunken; do you not, then, desire to be sober? Therefore, be ashamed! Henceforth, waking or sleeping, remember that you have seen the Son of Man, and spoken with him in person, and listened to him in person. Woe to those who have seen the Son of Man; blessed will they be who have not seen the man, and they who have not consorted with him, and they who have not spoken with him, and they who have not listened to anything from him; yours is life! Know, then, that he healed you when you were ill, that you might reign. Woe to those who have found relief from their illness, for they will relapse into illness. Blessed are they who have not been ill, and have known relief before falling ill; yours is the kingdom of God. Therefore, I say to you, 'Become full, and leave no space within you empty, for he who is coming can mock you.'"

(trans. Francis E. Williams, in Robinson, ed., *The Nag Hammadi Library in English*, pp. 30-31).

## 4. *John's Preaching of the Gospel, The Acts of John 87–105 (c. AD 150–200)*

*John's Preaching of the Gospel* stems from the second century and is part of the *Acts of John* (87–105), one of the earliest apocryphal Acts. It is a composite document containing a diverse range of materials, but mainly miracle stories. Due to the heightened gnostic tenor of *John's Preaching*, most scholars think that this section is a later addition into the *Acts*. Only a few fragmentary texts survive. The following excerpts show that Jesus was not really human and that he did not suffer.

93. "Another glory I will tell you, brethren. Sometimes when I meant to touch him, I met a material and solid body; and at other times again when I felt him, the substance was immaterial and bodiless and as if it were not existing at all. Now, if at any time he were invited by one of the Pharisees and went where he was invited, we went with him. And there was set before each one of us a

loaf of bread by our host, and he also received a loaf. And he would bless his own and divide it amongst us; and from that little piece each of us was filled, and our own loaves were saved intact, so that those who had invited him were amazed. And often when I was walking with him I wished to see whether the print of his foot appeared upon the earth—for I saw him raising himself from the earth—but I never saw it. Now, these things, dear brethren, I speak to you to encourage you in your faith towards him, for we must at the present keep silent about his mighty and wonderful works, inasmuch as they are mysteries and doubtless cannot be uttered or heard."

101. "Therefore I have suffered none of the things which they will say of me: that suffering which I showed to you and to the rest in dance, I wish it to be called a mystery. For what you are, you see that I showed you; but what I am, that I alone know, and no one else. Let me, therefore, keep that which is my own, and that which is yours you must see through me. As for seeing me I am in reality, I have told you this is impossible unless you are able to see me as my kinsman. You hear that I suffered, yet I suffered not; that I suffered not, yet I did suffer; that I was pierced, yet was I not wounded; hanged, and I was not hanged; that blood flowed from me, yet it did not flow; and, in a word, those things that they say of me I did not endure, and the things that they do not say those I suffered. Now what they are I will reveal to you for I know you will understand. Perceive in me the slaying of the Logos, the piercing of the Logos, the blood of the Logos, the wounding of the Logos, the hanging of the Logos, the passion of the Logos, the nailing of the Logos, the death of the Logos. And thus I speak, discarding manhood. Therefore, in the first place think of the Logos, then you shall perceive the Lord, and thirdly the man, and what he has suffered."
(trans. Elliott, *The Apocryphal New Testament*, pp. 318, 320-2).

## J. Conclusion

To conclude we may offer some observations by way of final evaluation. With respect to the study of the New Testament, the non-canonical gospels are not significant, except in a few instances, as sources for the reconstruction of the history described by the New Testament. By and large, apart from perhaps the *Gospel of Thomas*, the non-canonical gospels postdate the New Testament by many decades and are not greatly concerned about historical events. Recent calls for a reconstruction of the history of Jesus on the basis of the non-canonical gospels are not historically justifiable.[26] Rather, the non-canonical gospels are significant for students of the New Testament primarily in terms

---

[26] For example, the claims that the *Gospel of Mary*, a view promoted by Dan Brown's *The Da Vinci Code* (2003), and the recently discovered *Gospel of Judas* require a radical revision of our understanding of Jesus' life and death are historically uninformed. See James M. Robinson, *The Secrets of Judas: The Story of the Misunderstood Disciple and His Lost Gospel* (New York: HarperSanFrancisco, 2006), and compare Stanley E. Porter and Gordon L. Heath, *The Lost Gospel of Judas: Separating Fact from Fiction* (Grand Rapids: Eerdmans, 2007), and Bart D. Ehrman, *The Lost Gospel of Judas Iscariot* (New York: Oxford University Press, 2006).

of the questions they raise for New Testament theology. Although they reflect the world of the nascent Christian church, the questions they contain are still being raised today. Part of the early church's answer to those questions was the formation of the New Testament. Authentic Christianity does not consist in law or ritual, esoteric knowledge, the presence of the miraculous, or belonging to an established church. Rather authentic Christianity, or New Testament Christianity, is found in relationship with the historical Jesus who was crucified but then raised from the dead.

## Bibliography

Cameron, Ron. *The Other Gospels: Non-Canonical Gospel Texts*. Philadelphia: Westminster, 1982.

Charlesworth, James H. *The New Testament Apocrypha and Pseudepigrapha: A Guide to Publications, with Excursuses on Apocalypses*. Metuchen: Scarecrow Press, 1987.

Ehrman, Bart D. *Lost Scriptures: Books that Did Not Make It into the New Testament*. New York: Oxford University Press, 2003.

Elliott, James K. *The Apocryphal New Testament: A Collection of Apocryphal Christian Literature in an English Translation*. New York: Oxford University Press, 1993.

Evans, Craig. A. *Noncanonical Writings and New Testament Interpretation*. Peabody: Hendrickson, 1992.

James, Montague R. *The Apocryphal New Testament: Being the Apocryphal Gospels, Acts, Epistles, and Apocalypses with other Narratives and Fragments*. Oxford: Clarendon Press, 1924.

Klauck, Hans-Josef. *Apocryphal Gospels: An Introduction*, trans. Brian McNeil. London/New York: T. & T. Clark, 2003.

Koester, Helmut. *Ancient Christian Gospels: Their History and Development*. Philadelphia: Trinity Press International, 1990.

Pagels, Elaine, *The Gnostic Gospels*. New York: Random House, 1979.

Robinson, James M., ed. *The Nag Hammadi Library in English*. 3rd rev. ed. San Francisco: Harper & Row, 1990.

Schneemelcher, Wilhelm, ed. *New Testament Apocrypha. Volume One: Gospels and Related Writings*, English translation edited by R. McL. Wilson. Philadelphia: Westminster/John Knox Press, 1991.

# 10. The Historical Jesus

*Chris Forbes*

## A. The Question

What do historians mean when they talk about "the historical Jesus"? Versions of Jesus abound, each with its own emphasis. There is the Jesus of the gospels, whether the plain and forceful figure of Mark's Gospel or the majestic "word incarnate" of John. There is the Jesus of the great third and fourth century creeds of the churches, the unique "Son of God" and second person of the Trinity. There is the towering, distant heavenly figure of Byzantine and Medieval art, the far more approachable human figure of renaissance art and sculpture, and there is the "gentle Jesus, meek and mild" of the Victorian era. Our own age has various pop-culture versions of Jesus, whether they are the Christ-child of the Christmas story, the "superstar" of the 1971 musical, or the enigmatic figure alongside Mary Magdalene in the "Da Vinci Code."

All of these presentations take their starting point, in one way or another, from the Jesus of the gospels, the only Jesus to whom we have direct access. Many of them build on their predecessors, for we are separated from the Jesus of the gospels not only by nearly two thousand years, but also by multiple, often overlapping layers of interpretation.

The study of the "historical Jesus" attempts to see behind these layers of developing interpretation. Jesus himself lived and worked in Galilee and Judea in the first third of the first century AD. To understand the "historical Jesus" we attempt to situate him firmly in what can be known about early first century Galilee and Judea. We ask how he would have been perceived and understood by his first followers (and first opponents!), who, like him, were mostly Galilean Jews.

## B. The Problem

The gospels, the only substantial source of information we have about Jesus, were written between twenty-five and sixty years after Jesus' public career. During the years between Jesus and the gospels, a number of crucial developments had occurred, which changed the way Jesus was understood.

231

Some of the changes were subtle. Others were major.

The first and most obvious of these changes was that Jesus had been executed by crucifixion, and within only weeks some of his followers began to claim that he had risen from the dead. Those two facts forever changed the way Jesus was understood. In retrospect, Jesus' death came to be seen by many as the very center and purpose of his career. It is clear from the gospels that this was not how his followers understood him during his lifetime. Further, the claim that he had risen from the dead crystallized a whole range of new beliefs about Jesus: that God had vindicated him against his opponents, that he had been declared Son of God, Lord, Messiah, that his resurrection was the "first-fruits" of the resurrection of all humanity, an anticipation of God's final day of reckoning, and more. Such claims seem only to have been hinted at, or in some cases not mentioned at all, before his death. Beliefs about Jesus and his role in the plans of Israel's God grew rapidly. The earliest known Christian documents, the first letters of Paul, written only twenty years after Jesus' death, give him a role second only to God himself. They describe him as the Lord, Christ (1 Thess. 1:1),[1] they associate him with God as Judge (1 Thess. 3:13; cf. 2 Thess. 1:7-8), he is the one "in whom" Christians who have died "sleep" (1 Thess. 4:14), the one through whom salvation is received (1 Thess. 5:9), the revealer (Gal. 1:12), the one who lives in Christians (Gal. 2:20), who is being formed in Christians (Gal. 4:19), even while they are "in him" (1 Thess. 2:14; 3:8), and the Son of God who makes it possible for others to be sons of God through faith in him (Gal. 3:26). To what extent would these rapidly developing beliefs be "read back into" Jesus' own lifetime, as stories about him were remembered and retold?

Related to this general issue is a second, specific question. We know from a variety of sources that the early Christian movement had people who claimed to be directly inspired to speak "by the Spirit," who were often called "prophets." They spoke in the name of Jesus, and in some cases formed part of the leadership of Christian groups.[2] If they claimed to speak with Jesus' authority, were their sayings ever remembered as "things Jesus had said," possibly during his earthly life? Or were the sayings of Christian prophets carefully segregated from the sayings of Jesus passed on by tradition? The question is an important one. If prophetic sayings *were* widely accepted, Christians may not only have passed on, re-interpreted or modified sayings of Jesus: they may have created new ones as well.[3]

Second, the geographical and social location of the "Jesus movement"

---

[1] Indeed, so commonplace has the title "Christ" for Jesus become, that it is hardly even a title any longer. It has become virtually part of his name: Jesus (the) Christ is mostly simply "Jesus Christ."

[2] The best-documented individuals are Agabus (Acts 11:28; 21:10-11) and John of Patmos (Revelation).

[3] Of course, Christian prophets are not the only ones who could have created new Jesus-material. But they are the one clearly definable group within the movement who we know spoke directly in the name of Jesus/the Spirit, and hence may well have influenced the developing tradition.

shifted fundamentally. The focus of Jesus' activities had been the villages of rural Galilee, and his followers were predominantly small farmers or landless rural workers. After his death the movement that continued seems to have been based in Jerusalem. Those parts of the early Christian movement to which we owe the writings which became the New Testament were *urban*, not rural. That new geographical context would necessitate the re-interpretation of many sayings of Jesus, so that they made sense and remained relevant for the developing urban Jesus-movement. To what extent would this alter the picture of Jesus and his teachings, over time?

Third, the teachings of Jesus, and the stories about him, were translated from the original Aramaic into the international *lingua franca*, Koine (or "common") Greek. It is a matter of dispute how much Greek Jesus may have known, but few would doubt that the great bulk of the Jesus-tradition originally circulated in Aramaic. With the piecemeal translation of the tradition into Greek came the possibility of varying versions of the stories and sayings, or mistranslation, or more broadly, re-interpretation to fit the new linguistic and cultural context.

Fourth, and alongside this, the Jesus-movement began to spread from Galilee and Judea into the wider world of the Mediterranean coastlands. Here not only was the common language Greek, but the common culture was also based in Greek civilization. The Romans themselves, the overlords of the entire region, were themselves deeply influenced by Greek culture. Throughout the Mediterranean world there were communities of Jewish people, maintaining versions of their Jewish cultural and religious heritage, but doing so with Greek as their native language, and the Greco-Roman cities as their homelands. In order for the message about Jesus to make sense in this wider world, where Jewish terms like "Messiah" (and its Greek equivalent "Christ") had no obvious meaning, new terms and concepts would have to be found, or older ones adapted. How much re-interpretation would take place? And would the re-interpretation become so taken for granted that it would transform the rural Galilean Jesus and his story into something more culturally congenial to the sophisticated citizens of Ephesus and Corinth? To put it simply, to what extent would the message and stories of Jesus be "garbled in transmission"?

It is also important to remember that, for most of the period between Jesus' death and the writing of the first gospels, the Jesus-traditions were handed on piecemeal, by word of mouth. Perhaps some stories were written down early in this process, but we have no way of knowing for certain. Ancient civilization, even among the highly literate elite, was far more an oral culture than we often think. By and large people *preferred* oral communication. Even large books were usually written to be read aloud, and private silent reading was rare indeed. So if the stories of Jesus were passed on as an oral tradition, we need to ask how carefully that tradition was preserved in the telling, through the linguistic and cultural changes described above. Were the stories retold freely, with cheerful creative invention, or cautiously, with careful regard for the original setting? What "checks and balances," if any, might have applied to the process?

And then, at some unknown stage, a major shift occurred. Stories about Jesus began to be written down. Whether this happened first in Aramaic or in Greek we do not know. Neither do we know whether the first written collections were more like pamphlets or booklets. But when the process took hold, it fundamentally changed the way in which the Jesus-tradition was used. I do not mean that written gospels (or proto-gospels) *replaced* the oral tradition. Even as late as the early second century, the Christian leader Papias, bishop of Hierapolis in south-western Turkey and himself the author of five books, commented that he "did not suppose that what came out of books would benefit me as much as that which came from a living and abiding voice."[4] But the written gospels rapidly gained a place *alongside* the oral tradition, and by the mid-second century they had begun to displace its centrality. More importantly for our purposes, they provided a check on the development of the oral tradition: now there was a relatively fixed form, with which it could be compared.

The study of the historical Jesus, then, sets out to examine the gospels, and the few fragments of other information about Jesus, for material or ideas which seem to have survived the transmission process more or less intact. The aim is to "get behind the first Easter." It is to see behind the new perspectives and re-interpretations, to set aside the developing perspectives of the growing Christian movement. It is to look behind the Greek veneer of the gospels for the Galilean foundations. If the task can be achieved, we should be able to see Jesus without the benefits—and the distortions—of one to two generations of hindsight. We should be able to see him as a neutral but interested observer might have seen him during his lifetime, before his execution, and before the astounding beliefs of his early followers began to grow.

None of this presumes that the early Christians were wrong about Jesus, or had fundamentally misunderstood his intentions. Indeed, we would expect there to be a great deal of continuity between Jesus and the movement which (after all) he founded. But clearly there were changes as well as continuity. Historical Jesus studies must try to compensate for those changes, to see Jesus as he would have been seen by his first followers, his first opponents, and the merely curious among his contemporaries as well. Finally, and with some caution, we can also attempt to see him from his own point of view, and ask who he thought he was, and what he thought his public career was about.

## C. The Sources of Information

If we did not have the four "canonical" gospels, the short, semi-biographical works attributed to Matthew, Mark, Luke and John, collected together into

---

[4] Papias is quoted by Eusebius, the fourth-century church historian, in his *Hist. eccl.* 3.39. It is clear that Eusebius has access to a written copy of at least part of Papias' work, but no copy has survived into our own times. The translation cited is that of B. D. Ehrman, from the Loeb Classical Library edition of *The Apostolic Fathers,* vol. 2 (Cambridge: Harvard University Press, 2003), p. 99.

what eventually became known as the New Testament, we would know precious little about Jesus. If they had not survived, our earliest information about him would be (a) a few collections of sayings, mostly very brief, thought to be derived from him, written down more than a century after his death,[5] (b) one eighth century copy of a late first or early second century account of his passion and "resurrection,"[6] and (c) a few brief mentions of him, some controversial, in Roman and Jewish historians writing sixty years and more after his death.[7] All in all, we would probably know roughly as much about him as we now know about his contemporary, John "the Baptist." The gospels are our only substantial sources of information about Jesus, so our evaluation of their usefulness as historical sources is crucial. If they are not good sources of historical information, we have little else. So what *are* the gospels, and to what extent can we rely on the information they present about Jesus?

There are a range of things we do, and do not, know about the gospels, some of them a little surprising. For example, we do not know for certain who wrote them. The total evidence as to who wrote "Matthew's Gospel" is the title itself. There is no other certain information as to who this "Matthew" might have been. The theory that he is Matthew the tax-collector (Matt. 9:9) is based on nothing but the coincidence of the names. The only early evidence for the author of "Mark's Gospel" is the title, and one reference in the early second century church father Papias, quoted by Eusebius, *Hist eccl.* 3:39, as follows:

> When Mark was the interpreter [or translator] of Peter, he wrote down accurately everything that he recalled of the Lord's words and deeds—but not in order. For he neither heard the Lord nor accompanied him; but later, as I

---

[5] The earliest collections of sayings are the so-called *Gospel of Thomas* (the only substantial collection), Papyrus Egerton 2, published by H. I. Bell and T. C. Skeat as *Fragments of an Unknown Gospel and Other Early Christian Papyri* (London: British Museum, 1935), and P.Oxy 840. Later documents include the *Dialogue of the Savior* and the *Apocryphon of James* found among the Nag Hammadi documents. For a discussion of the non-canonical gospels, see chapter nine of this volume.

[6] The eighth-century account, discovered in 1886–87 in Egypt, is usually thought to be part of the so-called *Gospel of Peter*, probably written in the very late first or second century AD. The fragmentary papyri, P.Oxy 2949 and P.Oxy 4009 (third or possibly second century) *may* be other fragments of the same or a similar work, but this is far from certain.

[7] The brief mention of Jesus in Tacitus, *Ann.* 15:44 tells us only that the early Christian movement was named after him (Tacitus seems to presume that "Christ" is a name rather than a title), and that he was executed when Pontius Pilate was procurator (a minor error: Pilate was actually a prefect). Suetonius' *Life of Claudius* 25.4 mentions disturbances among the Jewish community in Rome "at the instigation of Chrestus." His *Life of Nero* 16:2 mentions the persecution of the Christians but says nothing directly about Jesus. Two passages in Josephus, *Ant.* (18.63-64 and 20.200) mention Jesus. The first gives considerable detail, whereas the second simply identifies James of Jerusalem as "the brother of Jesus, the so-called Christ." I say "controversial" because not all of these passages are certainly references to Jesus (that in Suetonius, *Claud.* 25.4 may not be) and some may have been inserted into the works in which they now appear, or modified, by Christian scribes (as in the case of the first of the two passages in Josephus).

indicated, he accompanied Peter, who used to adapt his teachings for the needs at hand, not arranging, as it were, an orderly composition of the Lord's sayings. And so Mark did nothing wrong by writing some of the matters as he remembered them. For he was intent on just one purpose: to leave out nothing that he heard or to include any falsehood among them.[8]

The evidence for Luke and John is a little stronger, but still disputed, and even if we knew the identities of the authors with certainty, we do not know where, or when, the various gospels were written. Matthew's Gospel *may* have been written in Antioch in north Syria. Mark's *may* have been written in Rome, and John's in or around Ephesus (on the coast of modern Turkey), but *none* of these locations is certain. The dates of writing are likewise uncertain, but to see why, we need to look in more detail at the question of the relationship between the gospels themselves.

It is clear from a close examination of the four canonical gospels that they contain some material which they all have in common, some material that two or three of them share, and some that is found in only one of them. It is also clear that Matthew, Mark and Luke share a good deal more material with each other than they share with John, which has more unique material than any other gospel.[9] Matthew, Mark and Luke also share a good deal more with each other in terms of structure and style than they share with John. These three are conventionally known as the "Synoptic" Gospels, the ones which can be "looked at together."[10] The complex pattern of similarities and differences between these Gospels invites the questions: do they share common sources? Do they copy from one another? Or are they essentially separate retellings of the same underlying Jesus-tradition?

The position taken up here is (deliberately) very much a mainstream one. It is that Mark wrote first, and that Matthew and Luke independently made use of both Mark, and another otherwise unknown source of information, as well as making their own independent contributions to how the story was told. Further, Matthew and Luke both had access to another early source of information, but which is now lost to us. It is represented in the many passages in Matthew and Luke which are very similar, or even virtually identical, but which are not to be found in Mark. This hypothetical source is known as "Q."[11] But it should be remembered that "Q" is only a

---

[8] Eusebius, *Hist. eccl.* 3:39, translated by B. D. Ehrman, in *The Apostolic Fathers*, vol. 2 (Cambridge: Harvard University Press, 2003), p. 103.

[9] The recognition that John's Gospel is strikingly different to the others in content and style can be documented as early as c. AD 200. Clement of Alexandria commented: "Last of all, John, perceiving that the external facts had been made plain in the gospel, being urged by his friends and inspired by the Spirit, composed a spiritual gospel" (quoted by Eusebius, *Hist. eccl.* 6.14.7). It is not clear quite what Clement meant by the distinction between "the external facts" and "a spiritual gospel," but it is clear that he makes the comment based on John's distinctiveness.

[10] The term "synoptic" originates with the title "Synopsis" for the multi-column parallel version of the "first three" gospels published by J. J. Griesbach in 1776 (though the term had been in use for at least 150 years before this). The use of the term "synoptic" as an adjective became popular in mid-nineteenth-century German scholarship, and spread from there.

[11] The groundwork for the "Q" hypothesis was laid by C. H. Weisse in his *Die evangelische*

"pronumeral," an "x," a label we give to the near-identical passages in Matthew and Luke.[12] We do not know with any certainty how much of "Q" Matthew and Luke preserve, whether they had access to exactly the same version of "Q," or whether parts of "Q" overlapped with Mark, and are thus undetectable. But despite the limits of our knowledge of "Q," we now have two early and independent sources of information, Mark's Gospel and "Q," underlying the three Synoptic Gospels. This position, adopted by a substantial majority of historical Jesus scholars, is commonly known as the "two document hypothesis."[13] There are several alternative theories which compete for second place,[14] but for our purposes the majority position is the best to follow.[15]

Most scholars argue, then, that Mark's Gospel was written first. It was probably written in the 60s or the early 70s of the first century. "Q" may have reached the form in which Matthew and Luke knew it a little earlier or a little later, but we cannot know for sure. Matthew and Luke were written some time afterwards, but we cannot know for certain exactly how much later, or which of them was written first. Depending on the date of Mark, they may have been written in the late 60s, the 70s or the 80s.

Finally there is John's Gospel. It is the view (once again) of a strong

---

*Geschichte* published in 1838, and further developed by H. J. Holtzmann in his *Die synoptischen Evangelien* published in 1863. In a recent book review, Jim West, of Quartz Hill School of Theology, aptly comments that: "Since its arrival on the scholarly horizon in 1838, this theory has been embattled, discarded, praised, ignored, reviled, adhered to, and rejected. No other theory, it seems, has provoked the slaughter of so many trees (for the production of paper) and the spilling of so much ink. It is the hypothesis that is neither settled, rebutted, nor completely convincing" (*Review of Biblical Literature* 1 [2007], reviewing E. Powell, *The Myth of the Lost Gospel*). A good example of both the potential, and the limits of the "Q" theory can be found in the well known story of Jesus' healing of the Centurion's servant, in Matt. 8:5-13 and Luke 7:1-10. The story has no parallel in Mark, and hence qualifies as "Q" material, but which of Matthew and Mark is closer to the original in "Q"? The "Q" hypothesis helpfully explains the obvious similarities between the two versions of the story (they depend on a common source), but doesn't tell us why they also differ on many small points. Either Matthew, Luke, or both have felt free to adapt the "Q" material, or they may have used different versions of it, or both.

[12] Even the origins of the use of "Q" as a term to designate material held in common by Matthew and Luke which they did not draw from Mark are obscure. It is normally said to derive from the German term "quelle", which means "source", and to be short for "Spruchquelle", "sayings source." There are, however, alternative views. See the discussion in L. H. Silberman, "Whence Siglum Q? A Conjecture," *Journal of Biblical Literature* 98, (1979), pp. 287-88, and J. J. Schmitt, "In Search of the Origins of the Siglum Q," *Journal of Biblical Literature* 100 (1981), pp. 609-11.

[13] K. Lachmann, writing in the 1830s, was one of the first to argue for the priority of Mark, the basis for the "two document hypothesis." B. H. Streeter gave the theory its definitive exposition in English in his work, *The Four Gospels: a Study of Origins* (New York: Macmillan, 1925).

[14] The best-known of these is the "Matthew first" position of J. J. Griesbach, dominant in the first half of the nineteenth century and revived in the twentieth century by W. R. Farmer and others. According to this view, Matthew wrote first, then Luke, making use of some of Matthew's material. Finally Mark produced an abridgment of Matthew, also using some material from Luke. More popular recently is the view of Austin Farrer, revived by Mark Goodacre, that Mark wrote first, Matthew next, and that Luke made use of both Matthew and Mark.

[15] The Synoptic Problem is also introduced in chapter 12 of this volume.

majority of historical Jesus scholars that John's Gospel can only be used to reconstruct the historical Jesus with the utmost caution. Though it shares a basic substructure of events and some particular stories with the Synoptic Gospels, it varies from each and all of them in so many details, large and small, that we are faced with a harsh choice. We can base our reconstruction of the Jesus of history on the Synoptics, or on John, but we cannot easily use both. The two pictures will not readily mesh. Further, John's Gospel is (probably) written later than at least Mark, and possibly later than Matthew and Luke as well, and there is a reasonably strong case that John wrote without having read a copy of any of the other three. And John's telling of the story of Jesus is so interwoven with his own meditations on its meaning that is often extremely hard to know where one ends and the other begins. There is no doubt that there is good historical tradition in John, but knowing where it begins and ends is an extremely difficult task. Most historians over the last century and a half have taken the view that Mark and "Q," being both earlier and less elaborately theological than John, should form the foundations for any reconstruction of the Jesus of history. To this foundation, material that is unique to Matthew, or to Luke, can sometimes be added, along with selected material from John.

But selected how? What is to stop the historian from being totally subjective, and simply constructing a Jesus to suit his own prejudices, by accepting as historical the material he prefers, and rejecting that which will not fit his personal biases? By what criteria is the historian to decide what is likely to reflect the historical Jesus, and what is more likely to be the product of the developing Christian movement's thinking about him?

## D. Criteria of Authenticity

Over the last century or so, Jesus-historians have developed a number of "criteria of authenticity," rules of thumb by which material in the Jesus-tradition can be evaluated for its historicity. There have been considerable debates as to which of these are the more logically valid, and the most practically useful. The list which follows is not exhaustive, but does represent the most commonly used "criteria." It is offered, not as a set of rules to be followed, but as a set of suggestions to be evaluated. As we will see, there is considerable debate about the various merits of these "rules of thumb."

### 1. "Literary Strata"

Historians commonly talk about the "strata" or "layers" of the synoptic tradition. The tradition is conceived of as an archaeological site, with "surface layers" and "deeper layers." On the very "surface" are editorial comments by the authors of the gospels. "Further down" is material which is found in only one of the later gospels (either Matthew or Luke, but not both: that would make it a candidate for "Q"). There is "triple tradition" material, which is represented in all three Synoptic Gospels. Material in Mark and "Q" are the "deepest layers" easily accessible. If material can be argued to be "pre-Markan," then it is "deeper still," and is presumed to be more likely to be historical.

But all this is metaphorical language, and could well be misleading. The "strata" may not be quite what they seem to be. They may be "literary strata" (remnants of the literary process which produced the gospels), but are they "historical strata"? Does their "stratum" determine their approximate "age," as it does in an archaeological dig? Not precisely, for these are not layers of soil laid down one upon another, one after another. We do not know which of Matthew and Luke is the earlier, and "triple tradition" material may simply be material which both Matthew and Luke found in Mark: it isn't "three times better" in any sense. No, these "strata" tell us only how material in the gospels is related in a *literary* sense: whether the selected passage occurs only in one gospel (or pre-gospel collection), or is used by one gospel writer directly from another, or by several dependent on one, or independently. And though these patterns are important and useful, the relationship between the "strata" and their general historical value is not a direct one. The "strata" of the synoptic tradition can still be thought of as layers, but they are not neat layers, each on top of its predecessor, and they are not datable in any direct sense. The "layer" tells us only at what literary stage/s the saying or story has been written into a gospel or gospels. On its own it tells us nothing about the historicity or the date of origin of the saying or story. It may help, but we ought not to let the "archaeological metaphor" persuade us without further evidence.

## 2. The Criterion of Multiple Independent Attestation

In its simplest form, this criterion argues that the more often a story or saying occurs in the synoptic tradition, the more generally likely it is to go back to the historical Jesus. There is good common sense here: a story or saying which is widely distributed may well be common because it has been in circulation for a longer period than one which is rare. It has had more time in which to spread. But the word "independent" is crucial. A saying or story which is in Matthew, Mark and Luke may only be "triply attested" because Matthew and Luke copied it from Mark. In such a case Matthew and Mark are not independent witnesses. But if a saying or story occurs in Mark and also in John (which is widely thought to be independent of Mark: that is, John has not read Mark), then that is double attestation. A saying or story which occurs independently in two or more different sources has a better claim to historicity than one which does not.

Now, all this is multiple attestation of sayings or stories, and it only gets us so far. Let's think about the case where a story occurred in Mark, but was also in "Q." We won't be able to tell for certain that it occurred in "Q," precisely because it is found in Mark (we can only detect "Q" as material in Matthew and Luke, which they did not get from Mark). But if the story in both Matthew and Luke differs *in the same way* from the one in Mark, then we have double attestation in both Mark and "Q" (unless the similarities in Matthew and Luke are a coincidence). But often it will be difficult to prove double attestation in such cases. If Matthew, Mark and Luke have the one saying or story in subtly different versions, how will we determine which differences are evidence of literary dependence, and which differences are just the "reporting style" of the individual writers?

The "multiple attestation" criterion works far better when it is used for ideas, not just sayings or stories. Let's take the idea, common in the gospels, that Jesus advocated and offered unconditional (or nearly unconditional) forgiveness, and acceptance into his circle, to people others would often not accept. This concept is found:

- In "triple tradition" material such as Mark 2:13 and parr. (the calling of Levi/Matthew), and in Mark 10:13-16 and parr. ("Let the children come"), and by implication in Mark 10:23-31 and parr. ("How hard it is for the wealthy to enter the Kingdom of heaven").
- In "Q" material such as Matthew 5:3-12 and Luke 6:20-26, the opening of the "Sermon on the Mount," and within the "Sermon" at Matt. 5:44 and Luke 6:32, and in the "Parable of the Lost Sheep," Matt. 18:12 and Luke 15:1.
- In "Matthew only" material such as Matt. 18:23-35 (the parable of the unforgiving servant), and Matt. 21:28-32 (the "parable of the two sons").
- In "Luke only" material such as Luke 7:36-50 (the sinful woman in the house of Simon the Pharisee), Luke 15:11-32 (the "parable of the prodigal son") and Luke 18:9-14 (the "parable of the Pharisee and the tax collector").
- For good measure, it is also in "John only" material such as John 1:11-13, John 4:1-42, and John 7:53–8:11, though admittedly the motif is not nearly so common in John.

Since the theme is to be found in virtually every "stratum" of the Jesus-tradition, it clearly has a considerable claim to historical authenticity.

Likewise, the idea that Jesus was a powerful exorcist is found in:

- Triple tradition material: Mark 1:32-34 and parr., Mark 5:1-20 and parr. (the "Gadarene demoniac"), Mark 3:14-19 and parr. (the appointing of the twelve disciples and commissioning them to cast out demons), and Mark 9:16-29 (their subsequent failure in the case of the son of the man who said "I believe; help my unbelief").
- Q: in Matt. 4:24 and Luke 6:18 (the summary statements just before the "Sermon on the Mount") and in Matt. 12:22-32 and Luke 11:14-23 (the dispute over the origins of Jesus' power, and the parable of the "strong Man").
- Mark 3:7-12.

- Luke 10:17, but, remarkably,
- The idea is never mentioned in John!

Another aspect of the argument from multiple independent attestation can be found where an idea occurs in the synoptic tradition in different literary forms. For example, the idea that Jesus announced the decisive intervention of God in human history, which he called "the coming of the kingdom of God," can be found not only in all the "strata" of the tradition, but also:

- In parables, which so often begin with the words "the kingdom of God is like . . ."
- In exorcism stories such as Matt. 12:28 / Luke 11:20.
- In isolated sayings such as Luke 17:20-21.

As such, this idea likewise has a considerable claim to be treated as authentic Jesus-tradition.

## 3. The Criterion of Dissimilarity

This criterion suggests that sayings or ideas attributed to Jesus in the gospels are more likely to be genuine if they are different from (dissimilar to) (a) the views of his Galilean and Judean contemporaries and/or (b) the views of the early churches (where those can be independently determined). The logic is simple: if Jesus' contemporaries or the early churches didn't make much use of an idea, they probably didn't invent it.

The two options within this criterion work rather differently. In the first case, the argument is as follows. If a saying or idea attributed to Jesus is unlike those of his contemporaries, it is unlikely that a well-known saying or idea has been "borrowed" by the early Christians and claimed as belonging to Jesus. It's unlikely precisely because the saying or idea *isn't* well-known. An example might be the intriguing claim attributed to Jesus that the Messiah could not be a descendant of David (Matt. 22:41-46; Mark 12:35-37; Luke 20:41-44), when most Jews presumed the Messiah would have at least a notional connection to David.

In the second case, if a saying or idea is unlike the ideas of the early churches, then it is unlikely that they "read it back" into the time of Jesus (perhaps to justify their beliefs by attributing them to him). A common example is the use of the phrase "Son of Man" by Jesus to refer indirectly to himself. Outside the gospels the phrase is used to refer to Jesus on only three occasions (Acts 7:56 and Revelation 1:13; 14:14), and even there it is a third-person reference, not Jesus applying it to himself. We can argue, therefore, that the early churches did not make much use of the phrase "Son of Man" as Jesus' form of self-description. Therefore it is highly unlikely that they invented the idea that he used it.

This criterion was used, particularly in the first half of the twentieth century, to establish a "critically assured minimum" of sayings and ideas which could be attributed to Jesus beyond reasonable doubt (because he was the *only* person known to have used them).[16] As such, it has considerable value. Over time, however, it has become clear that there are two related problems with this use of the criterion. The first is that the bar is being set too high. This criterion will exclude many sayings and ideas which probably *did* come from Jesus (but which were related to things his contemporaries said, or which the early churches remembered him saying, and therefore used).

Second, if used consistently, this criterion will necessarily create a portrait of Jesus which is seriously skewed. By excluding sayings and ideas similar to those of his Galilean and Judean contemporaries, this criterion will exaggerate the degree to which Jesus differed from them. It will create a "peculiar Jesus," a Jesus who was in all ways strikingly original. But the originality will be artificial, because points of similarity will have been systematically eliminated.

Similarly, if used consistently, this criterion will create a portrait of Jesus who made almost no impact on his subsequent followers in the early churches (by systematically excluding the cases where his sayings and ideas were taken up and used). Clearly such a portrait of Jesus is historically implausible: (a) Jesus was a first century Galilean, and probably shared many ideas with his contemporaries, and (b) it is highly implausible that the later Christian movement made him its central symbolic figure, but hardly picked up on any of his ideas or sayings.

As a result, many scholars have come to the view that the "criterion of dissimilarity" should be used only with considerable caution. It *can* be used to argue that a particular idea or saying most probably *did* originate with Jesus (because we know of no other plausible origin). But it ought *not* to be used negatively, to argue against the authenticity of sayings or ideas. Jesus was a person of his time, and his later followers most probably used some of his ideas. We ought, therefore, to expect some degree of "similarity," and not *require* dissimilarity.

More recently, N. T. Wright has argued for a more sophisticated version of this criterion, which he calls "double similarity and dissimilarity":

> When something can be seen to be credible (though perhaps deeply subversive) within first-century Judaism, *and* credible as the implied starting point (although not the exact replica) of something in later Christianity, there is a strong possibility of our being in touch with the genuine history of Jesus.[17]

But that is getting ahead of ourselves. Recent developments in methodology

---

[16] Thus J. D. G. Dunn: "The point was not that only sayings which satisfied this criterion should be recognised as authentic, but rather that such sayings will be the only ones we can *know* to be genuine." (*Jesus Remembered (Christianity in the Making: vol. 1)* [Grand Rapids: Eerdmans, 2003], p. 82).

[17] N. T. Wright, *Jesus and the Victory of God* (London: SPCK, 1996), p. 132.

will be dealt with further below.

## 4. The Criterion of Embarrassment

This criterion suggests that sayings or stories which run against the trend of the beliefs of the early churches are more likely to be historically authentic. In a sense, this criterion is a variant of the "criterion of dissimilarity." The early churches are hardly likely to have invented sayings or stories which ran counter to their own ideas. Such sayings and stories must have had great authority to have been retained in the tradition, and are therefore more likely to be authentic Jesus-material.

Three examples will illustrate the point. In Matt. 24:36 and Mark 13:32, discussing the "coming of the son of man," Jesus comments that "no-one knows that day or that hour, not even the angels of heaven, nor the Son, but only the Father." Now, this is a complex case, because the blunt use of the title "the Son" could be argued to show theological development from the early churches. But it is very hard to argue that the early churches would have invented the idea that there was something as important as the timing of his own return in glory (which is how they understood the "coming of the son of man"), that Jesus simply did not know. That Jesus didn't know such a thing would be a theological embarrassment. So it can be argued that such a saying would only have been retained in the tradition if the early churches were very certain Jesus had really said it.

This principle would apply even more to things Jesus seemed to know, but was wrong about. In Matt. 23:37 and Luke 13:34, Jesus is reported as lamenting over Jerusalem with the words "city that kills the prophets and stones those who are sent to it!" It seems most unlikely that the early churches would have invented this saying, because it could be understood to mean that Jesus, seeing himself as a prophet, expected to die by stoning. How Jesus actually died was too well known for that! It is entirely credible that Jesus could say such a thing, as a generalization, but not very credible that the saying was invented, and attributed to him by others.

And then there are other things that Jesus "shouldn't have said." In Matt. 12:31-32, Mark 3:28-29 and Luke 12:10, Jesus describes the "unforgivable sin." To many people's surprise, he says that "speaking/blaspheming against the Holy Spirit" is less forgivable than sin and blasphemy in general (Mark) or more specifically speaking against the Son of Man (Matthew and Luke, "Q"). This saying fulfils the criterion of embarrassment because it appears to make "speaking against the Holy Spirit" a worse offence than speaking against Jesus himself, whereas the tradition in general exalts Jesus above all others. Had such a saying been proposed within an early Christian group, it seems unlikely it would have been accepted except on the authority of Jesus himself.

Perhaps the most historically significant case-study for the criterion of embarrassment, however, is the foundational fact of Jesus' crucifixion. It is easy to forget that the fact that Jesus had been crucified was a problem for the early Christians, both from a Jewish and also from a Greco-Roman point of view. The "scandal of the cross" was that it marked Jesus as a condemned criminal, and strongly implied that he deserved his fate. The humiliation and horror of Jesus' death was something early Christians had to explain, both to themselves and to their critics, and the explanations they gave became central themes of their theology. But this "scandal" was not a puzzle that they set themselves. It was not an idea they invented, but one that was forced on them by the fact. And as a result, any reconstruction of Jesus must produce a Jesus who is "crucifiable." It must be historically credible that the Jesus we draw from the sources would be perceived by the Jerusalem authorities, and the Roman governor, not merely as a poetic preacher or a harmless nuisance, but as a serious threat. A Jesus not worth crucifying is not the historical Jesus.

## 5. The Criterion of Immediate Context

This criterion looks for evidence of a clear context in the career of Jesus which was unlikely to have been duplicated in later periods of the early Christian movement. An example of this might be the mention of "the Herodians" in Mark 3:6 (Matthew does not use the term in his version of this story, Matt. 12:14) and Mark 12:13-17 (which has Matt. 22:16-22, but no parallel in Luke). Who are "the Herodians"? In brief, we do not know for certain. They seem to be supporters of, or officials of, one of the "Herods," descendants of Herod the Great. These included Herod Antipas, Tetrarch of Galilee in Jesus' time, and Herod Agrippa, King of Judea in the early 40s AD. But whoever the Herodians were, Matthew is less interested in them than Mark, and Luke leaves them out altogether. The most likely reason is that the Herodians were either unknown to, or of no interest to, either them or their audience. The Herodians appear to be a phenomenon limited to Judea and Galilee. We have no evidence for them further afield. As such, the mention of them suggests at the least an historical memory of the Judean or Galilean context. But such cases are slippery. It is still possible that the mentions in Mark reflect disputes with supporters of a Herod later than Jesus' time.

## 6. The Criterion of Aramaic Context

This criterion looks for clear cases where the different forms of a saying in the gospels seem to go back to a mistranslation or pun in Aramaic. Jesus' instructions to his disciples are reported as follows:

| Matt. 10:9-10 | Mark 6:8-9 | Luke 9:3 |
|---|---|---|
| Take no gold, or silver, or copper in your belts, [10]no bag for your journey, or two tunics, *or sandals, or a staff*; for laborers deserve their food. | He ordered them to take nothing for their journey *except a staff*; no bread, no bag, no money in their belts; [9]but to *wear sandals* and not to put on two tunics. | He said to them, "Take nothing for your journey, *no staff*, nor bag, nor bread, nor money—not even an extra tunic." |

Note that while both Matthew's version forbids sandals, and both Matthew and Luke ("Q"?) rule out carrying a staff, Mark specifically permits both. It is argued that this could simply be because of a confusion in the translation of the Aramaic terms for "neither" (Matthew and Luke) and "except" (Mark).[18]

Compare Luke 11:39-41 with Matt. 23:23-5:

| Matt. 23:23-26 | Luke 11:37-41 |
| --- | --- |
| Woe to you, scribes and Pharisees, hypocrites! For you tithe mint, dill, and cummin, and have neglected the weightier matters of the law: justice and mercy and faith. It is these you ought to have practiced without neglecting the others. You blind guides! You strain out a gnat (*qalma*) but swallow a camel (*gamla*)![19] Woe to you, scribes and Pharisees, you hypocrites! You clean the outside of the cup and dish, but inside they are full of greed and self-indulgence. Blind Pharisee! First clean (*dakku*) the inside of the cup, so that the outside also may become clean. | While he was speaking, a Pharisee invited him to dine with him; so he went in and took his place at the table. The Pharisee was amazed to see that he did not first wash before dinner. Then the Lord said to him, "Now you Pharisees clean the outside of the cup and dish, but inside you are full of greed and wickedness. You fools! Did not the one who made the outside make the inside also? So give for alms [*zakku*]) those things that are within; and see, everything will be clean for you." |

There are two points here. First there is Matthew's pun on gnats and camels, which is apparent in Aramaic, but not in Greek or English. Second there is the discrepancy between Matthew's "clean the inside" and Luke's confusing "give what is inside to the poor." But in Aramaic the difference is a single letter.[20] Between them, these points make a strong case that the original saying arose in an Aramaic-speaking environment, and is therefore close to the context of Jesus.

The weakness of this criterion, however, is that it cannot distinguish between authentic sayings of Jesus and sayings which might have been invented or modified by his earliest, Aramaic-speaking disciples. An Aramaic substratum remains, however, a point (though not a decisive point) in favor of historicity.

A number of scholars take this approach a stage further. They attempt to deduce what the original Aramaic of sayings or stories may have been, and then find evidence of characteristic patterns of usage in them. Notably, J. Jeremias argued that a large number of sayings fell naturally into particular rhythms, or displayed antithetical parallelisms, which he believed were characteristic of "the voice of Jesus himself."[21] Most feel, however, that this

---

[18] M. Black, *An Aramaic Approach to the Gospels and Acts*, 3rd ed. (Oxford: Clarendon, 1967), p. 216. It should be noted that Black does not think Mark simply mistranslated the Aramaic. He thinks that "perhaps the ultimate source of the contradiction may have been in the confusion in Aramaic of the words for 'neither' and 'except' or 'but' and 'neither.' But it is likewise possible that Mark is here giving a purely Greek version of the saying. . ."

[19] Black, *Aramaic Approach*, pp. 175-76.

[20] Black, *Aramaic Approach*, p. 2.

[21] See most particularly J. Jeremias, *New Testament Theology, Vol. 1: The Proclamation of*

style of argument has too great a risk of subjectivity, and would use such arguments only with the greatest caution.

## 7. *The Criterion of Lack of Theological Point*

This criterion argues that a particular saying or story has no "theological agenda," and seems to have been recorded "just because it happened." An example often cited is the case of the young man wearing only a linen cloth at Jesus' arrest mentioned in Mark 14:51-52, who fled naked when one of the soldiers seized hold of the cloth. The weakness of all such cases, however, is that someone may *find* a theological point to the story, even one characteristic of the particular gospel author, at which point the argument collapses. Arguments "from silence" are always risky. Once again this criterion should only be used with great caution.

Various scholars have proposed various other criteria, but these are the ones which have been most widely discussed and adopted. Normally an argument for historicity will be based on a combination of factors. The "criteria" are not scientific tests. They are rules of thumb, allowing a historian to develop an argument based on probabilities. And, of course, they work in reverse. A saying in a late "stratum" of the tradition, which is *not* multiply attested, is less likely to be authentic (though it may be). A saying which has clear parallels in early Christian teaching must come under suspicion. A saying or story which particularly expresses the point of view of its gospel must be treated with greater caution, particularly if it is not attested elsewhere. Once again the argument is cumulative, not decisive. A gospel author could perhaps select an authentic story to make his point as easily as make one up. But a saying or story that reflects a later situation, or later interests, or shows theological development compared to its use in other gospels, loses historical credibility in precisely the same way that sayings and stories gain in credibility when they match the "criteria."

To go back to the archaeological metaphor, we may or may not be able to find "bedrock." But the archaeological metaphor has its limits. Perhaps the old saying, "There's no smoke without fire" can provide us with another metaphor. The gospels are like smoke. They both indicate that there is (or was) a fire, and suggest things about the kind of fire it was. They also obscure our direct view of the fire. But careful analysis of the "smoke" will tell us a great deal, and with luck, by following the trail of smoke, we may well get more than a glimpse of the fire as well.

## E. The Development of Historical Jesus Studies

The story of the rise and development of historical Jesus studies is far too complex to be told here in any but the most schematic outline. The story has

*Jesus* (London: SCM Press, 1971).

been surveyed many times, and accounts are easily accessible.[22] Simply to orientate ourselves, however, let me suggest a number of broad phases or stages through which our understanding of Jesus has passed, before focusing on the most recent developments.

## *1. The Pre-Modern Period*

Before the rise of modern historical study, the picture of Jesus accepted by most people in the western world was an easy-going blend of the Jesus of the gospels, the Jesus of the great creeds of the ancient church, and the Jesus of popular Christian piety. There were, naturally, non-standard views of Jesus held by some, and there were those among the intellectual elites who had doubts about aspects of the consensus. But Christian faith, of one variety or another, was part of the ideological bedrock of western culture. Jesus functioned as the great moral exemplar, the great moral teacher, and the primary mediator between God and humanity. He was simultaneously the ultimate expression of God's overwhelming love and self-giving for humanity, the awesome Son of God, Second Person of the Trinity, and the terrifying judge of the coming last day. Though some tension might be felt between these diverse roles, the figure of Jesus loomed large enough to unify them in his own person.

## *2. The Collapse of Consensus*[23]

Starting as early as the 1600s, and reaching a critical mass in the period broadly known as "The Enlightenment" (c. 1750–1800), a growing number of European intellectuals challenged the dominance of the orthodox Christian consensus. Their critique began with a questioning of the heritage of Greek and Roman philosophy. The great fathers of the church in the late Roman and early Medieval period had built up a remarkable creative synthesis between classical philosophy and Christian theology. Now that synthesis became vulnerable, as new, proto-scientific ideas began to take hold.

## *3. The "Liberal Jesus"*

As "Enlightenment" ideas gained strength at the level of philosophy and science, new, critical ideas about the study of history also began to develop. New ideas of historical method, based on rigorous comparison and analysis of the sources of historical information, were applied first to Greek and Roman

---

[22] Standard accounts include W. G. Kümmel, *The New Testament: The History of the Investigation of its Problems* (Nashville: Abingdon, 1972) and S. Neill and N. T. Wright, *The Interpretation of the New Testament, 1861–1986* (New York: Oxford University Press, 1988).

[23] See particularly for the period from 1450–1889, John Sandys-Wunsch, *What Have They Done to the Bible? A History of Modern Biblical Interpretation* (Collegeville: Liturgical Press, 2005). For the period since 1862 see the account of Neill and Wright.

history. But their sharp distinction between "what really happened" and "myth" was soon turned on the New Testament, and particularly on the gospel portraits of Jesus. Few if any of the new historians doubted Jesus' existence, but many of them believed that the early church's "mythical" interpretation of him had thoroughly obscured the real man beneath. If Jesus could be stripped of the supernatural trappings of the church's views, then the "historical Jesus" would remain. Perhaps surprisingly, few of these new historians set out to "debunk" Jesus himself. Most of them remained convinced that he was one of the truly great figures of human history, and if "properly" understood, could still function as an important role-model. His ethical teachings were often seen as his most lasting achievement. Out of a "scientific" dismissal of the supernatural aspects of the gospel stories, and a focus on Jesus as a teacher of abiding moral values, the "Liberal Jesus" was born.

As the nineteenth century progressed, more sophisticated literary analysis of the gospel traditions developed, and the relationship between Mark, "Q," and the later stages of the tradition were further analyzed. In Germany, long the pioneer in historical study of the New Testament, the dominant mid-nineteenth century "Tübingen school" of interpretation argued for mid to late-second century dates for the Gospels and Acts, and therefore for a long period of mythological development between Jesus himself and our sources of information about him.[24] In Britain more historically conservative views gained strength, with earlier dates for the gospels supported.[25] Meanwhile all sides were becoming aware of the importance of "apocalyptic" Judaism in the time of Jesus, and realizing that works such as the "Book of Enoch" (long known in Ethiopia, but only rediscovered by Europeans in the seventeenth century, and first published in Europe in 1821) might well hold the key to understanding crucial concepts in the teaching of Jesus.

One such concept was "the coming of the Kingdom of God." It had often been thought that the "kingdom" Jesus taught of was an interior, spiritual one ("the kingdom of God is within you," Luke 17:20-21), but now it appeared that he had preached the coming kingdom as the imminent end of all things, and the coming of God in judgment.[26] Further, his ethical teachings appeared to arise directly out of his eschatological views.[27] He urged people to repent,

---

[24] The rise and influence of the "Tübingen school" of New Testament interpretation is outlined by Neill and Wright, *Interpretation*, pp. 20-30, and covered in full detail by H. Harris, *The Tübingen School* (Oxford: Oxford University Press, 1975). The decline of the school as a result of the work of T. Zahn and J. B. Lightfoot on the writings of Clement and Ignatius is described by Neill and Wright, *Interpretation*, pp. 53-64.

[25] On the "Cambridge trio" of Lightfoot, Westcott and Hort see Neill and Wright, *Interpretation*, pp. 35-64.

[26] The work which did the most to cement in place this new understanding of "the coming of the kingdom" was J. Weiss' *Die Predigt Jesu vom Reiche Gottes* (Gottingen: Vandenhoeck & Ruprecht, 1892). This work has been translated into English as *Jesus' Proclamation of the Kingdom of God* (Chico: Scholars Press, 1985).

[27] The two terms "apocalyptic" and "eschatology" are often used in confusing ways. Throughout this survey, "apocalyptic" refers to a *genre of literature* which reports visions. "Eschatology," on the other hand, is a *set of ideas* to do with *ta eschata*, the last things, the final stages of God's purposes. Apocalyptic literature can have eschatological themes, but need not.

not simply in principle, but because "the kingdom of heaven/God is upon you" (Matt. 4:17; 10:7, Mark 1:15, Luke 10:8-11). His "good news" was precisely the news of the imminence of the kingdom. His parables were parables of the kingdom, and the "Lord's Prayer" was a prayer for the decisive coming of that kingdom, "on earth as in heaven." And yet the kingdom, it seemed, had not arrived. The problems this development brought were considerable. How could such a "primitive" mythological world-view be made credible for nineteenth-century man, whose belief in scientific and cultural progress was at its height? And how could a Jesus who had predicted the imminent end of the age retain any authority when his predictions had failed to eventuate? To many it seemed that, the more clearly Jesus was situated in his first-century context, the more foreign and the less comprehensible he became. Was it possible that the central, ethical "core" of his teaching could be separated from the outer, first-century eschatological "husk"? Could the teachings of Jesus be rescued from historical irrelevance? "Liberal" lives of Jesus' were many. Indeed, in an important sense there were too many. One critic commented scathingly that even the great Adolf Harnack, looking down the deep well of the past, saw at the bottom only a reflection of his own face and attitudes.[28]

At the very beginning of the twentieth century came another new development. Up to this point Mark's Gospel, as the earliest, had been used as the foundation of lives of Jesus. William Wrede analyzed the flow and development of Mark's Gospel, not simply as a source for the life of Jesus, but as a work in its own right, with its own interests and concerns. In Mark's Gospel he found a concern with the messianic identity of Jesus different from that in the other gospels. Wrede argued that Mark emphasized, more than the others and more consistently, that Jesus tried to hide the fact of his "Messiah-ship."[29] Wrede contended that this theme grew, not from the historical career of Jesus, but from the concerns of Mark himself and the early churches within which he worked. For Wrede, the theme developed because Jesus had *not* believed himself to be the Messiah, and had denied it on several occasions. But the early churches believed he *was* the Messiah, and so were faced with the problem of explaining his attitude. Mark's solution, Wrede argued, was to edit and arrange his material to show that Jesus was indeed the Messiah, but had wanted the fact kept secret. It was a conclusion based, not on history, but on Mark's theology. While Wrede's theory was subjected to considerable criticism, notably by Albert Schweitzer (below), it became widely influential. Probably more importantly, it suggested that the gospels could be studied, not simply as "sources," but as creative theological works. Though other trends

---

Eschatology may be visionary, but need not be.

[28] George Tyrrell, *Christianity at the Crossroads* (New York: Longmans, 1909), p. 49. The context makes it clear that Tyrrell had a particular concrete set of attitudes in mind: "The Christ that Harnack sees, looking back through nineteen centuries of Catholic darkness, is only the reflection of a liberal Protestant face, seen at the bottom of a deep well."

[29] W. Wrede, *The Messianic Secret* (London: James Clarke, 1971); the German original, *Das Messiasgeheimnis in den Evangelien,* was published in 1901.

would lead mainstream scholarship away from this approach, it would return in the second half of the twentieth century as "redaction criticism." But for the meantime, Mark's place as a secure foundation for studying Jesus' life had been undermined.

Famously, the "Liberal" phase of historical Jesus scholarship, with its emphasis on the abiding value of Jesus' moral teaching, effectively came to an end with the publication of Albert Schweitzer's *The Quest of the Historical Jesus: A Critical Study of its Progress from Reimarus to Wrede.*[30] Schweitzer surveyed the debate up to his own time, pointing out its unmistakable inadequacies. Like Weiss before him (see note 26, above), Schweitzer argued that the very core of Jesus' teaching was eschatological. Jesus expected the imminent, decisive intervention of God in human affairs. Indeed, he traveled to Jerusalem to bring on the crisis. But for Schweitzer, God did not act, and Jesus died in despair. Schweitzer faced squarely up to the problem of Jesus' first century eschatological world-view. The question remained: could the Jesus he described be of any value to modern humanity?

## 4. After Schweitzer: The Rise of "Form Criticism"

The most important development in the early part of the twentieth century was the rise of the method known as "form criticism." Scholars in several fields (particularly Homeric studies and the study of Scandinavian and other European sagas) had become aware of the importance of oral tradition in pre-literate and partly-literate societies. Now that realization was brought to bear on the gospel tradition. If Mark (and/or "Q") were the earliest written records of Jesus, what lay behind them? The answer suggested was: the oral tradition of the sayings and deeds of Jesus. But before Mark provided a narrative framework for those sayings and stories, it was argued, they circulated orally either as independent sayings, or short, topical collections, that fell into easily recognized types, or "forms." There were parables, miracle-stories, "pronouncement-stories" (stories told for the sake of the "pronouncement" Jesus made at the climax), beatitudes, controversy stories, wisdom sayings, apocalyptic sayings, and, depending on the scholar analyzing the material, a range of other "forms." Two of the most prominent of the early form-critics were Rudolf Bultmann and Martin Dibelius. Bultmann in particular dominated the field in the mid-twentieth century.

With this literary analysis came three further crucial steps of argument. First, comparison of the different editorial contexts of a saying or story in the different gospels would allow the form critic to "detach" the saying or story from the framework and context imposed on it by the gospel authors.[31] Second, the kinds of contexts in the life of the early churches in which

---

[30] The German original, *Von Reimarus zu Wrede: Eine Geschichte der Leben-Jesu-Forschung* (Tübingen: Mohr, 1906), made an immediate impact. It was first translated into English in 1910.

[31] This point was first clearly recognized by K. L. Schmidt, in his 1919 work, *Der Rahmen der Geschichte Jesu* (eng. *The Framework of the History of Jesus*).

different stories were handed down could be deduced. These might be liturgical settings, teaching settings, or in evangelistic or controversial contexts. But once this "life-situation" (German: *Sitz im Leben*) had been determined, it should also be possible, third, to tell how that context would (3) have shaped the telling of the saying or story in question. If the logic of this argument was good, then the scholar could hope to reconstruct the ways in which the oral tradition about Jesus developed in the period before the gospels were first written. The "form" of a saying or story would provide crucial clues about its prehistory.

D. F. Strauss, writing in the 1830s, had compared the stories of Jesus in the gospels to a handful of pearls.[32] Originally a lovely necklace, the breaking of the string had now left them separate and disorganized. To extend the metaphor, for much of the twentieth century the focus of scholarship was on the individual "pearls." But the question began to be: had the "pearls" themselves been polished into their present form by a long process of development? Was it still possible to tell what the original speck of historical grit had been, before the process began?

Three logically separate lines of argument were commonly added on to this basic form-critical methodology. One was the presumption that the oral ① gospel tradition developed similarly to the oral folklore in pre-literate societies, with considerable room for creative embellishment. The second was a dependence on the "criterion of dissimilarity" (see D.3 above) to determine ② a "critically assured minimum" of sayings and stories which could safely be considered authentic. The other was a sharp distinction between Judaic and ③ Hellenistic (Greek cosmopolitan) features of the gospel tradition. Hellenistic features were normally judged to be later, secondary developments making their way into the tradition from the churches of the "Gentile mission." The combination of these methods and presuppositions tended to create a strong climate of skepticism, so that a steadily diminishing proportion of the gospel tradition was judged to be authentic Jesus-material. The burden of proof was put firmly on those who wanted to argue for historical authenticity.

This combination of broad-scale skepticism and the intense focus on the literary development of the tradition directed many scholars away from studies of the historical Jesus. The (reconstructed) literature and ideas of the earliest churches seemed, for many, to be a more appropriate topic for study.

Protests against this mood certainly occurred. A school of Scandinavian scholars challenged the "oral folklore" approach to the gospel tradition with an intensive study of Rabbinic oral tradition.[33] They argued that the Rabbinic

---

[32] Neill and Wright, *Interpretation*, p. 254. I have been unable to locate the original quotation. The nearest analogy I have found is in Strauss, *The Life of Jesus Critically Examined*, vol. 1 (St. Clair Shores: Scholarly Press, 1970), p. 367, which was originally published in German in 1835: "The foregoing comparison shows us that the discourses of Jesus, like fragments of granite, could not be dissolved by the flood of oral tradition; but they were not seldom torn from their natural connexion, floated away from their original situation and deposited in places to which they did not properly belong."

[33] The most prominent figures in this "Uppsala school" were H. Riesenfeld (*The Gospel Tradition* [London: Mowbray, 1957]) and B. Gerhardsson (*Memory and Manuscript* [Lund:

literature of the second and third centuries AD showed clear evidence of formal memory-training: Rabbis taught their students to memorize considerable amounts of material "word-perfect." To what extent could this also have been true of the "rabbi" Jesus and his disciples, in the first century? For different reasons, scholars specializing in the Aramaic background of the gospels often critiqued the conclusions of the more skeptical among the form critics. J. Jeremias, in particular, argued that various features of the Greek of the gospels showed clear signs of the underlying Aramaic of Jesus and his earliest followers. He argued that, if the gospel tradition was back-translated into Aramaic, particular distinctive features of Jesus' own language (the *ipsissima vox Jesu*, the "voice of Jesus himself") could be detected and studied. Others such as Matthew Black, Joseph Fitzmyer and Max Wilcox, though less confident of Jeremias' program of back-translation into Aramaic, made real progress in the understanding of the Aramaic of Jesus and his earliest followers and the traces it had left in the Greek of the gospels. But for the majority of scholars, some version of form-critical method remained (and remains) a crucial weapon in the armory of the study of the historical Jesus. This was so because form criticism took seriously the process of primarily oral transmission of the Jesus-tradition in the period before the writing of the first gospels.

## 5. The "new quest" and the rise of the "third quest"

It was in Germany that form-critical method had been developed, and it was in Germany that it was most dominant. However, the mood of German scholarship began to change in the mid-1950s and early 60s. Scholars began to shift their focus again, from the development within the gospel tradition itself, either to its origins in the person of Jesus, or to its results in the written gospels. There were multiple reasons for these changes, which go far beyond the scope of a brief survey such as this, but it must be emphasized that they did not include a rejection of the basic insights of form criticism. Those were maintained, and became the premises of further work.

On the one hand, the change of mood took the form of the so-called "New Quest for the historical Jesus," and a range of new books on Jesus by leading continental scholars over the next ten to fifteen years. A broad consensus developed, suggesting that Jesus believed the coming "kingdom of God" should be understood as both imminent and in some sense already present. Jesus believed that his own mission *inaugurated* God's kingdom, but that this kingdom would only reach its goal when God himself intervened decisively in human history.[34] In some sense he believed his own authority was associated

---

Gleerup, 1961]).

[34] This balance between "future" and "realized" eschatology became one of the dominant positions in late twentieth-century historical Jesus scholarship, held by figures as radically different as J. Jeremias (*New Testament Theology*), N. Perrin (*Rediscovering the Teaching of Jesus* [New York: Harper & Row, 1967]), and G. E. Ladd (*The Presence of the Future* [Grand Rapids: Eerdmans, 1974]).

with the kingdom's dawning, and he put this authority into practice in his offer of forgiveness and fellowship.

On the other hand, the change of mood also led to the development of "redaction criticism."[35] This literary sub-discipline within gospel studies picked up where Wrede (see above) left off, and examined the gospels as theological statements in their own right. If the sayings and stories about Jesus were, as a result of their transmission, like a handful of pearls with a broken string, then it ought to be possible to study the ways in which they had been "re-strung" by the different gospel writers. The study of this editorial process allows us to ask about the characteristic ideas used by each individual gospel author to organize their material. It is like a more sophisticated version of the classical literary criticism which asks about the interests and themes of a particular author, but it presupposes the results of form criticism.

Over the same period, interest revived in trying to locate Jesus within the various strands of first-century Judaism known to us. At first this process was quite crude. People started with the Jewish historian Josephus' description of four "schools of thought" within the Judaism of his time.[36] Josephus spoke of the Pharisees, the Sadducees, the Essenes and the "fourth philosophy" (often misunderstood as the Zealots or "freedom fighters"), and various scholars tried to define Jesus' relationship with one or more of these groups. Thus S. G. F. Brandon argued that Jesus and the movement he founded should be understood as Zealots, and other scholars explored the similarities and differences between Jesus and the Pharisees or the Essenes. Over time it became clear that Josephus' description greatly simplified the complexity of first-century Judaism, and that the task of locating Jesus needed further refinement. The discovery of the Dead Sea Scrolls, and their ongoing publication through the 1960s, accelerated this development. However, the whole process remained focused on the level of *ideas*. Any attempt to locate Jesus within his broader socio-political framework was still very much in the background.

In the mid-1970s and early 1980s a series of new developments began which came to be labeled the "third quest of the historical Jesus."[37] Various starting points are suggested. For me, the first important steps were taken by the Hungarian Jewish scholar Geza Vermes in his book *Jesus the Jew* (London: Collins, 1973). Vermes set out to locate Jesus within the traditions of specifically Galilean piety, and drew a picture of Jesus as a *hasid*, a pious "proto-Rabbi" characterized by a strong prayer-life and reports of both miracle-working and tense relations with the Jewish establishment. Though the details of Vermes' portrait have been strongly contested, his approach set

---

[35] "Redaction," a word rarely used in English, is the equivalent to the German "Redaktion," which means the process of editing.

[36] Josephus' descriptions of these "schools of thought" can be found in his *J.W.* 2.119-66, and in his *Ant.* 13.171-73; 15.371 (very briefly); and 18.11-25.

[37] The phrase seems to have been invented by N. T. Wright, and is used, for example, in Neill and Wright, *Interpretation*, pp. 379-449. However, definitions of who is a "third quester" and who still really belongs to the second or "new quest" are subjective, and the issue ought not to concern us too much.

several trends.

First, he was confident that a persuasive, substantial historical portrait of Jesus could be constructed. After the intense skepticism of Bultmann, and the historical minimalism of much of the "new quest," the contrast was striking. Second, he was concerned to locate Jesus firmly within the broad spectrum of first-century Judaism, and to locate him within that spectrum as precisely as possible. Third, he was not very concerned with the traditional categories of theologically oriented Christian scholarship. It was indeed "Jesus the Jew" who was the focus.

There was more to come. In the same year as Vermes, Gerd Theissen had published an article on "itinerant radicalism" in early Christianity, and in 1977 the English translation of his *The First Followers of Jesus: A Sociological Analysis of Earliest Christianity* was published. This was followed the next year by his *Sociology of Early Palestinian Christianity*. Theissen was concerned to show that the social pattern of the early Christian movement focused around "wandering charismatics," people living a rootless, itinerant lifestyle, depending on the support of those to whom they preached. He argued that this pattern went back to the model of Jesus and his original followers. To Vermes' greater historical confidence and focus on the Jewish context, Theissen added a social-historical focus on the lifestyle of Jesus and his disciples. In 1979 Ben Meyer published *The Aims of Jesus*, with a strong critique of the over-use of the "Criterion of Dissimilarity," and a shift away from the saying-by-saying analysis of the Jesus-tradition. He asked, instead (as the title of his book suggests), the broad question as to Jesus' overall aims, within the context of Second Temple Judaism. In 1984 Marcus Borg published his *Conflict, Holiness and Politics in the Teachings of Jesus*, and in this and his later works began to develop what became an influential portrait of a Jesus who arose more out of the Israelite "Wisdom" tradition than out of apocalyptic. By contrast, in 1985 E. P. Sanders published his *Jesus and Judaism*, shifting the focus away from the difficult questions of the sayings-tradition, and concentrating on what could be known with confidence of Jesus' public *actions*. These he interpreted in terms of what he called "restoration eschatology," by which he meant Jewish views about how God would act to restore the fortunes of the nation of Israel. Once again, the focus had shifted towards the formation of broad historical hypotheses.

In the same year the Society for Biblical Literature, an international association of Biblical scholars based in the U.S.A., established a seminar on the question of the historical Jesus. This was not strange or unique: the society has numerous ongoing seminars which meet both at its international conferences and elsewhere. But this "Jesus Seminar" was to make quite a splash in the mass media.[38] As well as publishing individual and group academic projects, the movers within the seminar actively sought, and

---

[38] Any summary of the Seminar's work here must be brief to the point of caricature. For the seminar's own statement of the consensus methodology adapted by the members for their major publications, see R. W. Funk and R. W. Hoover, *The Five Gospels: The Search for the Authentic Words of Jesus* (New York: Macmillan, 1993), pp. 25-34.

achieved, considerable publicity for their enterprise. Most famously, they published an edition of the gospels, including the "Gospel of Thomas," with the various sayings and stories of Jesus color-coded into four categories based on the votes of the seminar-members. The categories were broadly described as follows: (1) *red*: Jesus undoubtedly said this or something very like it; (2) *pink*: Jesus probably said something like this; (3) *gray*: Jesus did not say this, but the ideas contained in it are close to his own, and (4) *black*: Jesus did not say this; it represents the perspective or context of a later or different tradition.[39]

It is important to emphasize that the "Jesus Seminar" was not a tight, unified group, but a diverse one, with members holding a range of views on many issues. That was why voting was necessary! However, the Seminar did publish a number of books containing what might be called its consensus views. Not all of these belonged to the scholarly mainstream, and some of their published views were tangential to what we have seen in the rest of the "third quest." Their critical methodology was more sceptical than many "third questers." Their emphasis on the importance of non-canonical sources (such as the *Gospel of Thomas*, which many of them believed embodied considerable amounts of early Jesus-tradition), went further than many others could accept. Their focus on the "Q" material was more mainstream, but one interpretation of it which was common among the members was more controversial. It was argued that the "Q" material gave us access to a different group of Jesus' disciples, one less interested in Jewish apocalyptic ideas, and more focused on Jesus' "subversive wisdom." However, what remained in the public mind was the color-coded "scholar's edition" of the gospels, and particularly the fact that so little of the gospel tradition made it into the red "Jesus almost certainly said this" category.

In 1987 R. A. Horsley published his *Jesus and the Spiral of Violence*, picking up where Gerd Theissen had left off. Where Theissen had focused on the "wandering charismatics" who he believed were the core of Jesus' followers, Horsley asked about the support base on which they relied, and to which their teaching was directed. He suggested that only a minority of Jesus' followers literally "followed him" around Galilee. The majority remained in their villages, and their new "communities of the kingdom" were the grass-roots of the Jesus-movement. For Jesus, the "coming of the kingdom of God" was not only a future prospect to be announced. It was also a present reality to be embodied, and lived out in community.

In 1991 J. D. Crossan became probably the best-known member of the "Jesus Seminar" with the publication of his *The Historical Jesus: the Life of a Mediterranean Jewish Peasant*. In the first half of the book Crossan mounted

---

[39] Funk and Hoover, *The Five Gospels*, pp. 36-37. Alternative definitions for the four positions were also given: (1) "I would include this item unequivocally in the database for determining who Jesus was"; (2) "I would include this item with reservations (or modifications) in the database"; (3) "I would not include this item in the database, but I might make use of some of the content in determining who Jesus was", and (4) "I would not include this item in the primary database."

a massive, sophisticated and well-written case, drawing on archaeology, cultural anthropology and Roman history to situate Jesus in his historical and cultural context. In the second half he focused on the gospel traditions themselves, basing his methodology heavily on the criterion of multiple attestation. He argued that *only* sayings and stories which were multiply attested in the tradition should be considered historical. But he also argued that attestations of a saying or story in non-canonical Christian writings, particularly the *Gospel of Thomas*, should definitely be included. In principle, the great majority of scholars would agree, but Crossan placed particular emphasis on such sources, arguing for very early dates for many of them.

The end result was a Jesus who Crossan describes as "an itinerant peasant Jewish cynic." "Cynic" is a term which needs some explanation. The Cynics (literally the "dog-men", so-called because they ignored or flouted the standards of polite behavior) were a loose school of non-conformist philosophers, tracing their origins back to Diogenes of Sinope (late fourth century BC). They are best described as parasitic critics of Greek urban culture, parasitic in the sense that they lived within and depended on urban society, while criticizing and satirizing its way of life. They advocated a deliberately simplified, highly individualistic life-style in reaction against the conformism, "consumerism" and elegance of urban life.[40] Crossan suggests that Jesus had been exposed to cynic ideas in cosmopolitan Galilee, and "re-invented the Cynic wheel" in peasant Jewish terms. In the (otherwise quite different) works of Borg and Crossan, a striking challenge was offered to the century-old consensus that Jesus and his proclamation of the "coming kingdom of God" was best understood against the background of Jewish apocalyptic literature. For Borg, and several others as different in their views as Ben Witherington III and Elizabeth Schüssler-Fiorenza, insufficient attention had been paid to the Jewish "wisdom literature" as a source for understanding Jesus. For Crossan, on the other hand, and others including F. G. Downing and B. L. Mack, the cosmopolitan background of popular Greek philosophy largely replaced apocalyptic as the matrix for understanding Jesus and his movement. Jesus' "kingdom-language" was understood as a metaphor for the privileges of the truly wise, those who had come to understand his counter-cultural message.

Several scholars attempted to balance the older "eschatological" consensus with the new emphasis on Wisdom traditions, describing Jesus as a "wisdom-prophet" or "prophetic sage."[41] Others, notably J. P. Meier and D. C.

---

[40] For a fuller explanation of the "cynic Jesus" hypothesis, see F. G. Downing, *Cynics and Christian Origins* (Edinburgh: T. & T. Clark, 1992), pp. 143-68, the critiques of H. D. Betz, "Jesus and the Cynics: Survey and Analysis of a Hypothesis," *Journal of Religion* 74.4 (1994), pp. 453-75; or P. R. Eddy, "Jesus as Diogenes? Reflections on the Cynic Jesus Thesis," in *Journal of Biblical Literature* 115.3 (1996), pp. 449-69; D. E. Aune, "Jesus and Cynics in First Century Palestine: Some Critical Considerations," in J. H. Charlesworth and L. L. Johns, *Hillel and Jesus: Comparative Studies of Two Major Religious Leaders* (Minneapolis: Fortress Press, 1997), pp. 176-92, and the response of F. G. Downing, "Deeper Reflections on the Jewish Cynic Jesus," *Journal of Biblical Literature* 117.1 (1998), pp. 97-104 .

[41] Thus B. Witherington III, *Jesus the Sage: The Pilgrimage of Wisdom* (Minneapolis:

Allison, strongly restated the traditional apocalyptic/eschatological view of Jesus,[42] while yet others re-interpreted Jesus' "inaugurated eschatology" along socio-political lines. We have already seen how R. A. Horsley argued that Jesus' "kingdom-language" was primarily a way of describing the movement of his village-based followers, understood as the restored and renewed people of God. Thus E. P. Sanders' "restoration eschatology" was given a concrete social form in the movement which Jesus created.

Meanwhile, two major British scholars were independently coming to similar conclusions about the nature of the pre-gospel oral tradition. The early form critics had postulated a freely-developing oral tradition of creative re-interpretation. Riesenfeld and Gerhardsson, by contrast, had argued for a formal process of memorization. Drawing on the work of K. E. Bailey, both N. T. Wright and J. D. G. Dunn argued that neither picture fits what we know about the early Christian churches, or the gospels as we have them. They argued that both kinds of evidence suggest rather an "informal, community-controlled" oral tradition, where marginal details may vary over retellings, but the central core of the sayings and stories is carefully preserved by a process of group memory.[43] Both Wright and Dunn argue that the "literary model" for understanding the gospels, with its archaeological metaphor of successive "layers," has been overdone. Rather than looking for a complex literary process whereby gospel writers have assembled and edited together material from various shadowy sources, they suggest that we need to take more seriously that the gospels could have reached their current form via the predominantly *oral* processes of community controlled retelling. A third British scholar, R. Bauckham, has added to the ferment by re-arguing the case for the importance of eye-witnesses in the transmission of the gospel tradition. All these conclusions are tentative, and have yet to be tested by detailed critical study, but they demonstrate the ways in which the debate is evolving.

Returning to the central theme of eschatology, N. T. Wright, in his *The New Testament and the People of God*, and *Jesus and the Victory of God*, accepted that Schweitzer was correct in basing his portrait of Jesus around apocalyptic ideas, but claimed that Schweitzer had seriously misunderstood them. For Wright, apocalyptic visions focus not on "the end of the world" understood in literal terms, but on the completion of God's saving purposes for his world and his people. He argues that a first-century Jew would have

---

Augsburg, 1994), pp. 147-208, and E. Schüssler-Fiorenza, *In Memory of Her* (New York: Crossroad, 1984), pp. 139-40, and *Jesus: Miriam's Child, Sophia's Prophet: Critical Issues in Feminist Christology* (New York: Continuum, 1994).

[42] J. P. Meier, *A Marginal Jew*, vol. 2 (New York: Doubleday, 1991), pp. 1044-47; D. C. Allison, Jr., "A Plea for Thoroughgoing Eschatology," *Journal of Biblical Literature* 113.4 (1994), pp. 651-68, and *Jesus of Nazareth: Millenarian Prophet* (Minneapolis: Fortress Press, 1998).

[43] Both Wright and Dunn cite K. Bailey's "Informal Controlled Oral Tradition and the Synoptic Gospels," *Asia Journal of Theology* 5 (1991), pp. 34-54. Wright has made the case his own in his *Jesus and the Victory of God*, pp. 133-36, and Dunn in his "Altering the Default Setting: Re-envisaging the Early Transmission of the Jesus Tradition," *New Testament Studies* 49 (2003), pp. 139-75, and *Jesus Remembered*, esp. pp. 205-10.

thought, not of the end of the world, but of the vindication of Israel against its enemies and the fulfilment of God's other promises of blessing. The prophetic promises of a glorious return from exile had not yet been truly fulfilled. The coming kingdom which Jesus announced would be that true return from exile. The imminent judgment of which Jesus warned was God's judgment on Israel's leaders and their policies, and it came to pass in AD 70, with the destruction of the temple by the Roman legions. To paraphrase Wright's teacher, G. B. Caird, it is not that Jesus predicted the end of the world, and was wrong. Jesus predicted the end of *his* world, and he was *right*. Here we see a further, highly original development of E. P. Sanders' concept of "restoration eschatology."

Two more individual contributions need to be commented on as this survey draws to a close. The first of these is the monumental work of J. P. Meier, whose four volume work, *A Marginal Jew: Rethinking the Historical Jesus* (1991–2009), is a veritable encyclopedia of historical Jesus scholarship.[44] After a thorough discussion of methods and criteria, Meier systematically examines the non-Christian, later Christian and canonical evidence in great detail. His work is remorselessly empirical, building up a broad picture bit by bit from individual sayings and stories deemed likely to be authentic. In some ways this approach feels dated, given the criticisms of Meyer, Sanders and Wright (among others), but there is no faulting his attention to detail and scrupulous fairness. His Jesus is first a disciple of John the Baptist, and later an independent eschatological prophet, modeling himself on the popular image of Elijah, proclaiming that God was about to act to gather the twelve tribes of Israel and set up his kingly rule in the world. He sees his own mission as a crucial inaugural stage in that process, and his circle of twelve disciples as symbolic of the gathering of the tribes. Further, Meier argues that late in his career Jesus also made symbolic claims to "Davidic messiahship."[45]

The second is the work of J. D. G. Dunn, *Jesus Remembered*. As with Wright and Meier, this is a multi-volume project which is still underway, so its full shape is not yet clear. As noted above, however, Dunn is particularly concerned with the nature of the oral tradition which preceded the written gospels. He urges forcefully that the Jesus who is remembered in the gospel tradition is not simply the risen Jesus of faith. He is also the earthly Jesus, whose impact on his disciples was clearly considerable, even before the rise of belief in his resurrection. They were, after all, *his* disciples. Dunn is (at least at this stage) more cautious than Meier about defining details of Jesus' self-understanding, but is none the less willing to argue that

> . . . Jesus was heard as speaking from God. . . for some at least as the

---

[44] At the time of writing, four volumes (vol. 1, "The Roots of the Problem", vol. 2, "Mentor and Message", vol. 3, "Companions and Competitors", and vol. 4, "Law and Love") have been published. So detailed and thorough is Meier's work that few will be surprised if the fourth volume grows into a fifth.

[45] Meier, *A Marginal Jew*, vol. 3 (New York: Doubleday, 2001), p. 634.

eschatological representative of God. Nor does it appear that this conviction arose only with Easter hindsight. . . It is hard to see how Easter faith could create such a weighty christological affirmation from the start, had the pre-Easter impact of Jesus not *already been measured in terms of divine authority and power.*[46]

## F. The Current State of the Discussion

Since 1973 we have seen a steady stream of new books on the historical Jesus, and there seems little prospect of it diminishing in the foreseeable future. Even when the widely varying positions we have surveyed are taken into account, the last thirty-five years of historical Jesus scholarship seem to be in broad agreement on a number of issues. There is a renewed confidence that a persuasive historical portrait of Jesus can be constructed. There is broad agreement that Jesus and his ideas are to be understood firmly within the framework of the Judaism of his time, rather than via the theological agendas of developed Christian theology. This is true whether the individual scholar focuses more on the apocalyptic literature, the wisdom literature, or a combination of the two. There is also a dissenting position which argues that Galilean Judaism, at least, was far more cosmopolitan and "Hellenized" than has normally been thought, and that Jesus is to be understood against the background of popular Greco-Roman thought. With the notable exception of J. P. Meier, there is a general move away from "bottom up," empirical approaches, in favor of the formation and testing of broad, contextually formed hypotheses. This approach has been argued for particularly by N. T. Wright and D. C. Allison, Jr. Allison has argued, with some force, that people are more likely to have remembered broad outline features of Jesus' teaching than particular fine details of wording. To focus on the details of particular isolated sayings, stripped of their literary context, he contends, is to start with the least certain historical material. We should look, instead, for broadly attested ideas.[47] There is a strong move away from the purely "history of ideas" approach to Jesus, which was primarily interested in his theological views, in favor of a broader social history perspective. There is a lively methodological debate, within which old methods are continually being challenged and refined, and new perspectives are being opened up. A number of the consensus positions of older generations of scholarship are now under challenge. For example, though some now make "Q" the main key to the interpretation of Jesus,[48] others raise new doubts about whether "Q" is a useful hypothesis at all.[49] In brief, to quote James H. Charlesworth, "Jesus

---

[46] Dunn, *Jesus Remembered,* p. 892.

[47] On this approach see D. C. Allison, Jr., *Jesus of Nazareth: Millenarian Prophet* (Minneapolis: Augsburg Fortress, 1998), and the summary in his essay, "The Historian's Jesus and the Church," in B. R. Gaventa and R. B. Hays, *Seeking the Identity of Jesus: a Pilgrimage* (Grand Rapids: Eerdmans, 2008), pp. 79-95, esp. pp. 84ff.

[48] A prominent example is J. D. Crossan, *The Historical Jesus* (San Francisco: Harper, 1991), pp. 227-64.

[49] A. Farrer, "On Dispensing With Q," in D. E. Nineham, ed., *Studies in the Gospels:*

research expands with chaotic creativity."[50]

It must be emphasized that any summary of the current state of historical Jesus studies can only be sketchy. In broad outline, however, several related models for understanding Jesus dominate the current debate, blurring and blending at the edges. A diagrammatic outline of these can be found in fig. 1 at the end of this chapter.

(1) The first of these models has been a major part of the debate for a century. This is the understanding of Jesus as a prophet of the imminent intervention of God, the "coming kingdom." Jesus is described as a "millennial prophet" or an "apocalyptic prophet." He predicts a great overturning of the world-order, accompanied by a "last judgment," and in some sense a "new world." This has long been, and still remains, the majority view.

(2) Related to this first model is the second, which agrees that Jesus predicted a great transformation of the world, but denies that he understood this as "the end of the world." Rather, it is argued, Jesus expected a social and political transformation. The people of Israel would be vindicated by their God, and their oppressors, both external and internal, would be decisively overthrown. Depending on the various versions of this model, the change might also bring a return to Eden-like conditions. It will be clear that there is room for considerable overlap between these first two views.

(3) Third, there is the model which understands Jesus primarily as a counter-cultural sage or holy man, someone who saw the expression of the "kingdom of God" mainly in terms of its effect on his own life, and on that of his groups of followers. This model draws much of its inspiration from the wave of new scholarship on the "wisdom-literature" of the Jewish tradition, and downplays the importance of eschatology for understanding Jesus. Here it is Jesus' social and ethical teachings that are in focus. His views on Israel's future, and on his own role in the plans of God, are less central.

(4) Fourth, there is the model which sees Jesus against the backdrop of counter-cultural traditions drawn from the wider Greco-Roman world. In this view, Jesus' Galilean environment was as much influenced by cosmopolitan urban culture as by parochially Jewish traditions. It is argued that Galilee's own regional culture, and the program of urbanization developed by Herod Antipas, opened the region to a wider range of cultural influences. Specifically, Jesus is seen as developing a set of teachings strikingly similar to those of the *kunikoi*, the Cynics. This loose school of non-conformist philosophers has been briefly discussed above, in the section on the work of J. D. Crossan. This interpretation of Jesus has the least in common with the two "prophetic" models, and only marginally more in common with the "sage" model. This Jesus may be ethnically Jewish, but he is deeply influenced by

---

*Essays in Memory of R. H. Lightfoot* (Oxford: Blackwell, 1955), pp. 55-88; M. Goulder, "Is Q a Juggernaut?" *Journal of Biblical Literature* 115 (1996), pp. 667-81, and M. Goodacre, *The Case Against Q, Studies in Markan Priority and the Synoptic Problem* (Harrisburg: Trinity, 2001).

[50] This is the title of Charlesworth's essay in J. H. Charlesworth and W. P. Weaver, eds., *Images of Jesus Today* (Valley Forge: Trinity Press International, 1994), p. 11.

trends from the wider Greco-Roman scene.

Alongside these four main models are numerous trends which have not yet achieved the same degree of momentum. The political dimensions of Jesus' activities are again under the spotlight. Anthropological and other social-scientific models are being applied. As we have seen, basic questions about the nature of the oral gospel tradition have been re-opened. Historical Jesus scholarship in the twenty-first century is far from simply a rehashing of old issues. New questions are being asked. New kinds of evidence are being examined. New hypotheses are being formed and tested. The quest (or quests) continue.

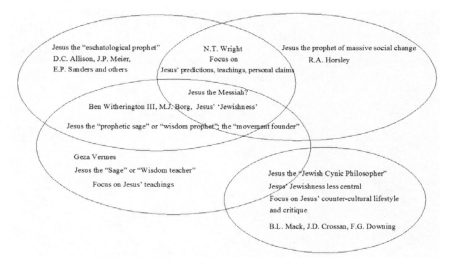

*Figure 1. Recent historical interpretations of Jesus.*

## Bibliography

Allison, Jr., Dale C. *Jesus of Nazareth: Millenarian Prophet.* Minneapolis: Fortress Press, 1998.

Borg, Marcus J. *Jesus in Contemporary Scholarship.* Valley Forge: Trinity Press International, 1994.

Charlesworth, James H., and Walter P. Weaver. *Images of Jesus Today.* Valley Forge: Trinity Press International, 1994.

Crossan, John Dominic. *The Historical Jesus: the Life of a Mediterranean Jewish Peasant.* San Francisco: HarperSanFrancisco, 1991.

Dunn, James D. G. *Jesus Remembered (Christianity in the Making: volume 1).* Grand Rapids: Eerdmans, 2003.

Dunn, James D. G. *The Evidence for Jesus.* Philadelphia: Westminster, 1985.

France, R. T. *The Evidence for Jesus.* Downers Grove: InterVarsity Press, 1986.

Freyne, Sean. *Jesus, a Jewish Galilean: A New reading of the Jesus Story.* London: T. & T. Clark International, 2004.

Gowler, David B. *What are They Saying About the Historical Jesus?* New York: Paulist Press, 2007.

Horsley, Richard A. *Jesus and the Spiral of Violence.* San Francisco: Harper & Row, 1987.

Kee, Howard Clark. *What Can we Know about Jesus?* Cambridge/New York: Cambridge University Press, 1990.

Meier, John P. *A Marginal Jew* (vol. 1, *"The Roots of the Problem,"* vol. 2, *"Mentor and Message,"* vol. 3, *"Companions and Competitors,"* and vol. 4, *"Law and Love").* New York: Doubleday, 1991-2001 (vols. 1-3) and New Haven: Yale University Press, 2009 (vol. 4).

Meyer, Ben F. *The Aims of Jesus.* London: SCM Press, 1979.

Neill, Stephen, and N. T. Wright. *The Interpretation of the New Testament, 1861–1986.* Oxford/New York: Oxford University Press, 1988.

Sanders, E. P. *Jesus and Judaism.* Philadelphia: Fortress Press, 1985.

Theissen, Gerd, and Annette Merz. *The Historical Jesus: A Comprehensive Guide.* Minneapolis: Fortress Press, 1998.

Vermes, Geza. *Jesus the Jew: A Historian's Reading of the Gospels.* London: Collins, 1973.

Weaver, Walter P. *The Historical Jesus in the Twentieth Century, 1900–1950.* Harrisburg: Trinity Press International, 1999.

Witherington III, Ben. *The Jesus Quest: the Third Search for the Jew of Nazareth.* Downers Grove: InterVarsity Press, 1995.

Wright, N. T. *Jesus and the Victory of God.* London, SPCK, 1996.

————. *The New Testament and the People of God.* London: SPCK, 1992.

# 11. The Markan Outline and Emphases

*Johan Ferreira*

## A. Why Did Mark Write His Gospel?

The Gospel of Mark, although containing little more than eleven thousand words, is arguably the most influential book that has ever been written. Mark, or the author of the Second Gospel, wrote his account of Jesus at least thirty years after Jesus' death. At that time Paul had already written his epistles and many other traditions about Jesus had become established and well-known. Why then did Mark decide, relatively late, to write an account of Jesus? The answer to this question involves a raft of scholarly issues.[1] However, most importantly, it brings us to the heart of New Testament theology as well as the belief and practice of Christianity. The Gospel of Mark is the shortest of the four canonical gospels. Most scholars are also convinced that Mark is the earliest gospel and that Matthew and Luke used Mark as the basis of their accounts of Jesus.[2] Therefore, the gospel form and indeed most of our knowledge of the life and teachings of Jesus are due to Mark. What motivated him to write his Gospel?

Early church tradition almost unanimously maintains that Mark, the disciple of Peter, wrote the Gospel in Rome.[3] This Mark is identified with the

---

[1] On the history of synoptic criticism, see D. L. Dungan, *A History of the Synoptic Problem: The Canon, the Text, the Composition, and the Interpretation of the Gospels* (New York: Doubleday, 1999). For general overviews see, K. F. Nickle, *The Synoptic Gospels: An Introduction* (Atlanta: John Knox, 1980) and R. H. Stein, *The Synoptic Problem: An Introduction* (Grand Rapids: Baker, 1987).

[2] This *consensus communis* in the main is based on the following observations: 1) Mark is the shortest and "crudest" of the gospels. Texts generally tend to grow and improve in linguistic quality over time. 2) Almost all the content of Mark is found in Matthew and Luke (only 6 percent of Mark is not found in Matthew). It is easy to explain these omissions if Matthew and Luke were dependent on Mark, but difficult to explain if Mark was dependent on Matthew and Luke. 3) When there is a similar sequence of events in Matthew and Luke, they follow the sequence in Mark. When the sequence of events disagrees in Matthew and Luke, they both depart from the sequence in Mark. This can be readily explained if Matthew and Luke depended on Mark. 4) The difference in wording of common units is best explained if Mark was the source. Matthew and Luke often improve the language of Mark.

[3] This tradition is preserved by Papias, Justin Martyr, the Muratorian Fragment, the Anti-Marcionite Prologues to the Gospels, Irenaeus, Clement of Alexandria, Origen, Tertullian, Epiphanius, Jerome, Augustine, and Eusebius. Only Chrysostom relates a tradition that Mark

John Mark of the New Testament.[4] Although the tradition cannot be verified beyond doubt, there are no compelling reasons to abandon it. Circumstantial evidence in support of the traditional view is strong. The earliest evidence of the tradition is preserved in Eusebius where he quotes the comment of Papias (c. AD 60–130) regarding the composition of the Gospel of Mark (*Hist. eccl.* 3.39.14).

> This, too, the presbyter used to say. "Mark, who had been Peter's interpreter, wrote down carefully, but not in order, all that he remembered of the Lord's sayings (λεχθέντα) and doings (πραχθέντα). For he had not heard the Lord or been one of His followers, but later, as I said, one of Peter's. Peter used to adapt his teachings to the occasion, without making a systematic arrangement of the Lord's sayings, so that Mark was quite justified in writing down some things just as he remembered them. For he had one purpose only—to leave out nothing that he had heard, and to make no misstatement about it."
> (trans. G. A. Williamson, *Eusebius: The History of the Church* [Harmondsworth: Penguin, 1965], pp. 103-4)

Markan scholars have been divided in their assessment of this tradition.[5] Apart from the problem of what is meant by Mark as the "interpreter" of Peter the statement itself is one or two stages removed from the composition of the Gospel. Papias grounds his remark on the authority of a certain presbyter (probably John, but not the Apostle), who in turn must have heard it from someone else. We have no knowledge about the reliability of this source. Yet, despite Eusebius' reservations about Papias' intelligence (cf. *Hist. eccl.* 3.39.13), one could judge that he would not have retained this tradition had he been suspicious of it.

The tradition of Markan authorship appears in various forms throughout the Mediterranean world, not all of them dependent on Papias. In an environment where apostolic authorship was one of the major arguments to support the canonicity of a document, there must have been weighty reasons for the prevalence of the tradition. In addition to the external evidence, the content of the Gospel also appears to support the tradition. Several passages contain information that implies the presence of an eyewitness. The author shows broad knowledge of Palestinian geography and customs. On the other hand, the lack of intra Jewish debates, the translation of Aramaic into Greek, and the prevalence of Latin loan words may imply a Gentile Roman audience.[6] Finally, the tradition also places the composition of the Gospel on

---

wrote the Gospel in Egypt. Evidence indicates that the appellation "According to Mark" was attached to the Gospel about the middle of the second century. See Martin Hengel, *Studies in the Gospel of Mark* (London: SCM Press, 1985), pp. 64-84.

[4] Cf. Acts 12:12, 25; 13:5, 13; 15:37, 39; Col. 4:10; 2 Tim. 4:11; Phlm. 24; 1 Pet. 5:13.

[5] Biblical scholars have tended to be extremely cautious about accepting the historicity of early traditions.

[6] For Aramaic words see Mark 3:17 (*Boanerges*); 5:41 (*Talitha koum*); 7:34 (*Ephphatha*); 9:5 (also 10:51; 11:21; 14:15) (*Rabbi*); 9:43 (*Gehenna*); 10:46 (*Bartimaeus*); 14:36 (*Abba*); 15:22 (*Golgotha*); 15:34 (*Eloi, Eloi, lama sabachthani?*). For Latin words see Mark 2:4, 9,11, 12

the eve of the Neronic persecution (AD 64), which accords well with the stress on suffering in the Gospel.[7] Therefore, the traditions that advocate the Markan authorship of the Second Gospel in all likelihood contain a factual historical core. Consequently, recent scholarship has taken the traditional view more seriously.[8] However, in the final analysis, certainty on these matters remains aloof.

However, the significance of Papias' statement for answering our question does not lie so much in what it says about authorship, but rather in the evidence it provides about the *Sitz im Leben* of the writing of the Gospel. According to the tradition, Peter had a repository of the Lord's sayings and doings at his disposal. A little further on in Eusebius, Matthew also is said to have made a compilation of the "reports" concerning Jesus. These statements reflect the situation in the middle of the first century when reports about Jesus' doings and sayings were circulating independently of one another. The other gospel accounts also show evidence of these unconnected stories, whether oral or written, being transmitted over a period of time. They contain collections of parables, miracles, sayings, and conflict stories, each category with its distinctive literary form.[9] Papias' statement informs us that in the context of these floating traditions, Mark put down what he "remembered." In other words, the author of the Gospel had a large body of material about Jesus at his disposal. His purpose, according to the presbyter, was somewhat nebulous: "to leave out nothing that he [i.e. Mark] had heard, and to make no misstatement about it." Rather, more to the point, the statement comes within the context of a debate concerning the disparity between the chronological orders of the different gospels. The presbyter was defending Mark's "inaccurate" order of events by laying the blame at Peter's door. However, the significance of the Gospel of Mark was not that it set out to preserve some of the doings and teachings of Jesus, nor that it intended to give a more accurate account, but that it placed these disconnected stories within a single narrative framework. Previously unrelated stories were now connected in an interrelated whole. Therefore, the significance of Papias' statement with respect to the purpose of Mark is that it shows that Mark was more than just a

---

(*krabbatos*); 4:21 (*modius*); 4:28 (*herba*); 5:9, 15 (*legio*); 6:27 (*speculator*); 6:37 (*denarius*) 7:4, 8 (*sextarius*); 12:14 (*census*); 12:42 (*quadrans*); 15:15 (*fragello*); 15:16 (*praetorium*), 15:39, 44, 45 (*centurio*). R. H. Gundry, *Mark: A Commentary on His Apology* (Grand Rapids: Eerdmans, 1993), pp. 1039-45. By and large the loan words are unique to Mark.

[7] Nero's persecution of the Christians is described in detail by Tacitus (*Ann.* 15.44).

[8] See Hengel, *Studies in the Gospel of Mark*, pp. 1-30; Gundry, *Mark*, pp. 1,026-45; J. R. Donahue and D. J. Harrington, *The Gospel of Mark*, Sacra Pagina Series 2 (Collegeville: Liturgical Press, 2002), pp. 38-46; and R. T. France, *The Gospel of Mark: A Commentary on the Greek Text* (Grand Rapids: Eerdmans, 2002), pp. 35-41. Also see the general overviews of P. J. Flanagan, *The Gospel of Mark Made Easy* (New York: Paulist Press, 1997) and P. J. Cunningham, *Mark: The Good News Preached to the Romans* (New York: Paulist Press, 1998).

[9] The most well-known of these sources is the so-called Q document, which contained the sayings (logia) of Jesus, used by the Gospel of Matthew and the Gospel of Luke, and the *Semeia* Source (Signs Source), which was a compilation of miracles, used by the Gospel of John. On the *Semeia* Source see R. T. Fortna, *The Gospel of Signs: A Reconstruction of the Narrative Source Underlying the Fourth Gospel* (Cambridge: Cambridge University Press, 1970).

collector but intentionally arranged the materials into one coherent story, chronological order being secondary.

The consequences of this process—Mark's collating, editing, and arrangement of traditions within one connected story—cannot be over estimated. After the formation of the Gospel, previously independent traditions about Jesus will be understood within the contours of the overarching story. Individual stories have become part of the whole and can only be understood in relation to the whole. What, then, was Mark trying to say with his new framework of the Jesus story? As we have pointed out, it was not that people had no recollections or "memoirs" of Jesus' ministry. There was a plethora of Jesus stories in existence. The importance of Mark does not consist in his provision of a large collection of Jesus traditions, but in his arrangement of these in one single narrative plot. Therefore, in order to understand the purpose of the Gospel of Mark, and consequently each individual story in the Markan outline, we need to ask the question regarding the Gospel's distinctive emphasis. Careful reading of the Gospel presents an unambiguous answer.

## B. What is the Center or Climax of Mark's Gospel?

Echoing Martin Kähler[10] at the end of the nineteenth century, many scholars have pointed out that the Gospel of Mark is basically a passion narrative with an extended introduction. Although individual pericopes in Mark touch on issues that are not directly related to Jesus' passion, the basic point of this observation is valid. The time that Mark allocates to Jesus' passion is noticeably disproportional to the rest of his ministry and life. The Gospel of Luke portrays Jesus as having had a life span of around thirty-three years (cf. Luke 3:23). Mark, however, is totally silent about the first thirty years of Jesus' life. He describes only the last three years of Jesus' life, or to be more exact, the period between his baptism and resurrection which can easily be confined to a time span of less than one year. Furthermore, looking more closely, Mark spends ten chapters (about 7,000 words) describing Jesus' ministry, and then six chapters (about 4,000 words) describing the last week of his life. The two longest chapters of Mark, chapters 14 and 15 (1,865 words), describe just the last two days of Jesus' life. In other words, Mark's use of narrative time clearly shows where his emphasis lay. Mark was captivated by the sufferings and cross of Jesus. Therefore, the center or climax of Mark's Gospel is to be found in the passion narrative. Mark has intentionally constructed his narrative plot to culminate in the death and resurrection of Jesus.

If our proposal is correct, then one will expect to see many allusions to the suffering of Jesus before the passion narrative in the Gospel. Indeed, that is what one finds. The Gospel's opening statement, especially the quotation

---

[10] Martin Kähler, *The So-called Historical Jesus and the Historic Biblical Christ* (Philadelphia: Fortress Press, 1964 [1892]), p. 80, n. 11.

from Isa. 40:3, recalls the schema of Second Isaiah, which culminates in the salvation brought by the servant of Yahweh through suffering and death (Isaiah 53).[11] Mark regards Jesus as none other than Isaiah's suffering servant, who died according to God's predetermined plan. According to Isaiah 53, despite appearances, the Yahweh handed over (παρέδωκεν, v. 6) the servant to bear the sins of many. The use of the Greek verb παραδίδωμι in the Septuagint is significant. It occurs three times in Isaiah 53 (once in verse six and twice in verse twelve). The term can either mean "to betray" or "to hand over." Mark uses the same term throughout his Gospel but especially within the passion narrative.[12] The term is used to describe Judas' betrayal of Jesus (cf. Mark 3:19). However, the Isaian context of the term also suggests that Mark had another connotation in mind. Jesus was not just betrayed but rather was handed over by God to die on the cross as a sacrifice for sin (cf. Mark 10:45). This Isaian motif is woven into the storyline in such a way that it binds the whole narrative together.[13]

Mark does not want the reader to miss the significance of the cross. The closer the reader comes to the passion the more emphasis is placed on the necessity of the cross. In the middle section of the Gospel, the journey to Jerusalem, Jesus predicts his death and resurrection no fewer than three times (Mark 8:31; 9:31; 10:33-34).[14] The first prediction occurs at a pivotal juncture within the text directly after Peter's confession that Jesus is the Christ. For the Markan Jesus, death on the cross is an indispensable part of what it means to be the Christ. It is what the Son of Man must (δεῖ) undergo. Although the resurrection is also an important aspect of the three predictions, it is the cross that is emphasized. Mark is intent to show his readers that Jesus' ministry reaches its fulfillment and culmination in the cross and resurrection, but especially the cross.

Likewise, the meaning of Jesus' teachings and miracles can be fully understood only by reference to the cross and resurrection.[15] The Parable of the Growing Seed (Mark 4:26-29), which is exclusive to the Gospel of Mark, is a parable about the kingdom and underscores that it will arrive paradoxically through Jesus' death on the cross. The small seed, automatically (αὐτομάτη), issues forth into a great harvest. The kingdom does not come through human muscle but through the supernatural events of the cross and

---

[11] Mark 1:2-3 is a conflation of Exod. 23:20; Mal. 3:1; and Isa. 40:3. Joel Marcus argues persuasively that Mark quotes OT texts with their wider contexts in view. See his *The Way of the Lord: Christological Exegesis of the Old Testament in the Gospel of Mark* (Louisville: Westminster/John Knox Press, 1992).

[12] Cf. Mark 1:14; 3:19; 4:29; 7:13; 9:31; 10:33; 13:9,11; 14:10, 11, 18, 21, 41, 42, 44; 15:1, 10, 15.

[13] Also see R. E. Watts, *Isaiah's New Exodus in Mark* (Grand Rapids: Baker, 2000).

[14] Both Matthew and Luke have retained the three passion predictions (cf. Matt. 16:21; 17:22-23; 20:18-19; Luke 9:22; 9:44; 18:32-33).

[15] Mark contains eighteen miracles (Mark 1:23-28, 29-31, 40-45; 2:3-12; 3:1-5; 4:35-41; 5:1-20, 22-24 [with 35-43], 25-34; 6:35-44, 45-52; 7:24-30, 31-37; 8:1-9, 22-26; 9:14-29; 10:46-52; 11:12-14) and about an equal number of extended metaphors, including the parables (Mark 1:16-17; 2:17, 19-20, 21, 22; 3:24, 25, 27; 4:2-8, 21-22, 26-29, 30-32; 7:14-23, 27; 8:14; 9:43-47; 12:1-9, 10-11; 13:28-29, 34-37).

resurrection. The miracles likewise point towards the cross and resurrection. The two feeding miracles (Mark 6:30-44 and 8:1-10) are directly linked with Jesus' death on the cross through his words at the Last Supper (cf. Mark 6:41; 8:6 and 14:22-24). Also characteristic of Mark is the large number of "raising" miracles in Jesus' ministry. Jesus raises (ἤγειρεν) Peter's mother-in-law, the fever leaves her (Mark 1:31). Rising does not have anything particularly to do with curing a high fever. The significance lies in the use of the same verb to describe the resurrection (Mark 14:28; 16:6).[16] The healing of Peter's mother-in-law points forward to the greater healing that will take place at the resurrection. All the doings and teachings of Jesus are placed within a narrative that points towards and climaxes in the cross and resurrection. Therefore, the Gospel of Mark reflects the basic structure of early Christian proclamation.[17] This proclamation, referred to by scholars as the *kerygma*, has been identified in some of the extant traditions contained in Acts and the epistles of Paul (cf. Acts 10:34-43; 1 Cor. 15:1-4). The primitive *kerygma* contained the following elements: (1) Jesus inaugurated the fulfillment of messianic prophecy; (2) he went about doing good and performing miracles; (3) he was crucified according to God's plan; (4) he was raised and exalted to heaven; (5) he will return to judge the world; (6) therefore, repent, believe, and be baptized. Mark's narrative in broad outline reflects a similar structure.[18]

Mark's intention is clear. If one wants to understand Jesus, he or she needs to understand the meaning of his suffering and death on the cross. Mark was more than a mere collector; he was a courageous theologian.[19] At the time of the writing of the Gospel, many traditions about Jesus were circulating and influencing Christian communities around the Mediterranean Sea. Depending on the traditions to which a community had access to, some were emphasizing Jesus as a teacher, others as a miracle worker, and in non-Christian circles as a tragic figure or as a troublemaker. Mark made a selection of these oral and written traditions and incorporated them within the narrative framework of his Gospel. By the imposition of this narrative framework, which culminates in the cross and resurrection, upon the traditions, Mark constructed an exclusive understanding of Jesus' ministry. Subsequently, when one reads or hears[20] a

---

[16] Also see Mark 2:9, 11, 12; 3:3; 5:41; 9:27; 10:49.

[17] Many scholars have discussed the related question regarding the genre of the Gospel of Mark. There has been a long tradition of comparing the gospels with other ancient writings, in particular: 1) Acts (πράξεις); 2) Memoirs (ἀπομνημονεύματα); and 3) Lives (βίοι). See G. N. Stanton, *Jesus of Nazareth in New Testament Preaching* (New York: Cambridge University Press, 1974); C. H. Talbert, *What is a Gospel? The Genre of the Canonical Gospels* (Philadelphia: Fortress Press, 1977); and R. A. Burridge, *What are the Gospels? A Comparison with Graeco-Roman Biography* (New York: Cambridge University Press, 1992). Yet, as a whole, the gospel is a distinct genre in ancient literature.

[18] See C. H. Dodd, *The Apostolic Preaching and its Developments* (London: Hodder & Stoughton, 1936). As such, the gospels should be seen as *kerygma* rather than biographies. The gospels are kerygmatic literature, reflecting the faith of the early Christians as it was proclaimed.

[19] Redaction critics have highlighted Mark's theological shaping of his traditions. See W. Marxsen, *Mark the Evangelist* (Nashville: Abingdon, 1969 [German orig. 1956]).

[20] C. Bryan has argued that the Gospel was written to be read out aloud. *A Preface to Mark:*

story in the Gospel, one will interpret that story under the shadow of the cross. In this way Jesus' parables demonstrate that he is not just a teacher of wisdom but the one through whose death God's kingdom will be established. Jesus' miracles demonstrate that he is not just a worker of powerful deeds, but that God's reign has dawned in the resurrection. Like Paul and Peter, Mark has found the meaning of the gospel in the cross and resurrection of Jesus. For Mark, therefore, without the cross there can be no gospel, and no satisfactory understanding of Jesus.[21]

## C. Jesus' Message of the Kingdom

The cross and resurrection stand at the centre of the Gospel of Mark. How does this, then, tie in with the message of Jesus as portrayed in the Gospel? Or, to frame the question in another way, how does the message of Jesus relate to the message of the Gospel? The Gospel's most important summary statement regarding the message of Jesus occurs at the beginning of Jesus' ministry (Mark 1:14-15):

> After John was put in prison, Jesus went into Galilee, proclaiming the good news (εὐαγγέλιον) of God. "The time has come," he said. "The kingdom of God is near. Repent and believe the good news!"

Jesus' proclamation is understood as "good news" or "gospel." The word "gospel" (εὐαγγέλιον) is a key word for Mark, occurring seven times (Mark 1:1, 14, 15; 8:35; 10:29; 13:10; 14:9).[22] Most scholars have associated the religious use of the term in the New Testament with the Roman imperial cult where it was used in connection with the proclamation of the emperor's appearance as the divine world-ruler and the inauguration of his reign.[23] This "news" was portrayed as tidings of joy. We judge this to be significant in explaining the prominence of the term in the New Testament.

However, more important for Mark is the Old Testament (OT) use of the related verb "to proclaim the gospel" (εὐαγγελίζω; *basar* in Hebrew), especially in Second Isaiah where the message of the coming reign of Yahweh is associated with the proclamation of the gospel (εὐαγγελιζόμενος;

---

*Notes on the Gospel in Its Literary and Cultural Settings* (New York: Oxford University Press, 1993). Only about ten to twenty percent of people around the Mediterranean were literate.

[21] So P. Achtemeier, "The cross therefore not only ends the career of Jesus, it also represents its culmination and the key to its meaning." *Mark* (Philadelphia: Fortress Press, 1986), p. 102.

[22] The term occurs four times in Matthew (4:23; 9:35; 24:14; 26:13), twice in Acts (15:7; 20:24), and sixty-two times in Paul. It does not occur in the Gospels of Luke and John.

[23] The term is found in several imperial inscriptions. The most famous of these is the inscription from Priene (9 BC) in Asia Minor, which celebrates the benefactions of Augustus to the world. It reads as follows: ". . . providence created the most perfect good for our lives. . . filling him [Augustus] with virtue for the benefit of mankind, sending us and those after us a savior who put an end to war and established all things. . . and whereas the birthday of the god [Augustus] marked for the world the beginning of good tidings [εὐαγγελία] through his coming."

*mĕbbasereth* in Hebrew, see Isa. 40:9; 52:7; also cf. 61:1). The content of the proclamation of the "good news" concerns the coming and rule of Yahweh, the dawn of a new age. In light of the prominence of Isaian themes in the Gospel, there can be no doubt that Mark sets Jesus' proclamation against the backdrop of Second Isaiah's proclamation of the reign of God. Indeed, Jesus can proclaim the "gospel" because he is not only the servant through whom it will be realized, but also Yahweh himself who has come to reign for his people. According to Isaiah and the Markan Jesus, the heart of the gospel message concerns the kingdom of God.[24]

In the OT the term "kingdom" (*malkuth* and *mamlakah*), when it refers to God's kingdom, denotes the rule of God. Aspects of realm or locality are secondary.[25] It may denote God's general sovereignty over all creation (Exod. 15:18; Ps. 103:19; 145:11-13). At times Israel is also presented as being the kingdom of Yahweh (Exod. 19:4-6; cf. Isa. 41:21; Jer. 8:19). However, most significant for the New Testament is the expectation of a future kingdom that is redemptive in nature. According to OT hope, the reign of God will create a universal righteousness, peace, and prosperity (cf. Ps. 24, 145; Isa. 2:2-4; 49:10-13; Jer. 9:24; 23:5-6; Daniel 2, 7). Furthermore, in several passages there is a connection between the coming of God's reign and the future Messiah. The Messiah is to be God's anointed one (so the meaning of the term), the appointed king who will establish God's rule and righteousness on the earth (cf. Isa. 9:1-7; 11:1-9; Psalm 72).[26] Therefore, John the Baptist's and then Jesus' proclamation of the imminent kingdom of God caused a stir among first-century Jews.[27]

Mark uses the term kingdom (βασιλεία) in Jesus' first utterance, summarizing Jesus' message in the Gospel.[28] A more literal translation of Jesus' words would read, "The time has been fulfilled and the reign of God has drawn near" (πεπλήρωται ὁ καιρὸς καὶ ἤγγικεν ἡ βασιλεία τοῦ θεοῦ). The juxtaposition of the two perfect verbs (πεπλήρωται and ἤγγικεν) emphasizes that the reign of God has approached in the ministry of Jesus and

---

[24] The expression "kingdom of God" occurs at Mark 4:11, 26, 30, and 9:1.

[25] Correspondingly, the OT focuses much more on God as king, *melek*, or on God as reigning than on the realm of God's reign. The terms *malkuth* and *mamlakah* (kingdom) occur eighty-nine and a hundred-and-seventeen times respectively in the OT, mostly referring to human political kingdoms. The Aramaic term *malku* (kingdom) occurs four times in Ezra and fifty-one times in Daniel.

[26] The term "messiah" (*mashiah*) occurs thirty-nine times in the OT. In most of these occurrences the word does not refer to an expected eschatological figure who will inaugurate the kingdom of God, but to a contemporary Israelite king. The term "messianic" is used in a broad sense to describe the general hope of a glorious future for the nation, as well as in the narrower sense of a personal Messiah who is to deliver the nation. Most passages that were later understood to be messianic by both Jewish and Christian sources do not contain the term (e.g., Num. 24:17; Gen. 49:10; Ps. 110; Isa. 9:5-6; 11:10; 32:1-8; Hos. 3:5 Amos 9:11-12; Mic. 5:1-5). Judaism espoused a range of views about the Messiah. See J. H. Charlesworth, ed., *The Messiah: Developments in Earliest Judaism and Christianity* (Minneapolis: Fortress Press, 1992).

[27] So much so, that it did not go unnoticed by Josephus, cf. *Ant.* 18.116-19.

[28] The term occurs twenty times in the Gospel, Mark 1:15; 3:24 (twice); 4:11, 26, 30; 6:23; 9:1, 47; 10:14, 15, 23, 24, 25; 11:10; 12:34; 13:8 (twice); 14:25; 15:43.

is increasingly making its presence felt. The time of the fulfillment of the OT promises has arrived. A new era is about to dawn. In the story of the strong man and robber (Mark 3:23-27) Jesus counters the accusation that he drives out demons by the power of Satan with the teaching that the authority (ἐξουσία) evident in his exorcisms demonstrates that a new kingdom is drawing near. Jesus is able to bind the strong man and rob his house because a new power is at work in his ministry. For Mark that kingdom arrives in power (ἐν δυνάμει) with the resurrection. The key passage is Mark 9:1. Jesus' pronouncement, coming halfway in the Gospel, is closely tied to the surrounding context. Jesus has just made his first passion prediction pointing to the culmination of his ministry in the cross and resurrection. Peter's objection is an indication of the mind of Satan on this issue. Ironically, the Son of Man is going to obtain victory through the path of suffering. This leads Jesus to say, "I tell you the truth, some who are standing here will not taste death before they see the kingdom of God come with power" (Mark 9:1). Jesus predicts the arrival of the kingdom with power within the lifetime of the disciples. Then follows the transfiguration, which is a foreshadowing of the resurrection glory of the Son of Man. The disciples are commanded "not to tell anyone what they had seen until the Son of Man had risen from the dead" (Mark 9:9). The full meaning of the transfiguration can only be understood after the cross and resurrection. In other words, Jesus' statement about the kingdom coming with power is sandwiched between two passages that point forward to the events of the cross and resurrection. Mark sees the arrival of the kingdom, or the dawning of the eschatological age, as coinciding with these events. It is also in this light that we can understand Mark's appropriation of the apocalyptic vision in Mark 13:24-27:

> But in those days, following that distress, the sun will be darkened, and the moon will not give its light; the stars will fall from the sky, and the heavenly bodies will be shaken. At that time men will see the Son of Man coming in clouds with great power and glory. And he will send his angels and gather his elect from the four winds, from the ends of the earth to the ends of the heavens.

The cross and resurrection of Jesus will be the beginning of this new world order—the new creation. This period will be characterized by Jesus' power and reign, evidenced by the ingathering of the elect from all parts of the world. For Mark this commences at the resurrection. On the first day of the week, the beginning of the new creation, the women were greeted with an open tomb and the words "he has risen." The new age of the kingdom has dawned. We may conclude our discussion so far by summarizing the Gospel of Mark's distinguishing emphasis by means of a theme: the kingdom of God is coming into the world with power through the suffering, cross, and resurrection of Jesus.

## D. What Does it Mean to Be a Disciple of Jesus?

The basic question Mark is addressing in his Gospel, amid a growing number of viewpoints, is what is Christianity? This question has two aspects: Who is Christ? And who is a Christian?[29] We have already discussed Mark's answer to the first question. The second question is closely related to the first. Mark defines the disciple, or the Christian, in terms of his portrayal of Christ. In short, for Mark a disciple is one who follows Jesus. The call of the first disciples consists of a command to follow Jesus. Simon and Andrew respond by following him (Mark 1:17-18). The term "to follow" (ἀκολουθέω) occurs eighteen times in Mark and designates the central trait of discipleship.[30] Closely related to the motif of following is the depiction of the "journey." Perhaps the journey metaphor encapsulates the heart of Mark's understanding of discipleship. Mark sets his teaching about discipleship within the framework of a journey. The disciple's life is like a journey, or more accurately, a disciple is one who follows Jesus along his journey. The journey passes through three geographical areas. Discipleship begins with the call that Jesus issues in Galilee. The disciples follow Jesus around Galilee and the surrounding Gentile areas. But then the journey extends beyond Galilee to Judea and finally reaches Jerusalem where the disciples need to face the challenge of the cross. Mark uses this basic geographical scaffold to construct his teaching on discipleship. For Mark, this pattern does not only have a spatial reference but also contains a symbolic or spiritual element.[31]

The disciples begin to follow Jesus in Galilee. Galilee is the place of action, powerful ministry, and success. In Galilee Jesus did many miracles. In Galilee Jesus revealed his power and glory. In Galilee the disciples began to believe in Jesus. It is a good place to stay. However, after Jesus' ministry in Galilee, he starts out on his journey to Jerusalem. Jerusalem represents the place of Jesus' suffering. Already early in the Gospel Mark is careful to portray Jerusalem as a place of opposition (cf. Mark 3:22; 7:1). The Jewish leaders who oppose Jesus live in Jerusalem. Therefore, when Jesus sets out for Jerusalem, the disciples are very reluctant. Being astonished and afraid they follow a long way behind (Mark 10:32). The disciples do not want Jesus to suffer (Mark 8:31-30; 9:5). Therefore, for the disciples Jerusalem presents threat, danger, and the prospect of failure. Indeed, for them the threat of suffering and death in Jerusalem presents a crisis of loyalty. Their Jerusalem

---

[29] Scholars agree that Mark's central concerns are Christology and discipleship. See R. T. France, *The Gospel of Mark*, p. 29. Several studies have dealt with the topic of discipleship in Mark. See especially E. Best, *Following Jesus: Discipleship in the Gospel of Mark*, JSNTSup 4 (Sheffield: JSOT Press, 1981).

[30] Mark 1:18; 2:14 (twice), 15; 3:7; 5:24; 6:1; 8:34 (twice); 9:38; 10:21, 28, 32, 52; 11:9; 14:13, 54; 15:41. The term "disciple" (μαθητής) occurs forty-six times in Mark.

[31] The use of geography to portray spiritual realities is a common feature of biblical literature. For example, Egypt is a metaphor for opposition and bondage (Isa. 19:6; Ezek. 19:4; Hos. 9:6; Joel 3:19); the desert is a metaphor for suffering and testing (e.g. Deut. 8:5; Ps. 63:1; Isa. 42:20); the mountain is a metaphor of God's presence (e.g. Exod. 3:1; 15:17; 24:12; Ps. 48:1).

experience serves to test their faith and commitment to Jesus (Mark 14:27-31). In Jerusalem what they feared comes upon them. Jesus is betrayed, arrested, abused, and finally put to death. The disciples, despite previous expressions of loyalty, scatter and flee. But that is not the end of their journey. Mark ends his Gospel very abruptly, but not without the promise to the disciples, and especially Peter, that he was going ahead of them to Galilee where they will see him just as he told them (Mark 16:7; cf. 14:28). Once they have passed through this crisis, they will see Jesus again in Galilee, the place of powerful and successful ministry. However, it is only by passing through the suffering of Jerusalem, or the way of the cross, that they will return there. Mark and his readers were certainly aware of the tremendous change effected in the disciples after the events of Easter. Whereas before the disciples were bewildered, weak, and unwilling to suffer, after Easter they became powerful witnesses of the gospel and even died for their faith. What changed them? For Mark, it was their journey with Jesus through Jerusalem.

As the cross lies at the center of Mark's Christology, so too the cross defines Mark's understanding of discipleship.[32] What is implicit in the journey narrative becomes explicit in Jesus' teaching in Mark 8:34: "If anyone would come after me, he must deny himself and take up his cross and follow me." It is significant to note that this passage comes immediately after the first passion prediction where the ministry of the Son of Man is inseparably linked with the cross. Jesus' teaching on discipleship immediately follows. If the cross was to play the key part in the mission of Christ, it means that the disciple, the follower of Christ, must also carry his cross. For Mark, then, since there can be no Christianity without the cross, so too there can be no genuine discipleship without suffering. Mark portrays the experience of the cross as the indispensable element for mature discipleship. At the beginning of their journey, the disciples often misunderstood Jesus because they did not understand that he had to suffer (cf. Mark. 4:13; 6:52; 7:18; 8:17; 9:32; 10:32). In fact, for Mark, true understanding, or *bona fide* discipleship, was impossible before the cross. They could not understand Jesus' teachings till then because they had not seen him on the cross. Their reaction to suffering in Jerusalem demonstrated that they were not mature disciples. They all ran away. They still had not come to grips with the centrality of the cross and consequently were unable to understand the full meaning of discipleship. It was only via the suffering of Jerusalem, or the way of the cross, that they would become mature disciples. The cross changed everything. It was only

---

[32] D. E. Nineham's comments on the genre of the gospels has an interesting bearing on the topic of discipleship: "It is striking that the Gospel does not tell us anything about Our Lord's appearance, physique, and health, or, for that matter, about his personality—whether, for example, he was a happy, carefree, placid man or the reverse. They do not even think to tell us definitely whether or not he was married! Likewise they give us no definite information about the length of his ministry or his age when he died, and there is no hint of the influence of his early environment upon him or of any development in his outlook or beliefs. From the point of view of the biographer the sheer *amount* of information the Evangelists give us is quite inadequate," *Saint Mark* [Harmondsworth: Penguin, 1963], p. 35. In other words, with respect to discipleship, these matters are not important.

after the experience of the cross that the disciples received the promise of the meeting in Galilee (Mark 16:7). Only then were they able to enter into more powerful and effective ministry. Mark did not have to spell out for his readers the tremendous effect of the disciples' ministry after the resurrection. Therefore, in Mark we find the following pattern of discipleship.

Galilee → Jerusalem → Galilee

Finally, in view of Mark's emphasis on carrying the cross, we may conclude our discussion on discipleship with the question, What does it mean for Mark to carry the cross? The biggest stigma or implication of the cross, as perceived in the first-century Greco-Roman world, was that of shame. Greco-Roman society functioned on the basis of the social values of honor and shame.[33] Execution by crucifixion was the pinnacle of dishonor and humiliation.[34] The challenge of discipleship is not to be ashamed of the cross-bearing Jesus (Mark 8:38). The concrete implications of the cross for discipleship are contained in the application that Jesus draws from the approach of the kingdom—repent and believe in the gospel. These commands, occurring in the present aspect of the verb, imply ongoing activity. Responding aright to the coming of the kingdom entails a life that is characterized by repentance and faith. First is repentance. As indicated by John's baptism, repentance involves confession of sin, which consists of self-denial and admission of personal wrong. In the context of Mark's Gospel, repentance calls for a change of mind, attitude, and behavior, especially in terms of relationships. It relates to changing one's view of God, oneself, others, and Jesus. One must be willing and ready to deny oneself and change (Mark 8:34). Secondly, the coming of the kingdom demands faith in the gospel, i.e. one must believe that God is acting in Jesus for the salvation of the world. Despite appearances to the contrary, one must believe that Jesus has come to give his life as a ransom for many (Mark 10:45). One must discard the unimpressive family background of Jesus (Mark 6:1-3) and confess that he is the Christ (Mark 8:27-29).[35] One must believe that Jesus, on the cross, is indeed the Son of God (Mark 15:32; cf. 15:39). Thus, values of honor and shame are radically redefined. The disciple must now live according to God's will (Mark 3:35), which is to love God above all and to love others as oneself (Mark 12:28-31). On the basis of Jesus' example, Mark especially emphasizes

---

[33] See J. G. Peristiany, ed., *Honour and Shame: The Values of Mediterranean Society* (London: Weidenfeld & Nicolson, 1965); D. Gilmore ed., *Honor and Shame and the Unity of the Mediterranean* (Washington: American Anthropological Association, 1987); B. J. Malina, *The New Testament World: Insights from Cultural Anthropology* (Atlanta: John Knox Press, 1981), pp. 25-50; and J. J. Pilch and B. J. Malina, eds., *Biblical Social Values and Their Meaning: A Handbook* (Peabody: Hendrickson, 1993), pp. 95-104.

[34] For a general description of the practice of crucifixion in the Roman world, see M. Hengel, *Crucifixion in the ancient world and the folly of the message of the cross* (Philadelphia: Fortress Press, 1977) and L. L. Welborn, *Paul, the Fool of Christ: A Study of 1 Corinthians 1–4 in the Comic-Philosophic Tradition* (London/New York: T. & T. Clark, 2005), pp. 124-46.

[35] Note Paul's statement in 2 Cor. 5:16.

that the disciple must serve and accept others. The one who wants to be great in the kingdom must become the servant of all (Mark 9:35; 10:43-44). Sectarianism is forbidden (Mark 9:38). Judgment must be suspended. In Mark we discover that often in the kingdom of God the most unsuitable people become model disciples whereas the most suitable, humanly speaking, fail in the moment of crisis. Those who may have been considered unsuitable for discipleship include women (Mark 5:28; 7:25; 14:3; 15:40-47; 16:1, 4), Gentiles (Mark 7:24-26), a widow (Mark 12:41), Simon of Cyrene (Mark 15:21), and the Roman centurion (Mark 15:39). Jesus' own disciples, on the other hand, fled at the prospect of suffering. Finally, of course, like Jesus, the cross may also imply the need to bear persecution. One must continue one's confession of and commitment to Jesus under maltreatment and ridicule.

## E. The Markan Outline

The diverse content of Mark's Gospel does not fit easily into a clearly defined structure. There are no unambiguous transitional markers or thematic groupings of material within the narrative. Consequently, attempts at imposing detailed structures on the Gospel have not been very successful. Rather, we find in Mark a relatively loose arrangement of materials but with a constant repetition of main themes throughout the narrative plot. When one reads the Gospel one is reminded of Papias' statement that Mark did not write "in order" and did not make a "systematic arrangement of the Lord's sayings." Accordingly, a number of outlines have been suggested for the Gospel. These range from very simple to highly structured schemas. For example, Nineham simply points to a shift in focus from Mark 8:31 onwards, whereas Mann discerns complex chiastic structures throughout the Gospel.[36] However, although elaborate outlines may be imposing a modern desire for structure onto the text, the Gospel does disclose a general order in the arrangement of its contents. Key to this structure is, as we have already observed, the development of the plot along geographic lines. The first part of Jesus' ministry is set in Galilee and the surrounding areas, which were mostly Gentile (Mark 1:14–9:50). The second part of Jesus' ministry is set along the journey through Judea and ends in Jerusalem (Mark 10:1–16:8). Associated with this geographic sequence is the shift in Jesus' teaching from focusing on the crowds to focusing on the disciples, and from revealing the power of the kingdom to revealing the necessity of his suffering. Most scholars will agree with this basic structure and change of emphasis. On the basis of these observations, we may suggest the following outline:

1. Title (1:1).
2. Jesus' Preparation (1:2-13).
3. Jesus' Ministry in Galilee and Surrounding Regions (1:14–8:21).

---

[36] Nineham, *The Gospel of St Mark*, p. 37; C. S. Mann, *Mark: A New Translation with Introduction and Commentary*, The Anchor Bible (New York: Doubleday, 1986), pp. 179-90.

4. Jesus' Journey from Galilee to Jerusalem (8:22–10:52).
5. Jesus' Ministry in Jerusalem (11:1–16:8).

## *1. Title (1:1)*

Mark commences his account of Jesus with a summary statement: "The beginning of the gospel about Jesus Christ, the Son of God."[37] The first line is not just an introduction to the ministry of John the Baptist, but introduces the whole story. For Mark, the story of Jesus culminating in his death and resurrection is just the beginning of the gospel. Mark's opening statement and his abrupt ending (Mark 16:8) imply that the gospel is continuing beyond the events described in the Gospel. Furthermore, the seven words of the Greek text (ἀρχὴ τοῦ εὐαγγελίου Ἰησοῦ Χριστοῦ υἱοῦ θεοῦ) recall the words that begin Genesis. With the beginning of the gospel, the start of a new creation is in view. In Mark "gospel" does not just mean "good news" or the message of Jesus, rather it refers to the transforming power of the kingdom which has come with Jesus. Mark's story describes how that power is beginning to have an affect in the lives of ordinary women and men and how it is confounding religious and political authorities.

## *2. Jesus' Preparation (1:2–13)*

The reference to the OT (Exod. 23:20; Mal. 3:1; and Isa. 40:3) sets the coming of John the Baptist and the ministry of Jesus against the backdrop of OT prophecy. The OT Scriptures are read in terms of salvation history as preparing the way for Jesus. Although apparently writing for Gentiles, Mark never loses sight of the OT, often alluding to it and quoting from it.[38] Mark's purpose for doing so becomes clear as the reader proceeds. It was very difficult for the early Christians to explain why their Messiah was crucified because it was against all Jewish expectation. By linking Jesus' ministry to OT prophecy, Mark shows that Jesus' coming and ministry was not by chance, but happened according to God's plan, especially his death on the cross.

As the OT served to prepare the way for Jesus, so too John the Baptist came to prepare the way for Jesus. John prepared the way by his baptism, his lifestyle, and his message. His baptism was "a baptism of repentance for the forgiveness of sins" (Mark 1:4). John's baptism reminded the people of their sins and their need for cleansing and a new beginning. Through his simple lifestyle—wearing clothing made of camel's hair and eating locusts—he

---

[37] Some manuscripts omit "Son of God."

[38] The number of OT quotations in Mark varies according the criteria applied. It varies from just above twenty to over seventy quotations. The number of OT allusions are of course much more but they are also more difficult to quantify. There are ten major quotations, cf. Mark 1:2-3; 4:12; 7:6; 9:48; 11:9-10; 11:17; 12:10-11; 12:36; 13: 24-25; 14:27. See also chapter seven of this volume.

prepared the people for Jesus' message which did not promise political or economic success but suffering in the way of the cross. His message prepared the way by exalting Jesus as the one expected.

The baptism and temptation of Jesus orient the reader to who Jesus is and to the significance of his ministry. It is hard to overinterpret these verses theologically. Clearly, Mark has reflected long and hard on Jesus' identity. His baptism and the subsequent endowment of the Spirit sanction him for his messianic ministry.[39] The voice from heaven legitimizes Jesus as God's appointed king. The story of Jesus' temptation in the desert recalls the temptation of Adam and Eve in Genesis 3. However, whereas Adam and Eve were in a delightful garden, Jesus was in a desert. Whereas Adam and Eve's temptation was a blatant attack on Yahweh's express command, Jesus' temptation was much more subtle. Yet, despite the odds stacked against Jesus, he overcame the tempter's advances. Through Jesus, the last Adam, humanity gains a new beginning. Thus, Jesus' baptism and temptation underscore both the messianic and universal scope of Jesus' mission.

### 3. Jesus' Ministry in Galilee and Surrounding Regions (1:14–8:21)

Jesus begins his ministry after the imprisonment of John the Baptist with the proclamation that the kingdom of God has drawn near. Mark is careful to place the beginning of Jesus' ministry after the activities of John in order to make a decisive break between the new epoch that Jesus is inaugurating and the prophets of old (cf. Mark 1:27; 2:21-22). Since he writes about the beginning of the gospel, Jesus' life before his baptism is not important. Mark presents Jesus as the preacher of the gospel, because he is not only its messenger but also its message. The basic message is that the kingdom of God has arrived with the coming of Jesus. The coming of the kingdom is so closely linked with the work and person of Christ that the proclamation of the gospel can only now begin. The response that is enjoined is repentance and faith. Repentance implies the reorientation of one's life according to the demands of the kingdom. Believing the gospel is synonymous with believing in Jesus (Mark 8:35; 10:29) and following him along the way (Mark 1:17; 2:14; 8:34; 10:21). This summary of Jesus' preaching provides a paradigm for subsequent Christian proclamation.

Jesus' proclamation is followed by the call to discipleship. His call is brief but powerful: "Come, follow me, and I will make you fishers of men" (Mark 1:17). The first disciples respond immediately. They leave their occupation and follow Jesus. Jesus acts similarly to the rabbis of the time in recruiting disciples, but, unlike them, Jesus chooses his. He does not lead a voluntary association that one may decide to join or not. There is no negotiation about the requirements. It is either acceptance or rejection. Moreover, in Jesus' call we notice the radical nature of Christian discipleship.

---

[39]There is not much doubt that Jesus was baptized by John. It is inconceivable that the early church would have invented such a story in view of the theological difficulties it caused.

Jesus does not call his disciples to learn or to follow a new doctrine: it is simply a matter of following "me." The boldness of Jesus' command is backed up with authority. The first disciples leave everything they have and follow Jesus.

After the recruitment of the disciples the narrative relates a number of Jesus' activities in quick succession. Mark uses the adverb "immediately" (εὐθύς) almost to the point of exhaustion in the Gospel. It occurs eleven times in the first chapter and forty times in the Gospel. The adverb adds a certain urgency and purpose to the narrative, creating an atmosphere of historical realism.[40] It is justly said that the Gospel of Mark highlights Jesus' works and that it is a gospel of action. The first miracle, an exorcism, is instructive. Here Mark begins to draw attention to Jesus' teaching activity. In fact, Mark's most common description for Jesus is "teacher" (διδάσκαλος).[41] The verb "to teach" (διδάσκω) occurs fifteen times in Mark.[42] Five times the Gospel refers to Jesus' teaching (διδαχή) (Mark 1:22, 27; 4:2; 11:18; 12:38). However, although Jesus is always engaged in teaching, Mark does not spend too much time on the content of his teaching (as Matthew does, for example), but highlights the power or the effect of Jesus' teaching in the lives of those who hear him. In addition, the more Jesus' ministry develops, the more Jesus himself becomes the subject of his teaching. Jesus' first exorcism is used to illustrate the authority of his teaching. People respond with amazement, a refrain that is repeated throughout the Gospel (cf. Mark 1:27; 5:20, 42; 6:51; 7:37; 9:15; 10:24, 26, 32; 11:18; 12:17, 37; 15:5, 44; 16:8).

Jesus' command to the demon to be quiet (Mark 1:25) introduces another important theme in Mark, which William Wrede labeled the "messianic secret."[43] Jesus regularly commands demons not to reveal his identity (Mark 1:25, 34; 3:12) and people whom he healed not to tell others (Mark 1:43-45; 5:43; 7:36; 8:26). According to Wrede, the historical Jesus never proclaimed himself to be the Messiah and so people had no knowledge of such a claim. Therefore, for apologetic reasons the author of the Gospel invented the secrecy motif to explain the subsequent Christian confession of Jesus as the Messiah. However, many scholars have pointed out that Wrede's position is problematic. Although Jesus tends to hide his true identity in the Gospel, word constantly gets out. More often than not those who are commanded not to make Jesus known, do exactly the opposite (cf. Mark 1:45; 7:36-37). Furthermore, on many occasions Jesus performs miracles in public and acts in such a way to draw attention to himself and his mission. In other words, even

---

[40] According to M. C. Tenney, "It conveys the impression that however varied and detailed Jesus' ministry may have been, he was hurrying toward some unseen goal that he envisioned, but that was hidden to most of his contemporaries and only faintly perceived by the disciples at those rare intervals when his words illumined their understanding." *New Testament Survey* (Grand Rapids: Eerdmans, 1985), p. 168.

[41] The noun διδάσκαλος (teacher) is applied twelve times to Jesus (Mark 4:38; 5:35; 9:17, 36; 10:17, 20, 35; 12:14, 19, 32; 13:1; 14:14).

[42] Mark 1:21, 22; 2:13; 4:1, 2; 6:2,6, 30, 34; 7:7; 8:31; 9:31; 10:1; 11:17; 12:14, 35; 14:49.

[43] *The Messianic Secret* (London: James Clark, 1971). Original German, *Das Messiasgeheimnis in den Evangelien* (Göttingen: Vandenhoeck & Ruprecht, 1901).

within Jesus' lifetime, as Mark recalls it, the so-called "secret" was not very well kept. Rather, it is more likely that other social and theological factors were behind the secrecy motif in Mark. Due to the tense political situation in Palestine Jesus may well have tried to avoid too much public attention. But perhaps most importantly the motif is connected with the understanding of the redemptive nature of Jesus' mission which was, according to Mark, fully revealed in the cross and resurrection. The demons did not recognize Jesus as the suffering Messiah and the worldwide proclamation of the gospel can strictly begin only after the events of Easter.[44]

With the healing of the paralytic man (Mark 2:1-12), Mark introduces a new theme—conflict with the religious authorities. Jesus' ministry is beginning to elicit opposition from the Jewish establishment. The story is used as an illustration that Jesus not only has the power to heal but also, more importantly, to forgive sins. Significant is the way in which Jesus links his authority to forgive sins with his identity as the Son of Man (Mark 2:10). The expression "Son of Man", used here for the first time in the Gospel, is the designation that Jesus most commonly uses to refer to himself.[45] Most probably, Jesus' use of the title is connected with the apocalyptic vision of Daniel 7:13-14 where a "Son of Man" is the portent of Yahweh's coming kingdom. However, more significant for Mark is the connection that Jesus makes between the Son of Man and suffering (Mark 8:31; 9:31; 10:33). The expression "Son of Man" is the title of Jesus that is most closely related to his death on the cross. Jesus' authority to forgive sins—a prerogative thought to belong to God alone—stems from his sacrificial death. Therefore, in the healing of the paralytic man there is a foreshadowing of the purpose of Jesus' mission, which draws opposition from the teachers of the law.[46]

The story of the healing of the paralytic man is followed by several controversy stories. Jesus is questioned about his association with sinners (Mark 2:13-17), about fasting (Mark 2:18-22), and about the Sabbath (Mark 2:23–3:6). These stories serve to highlight both the scope and the fundamental newness of Jesus' ministry. They also raise the question of Jesus' identity. Jesus' deeds and teaching unavoidably center on his own person. Chapter four provides the most comprehensive teaching of Jesus about the kingdom of God. The teaching comes in parables, which underscore the mysterious character of the kingdom. It is the longest teaching section in Mark. All the parables basically convey the same message—that the kingdom of God has come, albeit unobtrusively, in the person and work of Jesus. Although the kingdom has a small beginning it will have immense consequences. This is the secret of the kingdom that has been revealed to the disciples in this

---

[44] So J. C. Beker, "Mark employs the device of the messianic secret to emphasize that God's revelation in Jesus Christ can only be fully understood after the passion and resurrection of Christ." *The New Testament: A Thematic Introduction* (Minneapolis: Fortress Press, 1994), p. 76.

[45] In this respect the use of the expression in all four gospels is remarkably consistent.

[46] F. J. Moloney has described it as a "christological prolepsis." *The Gospel of Mark: A Commentary* (Peabody: Hendrickson, 2002), p. 62.

selection of parables (Mark 4:11). After the excursus on the kingdom there is a new cycle of miracles highlighting Jesus' supernatural power and the need for faith (Mark 4:35–6:6). The sending out of the Twelve marks a new stage in Jesus' ministry (Mark 6:7-12). In this section Jesus more and more reveals the purpose of his mission. He is portrayed not only as the healer of Israel but also of Gentiles. Jesus' frequent excursions into Gentile regions are significant and anticipate the future Gentile mission (Mark 7:24–8:13; also cf. 5:1-20). However, there is an underlying motif of misunderstanding (Mark 6:51-52; 7:18; 8:15). Thus, at the end of the first major section of the Gospel the disciples still do not understand (Mark 8:21).

## 4. Jesus' Journey from Galilee to Jerusalem (8:22–10:52)

The mid section of Mark's Gospel describes the disciples' journey with Jesus from Galilee to Jerusalem. This section contains instruction on what it means to follow Jesus. The journey started in Bethsaida, first proceeded northwards to Caesarea Philippi, then south to Capernaum, and next into Judea along the Jordan to reach Jericho. As many commentators have pointed out, there is both a geographical progression as well as a general shift in focus. Before the journey Jesus' teaching was largely directed towards the crowds; now it is addressed more and more to the disciples. Jesus increasingly reveals to them his true identity as the Son of Man and the purpose of his coming. All three passion predictions occur within this section. By locating most of his teaching on discipleship in this section, Mark emphasizes the fundamental importance of the cross for understanding discipleship.[47] The expression "on the way" is continually kept before the ears of the listener (Mark 8:27; 9:33-34; 10:17, 32, 52). It is Mark's central metaphor for discipleship.

Another point to observe is that the section is embedded within two miracle stories that relate the healing of a blind man. These stories have a symbolic significance for Mark. Before one can truly understand Jesus—or become a mature disciple—there needs to be enlightenment. In the first story a blind man is brought to Jesus. Perhaps most people's acquaintance with Jesus begins by "being brought" to Jesus, not quite sure what to expect. However, what stands out in this miracle is the man does not receive sight immediately but the restoration of sight happens in stages. Mark is saying that understanding occurs through a gradual process, not all at once. The description of the healing in the second story is much more succinct (Mark 10:46-52). Bartimaeus (evidently he and his family were known in the early Christian community) comes on his own volition and shows much more faith and eagerness to meet with Jesus. Even though others discourage him, he does not give up. His persistence pays off when Jesus calls him. Then after his request to have his sight restored, he is healed at once. Finally, the connection with discipleship is brought out by Mark's editorial comment: "Immediately

---

[47] It is interesting to note that Christians were first called those of the "Way" (cf. Acts 9:2; 19:9, 20, 23; 22:4; 24:14, 22).

he received his sight and followed Jesus along the road." Receiving sight and following Jesus along the way, the *via dolorosa*, are closely connected.

The healing of the blind man at Bethsaida (Mark 8:22-26) is followed by Peter's confession of Jesus as the Christ. Up till now the fundamental question has been intensifying all the time, "Who is Jesus?" (cf. Mark 1:22, 27, 45; 2:7, 12, 18; 3:8, 22; 4:41; 5:20, 42; 6:2-3; 7:37; 8:11). Peter's confession of Jesus as the Christ (Mark 8:29) comes as a defining moment in the Gospel. It is this confession of Jesus as the Christ that leads to further teaching about Jesus' identity as the Son of Man. He must suffer many things and even be killed (Mark 8:31). This statement turns all current understanding of the role of the Messiah on its head. Accordingly, Peter is not able to accept suffering as part of the Messiah's role and reproves Jesus. This reaction sets the stage for one of the Gospel's primary statements on discipleship: "If anyone would come after me, he must deny himself and take up his cross and follow me" (Mark 8:34). At this point the disciples still do not understand the nature of Jesus' mission or the implications of following Jesus. Jesus has to repeat his teaching on several occasions (cf. Mark 9:49; 10:29-30, 39, 43-44; 13:9, 13).

The transfiguration is another revelation to the disciples of Jesus' true identity. Indeed, is it also a foretaste of experiencing the power of the kingdom (Mark 9:1). However, the injunction to the disciples not to make it known shows that the true significance of the event can only be understood after the passion (Mark 9:9). This injunction comes right in the middle of the Gospel and in many ways forms the center point of the narrative. Jesus is destined for glory, but it is a glory that will come paradoxically by means of the cross.[48] The pattern for Jesus' life and of discipleship that is laid down here by Mark is also found in 1 Peter—it is one from suffering to glory (1 Pet. 1:6-8; 4:12-13; 5:10). Therefore, Mark does not replace a theology of glory with a theology of suffering, but rather integrates both aspects in Jesus' role as the Christ.[49] The transfiguration is closely connected with the surrounding narrative. The teaching on the necessity of suffering is followed by the experience of glory in the transfiguration of Jesus on the mountain. The appearance of Elijah and Moses, which recalls Israel's Sinai experience, highlights Jesus' eschatological role as the prophet (Deut. 18:15-19) and deliverer (Mal. 3:1 and 4:4-5) of his people. The voice from heaven, occurring a second time, legitimizes Jesus' identity not only as the prophet promised by Moses but also as God's Son (Mark 9:7).

Other stories within the travel narrative reveal particular ecclesiastical concerns. It appears that the community for which Mark was writing had disputes about superiority and control which led to disunity.[50] There was an argument "on the way" about who was the greatest (Mark 9:33-37). Jesus' pronouncement that anyone who wants to be first must be last and the servant

---

[48] According to Beker, "They fail to grasp that Jesus' glorification can only take place after his passion (9:10-13)." *The New Testament*, p. 77.

[49] So Gundry, *Mark*, pp. 1-26.

[50] These observations are all the more interesting in light of the suggested Roman provenance for the Gospel.

of all shows the incompatibility between Christian discipleship and worldly striving for greatness. Rather, by taking a child into his arms, Jesus teaches that in the new community the least, in terms of power and status, must be welcomed and favored as Jesus himself (Mark 9:37). In the next story the disciples are reprimanded for preventing others to minister on the basis that they did not belong to their group. Whereas the disciples' sanction of other ministries was conditional upon affiliation with them, Jesus is more tolerant and inclusive. "Do not stop him," Jesus commands (Mark 9:39). As long as others minister in Jesus' name and are not against the Twelve, they should not be hindered. The warning not to cause a little one to sin (Mark 9:42-49) should also be read within the context of community unity (cf. Mark 9:50). Causing a little one to stumble means not welcoming believers who are without status and social connection. Jesus' blessing of the children (Mark 10:13-16) further reinforces the need for a new perspective among the disciples. A disciple does not only need to welcome children (Mark 9:37), but also become like a child in order to enter the kingdom (Mark 10:15). Status in the ancient world was to a large extent determined by social connection. However, in the new community relationships are to be based on the association of these little ones to Christ. The old network of social status is replaced with a new one. Therefore, part of the cost of discipleship is coming under a new network of social obligation. Status in the kingdom is determined by a different set of values and behavior. The way to genuine greatness in the kingdom is via servitude, which is based on the pattern of Jesus (Mark 10:35-45). The message is counter cultural. Thus, Mark concludes Jesus' teaching on the journey with a statement on the purpose and nature of his coming—it is to give his life as a ransom for many (Mark 10:45).

## 5. Jesus' Ministry in Jerusalem (11:1–16:8)

The final section, Jesus' ministry in Jerusalem, is introduced with the triumphal entry into the city. Jesus enters Jerusalem, about a week before the major Jewish festival of Passover, riding on a colt. The episode is a prophetic enactment of Zech. 9:9-10. Jesus is carefully portrayed as making preparations to enter Jerusalem by riding on the colt. He is very aware of his identity and role as Israel's king. Unlike a military conqueror Jesus does not enter on a horse, an instrument of war, but a colt. His kingdom is not of this world. The crowd responds favorably by welcoming Jesus with the words of the last Hallel[51] psalm (Ps. 118:25-26). Jesus' symbolic action and the crowd's response in the context of the feast of Passover, which commemorated the deliverance from Egypt, carry very strong messianic overtones. Jesus is portrayed as Israel's deliverer and as the one who will establish the kingdom. The word "hosanna" is the Aramaic equivalent of the Hebrew *hoshi'na'* which is a prayer meaning "save us now." Jesus has indeed

---

[51] Hallel, meaning "praise," refers to six psalms (Psalms 113–118) often sung as a unit during Jewish holy days, especially Passover.

come to carry out their request, although not in the manner they anticipated. Jesus immediately enters the temple, but it is only on the following day that he cleanses it. In this way Mark portrays Jesus' actions in Jerusalem as deliberate and carefully orchestrated. He does not act out of impulse but according to a calculated plan. Jesus knows full well what he is doing.

In the cursing of the fig-tree (Mark 11:12-14, 20-21) and the parable of the Tenants (Mark 12:1-12) judgment is pronounced upon the Jewish leaders of Jerusalem. The fig featured as a symbol for Israel in the OT (Jer. 8:13; 24:1-10; Hos. 9:10, 16-17; Mic. 7:1). Jesus' apparently unreasonable act, in cursing the fig tree for not bearing fruit out of season, also suggests that his action is a symbolic gesture. The cleansing of the temple, being sandwiched within the story of the cursing of the fig-tree, is God's judgment on the corruption and commercialization of the temple worship. Likewise, the vine was a common symbol for Israel (Isa. 5:1-2; Ps. 80:8-13; Jer. 2:21). Despite God's patience and grace, Israel continues to reject God's purposes. The citation of Ps. 118:22-23 again shows the reader that Jesus is unwavering in approaching his destiny. These stories demonstrate to the reader that Jesus knows that he will be rejected and killed.

The discourse of chapter 13—sometimes referred to as the little apocalypse—has attracted much discussion in scholarly literature. It has even been referred to as the biggest "problem in the Gospel."[52] However, when one is cognizant of its socio-literary context it does not appear so strange. The discourse belongs to the genre of eschatological apocalypse, a distinct and common literary style of a number of Jewish writings of the period, which contained a range of characteristics—visions, colorful metaphors and imagery, and rich symbolism. The genre is characterized by a very pessimistic view of the present time, urgent eschatological expectation, and belief in the imminent coming of God's reign. It has often been described as a crisis literature whose main aim was to encourage a persecuted minority to persevere in their faith. In addition, the discourse of chapter 13 also reflects elements of the Farewell Discourse, another common literary genre in ancient texts.[53] These discourses occur in the context of the imminent departure of the community's leader, include predictions of the future, are replete with encouragement to those left behind, and contain final promises and commands. Their main purpose was to provide confidence and assurance to the community despite the departure of its leader. Mark's discourse can be divided into three sections. The first scene describes the persecution of the disciples (vv. 5-13), the second scene describes the tribulation that will come upon Jerusalem (vv. 14-23), and the third scene describes the final victory of

---

[52] A. M. Hunter, *The Gospel According to Saint Mark: Introduction and Commentary* (London: SCM Press, 1949), p. 122.

[53] H.-J. Michel has listed thirteen characteristics: (1) confirmation of approaching death; (2) address to a specific audience; (3) paraenetic expressions; (4) prophetic statements; (5) self-resignation; (6) the destiny of the followers; (7) the blessing; (8) the prayer; (9) the last command; (10) funeral directions; (11) promises and oaths; (12) further farewell gestures; (13) the end. *Die Abschiedsrede des Paulus an die Kirche Apg 20, 17-38: Motivgeschichte und theologische Bedeutung* (Munich: Kösel, 1973), pp. 48-54.

the Son of Man (vv. 24-37). The main purpose of the discourse is to assure the disciples of the success of the kingdom despite tribulation and to encourage them to persevere. The gospel will be preached to all nations (Mark 13:10). False prophets will not be able to deceive the elect (Mark 13:22). And, finally, the Son of Man will come with great power and glory (Mark 13:26). Therefore, the believing community only needs to be alert and watchful (Mark 13:5, 9, 23, 33, 35, 37). The passion of the Lord is already the beginning of these things.

The passion narrative contained in chapters 14 and 15, the climax of Mark's Gospel, relates the arrest, trial, and crucifixion of Jesus. Clearly it constitutes the most important part of the Gospel and of early Christian faith. The passion narrative is decidedly a more detailed and connected account than the preceding sequence of events. Furthermore, the more or less fixed outline of the passion narrative in all four gospels has led scholars to propose that it is the oldest written tradition and that Mark has adopted it as the basis of his narrative. Although it will always be difficult to arrive at certainty on particular details, it is easy to substantiate the necessity for an account of Jesus' death at a very early stage. The main point of the apostolic kerygma was that Jesus, the Messiah, was crucified under Pontius Pilate, but was raised from the dead.[54] The early Christian community had to address the obvious question—if Jesus was the Messiah, why was he executed like a common criminal under the sanction of the Sanhedrin, the highest Jewish religious authority, and the Roman provincial government? The earliest Christian preachers had to explain the paradoxical belief in a crucified Christ—a stumbling block to Jews and foolishness to Gentiles (1 Cor. 1:23). Therefore, there would have been considerable evangelical, theological, and apologetic reasons to construct a precise account, suffused with theological and apologetic significance, of the events that surrounded the crucifixion. This is exactly what we find when reading the passion narrative. Although the account reflects historical events, historical detail often gives way to theological and apologetic concerns.

Mark's primary theological motif for the passion is to show that the crucifixion happened according to God's predetermined plan and that Jesus willingly committed himself to it, and only secondarily to articulate the theological significance for Christ's death. Indeed, the main reason for Mark's Gospel can be seen as an apology for the crucified Christ. From the beginning of the Gospel, Mark carefully constructed his narrative to show the reader that the Christ had to suffer and die on the cross. This motif reaches a crescendo in the passion narrative. The anointing of Jesus is interpreted as pointing towards his burial (Mark 14:8). This event is so important that wherever the gospel is preached the action of the woman must also be told (Mark 14:9). Jesus knows what is going to happen. He knows that Judas is going to betray him and that Peter is going to disown him, yet he proceeds. Therefore, the events of the

---

[54] The centrality of this message can well be seen in the New Testament and the early church fathers.

passion are not accidental or unforeseen. During the Last Supper Jesus informs his disciples that "The Son of Man will go just as it is written about him" (Mark 14:21) and he proceeds to interpret his death as the establishment of the new covenant (Mark 14:22-25). The subsequent events are all interpreted in light of OT Scriptures. The shepherd must be arrested and his sheep scattered, a reflection on Zech. 13:7 (Mark 14:27). In the prayer in the Garden of Gethsemane Jesus again realizes that it is God's will for him to drink the cup of suffering and offers himself unreservedly. So, after the prayer he hands himself over to those who seek his downfall (Mark 14:41-42). The trials before the Sanhedrin and Pilate highlight Jesus' innocence. The accusations were both false and contradictory (Mark 14:56-59). When Jesus had the opportunity to extricate himself he remained silent (Mark 14:61; 15:5). The description of the crucifixion itself (Mark 15:21-41) is steeped in language from the OT, especially the Psalms describing the righteous sufferer.[55] Psalm 22 describes the suffering of the Righteous Servant, but also his vindication (vv. 21b-31). The contrast between the two halves of the Psalm is so stark that some scholars regard it as two separate psalms. For Mark, however, there is a link between the suffering of the servant and the eschatological coming of God's kingdom (cf. Ps. 22:27-28).[56] Therefore, Mark's use of the OT points to the divine purpose of Jesus' ministry. From the time of Mark onward, the story of Jesus could not be told except within the framework which saw in his death the climax of his mission. The cross was not his fate but his divine destiny. In the passion narrative Mark wants to show that Jesus dies "according to the Scriptures."

The related question of the theological significance of Jesus' death also receives attention in Mark, but not to the same extent as the scriptural necessity for his death.[57] Modern scholarship has down played Pauline interpretations of Jesus' death as a sacrifice for sins. However, although the central concern of the passion narrative does not lie here, a careful reading of the Gospel makes this interpretation unavoidable. The passion narrative should be understood in the context of the whole Gospel. It has already been hinted that Jesus is God's suffering servant according to the paradigm of Second Isaiah. Many passages in Mark carry clear sacrificial connotations; most perspicuous is Mark 10:45. Mark situates Jesus' death within the context of Passover, which celebrated the deliverance of Israel from Egypt with the slaughter the Passover lamb. Jesus' death at Passover, even though the authorities tried to avoid an execution at Passover, will naturally lead the reader to interpret Jesus' death in the same light. Jesus' words at the Last Supper make this interpretation explicit. Many interpreters have also seen in the release of Barabbas instead of Jesus an indication of substitutionary

---

[55] Compare Mark 15:23 and Ps. 69:21; Mark 15:24 and Ps. 22:18; Mark 15:31 and Ps. 22:7-8; Mark 15:34 and Ps. 22:1; Mark 15:36 and Ps. 69:21.

[56] Joel Marcus has shown that within the larger context of his Gospel, Mark is interpreting these allusions in an eschatological manner. *The Way of the Lord*, p. 181.

[57] For New Testament theologies of the cross, see J. T. Carroll and J. B. Green, eds., *The Death of Jesus in Early Christianity* (Peabody: Hendrickson, 1995).

atonement.[58] The imagery and irony of the crucifixion point in the same direction. Jesus is crucified as the "king of the Jews", amid sinners. The accusation is intended to mock Jesus, yet it reveals the divine intention of Jesus' mission. When the crowd jeered, "He saved others; but he cannot save himself" (Mark 15:31), they failed to realize that he was saving others precisely through his suffering and death. The tearing of the curtain of the temple not only pronounces judgment upon the temple but also announces that access to God has been obtained and that there is no longer any need for sacrifice. Thus, it is when the centurion "saw how he died" that he realizes Jesus' true identity and makes the first Christian confession, "Surely this man was the Son of God!" (Mark 15:39).

Mark ends his Gospel with the discovery of the empty tomb, the announcement of the resurrection, and the terrified response of the women. The major debate regarding Mark's resurrection narrative concerns the abrupt ending of the story, "because they were afraid" (16:8).[59] Since manuscript and literary data indicate that all longer endings were later additions to the Gospel and non-Markan, only three possibilities remain: Mark was interrupted and could not finish his Gospel; the original ending has been lost; or the abrupt ending is deliberate. It is very hard to postulate that for some unknown reason Mark could not finish the Gospel. There is also no supporting evidence that a part of Mark has been lost (e.g. in translations). The most likely scenario, then, is that the author intended to finish the account at verse 8. Upon reflection several theological reasons can account for the unexpected ending. First, the ending is linked with the Gospel's opening statement that the account is just the beginning of the gospel. Mark does not end the story with a well-rounded finale implying that the story is continuing to the time of the community that reads the Gospel. The gospel story will come to completion only when the apocalyptic vision of the Son of Man coming on the clouds with power and glory receives its full realization. Second, Mark's community would certainly have been aware of the resurrection appearances of Jesus and the transformation that occurred in the lives of the apostles (cf. Mark 9:9-10). The abrupt ending, therefore, is a means to highlight the transformative power of the cross and resurrection. It invites the reader to sense the reality of this power at work in the world. Third, the open-ended conclusion and the promise of a meeting with Jesus will encourage the reader to look for the resurrected Jesus in the context of his or her own life. In vv. 6-7 we see a crystallization of all the themes of the Gospel.

> Do not be alarmed [the young man said]; you are looking for Jesus of Nazareth, who was crucified. He has been raised; he is not here. Look, there is the place they laid him. But go, tell his disciples and Peter that he is going ahead of you to Galilee; there you will see him, just as he told you.

---

[58] For example E. Schweizer, *The Good News according to Mark* (Richmond: John Knox, 1970), p. 338, and J. R. Edwards, *The Gospel according to Mark* (Grand Rapids: Eerdmans, 2002), p. 461.

[59] The Greek text appears even more unnatural, ending with the conjunction "for" (γάρ).

In Mark, fear is often tied to unbelief (Mark 4:40; 5:36; 6:50; 9:32; 10:32). Although the women discovered the empty tomb, they did not believe nor tell anyone about it. Nonetheless, everyone knows that the story did not end there. The reader is left to ponder the logical inference—the promise of a meeting with the risen Lord must have been fulfilled.

## F. Conclusion

In summary, the Gospel of Mark contains at least seven basic emphases: (1) the centrality of the cross for Jesus' mission; (2) the importance of the cross for discipleship; (3) the presence of the power of God's kingdom; (4) the transformative impact of the gospel on people; (5) the demand for repentance and faith; (6) the opposition from religious and political authorities; and (7) the need to be open to unexpected surprises. These were the motivations behind the writing of the Gospel.[60] The Gospel reflects the historical situation of Christians undergoing persecution and of disunity within the Christian community. These observations accord with the early tradition of Markan authorship in Rome. The impact of the Gospel on the shape of subsequent Christianity cannot be overestimated. It is primarily due to the Gospel of Mark, appearing some time in the middle of the first century, that the cross and resurrection became the principal symbols of Christian doctrine and life.

## Bibliography

Achtemeier, Paul J. *Mark*. Philadelphia: Fortress Press, 1986.

Boring, M. Eugene. *Mark: A Commentary*. Louisville: Westminster John Knox, 2006.

Collins, Adela Yarbo. *Mark: A Commentary*. Minneapolis: Fortress Press, 2007.

Donahue, John R., and Daniel J. Harrington. *The Gospel of Mark*. Collegeville: Liturgical Press, 2002.

Edwards, James R. *The Gospel according to Mark*. Grand Rapids: Eerdmans, 2002.

Evans, Craig A. *Mark 8:27–16:20*. Nashville: Thomas Nelson, 2001.

France, R. T. *The Gospel of Mark: A Commentary on the Greek Text*. Grand Rapids/Carlisle: Eerdmans/Paternoster, 2002.

Guelich, Robert A. *Mark 1:1–8:26*. Dallas: Word Books, 1989.

Gundry, Robert H. *Mark: A Commentary on his Apology for the Cross*. Grand Rapids: Eerdmans, 1993.

Hooker, Morna D. *The Gospel According to St. Mark*. Peabody: Hendrickson, 1993.

Kelber, Werner H. *Mark's Story of Jesus*. Philadelphia: Fortress Press, 1979.

Moloney, Francis J. *The Gospel of Mark: A Commentary*. Peabody: Hendrickson, 2002.

Mann, C. S. *Mark: A New Translation with Introduction and Commentary*. Garden City: Doubleday, 1986.

Marcus, Joel. *Mark 1–8: A New Translation with Introduction and Commentary*. New York: Doubleday, 2000.

————. *Mark 8–16: A New Translation with Introduction and Commentary*. New

---

[60] The gospels are profound works of evangelistic theology. The early Christian communities did not write "systematic theologies" but, rather, on the analogy of the OT Scriptures, wrote "stories" diffused with theological meaning.

Haven: Yale University Press, 2009.

—————. *The Way of the Lord: Christological Exegesis of the Old Testament in the Gospel of Mark*. Louisville: Westminster/John Knox Press, 1992.

Senior, Donald. *The Passion of Jesus in the Gospel of Mark*. Wilmington: Michael Glazier, 1984.

Telford, W. R. *The Theology of the Gospel of Mark*. Cambridge/New York: Cambridge University Press, 1999.

Witherington III, Ben. *The Gospel of Mark: A Socio-Rhetorical Commentary*. Grand Rapids: Eerdmans, 2001.

# 12. Distinctive Features of the Gospels

*Timothy J. Harris*

Encountering four gospels with a common theme has been likened to entering an art gallery with a series of portraits of the same subject.[1] Each representation adopts an artistic style to highlight and develop particular features or characteristics. Rather than trying to blend the four accounts into one "super-gospel," there is great value in appreciating the distinctive contributions of each gospel as it stands.[2]

Yet the art gallery analogy only takes us so far. The gospels have qualities that are more akin to theater,[3] like four different stage plays, given the same basic plot and characters, but scope to explore things from distinctive perspectives. Indeed, it is increasingly recognized that the gospels were written with aural qualities, to be read aloud, to be "performed,"[4] and conversely to be heard and experienced. Perhaps the closest parallel is street theater, with its engaging qualities where the boundaries of stage and audience are broken down, and the observer becomes part of the scenario.

In this sense, the gospels were written to convey a profound vitality that surrounded the person of Jesus, an energy and dynamism that engaged with the fullness and realities of life—and death—as never before, all in the context of something new and transformative. The world has been changed, a new era in God's purposes has been inaugurated and windows to the future

---

[1] So Richard Burridge, *Four Gospels, One Jesus?*, 2nd ed. (London: SPCK, 1994), pp. 1-4; a variation of this image in reference to differing scholarly presentations of Jesus is found in N. T. Wright, *Who was Jesus?* (Grand Rapids: Eerdmans, 1992), pp. 1-2.

[2] Note especially Stephen C. Barton, "Many Gospels, one Jesus?" in Markus Bockmuehl, ed., *The Cambridge Companion to Jesus* (Cambridge: Cambridge University Press, 2001), pp. 170-83.

[3] In viewing Mark's Gospel through the category of theater, see G. G. Bilezekian, *The Liberated Gospel: A Comparison of the Gospel of Mark and Greek Tragedy* (Grand Rapids: Baker, 1977). Others do not take the comparison with Greek tragedy as far as Bilezekian, but the category of "drama" is well established, especially in regard to Mark's Gospel: see Ernest Best, *Mark: The Gospel as Story* (Edinburgh: T. & T. Clark, 1983), pp. 128-33.

[4] W. H. Kelber, *The Oral and Written Gospel: The Hermeneutics of Speakers and Writing in the Synoptic Tradition, Paul, and Q* (Philadelphia: Fortress Press, 1983); see also C. Bryan, *A Preface to Mark: Notes on the Gospel in Its Literary and Cultural Settings* (New York: Oxford University Press, 1993); and more recently Whitney Taylor Shiner, *Proclaiming the Gospel: First Century Performance of Mark* (Harrisburg: Trinity Press International, 2003) and Jonathan A. Draper, John Miles Foley and Richard A. Horsley, eds., *Performing the Gospel: Orality, Memory and Mark: Essays Dedicated To Werner Kelber* (Minneapolis: Fortress Press, 2006).

opened, revealing truths and happenings barely glimpsed before.

The category of *bioi* (ancient forms of biography) has gained increasing support in accounting for the form of the gospels.[5] The gospels were written primarily to present the life of Jesus. This sounds obvious, and of course it is.[6] But we need to keep our minds open to clues to this question as we explore distinctive features of the gospels. What are they trying to achieve, each in their own way?[7]

A form of *bios* yes, but not out of detached curiosity or to satisfy passing interest. The message has an urgency about it. They are written as part of the drama itself. Communicating the good news about this work of God engages the reader/hearer and calls for a response. Through the entry of Jesus of Nazareth and the events surrounding his life, death and resurrection, the kingdom-reign of God has undertaken its most profound development.

Thus the gospels—each in their own way—present us with Jesus as a man of flesh and blood, with a history, family and a people. Yet no ordinary man, but a man whose remarkable authority raises as many questions as it answers. As the narrative continues, claims concerning this authority are sharpened, and the accounts recorded serve to validate such claims. The gospel traditions present a Jesus who has the authority of God, a pivotal authority and place within the kingdom-reign of God that challenges and subverts any other claim.[8]

The purpose of this chapter is essentially descriptive—or better—observational. What we observe is of course subjective, reflecting our own interests and special concerns. Reading today, we stand as the "audience in front of the text," bringing with us our own assumptions and experiences.

---

[5] Note especially Richard Burridge, *What are the Gospels? A Companion with Graeco-Roman Biography*, SNTSMS 70 (Cambridge: Cambridge University Press, 1992). An important caveat is that the character of *ancient* biography is different in significant ways from modern forms of biography.

[6] An extensive debate underlies this statement. An influential axiom that prevailed for much gospel research of the latter half of the twentieth century assumed that the gospels were written in the context of specific church communities, addressing issues relevant to those church communities. The gospels are read as adopting a type of code or allegory through which these church communities can be discerned. This view has been substantially challenged in more recent times; see especially the essays contained in Richard Bauckham, ed., *The Gospels for All Christians: Rethinking the Gospel Audiences* (Edinburgh: T. & T. Clark, 1998).

[7] This chapter will focus primarily on the gospel texts as documents in themselves. We are not attempting a survey of research or methodological review. A socio-rhetorical approach will be adopted (viewing the gospels as documents that arose in and reflect a particular socio-cultural context, and reflect features as documents of that time and place), drawing on insights from narrative and discourse analysis (a "narrated" account with special interest in the shaping of the text around the interaction of characters, significant events and developing story-line located in a particular time and place). Although in reference specifically to Mark's Gospel, a helpful review of differing methodological approaches to gospel research applicable more generally is found in Peter G. Bolt, "Mark's Gospel," in Scot McKnight and Grant Osborne, eds., *The Face of New Testament Studies: A Survey of Recent Research* (Grand Rapids: Baker, 2004), pp. 391-413.

[8] In reference to Mark's Gospel, see Anne Dawson, *Freedom As Liberating Power: A Socio-Political Reading of the ἐξουσία Texts in the Gospel of Mark* (Freiburg: Universitätsverlag Freiburg Schweiz, 2000).

That said, there is much to be gained in seeking to survey the material before us as objectively as possible, if for no other reason than to ask "Do you see what I see?" Reading and observing can productively be a communal activity.[9] In surveying the texts as communally and objectively as possible, we may gather data that may lead on to more speculative and imaginative exercises: Why might the text be in this form? Why have these themes been highlighted? How might the intended audiences have influenced the material? What communities may be reflected, in the creation, concerns, and reception/preservation of the respective gospels? As a matter of methodological process, it is best to leave such questions and speculations to a later stage ("post-narrative"), seeking to explore distinctive features of the texts themselves as they strike us.

## A. Preliminary Issues

### 1. The Synoptic Problem

Any introduction to gospel studies soon encounters what is known as the "Synoptic Problem." Close similarities between Matthew, Mark and Luke at various points, including verbal parallels, make it clear that these three gospels stand in some sort of inter-relationship, and can be "viewed together" (hence "syn-optic"). The data is well known: about 97% of Mark's Gospel is reflected in Matthew, and about 88% paralleled in Luke. These three gospels share the same basic outline, and it seems that Matthew and Luke included extra material from their own sources. Various explanations have been proposed to explain this inter-relationship, and none is regarded as definitive or without difficulties. The majority approach[10] (and the one adopted here) is of "Markan priority"—that Mark's Gospel was written first, and that Matthew and Luke adopted Mark's basic outline and core material, and added extra material of their own. Where the three gospels touch on the same material (the "triple tradition") seldom do Matthew and Luke agree against Mark, whilst there are more Mark-Luke and Matthew-Mark agreements.

The picture is complicated by the fact that a significant portion of material (about 225 verses) is common to Matthew and Luke (the "double tradition"), but not found in Mark. While it is theoretically conceivable one

---

[9] Reading a chapter such as this in no way replaces the value of reading or hearing the gospels themselves, just as viewing a guide or synopsis about a piece of theater in no way replaces actually experiencing it.

[10] Alternate theories such as Matthean priority still have strong advocates and support, and caution is needed lest the issue be regarded as closed. For a concise outline of issues and proposals, see R. H. Stein, "Synoptic Problem," in Joel B. Green, Scot McKnight and I. Howard Marshall, eds., *Dictionary of Jesus and the Gospels* (Downers Grove: InterVarsity Press, 1992), pp. 784-92; and in more detail in R. H. Stein, *The Synoptic Problem: An Introduction* (Grand Rapids: Baker, 1987). In reviewing the options, see Craig A. Evans, "Sorting Out the Synoptic Problem: Why an Old Approach Is Still Best," in Stanley E Porter, ed., *Reading the Gospels Today* (Grand Rapids: Eerdmans, 2004), pp. 1-26; and the essays contained in David A. Black and David R. Beck, eds., *Rethinking the Synoptic Problem* (Grand Rapids: Baker, 2001).

writer drew on material from the other, it is more likely Matthew and Luke both used common material from another source, conventionally known as "Q" (from the German word *Quelle*, meaning "source"). This material is hypothetical to the extent that no actual document or collection of material of this nature survives, but the notion of Q is a viable one. About half of these verses have verbal correspondence (exact wording at times), and mostly comprise sayings and parables of Jesus.[11] They generally occur as blocks within Matthew's Gospel, and are more dispersed in Luke, and often follow the same general sequence in both Gospels.[12] The occasions where Matthew and Luke agree against Mark are problematical for the Marcan priority view, but may be explained by overlapping traditions—that Mark adapted some traditions or material (oral or written) also found in Q, and Matthew and Luke adopted the Q versions.

Material that is unique or distinctive to Matthew and Luke (sometimes designated M and L) is unlikely to have come from any single source, and may comprise other written material, oral traditions and personal experiences. In short, it is reasonable to recognize a range of influences resulting in some of the distinctive features of the gospels, as well as common traditions.

## 2. Oral Traditions

The existence of oral traditions predating written gospel traditions has been recognized from very early times. The excitement stirred by Jesus left people talking in his wake—despite many injunctions "not to tell anyone." The gospels themselves note that news about Jesus spread rapidly and widely. Two observations are especially relevant. First, the cultural context was essentially an oral one, with well recognized patterns of repetition, rehearsal and communal story-telling.[13] Yet the context of preserving teachings and traditions concerning Jesus has every appearance of being a disciplined one, subject to received traditions venerated within authoritative communities of faith.[14] While particular units appear to be based on received oral traditions,

---

[11] A helpful summary (in general terms) of the contents and character of "Q" may be found in David de Silva, *An Introduction to the New Testament: Contexts, Methods & Ministry Formation* (Downers Grove: InterVarsity Press, 2004), pp. 168-74.

[12] An introduction to these matters is found in Darrell Bock, "Questions about Q," in Black and Beck, *Rethinking*, p. 41-64.

[13] See especially Kenneth E. Bailey, "Informal Controlled Oral Tradition and the Synoptic Gospels," *Themelios* 20.2 (1995), pp. 4-11; James D. G. Dunn, *Jesus Remembered* (Grand Rapids: Eerdmans, 2003); and Martin Hengel, "Eye-witness Memory and the Writing of the Gospels," in Marcus Bockmuehl and Donald A. Hagner, eds., *The Written Gospel* (Cambridge: Cambridge University Press, 2005), pp. 70-98.

[14] The classic text is that of B. Gerhardsson, *Memory and Manuscript: Oral Tradition and Written Transmission in Rabbinic Judaism and Early Christianity* (Copenhagen: Ejnar Munksgaard, 1961), who particularly highlights the great respect shown by pupils towards the words of their Rabbi, and argues that at least the same measure of respect would be shown to the words of the one believed to be Messiah. See also the essays contained in Henry Wansbrough, ed., *Jesus and the Oral Gospel Tradition*, JSNTSup 64 (Sheffield: Sheffield Academic Press, 1991).

opinion differs to the extent such traditions can be retrieved.

A second observation is also significant. Early second-century accounts allude to close association between gospel traditions and apostolic witness. Papias (as noted by Eusebius, c. AD 260–340) is recorded as hearing from "the presbyter"[15] regarding sources of information associated with the "disciples of the Lord":

> But whenever someone arrived who had been a companion of one of the elders, I would carefully inquire after their words, what Andrew or Peter had said, or James or John or Matthew or any of the other disciples of the Lord, and what things Aristion and the elder John, disciples of the Lord, were saying. For I did not suppose that what came out of the books would benefit me as that which came from a living and abiding voice.
>
> Eusebius, *Hist. eccl.* 3.39.4 from *The Apostolic Fathers, Volume II*, edited and translated by Bart D. Ehrman, (Cambridge: Harvard University Press, 2003), p. 99.

In reference to Mark's Gospel, Papias is said to have reported that "the presbyter would say this":

> And this is what the elder used to say, "When Mark was interpreter [or translator] of Peter, he wrote down accurately everything that he recalled of the Lord's words and deeds—but not in order. For he neither heard the Lord nor accompanied him; but later, as I indicated, he accompanied Peter, who used to adapt his teachings for the needs at hand, not arranging, as it were, an orderly composition of the Lord's sayings. And so Mark did nothing wrong by writing some of the matters as he remembered them. For he was intent on just one purpose: to leave out nothing that he heard or to include any falsehood among them."
>
> Eusebius, *Hist. eccl.* 3.39.15 (trans. Ehrman, *Apostolic Fathers, Volume II*, p. 99.

This is a mixed report card in the view of the "presbyter." Mark is said to have interpreted and written the words of Peter accurately, but in an *ad hoc* order (following Peter). Whatever we make of the qualified support given to Mark,[16] the criterion for accepting such material is noteworthy: the material that ended up in Mark's Gospel was received from those with (at least) a credible chain of association with eyewitnesses, and especially in close association with the testimony of the Apostle Peter.

---

[15] The identity of "the presbyter" cannot be determined conclusively. Clearly a senior respected figure in the church; some speculate that it may have been John "the disciple of the Lord," others that there was another John familiar with the teachings of the apostle. Determining his identity is not vital, but the fact that this takes our evidence back one generation closer to the events themselves is significant.

[16] The qualified support is in itself a healthy sign, showing a discerning approach by Papias and the Presbyter: see Paul Barnett, *The Birth of Christianity: The First Twenty Years* (Grand Rapids: Eerdmans, 2005), p. 160. For a thorough treatment, see Martin Hengel, *Studies in the Gospel of Mark* (London: SCM Press, 1985), pp. 47-53.

## B. Distinctive Features

For the purposes of this chapter, the following pattern of approach will be employed:

Beginning and ending.
Settings, characters and encounters.
Form, shape and style.
Content and themes.
The person of Jesus.

The range of features reflected in this framework integrates exploration of the gospels as documents in their own right with the concerns of socio-historical and narrative approaches.

### 1. Mark's Gospel [17]

Not only is Mark the shortest of the canonical gospels, it has a very distinctive character. Overly neglected for many years ("why read Mark when you can get most of it in Matthew?"), appreciation for Mark's distinctive qualities has gained a strong following, reflected in specialist treatments of this Gospel. [18] Of the three Synoptic Gospels, it is the most akin in style to the street theater image proposed above. [19]

### (a) Beginning and Ending [20]

Mark begins abruptly and boldly. The opening affirmation sets the agenda for all that follows, and brings the narrative focus immediately to the person of Jesus. The first verse is ambiguous (perhaps deliberately so): "The beginning of the gospel of Jesus Christ" could refer either to the gospel concerning Jesus Christ, or the gospel conveyed by Jesus. In any event, the opening verse both declares Mark's belief and raises as many questions as it clarifies. The use of "gospel" would have surprised early readers. The term had yet to develop anything like its modern sense, and would not have denoted a category of

---

[17] Much of what is noted here in reference to Mark is also relevant to Matthew and Luke, and in some measure John as well. In identifying distinctive features of the gospels, we do not want to overlook key aspects they have in common. In addressing this, our treatment of Mark will be a little fuller than the other gospels.

[18] Among many, especially noteworthy are David Rhoads, Joanna Dewey and Donald Michie, *Mark as Story: An Introduction to the Narrative of a Gospel*, 2nd ed. (Minneapolis: Fortress Press, 1999), and David Rhoads, *Reading Mark: Engaging the Gospel* (Minneapolis: Fortress Press, 2004).

[19] See further Elizabeth Struthers Malbon, *Hearing Mark: A Listener's Guide* (Harrisburg: Trinity Press International, 2002).

[20] The significance of "beginnings" and "endings" is well recognized. See Morna D. Hooker, *Beginnings: Keys that Open the Gospels* (Harrisburg: Trinity Press International, 1997) and *Endings: Invitations to Discipleship* (Peabody: Hendrickson, 2003).

document. To Roman ears it was notably associated with proclamations concerning Caesar, military victories and all things imperial. Mark's use of the term in this preface is striking, pointing to one particular gospel, and orientates the *bios* as a form of proclamation with a message to convey.

The reference to Jesus as "Christ" ("anointed one") is also unexplained, and assumes some knowledge of the term in the context of the biblical narrative. As Mark continues, the episodes move from identifying Jesus to rethinking the type of Messiah Jesus was observed to be. A "messiah" denoted someone anointed by God for particular tasks, and stirred up a myriad of hopes and expectations. While there is some textual doubt over the addition of "the Son of God," the phrase is a significant one in Mark (note 1:11 and 15:39) and in keeping with what follows. Taken collectively, the opening verse is a stark and concise introduction, each term assuming a deeper significance as the narrative progresses. The use of "beginning" is more than a starting point in the story, and most likely refers to the book as a whole, especially the events describing the beginning of a new work of God through this person Jesus.

The prologue (1:1-13) moves into significant scriptural citation(s)[21] introduced by "as it is written." The scene is immediately set in the framework of promise and fulfillment. God is at work (note the implied "I") and preparations underway for the arrival of "the Lord" as long awaited. As significant a figure as is John the Baptist, to whom "all the country of Judea and all Jerusalem" were journeying, he is nonetheless located as a preliminary to the arrival of one "much mightier" than he.

Two features are especially worthy of note: the location is specifically "in the wilderness" (more on this below) and the Baptist's ministry was one of "repentance for the forgiveness of sins" (1:4). Such a baptism was not only a form of preparation in anticipation of the impending arrival, it was also a foreshadowing of a greater ministry about to unfold: "I have baptized you with water, but he will baptize you with the Holy Spirit" (1:8).

The introduction, outlining the necessary preparation for the arrival of the Lord, is short and sharply focused. It is onto this stage that Jesus is introduced, with no more background detail than "from Nazareth of Galilee." Like multitudes of others he was baptized by John in the Jordan, but from the point of his rising from the waters, "immediately" (εὐθύς) great happenings occurred: the "heavens opened," the "Spirit descending," and a "voice" came from heaven (as also in 9:7). While much of the narrative to follow will explore the question of Jesus' identity through the experiences of those who encountered him, here the reporting of the most profound voice of all leaves the reader/hearer in no doubt at all of the claims surrounding Jesus: "God's voice declares that Jesus is his son."[22] The statement evokes two images: the setting of Yahweh's appointed king on Zion (Ps. 2:6-7), and the sending of

---

[21] The quotation is a composite, mainly from Isa. 40:3, with elements from Mal. 3:1 and Exod. 23:20.

[22] R. T. France, *The Gospel of Mark: A Commentary on the Greek Text*, NIGTC (Grand Rapids: Eerdmans, 2002), p. 79.

God's chosen Servant (Isa. 42:1)—the servant King.

The account of the commencement of Jesus' public ministry (1:14-15) is characteristically forthright. Without any details at this point, it is noted specifically as following the arrest of John the Baptist. The transition is clearly important and the focus moves Jesus to center stage. The summary of Jesus' message ("the gospel of God") is likewise concise and enigmatic: "The time is fulfilled, and the kingdom-reign of God is at hand; repent and believe in the gospel." More of what is meant by this is explored in the gospel narrative that follows.

The ending of Mark is no less enigmatic. The longer ending (16:9-20) is most likely spurious, and a range of textual scenarios are canvassed (has the ending been lost or damaged at an early stage?). Suggestions concerning the appropriateness of the ending as it stands (at 16:8) have been multitudinous, and in the context of more contemporary narrative analysis show no sign of abating. The most plausible suggestions point to the open-ended nature of the Markan narrative. The opening words (in characteristic biblical style) announce the "beginning" of the gospel, while the end is over to the reader/hearer, those who respond to the call to ongoing discipleship. The next steps are for the audience to make.[23] Attractive as this may be in post-modern style, it falls short of providing a convincing explanation of authorial intent. More apposite is the recognition that the final note of "trembling and astonishment" does reprise a significant theme and narrative device throughout the Gospel. The impact of what has just occurred is frequently conveyed in Mark by a narratorial comment[24] in similar terms. As noted by Graham Stanton, for "the attentive reader the outcome of the story is clear,"[25] even if conveyed in enigmatic terms.

### (b) Settings, Characters and Encounters

Despite the terseness of Mark's Gospel, there is significance behind such detail as is given. The geographical settings[26] provide narrative shape to the Gospel.[27] The focus on Galilee, with the note at the outset about multitudes travelling *from* Jerusalem and Judea *to* the wilderness has a subversive undercurrent. Jerusalem was considered the hub of God's purposes, to which all people would be drawn. Yet here the movement is in the opposite

---

[23] "The ending Mark demands that *his readers* supply is the response of faith: it is only those who are prepared to believe and who set off on the journey of faith who will see the risen Lord," so Hooker, *Endings*, p. 23 (emphasis original).

[24] An implied "narrator" is not necessarily the same as the author. The distinction is most readily observed in the realm of theater. A narrator may be an entity in the production (on stage, or providing a "voice over"), while the author has written the script. The same dynamic works with texts, with an author creating an implicit persona within the text to provide commentary.

[25] Graham Stanton, *The Gospels and Jesus*, 2nd ed. (Oxford: Oxford University Press, 2002), p. 53.

[26] For detail, see Rhoads, Dewey and Michie, *Mark as Story*, pp. 63-72.

[27] France, *Mark*, pp. 13-14 shapes his outline around three acts, set in Galilee (1:14–8:21), on the way to Jerusalem (8:22–10:52), and in Jerusalem (11:1–16:8).

direction.[28] Reference to the "wilderness" (ἔρημος) is as much symbolic as geographic. It is a place of withdrawal, of preparation and of testing, but even more importantly it is a place of new beginnings and renewal for the people of God. It is significantly the location of Jesus' initial encounter with Satan (1:12).

As noted above, the geographical movement in Mark corresponds to three stages in narrative movement (Galilee, journey towards Jerusalem, and final week in Jerusalem). Much of the first half of Mark takes place in Galilee to the north, with representatives of authority in Jerusalem travelling to engage with Jesus from a distance (e.g. 3:22). Home base for Jesus is not his hometown of Nazareth, but Capernaum, a fishing village on the sea of Galilee. This locale becomes the center for the new "occupation" for the disciples as "fishers of people" (1:17). Travels out from Capernaum take Jesus and his growing retinue into neighboring towns and villages, beside the "sea"[29] (e.g. 1:16; 2:13; 4:1), on the sea (3:7-9), up on "the mountain" (3:13), and to "the other side of the sea" (5:1), into gentile territory. Jesus' return to "his own country" (6:1) is also largely symbolic, underscoring a theme of rejection and homelessness (note also the visit from his natural family in 3:31-35, redefining the identity of family[30]).

Alongside this geographical landscape (often specifically noted by Mark) are significant socio-cultural settings. Capernaum is not only a center of operations for Jesus' ministry, it is also the place where a new "home" is developed (3:20), most likely in the house of Simon and Andrew (1:29). The house and home is a fundamental and highly significant unit within the social world of this time, and this setting underscores a deeper spiritual motif woven in and through Mark's narrative (homelessness and the desire for "home"). Here it is a place of intimacy, and the developing of embryonic household families, representative of new community formation within the kingdom.[31] Yet they are also places of public engagement, with some of the houses in view likely to be of a size to allow a number of guests (a *domus* with *atrium*).

Adjacent to this setting of the home/household are episodes set within the synagogue. This provides the primary forum of engagement for the theological assertions of Jesus—his authoritative teaching. The synagogue was the domain of local authorities, a place of assembly for prayer, reading the Scriptures and teaching, as well as a type of local court. The interplay

---

[28] C. Myers, *Binding the Strong Man: A Political Reading of Mark's Story of Jesus* (Maryknoll: Orbis, 1988), pp. 125-26.

[29] The terminology (θάλασσα) seems a bit incongruous for what is really a lake (as in Luke), but this usage does follow the LXX and local usage. There are also symbolic overtones conveyed through the use of "sea," as a setting of disorder, chaos and spiritual challenge. A number of the settings recall Israel's past: the Jordan, desert, sea and mountain, as noted by Rhoads, Dewey and Michie, *Mark as Story*, pp. 69-70.

[30] On the profile of Jesus' family in Mark, note Stephen C. Barton, *Discipleship and Family Ties in Mark and Matthew*, SNTSMS, new ed. (Cambridge: Cambridge University Press, 2005).

[31] The household motif is explored by Michael F. Trainor in *The Quest for Home: The Household in Mark's Community* (Collegeville: Liturgical Press, 2001), with a special concern for Jesus' redefinition of household relationships.

between Jesus and religious authorities was in Mark invariably a public one, inviting those watching on (and through them, the reader/hearer) to form their own verdicts.

The same is true of one other significant setting: <u>public space</u>. This was the primary theater of social place and interaction, with strong conventions of order, boundaries and community life—a social world constructed by powerful perceptions of honor and shame. Particularly relevant here are conventions of "<u>challenge and riposte</u>." The former involves a gesture, statement or question which calls the object's honor into question, with the desire to bring about a public humiliation. "Riposte" is the response, often in the form of counter-challenge or rebuff. There are many examples in Mark.[32]

Within such contexts (both public and private), Jesus is presented as <u>challenging the</u> social world and the values that undergird it. He not so much flouts conventions, as exposes and subverts them. Whilst identifying with a community and people, and existing very much within and alongside them, he also rejected any claim to authority or power that failed to acknowledge the kingdom-reign of God. In the terminology of cultural anthropology, Jesus crossed boundaries, redefining notions of purity and defilement,[33] re-shaping the social world of those "in" and those "out," reversing the perceptions of those with high status and those with low. This is true of all the gospels, but it certainly is reflected in Mark distinctively.

One final setting is worthy of special note. Mark devotes significant space in his narrative to the <u>final week of Jesus</u> in Jerusalem, much of which takes place in and around the temple (from the new home-base of Bethany). After the defining moment of Jesus' enigmatic entry, Mark records in typical "sandwich style" (see below) the cursing of the fig tree, and the cleansing of the temple. The setting is profound at a number of levels: "Here was a man, proscribed by law . . . entering the capital city of the Jewish world, moving into its holiest place in a peaceful manner and making it his teaching seat. From another angle, we have the promised King entering Jerusalem, 'the City of the Great King,' taking his seat in the very house of God."[34]

Against the backdrop of these significant settings, Mark's narrative is developed through a series of encounters with a whole range of characters. The selection drawn by Mark serves both as a mirror through which to explore the person of Jesus (his character, identity, mission and authority) and a lens to highlight the journey of faith and the nature of discipleship. This has been a

---

[32] Three examples are of note: a challenge from the Pharisees and scribes (Mark 7: 5-9); the exchange with the Syrophoenician woman (Mark 7:24-38) and the series of challenges and responses in Mark 15 involving the arrest, trial and crucifixion of Jesus. See further Vernon K. Robbins, *Exploring the Texture of Texts* (Valley Forge: Trinity Press International, 1996), pp. 81-82.

[33] Note especially Rhoads, *Reading Mark*, ch. 6; and more generally J. H. Elliott, ed., *Social-Scientific Criticism of the New Testament and Its Social World*, *Semeia* 35 (Decatur: Scholars Press, 1986); David de Silva, *Honor, Patronage, Kinship and Purity: Unlocking New Testament Culture* (Downers Grove: InterVarsity Press, 2000).

[34] David Seccombe, *The King of God's Kingdom: A Solution to the Puzzle of Jesus* (Carlisle: Paternoster, 2002), pp. 509-10.

particularly productive area of recent scholarship.[35]

Jesus is the centrifugal point of the narrative: people are drawn to him (3:8). Discipleship is well recognized as a major motif, and perceptions on discipleship are reflected in both positive and flawed ways. The "failures" of the disciples are presented not as an indictment but as indicative of the disciple-making capacity of Jesus, despite such weaknesses. The disciples are in a profound process of learning and have some way to go. In a wider perspective, the presentation of the flawed disciples (notably including Peter) in such a gospel, based on the accounts and testimony of such disciples, is in itself a lesson in discipleship. Engagement with Jesus has the power to bring about forgiveness and transformation, especially as disciples persevere and learn the fundamental lesson of eschewing the saving of one's own life in favor of losing one's life for Jesus' sake and the gospel's (8:34–9:1).[36]

In this context, men and women disciples are presented as both fallible and faithful. It is striking however, that women "serve"[37] Jesus and in so doing, set an example of true discipleship. The telling presence of women at the end of the Gospel makes a significant statement—they have followed Jesus from beginning to end (underscored pointedly at 15:40-41).[38]

Other characters are presented collectively. Opposition to Jesus is primarily focused on Jewish leaders, described variously as scribes, Pharisees, Sadducees, Herodians and elders and Chief Priests.[39] The "crowd" (ὄχλος)

---

[35] Note especially two works by Elizabeth Struthers Malbon, *In the Company of Jesus: Characters in Mark's Gospel* (Louisville: Westminster/John Knox Press, 2000); and, on the various settings, *Narrative Space and Mythic Meaning in Mark* (Sheffield: Sheffield Academic Press, 1991).

[36] The centrality of this teaching in the narrative of Mark is developed by Rhoads, *Reading Mark*, ch. 3.

[37] Peter's mother-in-law is one example. After her healing, Mark notes with subtle poignancy "and she began to serve them" (1:31b). The use of διακονέω is rare in Mark (also 1:13; 10:45 and 15:41), and the association with "for even the Son of Man came not to be served but to serve, and to give his life. . ." (10:45) is telling: "In view of its connection here with the idea of dying or giving one's life, 'service' in the present story takes on the idea of total devotion to Jesus in response to being healed by Jesus," Graham H. Twelftree, *Jesus the Miracle Worker* (Downers Grove: InterVarsity Press, 1999), p. 60.

[38] A helpful balance is struck by Malbon: "although women characters are portrayed as followers in the Markan Gospel, minimal emphasis is placed on their fallibility as followers in comparison with the crowd and especially the disciples. . . Women characters of Mark are 'good' or 'positive' because they are followers or exemplify 'followership'—not because they are women. Women can be villains as well as heroes in the Gospel of Mark." The composite picture of those who follow Jesus underscores a twofold message: "anyone can be a follower, no one finds it easy," *Company*, pp. 65-67.

[39] These are noted sometimes as individual groups, sometimes collectively (in various combinations). Their presentation is as much a literary characterization as historical. They were far from a homogenous historical grouping, and Jesus had more than one class of opponent. There is much debate about the presentation of representatives of the Jewish religious and social establishment in the gospels. For a treatment approached from a narrative-literary perspective, see Malbon, *Company*, ch. 5. Malbon's three interpretive suggestions (pp. 148-58) are incisive: 1) where Jewish leaders are grouped together in the narrative, they are united in their opposition to Jesus; 2) the leaders are also distinguished within the narrative—in the earlier passages the main opposition comes from scribes and Pharisees (in the setting of Galilee and synagogues), later opposition closer to Jerusalem is focused on the chief priests, scribes and elders; and 3) the

also feature prominently in Mark, and in many ways the reader/hearer is invited to identify with this observers' perspective. It is to both the disciples and the gathered crowd that Jesus says, "Let anyone with ears to hear listen" (4:9). A particularly effective narrative device employed by Mark is the noting of the disciples' or crowd's response to all they hear or observe, characteristically expressed through terms of amazement, wonder, astonishment, fear and terror.[40] The impact of Jesus is presented as remarkable, and calls for an evaluation by the crowd and reader/hearer alike ("who is this man?") and response ("what does it mean to place faith in Jesus, and follow him?").

A succession of "minor" characters also play a significant narrative role in Mark, individuals who emerge from within the crowd. None are developed in any depth, few are named, and they do not play any ongoing part in the narrative. Yet collectively they serve to exemplify those who recognize some aspect of need within themselves, their household or circumstances. These "suppliants" are not presented as types, but as "person-like characters whom real readers could recognize as examples of people known to them from their real world," with a common underlying need in living under the shadow of death.[41]

### (c) Form, Shape and Style

The characteristic Markan outline is treated elsewhere in this volume (see the preceding chapter), and need not be rehearsed here. Significant transition points however are worthy of note, establishing pivotal developments in the Gospel narrative. From the earlier northern stage where Jesus publicly proclaims and enacts the kingdom-reign of God, he signals a new and necessary stage in his mission by turning towards Jerusalem and talking to the disciples of his coming death. The transition point comes dramatically on the way to the villages of Caesarea Philippi to the far north. Jesus is recorded by Mark (8:27-30) as asking a key question regarding who people say he is, followed by the more personally challenging "who do you say that I am?" Peter's famous reply "You are the Christ" speaks more broadly, for the disciples as a whole, but also as a conclusion to the series of encounters where onlookers (and through them the reader/hearer) have been asking themselves the same question—who is this man?[42] Clearly it is a watershed moment, both

---

exceptional response of some Jewish leaders points to a more complex picture and positive examples (e.g. The scribe who is "not far from the kingdom of God," 12:34; Joseph of Arimathea and Jairus).

[40] A useful list of such terms and their context is provided by Malbon, *Company*, pp. 85-86.

[41] Peter G. Bolt, *Jesus' Defeat of Death: Persuading Mark's Early Readers*, SNTSMS 125 (New York: Cambridge University Press, 2003), pp. 269, 271.

[42] There is much debate about the authenticity of these verses. The exchange here between Jesus and Peter clearly fits Mark's redactional purposes (identifying Jesus as Messiah, and the ongoing confrontation with Satan). Such an exchange is also credible within the context of Jesus' ministry, with the desire to avoid limited or misconceived notions of messiahship, as well as directing attention to the mission he came to fulfill.

in the recollection of the disciples, and in Mark's narrative composition of his Gospel (picking up and addressing the belief reflected in the introduction, 1:1).

The turning point is stark and multifaceted. With the charge to keep this central proof private, the direction moves from addressing that question to a greater work necessary for Jesus' mission (note also 9:30). He speaks for the first time in this narrative of his impending death and resurrection, and in this context issues the ultimate challenge of discipleship—who is prepared to follow? Again the question applies more broadly, not only to the immediate audience, but to all who read or hear of this declaration: "If anyone would come after me. . ." (8:34), with the ensuing teaching focusing on the cost of discipleship.

The change in atmosphere is equally abrupt. The tone shifts in turn from the rebuking of Jesus by Peter, the bluntest of replies ("Get behind me, Satan!" 8:33), to a sense of foreboding and fear on the part of the disciples to explore the question of Jesus' death further, having been raised by Jesus on two other occasions in this section (9:30-32; 10:32-34).[43] The journey to Jerusalem is framed clearly in terms of Jesus' awareness of what is to come.

Parallel to Peter's Caesarea Philippi confession, and following on from Jesus' pronouncement about seeing the kingdom-reign of God coming with power (9:1), stands the account of the transfiguration. This remarkable episode is highly evocative without elaboration. The heavenly "voice" speaks once again: "This is my beloved Son; listen to him" (9:7), forming the centerpiece of the unit. This cryptic passage conveys an assurance of God's hand behind this new direction to Jesus' mission, and in doing so raises the context dramatically to the cosmic realm and the anticipation of a greater glory. In narrative terms the whole episode places the story of Jesus against the backdrop of the greater—and ongoing—narrative of the Bible.

As profound and distinctive as the shape of Mark's Gospel is the style through which it is conveyed. Lacking the polish of Matthew and Luke, or the extended discussions of John, Mark has a sense of movement, engagement and overriding purpose.

A number of stylistic features have been identified, with the frequency of εὐθύς particularly noteworthy.[44] This adverb is generally translated "immediately" or "at once," although it can also denote a milder "then." Its use in Mark generates a sense of activity and drama, of movement and developing events. Complementing this term is Mark's use of the "historic present," using the present tense when retelling a story as if it was happening currently, conveying a more vivid perspective. The connections between events are purposeful—one event leading to the next. Stylistically this is reinforced by the frequent use of καί ("and") to start sentences.

Another feature in Mark's story-telling is the "sandwich technique." After

---

[43] "Their failure to understand is only partial: they understand enough to be afraid to ask to understand more," so Ernest Best, *Following Jesus: Discipleship in the Gospel of Mark,* JSNTSup 4 (Sheffield: JSOT Press, 1981), p. 73.

[44] Forty times in Mark, eleven of which are in chapter 1.

commencing one story or pericope, an interruption or second episode occurs, before the first story is resumed (an A$^1$-B-A$^2$ sequence). The interspersing of events highlights common themes or concerns like a thread. One well recognized instance is found in the second half of Mark 5. This section starts with the encounter with Jairus and his concern for his daughter (5:21-24). While responding to this request, Jesus is approached and touched by the woman afflicted with a flow of blood, and concludes with Jesus' statement "Daughter, your faith has made you well. . ." (5:34a). At this point the narrative returns to the first storyline, with news that Jairus' daughter is dead. Jesus eventually enters the house and raises the girl, but before doing so he gives the assurance "Do not fear, only believe" (5:36). Both stories have remarkable healings in common, but the underlying thread focuses on faith.[45]

### (d) Content and Themes

A significant proportion of Mark's Gospel involves miracles, healings and exorcisms—about one third of the Gospel, and over half of the first ten chapters. At one level, these episodes testify to Jesus' authority and power (δύναμις, "power," "might," "strength" is Mark's preferred term for miracle; see especially 5:30). Yet they are more than that. They affirm Jesus' connection with the power of God and the inauguration of the kingdom-reign of God.[46] Satan and all other powers are overthrown, and God's purposes in restoration, salvation and *shalom* are realized (5:34). In Mark's account, the first day of public ministry following the call of the disciples was a full one (1:21-34), involving the healing of the man with an unclean spirit (notably on the Sabbath, in the synagogue at Capernaum), Simon's mother-in-law, and at sundown "all who were sick or oppressed by demons" (1:32).

There is a certain irony in the presentation of Jesus as teacher and preacher, for Mark contains little of the actual teachings of Jesus. Mark's profile of Jesus is as a man of action, and that activity frequently included teaching and proclamation. The morning following Jesus' first day of public ministry, Mark notes Jesus speaking to his disciples with the resolve: "Let us go on to the neighboring towns, so that I may proclaim the message there also" (1:38). The "also" is significant: the activity of the previous day was proclaiming the message. Rather than subsuming miracles to the priority of teaching, this verse identifies Jesus' message with his actions.[47]

The teaching of Jesus in Mark touches upon faithful discipleship in the context of community and daily life, including divorce, forgiveness, status and humility, trust and prayer. Of particular interest are occasions when Mark notes issues of contention, from questions about fasting, Sabbath day observance and ceremonial defilement. Consideration of those included within

---

[45] Other examples may be found in 3:20-35; 4:1-20; 6:7-30; 11:12-21; 14:1-11; 14:17-31; 14:53-72; 15:40-16:8.

[46] See further Twelftree, *Miracle Worker*, ch. 3.

[47] Twelftree, *Miracle Worker*, p. 61: "both the message and the healings are the message of Jesus."

the people of the kingdom-reign of God also runs throughout the Gospel. The explanation concerning speaking in parables[48] is identified as being "given the secret of the kingdom of God" (4:11) for those who perceive, understand, repent and receive forgiveness. The enigmatic exhortation "Let anyone with ears to hear listen!" (4:23) anticipates a polarized response. Those who do understand receive insight into the mission of Jesus, whilst for others it flags controversy and hostility (see also 7:14; 8:1; 10:42; 12:43).

The final week in Jerusalem prior to the crucifixion receives a special focus in Mark (chapters 11–13). The challenge to the religious hierarchy is highlighted through the cleansing of the temple (11:15-19)—recorded in John's Gospel earlier in Jesus' ministry (John 2:13-22)—bracketed by the cursing and withering of the fig tree (11:12-14; 20-25). The profile in Mark underscores the impending showdown between the religious establishment and Jesus' claims to authority (in view from the outset, 1:27; 12:6-7) and it is this issue that runs through the encounters that follow (see especially 11:27-33).

We have already drawn attention to the themes of <u>discipleship and faith</u> in Mark.[49] These motifs are drawn together by the direction of the narrative. Discipleship involves responding to the call to follow in the steps of Jesus (8:34), a journey shaped by the denial of self-interest and the taking up of a cross. There is a corresponding purposefulness and sense of mission in the path that led to Jesus' betrayal, treatment before Jewish and Roman authorities, and the crucifixion. The language that describes this sense of purpose is distinctive in Mark: a life given as a "ransom" ($\lambda \acute{u} \tau \rho o \nu$) on behalf of ($\dot{a} \nu \tau \acute{i}$) many (10:45).[50]

It is often said of Mark that it is a "passion-narrative with a long introduction." That is certainly an overstatement, but like all good caricatures it brings notable features into stark relief. There is no doubt that the shadow of the cross grows darker as the narrative continues.

Events move in a climactic and cataclysmic direction. A showdown looms that has been building in intensity since the "testing" of Jesus by Satan noted in 1:13. Challenges and confrontation with the realm of evil spirits are woven throughout the narrative fabric (see especially 8:33), and Jesus places the events about to unfold against the backdrop of cosmic history itself (Mark 13). Yet not only are the events of Jesus' crucifixion, death and resurrection a

---

[48] For further discussion of parables, see chapter 14 in this volume.

[49] See further Christopher D. Marshall, *Faith as a Theme in Mark's Narratives* (New York: Cambridge University Press, 1989).

[50] Also paralleled in Matt. 20:28. Much debate surrounds the significance of this term. For an incisive review and treatment, see France, *Mark*, pp. 420-21. A $\lambda \acute{u} \tau \rho o \nu$ would be readily understood in the Hellenistic and Roman periods as a payment to secure release from prison, captivity or slavery. There is also evidence of such an offering being made to gods in which offences are expiated; see further the inscriptional examples covered in G. H. R. Horsley, *New Documents Illustrating Early Christianity*, Volume Two (Sydney: Ancient History Documentary Centre, Macquarie University, 1982), p. 90 and especially Volume Three, pp. 72-75; and A. Y. Collins, "The Significance of Mark 10:45 among Gentile Christians," *Harvard Theological Review* 90 (1997), pp. 371-82.

cosmic showdown within the purposes of the Father who sent his Son (highlighted in the intensive prayers in Gethsemane), they provide a meta-narrative in which the realities of life find some measure of meaning. Human authorities act out of fear and rivalry, plotting and manipulating processes for a range of unworthy—and quite unjust—motives. For all his resolve to be obedient to his "Abba, Father" (14:36), Jesus did not deserve his betrayal by a companion and the brutal, contemptuous, vindictive hostility culminating in crucifixion.

The kingdom-reign of God is established in and through the harsh realities of human experience, with the greatest anguish of all glimpsed briefly in the view "from a distance" (15:40) of Jesus' cries of forsakenness from the cross (15:34).[51] Hope beyond such darkness is characteristically understated in the deceptively simple announcement in the quiet of the empty tomb, but no less powerful in the enormity of its implications: "Do not be alarmed; you are looking for Jesus of Nazareth, who was crucified. He has been raised; he is not here" (16:6). Without the benefit of explicit explanations, the reader/hearer is thrown back along with the women and other early disciples to make sense of such stupendous news. The narrative has prepared the way: not only did Jesus alert his followers to the impending horrors of his death, but also to the ultimate new reality of his rising after three days (8:31; 9:31; 10:34).

Against the intensity of Jesus' experiences narrated by Mark, the reader-hearer can begin to identify commonalities at the most fundamental level. Life is not fair, and frequently unjust. Evildoers appear to flourish and triumph. Weakness and vulnerability is often exploited, and society is invariably shaped by an elite who reinforce their position by excluding or removing those who threaten them or fall out of favor. How the God who stands behind the gospel of Jesus can further the work of the kingdom-reign, despite such realities, would have made a poignant message to Mark's early audience, especially the followers of Jesus fearing or experiencing the horrors of persecution as a public spectacle in Rome at the direction of Nero (see Tacitus, *Ann.* 15.44).

## (e) The Person of Jesus

On the basis of the evidence of the gospel traditions, Jesus' preferred title is the elusive "Son of Man." Unlike the expectation-laden identity of the Messiah, the designation "Son of Man" can be little more than a form of self-reference, akin to "one" in English. Yet as presented in Mark, the term suggests a figure of authority. At times there is a probable allusion to the heavenly figure of Dan. 7:13, although this was not highly developed by the time of Jesus and therefore more congenial to reflect the enigmatic, yet progressively meaningful sense as the Gospel narrative develops (note

---

[51] See especially Peter G. Bolt, *The Cross from a Distance: Atonement in Mark's Gospel* (Downers Grove: InterVarsity Press, 2004), pp. 127-45.

especially the "christological climax" of 14:62, together with Messiah and Son of God[52]). Jesus brings unique meaning to the term.[53]

For all the recognition of the exceptional nature of Jesus, it is also important to observe his solidarity with humanity. Jesus is presented in Mark in very human terms, with notes of his compassion (1:41, or possibly anger), anger and grief (3:5), tiredness (4:38), amazement (6:6), sighing or groaning (7:34; 8:12), annoyance (10:14). Such observations are not cause in Mark for theological reflection as to Jesus' being, but are part and parcel of the narrative.

Mark employs a range of hints, echoes and suggestive allusions, and collectively presents Jesus as the key figure within a greater biblical narrative. He is repeatedly misunderstood by family, neighbors, religious leaders and followers, but the narrative guides the reader/hearer through a range of appellations, from teacher, rabbi, lord, to a carefully nuanced messianic figure, son of David, the Father's Son, Son of God, son of man, one who suffers, with Isaianic servant echoes throughout. A defining moment in resolving the question of Jesus' identity comes with the climactic declaration at the cross from the mouth of the centurion in charge of the execution squad: "Truly this man was God's Son!" (15:39). The significance is multilayered, for the centurion would not have perceived any theological sense, but quite possibly a political statement (since Augustus the appellation "son of god" was a special claim of Caesar). For the reader/hearer, however, the term takes on a more profound sense: the centurion has spoken a truth beyond his knowing.

In all this, Mark's perspective on Jesus cannot be discerned without reference to his suffering. The issue is not so much *who* is Jesus, but *what* is central to Jesus' identity, and this can only be perceived with reference to his relationship with the Father (note that the combined Aramaic/Greek combination "Abba, ὁ πατήρ is unique in the gospels to Mark, 14:36). As the reader/hearer of Mark encounters these claims, the issue of Jesus' identity likewise is framed in relational terms, with a call to follow and in so doing enter the kingdom-reign of God. The audience is urged to join the drama.

## 2. Matthew's Gospel

Our longer treatment of Mark's Gospel has laid the foundation and superstructure for the other two Synoptic Gospels, and is intended to complement the exploration of their respective distinctive characters and themes. Much of Matthew's more distinctive material is reflected in the earlier chapters (1–11): from chapter 12 on it resumes the Markan narrative with few rearrangements or omissions. Matthew treats his received traditions with care, but pursues an independence and creativity where it serves his

---

[52] France, *Mark*, p. 610.

[53] I. Howard Marshall provides a concise summary and evaluation of this extensive area of debate in *DJG*, s.v. "Son of Man."

particular concerns.[54] The Gospel is to be read as a whole, where earlier pericopes prepare the way for later episodes that provide new perspectives on related questions. Matthew is regarded as the most Jewish of the gospels, with a concern to articulate the story of Jesus in terms of the fulfillment of Old Testament promises and hopes. Yet Matthew's concerns in regard to formative Judaism[55] are complex, and will be considered further below.

### (a) Beginning and Ending

The beginning and ending of Matthew are particularly telling. He sets aside Mark's reference to "gospel," and opens instead with "[a] book of the genealogy of Jesus the Messiah. . ." (1:1), a form of words that recalls Gen. 2:4 and 5:1. Jesus' origins are set against the backdrop of the biblical narrative reaching back to the very beginning and the story of creation itself. This genealogy is directed towards the concluding reference to "Jesus. . . called the Messiah" (1:16). Three segments of biblical history are covered, with pivotal stages turning around David and the Babylonian exile. These three periods are specifically styled as comprising fourteen generations (1:17), possibly reflecting the numeric value of David's name in Hebrew (each letter also represents a number). More plausible is the suggestion that the genealogy reveals a veiled pattern of six sevens (structured around the three major periods of history), with the story of Jesus inaugurating a climactic new era in the biblical story.

The selection of the names within this genealogy is also revealing, especially the unexpected inclusion of Tamar, Rahab, Ruth and "the wife of Uriah" (Bathsheba). It is not their gender as such—women were included in genealogies where there was particular cause. While a Davidic royal association is underscored ("King David" 1:5), Matthew goes out of his way to name the proverbial "family skeletons in the closet." Not only are their stories associated with sexual impropriety by way of occupation (Rahab) or treatment, of equal interest is the non-Jewish identity of the first three.

Perceived social and cultural irregularities in the genealogy from the stance of religious purists are undermined by the schematized presentation: God's purposes are unfolding according to plan. The stage is also set for the irregular circumstances of Mary's pregnancy and the assurance that despite the potential for public disgrace, the birth of Jesus conforms to a greater act of divine intervention. God's provision of salvation emerges from circumstances that might otherwise be considered morally deviant.[56] Yet any such perception is rendered redundant in the revelation to Joseph that the conception and birth

---

[54] See further Ulrich Luz, *Studies in Matthew* (Grand Rapids: Eerdmans, 2005), pp. 20-25.

[55] The period leading up to the Jewish Revolt in AD 66–70 is conventionally known as "Second Temple Judaism," while the century or so following the Revolt is known as "Formative Judaism." The Judaism of Jesus' day is the former, while that of the author of Matthew was most likely the latter.

[56] So W. D. Davies and Dale Allison, *A Critical and Exegetical Commentary on the Gospel according to Saint Matthew*, vol. 3 (Edinburgh: T. & T. Clark, 1997), pp. 171-72.

of Jesus is fully in accord with prophecy, and the essential truth lies in the child's name: "Emmanuel," which as Matthew explains to the reader means "God is with us" (1:23).

The final verses of Matthew revisit these motifs, and form an effective *inclusio*. Indeed Matthew reflects a number of "bookends" in his opening and closing sections. The commanding place of Jesus in God's purposes is stated in uncompromising terms: "All authority in heaven and on earth has been given to me" (28:18). The passive "has been given" indicates another intervention of God through the resurrection of Jesus. The few verses that follow may be brief in expression, but enormous in implication. The eleven disciples, summoned as the nucleus of the embryonic church, are charged to "go therefore and make disciples of all nations." God's saving purposes embodied in the person and work of Christ are not to be limited to the people of Israel. And the foundational truth revealed at the entry of Jesus in flesh and blood into this world ("God is with us") is revisited at his departure: "I am with you always, to the end of the age" (28:20b).

### (b) Settings, Characters and Encounters

Matthew sets his gospel drama against the backdrop of a much bigger stage and cast. Early in the narrative characters appear from further afield, especially in the form of the magi visiting from the East in search of "the child who has been born king of the Jews" (2:1-2). After the visit of the magi and guided by an "angel of the Lord," Joseph took Mary and the child and fled to Egypt (a Roman province beyond Herod's jurisdiction), where they remained until the death of Herod.[57] Matthew's purposes however are more than dramatic. His editorial comment at Matt. 2:15 notes: "This was to fulfill what had been spoken by the Lord through the prophet, 'Out of Egypt I have called my son'" (see Hos. 11:1). The life-story of Jesus is presented as paralleling the journeys of the people of Israel at the time of the Exodus.

While geographical details associated with the return from Egypt (choosing Nazareth rather than Judea) are identified with political concerns (Matt. 2:22), they are similarly associated in Matthew's view with the fulfillment of prophecy (2:23). Following Jesus' move from Nazareth to Capernaum to establish a new home (4:12), the Galilean district assumes theological significance as the location in which a great light will emerge for those "in darkness. . . the shadow of death" (4:15-16).

The stage is set with the calling of the disciples, and the movement of "great crowds" traveling from all directions drawn by the growing fame of Jesus. At this point in the narrative one of the most distinctive units associated with Matthew is introduced by topological reference: Jesus, accompanied by his disciples ascended the mountain, sat down (the posture of a rabbi) and began to teach them (5:1-2), with the crowds listening (7:28). We shall

[57] Archelaus, a son of Herod, ruled in Judea (but not in Galilee), and appears to have influenced the family's return to the northern region (2:22).

explore the "sermon on the mount" material shortly, but for now we note the reference to "the mountain." Allusions to mountains in Matthew are noteworthy,[58] and may be suggestive of a Moses-like figure gathering God's people (as at Mt Sinai) and delivering a new or fulfilled form of the Torah.[59] Caution is needed in drawing such conclusions, but the mountain top setting for a significant revelation of God's purposes, in which disciples are called to respond, is characteristic of Matthew.

The profile of the disciples is different to that found in Mark. Matthew mutes references to the Markan motif of the disciples' failure to understand. In Matthew, the disciples, while being of "little faith" (8:26; 14:31; 16:8; 17:20), receive special explanations, and their resultant growth in understanding (albeit still limited) reflects effective instruction by Jesus.[60] Yet in narrative terms the disciples are presented as relatively "flat,"[61] reflecting both positive and negative examples. The focus on true discipleship is located in the teachings of Jesus and exemplified in his pattern of life.[62] It is from identifying with the curious crowds attracted to Jesus that the reader/hearer is challenged to step out in discipleship.

The other significant grouping in Matthew is the religious leaders. As in Mark, encounters between Jesus and religious leaders are frequently characterized by conflict and plotting to kill him. In narrative terms, the leaders are undeveloped as characters, and exemplify opposition to the mission of Jesus. As such they are designated with a core trait of being "evil" (12:34), or more evocatively "a brood of vipers" (3:7; 12:34; 23:33). This fundamental trait is elaborated through a relentless list of indictments: they are hypocrites (15:7-9; 23:3, 13, 23, 25, 27, 29), ignorant and dangerous teachers (16:12; 22:29), blind guides (15:14; 23:16-19), and the implied targets of those who exercise false piety for public display (6:1-5).[63] A clue to the pedagogical intent of these fierce denunciations and warnings is detected in 23:1. Jesus addresses both the crowds and his disciples, and in recording Jesus condemning so strongly the community leadership of his day, Matthew may

---

[58] Matt. 4:8; 5:1 and 8:1; 17:1; 24:3 and 28:16; see further Terence L. Donaldson, *Jesus on the Mountain: A Study in Matthean Theology* (Sheffield: JSOT Press, 1985).

[59] "[E]very major event in Matt. 1-5 apparently has its counterpart in the events surrounding Israel's exodus from Egypt. Moreover, the order of events in Matthew lines up with the chronological order of events in the Pentateuch. . . when Jesus goes up on the mountain to utter the Sermon on the Mount, he is speaking as the mosaic Messiah and delivering the messianic Torah," W. D. Davies and Dale C. Allision, *Matthew: A Shorter Commentary* (New York: T & T Clark, 2004), p. 64.

[60] Luz, *Studies*, pp. 121-25; see also Michael J. Wilkins, *Discipleship in the Ancient World and in Matthew's Gospel*, 2nd ed. (Grand Rapids: Zondervan, 1995).

[61] In the terminology of narrative criticism, a "flat" character is one presented without much detail.

[62] See further Jeannine K. Brown, *The Disciples in Narrative Perspective: The Portrayal and Function of the Matthean Disciples*, Academia Biblica 9 (Atlanta: Society of Biblical Literature, 2002).

[63] Jack Dean Kingsbury, *Matthew as Story*, 2nd ed. (Philadelphia: Fortress Press, 1988), pp. 17-24; and more extensively, Warren Carter, *Matthew: Storyteller, Interpreter, Evangelist* (Peabody: Hendrickson, 1996), pp. 119-241.

be projecting such warnings in the direction of church leaders of his day.[64]

The audience is drawn into the perspective of the storyteller. The conflict with religious authorities at the socio-political level (assisted by the Roman Prefect) is but an outworking of a greater cosmic battle between God and Satan.[65] The cosmic atmosphere accompanying the climactic showdown at the passion of Jesus reflects a characteristic Matthean "deeper reality" perspective: earthquake, splitting rocks, tombs opened and a resurrection of many saints (27:51-52).

It is beyond our scope to explore the question of an intended audience, but it has been well observed that the gospels have a community building function, and Matthew in particular both encourages and challenges believers at the time of its composition and early readers/hearers.[66] In identifying spiritual fault with those who oppose Jesus and especially in the manner of their leadership, a powerful message is sent to the church of Matthew's time. It is probable that in composing his *bios* of Jesus Matthew was especially mindful of bitter tension between the synagogue and Christian communities of his day, and the association with conflict between Jesus and Jewish leaders assumed an ongoing relevance.

### (c) Form, Shape and Style

Matthew is the most structured of the Synoptic Gospels. Five main blocks of discourse are presented, each ending with "when Jesus had finished these sayings" or similar words.[67] To achieve the emphasis on Jesus as authoritative teacher, Mark's narratives are abbreviated (and at points relocated) to allow for much more extensive accounts of Jesus' teachings. Matthew's style is compact and with singular focus on the essential issues—he gets to the point concisely.[68] The discourse sections are matched by blocks of ongoing narrative, which place the content of Jesus' teachings in the wider context of his presence and engagement with communities and individuals that reflect the whole spectrum of social status and human experience. The teaching is grounded in real life encounters and observations, words are matched with action.

Matthew is also renowned for plentiful references to Scripture (over sixty), frequently with a formulaic introduction "this was to fulfill. . ." (a

---

[64] Note especially D. E. Garland, *The Intention of Matthew 23*, NovT Supp 52 (Leiden: Brill, 1979).

[65] "To welcome or follow Jesus is to agree with God. To oppose Jesus is to oppose God and side with Satan (4:1-11)." Warren Carter, *Matthew and the Margins: A Sociopolitical and Religious Reading* (Maryknoll: Orbis, 2000), p. 3.

[66] Stanton, *Gospels and Jesus*, p. 28.

[67] The discourse blocks may be identified as 5:1–7:27 (Sermon on the Mount); 9:39–10:42 (laborers sent out into the harvest); 13:1-52 (parables of the kingdom-reign of heaven); 18:1-35 (relationships within the kingdom-reign of heaven); and 24:1–25:46 (Olivet discourse).

[68] Matthew's style is especially well addressed in R. T. France, *Matthew: Evangelist and Teacher* (Exeter: Paternoster, 1989), pp. 128-41.

passive form of πληρόω).[69] These have the form of a narrator's explanatory aside to the audience, and keeps the theme of promise and fulfillment to the fore throughout the narrative. References to Scripture come either as recitation or as more general reference.[70] The degree to which Scripture is being reinterpreted or reworked as *pesher*[71] is strongly debated, but it is clear that Matthew at least re-contextualizes such passages with a view to fulfillment to be discerned in the gospel story of Jesus.

A creative literary artistry has been detected in the subtle use of patterns and groupings, even to the point of being described as poetic. There is a possible liking for sequences of seven (seven parables in ch. 13, seven woes in ch. 23). Others have noted groupings of three and triadic forms, as well as chiasm, repetition, *inclusio* and thematic juxtaposition.[72] In stark contrast to Mark, there is little attention to chronology, with arrangement shaped more by thematic interests.

### (d) Content and Themes

The Jewish character and interests of Matthew's Gospel are well recognized. The author is almost universally believed to be a Jew, and (as noted above) writes in the context of the greater narrative of received Scripture, which assumes the intended audience shared such interests. The preference for the Jewish expression "kingdom-reign of heaven" is but one example of this character. Indeed, reference to the "kingdom" is about three times that found in Mark, and is uniquely designated "the gospel of the kingdom" (4:23; 9:35; 24:14). The coming of Jesus fulfils the promise of the kingdom-reign and inaugurates the epoch it represents, while still retaining a future expectation.

Jesus' relationship to the law is a major interest in Matthew. The clearest expression of this is found in 5:17-18, and the affirmation from Jesus that he came not to abolish, but to fulfill the law and the prophets. The nuance of "fulfill" here can denote completion, in the sense of "to bring to its intended meaning."[73] The fuller sense of the law is expounded in the teachings that follow, and especially in the treatment of "righteousness" (in Matthew almost unique amongst the Synoptic Gospels) and "the righteous." The former term is used in Matthew with ethical import to denote a godly manner of life[74] or one in accord with God's purposes. The Sermon on the Mount is framed by exhortations to righteousness and a piety that comes from the heart. The opening beatitudes (5:3-12) adopt a common form of expression commencing with μακάριος ("blessed"), a term conveying deep happiness, but primarily an

---

[69] At least ten occasions (1:22; 2:15, 17 23; 4:14; 8:17; 12:17; 13:35; 21:4; 27:9). Reference to fulfillment is also attributed to Jesus (5:17; 26:54, 56).

[70] A helpful list is provided by de Silva, *Introduction*, p. 247.

[71] A Hebrew word meaning "interpretation," a style of commentary.

[72] See further Donald A. Hagner, *Matthew 1–13* (Dallas: Word, 1993), pp. lii-liii.

[73] So Hagner, *Matthew 1–13*, pp. 105-6.

[74] The major monograph on this theme is by B. Przybylski, *Righteousness in Matthew and His World of Thought* (New York: Cambridge University Press, 1980).

assured relationship with God that brings such blessing. While the Sermon starts with declarations in the beatitudes, it concludes with a strong injunction not only to hear the words of Jesus, but to do them (7:24, cf. 7:21).

Matthew is also the only gospel to refer to the church (16:18; 18:17 twice). Authority transferred to the disciples in the context of their mission (10:1) is especially associated with Peter (16:19), and extended to the sphere of church discipline in 18:18. Peter's foundational role in establishing the church is subject to much debate, but he clearly is given a position of foundational leadership. The church is not presented as an institution as such, but the gathering of those who follow Christ is foreshadowed in relational terms: "*my* church." The building of a community does not replace the people of Israel, but is in continuity with the developing story of salvation brought into a new epoch through the coming of Jesus.

Tellingly, the phrase "all nations" in the later chapters of Matthew includes both Jews and Gentiles. The scene (unique to Matthew) of "all the nations" gathered before the Son of Man in glory, and in which a separation will occur revealing and separating the righteous from the cursed (25:31-46), is framed in intimately relational terms. Actions done to others are done also to Jesus. Relationship to Jesus is fundamental to being identified as one of God's people (see also 10:32, 40).

One of the foremost interpretive challenges in reading/hearing Matthew is in gaining perspective on the relationship between Jesus and the Judaism of his time (as well as between Christians and formative Judaism/synagogues of the later period). As is well recognized, much of the critical focus falls upon the failures and opposition of the Jewish leaders (see above). A distinctive departure from Mark's version of the final week in Jerusalem is seen in Matthew's insertion of a sequence of parables (25:1-30; 21:28-45; he also relocates related parables) pointedly condemning the leaders for their failures as workers, managers, guests and ill-prepared virgins awaiting their bridegroom.

The broader cosmic sweep of Matthew includes all who reject or oppose Jesus, and it is in this context that the Jewish crowd assumes a measure of responsibility as well, notably in the declaration "His blood be upon us and our children" (27:25). Most interpreters exercise great care in clarifying the Matthean context as distinct from broader anti-Semitic sentiments.[75] The complex relationship with various stages and forms of Judaism reflects both a family affinity with the same forebears, and a distancing if not complete break in association.[76] As Matthew's Gospel combines both old and new (9:16-17; 13:52), the emergent entity is constituted wholly in and through the person of Jesus. The climactic rending of the temple curtain in two at the precise moment of Jesus' death, from top to bottom (27:51), is symbolic of a new era in God's covenantal purposes that transcends the former. End-time

---

[75] See especially Donald A. Hagner, "Matthew: Christian Judaism or Jewish Christianity?" in McKnight and Osborne, *Face of New Testament Studies*, pp. 274-78.

[76] Note Brendan J. Byrne, *Lifting the Burden: Reading Matthew's Gospel in the Church Today* (Collegeville: Liturgical Press, 2004), pp. 1-8.

expectations of resurrection are rehearsed, with the promise of more to come in the new life that flows from Jesus' death (and resurrection, as foreshadowed in 27:53). Such dramatic events are indicative of a greater work of God on a cosmic scale underway through the story of Jesus. Matthew again characteristically widens the scene and evocatively intensifies the atmosphere.

### (e) The Person of Jesus

Matthew's presentation of the person of Jesus is distinctive more by way of shading than stark contrast. He adopts the same essential christological focus as Mark, with the notable addition of "Emmanuel" in 1:23. Jesus is presented as king, but in Matthew there is an emphasis on the character of his kingship, and especially his "meekness." On the entry of Jesus to Jerusalem, Matthew adds (in fulfillment of prophecy) "behold your king is coming to you, meek, and riding on a donkey." The same quality of kingship is found in 11:29 ("for I am meek and lowly in heart" [KJV]).[77]

One of the most distinctive aspects of Matthew's profile of Jesus relates to his role as authoritative teacher, and especially as interpreter of the Torah within the wider purposes of God. As the Torah was central to the covenantal identity of Israel, in Jesus it becomes subordinate to his greater mission and the inauguration of the kingdom-reign of heaven through his presence. It is in being identified with Jesus, someone greater than Solomon (12:42), greater than the temple (12:6), someone who mediates between people and God (10:32), that a newly constituted people consisting of both Jews and Gentiles is created.[78]

As in the other gospels, Jesus is central and pivotal to the whole narrative. If anything, in Matthew the backdrop is more sweeping, and the recognition of the authority and homage due to Jesus is shared by a wider cast. Subtly the centurion is joined by "those who were with him" in being filled with awe and affirming that "Truly this was the Son of God!" (27:54).

### 3. Luke's Gospel

The Gospel of Luke is distinctive in being the first volume of a two-volume work (Luke-Acts). As such, its vision looks further over the horizon and anticipates the ongoing work of God through the apostolic mission empowered by the Holy Spirit. Particularly characteristic of Luke is the identification of God's plan of salvation, with Jesus challenging, even subverting the world in every dimension. Jesus is at the margins of society,

---

[77] "Meek" (πραΰς) and "humble" are unfortunately confused in many recent translations. The former was a positive term, often conveying an attribute of rule or kingship (kind and gentle, in contrast to tyrannical or angry). By contrast "humility" was seen as abject and shameful; see further Deirdre J. Good, *Jesus the Meek King* (Harrisburg: Trinity Press International, 1999), and E. A. Judge in Horsley, ed., *New Documents*, volume 4, pp. 169-70.

[78] Byrne, *Lifting the Burden*, p. 270.

ignoring conventions of honor and shame in establishing an alternative realm and order, with an alternative value system that brings peace to those otherwise labeled sinners or outcasts. Jesus is a man with a mission, and that mission evokes scandal in some quarters, but heartfelt devotion in others.

## (a) Beginning and Ending

The opening dedication to "most excellent Theophilus" (1:3) is informative as to Luke's intention and approach. Not being himself an eye-witness, Luke is aware of other (apparently well known) accounts describing "events that have been fulfilled among us," and after careful investigation sets about to write "an orderly account . . . that you may know the truth. . ." (1:3-4), his narrative reflecting contemporary Greco-Roman historiographical conventions.[79] Careful and orderly are the standards Luke sets for his narrative.

This narrator's prologue prepares the way for the opening of the narrative proper in 1:5. Preparation for the coming of Jesus through the birth of John the Baptist is given its most extended treatment among the gospels, an account that runs in tandem with the storyline regarding the conception and birth of Jesus. Similarities between the two storylines is underscored by special announcements, angelic assurance that this is "good news" (1:19; 2:10), and the three subsequent songs of praise (Zechariah, Mary, and Simeon). Tucked away in this opening section are two references to God's faithfulness to the promises made to Abraham (1:55, 73), with echoes of the narratives in Genesis 11–21.[80]

The opening passage also paints another backdrop to the stage. John and Jesus enter a socio-political world of the Caesars (Emperor Augustus, 2:1), and those in power under their patronage: notably King Herod of Judea (1:5). The first reference to Augustus is in the context of his control and decree over "all the world" (2:1), while Mary's song points the way to a great reversal: "[the Lord] has brought down the powerful from their thrones, and lifted up the lowly" (1:52).

While Luke provides more than any other canonical gospel about Jesus' childhood and family life, his narrative also engages more directly with the call to "John, son of Zechariah," and the subsequent mission of Jesus in 3:1. Here again the stage is set with detailed reference to political power and governance, together with religious authority in the form of the high priests (3:1-2).

The Gospel concludes with a prolonged account of resurrection appearances, and a brief note recording the ascension near Bethany (24:50-51—unique in the gospels). Without any mention of a subsequent work that will resume the narrative, the references to returning to Jerusalem and being in

---

[79] See especially Loveday Alexander, *The Preface to Luke's Gospel: Literary Convention and Social Context in Luke 1.1-4 and Acts 1.1*, SNTSMS 78 (Cambridge: Cambridge University Press, 1993).

[80] See especially Joel Green, *The Gospel of Luke* (Grand Rapids: Eerdmans, 1997), pp. 52-58.

the temple (24:52-53) have the hallmarks of an intermission, and set the scene for the resumption of the narrative in Acts. Of particular significance however are the preceding words of instruction (24:44-49) regarding the opening of their minds to understand Scripture (especially concerning Jesus), and the commission "that repentance and forgiveness of sins is to be proclaimed in his name to all nations, beginning from Jerusalem" (24:47). The sense of anticipation is further struck by the promise "I am sending upon you what my Father promised" (24:49).

Although it is beyond the scope of this chapter, we should note the book of Acts concludes not only with the gospel witness having reached Rome, but also with the theme of a rejected prophet: the leaders of the Jewish community in Rome listened to Paul trying to convince them concerning Jesus from the law of Moses and the prophets. Some were convinced, others refused to believe. As a result of such rejection, Paul concluded: "Let it be known to you then that this salvation of God has been sent to the Gentiles; they will listen" (Acts 28:28). In many ways, this forms a conclusion to both Luke and Acts.

### (b) Settings, Characters and Encounters

Luke presents Jesus on the move. His sense of mission and teaching is woven into a continual series of encounters with a diverse cast of people. The nativity narrative immediately reflects this diversity, from the low social status shepherds (2:8) to the angelic messenger accompanied by a "multitude of the heavenly host" (2:13). The faithful within Israel are also drawn into a select circle of those who recognize the significance of Jesus, from Simeon ("righteous and devout, looking forward to the consolation of Israel," 2:25), to "a prophet, Anna . . . of great age" (2:36). Luke's intention at this point is clear: Jesus was of great significance and delight for "all who were looking for the redemption of Jerusalem" (2:38).

At this point in the narrative Jesus has a background role. The family pilgrimage to Jerusalem when Jesus was twelve is viewed through his parents' anxious experiences, with the only recorded words of Jesus highlighting the question of his ultimate identity and loyalty ("Did you not know I must be in my Father's house?" 2:49). There is no suggestion of disrespect for his parents, for he submitted himself to them (2:51). Other than this and the amazement at his understanding and answers (2:47), Jesus' childhood is otherwise summarized with reference to his growing wisdom and divine and human favor (2:40, 52).

A transition from the early focus on John the Baptist occurs with a scene change between 3:18-20, where John is taken off-stage, and 3:21 where Jesus takes center stage. It is only at this point that Luke introduces the adult Jesus ("about thirty years old") through a brief account of his baptism and anointing with the Spirit (divine confirmation and empowerment), and more extensively through his genealogy. A genealogy was a significant marker of social status and position, and Luke's version starts with a passing reference to perceptions that belie the truth: "He [Jesus] was the son (as was thought) of Joseph son of

Heli" (3:23). It is a broad hint that there is more to Jesus' social standing than appears at first glance. For those who share the narrator's understanding of Jesus' conception, a deeper truth is underscored at the climax of the genealogy, with its less than subtle ambiguity: ". . . son of Adam, son of God" (3:38). Juxtaposed with the preceding baptismal affirmation "you are my Son" (3:21), this alerts the reader/hearer that there is more to be revealed than appears in the standard socio-cultural perspective.

Luke has a very active role played by the Holy Spirit (in similar terms in both the Gospel and Acts).[81] Returning from his baptism, this intimate relationship is doubly underscored: "Jesus, full of the Holy Spirit. . . was led by the Spirit" (4:1).

Two scenes run in tandem to introduce the commencement of Jesus' adult ministry. In one, Jesus is put to the test by the devil; in the other, Jesus returns to his home town to announce the focus of his mission. Both scenes reflect dimensions of the one mission, with the temptation narrative brought to the foreground as a necessary preparation for all that is to follow. The final verse of this unit sends the devil to a position behind the scenes, to re-emerge later (4:13).

The selection of Jesus' return to Nazareth as the first detailed account of Jesus' public ministry signals an episode of special importance. It occurs on the Sabbath day, in the synagogue. We shall return to this pericope below, but for now we note the dramatic focus: "the eyes of all in the synagogue were fixed upon him" (4:20). Jesus is not only center stage in Luke's narrative; he is now under the closest of scrutiny by the communities in which he moves.

Luke's Jesus shares the cast with those also found in Mark and Matthew. Our attention is drawn to some noteworthy exceptions. A change in scene occurs with Jesus traveling to Nain at 7:11, with echoes of both the Nazareth sermon (4:16-30), and beyond that to Elijah in 1 Kings 17:8-24. The woman Jesus meets at Nain is doubly vulnerable. She is a widow and has now lost her only son. The mid point of the narrative highlights Luke's primary concern: "When Jesus saw her, he had compassion on her and said to her, 'Do not weep'" (7:13). The episode provides a window into Jesus' greater mission and his "seeing" of people that characterizes it. Jesus is someone with his eyes open to the realities of the world around him.

Another profound episode is recorded at length soon after: the "sinful" woman at the Pharisee's house (7:36-50). It is so emblematic of Luke's distinctive style, setting and focus we shall treat it at slightly greater length. The episode opens in the cursory form. A Pharisee invites Jesus to dine with him; Jesus went into his house and took his place at the table (7:36). The meal-setting, and especially a banquet with some affinity to Greco-Roman *symposia*, is a microcosm of the social world of that community.[82] There are

---

[81] On this extensive theme and area of debate, see Max Turner, *Power from on High: The Spirit in Israel's Restoration and Witness in Luke-Acts*, JPTSup 9 (Sheffield: Sheffield Academic Press, 1996), and Ju Hur, *A Dynamic Reading of the Holy Spirit in Luke-Acts*, JSNTSup 211 (Sheffield: Sheffield Academic Press, 2001).

[82] On the significance of meals throughout Luke, see Arthur A. Just Jr., *The Ongoing*

clear rules of decorum and social place. Luke assumes the reader-hearer is quite familiar with the scene. The matter of fact style of Luke belies the jaw-dropping nature of his account as it moves to the socially bizarre. A woman with a notorious reputation as a "sinner" enters uninvited with the purpose of engaging Jesus. Her own story is not told, but it is most likely she gained her livelihood by selling sexual favors. In the social perspective of her world, she is the wrong person at the wrong place.

The narrative lingers at each scandalous detail, accentuated by the repetitive use of "and." There is no attempt to move on quickly or hide the scandal. Her appearance appeared to reinforce her reputation, for to have hair loose in such a context is to be seductively provocative, akin to being topless in western culture today. The scene confronts every sense of decorum: a fallen woman, dressed shamefully, fondles Jesus' feet as he reclines at table. Original hearers would be in agreement with the Pharisee. Jesus, if he had any sort of discernment, must know that not only is this conduct dishonorable, in terms of ritual purity he is being polluted by someone who carries the social label of "sinner" (7:39).

The shape of the narrative opens up a triadic dynamic. It is only at this point that the Pharisee is named as Jesus challenges Simon to look again at the scene: "Do you see this woman?" (7:44). Applying the values of cancelled debt to the realm of forgiveness, he publicly declares what was otherwise a private matter between him and the woman: "I tell you, her sins, which were many, have been forgiven; hence [or possibly "because"] she has shown great love" (7:47). Not only does the alternative view of the scene touch the woman, it includes Simon himself, who by the same cultural standards has offended Jesus and is in need of forgiveness (7:44-45). Yet the narrative has yet to make the final challenge. Jesus speaks to the woman, but does so specifically in the hearing of all those at the table. In his declaring her sins forgiven, her label "sinner" is publicly removed. The final words are especially telling of Luke's narrative purpose: "Your faith has saved you; go in peace." Salvation is expressed in terms of forgiveness, and the outcome is an assurance of peace that encompasses both spiritual and social dimensions. The reader-hearer is not told of the outcome of all this, but the challenge is stark: will they look again at societal labels and attitudes, recognize the authority of Jesus in the removal of sin and associated labels, and allow those forgiven to "go in peace" in their own contexts? It is no coincidence that this encounter is followed by reference to a number of women included in the circle around Jesus, some named, as well as "many others" who provided for Jesus (8:2-3).[83]

Other notable encounters include the lawyer intent on testing Jesus (10:25), resulting in the parable of the Samaritan who attended to the needs of

---

*Feast: Table Fellowship and Eschatology at Emmaus* (Collegeville: Liturgical Press, 1993), and on the theme of hospitality in Luke more generally, Brendan Byrne, *The Hospitality of God: A Reading of Luke's Gospel* (Collegeville: Liturgical Press, 2000).

[83] On the place of women within the narrative of Luke, see Barbara E. Reid, *Choosing the Better Part? Women in the Gospel of Luke* (Collegeville: Liturgical Press, 1996).

the traveler on the road to Jericho. Luke 14 has a series of units that continue reflections upon meals and banquets and associated conventions.[84] In Luke 18 we see the juxtaposition of the place of children within the kingdom-reign of God on the one hand (18:15-17), and the wealthy ruler on the other (18:18-25). A <u>transfer in social values</u> is underscored. Children "such as these" are affirmed in "receiving" the kingdom-reign of God, while the rich man failed the litmus test of foregoing his wealth by trusting God's provision. The blind beggar outside Jericho (18:35-43) was from the lowest strata of social order, yet has great insight into Jesus' mission. Zacchaeus (19:1-10), a wealthy district tax collector, accrued a doubly despised stigma. As a class, tax collectors were notoriously corrupt, exploiting the private contractor's system for gain, while also working for the Roman administration as part of an economic regime that oppressed the peasants.[85] It is the outcast Zacchaeus that Jesus assures with the words: "Today salvation has come to this house"; concluding with: "the Son of Man came to seek out and save the lost" (19:9-10).

The ultimate encounter with an outcast with no social place whatever occurs at the crucifixion. It is Luke who records the exchange with the criminal at the cross, and the remarkable assurance that "today you will be with me in Paradise" (23:43).

### (c) Form, Shape and Style

Much of Luke's form, shape and style can be seen in the encounters noted above. The narrative embodies the mission focus of Jesus. There are three distinctive aspects to the shape of Luke's Gospel. We have touched upon the first already. In choosing to highlight Jesus' return to his home town and especially the sermon in the synagogue as the first detailed account of his public ministry, Luke has elevated this episode and made it programmatic of Luke-Acts as a whole. The care taken in finding the passage from Isaiah 61 makes this citation fundamental to Jesus' missionary program. Through the anointing of the Spirit, <u>Jesus came to "bring good news to the poor,"</u> "proclaim release to the captives," "recovery of sight to the blind," and to "let the oppressed go free." Echoes of the Jubilee injunctions (Leviticus 25) are reflected throughout, and especially in the concluding "to proclaim the year of the Lord's favor" (4:19). The pivotal moment in the episode is not in this missionary charter or claim to fulfill its promise, nor even the familiarity of his home town, but in the claim that his home town will be passed over while good news to the poor would embrace the likes of "the widow, the unclean, the Gentile, those of low status."[86] This unit has a <u>proleptic function</u> in anticipating themes developed further as Luke-Acts proceeds. As Jesus was

---

[84] For conventions in the issuing of invitations, see examples in S. R. Lewelyn, *New Documents*, Volume 9, pp. 62-66.

[85] Ernst Badian, *Publicans and Sinners: Private Enterprise in the Service of the Roman Republic* (Ithaca: Cornell University Press, 1983).

[86] Green, *Luke*, p. 218.

rejected at the synagogue in his home town, so the gospel message is taken first to the synagogue throughout Luke and Acts, and when rejected is then taken to the Gentiles.

Second, Jesus is frequently on the road in Luke, encountering people as he moves in and out of towns and villages. The long central section of Luke (9:51–19:48), sometimes called the Travel Narrative, contains some of the most distinctive elements associated with Luke. The focus is less on the identity of Jesus or his mission, but the outworking of that mission in the context of the communities in which he engages. Responses to Jesus are increasingly polarized, and Jesus' journey is leading towards greater hostility and the journey's destination in Jerusalem (signaled at the outset, 9:51). And as is frequently the case, Jesus' own steps towards Jerusalem are accompanied with a challenge for those who would follow him, the cost of discipleship (9:57-62).

The final notable feature of Luke's Gospel is the inclusion of many parables unique to Luke. These are dealt with elsewhere in this volume so we shall not explore them in depth here, other than to note their careful thematic juxtaposition. Luke 15 is a well recognized example, with a highly significant introduction setting the scene and audience. Jesus speaks in the hearing of Pharisees and scribes grumbling at his association with tax collectors and sinners (15:1-2), and as a rejoinder presents a sequence of three parables concerning lost-ness, and the response of joy and celebration when what was lost is discovered and returned home.[87] The parables in Luke reflect a variety of features, from taking unlikely characters as object lessons in some particular quality (e.g. the self-interested and corrupt manager in 16:1-9), to parables of reversal (e.g. the rich man and Lazarus in 16:19-31), parables in which a crisis is pending (e.g. the rich fool in 12:13-21; cf. 16:1-9), and parables featuring an absent authority and a return bringing a call to account (e.g. the parable of the ten *minas* in 19:11-27; cf. 20:9-19).

### (d) Content and Themes

A number of key themes have been already noted: anticipated rejection by Jesus' own people and the inclusion of Gentiles; the bringing of good news to the poor, accompanied by warnings to the wealthy;[88] Jesus' mission to seek and save the lost.

The motif of reversal is also starkly presented in Luke.[89] The story and song of Mary exemplifies the hope of vindication already present in the scriptural traditions. Mary describes herself as of low estate and a "slave"

---

[87] The classic treatment of these parables is by Kenneth E. Bailey, *Poet and Peasant and Through Peasant Eyes: A Literary-Cultural Approach to the Parables in Luke* (Grand Rapids: Eerdmans, 1983).

[88] Note especially Halvor Moxnes, *The Economy of the Kingdom: Social Conflict and Economic Relations in Luke's Gospel* (Philadelphia: Fortress Press, 1988).

[89] See further John O. York, *The First Shall be the Last: The Rhetoric of Reversal in Luke*, JSNTSup 46 (Sheffield: Sheffield Academic Press, 1991).

(δούλη, 1:48), but her hope lies in being treated with "favor" in the purposes of God, and she will be called "blessed." The Mighty One has done great things for this person of low estate. The reversal of position motif is clearly in evidence, and is underscored in the second half of the song, as already noted above. Luke 14 similarly addresses conventions of rank and status and the value systems by which people are considered. The elite are supplanted, and those otherwise regarded as being of no status or having no place are brought into the inner circle of a community in which there is no regard for boundaries or insider/outside categories.[90]

The topic of Lukan eschatology has been a matter of extensive debate. In Jesus, the kingdom-reign of God had come into the midst of the communities in which he moved (17:21). The salvation brought by Jesus had very immediate spiritual, social, communal, physical and material expression, as well as future dimensions and expectation still to be consummated. It is both a present reality and a future hope.[91]

### (e) The Person of Jesus

The Jesus of Luke's Gospel draws on a similar christological matrix to the other Synoptic Gospels. Jesus the Savior (2:11) is presented in fully human terms, with historical, social and familial identity. His entry is cast strongly in Messianic terms and expectations. His story includes temptations and very human needs. His character is marked by compassion and attentiveness to relationships—to "seeing" people. The strongest aspects in Luke's portrait of Jesus are his roles as teacher and prophet, and especially a prophet who must suffer rejection and violence (9:18-24). Other dimensions are more subtle. Jesus is a vindicator of the poor and friend of sinners.[92]

Yet in many ways the Jesus of Luke defies neat categorization, but is a Jesus who is glimpsed in memorable cameo moments. Jesus is capable of such intimacy at the Passover/last supper (his "deep desire" to share the meal with his disciples), while uttering words that came at enormous cost: "This cup that is poured out for you is the new covenant in my blood" (22:20). The assurance of forgiveness of sin so frequently noted in Luke's Gospel drives Jesus to a death that carries far-reaching significance. Luke's Jesus on the Mount of Olives is a man of prayer, in the midst of a mighty contest.[93] The post-resurrection Jesus is also elusive, initially glimpsed only fleetingly, before (characteristically) sharing a meal. Yet the most notable feature of Luke's

---

[90] Willi Braun, *Feasting and Social Rhetoric in Luke 14*, SNTSMS 85 (Cambridge: Cambridge University Press, 1995).

[91] Note especially the careful treatment by Robert Maddox, *The Purpose of Luke-Acts* (Edinburgh: T. & T. Clark, 1982), pp. 100-157, which deals also with the question of the "delay of the *parousia*" and its possible influence on Luke's writings.

[92] Wilfred J. Harrington, *Luke: Gracious Theologian. The Jesus of Luke* (Dublin: Columba Press, 1997), pp. 58-86.

[93] "Agony" (ἀγωνία, 22:44) here denotes more a struggle for victory than anxiety: Byrne, *Hospitality*, p. 175. Note also that these verses do not appear in some texts.

presentation of Jesus develops incrementally, as references to God as "the Lord" are joined by parallel references to Jesus in the same terms. For Luke, the presentation of Jesus will take a higher profile in the gospel proclamations recorded in Acts, but the foundations for these gospel traditions are clearly laid in Luke's "first book" (Acts 1:1).

Luke's closing scene before intermission has the disciples in a state of great joy despite the departure of the one around whom the whole drama has unfolded. They exit the stage as instructed to Jerusalem, awaiting the promised power, "continually in the temple and praising God" (24:53).

## 4. John's Gospel

While the traditional image of an eagle for the Gospel of John has no direct basis in the text, it does convey something of the soaring perspective that is so distinctive of the Fourth Gospel. Critical issues relating to the one non-Synoptic Gospel in the canon are many, varied and frequently contested.[94] Our focus here will be on distinctive features of the text as we now have it, rather than speculation as to the possible processes that may have shaped its composition. Some processes of development are inevitable, and recent work has highlighted the vibrant character of oral traditions and "social memory" that may account for some of John's distinctive features.[95] We also set aside the issue of authorship, other than noting the distinctions drawn between the "fourth evangelist" (author or editor), the community in which the Johannine tradition was affirmed, and a possible redactor (or redactors) responsible for revisions of such traditions. In speaking here of "John," we here mean the collective influences that shaped the entity we know as the Gospel of John, without any conclusion as to identity or development process.

### (a) Beginning and Ending

The prologue to John's Gospel (1:1-18) has a relative simplicity of style and language, yet a sweeping and far reaching field of vision. It is here that the *logos* terminology[96] in the first verse points to a profound association with

---

[94] A well selected cross section of major perspectives is gathered in John Ashton, ed., *The Interpretation of John*, 2nd ed. (Edinburgh: T. & T. Clark, 1997); see also Robert Kysar, *The Fourth Evangelist and His Gospel: An examination of contemporary scholarship* (Minneapolis: Augsburg, 1975); more recent approaches are reflected in Robert T. Fortna and Tom Thatcher, eds., *Jesus in Johannine Tradition* (Louisville: Westminster/John Knox Press, 2001). A number of classic commentaries are devoted to John's Gospel, including those by Westcott (1881), Brown (1966, 1970), Bultmann (1971), Barrett (2nd ed., 1978), and Schnackenburg (1980, 1982).

[95] See especially Tom Thatcher, *Why John WROTE a Gospel: Jesus-Memory-History* (Louisville: Westminster/John Knox Press, 2006).

[96] The background to λόγος terminology is a significant area of research. It appears to have drawn on the two streams of Hellenistic thought and Jewish faith, merged into the type of composite notion reflected in Philo of Alexandria, and most likely indicative of wider familiarity with such a term. In the Fourth Gospel the notion of Logos is multidimensional, including God's

"God" ("the Word with God, and the Word was God"), and in keeping with the opening words ("In the beginning . . ."), places the narrative to follow in the context of a beginning with God prior to the creation of life and all things.

Precedents for a genre of prologue can be found in Greek religious theater, with an introduction providing "verbal scenery" for all that is to follow.[97] Major characters are introduced: the *logos* who is Jesus Christ, the Word become flesh (1:14), the only Son (1:18); a second major character in the form of a "man sent from God whose name was John," a witness whose role it is to testify to the light (1:7); and finally Moses (1:17), representing the received traditions that shaped the community of faith to this point in time.

Notwithstanding the allusions to the historical realities that lie behind these events, the prologue to John's Gospel is more by way of a theological presentation than narrative such as found in the other gospels. Each word and phrase is carefully weighed, preparing the way for the exposition of such themes in the body of the work, especially the polarities of belief and unbelief (1:10-12).

The ending of John's Gospel is ambiguous—it appears to have two endings. An appropriate ending is found in 20:30-31, with the disclaimer that much more could be written about Jesus, yet this account has been selected and presented "so that you might come to believe that Jesus is the Messiah, the Son of God, and that through believing you may have life in his name." Having reached such a point, it is a little surprising that the narrative then continues with what is now the final chapter. There is no textual evidence for the text without chapter 21, and it is best viewed as a form of epilogue to the Gospel as a whole. The focus on Peter's restoration, prophecy concerning the manner of his death, and expectations concerning the beloved disciple may indicate that this material (notably 21:15-23) was added to clarify issues current at a later stage.[98]

### (b) Settings, Characters and Encounters

While details of geographic location occupy a low profile within the presentation of John's Gospel (often at the end of a unit: 1:28; 6:59; 8:20; 11:54), there is widespread recognition that the Gospel reflects an informed knowledge of Palestine and various traditions associated with Jewish customs.[99] The pattern of movement is significantly different to that of the Synoptics, and especially so in respect to Jerusalem. John records earlier visits

---

self-revelation, creative power and energy, wisdom and Torah, the expression and embodiment of the gospel message in the person of Jesus.

[97] Elizabeth Harris, *Prologue and Gospel: The Theology of the Fourth Evangelist*, JSNTSup 107 (Sheffield: Sheffield Academic Press, 1994), pp. 12-16.

[98] Note especially Richard J. Cassidy, *John's Gospel in New Perspective: Christology and the Realities of Roman Power* (Maryknoll: Orbis, 1992), pp. 69-79, who notes the growing pressures on followers of Jesus in political-theological conflict with Roman authorities.

[99] Martin Hengel, *The Johannine Question* (Philadelphia: Trinity Press International, 1989), p. 110.

to Jerusalem (2:13; 5:2; 7:10), and three Passovers (2:13; 6:4; 11:55), suggesting a longer period of time for Jesus' public ministry. Whatever may be concluded about the underlying historical realities of Jesus' movements, John's Gospel is largely structured around themes, signs and associated passages of discourse.[100] Strict chronology is not a major feature shaping the Fourth Gospel.

The profile given to particular scenes and characters does drive the narrative: notably the wedding in Cana of Galilee and the mother of Jesus (2:1-11); the visit at night by Nicodemus (3:1-21); the encounter at Jacob's well at noon with the woman of Samaria (4:1-42); the healing at the pool by the Sheep Gate (5:2-9); the roadside healing of the man born blind (9:1-12); the delayed graveside meeting with those mourning Lazarus' death (11:1-44); and interaction with Mary, Martha and Lazarus within the home at Bethany[101] (12:1-11). The post-resurrection appearances in the final two chapters similarly have an episodic feel, with special attention given to Thomas (20:24-29) and Simon Peter (21:15-19).

Women feature in noteworthy ways throughout John, portrayed in real and non-stereotypical terms as individuals in their own right. As disciples, they are profiled with comparable standing to male disciples, and within the composition of the text are presented as "gender pairs" that reinforce a "genuine discipleship of equals."[102]

Other than Jesus, in narrative terms three other characters feature with particular significance in John's Gospel. First, John the Baptist receives distinctive attention in John (1:6-8, 15, 19-28, 30; 3:22-30; 5:33-36; 10:40-42), with additional information apparently independent of the Synoptic Gospels. The Baptist's relationship to Jesus is carefully focused on witnessing to Jesus as Messiah,[103] and the priority of Jesus ("He must increase, but I must decrease," 3:30). The "disciple whom Jesus loved" is another notable identity in John, referred to four times (13:23; 19:26-27; 20:2-10; 21:7, 20-23), and implied in another (21:24; possibly also 1:35-36; 18:15-16). This disciple is clearly very important to the gospel traditions underlying John's Gospel, not only as an eyewitness but also as a trusted member of the circle closest to Jesus (note especially 19:35; 21:24).[104] As presented in John's Gospel, the

---

[100] In reference to the temple encounter in John 2:13-22, see Mark A. Matson, "The Temple Incident: An Integral Element in the Fourth Gospel's Narrative," in Fortna and Thatcher, *Jesus*, pp. 145-53.

[101] Mark W. G. Stibbe draws attention to the insiders' perspective reflected in the narrative set in and around Bethany, and proposes a "Bethany Gospel" based on the eyewitness testimony of Lazarus, *John as Storyteller: Narrative Criticism and the Fourth Gospel* (New York: Cambridge University Press, 1992), pp. 77-82.

[102] Margaret M. Beirne, *Women and Men in the Fourth Gospel: A Genuine Discipleship of Equals*, JSNTSup 242 (New York: T. & T. Clark International, 2003), especially pp. 220-21. Beirne argues rightly that the profile given to women is not to be discerned in isolation, but in reference to relationships and alongside males. She identifies six such gender pairs.

[103] This "witness motif" is well summarized in John W. Pryor, *John, Evangelist of the Covenant People: The Narrative and Themes of the Fourth Gospel* (Downers Grove: InterVarsity Press, 1992), pp. 11-15.

[104] The beloved disciple is traditionally identified as John bar Zebedee; for a stimulating

beloved disciple is given a very positive profile and exemplifies the best of committed discipleship.

The final and major entity in John's Gospel is God. All other aspects of the Gospel, including its Christology, are to be understood in reference to the *theo*centric core that is woven into the fabric of the whole document.[105] In a sense, the entire Gospel is an explication of the first verse, and especially as elaborated in 1:14 and 18. References to God in John work in a number of directions: such a God is clearly the God of Israel who created the world and entered into a covenant relationship with his people.[106] This is the same God whom Jesus calls "my Father" and is depicted as the source and origin of Jesus' ministry. "God is known as the Father through the Son, and God is known as the Father of the Son"—the relationship that underscores the essential portrayal of God in the Gospel of John.[107] It is in precisely this same relational context that the Spirit (1:33; 14:26 and 20:22) and "the Paraclete" (14:16, 26; 15:26; 16:7) are to be understood.[108]

In John the Spirit is not "poured out" or said to fill people (as in Luke-Acts), but particularly in the later sections of the Gospel relates to a number of functions such as teaching and enabling the disciples to recall Jesus' words, to be guided into all truth, and to bear witness to such truth. The Spirit is the Spirit of Truth (14:17; 15:26; 16:13).[109] Yet the Spirit is also identified with various activities of God, and especially bringing life and new life from above (3:5-8). The Spirit is an agent of renewal. In the post-resurrection narratives the Spirit is "breathed on" the disciples, an experience that is associated with the authority to pronounce the forgiveness of sins (20:22-23).

### (c) Form, Shape and Style

The distinct writing style of John permeates the whole document. It is exceedingly difficult to distinguish between redaction and received tradition. Put starkly, we are given an account of the teachings of Jesus largely expressed in John's words. John explores his scenes at greater length than the other gospels, and weaves narrative with theological discourse and interpretation. He has a liking for elemental terms, often paired in antithetical symmetry: light and darkness, above and below, truth and falsehood, flesh and Spirit, belief and unbelief, death and life. At times John's style of discourse is

---

(but not entirely convincing) alternative identification as Lazarus, see Stibbe, *John as Storyteller*, pp. 77-81. See also James H. Charlesworth, *The Beloved Disciple* (Valley Forge: Trinity Press International, 1995). For Charlesworth, the Beloved Disciple is the witness who validates the Gospel of John.

[105] Marianne Meye Thompson, *The God of the Gospel of John* (Grand Rapids: Eerdmans, 2001).

[106] Pryor, *Covenant People*, pp. 158-60.

[107] Thompson, *God*, p. 229.

[108] See further Gary Burge, *The Anointed Community: The Holy Spirit in the Johannine Tradition* (Grand Rapids: Eerdmans, 1987); and the treatment in Thompson, *God*, ch. 4.

[109] References to the Holy Spirit (other than 1:33), the Spirit of Truth and the Paraclete occur only in the Farewell Discourses (chs. 14–17).

cryptic, with statements or "riddles" that raise as many questions as they answer.[110] At other points a deliberate ambiguity can be detected, a form of ironical double entendre with deeper significance to be detected by the alert hearer/reader. One of the more obvious examples involves the "blind" and those who "see" in 9:39.[111] Although repetitions are often found, they are usually in the form of carefully constructed variations on a theme, and overall the narrative is expressed with poetic artistry and theological sophistication. The distinctive "truly, truly" phrasing (ἀμὴν ἀμήν) reflects a rhetorical flourish, and most likely can be attributed to the oral tradition that underlies John's Gospel.[112] It serves to underscore traditional sayings attributed to Jesus as being particularly profound and authoritative.

John is essentially divided into two main sections, known as the "Book of Signs" (1:19–12:50) and the "Book of the Passion" (13:1–20:31). The former section is largely shaped episodically and thematically, and will therefore be discussed below.

### (d) Content and Themes

The description of miraculous happenings as "signs" (σημεῖα) is one of the most distinctive features of John's Gospel. It first occurs at the conclusion of Jesus' turning water into wine: "Jesus did this, the first of his signs, in Cana of Galilee, and revealed his glory; and his disciples believed in him" (2:11). If walking on the sea of Galilee is included, then seven signs can be noted:

Water into wine at Cana (2:1-11).
Healing the official's son (4:46-54).
Healing of the paralytic man (5:2-9).
Feeding the crowd (6:1-14).
Walking on the sea of Galilee (6:15-21).
Giving the blind man sight (9:1-7).
Raising Lazarus from the dead (11:1-44).

Another sign is found in the concluding chapter, namely, the abundant catch of fish (21:1-14). The prominence of the sign motif has led to elaborate reconstructions of some form of "signs source" or "signs gospel."[113]

The miracles as signs reveal God's glory, and are intended to lead to faith.

---

[110] Tom Thatcher, "The Riddles of Jesus in the Johannine Dialogues," in Fortna and Thatcher, *Jesus*, p. 263-80.

[111] Compare also the ambiguous dialogue between Jesus and Nicodemus in chapter 3. In relation to the use of irony, see Gail R. O'Day, *Revelation in the Fourth Gospel Narrative Mode and Theological Claim* (Philadelphia: Fortress Press, 1986).

[112] The double form occurs twenty-five times in John, but not in the other gospels, which have the singular form ("truly").

[113] The classic treatment is by Robert Fortna, *The Gospel of Signs: A Reconstruction of the Narrative Source Underlying the Fourth Gospel*, SNTSMS 11 (New York: Cambridge University Press, 1970); see also Sara C. Winter, "Little Flags: The Scope and Reconstruction of the Signs Gospel," in Fortna and Thatcher, *Jesus*, p. 219-35.

In and around these episodes are interpretive discourses on related themes. The structure is not as neat as some proposals would have it, but the broad shape can be discerned in which discourses reflect on various events.[114]

Particularly distinctive are the seven "I am" sayings. Three relate directly to signs: "I am the bread of life" (6:35, note feeding of the crowd); "I am the light of the world" (8:12, note the giving of sight to the blind man); and "I am the resurrection and the life" (11:25, note the raising of Lazarus from the dead). The other four arise in the context of providing commentary on various motifs: "I am the door of the sheep" and "I am the good shepherd"; "I am the way, the truth, and the life"; "I am the true vine." The person of Jesus is presented in evocative and compelling terms, and each calls for a response of belief by the hearer/reader.

The second major section of John's Gospel has three phases. The first takes place in the upper room, and includes the washing of the disciples' feet as an example of taking the role of a slave (13:15). There follows a series of discourses, with the atmosphere becoming more tense and fearful (hence "do not let your hearts be troubled," 14:1), and the extended prayer in chapter 17. The Passion Narrative includes some material unique to John, but largely contains similar features to the Synoptic Gospels.

An appendix on distinctive Johannine vocabulary in Raymond Brown's commentary provides samples of John's thematic concerns: love, truth/true, to see, glory, command/commandment, life, world, to abide, to believe, light and darkness, hour.[115] John's eschatological perspectives are integrated into a number of the list above, and especially in the use of "hour" (note 2:4; 7:30 and 8:20; compare 12:23, 27; 13:1; 17:1), as well as "the day," "now" and "already." The expression "the hour is coming and now is" (4:23; 5:25) expresses the temporal paradox that epitomizes Johannine eschatology. The present and the future converge in the salvation uniquely achieved through Christ.

There is one other carefully nuanced pattern of expressions that relate to the Gospel's main purpose: to encourage (that is, both elicit and confirm) faith (20:31). Throughout the Gospel a range of unbelief and belief can be discerned.[116] At one level, there are those whose unbelief drives them to determined opposition to Jesus (e. g. 3:19-20; 11:47). There are others who see the signs and wonders and believe in Jesus as a wonder-worker sent by God—but no more than that. Jesus refused to trust himself to such people, and such limited faith is regarded as inadequate (2:23-25; 3:2-3; 4:45-48; 7:3-7). A third type of response is regarded as genuine and acceptable: those who recognize the true significance of the signs and come to believe in Jesus and his mission as an activity of God (e.g. 4:53; 6:69; 9:38; 11:40). Finally, there is a higher form of faith recognized in those who do not see the actual signs or witness Jesus directly, but believe on the basis of the testimony of those who

---

[114] A judicious assessment is provided by Pryor, *Covenant People*, pp. 95-100.

[115] Raymond E. Brown, *The Gospel according to John: Introduction, Translation and Notes,* 2nd ed., vol. 1 (Garden City: Doubleday, 1981), pp. 497-524.

[116] This paragraph is drawn essentially from Brown, *John*, Volume 1, pp. 530-31.

were eyewitnesses (17:20; 20:29). There are significant implications in all this for discipleship within a community of faith and shared experiences that are grounded in reliable eyewitness traditions concerning Jesus.

### (e) The Person of Jesus

We have already touched on a variety of ways in which John presents Jesus as the *logos* who was "with God and. . . was God" with the authority to create and to rule, the Word who takes human form and dwells among his people. In addition to the "I am" statements noted above are the "I am" statements without predicate (8:24, 28, 58), to be identified with the name of God (Exod. 3:14). It is not so much that Jesus claims directly to be Yahweh, but that he alludes to an essential identification with God, reinforced by the sharing in a number of exclusive divine prerogatives.[117]

A number of the titles and roles attributed to Jesus are shared with the Synoptic Gospels, albeit with some distinctive aspects evident in John's Gospel. The "son of man" references in John are without parallel, and do not carry the apocalyptic imagery of "coming on the clouds of heaven" found in the Synoptics. Instead, the title highlights Jesus' exalted position in God's purposes.[118] Especially characteristic of John is Jesus having been sent into this world by the Father (3:16), and of having come "from above" intent on doing the work of God. Jesus enters the world as an agent about the Father's mission (6:38; cf. 5:30; 17:4).[119]

Affirmations about the sovereignty of Jesus permeate the whole Gospel, and were originally expressed in a socio-political context where to confess allegiance to Jesus as the "Savior of the world" (4:42), "Lord," and especially "my Lord and my God" (20:28) brought significant tension and pressure before the Roman authorities.[120] Seen in this context, the purpose of John's Gospel in urging belief in Jesus as the Christ, the Son of God, and especially the emphasis on remaining with Jesus recognizes very real issues and challenges for the early reader-hearers.

## C. Conclusion

I started this chapter by noting its inevitable limitations. It is no more than a brief guide, pointing out distinctive features here and there. Yet such observations do not do justice to the richness and creativity of the original materials, especially in the dramatic and engaging manner in which they

---

[117] Thompson, *God*, pp. 87-92.

[118] Walter Wink, "The 'Son of the Man' in the Gospel of John," in Fortna and Thatcher, *Jesus*, pp. 117-23.

[119] David Rensberger, "The Messiah Who Has Come into the World," in Fortna and Thatcher, *Jesus*, pp. 15-23.

[120] Cassidy, *New Perspective*, pp. 33-39, with attention given to the perceptions reflected in the correspondence between Pliny the Younger (governor of Bithynia-Pontus) and the Emperor Trajan.

present the gospel traditions concerning Jesus of Nazareth. They make no attempt to be dispassionate accounts, but come with the integrity of personal commitment: the writers believe in their subject matter, not out of intellectual curiosity or interest, but with the zeal of those who are devoted to the one who stands at the center of their world, and ours. As with all forms of documentary study, nothing replaces the importance of reading (or hearing) the documents themselves.

That each gospel has a quality and complexity of its own underscores the enigmatic character of the gospel traditions. This diversity of perspective in itself reflects the undoubted impact of the person of Jesus that eludes being reduced to neat categories. While there is compelling testimony to the centrality of Jesus in the unfolding purposes of God, the diverse gospel traditions take the hearer-reader in directions that are at once memorable yet continue to surprise.

Fresh approaches to exploring the gospels continue to reveal new dimensions to their distinctive features. Without pushing the theatrical imagery too far, there is a sense in which the creative diversity of the gospels, open as they are to new readings, are akin to classic texts being revisited and expressed in new productions. Qualities emerge that are capable of conveying integrity to the gospel traditions, while re-expressing familiar material in striking and challenging terms.

The strength of the persona of Jesus, found on every page of the gospels, brings a unity of purpose and devotion seen through the eyes of a diverse community of witnesses. That very diversity serves the audience well, and in large measure the enduring capacity of the gospels to engage such diverse readership testifies to their remarkable capacity to convey the richness of the traditions about Jesus.


## Bibliography

Ashton, John ed. *The Interpretation of John*. Second Edition. Edinburgh: T. & T. Clark, 1997.

Aune, David E. ed. *The Gospel of Matthew in Current Study: Studies in Honor of William G. Thompson*. Grand Rapids: Eerdmans, 2001.

Bauckham, Richard ed. *The Gospels for All Christians: Rethinking the Gospel Audiences*. Edinburgh: T. & T. Clark 1998.

Green, Joel B., and Scot McKnight, eds. *Dictionary of Jesus and the Gospels*. Downers Grove: InterVarsity Press, 1992.

Bockmuehl, Markus, and Donald A Hagner, eds. *The Written Gospel*. Cambridge: Cambridge University Press, 2005.

Burridge, Richard A. *Four Gospels, One Jesus? A Symbolic Reading*. London: SPCK, 1994.

Byrne, Brendan J. *The Hospitality of God: A Reading of Luke's Gospel*. Collegeville: Liturgical Press, 2000.

Carter, Warren. *Matthew: Storyteller, Interpreter, Evangelist*. Peabody: Hendickson, 1996.

deSilva, David A. *An Introduction to the New Testament: Contexts, Methods & Ministry Formation*. Downers Grove: InterVarsity Press, 2004.

Horsley, Richard A., Jonathan A. Draper, and John Miles Foley, eds. *Performing the Gospel: Orality, Memory and Mark*. Minneapolis: Fortress Press, 2006.

Fortna, Robert T., and Tom Thatcher, eds. *Jesus in Johannine Tradition*. Louisville: Westminster John Knox, 2001.

Harris, Elizabeth. *Prologue and Gospel: The Theology of the Fourth Evangelist*. New York: T. & T. Clark International, 2004.

McKnight, Scot, and Grant R. Osborne, eds. *The Face of New Testament Studies: A Survey of Recent Research*. Grand Rapids: Baker Academic, 2004.

Porter, Stanley E. ed. *Reading the Gospels Today*. Grand Rapids: Eerdmans, 2004.

Rhoads, David. *Reading Mark: Engaging the Gospel*. Minneapolis: Fortress Press, 2004.

Shiner, Whitney Taylor. *Proclaiming the Gospel: First Century Performance of Mark*. Harrisburg: Trinity Press International, 2003.

Stanton, Graham N. *The Gospels and Jesus*. Second Edition. New York/Oxford: Oxford University Press, 2002.

# 13. The Kingdom of God in the Proclamation of Jesus

*Stephen Voorwinde*

The kingdom of God was the grand theme of Jesus' preaching. Particularly in the Synoptic Gospels, it forms the focal point for both his teaching and his miracles. Yet the kingdom is also the great paradox in Jesus' ministry. It seems to arrive at the commencement of his mission and at the same time it is portrayed as still to come. To complicate matters further, the Greek word βασιλεία *(basileia)*, commonly translated "kingdom" in the gospels, has a far broader range of meaning than our English term. The same is true of the Hebrew and Aramaic words that lie behind the New Testament (NT) usage. They all mean "kingship" in its various nuances, such as the exercise of kingship (or "reign") and the territory ruled over (or "kingdom").[1] Depending on the context, the word *basileia* can have either a dynamic or a concrete meaning, i.e., the king's rule or his realm.

## A. The Setting for Jesus' Kingdom Proclamation

In spite of these complexities in its meaning, the Synoptic Gospels report that the proclamation of the kingdom always drew a crowd (e.g. Matt. 3:5; 4:25). But why did no one ask Jesus or John the Baptist what they meant by the *basileia*? How would their contemporaries have understood their kingdom message? The answers to these questions lie in the OT background and in developments within Judaism during the Second Temple period.

### 1. Old Testament (OT) Background

The word *basileia* is found in the canonical books of the LXX no fewer than 400 times. In all but a dozen cases it translates the *mlk* word group in Hebrew and Aramaic. The technical term "kingdom of God," while common in the Synoptics, does not occur in the Hebrew Bible or the LXX, although there are passages that speak about God ruling (e.g. Psalms 93, 96, 99). The *mlk* word group has a wide range of meanings, including "kingship," "royal power," "royal dignity," "dominion" and "kingdom." In the last sense it can refer to

---

[1] Thus James D. G. Dunn, "Jesus and the Kingdom: How Would His Message Have Been Heard?" in David E. Aune, Torrey Seland and Jarl Henning Ulrichsen, eds., *Neotestamentica et Philonica: Studies in Honor of Peder Borgen* (Leiden: Brill, 2003), p. 3.

the following:

### (a) Non-Israelite Kingdoms

Examples of such foreign kingdoms range from the tiny principalities of Sihon and Og (Num. 32:33; Deut. 3:4, 10, 13) to the mighty Babylonian and Persian empires (Dan. 1:20; 2:1; Ezra 4:24; Neh. 12:22). Significantly these OT references culminate in the kingdoms represented by the giant colossus of Nebuchadnezzar's dream (Dan. 2:36-44) and by the four beasts of Daniel's vision (Dan. 7:2-8, 23-24). Such references to non-Israelite kingdoms make up the most common usage of *mlk/basileia* in the OT.

### (b) The Kingdom of Israel/Judah

The next most frequent set of references is to the theocratic kingdom. This kingdom was established at Sinai (Exodus 19–24) with the Lord as its acknowledged King (Exod. 15:18; cf. Deut. 17:14-17). It was founded on the Ten Commandments and the laws of the Book of the Covenant (Exod. 20:1-17; 24:1-8; cf. Deut. 17:18-20). Compared to foreign kingdoms Israel was to be a kingdom of priests bound by covenant to Yahweh (Exod. 19:6). The covenant was later enacted more specifically with David and his descendants (2 Sam. 7:12-16; 2 Chron. 17:11-14). The terms of the Davidic covenant spell out quite emphatically that David's kingdom shall be established forever, a point reiterated with Solomon at the dedication of the temple (2 Chron. 7:18; cf. 1 Kings 9:4-5). Solomon, however, failed to keep the terms of the covenant, so the kingdom was torn away from him (1 Kings 1:11), yet not completely because of God's unconditional promise to David (1 Kings 11:13). Hence the many references to Judah as the "kingdom" of Solomon's descendants (e.g. 2 Chron. 14:5; 21:3-4).

### (c) God's Kingdom

Compared to the many OT references to the theocracy and the kingdoms of the nations, the references to God's rule are relatively few. Nouns which refer to the rule or royal dignity of God occur only fourteen times.[2] Although occurrences are sparse, they are significant as well as diverse in meaning. Occasionally God's kingdom is simply identified with the theocracy (1 Chron. 17:14; 28:5; 2 Chron. 13:8). This identification, however, can serve as no more than a starting point. A distinction is commonly made between God's kingdom as (a) his providential and moral government or the exercise of divine sovereignty (1 Chron. 29:11; Ps. 103:19; Dan. 4:3, 34; 6:27), and (b) God's extending his redemptive rule over the whole world (1 Chron. 28:5; 2

---

[2] Thus H. G. L. Peels, "The Kingdom of God in the Old Testament," *In die Skriflig* 35 (2001), p. 176.

Chron. 13:8; Ps. 22:29; Obad. 21; Dan. 7:27).[3] Although in most cases this distinction is clear-cut, this is not always the case. At times the sphere of God's sovereignty and the sphere of his redemption are difficult to distinguish. This is the case, for example, in Ps. 145:11-13:

> They shall speak of the glory of your kingdom, and tell of your power, to make known to all people your mighty deeds, and the glorious splendor of your kingdom.
> Your kingdom is an everlasting kingdom, and your dominion endures throughout all generations. The LORD is faithful in all his words, and gracious in all his deeds.[4]

The ambiguity is intentional as eventually the sphere of God's sovereignty and that of his redemption will be one and the same. The redemptive sphere which began with the theocracy will eventually encompass the earth (Dan. 7:27). This expectation shades into the next category.

### (d) The Kingdom to Come

The future dimension of the kingdom is one that develops gradually within the OT. Three stages can be detected:

1. The Sinai covenant casts the theocratic ideal in the future tense. God declares to Israel that "you shall be for me a priestly kingdom and a holy nation" (Exod. 19:6). Needless to say, this theocratic ideal was never realized in the historical nation of Israel. Nevertheless, as prophesied by Balaam, Israel's "kingdom shall be exalted" (Num. 24:7).
2. This prophecy finds an early fulfillment in the reign of David (1 Chron. 14:2), and it is in him that the covenant with Israel enters its next phase. Prior to the monarchy God was regarded as the sole ruler of the kingdom of Israel. With the institution of the kingship God hands over the rule of Israel to a human king. After the rejection of Saul, "the LORD lays the foundation for the future course of history in his covenant with David to establish David's house forever over his kingdom" (2 Sam. 7; 1 Chron. 17; Ps. 89).[5] This promise of a Davidic dynasty is the seedbed from which later messianic expectations would grow (e.g. Isa. 9:1-7; 11:1-10; Amos 9:11-15).[6]

---

[3] See Murray Adamthwaite, "The Kingdom from an Old Testament Perspective," *Vox reformata* 64 (1999), p. 6; cf. Peels, "Kingdom in OT," p. 185, who claims that the OT "may speak both in universalist and particularist terms of the kingdom of God." These elements are not in tension, but complement one another, e.g. 2 Chron. 20:6; Ps. 95.

[4] See also Ps. 22:29; 93:1-2; 95:1-5; Obad. 21; see also the Songs of the Sabbath Sacrifice among the corpus of the Dead Sea Scrolls (4Q400-407, 11Q17).

[5] Bruce Waltke, "The Kingdom of God in Biblical Theology," in David W. Baker ed., *Looking into the Future: Evangelical Studies in Eschatology* (Grand Rapids: Baker, 2001), p. 25.

[6] Cf. Wolter Rose, "Messianic Expectations in the Old Testament," *In die Skriflig* 35

Because this promise is unconditional and has the character of an everlasting covenant, it provides the framework for the prophetic anticipation of the kingdom of God.[7]

3. With the exile the Davidic dynasty goes into eclipse, and yet it is precisely at the time of the Babylonian captivity that the clearest prophecies/promises are to be found, especially in Daniel 7. It is in this chapter that we find the sharpest antithesis between worldly kingdoms (depicted as monstrous secular empires) and the kingdom of God. Hence there is a redemptive-historical build up in the OT that culminates in Daniel. It begins with the covenant at Sinai, gains momentum with the promise to David, and climaxes paradoxically in Daniel at a time when the Davidic kingdom has ceased to be.

The kingdom of God can be both contrasted to and compared with Daniel's four earthly kingdoms. For our purposes this is highly instructive. The kingdom of God is neither other-worldly nor necessarily to be understood as an end-of-the-world apocalyptic event. Like those worldly empires it has a historical and temporal manifestation, but unlike them it is not short-lived but endures forever (Dan. 2:44; 4:3, 34; 7:27).[8] While Daniel provides the high point of OT kingdom theology, it also serves as the starting point for Jesus' understanding of the kingdom. His kingdom proclamation in the Synoptic Gospels undeniably drew its inspiration from the kingdom visions in Daniel.[9]

As Jesus' native language was Aramaic, he may have felt naturally drawn to the Aramaic section of Daniel (2:4b–7:8). It is precisely there that the clash of the kingdom of God with the kingdoms of this world is most graphically portrayed. At the climax of this section the reader is introduced to the enigmatic Son of Man and his mysterious kingdom. Did Jesus see himself and his mission as the fulfillment of this grand vision? This will be a pivotal question in our consideration of the gospel data. These materials must, however, also be understood in their more immediate historical context. This is provided in the developments that took place during the Second Temple period. Whether these developments influenced Jesus' understanding of the kingdom is a matter of debate. Of their influence on the views of his contemporaries there can be no doubt.

## 2. The Second Temple Period

During the Second Temple period the vicissitudes of Judah's political fortunes affected the people's hopes for the future, particularly their understanding of the coming kingdom. Apart from a relatively brief period of independence

---

(2001), pp. 282-83.

[7] Thus Adamthwaite, "OT Perspective," p. 10.

[8] See Craig A. Evans, "Daniel in the New Testament: Visions of God's Kingdom," in John J. Collins and Peter W. Flint, eds., *The Book of Daniel: Composition and Reflection*, vol. 2 (Leiden: Brill, 2001), pp. 500-501.

[9] Evans, "Daniel in NT," p. 521.

under the Hasmoneans (142–63 BC), the Jews suffered varying degrees of oppression under successive empires. Kingdom expectations continued to rise. By the time of the Roman occupation these reach fever pitch as evidenced by the number of messianic pretenders that appear during this period (e.g. Acts 5:36-37).[10] By the first century of our era the national context was charged with kingdom expectations. As to the nature of that kingdom, however, there was by no means a unified concept or a single school of thought. The following tendencies may be observed in the literature.

### (a) The Apocrypha/Pseudepigrapha

Some of these writings follow the OT pattern of thought about the kingdom of God.[11] In Tobit 13:1, for example, God's kingdom is synonymous with his eternal sovereignty: "Blessed be God who lives forever, because his kingdom lasts throughout all ages." At times, however, *basileia* also takes on an ethical meaning. Thus in 4 Macc. 2:23 the kingdom is described as "temperate, just, good, and courageous." Wisdom 6:20 claims that "the desire for wisdom leads to a kingdom."[12]

In other writings three further strands can be detected:

1. The kingdom is viewed as a purely earthly state of affairs. The emphasis is very nationalistic and particularistic. Nothing is said of a future world or of supernatural, divine intervention. The Psalms of Solomon (late first century BC) includes a prayer for an earthly Davidic king who will both reign over Israel and have the Gentiles serve under his yoke (17:21-25). The Lord's goodness is over Israel (5:18), while "the kingdom of our God is forever over the nations in judgment" (17:3).
2. One of the themes of the Testaments of the Twelve Patriarchs (c. 200 BC–AD 100) is the kingdom that God has chosen to give to Judah (T. Iss. 5:7). Not surprisingly, it is in the Testament of Judah that the

---

[10] In Acts 5:37 Gamaliel mentions the revolt of Judas the Galilean. According to Josephus this Judas "prevailed with his countrymen to revolt; and said they were cowards if they would endure to pay a tax to the Romans, and would, after God, submit to mortal men as their lords" (*J.W.* 2:118). Martin Hengel, *The Zealots: Investigations into the Jewish Freedom Movement in the Period from Herod I until 70 A.D.*, trans. David Smith; Edinburgh: T. & T. Clark, 1989), p. 93, explores the kingdom expectations behind Judas' uprising: "In common with other pious Jews of his own period, he certainly expected the kingdom of God and Israel to be realized as a miraculous eschatological act of God. At the same time, however, he also rejected a purely passive and quietest hope and believed that God would only bring about his kingdom and with it the kingdom of his people in the world if Israel acknowledged his absolute claim to rule here and now, with no reservations whatever."

[11] B. Klappert, "King, Kingdom," in Colin Brown, ed., *New International Dictionary of the New Testament Theology*, 4 vols. (Grand Rapids: Zondervan, 1975-85), vol. 2, p. 377.

[12] The Wisdom of Solomon dates back to the first century BC and 4 Maccabees to the period between 63 BC and AD 70. Both were probably originally composed in Greek. Tobit was written in Hebrew during an earlier period. The exact date is disputed.

term basileia features most prominently.13 Because of his promiscuity, Judah confesses that he was divested of his kingship (T. Jud. 15:2, 3; 17:3). Nevertheless, God has granted him an earthly kingdom (21:2-4), but because of disobedience his rule will be "terminated by men of alien race, until the salvation of Israel comes, until the coming of the God of righteousness" (22:2). God will then usher in a period of universal peace to be enjoyed by both Israel and the nations. With this prospect in view, Judah declares: "He shall preserve the power of my kingdom forever" (22:3). From the root of this kingdom "will arise the rod of righteousness for the nations, to judge and save all that call on the Lord" (24:5-6). In these pronouncements that the writer places in the mouth of the patriarch Judah a dualism can be detected between national, earthly expectations on the one hand and universal-cosmic ones on the other.

3.  Some works therefore attempt a synthesis of these two strands. In 4 Ezra 7:26-44,14 for example, the earthly messianic kingdom serves as a transition to the transcendent heavenly kingdom which is introduced by the resurrection of the dead and the judgment of the world. This becomes particularly clear in vv. 28-33 where the messianic kingdom of Israel becomes a provisional phase in eschatology:

[28] For my son the Messiah shall be revealed with those who are with him, and those who remain shall rejoice four hundred years.
[29] After those years my son the Messiah shall die, and all who draw human breath.
[30] Then the world shall be turned back to primeval silence for seven days, as it was at the first beginnings, so that no one shall be left.
[31] After seven days the world that is not yet awake shall be roused, and that which is corruptible shall perish.
[32] The earth shall give up those who are asleep in it, and the dust those who rest there in silence; and the chambers shall give up the souls that have been committed to them.
[33] The Most High shall be revealed on the seat of judgment, and compassion shall pass away, and patience shall be withdrawn.
(trans. Bruce M. Metzger, in James H. Charlesworth, *Old Testament Pseudepigrapha*, vol. 1, pp. 537-38)

*(b) The Targums*

In the Aramaic-speaking synagogue the targums (Aramaic translations/ interpretations of the Hebrew text) often replace the OT verbal expression "God reigns" by "the kingdom of God."[15] The expression "the kingdom of the

---

[13] See, e.g., *T. Jud.* 1:6; 24:1-6.
[14] 4 Ezra 3–14 is a Jewish work written at the end of the first century AD.
[15] For example, *Tg. Onq.* Exod. 15:18; *Tg. Isa.* 24:23.

Lord" occurs in the targums of Isa. 24:23; 31:4; Obad. 21; Mic. 4:7; and Zech. 14:9. These targumic expressions may well provide significant background to Jesus' frequent use of "the kingdom of God" which, as we have already seen, is not found in the OT.

### (c) Tannaitic Literature

In later Jewish literature there emerges the abstract expression *malkuth shamaim* ("kingdom of heaven"). This expression owes its origin to the tendency in Rabbinic Judaism to find an alternative to the divine name. It is therefore synonymous with "kingdom of God." The term implies the essential idea that "God rules as King."[16] It refers to his kingly being or kingship, rather than to the territory ruled by him.[17] In this literature the expression has a twofold meaning:

1.  For the rabbis the *malkuth shamaim* denoted the moral dominion of God. To accept the yoke of the *malkuth shamaim* is to acknowledge God as one's King and Lord. It is the confession of monotheism as expressed in the Shema (Deut. 6:4-8) and implies that the confessor, to quote the Mishnah, "afterwards take upon himself the yoke of the commandments" (*m. Ber.* 2.2).
2.  In the second sense the *malkuth shamaim* has a far wider application. In the theology of later Judaism it is a purely eschatological concept.[18] This perspective comes to expression, for example, in the opening lines of an early Hebrew prayer, the *Qaddish*: "Glorified and sanctified be his great name in the world he has created according to his own pleasure. May he establish his royal dominion and start his deliverance of his people, and may he bring his Messiah and redeem his people. . ." Finally the whole world will recognize the kingship of God over all humankind.

At the time of Jesus there was therefore a great diversity of conceptions of the kingdom of God.[19] Nevertheless the Second Temple period provides a matrix in which Jesus can proclaim his kingdom message with maximum effectiveness. Although there were deep-seated misunderstandings about the kingdom (Acts 1:6), Jesus and John the Baptist had a ready platform for their preaching. With the kingdom of heaven as their subject they could expect a ready audience. In their day it was a hot and controversial topic. To announce the arrival of the kingdom was to say that Israel's hopes and the prophecies of

---

[16] B. Klappert, "King, Kingdom," p. 377.

[17] K. L. Schmidt, "βασιλεύς," in G. Kittel and G. Friedrich, eds., *Theological Dictionary of the New Testament*, 10 volumes (Grand Rapids: Eerdmans, 1964-1976), vol. 1, pp. 571-72.

[18] See Herman Ridderbos, *The Coming of the Kingdom*, trans. H. de Jonste; ed. Raymond O. Zorn (Philadelphia: Presbyterian & Reformed, 1969), p. 9.

[19] According to Dunn, "Jesus and the Kingdom," p. 23, "there was no single comprehensive grand narrative shaping the thought of Jesus' contemporaries."

the OT were now being fulfilled. At last the kingdom had come. Or had it?

## B. The Content of Jesus' Kingdom Proclamation

Did Jesus proclaim a kingdom that was already present or still future? Was it a present reality or a future hope? This question launched a scholarly debate that lasted for most of the twentieth century. It is now generally agreed that earlier scholars who regarded Jesus' view of the kingdom as either exclusively present[20] or absolutely future[21] failed to do justice to all the gospel data. Scholarship has had to learn to live with the eschatological tension created by the "already" and "not yet" dimensions of the kingdom. In an effort to resolve this tension some scholars have spoken of "an eschatology that is in process of realization."[22] It is probably wisest, however, to leave the tension unresolved and recognize the temporal paradox for what it is, namely that the kingdom is both present and future at the same time.[23]

In Jesus' teaching the kingdom of God is therefore truly multi-dimensional in character. It manifests itself as both rule and realm, as both present and future. Yet even here the connections are neither simple nor uniform. Our understanding cannot simply be reduced to a present rule contrasted to a future realm. Again the concept is too elastic and elusive to allow itself to be simplified so readily. There is also a sense in which God's realm is present and his reign still future. But how? The time has come to let the gospel writers speak for themselves. It is also time to ask whether each has his own way of presenting (and perhaps even unraveling) the paradox of the kingdom.

As a preliminary observation, it should be noted that the number of references to the kingdom of God/heaven varies significantly from gospel to gospel. Matthew has fifty occurrences, Mark fourteen, Luke thirty-nine, and John merely five.[24] Statistics, however, seldom tell the whole story, although in this case the discrepancies—particularly between John and the Synoptics—are rather wide. What do these numerical differences indicate? Is the kingdom

---

[20] For example, Albrecht Ritschl, *The Christian Doctrine of Justification and Reconciliation: The Positive Development of the Doctrine*, trans. H. R. Mackintosh and A. B. Macaulay (Edinburgh: T & T Clark, 1900), pp. 280-82; C. H. Dodd, *The Parables of the Kingdom* (London: Fontana, 1961 [originally published in 1935]), p. 7.

[21] Thus Johannes Weiss, *Jesus' Proclamation and the Kingdom of God*, trans. Richard H. Hiers and David L. Holland (Philadelphia: Fortress Press, 1971), pp. 129-30. This work appeared originally in German in 1892. Several years later (1906) came the even more influential monograph by Albert Schweitzer, *The Quest of the Historical Jesus: A Critical Study of Its Progress from Reimarus to Wrede*, trans. W. Montgomery (New York: Macmillan, 1962); see esp. pp. 370-71.

[22] E.g. J. Jeremias, *The Parables of Jesus*, trans. S. H. Hooke, rev. ed. (New York: Charles Scribner's Sons, 1963), p. 230.

[23] Thus Ridderbos, *Coming of the Kingdom*, p. 106: "The fulfillment is here, and yet the kingdom is still to come. The kingdom has come, and yet the fulfillment is in abeyance."

[24] C. C. Caragounis, "Kingdom of God/Kingdom of Heaven," in J. B. Green and S. McKnight, eds., *Dictionary of Jesus and the Gospels* (Downers Grove: InterVarsity Press, 1992), p. 426.

more central to some gospels than to others? Or do the four simply present complementary perspectives on the kingdom? Only a closer examination of the gospel data will begin to answer such questions, as we shall see.

## 1. The Kingdom in Mark

In his references to the kingdom Mark consistently uses the phrase "the kingdom of God."[25] In his use of this expression Mark is unique, not just among the Evangelists but in the NT as a whole. Moreover, no one in this Gospel uses this phrase or refers to it except the narrator and Jesus himself. The kingdom is preached by Jesus, and only by Jesus. In this Gospel "king" and "kingdom" are bound together.[26] Only the King announces the kingdom.

After a brief introduction where he sketches the ministry of John the Baptist and Jesus' temptation, Mark presents his account along broadly geographical lines. The narrative quickly moves away from the Jordan and the wilderness (1:1-13) and moves to Galilee (1:14–8:26), through a journey section (8:27–10:52), and on to Jesus' destination in Jerusalem (11:1–16:8). It will be most fruitful to consider Mark's kingdom references in the light of this basic outline.

### (a) Galilee (1:14–8:26)

For Mark's Gospel it is no doubt significant that the very first words attributed to Jesus have to do with his kingdom proclamation: "The time is fulfilled, and *the kingdom of God* has come near; repent, and believe in the good news" (1:15). This statement provides the key not only to Jesus' Galilean ministry, but indeed to Mark's theology as a whole.

The immediately preceding context also throws light on this announcement. Jesus was baptized by John in 1:9. Although Mark does not dwell on the point, it is clear that by submitting to John's water baptism Jesus is identifying with the penitent sinners who were preparing themselves for his coming (vv. 4-8). More explicit, however, for an understanding of Jesus' identity is the pronouncement from heaven, "You are my Son, the Beloved; with you I am well pleased" (1:11). In the OT it was Israel and, more specifically, Israel's king who was the son of Yahweh (Exod. 4:22, 23; 2 Sam. 7:14; Ps. 2:7; Hos. 11:1). Hence as God's beloved Son Jesus is Israel's anointed king. Moreover, the baptismal pronouncement is also an allusion to

---

[25] The only exception is found in Mark 11:10 where the crowd chants: "Blessed is the coming kingdom of our father David." Mark may be suggesting that the nationalistic kingdom expected by the crowd was not the kingdom proclaimed by Jesus.

[26] Both Mark's use of the fixed phrase "kingdom of God" and its restriction to the spoken words of Jesus (except for the single narrative occurrence in Mark 15:43) are unique features identified by M. E. Boring, "The Kingdom of God in Mark," in Wendell Willis, ed., *The Kingdom of God in 20th-Century Interpretation* (Peabody: Hendrickson, 1987), pp. 137-38.

Isa. 42:1 which introduces the Lord's Servant in whom his soul delights and upon whom he has put his Spirit.[27] This is of course the very same Servant who will later become the suffering Servant who is foreshadowed in Isa. 52:13–53:12. The stage for Jesus' ministry has therefore been set. He is both the King of Israel and the Servant of the Lord. In Mark's Gospel he will fulfill both roles. It is therefore as the Servant King that he announces the kingdom. As the promised Davidic King and Isaianic Servant, it is small wonder that Jesus can declare, "The time is fulfilled." God's great future has finally arrived. OT prophecies are being fulfilled at last.

That Jesus should strike a note of fulfillment at this point in time is relatively easy to comprehend. More difficult is the statement that immediately follows: "The kingdom of God has come near" (Mark 1:15b). Side by side, these two pronouncements express the present-future paradox with the utmost clarity at the very outset of Jesus' kingdom proclamation. It will not do to reduce the one statement to the confines of the other. Jesus' two declarations, though intimately related, are not synonymous. The time has come and the in-breaking of the kingdom is imminent. The tension between the "already" and the "not yet" must be allowed to retain its full force.

This of course raises the all important question: If even at this crucial juncture of Jesus' ministry the kingdom is no more than "near," when does it finally arrive? If now it can be described as "at hand," when can it be said to have come? With the anointed King on the scene, the kingdom is obviously dawning and imminent, but when—in Mark's scheme of things—does it make its definitive appearance?

While the other Synoptics give detailed accounts of Jesus' temptations in the wilderness, Mark mentions them only in passing without so much as recording the final outcome. The subsequent narrative, however, leaves the reader in no doubt. Three of the four exorcisms in Mark are found in the Galilee section (1:21-28; 5:1-20; 7:24-30). In these exorcisms we witness clashes of kingdom proportions. Jesus is doing battle on behalf of the kingdom of God and is making God's rule on earth a reality. As Kelber points out: "Exorcisms and healings are the principal approaches used to translate the kingdom program into action. In both cases, Jesus intrudes upon enemy territory, challenges and subdues the forces of evil which are in the way of the fulfillment of the kingdom of God."[28]

If Jesus' healings and exorcisms are evidence of the kingdom's dawning, his parables illustrate the nature of the kingdom. Yet even the parables cannot be understood apart from the clash of the kingdoms. It is no coincidence that the cluster of parables in Mark 4:1-34 follows hard on the heels of the "Beelzebub controversy" of Mark 3:20-30. As part of his defense Jesus

---

[27] In its "Index of Allusions and Verbal Parallels" UBS[4] detects allusions to Ps. 2:7 in Matt. 3:17, Mark 1:11 and Luke 3:22 (p. 895) and to Isa. 42:1 in Matt. 3:17, Mark 1:11 and Luke 9:35 (p. 897). The baptismal pronouncement identifying Jesus as God's Son is therefore worded in such a way as to suggest that he is also the King of Israel and the Servant of the Lord.

[28] Werner H. Kelber, *The Kingdom in Mark: A New Place and a New Time* (Philadelphia: Fortress Press, 1974), p. 17.

explains his exorcising activity in kingdom terms (3:24). Little wonder that Jesus' first parable (the Sower) has to do with people's response to the message of the kingdom (4:1-20). It is precisely between this parable and its interpretation that Jesus makes the strongest possible connection between parables and the kingdom: "To you has been given the secret of the kingdom of God, but for those outside, everything comes in parables" (4:11; cf. Matt. 13:11; Luke 8:10). This is the key to parable interpretation, as the meaning of the parables can only be understood by those to whom the secret or mystery of the kingdom has been given.

From the parables in Mark 4 we get the first indication that Jesus' kingdom teaching comes by way of illustration rather than by way of definition. Neither in Mark nor in the other gospels does he ever define what he means by "kingdom." Rather he presents his listeners with a variety of pictures—the snapshot, the portrait, the still life, the panorama, even the moving picture. The genius of this teaching style is that in the hands of Jesus the tensions inherent within the kingdom concept (rule-realm, present-future) are readily dissolved. His seemingly simple stories and vignettes brilliantly embrace the multi-dimensional character of the kingdom. The kingdom parables in Mark 4 are a case in point.

Each of these three parables in its own way demonstrates the comprehensive character of the kingdom (vv. 3-32). Viewed together, however, their complementary emphases become apparent. The Sower focuses on its beginning (the sowing), the Seed Growing Secretly on its development (the growth), and the Mustard Seed on the final stage (the tall shrub affording shelter to the birds). By using the language of the land Jesus has indicated the significance of his preaching, healings and exorcisms in Galilee—the universal reign of God is beginning to break into the present world order!

### (b) The Journey (8:27–10:52)

With Peter's confession at Caesarea Philippi (8:29) Mark's Gospel reaches both a preliminary climax and a dramatic turning point. Up till now, at least in geo-political terms, the kingdom has been advancing in unspectacular fashion. Nevertheless Jesus' ministry has been crowned with some dazzling successes. Throughout the Galilean phase he seems to enjoy success upon success. He attracts disciples, draws crowds, exorcises demons, works miracles, teaches with authority and outwits opponents in debate. As Robert Gundry declares, "this material teaches a theology of glory."[29] It is this successful and glorious Jesus whom Peter hails as the Messiah. But in a few moments all of this is going to change radically. The theology of glory must make way for a theology of suffering. With little warning the triumphant Messiah becomes the suffering Servant, a change of role for which the disciples were obviously

---

[29] Robert H. Gundry, *Mark: A Commentary on His Apology for the Cross* (Grand Rapids: Eerdmans, 1993), p. 2.

quite unprepared. The Galilean mission had given little hint of the dramatic turn-around that was about to take place. No sooner has Peter made his confession (8:29) than Jesus begins to predict his own sufferings (8:31-33) and to issue a call to discipleship precisely on that basis (8:34-38).[30] Discipleship involves cross bearing. The journey to Jerusalem has begun.

As though to reassure his stunned disciples Jesus concludes his summons with a promise: "Truly I tell you, there are some standing here who will not taste death until they see that the kingdom of God has come with power" (9:1). The statement is puzzling, but its underlying assumption is clear enough—the kingdom of God has not yet come with power. The question raised by Jesus' original proclamation that the kingdom was at hand (1:15) still remains unanswered. This time, however, the readers are not left in total suspense. They are given a clue. The kingdom will come in power during the life-time of at least some of the bystanders. Yet even this clue still begs the question.[31]

### (c) Jerusalem (11:1–16:8)

As he approaches Jerusalem, Jesus is welcomed by enthusiastic supporters, but in Mark's account of the entry Jesus is never actually proclaimed king (cf. Matt. 21:5; Luke 19:38; John 12:13). The closest the crowds come is when they chant: "Blessed is the coming kingdom of our ancestor David!" (11:10), a declaration probably best understood in nationalistic and possibly even militaristic terms.[32] If this was their meaning, Mark could well be lacing their words with irony. The kingdom of David was coming, but in a way that was beyond their wildest patriotic dreams.

The remaining direct references to the kingdom of God in the Jerusalem context reveal an understanding of the kingdom in the best Jewish tradition. When a scribe recognized that the heart of true religion lay in undivided devotion to God, Jesus told him that he was not far from the kingdom (12:34). At the Last Supper Jesus refers to the eschatological feast in the kingdom of God (14:25). Finally, Joseph of Arimathea is described as waiting for the kingdom of God (15:43).

Thus we come to the end of the occurrences of "the kingdom of God" in Mark. Our questions about the kingdom's arrival and its coming in power are still left tantalizingly unanswered. There are hints, but little more. Yet suddenly light shines from an unexpected quarter. Not the word "kingdom"

---

[30] Beyond 9:1, the remaining references to the kingdom of God in the journey section (9:47; 10:14-15, 23-25) should be read in terms of the call to discipleship issued here. In each case the cost of discipleship is spelled out. See further n. 36 below.

[31] Thomas R. Hatina, "Who Will See 'The Kingdom of God Coming with Power' in Mark 9,1—Protagonists or Antagonists?" *Biblica* 86 (2005), p. 21, argues from the use of the word "power" in the apocalypses in Mark 13:26 and 14:62 that the bystanders in Mark 9:1 are antagonists. This makes Jesus' prediction of the kingdom coming with power a threat of divine judgment. What Hatina fails to say, however, is when this judgment is likely to come.

[32] Cf. *Pss. Sol.* 17:21-25 (and note section A.2 [a] 1 above).

(*basileia*), but its cognate "king" (*basileus*) holds the key to our quest. Jesus is never called "king" in Mark prior to chapter 15. Now he is proclaimed king no fewer than six times, but always in mockery, jest, ridicule, and accusation (vv. 2, 9, 12, 18, 26, 32). This is the ultimate stroke of irony in Mark's Gospel. Never has the truth so poignantly been spoken in jest. Paradoxically, Mark is claiming that all the false accusations are true! Pilate, his soldiers, the chief priests and the scribes spoke more than they knew, or were prepared to admit. In spite of themselves they proclaim what Mark has been seeking to demonstrate all along. Jesus *is* the King of the Jews, the King of Israel.

Mark therefore has an incredible surprise in store at the end of his Gospel. He does in fact answer the questions relating to the kingdom's arrival (1:15) and coming in power (9:1). But the answer is totally unexpected and paradoxical.[33] The climax of the kingdom comes when the king is crucified.  His execution is his coronation and his throne a cross.[34]

On the cross Jesus fulfils the dual role of suffering Servant and anointed King. For Mark this is the supreme moment of the kingdom's manifestation. This is the heart of his kingdom message. Can the same also be said of the other evangelists?

## 2. The Kingdom in Matthew

Compared to Mark the references to the kingdom in Matthew are more frequent, more varied and more nuanced. Matthew's favorite expression is "the kingdom of heaven" which he uses thirty-one times.[35] Only rarely does he use "the kingdom of God"—merely four times, and then, it has been suggested, for the sake of emphasis (12:28; 19:24; 21:31, 43).[36] On thirteen

---

[33] Thus Michael Bird, "The Crucifixion of Jesus as the Fulfillment of Mark 9:1," *Trinity Journal* (new series) 24 (2003), p. 35: "Mark regarded the crucifixion as the kingdom of God coming in power. Mark's kingdom theology directs us unequivocally to the cross as the central symbol of its arrival. . . The nature of Jesus' death is portrayed in such a way that it may appropriately be called power in powerlessness."

[34] See Paul W. Barnett, *The Servant King: Reading Mark Today* (Sydney: Anglican Information Office, 1991), pp. 29-30. This is not to suggest that there is no further fulfillment at the end of time when the kingdom comes not only in power but also in glory (see 4:26-32; 8:38; 10:37; 13:24-37), but it does mean that in Mark's development of the kingdom theme the cross is climactic. This point is driven home further by the centurion's declaration at the cross: "Truly this man was God's Son!" (15:39). This is the title by which Jesus was introduced (according to some of the earliest and most reliable manuscripts) at the beginning of the Gospel (1:1). He was also identified as such by the heavenly voice both at his baptism (1:11) and at the Transfiguration (9:7). The title has significant kingdom connotations since the king of Israel was regarded as God's son in the OT (2 Sam. 7:14; Ps. 2:7; 89:26-27).

[35] It is generally assumed that Matthew uses this expression in an effort to find a circumlocution for the divine name, in much the same way as the rabbis (see discussion above). Recently, however, a more compelling explanation has been suggested. Robert Foster, "Why on Earth Use 'Kingdom of Heaven'?: Matthew's Terminology Revisited," *New Testament Studies* 48 (2002), p. 489, argues that this expression forms "part of a larger 'heavenly' discourse in the Gospel. He uses this 'heavenly' speech to support his strategy of reaffirming the disciples of Jesus as the true chosen people of God."

[36] J. C. Thomas, "The Kingdom of God in the Gospel according to Matthew," *New*

occasions the kingdom is referred to in other ways. Although mostly found on the lips of Jesus, references to the kingdom are also made freely by others, e.g. the narrator (4:23; 9:35), the disciples (10:7; 18:1) and John the Baptist (3:2). Matthew shares nine kingdom sayings with Mark, and has nine further sayings in common only with Luke.[37] Most of his references to the kingdom are therefore unique to his Gospel.

Following a simple geographical outline (as with Mark) will hardly do justice to the wealth and variety of the Matthean material. In this case it is probably best to arrange the data under subject headings that are particularly relevant to our topic and highlight some of the unique features of Matthew's presentation.

### (a) John the Baptist

In Matthew's kingdom presentation John the Baptist stands as a landmark figure. In fact, the opening announcement of the kingdom's imminent arrival comes not from Jesus but from John: "Repent, for the kingdom of heaven has come near" (3:2). Endorsing John's declaration Jesus commences his own preaching ministry using these very words (4:17). There is every suggestion of continuity between the ministry of John and that of Jesus. The fact that both preach the same message, however, should not be allowed to mask the differences between them which are epochal in character. John's work is preparatory and his ministry anticipatory. His message is one of pure promise. He is the forerunner. Jesus, on the other hand, is the fulfiller—a recurring theme in Matthew's Gospel.

When John sends a delegation to ask whether or not Jesus is the Coming One,[38] he does not get a straight answer. Jesus appeals to some of his miracles—the blind see, the lame walk, lepers are cleansed, the deaf hear and the dead are raised up. Moreover, the poor have the gospel preached to them (11:4, 5). The point is not that he is performing miracles, but that he is performing precisely those miracles, and engaging in exactly that kind of activity, that had been prophesied of the Messiah (Isa. 35:5, 6; 61:1). Although his answer may at first seem rather cryptic, it is nothing less than a strong affirmation that he is in fact the Coming One. It is precisely in this capacity that Jesus ushers in the kingdom.

Having answered John the Baptist, Jesus then defends him (11:7-15), and in the most extravagant terms. He does not hesitate to heap on John one

---

*Testament Studies* 39 (1993), p. 141. Foster, "Why on Earth?," pp. 494-95, observes that Jesus uses "kingdom of God" only when speaking to or about those who reject him and that in each case the phrase carries a certain "shock value".

[37] Caragounis, "Kingdom of God/Heaven," p. 427.

[38] John's question does not necessarily suggest that he was expecting a geo-political demonstration of Jesus' kingly authority after the manner of *Pss. Sol.* 17. The motivation for his question probably lies closer at hand, namely in his own prediction that Jesus would baptize with the Holy Spirit and with fire as a way of ushering in his messianic kingdom (Matt. 3:11-12). In spite of the spectacular miracles Jesus was performing, there was as yet no evidence for either of these baptisms.

accolade after another. John was neither fickle (v. 7) nor "posh" (v. 8), but rather a prophet and more than a prophet (v. 9). To him had been granted the unspeakable privilege of heralding the Messiah (v. 10). This made him the greatest man who had ever lived (v. 11)! Yet in spite of having carried out such a high calling John has now been eclipsed. In him the succession of OT prophets has reached both its climax and its conclusion. John stands at the high water mark of the old era, but that era has now passed. Therefore "the least in the kingdom of heaven is greater than he" (v. 11). The comparison is of course not based on character, but on the responsibilities and privileges conferred by the kingdom.[39]

John's crucial role in salvation history is underscored by the fact that his day marks a new period in the realization of the kingdom. His ministry was a catalyst. As Jesus states in v. 12: "From the days of John the Baptist until now, the kingdom of heaven has been forcefully advancing, and forceful men lay hold of it" (NIV). Since the days of John[40] the kingdom has been proclaimed and is being stormed by those eager to get in. The strong assumption behind Jesus' observation is that the kingdom is a present reality that can be grasped in a way that was not yet possible in the days of John. With Jesus the kingdom has not only drawn near, it has come.

But what was it that since the days of John the Baptist made the kingdom a present reality? What constituted the great change? What was the decisive impulse? How exactly did the kingdom of God come with the activity of Jesus?

### (b) The Devil and Demons

In Matthew's account of the Beelzebul controversy (12:22-37) Jesus defends himself against his critics by putting the debate in a broad kingdom perspective. He makes the reasonable observation that Satan's kingdom is not a "house divided" (vv. 25-27). Therefore it is logically impossible for Jesus to be casting out demons by Beelzebul, the prince of demons. His power to exorcise must therefore be divine rather than demonic. By sheer force of logic he can insist that "if it is by the Spirit of God that I cast out demons, then the kingdom of God *has come* to you" (v. 28, cf. Luke 11:20). Here Jesus speaks quite emphatically of the presence of the kingdom. The kingdom is not just "near" or "at hand." It has definitively arrived. Moreover, Jesus' exorcisms are proof positive of its arrival.

---

[39] See D. A. Carson, *The Expositor's Bible Commentary: Matthew*, vol. 8, F. E. Gaebelein et al., eds. (Grand Rapids: Zondervan, 1984), p. 265.

[40] For our purposes the time indicated by the expression "from the days of John the Baptist" is important. If the phrase "until John" in the next verse means that all the prophets and the law prophesied *up to and including John* (as seems likely), then Jesus is indeed thinking of developments that have occurred *since* the days of John. Jesus is therefore not suggesting that John inaugurated the kingdom, but only that it was inaugurated during the time of his ministry. As Carson argues: "The expression does not even assume John's death; it only assumes that the crucial period of his ministry during which the kingdom was inaugurated lies in the past" (*Matthew*, p. 266).

The exorcisms are not isolated events. Jesus drives home his point with the illustration that immediately follows: "Or how can one enter a strong man's house and plunder his property, without first tying up the strong man? And then he will plunder his house" (v. 29; cf. Mark 3:27). Jesus' words would seem to imply a twofold action: *first* the strong man is bound, and *then* his house is plundered and his property carried off. This observation would appear to weaken those interpretations which understand this verse as simply illustrating what happens at an exorcism.[41] More convincing is the explanation that, with the binding of the strong man, Jesus is referring to the temptations in the desert (4:1-11). As a consequence of his triumph on that occasion he is able to drive out demons to which he refers metaphorically as plundering the strong man's house and carrying off his property. In the desert Jesus was therefore able to achieve a preliminary binding of Satan. Moreover, as Ridderbos has pointed out,[42] the temptations have kingdom dimensions. This becomes particularly clear when the devil offers Jesus all the kingdoms of the world and their glory (4:8, 9). Universal, cosmic lordship is on the line. Jesus has come to set up his kingdom and to destroy the kingdom of Satan. The first showdown comes with the temptations in the wilderness. Satan suffers his first major defeat. From this titanic victory in the desert Jesus follows through with his numerous expulsions of demons (4:23-25; 8:16-17, 28-34; 12:22; 15:21-28; 17:14-21).

The exorcisms performed by Jesus therefore provide incontrovertible proof that the kingdom has indeed arrived. They show that in and through him the eschatological rule of God is present among men.[43] They further prove Jesus' victory over the devil and thus the decisive breakthrough by the kingdom of heaven.[44]

Yet the very clarity of the evidence indicating the arrival of God's kingdom presents us with problems of its own. This evidence stands side by side with equally clear evidence that the kingdom is still "near" or "at hand." It is *after* his triumph in the desert that Jesus so precisely echoes the words of John the Baptist: "Repent, for the kingdom of heaven has come near" (4:17). Nor is this the last reference to the kingdom's nearness in Matthew's Gospel. Before commissioning his disciples on a preaching tour, Jesus instructs them to proclaim, "The kingdom of heaven has come near" (10:7). Then in the very next breath he tells them to "cure the sick, raise the dead, cleanse the lepers, cast out demons" (10:8). So here exorcisms are not seen as signs of the kingdom's arrival but of its nearness. Jesus can therefore appeal to his victories over Satan and the demons as evidence *both* of the kingdom's nearness *and* its arrival. For a tidy mind this is not a comfortable observation.

---

[41] So Graham H. Twelftree, *Jesus the Exorcist: A Contribution to the Study of the Historical Jesus* (Peabody: Hendrickson, 1993) p. 112. Twelftree suggests that "what we have here [in Mark 3:27] is a *parable of an exorcism.*"

[42] Ridderbos, *Coming of the Kingdom*, p. 62.

[43] Thus G. R. Beasley-Murray, *Jesus and the Kingdom of God* (Grand Rapids: Eerdmans, 1985), p. 75.

[44] So Twelftree, *Jesus the Exorcist*, p. 170: "In short, *in themselves the exorcisms of Jesus are the kingdom of God in operation*" (author's italics).

It leaves our discussion with some awkward loose ends. Various kingdom sayings in Matthew's Gospel must be left unreconciled. The eschatological tension sensed between them must be left intact and not be minimized.

On a broader canvas, Matthew's and Mark's kingdom perspectives must not be artificially harmonized. For all the ironies and paradoxes that make his account so intriguing, Mark nevertheless draws a straight line from the kingdom's dawning at Jesus' baptism to its inauguration at his trial and crucifixion. This is at least partly due to his playing down the significance of the temptations in the desert and lack of further reflection on the ministry of John the Baptist. But Matthew's Jesus is the Teacher who pauses to explain the implications of earlier events. This makes Matthew's presentation of the kingdom richer and more nuanced than Mark's, but it does leave certain tensions unresolved and thus acutely felt by the sensitive interpreter. Nevertheless it is these very tensions between the kingdom's imminence and its arrival, between the present and the future, that provide the only plausible framework for understanding Matthew's further references to the kingdom.

### (c) Jesus' Proclamation

Of decisive importance for our understanding of the early chapters of Matthew are two summary statements of Jesus' ministry where his proclamation of the gospel of the kingdom occupies a prominent position. Just prior to recording the Sermon on the Mount, Matthew reports that Jesus "went throughout Galilee, teaching in their synagogues, and proclaiming the good news of the kingdom and curing every disease and every sickness among the people" (4:23). These words are repeated almost verbatim in 9:35 before the next major discourse in chapter 10. By thus making use of the literary device of inclusio, the evangelist groups together Jesus' preaching in chapters 5–7 and his miracles in chapters 8–9.

In the Sermon we have Matthew's most detailed account of Jesus' kingdom proclamation. It is essentially the charter of the kingdom. It speaks of the character, standards and way of life in the kingdom being ushered in by Jesus. The complementary aspects of rule and realm, the eschatological tension between the present and the future, all of which are so crucial to Matthew's presentation of the kingdom, are equally crucial to the ethical teaching of the Sermon on the Mount (5:3, 10, 19, 20; 6:10, 13, 33; 7:21). In it the multi-dimensional nature of the kingdom is given eloquent expression. Jesus is proclaiming the gospel of the kingdom and teaching an appropriate response ethic.[45] True to Matthean form that kingdom is already here and is yet to come.

---

[45] See Ron Farmer, "The Kingdom of God in the Gospel of Matthew," in Willis, ed., *The Kingdom of God*, p. 127: "What this means is that the ethic of Jesus is neither a call to repentance in light of an imminent, future kingdom nor is it a blueprint for bringing about the perfect society on earth. Rather, Jesus' ethic is a response ethic, the proper response of people who have experienced the gracious, saving activity of God. . . The Matthean ethic is indeed a response to grace."

The rich variety of Matthew's kingdom motifs is further illustrated by an abundance of specifically designated kingdom parables. As with Mark, Matthew's major collection of kingdom parables (13:1-52) follows soon after the Beelzebul controversy (12:22-37). Again the series begins with the parable of the Sower (13:1-23). Beyond this, Mark and Matthew share only one more parable in this context, namely that of the Mustard Seed (13:31, 32). Matthew pairs it with the parable of the Leaven, ostensibly to illustrate the extensive and the intensive growth of the kingdom respectively.[46]

As the parables of Jesus receive separate treatment elsewhere in this volume, detailed discussion of the Matthean parables would be superfluous at this point. In some of these parables the kingdom is clearly portrayed as present (13:44-46; 21:28-46), and in others as yet future (25:1-46). Still others embrace both the present and future dimensions of the kingdom (13:24-31, 36-43, 47-50; 18:21-35).

## *(d) Jesus as King*

For Matthew, as for Mark, Jesus is the suffering Servant, a role he fulfils supremely in his death (20:28). Again it is within the context of his trial and crucifixion that his kingship is mockingly proclaimed (27:11, 29, 37, 42). But in Matthew the ironic twist is not as sharp. He does not wait till the passion to have Jesus proclaimed king. Time and again the reader has been reminded of Jesus' royal status—at his birth (2:2), at his triumphal entry (21:5) and at the last judgment (25:34, 40).

Moreover, Jesus' role as suffering Servant has been overlaid with a more dominant motif, namely his identification as the son of David. This title, conferred on Jesus only three times in Mark (10:47, 48; 12:35), is ascribed to him no fewer than eight times in Matthew (1:1; 9:27; 12:23; 15:22; 20:30, 31; 21:9, 15). In fact, the designation is found in the very opening verse of this Gospel: "An account of the genealogy of Jesus the Messiah, *the son of David*, the son of Abraham." The tripartite structure of the genealogy that follows is arguably arranged according to the fortunes of the house of David—its rise (1:3-6), its decline (1:6-11), and its apparent eclipse (1:12-16). At the conclusion of the genealogy there is already a hint that, with Jesus as the Messiah, the house of David will be restored (1:16, 17). Jesus' Davidic descent remains a strong theme throughout this Gospel. Joseph is addressed by the angel as "son of David" (1:20). Jesus is hailed with this title again and again—by those who plead with him for mercy (9:27; 15:22; 20:30, 31), by the crowds (12:23; 21:9) and by the children in the temple (21:15). In Jerusalem he checkmates his opponents, reducing them to silence, by asking astute questions about the role of David's son (22:41-46).

Matthew accents the theme of Jesus' royalty by stressing the homage paid to him, a feature virtually absent from Mark. The first so to worship him are, remarkably, magi from the Gentile world (2:2, 11). Perhaps significantly

---

[46] Thus S. Kistemaker, *The Parables of Jesus* (Grand Rapids: Baker, 1980), pp. 47, 50.

another Gentile, the Canaanite woman, is one who both worships Jesus and calls him "son of David" (15:22, 25). Both this woman and the magi are indications that Jesus is the Davidic king who has come to establish an empire that will span the globe (cf. Dan. 7:14, 27). As the risen one he has the power to do exactly that. On this note the Gospel draws to a triumphant close (28:18-20).

## 3. The Kingdom in Luke

Like Mark, Luke prefers to refer to the kingdom as "the kingdom of God" and does so thirty-two times. Most frequently, though not exclusively, the expression is used by Jesus and the evangelist. On seven further occasions the kingdom is referred to in other ways. At a formal level Luke therefore resembles Mark. Conceptually, however, he has far greater affinities with Matthew.

### (a) The King

From the very outset Jesus is introduced as a Davidic king. The first to announce the kingdom in Luke is neither Jesus nor John the Baptist, but the angel Gabriel who does so in terms strongly reminiscent of the Davidic covenant (1:32, 33; cf. 2 Sam. 7:12-16). Throughout Luke's account of the nativity Jesus' Davidic descent is repeatedly emphasized (1:27; 2:4, 11). He is again addressed as "son of David" (18:38, 39) and uses the title to refute his opponents in debate (20:41-44).

When we turn to Luke's sequel in the book of Acts the words of the Davidic covenant alluded to by the angel take on a deeper significance.[47] Particularly impressive is the strong emphasis on it in Peter's Pentecost address (Acts 2:30-36). The oath to David guaranteed that there would be a descendant on his throne. This promise, reaffirmed by the angel to Mary, has now been fulfilled in the exaltation of Jesus.[48] Jesus' enthronement as the eschatological Davidic king is confirmed by his resurrection (vv. 30-32), ascension and Pentecost (v. 33).[49] Thus the angelic announcement and Peter's sermon are to be read in tandem. The statements are parallel and both focus on the work of the Holy Spirit (Luke 1:35; Acts 2:33). Together they provide the framework within which the Gospel of Luke is to be read.

The importance that Luke attaches to the Davidic covenant is highlighted

---

[47] Michael Wolter, "'Reich Gottes' bei Lukas," *New Testament Studies* 41 (1995), p. 541, argues that Luke's presentation of the kingdom of God in the Gospel cannot be understood without Acts. A framework for Luke's kingdom references is provided by Luke 4:43 and Acts 28:31, with Acts 1:3, 6 acting as a hinge.

[48] See R. O'Toole, "The Kingdom of God in Luke-Acts," in Willis, ed., *The Kingdom of God*, p. 149.

[49] After the death, resurrection and ascension of Jesus, and in accord with the Father's promise (Luke 22:29), the kingdom of God becomes the kingdom of the exalted Jesus. See Wolter, "'Reich Gottes,'" p. 550.

by the fact that not only Peter's first sermon but also Paul's draw attention to it. Speaking in the synagogue at Pisidian Antioch, Paul first underscores Jesus' Davidic descent (Acts 13:22, 23) and then describes Jesus' resurrection in terms of the enthronement of a Davidic king (Acts 13:30-37). It is therefore in Jesus that God's promise of an everlasting kingdom to David is ultimately realized. Not only that, but at the Jerusalem Council James recognizes that the house of David, which had gone into eclipse almost beyond recovery, has now been immeasurably extended through the inclusion of the Gentiles (Acts 15:16). As the apostles carry out the great commission, new vistas of Christ's reign lie before them. The kingdom that they had once considered to be restricted to Israel (1:6) is now proclaimed throughout the world to Jews, Samaritans and Gentiles (Acts 8:12; 14:22; 19:8; 20:25; 28:23).[50] Even under house arrest in Rome, Paul was able to preach the kingdom of God "with all boldness and without hindrance" (Acts 28:31). It is with this suggestion of still further horizons opening up for the kingdom that Luke draws his two-volume account to a close. There is every indication that, as the angel said, this new Davidic kingdom will have no end (cf. Dan. 7:14, 27).

Because the Third Gospel has its continuation in Acts, Luke is able to bring out dimensions of the kingdom of God that Matthew could only hint at. What is implicit in Matthew becomes explicit in Luke-Acts. While Matthew can refer to the church as a future expression of the kingdom (Matt. 16:18-19), Luke can give an account of its birth and its progress from Jerusalem to Rome. Matthew ends with the commission to evangelize Gentiles (Matt. 28:18-20), while the book of Acts shows how this commission was carried out (Acts 1:8).

In Luke-Acts, as in Matthew, Jesus' role as the Davidic king overshadows that of the suffering Servant. Nevertheless this perspective is by no means eclipsed.[51] Again Jesus is referred to as king in the context of his passion, but in Luke's Gospel all traces of irony have disappeared. In his account of Jesus' trial Luke is more at pains to point out Jesus' political innocence and the hypocrisy of his accusers. The members of the Sanhedrin had found Jesus guilty of blasphemy (22:66-71), while before Pilate they subtly transform this verdict into a charge of treason (23:2, 3). They accuse him of being a "king" in the sense of being a Jewish upstart against Roman rule. Throughout Luke's trial scene the title is purely a political term, without any religious overtones. Luke has already established the true nature of Jesus' kingship—even before his birth (1:33) and again at the triumphal entry (19:38). Ironically, it is not the religious leaders but a criminal who has genuine insight into the character of Jesus' kingdom (23:42).

---

[50] Wolter, "'Reich Gottes,'" pp. 552-58, argues that in Acts a semantic shift has taken place in that the traditional Jewish particularistic understanding of the kingdom of God has been replaced by a universal understanding which includes the Gentiles in the kingdom. This shift has been carefully anticipated by Jesus' teaching in such passages as Luke 4:25-27; 13:28-29; 14:15-24. Hence Jesus redefines the traditional Jewish kingdom expectation in anticipation of the universal kingdom proclamation in Acts.

[51] For example, Luke quotes directly from Isaiah 53 in Luke 22:37 and Acts 8:32-33, and alludes to this chapter in Luke 23:33-34; 24:27, 46 and Acts 10:43.

### (b) Affinities with Matthew

With their common presentation of Jesus as the son of David, it is not surprising to discover that Luke develops the kingdom concept along similar lines to Matthew. Their affinities can be summarized as follows.

John the Baptist is seen as a crucial player in the unfolding drama of the kingdom. Luke's account is less nuanced than Matthew's in that there is no reference to John's message of the kingdom being at hand. John is simply grouped with the law and the prophets (Luke 16:16) and distinguished from those in the kingdom (7:28). The devil and demons are defeated and cast out (4:1-12; 11:14-26), a sure sign that the kingdom of God has come (11:20). Jesus' proclamation is often summarized in kingdom terms (4:43; 8:1; 9:11). The rich are warned (18:24, 25) and would-be disciples are challenged to enter the kingdom as children (18:16, 17). The Sermon on the Plain opens with a reference to the kingdom (6:20). Parallels to kingdom references in Matthew's Sermon on the Mount are also found in other contexts (11:2; 12:31). Parables are used to illustrate the kingdom, but only on three occasions is the connection specifically made. The parables of the Mustard Seed and the Leaven (13:18-20) are paralleled in Matthew, while that of the Minas (19:11-27) shares some common features with Matthew's parable of the Talents. The future kingdom is portrayed under the imagery of an eschatological banquet (13:29; 14:15; 22:15-18).

### (c) Unique Features

Although Matthew and Luke have much in the way of a common perspective, the eschatological tension inherent within the kingdom comes to expression in Luke in slightly different ways. Although the place of John the Baptist is more simply defined, there are other ways in which Luke's Gospel presents its own complications.

Although Luke views the kingdom as present in the ministry of Jesus, particularly through his exorcisms, one of his statements on the presence of the kingdom has proved something of a *crux interpretum*. In answering the Pharisees' question as to when the kingdom of God would come, Jesus declares: "The kingdom of God is not coming with signs that can be observed; nor will they say, 'Look, here it is!' or 'There it is!' For, in fact, the kingdom of God is among you" (17:20-21). The last phrase could also be translated "within you." Problematic though this pronouncement is, it is a clear indication of the presence of the kingdom. The future kingdom is the subject of the verses that follow (17:22-37).

Luke does not present John the Baptist as making any direct kingdom declarations. Rather, his message that the kingdom is near is to be announced by Jesus' disciples. In commissioning the seventy Jesus tells them that whether a city receives them or not, they are to say, "The kingdom of God has come near" (10:8-11). For those who hear the disciples' preaching this is their day of opportunity. To reject the message of the kingdom has serious consequences.[52] Jesus uses a similar expression in a more futuristic sense when he predicts eschatological signs: "So also, when you see these things taking place, you know that the kingdom of God is near" (21:31). These two passages viewed together eloquently capture the eschatological tension in Luke. The kingdom is near in the mission of the seventy; it can still be described as "near" just prior to the Parousia.

This tension comes to expression in a unique and fascinating way in the parable of the Minas (19:11-27), the very parable commonly appealed to in an effort to suggest that Luke's eschatological scheme is different from that of the other gospels. This is one of the few occasions where the purpose of a parable is explicitly stated: "He went on to tell a parable, because he was near Jerusalem, and because they supposed that the kingdom of God was to appear immediately" (19:11). Partly on the basis of this verse Conzelmann has argued against Luke's expectation of an imminent Parousia, replacing it with a lengthy period of delay.[53] This understanding, however, ignores the larger context of the parable. In the narrative that follows the parable, Jesus is given a regal welcome into Jerusalem, the crowds joyfully hailing him as king (19:37, 38). Luke has so crafted his material that in adjoining pericopes he juxtaposes the kingdom as both a future hope and a present reality. Rather than disproving, the parable of the Minas rightly understood epitomizes the eschatological tension in Luke's presentation of the kingdom.[54]

## 4. The Kingdom in John

Kingdom terminology is almost completely absent in John. The Evangelist's functional equivalent is (eternal) life.[55] In the Fourth Gospel this is the vehicle by which the eschatological tension in Jesus' teaching is primarily carried.[56]

---

[52] Thus Leon Morris, *The Gospel according to St. Luke: An Introduction and Commentary* (Grand Rapids: Eerdmans, 1974), p. 183.

[53] Hans Conzelmann, *The Theology of St. Luke*, trans. G. Buswell (New York: Harper, 1961), p. 113.

[54] See Laurie Guy, "The Interplay of the Present and the Future in the Kingdom of God (Luke 19:11-44)," *Tyndale Bulletin* 48 (1997), p. 137: "We need to recognize the paradoxical nature of Luke's language about the kingdom of God. It is nuanced rather than straight-forward language. Earlier, in 9:27 and in 17:20-21, Luke has referred to a kingdom which, while future, also has present or near-present dimensions. Despite reference to futurity in 19:11, the subsequent material points in some sense to the presence or immediacy of the kingdom. . . There is not yet a kingdom, and yet there is a kingdom. Luke 19:11 points to a future kingdom, but this does not negate its present coming."

[55] C. K. Barrett, *The Gospel according to St John: An Introduction with Commentary and Notes on the Greek Text* (London: SPCK, 1955), p. 179, notes in his exposition of John 3:15 that "in John eternal life is first mentioned after the only references in the Gospel to the kingdom of God (3.3, 5). It is clear. . . that the concept retains something of its original eschatological connection, but also that it may equally be thought of as a present gift of God; in this, ζωὴ αἰώνιος in John resembles 'kingdom of God' in the Synoptic Gospels. That which is properly a future blessing becomes a present fact in virtue of the realization of the future in Christ."

[56] George E. Ladd, *A Theology of the New Testament*, rev. ed. (Grand Rapids: Eerdmans, 1993), notes that "while the idiom is different, and we are not to identify the Kingdom of God

Nevertheless in the five references to the kingdom in John (3:3, 5; 18:36 [*3x*]) the present reign and the future realm receive equal attention.

In Jesus' conversation with Nicodemus on the subject of the new birth, Jesus insists that without such a supernatural rebirth no one can either see or enter into the kingdom of God (John 3:3, 5). The reference is to eschatological salvation as a future realm that can be both seen and entered.[57] The concrete and static meaning of *basileia* would seem to fit best here.

On the other hand, in Jesus' declaration before Pilate that his *basileia* is not of this world (John 18:36) the idea of a present rule or kingship would seem to fit best. As in Mark, there is once again a strong connection between king (*basileus*) and kingdom (*basileia*). The reign of this other-worldly king comes to expression in a highly paradoxical way. Here again we have a passion account that is laced with a strong sense of irony. In the Fourth Gospel Jesus is supremely declared king by the trilingual inscription fixed to his cross (John 19:19, 20). As in Mark, Jesus' kingship is established through his suffering and sacrificial death.[58] Although John's references to the kingdom are indeed sparse, they carry the same tensions and nuances as the more frequent occurrences in the Synoptics.

## C. Conclusion

The gospels present complementary perspectives on the kingdom. Even though the paradoxical tension between the "already" and the "not yet" can at times be acutely felt, there are no competing eschatologies in the gospels. All four evangelists also provide evidence for both the "rule" and "realm" dimensions of the kingdom. This does not, however, eliminate differing nuances between them. This is particularly so in the Synoptics, where Jesus' ministry is carried out in terms of his identity as the beloved Son in whom God is well pleased. The OT figures alluded to in the baptismal pronouncement[59] find their fulfillment in varying ways. Introduced in these terms, Jesus is both the Davidic King who fulfils Daniel's vision of universal kingship and the servant of the Lord who is also a righteous sufferer. While these two are not in tension, each of the gospels highlights them in different ways and thus brings out differing aspects of Jesus' kingship. Davidic royalty is highlighted by Matthew and Luke, while it is the suffering sovereign who receives the kingdom in Mark and John.

A final feature not to be forgotten is the fact that Jerusalem is "the city of

---

and eternal life, the underlying theological structure is the same, though expressed in different categories. If eternal life is indeed the life of the eschatological Kingdom of God, and if the Kingdom is present, it follows that we might expect the Kingdom to bring to human beings a foretaste of the life of the future age."

[57] Thus Hans Kvalbein, "The Kingdom of God and the Kingdom of Christ in the Fourth Gospel," in David E. Aune, Torrey Seland and Jarl Henning Ulrichsen, eds., *Neotestamentica et Philonica: Studies in Honor of Peder Borgen* (Leiden: Brill, 2003), p. 222.

[58] For a more detailed discussion of this point see Stephen Voorwinde, *Jesus' Emotions in the Fourth Gospel: Human or Divine?* (London: T. & T. Clark, 2005), pp. 104-06.

[59] See n. 27 above.

the great King" (Ps. 48:2; Matt. 5:33). In each of the Synoptics Jesus' ministry moves towards Jerusalem as its final destination. It is there that matters come to a head and to a climax. But what Jesus the king actually does when he arrives in his royal city is presented differently by each gospel writer. On the assumption that Mark ends at 16:8, Jesus goes to Jerusalem to die—hence Mark's presentation of Jesus as the suffering Servant. In Matthew Jesus not only dies in Jerusalem, but he also rises from the dead. In Luke-Acts he does even more. He dies, rises, ascends and sends his Spirit. For Matthew and Luke Jesus is therefore also the Davidic king whose kingdom comes not so much in his death as in the triumph of his exaltation.

## Bibliography

Adamthwaite, Murray. "The Kingdom from an Old Testament Perspective." *Vox reformata* 64 (1999): 6-20.

Beasley-Murray, George R. *Jesus and the Kingdom of God*. Grand Rapids: Eerdmans, 1985.

Bird, Michael. "The Crucifixion of Jesus as the Fulfillment of Mark 9:1." *Trinity Journal* (new series) 24 (2003): 23-36.

Caragounis, Chrys C. "Kingdom of God/Kingdom of Heaven." In *Dictionary of Jesus and the Gospels*, edited by Joel B. Green and Scot McKnight, pp. 417-30. Downers Grove: InterVarsity Press, 1992.

Chilton, Bruce. "The Kingdom of God in Recent Discussion." In *Studying the Historical Jesus: Evaluations of the State of Current Research*, edited by Bruce Chilton and Craig A. Evans, pp. 255-80. New York/Leiden: Brill, 1994.

Dunn, James D. G. "Jesus and the Kingdom: How Would His Message Have Been Heard." In *Neotestamentica et Philonica: Studies in Honor of Peder Borgen*, edited by David E. Aune, Torrey Seland and Jarl Henning Ulrichsen, pp. 4-36. Boston/Leiden: Brill, 2003.

Evans, Craig A. "Daniel in the New Testament: Visions of God's Kingdom." In *The Book of Daniel: Composition and Reflection*, edited by John J. Collins and Peter W. Flint, 2:491-527. Leiden: Brill, 2001.

Foster, R., "Why on Earth Use 'Kingdom of Heaven'? Matthew's Terminology Revisited." *New Testament Studies* 48 (2002): 487-99.

Guy, L. "The Interplay of the Present and the Future in the Kingdom of God (Luke 19:11-44)." *Tyndale Bulletin* 48 (1997): 119-37.

Kelber, Werner H. *The Kingdom in Mark: A New Place and a New Time*. Philadelphia: Fortress Press, 1974.

Klappert, B. "King, Kingdom." In *New International Dictionary of the New Testament Theology*, 2:372-89. 4 vols. Grand Rapids: Zondervan, 1975-1985.

Peels, H. G. L. "The Kingdom of God in the Old Testament." *In die Skriflig* 35 (2001): 173-89.

Ridderbos, Hermann. *The Coming of the Kingdom*. Translated by H. de Jongste and edited by Raymond O. Zorn. Philadelphia: Presbyterian & Reformed, 1969.

Rose, Wolter. "Messianic Expectations in the Old Testament." *In die Skriflig* 35 (2001): 275-88.

Schmidt, K. L. "βασιλεύς." *Theological Dictionary of the New Testament*, 1:564-93. Edited by G. Kittel and G. Friedrich. Translated by G. W. Bromiley. 10 vols. Grand Rapids: Eerdmans, 1964-1976.

Seybold, K. "Melek." *Theological Dictionary of the Old Testament*, 7:346-74. Edited by G. J. Botterweck and H. Ringgren. Translated by J. T. Willis, G. W. Bromiley, and D. E.

Green. 8 vols. Grand Rapids: Eerdmans, 1974-.

Thomas, J. C. "The Kingdom of God in the Gospel according to Matthew." *New Testament Studies* 39 (1993): 136-46.

Twelftree, Graham H. *Jesus the Exorcist: A Contribution to the Study of the Historical Jesus.* Tübingen: Mohr (Siebeck), 1993.

Voorwinde, Stephen. *Jesus' Emotions in the Fourth Gospel: Human or Divine?* New York: T. & T. Clark International, 2005.

Vos, Geerhardus. *The Teaching of Jesus concerning the Kingdom of God and the Church.* Grand Rapids: Eerdmans, 1951.

Waltke, Bruce. "The Kingdom of God in Biblical Theology." In *Looking into the Future: Evangelical Studies in Eschatology*, edited by David W. Baker, pp. 15-27. Grand Rapids: Baker Academic, 2001.

Weiss, Johannes. *Jesus' Proclamation and the Kingdom of God.* Translated, edited, and with an introduction by Richard Hyde Hiers and David Larrimore Holland. Philadelphia: Fortress Press, 1971.

Willis, W. ed. *The Kingdom of God in 20th-Century Interpretation.* Peabody: Hendrickson, 1987.

Wolter, Michael. "'Reich Gottes' bei Lukas." *New Testament Studies* 41 (1995): 541-63.

Zorn, Raymond O. *Christ Triumphant: Biblical Perspectives on His Church and Kingdom.* Edinburgh: Banner of Truth, 1997.

# 14. The Parables

*Greg W. Forbes*

The parables are probably the most well-known and most loved aspects of the teaching of Jesus. In fact, a number of proverbial expressions used in Western culture stem from the parables. One who offers timely assistance may be referred to as a "good Samaritan," or a wayward boy is known as a "prodigal son." Many outside of Christian circles are unaware of the original story, and would be quite surprised to know the identity of the storyteller![1]

The purpose of this chapter is to examine the parables of Jesus and their interpretation. Parable research has been a most attractive and fruitful aspect of New Testament (NT) scholarship since the beginning of the twentieth century. As biblical research is about investigating problems in the meaning and interpretation of the text, the parables provide a fertile soil for discussion because of the number of critical issues their investigation raises. Matters such as authenticity, literary genre, theology, historical setting, transmission, and modern relevance continue to be debated with only a limited consensus in certain areas. Our study will begin with the vexing question of whether the parables are to be regarded and interpreted as allegory, before moving on to examine some of the wider interpretive issues. We will conclude with a discussion of why Jesus chose to use such stories, which are at one level so simple yet at another so profound and enigmatic.

## A. The Parables as Allegory

There is no doubt that the main interpretive issue with respect to the parables of Jesus is the extent to which they should be considered allegorical. It should be stressed at the outset that the allegorical interpretation of biblical texts was not a novel innovation of the Christian church. It was the principal exegetical method employed by Philo of Alexandria (c. 20 BC–AD 50), and was a common approach taken by the Qumran sectaries in their interpretation of scripture (an approach known as *pesher*).[2] Underlying this approach was a

---

[1] This assumes essential authenticity of the parables. See further section C, below.

[2] See K. R. Snodgrass, "From Allegorizing to Allegorizing: A History of the Interpretation of the Parables of Jesus," in J. D. G. Dunn and S. McKnight, eds., *The Historical Jesus in Recent Research* (Winona Lake: Eisenbrauns, 2005), p. 249. As an example of *pesher* approach used at Qumran, note the commentary on Hab. 2:2 in 1QpHab 7.1-5: "And God told Habakkuk to write

conviction that Scripture speaks to the concerns of the contemporary era, and thus correspondence was sought between the details of the text and some contemporary reality.

For the church fathers, these concerns centered on elucidating the gospel message, or stressing some aspect of Christian doctrine or practice. Thus many of the Fathers, including Irenaeus, Tertullian, Clement of Alexandria, Origen, and Augustine, understood the parables as detailed allegories that illuminated the above concerns. This gave rise to quite novel interpretations from our point of view,[3] interpretations which varied considerably from one expositor to the next.[4] Voices of protest were heard from the Antiochene Fathers, especially John Chrysostom, but the allegorical method continued unabated.

This approach continued through the medieval period[5] up to the reformation, when it was strongly denounced by Luther and Calvin.[6] In the post-reformation period allegory still prevailed in some circles, while there also appeared what became known as the "historico-prophetical school," where the gospel parables (like the book of Revelation) were seen to contain a prophecy of church history to the present day.[7]

At the end of the nineteenth century, parable research entered a new epoch with the publication of Adolf Jülicher's work *Die Gleichnisreden Jesu*.[8] Jülicher began by drawing a distinction between *simile* and *metaphor*. A *simile* needs no interpretation; its comparison is stated and is obvious. On the other hand a *metaphor* requires interpretation, for it says one and thing but points to another. An *allegory* is an arrangement of metaphors in a narrative, while a *similitude* (*Gleichnis*) is an expanded simile.

Jülicher argued that most parables are similitudes. They are definitely not allegories. Because Jesus' purpose was to instruct the common folk he would not have spoken in such cryptic terms. Moreover, a parable has one point of

---

what was going to happen to the last generation, but he did not let him know the end of the age. And as for what he says: 'So that the one who reads it may run', its interpretation concerns the Teacher of Righteousness, to whom God has disclosed all the mysteries of the words of his servants, the prophets." F. G. Martínez, *The Dead Sea Scrolls Translated: The Qumran Texts in English*, Second Edition (Leiden: Brill, 1994), p. 200.

[3] For example, the often quoted interpretation by Augustine (*Sermons* LX) of the Good Samaritan, where the wounded traveler is fallen man, the robbers are the devil and his angels, the priest and the Levite correspond to the priesthood and ministry of the OT, the innkeeper is the apostle Paul, the inn is the Church, the two coins relate to the two commandments of love, and the binding of the wounds refers to Christ's restraint of sin.

[4] For a fuller treatment of this period, see A. M. Hunter, *Interpreting the Parables* (London: SCM Press, 1960), pp. 21-41; W. S. Kissinger, *The Parables of Jesus: A History of Interpretation and Bibliography* (Metuchen: Scarecrow, 1979), pp. 1-71; R. H. Stein, *An Introduction to the Parables of Jesus* (Philadelphia: Westminster, 1981), pp. 42-52.

[5] For parable interpretation during the medieval period, see S. L. Wailes, *Medieval Allegories of Jesus' Parables* (Berkeley: University of California Press, 1987).

[6] Although ironically Luther continued to use this method himself. See Kissinger, *Parables*, pp. 44-56.

[7] See Hunter, *Interpreting*, p. 35.

[8] A. Jülicher, *Die Gleichnisreden Jesu*, two vols. (Tübingen, J. C. B. Mohr, 1888–1899). This work has never been translated into English.

comparison only (the *tertium comparationis*—literally "the third part of the comparison"—i.e. the point that the two items being compared have in common) which is self explanatory, while other details are simply stage props. Jülicher realized that this reasoning had important ramifications for the interpretations that were appended to some of the synoptic parables, for these interpretations treat the parable as an allegory (e.g. Mark 4:13-20, the Sower). Consequently, he proposed that the parables have an authentic core that goes back to Jesus, but they have been heavily influenced by the evangelists who saw a need to interpret them allegorically.[9]

Jülicher left an enduring legacy. A reluctance to view the parables as allegories in any sense, coupled with an interpretive approach centered on the *tertium comparationis*, persisted in the influential works of C. H. Dodd and J. Jeremias.[10] Although the parables continued to be interpreted at least partly in an allegorical fashion in popular Christianity, allegorical interpretation became decidedly unfashionable in the scholarly guild.[11] This is evident today in some circles, and is typified by the work of the Jesus Seminar[12] as a whole and its various participants who have written individually on the parables.[13] In general terms, the rejection of allegory tends to go hand-in-hand with the contention that the literary setting for the parables provided by the gospel writers is artificial.

Winds of change were evident in the 1970s, when the insights of literary criticism were brought to bear on parable research. Most influential was the study by Madeleine Boucher,[14] who argued that allegory is nothing more than an extended metaphor in narrative form. This narrative may or may not consist of a series of individual metaphors, but this is unimportant. What is important is that the whole meaning of the narrative is a metaphor for something. In other words, any parable that has both a literal and metaphorical meaning should be termed an allegory. Thus the Prodigal Son (Luke 15:11-32) is an allegory, for it refers to more than a son coming home to his father.

---

[9] Jülicher, *Gleichnisreden*, vol. 1, pp. 1-148.

[10] On Dodd and Jeremias, see below.

[11] Some concessions were granted when literary critical approaches began to emphasize the parables as metaphor, whereby metaphor becomes a revelatory image. Nevertheless, interpreters such as D. O. Via, G. V. Jones, and N. Perrin continued to avoid speaking of the parables as allegories.

[12] The Jesus Seminar was convened in 1985 in the USA, and comprises a group of gospel specialists from a particular scholarly persuasion who rated the authenticity of the parables of Jesus. Besides a general tendency to see the framework and interpretation of the parables as secondary, certain parables (e.g. the Rich Man and Lazarus, the Dragnet, the Wheat and Tares) are considered unauthentic as a whole. Furthermore, in all instances the *Gospel of Thomas* version of a parable is preferred. See R. W. Funk, et. al., *The Parables of Jesus: Red Letter Edition* (Sonoma: Polebridge, 1988) and the finalized work of the seminar regarding the sayings of Jesus in Funk, R. Hoover & The Jesus Seminar, *The Five Gospels: What did Jesus Really Say?* (San Francisco: Macmillan, 1993).

[13] See, for example, J. D. Crossan, *In Parables: The Challenge of the Historical Jesus* (San Francisco: Harper and Row, 1985); B. B. Scott, *Hear Then the Parable: A Commentary on the Parables of Jesus* (Minneapolis: Fortress, 1989).

[14] M. Boucher, *The Mysterious Parable: A Literary Study*, CBQMS 6 (Washington: Catholic Biblical Association, 1977).

Similarly, the Friend at Midnight (Luke 11:5-10) is an allegory, for it is more than a story about a neighbor wanting bread.[15] So ~~every parable has two levels~~ of meaning and is therefore allegorical.[16]

The upshot of this approach is that any *a priori* rejection of the parable framework as unauthentic due to the presence of allegory is illegitimate. The frames or parable interpretations may well stem from the evangelist rather than Jesus, but other criteria must establish whether this is the case. Furthermore, even if an interpretation does not go back to Jesus himself, it does not necessarily misread the original meaning of the parable. Rather, the interpretation adapts the parable to a new setting. For instance, the explanation to the Sower (Mark 4:1-9, 13-20) does not transform the parable into an allegory. The parable is already an allegory as it refers to something to do with the kingdom of God, not to sowing literal seed. The interpretation merely restates the parable in explicit literal terms, which is a legitimate exercise undertaken by both exegetes and pastors.[17] This interpretive practice is given further credence by the fact that interpretations to parables and fables, even allegorical interpretations, are not uncommon in rabbinic, other Semitic, or classical literature.[18]

Other important studies have supported the conclusions drawn by Boucher.[19] These studies, together with the growing awareness of the similarity between the rabbinic parables and the parables of Jesus,[20] have meant that many recent interpreters no longer support Jülicher's categorical rejection of allegory. Nevertheless, consensus still does not exist as to whether or not the parables should be considered as allegories *per se*. One extreme is epitomized by the Jesus Seminar, where the allegorical features of the parables are universally seen as reflecting the later situation and interpretive

---

[15] Boucher, *Mysterious Parable*, pp. 20-21. Boucher contends that the problem in the past has been that allegory has been incorrectly defined as a literary genre, when, in fact, it is only a device of meaning or mode. The genre is *parable*, which, in turn, sometimes uses allegory as a mode.

[16] Boucher, *Mysterious Parable*, pp. 22-24.

[17] Boucher, *Mysterious Parable*, pp. 23, 28, 30-31, 40-41. Boucher does not deny that some of the power of the parable is lost when an interpretation is given.

[18] Boucher, *Mysterious Parable*, p. 31.

[19] Hans-Josef Klauck, *Allegorie und Allegorese in synoptischen Gleichnistexten*, NtAbh 13 (Münster: Aschendorff, 1978); H. Weder, *Die Gleichnisse Jesu als Metaphern* (Göttingen: Vandenhoeck & Ruprecht, 1980); M. C. Parsons, "Allegorising Allegory: Narrative Analysis and Parable Interpretation," *PRS* 15 (1988), pp. 147-64; J. M. Ford, "Towards the Restoration of Allegory: Christology, Epistemology and Narrative Structure," *SVTQ* 34 (1990), pp. 161-95; R. L. Wilken, "In Defence of Allegory," *ModTh* 14 (1998), pp. 197-212.

[20] A selection of the more recent literature on this relationship includes, P. Dschulnigg, *Rabbinische Gleichnisse und das Neue Testament* (Bern: Peter Lang, 1988); B. H. Young, *Jesus and his Jewish Parables: Rediscovering the Roots of Jesus' Teaching* (New York: Paulist Press, 1989); H. K. McArthur & R. M. Johnston, *They Also Taught in Parables* (Grand Rapids: Academie Books, 1990); D. Stern, *Parables in Midrash: Narrative and Exegesis in Rabbinic Literature* (Cambridge: Harvard University Press, 1991); C. L. Blomberg, *Interpreting the Parables* (Downers Grove: InterVarsity Press, 1987), pp. 158-68; C. A. Evans, "Parables in Early Judaism," in R. N. Longenecker, ed., *The Challenge of Jesus' Parables* (Grand Rapids: Eerdmans, 2000), pp. 51-75.

stance of the early church. At the other end of the spectrum of modern scholarship, Craig Blomberg proposes that the parables are more allegorical than is normally acknowledged, although they are not necessarily allegorical in every detail. The parables derive their allegorical nature both from the fact that they refer to realities outside of the story, and from the main characters in the story itself, particularly when that character engages in some shocking or extraordinary behavior.[21] Blomberg proposes that we should speak of an *allegory continuum*, with some stories containing a greater percentage of metaphorical referents than others. In fact, part of the artistry of a parable is to leave the audience wondering about which specific details do have a double meaning. Furthermore, the key to interpreting the parables as allegories lies in recognizing the key referents that would have been intelligible to a first century Palestinian audience.[22]

In concluding this part of the discussion, it is difficult to avoid the conviction that not only do the parables contain allegorical details, they may also be considered as allegories at the level of composition. On the one hand, this has been ably demonstrated by literary studies that have shown that the rejection of allegory is based on a narrow and deficient understanding of its function. Allegory is a diverse phenomenon that goes far beyond the level of cryptogram. On the other hand, we need to recognize that Jesus intended to communicate truth about God and humanity through his parables. In other words, the details of a parable have meaning within the story, but some of these details point beyond themselves to higher realities.[23] This explains the quite ironical situation whereby many who deny the existence of allegory still conclude with an allegorical interpretation of some parables.[24]

The acceptance of allegory in the parables of Jesus gains even more credence when the Jewish parallels are examined. Although the rabbinic parables are generally from a period later than the first century they are not irrelevant to the discussion, and there is ample evidence from the parables in the Old Testament (OT) that allegory is not foreign to them.[25] Despite this we

---

[21] Blomberg correctly perceives that the shock element of a parable—e.g. self-respecting middle eastern fathers do not run (cf. Luke 15:20)—can only be resolved by recognizing the allegorical nature of the story. When it is understood, for instance, that the father represents God in his "amazing and love for his ungrateful children" (Blomberg, *Parables*, p. 176) the problem disappears.

[22] Blomberg, *Parables*, pp. 29-69, 133-63. See also *idem*, "Interpreting the Parables of Jesus: Where are we and where do we go from here?" *CBQ* 53 (1991), pp. 63-75. J. W. Sider, "Proportional Analogy in the Gospel Parables," *NTS* 31 (1985), pp. 1-23, also concludes that parable and allegory are one and the same.

[23] "One must conclude that the allegorical features are primarily due to the parable's interconnectedness with the larger story of the gospel." W. Kelber, *The Oral and Written Gospel: The Hermeneutics of Speaking and Writing in the Synoptic Tradition, Mark, Paul and Q* (Philadelphia: Fortress, 1983), pp. 63-64. Kelber is speaking specifically of the parable of the Wicked Tenants (Mark 12:1-12), but the point is applicable generally.

[24] For instance, see J. Jeremias, *The Parables of Jesus* (London: SCM Press, 1963), p. 128, and Hunter, *Interpreting*, pp. 62-63, who both acknowledge that the father of the prodigal son represents God.

[25] See note 20 above for the most recent studies of the relevant Jewish literature.

should not, however, return to the allegorizing exegesis of the Fathers. Such an approach sheds more light on the concerns and teaching of the church, than it does on the concerns and teaching of Jesus.[26] Parables do contain allegorical features, but many of the details of the story are simply stage props and perform no function outside of the story world.

This now leads us into a more general examination of the main interpretive approaches to the parables.

## B. Main Interpretive Approaches to the Parables

Obviously, the issue of whether the parables should be considered allegorical or not is absolutely critical to their interpretation. However, there are also other methodological issues that govern parable interpretation. A common dispute centers on how many points a parable may legitimately make. We begin again with Jülicher.

Jülicher, as we saw above, maintained that a parable has only one point of comparison, the *tertium comparationis*. However, influenced by his liberal theology, Jülicher tended to define the *tertium comparationis* in terms of a general moral truth. This liberalizing tendency was corrected by C. H. Dodd[27] and J. Jeremias,[28] who argued that the parables need to be understood in an eschatological framework (although their understanding of this framework differed), for eschatological crisis was characteristic of their original setting.[29] Jeremias also stressed the importance for parable interpretation of studying the first century Palestinian milieu. The Dodd/Jeremias tradition continued to exert influence over such prominent interpreters such as A. M. Hunter[30] and R. H. Stein. Nevertheless, these interpreters followed Jülicher in seeking for a single point of comparison in the parable.

The idea of a single *tertium comparationis* began to be challenged on a number of fronts, first by what became known as *the new hermeneutic*.[31] This interpretive approach explores the function of speech and word, viewing language as existential address. As such, Jesus' words (especially the parables) are considered as language events which encounter the reader afresh in a new situation, confronting them with a decision regarding authentic

---

[26] Snodgrass, "From Allegorizing to Allegorizing," p. 250.

[27] C. H. Dodd, *The Parables of the Kingdom* (London: Fontana, 1961 [orig. 1935]).

[28] Jeremias, *Parables*. See also his *Jerusalem in the Time of Jesus* (Philadelphia: Fortress, 1969).

[29] However, whereas Dodd interpreted the eschatology of the parables in a fully "realized" sense, J. Jeremias presented a more balanced approach, recognising that eschatology was in the process of being realized.

[30] Hunter, *Interpreting*, esp. pp. 42-91. See also Hunter, *The Parables Then and Now* (London: SCM Press, 1971), pp. 108-121.

[31] On the new hermeneutic in general, see P. J. Achtemeier, *An Introduction to the New Hermeneutic* (Philadelphia: Westminster, 1969); J. M. Robinson and J. B. Cobb Jr., eds., *New Frontiers in Theology II—The New Hermeneutic* (New York: Harper & Row, 1964); A. C. Thiselton, "The New Hermeneutic," in I. H. Marshall, ed., *New Testament Interpretation: Essays on Principles and Methods* (Exeter: Paternoster, 1977), pp. 308-33; A. C. Thiselton, *The Two Horizons* (Grand Rapids: Eerdmans, 1980).

existence. The parables show that God and the kingdom are to be experienced existentially in the ordinary aspects of life, yet their radical aspect leaves us "naked" before their challenge. In this sense the parable becomes, in Norman Perrin's words, "almost impossible to live with."[32] Thus the parables do not teach something about the kingdom, they provoke an experience of the kingdom. The ultimate task of the interpreter is, therefore, to allow the story to speak for itself without attempting to draw lessons from it.[33]

Other voices were being raised against the one point interpretive method championed by Jülicher. For those who were interested in the parables from more of an aesthetic perspective, this model was far too restrictive.[34] This concern was also echoed by those working from a reader-response model.[35] Reader response criticism, a form of post-structuralism, repudiates some of the key features of structuralism.[36] In particular, it argues that there is no objective meaning to a text, for meaning is not dependent on authorial intent but arises out of an interaction between text and reader. In other words, meaning is the subjective creation of the reader, for a text may legitimately say something different to, or more than, the author intended. This is particularly so for the parables, which are polyvalent (i.e. they evidence the ability to interact with readers in different ways) by nature. Not only is all language in itself polyvalent, the metaphors contained in the parables are ubiquitous and untranslatable.[37] When a parable is viewed in these terms, allegory is a possibility, though of course it is not the only possibility.

---

[32] N. Perrin, *Jesus and the Language of the Kingdom: Symbol and Metaphor in New Testament Interpretation* (London: SCM Press, 1976), p. 200.

[33] Perrin, *Language*, pp. 194-205. The key figures of the new hermeneutic regarding the parables of Jesus were Ernst Fuchs, and his students Eberhard Jüngel and Eta Linnemann, although Linnemann sought to combine the historical-critical approach of Jeremias with an existential interpretation. She also followed Jülicher in insisting that a parable has only one point of comparison.

[34] See, for example, D. O. Via, *The Parables: Their Literary and Existential Dimension* (Philadelphia: Fortress, 1977); R. W. Funk, *Language, Hermeneutic and the Word of God: The Problem of Language in the New Testament and Contemporary Theology* (New York: Harper & Row, 1966), pp. 136-47; S. McFague, *Speaking in Parables: A Study in Metaphor and Theology* (Philadelphia: Fortress, 1975), pp. 71-79.

[35] On reader-response criticism, see R. M. Fowler, "Who is 'The Reader' in Reader Response Criticism?" *Semeia* 31 (1985), pp. 5-23; J. P. Tompkins, ed., *Reader-Response Criticism* (Baltimore: Johns Hopkins University Press, 1980); W. W. Klein, *et. al.*, *Introduction to Biblical Interpretation* (Dallas: Word, 1993), pp. 138-45, 438-40.

[36] Structuralism is concerned to analyse the deep structures of language which lie below the surface of narrative fiction and operate in the author's mind at a subconscious level. In contrast to the approach of the new hermeneutic, structuralism assumes that the text has a fixed meaning which can be ascertained. On post-structuralism in general, see D. S. Greenwood, "Poststructuralism and Biblical Studies: Frank Kermode's *The Genesis of Secrecy*," in R. T. France and D. Wenham, eds., *Gospel Perspectives III* (Sheffield: JSOT Press, 1983), pp. 263-88. Greenwood examines the notion of freeplay (the liberties available to the reader), deconstruction (how a literary text dismantles itself) and also looks at the institutional control of interpretation. For a helpful, non-technical summary of post-structuralism and reader-response criticism, see Blomberg, *Parables*, pp. 152-61.

[37] J. D. Crossan, *Cliffs of Fall: Paradox and Polyvalence in the Parables of Jesus* (New York: Seabury, 1980), p. 8.

Others, however, are more cautious of reader-centered models. Blomberg points out that we need to draw the distinction between an objective meaning governed by the original setting of a parable, and multiple contexts for application. The latter is created by the reader but the former is not. To the extent that reader-response criticism emphasizes the freedom and power of the reader to translate the parable into a new context, it is invaluable. However, this is not usually how the discipline advertises itself.[38] A. C. Thiselton contends that reader-response criticism is valuable in the sense that: (1) it deals with different perspectives on a parable; (2) it frees the text from the time bound constraints imposed by the historical-critical model; and (3) it cuts through the false assumption that a text has an obvious meaning apart from the stance and expectations of the interpreter. However, it is inadequate when used in isolation as a single hermeneutical model, for this will inevitably lead to hermeneutical radicalism and interpretive anarchy.[39] Thiselton also notes that the inherent danger of an autonomous text (where meaning is achieved solely by an interaction between text and reader), is that ultimately there is no necessity for the reader (or reading community) to be challenged or transformed by the text. Furthermore, if a text has no objective meaning, then there is no definite Christian message to proclaim, for the principles of revelation and grace have been undermined. Rather, as Thiselton remarks, when meaning is created in the interaction of text and reader, reading the scriptures becomes a process of "religious self discovery" which is "potentially idolatrous."[40]

In the past two decades, scholarly literature on the parables has shown little signs of waning. Given the confines of this study, we will only discuss some of the more significant and relevant contributions.[41] In line with the trend towards a sociological analysis of the NT writings, W. R. Herzog wishes to demonstrate how the parables are a comment on the oppression of the peasant class by the aristocratic ruling class.[42] They do not, therefore, depict the kingdom of God, but are an analysis of the contemporary social situation

---

[38] Blomberg, *Parables*, pp. 152-60.

[39] A. C. Thiselton, "Reader Responsibility Hermeneutics, Action Models and the Parables of Jesus," in Thiselton, et. al., *The Responsibility of Hermeneutics* (Grand Rapids: Eerdmans, 1985), pp. 79-113. An example of such anarchy may be seen in D. O. Via, "The Prodigal Son: A Jungian Reading," *Semeia* 9 (1977), pp. 21-43, where he believes that the parable can be read in terms of the alienation of the ego to self and its subsequent reconciliation. M. A. Tolbert, "The Prodigal Son: An Essay in Literary Criticism from a Psychoanalytical Perspective," *Semeia* 9 (1977), pp. 1-20, believes that the parable illustrates the conflict and desire for resolution that forms the fabric of daily social life.

[40] See A. C. Thiselton, *New Horizons in Hermeneutics* (Grand Rapids: Zondervan, 1992), esp. pp. 546-50. Thistelton's point is this: readers who create meaning will tend to find meaning congenial to them, and thus are in the dangerous position of not being open to challenge, rebuke or change.

[41] For a comprehensive overview of parable research from 1980 to 1994, see Blomberg, "Current Trends," pp. 231-54. For more up-to-date overview, see Snodgrass, "From Allegorising to Allegorising," pp. 248-68.

[42] W. R. Herzog, *Parables as Subversive Speech: Jesus as the Pedagogue of the Oppressed* (Louisville: Westminster/John Knox Press, 1994).

of Jesus, designed to provoke social analysis.

Luise Schottroff[43] is also interested in pursuing a sociological analysis of the parables, but in contrast to Herzog is still concerned to retain the literary setting or the parable frames. Schottroff is opposed to dualistic[44] parable interpretation which helps legitimate oppressive power structures and the gospel for the rich. Parables must not be understood as mere metaphors depicting an external reality, but use everyday language and scenarios in order to demonstrate how those who would live in the kingdom of God are to orientate their lives in the midst of such scenarios.[45] Thus, in agreement with Herzog, wealthy landowners (e.g. Luke 19:11-27) are not pictures of a God who is to be obeyed, but are realistic portrayals of an oppressive economic system that needs to be opposed.

A study which rejects the common consensus that the parables are concerned with the kingdom of God is that presented by C. W. Hedrick.[46] Hedrick believes that the parables must be understood as poetic fiction, that is, simple stories that need no external referents such as the kingdom of God. He contends that the original understanding of the parables was lost very early in the tradition, and consequently allegory and metaphor were utilized to make them comprehensible. Thus Hedrick rejects all the gospel contexts as secondary.[47] As an example of Hedrick's approach, the Good Samaritan (Luke 10:25-37) is understood as an example of what it means to be a righteous man,[48] while the Judge and the Widow (Luke 18:1-8) shows that true righteousness must include proper motives.[49]

While it was the literary critics such as Wilder and Ricoeur who first discussed how Jesus utilized the non-conventional in his parables, more recent studies have pursued this further. G. Aichele looks at the realm of the "fantastic,"[50] while A. Parker examines the disturbing aspects of the parables in terms of cognitive dissonance.[51] Parker argues that the parables are not meant to conceal but to be clearly understood. The aim is to stimulate awareness and to correct attitudes. Thus the parables perform a therapeutic function.

The background for the parables of Jesus has been the attention of several major works. Brad H. Young examines the extant rabbinic parables and

---

[43] L. Schottroff, *The Parables of Jesus* (trans. L. Maloney; Minneapolis: Fortress, 2006).

[44] By this she means a hermeneutical approach where the various metaphors in a parable are always conceived as pointing to another, higher reality.

[45] Schottroff labels this an "eschatological" approach, which is a little confusing. By "eschatology" she means the reign of God impacting life, values and culture in the present.

[46] C. W. Hedrick, *Parables as Poetic Fictions: The Creative Voice of Jesus* (Peabody: Hendrickson, 1994). At a more popular level, see his more recent book *Many Things in Parables: Jesus and His Modern Critics* (Louisville: Westminster/John Knox Press, 2004).

[47] Hedrick, *Poetic Fictions*, pp. 3-89.

[48] Hedrick, *Poetic Fictions*, pp. 113-16.

[49] Hedrick, *Poetic Fictions*, pp. 205-07.

[50] G. Aichele, "The Fantastic in the Parabolic Language of Jesus," *Neot* 24 (1990), pp. 93-105.

[51] A. Parker, *Painfully Clear: The Parables of Jesus* (Sheffield: Sheffield Academic Press, 1996).

concludes that the parables of Jesus and the rabbis reflect a common didactic method employed by Jewish teachers during the Second Temple period.[52] E. Rau, on the other hand, probes beyond late Israelite religious thought and examines the substantial influence of Hellenistic-Roman rhetoric.[53]

Two recent commentaries on the entire corpus of synoptic parables are worthy of mention. Although sharing much in common with J. D. Crossan and other members of the SBL Parables Seminar and the Jesus Seminar, B. B. Scott also advances the view that parables are not just illustrations, but an example of the way in which oral cultures think. Stories become vehicles for thought. Therefore, it is misguided to seek the original form of a parable for Scott considers that "because the parable was oral . . . it passed out of existence as soon as it was spoken."[54] One cannot "possess" an original parable; in oral cultures it is the basic outline or structure that is remembered and performed anew.[55] Parables thus take priority over their context. Consequently, it is unproductive to search for an original setting. A parable indeed had many settings, even in the ministry of Jesus, for Jesus no doubt employed a parable more than once. Scott makes the reasonable observation that "[s]torytellers develop a corpus of stories that they employ in a variety of situations."[56]

Scott also discusses how parables are "antimyth," in that they shatter the world of myth which seeks to overcome life's contradictions.[57] In this sense he agrees with Crossan and Parker, showing how a parable provides new, often novel insights. This is done by employing both resemblance and dissimilarity in order to challenge the preconceived notions of the hearers, thereby forcing them to redefine cherished beliefs and notions.[58]

The work of Craig Blomberg has been referred to on a number of occasions already, and it is perhaps appropriate to conclude this section by summarizing his findings. In line with his basic thesis that the parables are more allegorical than is normally acknowledged, Blomberg is critical of methods which either limit a parable to one meaning or refuse to allow a parable to have any concrete meaning. He points out that if the parables are truly language events that challenge existing belief, then this challenge must be felt as propositional communication. If not, there will be continued

---

[52] B. H. Young, *Jesus and his Jewish Parables: Rediscovering the Roots of Jesus' Teaching* (New York: Paulist Press, 1989). Young's study is marred by his tendency to interpret Jesus and the Synoptic Gospels through the lens of rabbinic Judaism. For example, he argues that the kingdom was not an eschatological but a moral concept. However, this ignores the influence of the prophetic tradition and apocalyptic Judaism. See also the literature cited in note 20, above.

[53] E. Rau, *Reden in Vollmacht: Hintergrund, Form und Anliegen der Gleichnisse Jesu* (Göttingen: Vandenhoeck & Ruprecht, 1990).

[54] Scott, *Hear*, p. 40.

[55] Scott, *Hear*, pp. 37-40.

[56] Scott, *Hear*, p. 42. Note that here Scott also rejects the notion that the original setting was one of conflict with the Pharisees.

[57] Scott, *Hear*, pp. 37-39. At this point Scott interacts with the thought of Lévi-Strauss regarding myth.

[58] Scott, *Hear*, pp. 42-62.

uncertainty about how to respond.[59]

Building on the earlier observation of Funk, Blomberg shows how an analysis of surface structure reveals that a number of the parables reflect a simple triadic structure. Normally this structure embodies a master figure and two subordinates, which equate roughly to God (or his representative), his followers, and his antagonists. The main points of the story align with each main character. Blomberg concludes that each parable tends to make one point per main character (there are usually two or three), and it is the main characters who normally give the parable its allegorical nature.[60]

It is evident that the precise function of the parables remains a debated issue. While it is generally recognized that the parables can no longer be considered merely as simple stories designed to illustrate and educate, clearly this is one of their intended functions.[61]

To some extent, one's understanding of function is determined by how one interprets the enigmatic statement of Mark 4:10-12.[62] Apart from this, however, there is still a limited consensus. While the parables disarm the hearer/reader by their everyday realism and simplicity, the use of hyperbole, extravagance, and the unusual are obviously designed to shock. This shock element is, in turn, designed to challenge and provoke a certain response. Nevertheless, there is disagreement as to whether the majority of the parables should be understood in the context of conflict, or in terms of an existential challenge to the disciples. Perhaps the answer lies not in either/or but in both/and.

A final methodological issue concerns the distinction that is sometimes drawn between a parable proper and the so-called *example stories*. This latter category relates particularly to four parables unique to Luke's Gospel—the Good Samaritan (10:25-37), the Rich Fool (12:13-21), the Rich Man and Lazarus (16:19-31) and the Pharisee and the Tax Collector (18:9-14). Following Jülicher, these four stories were seen as distinct from the other narrative parables on the ground that they contain no obvious metaphors but rather teach a direct moral truth. However, Boucher's study questions this distinction on the ground that the parable as a whole is a metaphor because it points to something beyond itself. Whether there are individual metaphors within the story or not is irrelevant to genre classification. It has also been demonstrated from an analysis of ancient rhetorical treatises that all parables should be considered examples of something (e.g. behavior), while those labeled *example stories* by modern scholars could easily be termed *parables* by ancient authors. Thus the distinction is an artificial scholarly construct.[63]

---

[59] Blomberg, *Parables*, pp. 133-44.

[60] Blomberg, *Parables*, pp. 162-63.

[61] B. Gerhardsson, "If we do not cut the Parables out of their Frames," *New Testament Studies* 37 (1991), pp. 321-28, argues that when we treat the parables in the frames in which they come, we see that their main function is to clarify and teach. Sometimes they may attack or defend, but this is a secondary aim only. He states, "they are designed by a man with a message which he wants to elucidate." (p. 328).

[62] The main lines of interpretation are discussed in section D, below.

[63] J. T. Tucker, *Example Stories: Perspectives on Four Parables in the Gospel of Luke*,

From the survey presented above, it can be seen that it has become fashionable in recent times to deny the validity of interpreting the parables, at least in terms of propositional speech. It is argued that we must simply let the parables speak, for they cannot, by their very nature, be cast into a propositional mould. Others emphasize the polyvalent nature of the parables, refusing to concede that a text has an objective, fixed meaning.

Although it is definitely true that a parable has a certain intrinsic force when it remains a parable, every reader comes to the text with the goal of interpretation. No text speaks of itself. Furthermore, Jesus obviously meant to communicate something tangible, not to offer unlimited possibilities.[64] While it may be difficult to regain Jesus' precise intention in certain instances (e.g. Luke 16:1-8, The Dishonest Manager), the synoptic evangelists certainly understood the tradition in a particular way. They attempted to communicate their understanding of the significance of that tradition by placing it in a given setting and providing interpretive comments either drawn from the tradition or provided by themselves (e.g. Luke 16:8b-13; 18:1, 14). In other words, the evangelists want their readers to learn something concrete from the text.

The dangers of reader-response method have already been discussed. Consequently, while not wanting to downplay the importance of the pre-understanding of the reader, reader-response needs some regulation if it is going to avoid the pitfalls of interpretive anarchy or listlessness. This control is best provided by the historical-grammatical meaning of the text, with particular attention paid to the literary context. There is no doubt that the more one is inclined to reject the literary context provided by the gospels the more loose and nebulous parable interpretation becomes.

It would also appear to be methodologically unsound to ignore the OT and rabbinic parallels in favor of modern literary-critical fashions. Indeed, the more novel interpretations proposed in recent times seem more indebted to a personal ideology than a concern for accurate historical analysis or exegesis. As one observer has recently noted, many interpreters have shifted from being hearers and interpreters of the parables, to become authors of parables instead.[65]

The sociological approach of Herzog and Schottroff is certainly gaining in popularity. This is the result not only of a more informed understanding of first-century Palestinian society and the Greco-Roman world but also of a more diverse range of contemporary NT scholars able to identify with the oppressive structures of that society and world. However, although Herzog's work is insightful in many respects, it is ultimately marred by his unilateral rejection of the literary setting given by the gospel writers. Once this is jettisoned, any ideological approach is possible. Schottroff is on firmer ground

---

JSNTSup 162 (Sheffield: Sheffield Academic Press, 1998).

[64] Stein, *Parables*, pp. 68-69. See also his discussion of parable genre and assessment of the strengths and weaknesses of the ascetic and existential approaches to parable interpretation in R. H. Stein, "The Genre of the Parables," in R. N. Longenecker, ed., *The Challenge of Jesus' Parables* (Grand Rapids: Eerdmans, 2000), pp. 30-50.

[65] Snodgrass, "From Allegorising to Allegorising," p. 263.

in advocating retention of the parable frames and literary setting, although the retention of this setting at times ironically supports an interpretation of the parable that she rejects.[66]

## C. The Authenticity of the Parables

The matter of authenticity has surfaced at times throughout our discussion. Here we will attempt an overview and an assessment of the current situation.

It has been the general consensus of twentieth century scholarship that the parables are the closest we come to the *ipsissima vox* (authentic voice) of Jesus. This is so because of their reflection of a Palestinian background, their use of Aramaic idiom, and their tendency to satisfy the other so-called criteria for authenticity.[67] However, it has been an enduring legacy of Jülicher that an authentic core of a parable is often separated from the appended framework. The latter, which often does not appear to capture the central feature of a parable, is seen as the work of the early church or the evangelists, who sought to interpret the parables along allegorical lines.

The above approach is fairly representative of modern scholarship, and has been popularized in recent times by the Jesus Seminar. However, those scholars who are willing to concede that the parables are allegories in one form or another are also more willing to view the interpretations as authentic. Blomberg, for example, points out that as parables should be considered as allegories, their interpretations are consistent with this fact. Furthermore, most parables make more than one point. Thus the logia that surround a parable in its literary context relates to a point that can be legitimately derived from the parable.[68] Moreover, the OT and rabbinic parables reflect a tendency for explanations to be appended, and we should not underestimate the authenticity of their presence in the synoptic parables.[69]

J. W. Sider has also produced a forceful and well-argued attack on the

---

[66] For instance, Schottroff, *Parables*, p. 56, regards the parable of the Great Feast (Luke 14:15-24) as a challenge to the meal practice of the hearers and the need for them to consider the rights of the poor. However, the literary setting (v. 15) clearly points to the feast being understood as a metaphor for the messianic banquet.

[67] Apart from Palestinian background, the criteria for authenticity are normally seen as dissimilarity, multiple attestation and coherence. For a discussion of these criteria, see R. H. Stein, "The 'Criteria' for Authenticity," in R. T. France and D. Wenham, eds., *Gospel Perspectives I* (Sheffield: JSOT Press, 1980), pp. 225-63; S. C. Goetz and C. L. Blomberg, "The Burden of Proof," *JSNT* 11 (1981), pp. 39-63; C. L. Blomberg, *The Historical Reliability of the Gospels* (Downers Grove: InterVarsity Press, 1987), pp. 246-54. For acceptance of the originating structure of the parables because of dissimilarity see Scott, *Hear*, pp. 63-64.

[68] Blomberg, *Parables*, p. 93. For example, he notes how the three appendices to Luke 16:1-8 (The Dishonest Manager) each fit a particular theme: God's commendation, the steward's cleverness and the heavenly reception. In addition, he argues that most parables have some kind of interpretation, no matter how brief.

[69] Based on a study of Jewish parables, C. H. Cave, "The Parables and the Scriptures," *NTS* 11 (1964-65), pp. 374-87, shows the importance of examining the literary context for parable interpretation.

Jeremias tradition.[70] He argues that hypothesis builds on hypothesis to produce a supposed reconstruction of the original text that is, at best, subjective and dubious. Finding support from secular literary critics such as Northrop Frye, he claims that we must deal with the texts as they stand in the gospels. While those texts may not be totally authentic, they are more reliable than any proposed reconstruction.[71]

In his later work on the parables of Luke 15, Bailey makes some further important contributions to the study of the parables. He contends that Jesus of Nazareth must be seen not merely as a storyteller or an example of love, but as a serious theologian with a powerful and astute mind. Furthermore, in telling his parables Jesus stood in the OT and wider Middle Eastern tradition where metaphor and simile were the primary focus of speech, creating meaning rather than merely illustrating a concept. This is the opposite of Western thought where a concept is proposed with the option of illustrating that concept if so desired. Nevertheless, it is significant that in Middle Eastern thought metaphor and simile do not stand alone. In many cases the metaphor is enclosed within, or is followed by, a conceptual interpretation. Thus, although the conceptual interpretation is of secondary importance, it is still a legitimate component of thought.[72]

This, of course, has enormous implications for the authenticity of the interpretations attached to the gospel parables. It can no longer be simply assumed that such interpretations are unauthentic creations of the early church or of the evangelists, because the method of metaphor with interpretation has firm roots in both OT tradition and in the cultural milieu.[73]

It appears then, that once a *prima facie* case for understanding the parables as allegory in some measure is established, much of the rationale for considering their interpretive framework as secondary disappears. In addition, once it is recognized that metaphor and interpretation are a common feature of

---

[70] The Jeremias tradition is that which works from a reconstruction of a supposed original parable rather than from the form found in the literary setting. Sider includes in this tradition such scholars as Hunter, Linnemann, Funk, Via, and Crossan.

[71] J. W. Sider, "Rediscovering the Parables: The Logic of the Jeremias Tradition," *JBL* 102 (1983), pp. 61-83. Thiselton, "Reader Responsibility," pp. 100-101, is critical of Sider for polarising history and literature. He points out that not all historical inquiry is sceptical, nor does it work at cross purposes to the task of doing justice to the text. This criticism of Sider appears somewhat harsh. Sider is not denigrating all historical inquiry, merely that which presumes unauthenticity then believes that it can offer an objective reconstruction.

[72] K. E. Bailey, *Finding the Lost: Cultural Keys to Luke 15* (St Louis: Concordia, 1992), pp. 15-28.

[73] Bailey offers Isa. 55:8-9 as one example of parable enclosed within conceptual thought:

For my thoughts are not your thoughts,
nor are your ways my ways, says the Lord.
For as the heavens are higher than the earth,
so are my ways higher than your ways
and my thoughts than your thoughts.

Note also Isa. 5:1-7, where the Song of the Vineyard is followed by an explanation to the effect that the vineyard is to be understood as the nation of Israel who had failed to yield justice and righteousness.

OT literature, Middle Eastern tradition and the rabbinic parables, it becomes intellectually untenable simply to ignore the appended framework. Of course, this does not prove that such framework originates with Jesus, for in many cases it clearly does not (e.g. Luke 18: 1, 9). However, the issue must be decided by contextual factors and no longer dismissed on *a priori* grounds.[74] In any case, the framework gives the reader a clear understanding of how the Evangelist wants the parable to be understood, and if our goal is to interpret the parables in their literary and theological setting, the interpretations become indispensable.

## D. The Role of the Parables in the Teaching of Jesus

Given that roughly thirty-five percent of the content of Jesus' teaching in the Synoptic Gospels is in parables, it is important to determine why Jesus used this particular method. Although Jesus was not unique in the use of parables, his parables themselves are unique with respect to their number and their vividness.[75] What was he actually trying to achieve with these simple, yet strikingly profound picture stories? Here we draw on the history of interpretation surveyed above, and also introduce some new factors.

The first thing that can be said is that the parables are not simply illustrations of more direct teaching given elsewhere. Nor are they exegetical in the sense of being concerned with scriptural exposition. Rather, in the words of Hultgren, "the parables are themselves front and center bearers of the message of Jesus."[76] This message is primarily the kingdom of God. They describe the kingdom of God in terms of its timing, its nature, and the response it demands. With respect to its timing, the parables of growth (Mark 4:26-32) highlight the veiled nature of the kingdom. It is inconspicuous at present, but is growing to fulfillment. God's rule has been inaugurated, but the final harvest awaits. But this future harvest has a dual outcome; consequently there is the need for decision (Matt. 13:24-30, 47-50). The kingdom demands a response, and entry is only via repentance and faith. Participants in the messianic banquet are not chosen on the grounds of physical descent or racial identity (Luke 13:6-9; 14:15-24; 16:19-31), but all who accept the invitation

---

[74] Another factor that has a bearing on the authenticity of the parables and their interpretations is the issue of gospel genre. Until recently this has been a rather unfruitful area of gospel research, with no consensus reached (except, perhaps, that the gospels present an entirely new genre). However, the recent work of R. A. Burridge, *What are the Gospels? A Comparison with Graeco-Roman Biography*, SNTSMS 70 (Cambridge: Cambridge University Press, 1992) has demonstrated that the gospels should be considered as an example of the Greco-Roman βίος, which aims to preserve the memory of a central figure. (While there are some unique features in the gospels, the difference between them and the βίοι are no greater than those in the βίοι themselves). In the gospels, the central figure is Jesus, and as the gospels were written within the lifetime of Jesus' contemporaries, there would certainly have been restriction on free composition.

[75] A. J. Hultgren, *The Parables of Jesus: A Commentary* (Grand Rapids: Eerdmans, 2000), pp. 8-10 discusses what he regards as other unique features of Jesus' parables.

[76] A. J. Hultgren, *Parables*, p. 8.

are welcome including outcasts, sinners, the marginalized—even Gentiles (Mark 12:1-12; Luke 14:15-24; 15:1-3).

In view of the imminent consummation of the kingdom there is a need for watchfulness (Matt. 25:1-13), and watchfulness entails the servants of the kingdom using their time wisely and productively (Luke 12:35-48). Of course there are various obstacles to entering the kingdom (Mark 4:1-9, 13-20), but whatever cost one pays for a reorientation of values, or a re-prioritization of time, is ultimately worth it. The value of the kingdom is priceless; it is worth giving up all to enter (Matt. 13:44-46). The kingdom also carries with it ethical demands. The servant of the kingdom must live simply and care for the poor (Luke 12:13-21; 16:19-31), loving one's neighbor as oneself (Luke 10:25-37).

The parables also give instruction regarding the nature of the God of the kingdom.[77] In this way insight is gained as to the motivation for the kingdom's presence. God is approachable and answers prayer (Luke 11:5-8; 18:1-8). He is merciful (Luke 13:6-9; 18:9-14), and is prepared to engage in radical behavior in order to seek out the lost so they may participate in his kingdom (Luke 15:1-32). In fact, it is at this point that we encounter some of the most radical features of the parables, for God is sometimes portrayed in extravagant ways and by means of atypical (Matt. 22:1-10; Luke 14:15-24) or even unscrupulous characters (Luke 18:1-8).

There is no doubt that Jesus creatively used his cultural and life experiences in the formation of his parabolic stories. And it is here that we see the value of story as a didactic method. Not only are stories vivid, they draw on a shared cultural experience and thus create immediate rapport with the hearer.[78] Furthermore, stories are easy to remember and lead to a thirst for more. There is the additional benefit for the storyteller insofar as the audience is able to identify more clearly in story than in propositional speech. Whereas the latter can lead to the erection of protective barriers, stories have potential to bypass them.[79]

Possibly one of the reasons that Jesus was able to avoid arrest for so long was that he was able to disarm his opponents by the use of parables. The story elicits agreement, then confronts them with the reality of their own condition. In the OT we have a splendid example of this strategy in Nathan's entrapment of David in 2 Sam. 12:1-15. In the gospels, such a situation occurs in the telling of the parable of the Two Sons (Matt. 21:28-32). This approach is not only effective in disarming opponents, but also in prompting the recalcitrant.

At other times Jesus apparently states that the function of his parabolic teaching is to conceal. Crucial here is the disputed text Mark 4:10-12. The

---

[77] See Greg W. Forbes, *The God of Old: The Role of the Lukan Parables in the Purpose of Luke's Gospel* (Sheffield: Sheffield Academic Press, 2000), pp. 225-306.

[78] This rapport is also created by means of the common introductory formula "Which one of you. . .?"

[79] On storytelling and the value of story, see W. J. Bausch, *Storytelling: Imagination and Faith* (Connecticut: Twenty-Third Publications, 1984); R. L. Lewis, & G. Lewis, *Learning to Preach Like Jesus* (Westchester: Crossway, 1989); N. Mellon, *Storytelling and the Art of Imagination* (Rockport: Element, 1992).

main lines of interpretation are as follows. First, Mark has misunderstood the use of παραβολή in the narrow sense of *parable* when in fact it means *riddle/secret*. Consequently these verses belong to another context and refer to Jesus' proclamation as a whole.[80] Second, the force of ἵνα should be reduced to mean *unless* or *because* (following *Tg. Isa.* 9:6-10 which Mark's quote most closely resembles). Third, there was a mistranslation of the Aramaic *de* which should read *who*.[81] Fourth, ἵνα introduces the OT quote.[82] Fifth, the verses reflect a setting in the early church and show why the Jews rejected Jesus.[83] Sixth, the saying relates only to the parable of the Sower.[84] Seventh, the saying is authentic in this context and differentiates between cognitive hearing only (i.e. *those outside*) and true hearing.[85] The latter option seems to be the most natural solution to the problem as it fits with the repeated commands to *listen* in vv. 3, 9, 23, and 33. Consequently, the parables appear as riddles to the spiritually obtuse, thus further cementing their fate.

As various recent scholars have noted, it is too simplistic to regard Jesus' parables merely as nice stories designed to educate. They are meant to evoke a response, and as such frequently have "shocking" elements. Not only are there some unscrupulous characters, such as an unjust judge (Luke 18:1-8) and a dishonest manager (Luke 16:1-8), some parables have quite unexpected plot development and outcomes. A couple of examples will suffice.

In the parable of the Lost Sheep (Luke 15:4-7) Jesus invites his audience to assume the role of a shepherd. But according to the literary context his prime audience is the religious authorities. What is shocking for them is that they are being asked to imagine themselves in an unclean occupation. However, the irony is they actually are shepherds of the nation (cf. Ezek. 34:1-31), and are now confronted with the humiliating charge that they have lost part of the flock! A further shock element is evident in the image of God seeking out the lost and rejoicing over those being brought home. While the religious authorities would have found no problem accepting that the lost could repent, that God would go and seek them out is another thing altogether.[86]

Another example of the shock factor of the parables is evident in the parable of the Pharisee and the Tax Collector (Luke 18:9-14). The Pharisee was a highly regarded member of Jewish society,[87] and on the surface his prayer is nothing but a factual statement of his own position. A tax collector,

---

[80] Jeremias, *Parables*, pp. 13-18

[81] T. W. Manson, *The Teaching of Jesus* (Cambridge: Cambridge University Press, 1935), pp. 78-80.

[82] W. L. Lane, *The Gospel of Mark*, NICNT (Grand Rapids: Eerdmans, 1974), p. 159.

[83] Dodd, *Parables*, pp. 13-15; C. E. Carlston, *The Parables of the Triple Tradition* (Philadelphia: Fortress, 1975), pp. 97-109.

[84] G. V. Jones, *Art and Truth*, pp. 225-30.

[85] Boucher, *Mysterious Parable*, pp. 42-63; Klauck, *Allegorie*, p. 251; S. J. Kistemaker, *The Parables of Jesus* (Grand Rapids: Baker, 1980), pp. xviii-xix; Blomberg, *Parables*, pp. 40-41; J. Marcus, *The Mystery of the Kingdom of God* (Atlanta: Scholars Press, 1986), pp. 73-123.

[86] Forbes, *God of Old*, pp. 113-24.

[87] See Josephus, *J.W.* 1.110; 2.162; *Ant.* 18.14-15.

on the other hand, was a despised occupation due to the propensity for dishonesty, not to mention the need for collaboration with the Romans. No doubt the original audience would have been profoundly shocked at the pronouncement of Jesus. The Pharisee had merely told the truth, whereas the tax collector had asked for forgiveness, but had done nothing in the form of offering restitution as a tangible sign of repentance. Of course the audience is being asked to re-evaluate not only their understanding of true piety but also to recognize that comparing oneself to others is of little value in the economy of God. Moreover God accepts anyone on the basis of a repentant heart.[88]

## E. Conclusion

The winds of change have certainly blown strongly over the last century with respect to parable interpretation, and it would probably be most unwise to think that all available avenues for study have been exhausted.[89] Progress has been made, with limited consensus in certain areas. Allegory is no longer the object of horror that it once was, although there is little agreement on precisely how much allegory the parables of Jesus contain. Most agree that in the parables we come as close as anywhere to the authentic voice of Jesus, although some would want to differentiate between an authentic parable core and the secondary nature of the appended framework.

While there is a certain value in the parable remaining parable, there seems little value in the approaches that seek to deny the validity of concrete interpretation. Yes, the parables may be polyvalent to some extent, but it is hard to escape the conclusion that Jesus did intend to convey some meaning or evoke some response from his hearers.

What is certain is that the parables are not to be regarded merely as simple stories designed to educate. They do that, but they do much more. They confront, challenge and regularly shock the hearer by the use of atypical characters or unexpected conclusions. Often these features are neglected or missed because they demand a certain familiarity with first century Palestinian culture, or have been sanitized by centuries of use in an ecclesiastical setting.

A final word regarding the teaching and preaching of the parables in the contemporary church. There is anecdotal evidence that the parables have been somewhat ignored from the pulpit in recent years due to the sheer difficulty of knowing how to treat them. If the scholarly world presents such a huge diversity of opinion on parable interpretation, then the easiest way out is probably to look elsewhere for sermon material. But this would be a shame, for if Jesus used the parabolic medium to convey the essence of his teaching—the kingdom of God—then the church as a proclaimer of the kingdom can only ignore the parables to its own detriment.

---

[88] Forbes, *God of Old*, pp. 211-21.

[89] As did G. V. Jones, *The Art and Truth of the Parables* (London: SPCK, 1964), p. x: "I doubt, moreover, if many further lines of interpretation can be explored than those which have already been established."

## Bibliography

Bailey, Kenneth E. *Finding the Lost: Cultural Keys to Luke 15*. St Louis: Concordia, 1992.

Blomberg, Craig. L. *Interpreting the Parables*. Downers Grove: InterVarsity Press, 1990.

Boucher, Madeleine. *The Mysterious Parable: A Literary Study*. Washington: Catholic Biblical Association, 1977.

Crossan, John Dominic. *Cliffs of Fall: Paradox and Polyvalence in the Parables of Jesus*. New York: Seabury, 1980.

————. *In Parables: The Challenge of the Historical Jesus*. San Francisco: Harper and Row, 1985.

Evans, Craig. A. "Parables in Early Judaism." In *The Challenge of Jesus' Parables*, edited by Richard N. Longenecker, pp. 51-75. Grand Rapids: Eerdmans, 2000.

Forbes, Greg W. *The God of Old: The Role of the Lukan Parables in the Purpose of Luke's Gospel*. Sheffield: Sheffield Academic Press, 2000.

Hedrick, Charles W. *Parables as Poetic Fictions: The Creative Voice of Jesus*. Peabody: Hendrickson, 1994.

————. *Many Things in Parables: Jesus and His Modern Critics*. Louisville: Westminster John Knox Press, 2004.

Herzog, William R. *Parables as Subversive Speech: Jesus as the Pedagogue of the Oppressed*. Louisville: Westminster John Knox Press, 1994.

Hultgren, Arland J. *The Parables of Jesus: A Commentary*. Grand Rapids: Eerdmans, 2000.

Jones, Geraint Vaughan. *The Art and Truth of the Parables: A Study in their Literary Form and Modern Interpretation*. London: SPCK, 1964.

Kissinger, Warren S. *The Parables of Jesus: A History of Interpretation and Bibliography*. American Theological Library Association; Metuchen: Scarecrow Press, 1979.

Marcus, Joel. *The Mystery of the Kingdom of God*. Atlanta: Scholars Press, 1986.

McArthur, Harvey K., and Robert M. Johnston. *They Also Taught in Parables: Rabbinic Parables from the first Centuries of the Christian Era*. Grand Rapids: Academie Books, 1990.

McFague, Sallie. *Speaking in Parables: A Study in Metaphor and Theology*. Philadelphia: Fortress Press, 1975.

Parker, A. *Painfully Clear: The Parables of Jesus*. Sheffield: Sheffield Academic Press, 1996.

Perrin, Norman. *Jesus and the Language of the Kingdom: Symbol and Metaphor in New Testament Interpretation*. London: SCM Press, 1976.

Schottroff, Luise. *The Parables of Jesus*. Translated by Linda Maloney. Minneapolis: Fortress Press, 2006.

Scott, Bernard Brandon. *Hear Then the Parable: A Commentary on the Parables of Jesus*. Minneapolis: Fortress Press, 1989.

Stein, Robert H. *An Introduction to the Parables of Jesus*. Philadelphia: Westminster Press, 1981.

————. "The Genre of the Parables." In *The Challenge of Jesus' Parables*, edited by Richard N. Longenecker, pp. 30-50. Grand Rapids: Eerdmans, 2000.

Stern, David. *Parables in Midrash: Narrative and Exegesis in Rabbinic Literature*. Cambridge: Harvard University Press, 1991.

Tucker, Jeffrey T. *Example Stories: Perspectives on Four Parables in the Gospel of Luke*. Sheffield: Sheffield Academic Press, 1998.

Via, Dan O. *The Parables: Their Literary and Existential Dimension*. Philadelphia: Fortress Press, 1980.

Young, Brad H. *Jesus and his Jewish Parables: Rediscovering the Roots of Jesus' Teaching*. New York: Paulist Press, 1989.

# 15. The Ethics of Jesus

*Brian Powell*

This chapter will address this topic with some secondary attention to the actions of Jesus, since the gospel writers do make some significant connection between the two. Relevant material from all the canonical gospels, but mainly the Synoptic Gospels, will be considered, but particular attention will be given to the Sermon on the Mount (Matthew 5–7), since it is at once an especially rich source of ethical teaching and especially challenging to those who seek to interpret it.

It is no easy task to provide a coherent account of Jesus' ethical teaching. In fact, many Christians have found it so difficult that Glen Stassen and David Gushee are able to argue, with at least some measure of justice, that the history of Christian ethics has frequently been marked not by its building on the foundation of Jesus' teaching and practice but by its evasion of that teaching and practice. More specifically, they observe that the Sermon on the Mount has seldom figured prominently in textbooks on Christian ethics.[1]

The difficulty is certainly not lessened if one attempts to provide such an account within the confines of a single chapter within a more general book. Robert Stein begins such an attempt by identifying four major problems and several lesser interpretive issues.[2] The first major problem which he identifies is that the record of Jesus' ethical teachings in the gospels is unsystematic and scattered. The second is that many ethical issues are either not addressed or addressed only very briefly, at times simply in passing. The third is the apparently contradictory nature of some of his teachings. Here Stein offers as examples Jesus' apparent attitude to the Jewish law and the apparent conflict between his words on reward and his emphasis on grace. The fourth is the apparent impossibility of his ethical demands. There is general recognition of these four problems, but disagreement over their magnitude, and over the extent to which they can be resolved.

There have been varied responses to these and other perceived problems by scholars, to which we shall now turn.

---

[1] See the preface (pp. xi-xvi) to their *Kingdom Ethics: Following Jesus in Contemporary Context* (Downers Grove: InterVarsity Press, 2003).

[2] See his *The Method and Message of Jesus' Teachings*, rev. ed. (Louisville: Westminster John Knox Press, 1994), ch. 6 entitled: "The Content of Jesus' Teaching: the Ethics of the Kingdom." The introductory remarks mentioned are found on pp. 90-91.

## A. Survey of Scholarship

This survey is deliberately brief so as to avoid devoting an excessive proportion of the chapter to it. Such surveys are available.[3]

One approach, which has sought to deal particularly with the difficulty of the perceived extremity of Jesus' demands and with the tension between grace and reward, has been that of distinguishing between two levels of discipleship, an approach particularly associated with Roman Catholicism but by no means unknown among Protestants. Some of Jesus' ethical teachings, such as the commandment to love God and one's neighbor, are seen as applicable to all Christians. But others, such as the call to surrender all personal possessions, are seen as applicable only to some Christians, those who are living in some way at a "higher" level. This approach has the merit of attempting to give practical relevance to all of Jesus' ethical teachings without undermining the gracious offer of salvation to all who repent and believe.

But it is difficult to find a basis for this distinction in the gospel records. Matthew introduces the Sermon on the Mount (5:1-2) by saying that Jesus was teaching "his disciples," without any suggestion of restriction, and some of Jesus' most demanding sayings are clearly recorded in inclusive terms. For example, Mark records Jesus as saying that "any" who want to follow him are to "deny themselves and take up their cross" (8:34), and Matthew's slightly different wording (10:38) is equally inclusive. Similarly, Luke records the subjects addressed by the confronting demand to "hate" one's family as "whoever" comes to Jesus to be his disciple.

Another way of restricting the applicability of Jesus' ethical demands is found in the approach which limits the period to which they apply. The most influential version of this approach is the one developed by Johannes Weiss and Albert Schweitzer. They emphasized the eschatological character of Jesus' teaching, and saw him advocating an "interim ethic," a temporary ethic for the brief period which he expected to elapse between the beginning of his public ministry and the coming of the kingdom of God in its full reality. Thus Jesus' radical ethical demands are not directly applicable to the historical circumstances which have actually come to pass.

This approach rightly connects Jesus' ethical teaching with his proclamation of the kingdom, but it relies on an understanding of that proclamation which gives exclusive credence to the note of an imminent future in the gospel record at the expense of other features. Moreover, it is not characteristic of Jesus' ethical teaching to appeal to an imminent crisis as the ground for action. More often he appeals to grounds of a quite different kind, such as the character of God (e.g. Luke 6:32-36) or God's will as expressed in creation (e.g. Mark 10:2-9). An example of an appeal to an imminent crisis is when Jesus instructs his disciples to move on to another town when

---

[3] This survey largely follows that of Stein in *Method and Message*, pp. 91-99. Dale Allison provides one focused specifically on the Sermon on the Mount on pp. 1-7 of his *The Sermon on the Mount* (New York: Crossroad, 1999). Stassen and Gushee provide a survey which traces the history of the church on pp. 128-32 of their *Kingdom Ethics*.

persecuted, since they "will not have gone through all the towns of Israel before the Son of Man comes" (Matt. 10:23). But this is "ethical" instruction only in a rather restricted sense, and the meaning of the reference to the coming of the Son of Man is subject to considerable scholarly debate.[4]

An approach which contrasts with both the previous two is that which declares that Jesus' ethical teachings are applicable to all Christians of all times, to be understood literally and obeyed. Such an approach has been followed by a number of groups and individuals across history, such as the Anabaptists and Leo Tolstoy. This approach deserves respect for its earnest desire to take Jesus' teaching seriously, but it is vulnerable to criticism on two fronts. It can be criticized on the pragmatic basis that human beings have consistently failed to live in the fashion envisaged by this approach, even within groups which have embraced the challenge. More seriously, perhaps, it is by no means evident that this approach does the justice to Jesus' intent which it desires to do. Is literalism consistently the way to take seriously a teacher who readily employed figurative language and hyperbole? And does their emphasis on the demands made by Jesus do justice to his gracious welcoming of sinners, or his patience with the failures of his disciples?

A fourth approach, which is associated particularly with Lutheranism, agrees with the previous one that full weight should be given to the high demand embodied in Jesus' ethical teaching, but disagrees that this is to be done by obeying his teachings. Rather, to take Jesus' ethical demands seriously is to confront one's own incapacity to obey and thus to be driven to the proper response of repentance and reliance in faith upon the righteousness of Jesus. This approach is realistic about human weakness and emphasizes the grace of God. But does it reflect the way in which Jesus' ethical teaching is presented in the gospels? There is certainly no positive encouragement for this interpretation, and the fact that much of Jesus' ethical teaching is said to be addressed to disciples (e.g. Matt. 5:1; Luke 6:20) seems to tell against it. Moreover, Jesus is recorded in several places as expecting that his disciples will act in accordance with his teaching (e.g. Matt. 7:24-27; Mark 10:41-45; Luke 6:43-49).

Another approach is to identify the enduring essence of Jesus' ethical teaching. One version of this approach, which is often termed the "liberal" approach, identifies that enduring essence as an inner disposition of love. Another version, which is often termed "existentialist," identifies it as a call for radical personal decision to follow Jesus. Both versions tend to minimize the importance of specific ethical teachings. Both are successful in highlighting important dimensions of Jesus' teaching. It is clear that he did give importance to one's inner disposition and to love of God and neighbor, and that he did call for a decision to follow him. But Jesus did also show a concern for actions as the fruit of right disposition (Matt. 7:15-20; Luke 6:43-45). And he addressed numerous specific ethical issues, often in a fashion

---

[4] See, for example, John Nolland's discussion on pp. 426-29 of his *The Gospel of Matthew* (Grand Rapids: Eerdmans, 2005) and that of Ulrich Luz on pp. 91-94 of his *Matthew 8–20* (Minneapolis: Fortress Press, 2001).

which seems to give importance to actions in these specific areas as an expression of discipleship. Possible examples include the right way to give alms (Matt. 6:2-4), forgiving offences (Mark 11:25) and showing love of enemies through one's actions (Luke 6:27-31).

No approach is likely to resolve all difficulties associated with understanding the ethics of Jesus. But Scot McKnight is right when he insists that the ethic of Jesus has "its moorings in what he affirmed about God and the kingdom."[5] Further, if we accept that Jesus proclaimed the kingdom of God as at once present and future,[6] then his ethical teaching must be understood within this context. If so, then it makes real demands on his disciples in the world as it is now, but their response to these demands is affected by the tension between living under God's rule as having come in Jesus and living as imperfect disciples in a world which still awaits the final consummation of God's rule. The remainder of this chapter represents an attempt to approach the ethics of Jesus in such a way, and accordingly begins with a consideration of their relationship with the kingdom of God.

## B. Keys to Interpretation

After he has surveyed various approaches to the Sermon on the Mount, Dale Allison remarks that they generally err by being one-sided and unduly simplifying. Accordingly, he then sets out not to offer a fully integrated approach of his own but rather "several generalizations" which "may serve us as exegetical guidelines."[7] This wise humility can be applied more generally to the ethics of Jesus, and what follows at this point is an attempt to identify principles which might guide a right understanding of the ethics of Jesus.

## *1. The Ethics of Jesus and the Kingdom of God*

There is wide support among recent scholars for the proposition that the ethics of Jesus must be considered in close connection with his proclamation of the kingdom of God.[8] N. T. Wright, for example, argues that Jesus' ethics must be understood in relation to his "kingdom-story," and hence as "the god-given

---

[5] See *A New Vision for Israel: The Teachings of Jesus in National Context* (Grand Rapids: Eerdmans, 1999), p. 156. Luz argues that Matt. 10:23 was "corrected" by the Great Commission of Matt. 28:18-20, as was 10:5-6.

[6] As many scholars now do, including McKnight himself, whose two chapters on "The Ethic of Jesus," in *A New Vision for Israel* are preceded by two chapters entitled "The Kingdom Now Present" and "The Kingdom Yet to Come."

[7] See *Sermon on the Mount*, p. 7. His guidelines follow on pp. 7-25.

[8] Apart from McKnight, who is mentioned above, examples include: Allen Verhey (*The Great Reversal: Ethics and the New Testament* [Grand Rapids: Eerdmans, 1984]); Bruce Chilton and J. I. H. McDonald (*Jesus and the Ethics of the Kingdom* [Grand Rapids: Eerdmans, 1987]); Wolfgang Schrage (*The Ethics of the New Testament* [Edinburgh: T & T Clark, 1988]); Eduard Lohse (*Theological Ethics of the New Testament* [Minneapolis: Fortress Press, 1991]); N. T. Wright (*Jesus and the Victory of God* [London: SPCK, 1996]); Glen Stassen and David Gushee (*Kingdom Ethics* [Downers Grove: InterVarsity Press, 2003]).

way of life for those caught up in this renewal," that is, "the rescue and renewal of Israel and hence of the world."[9] He proceeds to propose a parallel with Jesus' recorded words concerning the connection between the casting out of demons and the coming of the kingdom (Mark 12:28; Luke 11:20). He says that "it is as though Jesus were to say, 'If I command you to behave as those with renewed hearts, then the kingdom of god [*sic*] has come upon you.'"[10] Other scholars who agree about the importance of this link formulate the nature of the connection in other ways.

The foundation for insisting on this connection is not purely a matter of explicit verbal connections in the gospel records, and it is certainly true that many of Jesus' recorded ethical teachings contain no reference to the kingdom of God, but there are a number of telling verbal connections. Each of the Synoptics asserts that Jesus' proclamation of the coming near of the kingdom of God was accompanied by a call to repentance (Matt. 3:2; 4:17; Mark 1:14-15; Luke 10:13). They do not all make explicit the ethical implications of this assertion, but Luke does so in his record of John the Baptist's call to repentance,[11] and it is hard to imagine any understanding of "repentance" in a setting where the Old Testament (OT) prophets were known which would not have included ethical implications of some kind. Again, all the Synoptic Gospels record Jesus demanding that the kingdom of God be given a practical priority, sometimes in association with a demand to put aside those things which constitute obstacles to such a priority (Matt. 6:25-33; 13:44-46; Mark 9:42-48; Luke 9:57-62; 12:22-34). For example, in Matt. 6:25-33 and Luke 12:22-34 striving for the kingdom entails not striving for material possessions. Mark 12:28-34 records the case of a scribe whose endorsement of Jesus' emphasis on the commandments to love God and one's neighbor prompts Jesus' pronouncement that he is "not far from the kingdom of God." Other passages containing these commandments do not make this connection, but even a lone example suggests that it is not inappropriate to think of these commandments, which are generally seen as occupying a key place among Jesus' ethical teachings, as having a kingdom connection.

The connection between ethics and kingdom can also be established on broader conceptual grounds. When Jesus proclaimed that the kingdom of God had come near he inevitably did so against the background of Jewish thinking about the kingship of God, including especially references to God's kingship in the Scriptures. This was a kingship which involved strong ethical demands. When he associated that proclamation with a call for repentance, and with other demands for people to respond and live in particular ways, he inevitably did so against the background of the Jewish prophetic tradition, including especially the prophets recorded in the Scriptures. Certainly these prophets frequently made ethical demands on the basis of the kingly authority of God.

More specifically, a good case can be made for a particularly strong link

---

[9] See *Jesus and the Victory of God*, pp. 279-82. The quoted words occur on pp. 279, 280.

[10] *Jesus and the Victory of God*, p. 282.

[11] Luke 3:7-14. Matthew lacks Luke's detail but his account also includes the demand to "bear fruit worthy of repentance" (3:8).

between Jesus' proclamation of the kingdom and Isaiah. Glen Stassen and David Gushee identify seven "clues" which point to Isaiah as the primary background of Jesus' teaching on the kingdom.[12] These seven include the passages in Isaiah that refer to the kingship of God and to his coming reign, the prominence of Isaiah among the recorded scripture citations by Jesus, the possible dependence on Isaiah of the specific gospel passages where Jesus announces the kingdom of God,[13] and the fact that four passages in the Aramaic Targum of Isaiah contain the phrase "kingdom of God" (and one has "the kingdom of the Messiah").[14] They then proceed to derive from Isaiah "the seven marks of God's reign."[15] The two most prominent of these are God's deliverance from oppression and the manifestation of his righteousness, both of which clearly have ethical implications. Consequently, a valid account of the ethics of Jesus must make take its rise from Jesus' proclamation of the kingdom of God. The kind of effect which this reference has will, of course, depend on one's understanding of the kingdom of God.[16]

## 2. Interpreting Exegetically in Context

The Sermon needs to be interpreted with an appreciation of its character. In particular, as Dale Allison points out,[17] it needs to be noted that the Sermon is partly a poetic text, and contains both metaphor and hyperbole. For example, it is unlikely that Matt. 5:23-24 literally envisages an interrupting of temple worship. Rather, it is a vivid pictorial way of saying that an essential requirement of offering acceptable worship to God is seeking reconciliation with people.

Specific sections of the Sermon need to be interpreted in relation to other sections. It is important, for example, to weigh carefully the fact that the Sermon begins with the Beatitudes (5:3-12). The Beatitudes are properly seen as prophetic words of grace.[18] This is particularly obvious with the earlier pronouncements. Three of the first four are pronouncements of blessing upon those who lack: those who are "poor in spirit" rather than rich, those who mourn rather than those who rejoice and those who "hunger and thirst for righteousness" rather than those who are already full of righteousness. The

---

[12] *Kingdom Ethics*, pp. 22-25. In making their case, they draw on the work of several other scholars, particularly Bruce Chilton.

[13] Stassen and Gushee cite Matt. 8:11; Mark 1:15; 9:1; Luke 4:18, 19, 21; 16:16. This is one point where they acknowledge their debt to Chilton.

[14] They cite the *Tg. Isa.* 24:23; 31:4; 40:9; 52:7 and 53:10, again acknowledging a debt to Chilton. They date three of these (24:23, 52:7 and 53:10) to early in the Tannaitic period (c. AD 100) and the other two to the early Tannaitic period or later.

[15] Stassen and Gushee, *Kingdom Ethics*, pp. 25-28.

[16] See ch. 13 of this volume.

[17] Allison, *Sermon on the Mount*, pp. 11-12.

[18] Stassen and Gushee, *Kingdom Ethics*, pp. 33-37. Both writers acknowledge a debt to Robert Guelich's *Sermon on the Mount* (Dallas: Word, 1982). A major part of their argument consists of identifying echoes in the Beatitudes, chiefly the first four pronouncements, of Isaiah 61.

third Beatitude, the blessing of Matt. 5:5 on those who are "meek" (οἱ πραεῖς), could be read as commending a laudable virtue. However in the Septuagint "meek" often denotes those who are poor or afflicted. Therefore it may well refer in Matt. 5:5 to those who rely on God for justice, rather than claiming it through their own assertion of power or by relying on a human benefactor. Thus the Sermon on the Mount begins with the gracious pronouncement of blessing and divine grace upon those who lack. This directs us away from any interpretation of the Sermon which views it as a series of heavy demands for human achievement. The other Beatitudes, incidentally, do seem to make some demands on the hearers, but these need to be read in context with the earlier ones as responses to God's grace. Drawing on Dietrich Bonhoeffer, the term which Stassen and Gushee use is "participative grace." Another example is to be found in the contiguity of 5:17-20 and 5:21-48. The positive view of "the law and the prophets" in the first passage should restrain us from reading the ensuing one as a straightforward overthrowing of the law. Conversely, the second passage should prevent us from reading the first as a declaration that honoring the law requires that there be no change in its application.[19]

There are considerations which go beyond the relationship between sections of the Sermon. One of these is that Jesus is the speaker. Thus Jesus' words and behavior recorded elsewhere should influence our interpretation of his words as recorded in this place. For example, the fact that Jesus is recorded in Matt. 11:29 as describing himself as "meek" (KJV, ASV) (πραΰς)[20] should influence our understanding of the meekness commended in 5:5. Consequently Jesus' own behavior, especially but not exclusively as recorded by Matthew, indicates that this meekness is compatible with assertiveness and even a readiness to be provocative.[21] Another consideration, which has already arisen by implication, is the broader context of Matthew's Gospel as a whole. For example, the use of the word "perfect" (τέλειος) in 19:21, where Jesus is calling upon a rich young man to sell his possessions and follow him, suggests that the same word in 5:48 is more likely to be about thoroughgoing discipleship than about sinlessness.[22]

---

[19] These remarks do not assume that the placement of these passages necessarily reflects the timing of Jesus' speaking, but that Matthew is a trustworthy guide to the meaning of Jesus' teaching. Those who disagree with this assumption may, of course, reach different conclusions.

[20] The NRSV has "gentle," but it is the same Greek word translated "meek" in Matt. 5:5. Moreover, Deirdre Good argues at length in her *Jesus the Meek King* (Harrisburg: Trinity, 1999) that Jesus is portrayed deliberately in the Gospel of Matthew as "the meek king," one who embodies an ideal of gentle kingship and exemplifies a quality of meekness to be imitated within community life.

[21] Dale Allison uses this example on p. 20 of his *Sermon on the Mount*, but also discusses the significance of the person of Jesus for interpretation of the Sermon at much greater length on pp. 15-25.

[22] Another significant consideration which has not been canvassed, for reasons of space, is that of the audience and situation addressed by Jesus and Matthew. One helpful discussion of this in relation to the Sermon on the Mount is to be found in Wright's *Jesus and the Victory of God*, pp. 287-92.

## 3. Balancing Continuity and Discontinuity

It has already been noted in relation to the contiguity of Matt. 5:17-20 and 5:21-48, that these passages need to be considered in a way that rules out both unqualified continuity and unqualified discontinuity between the law and Jesus' ethical teaching. The need for a balanced view has been recognized by many recent scholars.[23]

On one hand, there is considerable evidence for a measure of continuity between previous Jewish thought, especially as found in the OT, and the ethical teaching of Jesus. Most explicitly, there is, as already mentioned, the statement found in Matt. 5:17-20, together with a comparable, although briefer and less emphatic, statement in Luke 16:17. But this is not all we have. Eduard Lohse offers several parallels in Jewish teachings to the ethical teachings of Jesus,[24] among which, and perhaps the most interesting, are two parallels to what is commonly known as the Golden Rule (Matt. 7:12; Luke 6:31). One of these is negative in form, but the other, from the *Letter of Aristeas* (c. 200 BC–AD 100), is positive, counseling that one's desire to be a partaker in good things should guide one's behavior toward others. It is more obvious, and certainly significant, that the twin commandments to love God and neighbor, which clearly occupied an important place within the ethical thought of Jesus, make use of two quotations from the OT.[25]

On the other hand, there is also considerable evidence for a measure of discontinuity. To begin with Matt. 5:21-48, there is room for debate over whether OT teachings are abrogated, but certainly this material is framed in such a way as to draw attention to a contrast between Jesus' teaching and some teachings to be found in the Judaism of this time. And all four canonical gospels record Jesus as coming into conflict with Jewish teachers through his rejection of strict restrictions upon working on the Sabbath. In addition, Jesus' teaching on love of other people contains elements of discontinuity as well as continuity. In particular, his strong call for love of one's enemies, although some limited encouragement might be found for it in the OT,[26] seems to have clearly challenged the conventional thinking of his own day. The challenge is made discomforting by the fact that Jesus promotes love of one's enemies beyond the realm of abstraction. Among the concrete examples of loving one's enemies which Jesus provides is that in Matt. 5:41 of going "the second mile" when forced to go one, an example which is generally agreed to refer to the right of soldiers to compel unpaid service.[27] Love of one's enemies included love of the Roman oppressor.

Both continuity and discontinuity are to be found in the parable of the

---

[23] For example: Verhey, *The Great Reversal*; Schrage, *The Ethics of the New Testament*; Lohse, *Theological Ethics*; Stein, *Method and Message*; N. T. Wright, *Jesus and the Victory of God*; Stassen and Gushee, *Kingdom Ethics*.

[24] *Theological Ethics*, pp. 67-68.

[25] Mark 12:28-34 and parallels; cf. Deut. 6:5; Lev. 19:18.

[26] Chiefly in Exod. 23:4-5 and Prov. 25:21-22.

[27] For example, see the commentaries on Matthew of both Craig Keener (Grand Rapids: Eerdmans, 1999), pp. 199-200; and Nolland, pp. 259-60.

Good Samaritan (Luke 10:25-37), as N. T. Wright has shown.[28] The passage begins with a normal Jewish question, about having a share in the age to come. Jesus' answer is also in continuity with Jewish tradition, in that he directs his questioner to Scripture by asking, "What is written in the law? What do you read there?" The lawyer's answer quotes two scriptural passages (Lev. 19:18; Deut. 6:5) and earns Jesus' commendation. The lawyer then asks an interpretive question based on his quotation of Leviticus. This is again good Jewish practice, especially if Wright is correct in seeing this question as concerned with drawing the boundaries of covenant at the appropriate place, so as to include those like himself and exclude unacceptable persons.[29] The break with traditional Jewish thought comes with Jesus' story. As has often been noted, he shifts attention from the restrictive question, "Who is my neighbor?" to the unrestricted demand to imitate the Samaritan of the story in acting out the part of neighbor. His choice of a Samaritan as exemplar is deliberately provocative, and serves to rule out any appeal to covenant boundaries in order to limit the scope of the commandment to love one's neighbor.

It is no simple matter, of course, to formulate satisfactorily this balance between continuity and discontinuity, but it is clear that such a balance is required.

## 4. Balancing Grace with Demand and Reward

Many commentators have perceived a contradiction between the strength of demand in much of Jesus' ethical teaching, as recorded in the gospels, and the strong note of grace elsewhere in his teaching. Similarly, a contradiction has been perceived between the motif of reward in his ethical teaching and this strong note of grace. Those who do not agree that there is a contradiction generally accept that there is a tension. When this position is taken, as it is in this chapter, there is again a need for balance.

Grace certainly is a strong note in the gospel records of Jesus' actions and teachings. Jesus' readiness to associate with the marginalized, and specifically with "sinners," is recorded repeatedly in the Synoptic Gospels—in material of varied character and, according to most views, from diverse sources. They also record Jesus' readiness to offer forgiveness to sinners. There are different views about the significance of these features. N. T. Wright, for example, argues that the offence caused by Jesus' behavior lay primarily in his welcoming unexpected people into the kingdom, as "part of the restored people of YHWH,"[30] whereas it has been more common in the past to emphasize individual forgiveness.[31] Under any view, however, these features

---

[28] *Jesus and the Victory of God*, pp. 304-07.

[29] *Jesus and the Victory of God*, p. 306. He cites Kenneth Bailey (*Through Peasant Eyes*, p. 43, combined in the 1983 edition with *Poet and Peasant*), who appeals to Sir. 12:7 ("Give to the one who us good, but do not help the sinner") in support.

[30] *Jesus and the Victory of God*, p. 272.

[31] The need to balance the individual and corporate dimensions is taken up in the next

of the gospel records demand acknowledgment.

In addition, this strong note of grace is not unconnected with Jesus' ethical teaching. [If, as has already been argued, Jesus' ethical teaching is properly to be understood in connection with his proclamation of the kingdom of God, then it is connected also with grace, since grace is one prominent feature of that proclamation.] Here is how Wolfgang Schrage characterizes Jesus' proclamation of the kingdom:

> His message, however,[32] puts primary emphasis on the salvific nature of the kingdom of God, displayed in the message of salvation and the forgiveness of sins, in healings and exorcisms, in table fellowship with sinners and tax collectors, in fulfillment of the prophets' promises . . .[33]

Jesus' proclamation of the kingdom is a gracious invitation, although an invitation which calls for repentance and faith. The connection between grace and ethics is also established by the key placement of the Beatitudes at the beginning of Matthew's Sermon on the Mount, which has been discussed above, and their similar placement in Luke's Sermon on the Plain.[34] So how do we balance demand and reward with this emphasis on grace?

The primary factor with respect to our question is that Jesus' gracious invitation expects a response which includes gracious behavior, that is, behavior prompted and shaped by the grace of God. In Luke 7:36-50, for example, Jesus seizes on the actions of the sinful woman who bathes and anoints his feet to teach that those who know that they have been forgiven much will love much and will demonstrate that love in action. Elsewhere he teaches that those who have accepted the forgiveness of God are expected, indeed required, to forgive others. This is taught with particular force in the parable usually known as the Parable of the Unmerciful Servant, and the teaching which surrounds it.[35] Glen Stassen and David Gushee put forward the concept of "transforming initiative."[36] This concept springs from an analysis of much of the Sermon on the Mount, especially but not only the "antitheses" of Matt. 5:21-48, as consisting of triads in each of which the third and climactic component consists of this transforming initiative. Whether or not we accept this analysis, there is value in their suggestion that Jesus is not imposing an impossible demand, but teaching "regular practices," practices which will transform both the person who engages in them and their

---

section of this chapter.

[32] The implied contrast is with John the Baptist. Schrage has just asserted that John's focus is on God's judgment, whereas Jesus integrates the idea of judgment into a message which places the emphasis elsewhere.

[33] *Ethics of the New Testament*, p. 23. In support he cites Ulrich Luz's assertion (in his article "basileia," in *Exegetisches Wörterbuch zum Neuen Testament* [Stuttgart: Kohlhammer, 1980–83]) that the coming of the Kingdom of God is to be interpreted "as God's unlimited and boundless love for the outcasts and marginal people of Israel."

[34] In Luke 6:20-23, followed by the "woes" of vv. 24-26, then the rest of the Sermon, which has strong ethical content, in vv. 27-49.

[35] Matt. 18:21-35. See also Matt. 6:12,14-15; Mark 11:25; Luke 6:37; 11:4.

[36] *Kingdom Ethics*, pp. 132-43.

relationships with others. Also potentially helpful is the suggestion of Chilton and McDonald that the word "child" (παιδίον) in several of Jesus' sayings about the kingdom has behind it the Aramaic *talya*, which can also be translated as "servant" (διάκονος) with the result that there is a merging of the images of child and servant.[37] If they are right, we observe a verbal bridge between grace and demand: one must enter the kingdom through the empty-handed receptivity of the child, but assume the role of humble service.

We need to turn now to consider the concept of grace and reward. Jesus is recorded on numerous occasions as speaking of God's rewarding of faithful disciples. Sometimes this is a reward within this life to be experienced in God's provision (Matt. 6:25-34; Luke 12:22-31) or in belonging to the new community of faith (Mark 3:31-35; 10:28-30). More often it is an eschatological reward, which may be spoken of simply as God's "reward" (as in Matt. 6:2-4; Luke 14:14) or in a variety of terms such as "eternal life" (as in Mark 10:30) or eschatological table fellowship (as in Matt. 8:1; Luke 13:28) or entering the kingdom (as in Matt. 7:21; Mark 10:15). Such rewards, however, are not to be understood as payment which God is obligated to make, but as the gracious acts of the God who delights to give good things to his children.[38] Moreover, Jesus is recorded as teaching explicitly that nobody can put God in his or her debt any more than the slave can the master (Luke 17:7-10). Also relevant is the parable of the workers in the vineyard (Matt. 20:1-16). This parable underlines the sovereign generosity of God's rewards. If, as seems reasonable, the full day's wage is to be identified with eschatological reward then it is arguable that the first group of workers is a hypothetical group, that is, no disciple of Jesus can actually claim to have served a "full day" so as to merit entry into the kingdom. As Robert Stein puts it, "what believers receive from God for faithful service is therefore not merited pay but the gracious blessing of their heavenly Father."[39]

## 5. Balancing the Individual and the Corporate

Scholars in the Reformation tradition have generally tended to emphasize the individual dimension of Jesus' ethics, beginning with an individual understanding of repentance and faith. But several recent scholars have challenged this emphasis and argued in particular for the primacy of a corporate understanding of repentance and faith. N. T. Wright, for example, argues on the basis of what it meant to proclaim the kingdom of God in a Jewish context that repentance meant fundamentally "what Israel must do if her exile is to come to an end."[40] Similarly, he interprets the call for faith as a call to Israel to believe that "Israel's God is acting climactically in the career

---

[37] *Jesus and the Ethics of the Kingdom*, pp. 80-89.
[38] As God is depicted in Matt. 7:11, for example.
[39] *Method and Message*, p. 109.
[40] *Jesus and the Victory of God*, p. 248. His discussion of repentance occupies pp. 246-58. McKnight takes a similar view of repentance in his *A New Vision for Israel*, pp. 172-76.

of Jesus himself."[41] More broadly, he sees Jesus' ethics as a "praxis of the kingdom" to be <u>practiced within the setting of groups of people who had responded to Jesus with repentance and faith</u>.[42] Nevertheless scholars such as Wright do find a place for an individual dimension, just as those who before them had emphasized that dimension normally found a place for a corporate dimension. The debate is not between two mutually exclusive views, but between two different emphases.

If we are to choose between these emphases we need to reflect on the way in which the concepts of repentance and faith are employed in the gospels. The concept of repentance first occurs within the Synoptic Gospels in the context of the ministry of John the Baptist (Matt. 3:2; Mark 1:4; Luke 3:3). In each instance both the corporate and the individual dimensions are clearly significant, since each gospel associates the call for repentance with a citation of Isaiah concerning God's restoration of his people coupled with the individual act of baptism. Both dimensions are also clearly present when Jesus is recorded calling for repentance. Both Mark and Matthew characterize Jesus' early preaching as involving a call to repentance, and both associate this with the proclamation of the kingdom of God as having drawn near (Mark 1:14-15; Matt. 4:17). Matthew makes it clear that this message concerns Israel by placing a citation of Isaiah before it, but even without this guidance this would be a natural inference. One might also imagine that there is a need for an individual response since there was with John, and this is encouraged by the fact that the next pericope in Matthew and Mark concerns the calling of individual disciples. This is not paralleled in Luke, but other instances of the language of repentance in that Gospel do suggest that both individual and corporate dimensions had a place within Luke's understanding of Jesus' teaching (see Luke 13:1-5; 16:30; 17:1-4). Most helpful in this regard is the story of Zaccheus in Luke 19:1-10. Although the word "repentance" is not used, this is clearly an account of a decisive turning away from the old life in response to Jesus. Here we certainly have the act of an individual, but he demonstrates his repentance through acts toward many people. Jesus' commendation of him contains a strong corporate note in designating him "a son of Abraham" (v. 9).

The individual dimension is often to the fore where faith is mentioned. This is the case in several instances where individuals are called upon to show faith, or are commended for showing faith (see Matt. 8:13; 9:28; Mark 5:36; 9:23-24; Luke 8:50). But groups are also sometimes addressed concerning faith. In Mark 11:20-24 Jesus teaches his disciples about believing prayer.[43] There is nothing to restrict this teaching to individual or corporate prayer, and it seems reasonable to apply it to both. In Mark 9:42 (= Matt. 18:6) the expression "these little ones who believe in me" is used to identify a group, in the context of teaching concerning right behavior within the community of

---

[41] *Jesus and the Victory of God*, p. 262 within a section on faith occupying pp. 258-64.

[42] *Jesus and the Victory of God*, pp. 296-97.

[43] Apart from the examples which follow, consider Matt. 21:32; Mark 11:31; Luke 8:12-13; 20:5; 22:67.

those who follow Jesus. A merely verbal analysis might lead one to conclude that the individual dimension is clearly primary. But one has to weigh the contention of Wright that the context provided by Jesus' proclamation of the kingdom gives any call to place one's faith in him a strong corporate dimension.

What is clear is that both dimensions have to be given a significant place in relation to repentance and faith, and that this should lead one to expect there to be both individual and communal aspects to Jesus' ethical teaching in general.

## C. Prominent Features of the Ethics of Jesus

The following discussion identifies a number of features of Jesus' ethical teaching which are found consistently, and therefore can be used to characterize that teaching in general.

### 1. Love

The Synoptic Gospels record Jesus giving great importance to the dual commandment to love God and neighbor (Matt. 22:34-40; Mark 12:28-34; Luke 10:25-28). Mark and Matthew both record the dual commandment as Jesus' response to a scribe's question concerning which commandment is the greatest, while Luke records Jesus commending the same pair of commandments enunciated by a teacher of the law as what must be done to inherit eternal life. Numerous scholars accord the dual commandment a prominent place in their understanding of the ethical teaching of Jesus.[44] This emphasis on love of God and neighbor is reflected elsewhere in the Synoptic Gospels.

The commandment to love God with one's whole being is reflected particularly in Jesus' calling for an overriding allegiance to God. This connection is particularly clear in Matt. 6:24, where Jesus declares in proverbial language that "no one can serve two masters," or love two masters, then draws the conclusion that "one cannot serve God and wealth." Luke 9:62 concludes a passage where declarations of a desire to follow Jesus are qualified by the saying that "no one who puts a hand to the plow and looks back is fit for the kingdom of God." Here the word "love" is not used, but the call for unqualified allegiance to the kingdom of God may well imply the same love which is ready to serve God alone. There are passages where Jesus demands love and allegiance toward himself.[45] In Matt. 10:37-49 Jesus declares that his disciples must love him more than parents and children, or even their own lives. It seems that love and allegiance toward God merge into

---

[44] For example: Chilton and McDonald, *Jesus and the Ethics of the Kingdom*, pp. 92-95; Lohse, *Theological Ethics*, pp. 52-59; McKnight, *A New Vision for Israel*, pp. 206-10; Schrage, *The Ethics of the New Testament*, pp. 81-85; Stein, *Method and Message*, pp. 103-05.

[45] Apart from Matt. 10:37-49, see Luke 9:23-26; 14:25-33.

love and allegiance toward Jesus himself.

The commandment to love one's neighbor as oneself is elaborated upon by Jesus in terms of doing good to others. This elaboration is particularly obvious in Luke 10:29-37 where this commandment to love is explicitly amplified by means of the parable of the Good Samaritan. The question which prompts the parable is "who is my neighbor?" Rather than answering this question, the parable implies that the proper question is: "How am I to be the neighbor who loves?" The Samaritan of the parable embodies the answer to this question. Elsewhere Jesus' emphasis on doing good to others is clearly expressed in what is commonly known as "the Golden Rule," the injunction to do to others as we would have them do to us (Matt. 7:12; Luke 6:31). It is also prominent in the gospel records of Jesus' defense of his healing on the Sabbath, both verbally in language of "doing good on the Sabbath" (Mark 3:4; Luke 6:9) and implicitly in the necessity accorded acts of practical compassion (Luke 13:10-17; 14:1-6). In Jesus' teaching, as Stein comments, "love is to be understood as love demonstrated by actions."[46] This should not, however, be understood in such a way as to exclude the emotions. As Chilton and McDonald point out, the pairing of this commandment with the commandment to love God implies that we should also love others with our whole person. Action is primary, but emotional involvement is not excluded.[47]

The other leading feature of Jesus' elaboration of the principle of love of one's neighbor is his insistence that such love must extend to one's enemies. This is implicit in his choice of a Samaritan to embody practical love towards the man, presumably a Jew, who went down from Jerusalem to Jericho and fell into the hands of robbers. It is explicit in Matt. 5:43-48, where Jesus rejects the view that one should love one's neighbor and hate one's enemy, and instead says, "Love your enemies and pray for those who persecute you" (see also Luke 6:27-36). Several scholars have identified the call to love one's enemies as the one clearly unusual and confronting element in Jesus' understanding of the love of one's neighbor.[48]

## 2. The Character and Action of God

The call to love one's enemies also provides a link with a second prominent characteristic of Jesus' ethical teaching, that is, his grounding of that teaching in the character and action of God. The call to love one's enemies is so grounded both in Matt. 5:43-48 and Luke 6:35-36. In Matthew's account, Jesus says, "Love your enemies and pray for those who persecute you, so that you may be children of your Father in heaven; for he makes his sun rise on the evil and on the good, and sends rain on the righteous and on the unrighteous." At the end of the passage he adds, "Be perfect, therefore, as your heavenly Father is perfect." The adjective "perfect" translates the Greek τέλειος, which

---

[46] In his *Method and Message*, p. 104.

[47] *Jesus and the Ethics of the Kingdom*, p. 94.

[48] For example, McKnight, *A New Vision for Israel*, pp. 218-24 and Schrage, *The Ethics of the New Testament*, pp. 73-79.

might be better rendered here as "whole" or "complete,"[49] or understood in the light of the use of the word in the Greek version of Deut. 18:13 to mean wholeheartedness or, on the human side, complete loyalty to God.[50] In Luke 6:35, Jesus says that those who love their enemies "will be children of the Most High, for he is kind to the ungrateful and the wicked," and concludes by saying, "Be merciful, just as your Father is merciful" (v. 36).

But it is not only love of enemies that is grounded in the character and action of God.[51] It is not surprising that acting in love toward other believers is also taught with reference to the attitude of God himself. In Matt. 18:10 Jesus is recorded exhorting his disciples to "take care that you do not despise one of these little ones." The identity of "these little ones" is presumably defined by the longer expression which occurs a few verses earlier (Matt. 18:6), "these little ones who believe in me." This exhortation is supported by two explicit references to God as "Father" with a brief parable in between. Jesus first declares that "in heaven their angels continually see the face of my Father in heaven" (v. 10), then tells the story of the shepherd who searches for one lost sheep with that story's declaration that "it is not the will of your Father in heaven that one of these little ones should be lost" (18:14). It is God's love for those who believe in Jesus, and perhaps especially those believers who are weak and vulnerable, which requires that they be treated with loving care.

Similarly, God's forgiveness demands that those who heed Jesus' teaching also be prepared to forgive. In both versions of the Lord's Prayer (Matt. 6:9-15; Luke 11:2-4), a strong connection is made between receiving God's forgiveness and readiness to forgive others. This connection is made with particular forcefulness in the parable recorded in Matt. 18:23-35. Jesus tells the story of a slave who is forgiven an enormous debt by a king, but refuses to do the same for a fellow slave who owes him a much smaller amount. The king then condemns the unforgiving slave with the words, "Should you not have had mercy on your fellow slave, as I had mercy on you (v. 33)?" Jesus then describes the king's punishment of this slave before explicitly applying the parable by saying, "So my heavenly Father will also do to every one of you, if you do not forgive your brother or sister from your heart" (v. 35).

God provides the pattern for his people to imitate. But it is also the case that those who have found acceptance with God by being forgiven have placed themselves under a binding obligation to forgive one another. There is, then, a direct connection between this reason for forgiving others and Jesus' mission.[52] The demand to forgive as the Father forgives comes from the one whose mission was to be the agent of that forgiveness and "to call not the righteous but sinners" (Mark 2:17).[53]

---

[49] One who takes this view is Keener, in his *A Commentary on the Gospel of Matthew*.

[50] One who takes this view is Nolland, in his *The Gospel of Matthew*, p. 271.

[51] McKnight, *A New Vision for Israel*, p. 236.

[52] Schrage, *The Ethics of the New Testament*, p. 31.

[53] See also Matt. 9:13; Luke 5:32.

## 3. The Person of Jesus

The most obvious connection between the person of Jesus and his ethical teaching is to be found in his authority. The gospels depict Jesus as someone who taught with authority. The Synoptics explicitly declare that his hearers were struck by the authoritative character of his teaching.[54] The connection between the authority of Jesus and his ethical teaching is especially clear in the Sermon on the Mount.[55] Within the three chapters of the Sermon, and often in introducing ethical teaching, Jesus is recorded thirteen times as using the expression "I say to you."[56] In addition, a majority of these instances are emphatic in form. On six occasions (Matt. 5:22, 28, 32, 34, 39, 44) the expression occurs in the context of contrasting what Jesus says with what others have said, and in these six instances the use of the pronoun ἐγώ, which is not necessary in Greek, underlines the contrast. On four other occasions emphasis is provided by the addition of "truly" (ἀμήν) (5:18; 6:2, 5, 16).

Closely related to Jesus' authority is his expectation of obedience. It is implicit in the giving of authoritative instruction about how to live that this instruction should be obeyed. This expectation is implicit also in the way in which he speaks to people. He calls disciples expecting them to follow him; he authoritatively gives directions to them; he addresses those whom he heals expecting to be heeded.[57] Such expectations become explicit in Matt. 7:21-27 and the parallel passage in Luke 6:46-49. In Matthew's version Jesus is recorded as saying that not all who call him "Lord" will enter the kingdom of Heaven, but only those who do the will of his Father in heaven. Essentially this is a demand for obedience toward God rather than a direct claim by Jesus of personal authority. Nonetheless, calling Jesus "Lord" is viewed as insufficient, not as inappropriate. In addition, Jesus refers to God as "my Father" and presents himself as the one who will utter the final word of judgment upon those who do not obey. These features combine to suggest that obedience toward God is expressed by obedience toward Jesus. This is confirmed by what follows: Jesus uses the parable of the Wise and Foolish Builders to teach that it is necessary to hear his words and act upon them.

Finally, Jesus the ethical teacher is also the exemplar of his own teaching. This expectation is most clearly propounded in Mark 10:35-45 and the parallel passages in the other Synoptic Gospels (Matt. 20:20-28; Luke 22:24-27). Mark records Jesus as responding to his disciples' desire for the places of eminence by teaching them that they are not to seek high status, as the Gentiles do, but rather to embrace the lowly place of serving others, even serving in the fashion of a slave. This teaching is brought to a conclusion by Jesus' putting himself forward as the example of such voluntary servanthood

---

[54] Mark 1:22; Matt. 7:28-29; Luke 4:31-32; John 7:46.

[55] See Allison's *The Sermon on the Mount*, pp. 24-25.

[56] Matt. 5:18, 20, 22, 28, 32, 34, 39, 44; 6:2, 5, 16, 25, 29.

[57] Confining our examples to the first half of Mark, we have the following. Of calling disciples: 1:16-20; 2:13-14. Of directing disciples: 3:9; 3:14; 6:7-11; 6:45. Of addressing those whom he heals: 3:1-6; 5:19; 5:43; 8:26.

as the Son of Man who "came not to be served but to serve, and to give his life a ransom for many" (Mark 10:45). The force of this statement is increased by the fact that it follows immediately after the prediction of his going up to Jerusalem to be handed over to be killed (Mark 10:33-34). The Gospel of John has no direct parallel. However, in John 13:1-16 Jesus voluntarily takes upon himself the lowly servant role of washing his disciples' feet, and then tells them that this is an example for them to follow.

Dale Allison makes a good case for the proposition that Matthew tells the story of Jesus in such a way as to show him to be the exemplary embodiment of his ethical teachings as recorded in the Sermon on the Mount.[58] It would not be difficult to argue for something similar in the other Synoptics. The Jesus of Mark and Luke might well be seen as one who lived in accordance with the commandment to love God and neighbor, who acted in conformity with the character and actions of the God whom he called "Father" and who clearly did embody the servanthood which he claimed to exemplify.

## 4. Integrity

It must be acknowledged that the term "integrity" cannot be derived directly from the language of the gospels. But it can be justified as a word which sums up several related features of Jesus' ethical teaching as recorded in the Synoptics. One of these features, which has been noted by numerous scholars, is a concern for the inner person.[59]

The passage to which appeal is most frequently made n this regard is Mark 7:14-23 and its parallel in Matt. 15:10-20. Mark begins by recording Jesus' declaration that "there is nothing outside a person that by going in can defile, but the things that come out are what defile." This follows the record of an exchange between Jesus and some scribes and Pharisees who have noticed some of his disciples eating with "defiled," that is, unwashed, hands. The verses that follow record a reiteration and elaboration of that declaration. A person is not defiled by those things that go into a person (v. 18) but rather by the things that come out of person (v. 20), that is, by the actions which spring from the vices resident in the human heart.

The presence of "murder" and "adultery" in Mark 7:21-22 creates a verbal link with Matt. 5:21-30. Here Jesus is recorded as internalizing the established prohibitions of murder and adultery. Jesus moves from murder to anger, specifically that kind of anger which is akin to murder in its hostility toward the brother or sister. Similarly he moves from adultery to lust. There is no suggestion here that Jesus has revoked commandments against the outward acts of murder and adultery. Rather, he has intensified these prohibitions by extending them to the inner conditions which lead toward the outward acts.

Therefore McKnight and others are right who reject a sharp opposition

---

[58] In his *The Sermon on the Mount*, pp. 19-24.

[59] McKnight, *A New Vision for Israel*, p. 213. "Jesus called those who saw in him the fulfillment of what Jeremiah anticipated [see Jer. 31:31-34] to be transformed from the inside out."

between the inward and outward in Jesus' ethical teaching in favor of a union of the two.[60] This finds further support in what Jesus says about "fruit" in Matt. 12:33-37 and Luke 6:43-45. Both passages affirm that only a good tree can bear good fruit. Both passages relate the character of a tree to the inner character of a person, that is, to the "heart." So the good heart produces good things, but it is also the good things produced which demonstrate the reality of such a heart. A concern for good acts is also evident in the parable of the Two Sons in Matt. 21:28-32. Jesus elicits from his hearers the recognition that it is the son who acted in obedience, despite earlier verbal refusal, who "did the will of his father," rather than the son who spoke obediently but failed to act. The contrast, of course, is not between outward act and inner attitude but between act and empty word.

This brings us back to the term "integrity." This term fits Jesus' image of the healthy tree, whose observable fruitfulness bears witness to an inner health. It also fits other elements in Jesus' teaching. Negatively, there are Jesus' numerous attacks on hypocrisy which are recorded in the Synoptics, Matthew especially.[61] Jesus consistently challenges outward show which does not correspond to inner reality, and he attacks inconsistency in people's actions. In Matt. 6:5-6, for example, Jesus condemns those whose prayers are not genuinely directed to God but are performed publicly in order to gain the respect of other people. In Matt. 23:23-24 he condemns the inconsistency of those scribes and Pharisees who punctiliously tithe but "neglect the weightier matters of the law: justice and mercy and faith." These passages might be taken to imply a contrasting positive picture, of a person who is all of one piece, acting consistently in line with a genuine goodness of heart. Such an inference is encouraged by Matt. 5:33-37. Here Jesus goes beyond the prohibition of false swearing to oppose all swearing. He initially supports this by exemplifying those things normally invoked in oaths, and demonstrates the connection of each one with God. This seems to imply that there is lack of reverence for God in indirectly invoking his authority to provide assurance of our veracity. But Jesus then says, "Let your word be 'Yes, Yes' or 'No, No'; anything more than this comes from the evil one" (Matt. 5:37). This could be seen as merely reinforcing the prohibition against swearing but, in the light of the passages already considered, it is attractive to see the sufficiency of simply saying "Yes" or "No" as characteristic of the honest person, the person of integrity, whose bare word can always be trusted.

## D. A Specific Ethical Issue: Marriage and Divorce

The length of a single chapter does not make it possible to discuss a range of specific ethical issues at a helpful level. Accordingly, one issue, marriage and divorce, will be considered briefly. It has been chosen for several reasons. It

---

[60] For McKnight see *A New Vision for Israel*, pp. 213-15. See also Schrage, *The Ethics of the New Testament*, pp. 40-46; Stein, *Method and Message*, pp. 101-3; Wright, *Jesus and the Victory of God*, pp. 282-87.

[61] See Matt. 6:1-6, 16-18; 7:1-5; 23:13-36. But also Mark 7:1-13; Luke 6:39-42; 20:45-47.

illustrates both how the characteristics of Jesus' ethical teaching in general can be seen to be at work in a specific area and how there are likely to be complications involved in interpreting and applying Jesus' teaching. It is also an issue which continues to be debated among Christians. And the amount of relevant material in the gospels is sufficient to exemplify the process of drawing together material from several contexts, without being so great as to be overwhelming for a brief treatment.[62]

When one compares the relevant gospel passages a common feature can readily be discerned. They all view divorce negatively and strongly discourage it. This is true even of those passages which seem to allow for divorce under some circumstances (Matt. 5:31-32; 19:3-9). In addition, the two longer and more detailed passages (Matt. 19:3-9; Mark 10:2-12) provide a common view of marriage which seems to underlie this negative view of divorce. Marriage is based on God's creation of human beings as male and female and to be in God's purpose a joining together of a man and a woman as "one flesh," so that no human being should separate what God has made one.

Two of the four general characteristics of Jesus' ethical teaching noted earlier in this chapter are clearly present in this specific area, while the other two might possibly be discerned as implicit. First, while love of God and of ① neighbor are not obviously invoked, the emphasis on respect for God's purpose might be seen as implying love of God, and the concept of two becoming one flesh might be seen as demanding love of one another.[63] Second, the positive teaching on marriage is firmly based on the action of God ② in creating people male and female with an innate desire for union. It is because of God's purpose for marriage and his "joining together" of a man and a woman in a binding relationship that marriage must be strongly upheld. ③ Third, Jesus' authority plays an important role in this teaching. Both the Matthean passages contain the formula "I say," and all four passages are authoritative in tone. Furthermore, the manner in which Paul invokes the teaching of Jesus in 1 Cor. 7:10[64] reflects the great importance and authority which he attributed to such teaching. Fourth, the principle of integrity is not ④ clearly present, but the opposition to divorce might be seen as demanding that married persons, both men and women alike, act in a manner consistent with their commitment to one another.

There are, of course, significant difficulties involved in deriving a coherent view of divorce from these passages. One difficulty is the fact that the two passages in Matthew qualify the prohibition of divorce by adding "except for unchastity" (Matt. 5:32; 19:9), whereas those in Mark and Luke do not. Associated with this difficulty is the debate over whether Jesus is to be seen as abrogating Moses' provision for divorce. A likely explanation is that the exception was known to the authors of the other two gospels, but viewed

---

[62] Matt. 5:31-32; 19:3-9; Mark 10:2-12; Luke 16:18. Some scholars also consider 1 Cor. 7:10-16 because it contains, in v. 10, a reference to a command of "the Lord."

[63] The latter inference is in fact made in Eph. 5:28-31.

[64] "To the married I give this command—not I but the Lord."

as a minor note, and that they were satisfied that the main thrust of Jesus' opposition to divorce could be conveyed without including this qualification. This is relatively easy to imagine in the instance of the very brief teaching contained in Luke 16:18. Its absence from Mark 10:2-12 is more of a problem given the greater length of that passage, but one might argue that this absence reflects a focus on the main thrust of Jesus' teaching rather than ignorance or rejection of the qualification.[65] Another possible explanation is that the qualification is an interpretive addition on the part of Matthew conveying the intent of Jesus' teaching.[66]

Should Jesus, then, be seen as abrogating Moses' provision for divorce? Much depends on what one makes of Jesus' comment, as recorded in both the longer passages, that Moses made this provision because of hardness of heart. It is certainly not justifiable to interpret this as equivalent to rejection of what Moses allowed, since the words themselves do not require this and the context of the Gospel of Matthew, in which Jesus' respect for Scripture is clearly affirmed, tells strongly against it. The contention that Jesus is saying that the provision is no longer required deserves more serious consideration.[67] But it is questionable whether Jesus brought new conditions such that any provision for hardness of heart could be set aside. Much of the immediately preceding chapter of Matthew's Gospel could be considered to be such provision. This is certainly true of Matt. 18:15-35. This passage envisages one "brother" or "sister" sinning against another, difficulty in dealing with such sin, the need for forgiveness between brothers and sisters and the reluctance of some to forgive.

If, then, we consider Moses' provision for divorce still relevant and the qualification of Jesus' prohibition of divorce in Matt. 5:32 and 19:9 valid, we will still have to decide how to interpret and apply these. In particular, what is the meaning in context of the Greek word πορνεία translated by the NRSV in both passages as "unchastity"? It is a general word for sexual immorality, but is used here in the context of marriage. Some have therefore understood it to refer specifically to adultery. But the word μοιχεία was available to Matthew to convey this clearly, and it seems unlikely that he would have overlooked the distinction, since he uses the two words in the vice list of 15:19. This suggests a broader meaning for πορνεία, but it is not easy to determine what this might cover in the context of marriage. Then there remains the question of application. Should we simply carry our understanding of this qualification over into contemporary practice, or does it constitute an instance of some broader principle, such as breaking the marriage covenant?

---

[65] David Instone-Brewer, in his *Divorce and Remarriage in the Bible* (Grand Rapids: Eerdmans, 2002), a very thorough treatment of this ethical issue in the light of historical context, argues persuasively that both Mark and Matthew have selectively but accurately reported the original debate. See especially pp. 171-75.

[66] Again, Instone-Brewer expresses the opinion that Matthew did make some small additions, but that these accurately conveyed information that would originally have been assumed.

[67] This is the contention, for example, of Wright in his *Jesus and the Victory of God*, pp. 284-86.

It would be foolish to attempt to resolve this difficulty in a few words, so readers of this chapter are invited to read and reflect further.[68] Any resolution, however, must respect what is clear in the gospels on this matter. Marriage, therefore, must be held in high regard, and divorce cannot be treated casually. The broader character of Jesus' teaching and actions must also be respected, which rules out any position which fails to show compassion to those who are divorced or in difficult marital situations.

## E. Conclusion

The preceding section has illustrated the fact that it is not always easy to engage with Jesus' ethical teaching. Even where interpretation and application of his teaching is not difficult, and perhaps especially then, it may not be easy to live in conformity with his teaching. But because ethical teaching constitutes a large proportion of Jesus' teaching as recorded in the Synoptic Gospels it demands our attention.

This chapter seeks to provide readers with a basis for beginning to give serious attention to the ethical teaching of Jesus in a rigorous and potentially fruitful way. That it begins with a survey of different approaches constitutes recognition that such serious attention must include a readiness to consider and learn from a variety of perspectives. This survey also serves to illustrate the importance of weighing all the relevant evidence in the gospels.

The approach to the study of the ethics of Jesus espoused within the chapter itself is based on an understanding of the kingdom of God proclaimed by Jesus as at once present and future. It attempts not only to hear in his teaching a real demand upon disciples today but also to give due weight to the reality that we are imperfect people living in a world which still awaits the final consummation of God's rule. The author's conviction is that this approach best reflects the character of all the relevant material in the gospels. But this implies no claim that this approach resolves all difficulties.

Nonetheless, five principles are advanced with some confidence that they lead towards a right understanding of the ethics of Jesus. These are: the connection between the ethics of Jesus and the kingdom of God; the need to take context seriously; the recognition of both continuity and discontinuity between the teaching of Jesus and previous Jewish thought; the balance between grace and both demand and reward; and the recognition of both individual and corporate dimensions.

Four prominent features of Jesus' ethical teaching are also identified with a considerable degree of confidence. These are: the prominence given to love of God and neighbor; the grounding of Jesus' teaching in the character and action of God; the close connection between Jesus' teaching and his person; and an emphasis on integrity.

---

[68] A good place to start would be the chapter on marriage and divorce in Stassen and Gushee, *Kingdom Ethics*, pp. 271-89. This chapter provides numerous references which could lead into other reading. Those willing to read at length are referred to Instone-Brewer's, *Divorce and Remarriage in the Bible*.

*Brian Powell*

There is much that is clear in the ethical teaching of Jesus and much that makes distinct demands on his disciples. This is not to deny that some difficult issues remain, as exemplified in the exploration of the issue of marriage and divorce, but clear teaching does provide a basis for wrestling with these issues in a fashion which itself expresses respect for the ethics of Jesus.

## Bibliography

Allison, Dale C., Jr. *The Sermon on the Mount: Inspiring the Moral Imagination.* New York: The Crossroad Publishing Company, 1999.
Chilton, Bruce and McDonald, J. I. H. *Jesus and the Ethics of the Kingdom.* Grand Rapids: Eerdmans, 1987.
Davies, W. D. *The Sermon on the Mount.* Cambridge: Cambridge University Press, 1966.
Good, Deirdre J. *Jesus the Meek King.* Harrisburg: Trinity Press International, 1999.
Hays, Richard. *The Moral Vision of the New Testament.* New York: HarperCollins, 1996.
Instone-Brewer, David. *Divorce and Remarriage in the Bible.* Grand Rapids: Eerdmans, 2002.
Lohse, Eduard. *Theological Ethics of the New Testament.* Minneapolis: Fortress Press, 1991.
McKnight, Scot. *A New Vision for Israel: The Teachings of Jesus in National Context.* Grand Rapids: Eerdmans, 1999.
Schrage, Wolfgang. *The Ethics of the New Testament.* Edinburgh: T. & T. Clark, 1988.
Stassen, Glen and Gushee, David. *Kingdom Ethics: Following Jesus in Contemporary Context.* Downers Grove: InterVarsity Press, 2003.
Stein, Robert H. *The Method and Message of Jesus' Teachings.* Louisville: Westminster John Knox Press, 1994.
Verhey, Allen. *Remembering Jesus: Christian Community, Scripture and the Moral Life.* Grand Rapids: Eerdmans, 2002.
Wright, N. T. *Jesus and the Victory of God.* London: SPCK, 1996.

# 16. The Miracles of Jesus

*Evelyn Ashley*

Exclusive of parallels, the gospels record Jesus performing over thirty miracles.[1] Additionally, there are numerous summary statements that refer to Jesus performing miracles, especially healings and exorcisms. These accounts are distributed through all strata of the gospel material—in both Mark and Q[2] as well as in material found exclusively in Matthew, or Luke, or John. Thus the miracle stories are an integral part of the gospel accounts of Jesus' life and as such cannot be ignored.

However, these miracle stories form a topic on which there are significant differences of opinion.[3] For some, Jesus' miracles are simply taken for granted; for others the whole concept of miracles is a matter for debate. Much of the discussion, and thus much of the written material, revolves around four questions.

First, there is the philosophical question: Can miracles happen and do they happen? These are underlying questions, the answers to which will impact the answers to all the other questions regarding Jesus' miracles. If it is concluded that miracles cannot happen, then clearly there must be some explanation for the stories of Jesus' miracles other than that they were real miracles that actually occurred. On the other hand, if it is accepted that miracles can occur, then it becomes possible at least to consider that the stories of Jesus' miracles go back to real events.

Second, there is the historical question: Did Jesus' miracles occur? Even if it is conceded that miracles can occur, there is still the question of whether the stories presented in the gospels are historically accurate. Were the miracles stories created by the early church to make a point? Or are the gospel accounts embellishments of real events or stories about the types of things Jesus did but not reports of specific events? Or did the miracles in fact occur as they are recorded in the gospels?

---

[1] It is outside the scope of this chapter to discuss the miracles of which Jesus was the subject, that is, his birth, baptism, transfiguration and resurrection.

[2] Without entering the discussion regarding the possible existence, composition, history, etc. of "Q," it can, at a minimum, be used as a shorthand designation for the material that is common to Matthew and Luke, but not found in Mark.

[3] The bibliography at the end of this chapter provides a small sample of what has been written on the topic and forms a starting point for further research. Most of the entries include bibliographies which widen the scope for research.

(3)    Third, there is the literary question: What did the evangelists intend when they narrated the miracles of Jesus? Clearly, any interpretation of the evangelists' intent will be significantly impacted by the conclusions arrived at for the previous two questions. If the stories are regarded as historically accurate, or at least based on historical reality, then the intent of the evangelists will be understood very differently than if the stories are regarded as fictional or mythical.

(4)    And finally, there is the theological question: What is the significance of Jesus' miracles? This poses two further questions: What was Jesus' own understanding of the miracles? and what was the understanding of the early church, including those who wrote the gospels? These questions have a significant overlap with the previous group of questions, but they lead into a third question: What is—or perhaps, what should be—our understanding of, and thus our response to, the miracle stories?

This chapter will consider each of these questions in turn, briefly surveying the various types of answers that have been given to each.

## A. The Philosophical Question: Can Miracles Happen?

While there have always been some who have questioned the possibility of miracles and thus the reality of Jesus' miracles, for most of the history of the church Jesus' miracles, as recorded in the gospels, have been taken for granted. This, however, changed significantly with the coming of the Enlightenment and the rise of Rationalism and Empiricism. The questioning of the possibility of miracles and, in turn, the reliability of the biblical accounts of miracles became not only permissible, but widespread.

In coming to a conclusion regarding the possibility, or otherwise, of miracles, two factors are significant: (1) the chosen definition of "miracle," and (2) the person's underlying worldview. The interplay of these two factors can be seen in the various views presented below.

Benedict Spinoza was an early Rationalist whose *Theologico-Political Treatise* (1670) was circulated in the late seventeenth century. He espoused a pantheistic view of God, understanding God and the universe to be of the same substance. He concluded that it was impossible for miracles to occur because it was impossible for God to act outside of creation. Spinoza understood the laws of nature to be the result of God's will, so for God to intervene in the laws of nature would be for God to violate his own will, something that was not possible.[4] His definition of miracles as "violations" of "natural laws" which are "immutable," and thus contrary to the "will of God," made the possibility of miracles appear irrational. Geisler summarizes Spinoza's argument against miracles in this fashion:

1. Miracles are violations of natural laws.

---

[4] C. John Collins, *The God of Miracles: An Exegetical Examination of God's Action in the World* (Wheaton: Crossway Books, 2000), p. 162.

2. Natural laws are immutable.
3. It is impossible to violate immutable laws.
4. Therefore, miracles are impossible.[5]

Spinoza's rationalistic, deterministic, and pantheistic presuppositions meant that the only conclusion he could come to was that miracles could not happen.

Perhaps the best known writer on the topic of the possibility of miracles is David Hume (1711–1776). Much of what has been written on the topic of miracles in the last two hundred and fifty years has, in one way or another, been written in response to his argument. In his *Enquiry Concerning the Human Understanding*[6] he included a section entitled "Of Miracles," which had the purpose of denying both the possibility of miracles and the possibility of determining that a miracle had occurred.

Instead of the rationalistic approach taken by Spinoza, Hume took an empirical approach in which the relationship between cause and effect was integral to his argument. From repeated experience, people conclude that certain events will happen in a predictable way. For example, it is not possible to be certain that the sun will rise tomorrow, but the experiential evidence is so strong that it is reasonable to believe that it will rise and foolish to believe that it will not. This "uniform experience" reaches the level where there is no room for doubt. By contrast, the evidence for miracles can never be strong enough to conclude that a miracle has occurred because "uniform experience" indicates that they do not. Geisler summarizes his argument thus:

1. A miracle is by definition a rare occurrence.
2. Natural law is by definition a description of regular occurrence.
3. The evidence for the regular is always greater than that for the rare.
4. Wise individuals always base belief on the greater evidence.
5. Therefore, wise individuals should never believe in miracles.[7]

Once again assumptions have played a key role in the outcome of the argument. Because, generally, experience is strongly against miracles, Hume assumed that there can never be *enough* evidence to support the occurrence of a miracle. It was logical to assume therefore that *all* reports of miracles must be *false*. But as Collins concludes:

From a literary point of view, Hume's reasoning overlooks one very important fact, namely, the normal reason for telling a story is to report "interesting" or "tellable" events, not the *usual* ones. This means that a narrative will not be about what we all know about already. This leads to another flaw in Hume's case: a consistent application of Hume's ideas would

---

[5] Norman L. Geisler, *Miracles and the Modern Mind* (Grand Rapids: Baker, 1992), p. 15.

[6] The first edition was published in 1748, with a second published posthumously in 1777. In addition to a number of reprints of the whole work, the section "Of Miracles" has been reprinted in part or in whole in numerous publications.

[7] Geisler, *Miracles*, pp. 27-28.

have us doubting *all* historical accounts of unusual things.[8]

In addition to arguing that the *amount* of evidence was insufficient to support belief in miracles, Hume also argued that the *kind* of testimony given in favor of miracles was insufficient. In his estimation, not enough people of "good sense, education, learning, integrity, and reputation" had witnessed any particular miracle in history for the evidence to be taken seriously, nor had miracles been performed "in such a public manner and in so celebrated part of the world, as to render detection unavoidable."[9] He noted that reports of miracles are more prevalent among "ignorant and barbarous" people and concluded that "civilized" people only believed in miracles when they had received the accounts from their "ignorant and barbarous ancestors."[10] Consequently, according to these criteria, the only accounts of history of any kind that could be regarded as reliable are those which came from large urban centers of the Western world in the last few centuries.

C. S. Lewis sought to counter Hume's argument in the following way. For Lewis the issue was not how much evidence or what type of evidence there might be for any given miracle, but rather the way in which the evidence was approached. This led him to define a miracle differently to Hume as "an interference with Nature by supernatural power."[11] For him, a miracle did not set aside nature or break the laws of nature. Rather he understood God to be acting to initiate a miracle. The principles of nature continue to work in a way that is analogous to the actions of a human's altering of the course of nature, though on a lesser scale.

Lewis saw a category of some of Jesus' miracles as parallel to the way God acts in nature. He labeled miracles such as the feeding of the five thousand, the turning of water into wine, and healings as "Miracles of the Old Creation" since, as he puts it, "they reproduce what we experience in the natural order."[12] On the other hand, Lewis labeled miracles such as the raising of Lazarus and of Jairus's daughter, Jesus walking on water and Jesus' resurrection as "Miracles of the New Creation," as these were not things that could happen through natural processes but heralded a new order, a new creation. But he did not view these as random events or violations of the order of nature.

More recently Corner has argued that understanding miracles as "interventions" implies that God is only active in miracles and not at other times. He differentiates between "general divine action" and "special divine action." He defines "general divine action" as "those actions of God that pertain to the whole of creation universally and simultaneously—effectively

---

[8] C. J. Collins, *God of Miracles*, p. 167.

[9] David Hume, *Enquiries Concerning the Human Understanding and Concerning the Principles of Morals*, reprinted from the posthumous edition of 1777 and edited with Introduction, Comparative Table of Contents, and Analytical Index by L. A. Selby-Bigge (London: Clarendon Press, 1975), pp. 116-17.

[10] Hume, *Enquiries*, p. 119.

[11] C. S. Lewis, *Miracles* (London: Geoffrey Bles, 1947), p. 15.

[12] Lewis, *Miracles*, p. 162.

God's action in creating and sustaining the world." "Special divine action" is the activity of God that pertains "to one particular time and place as opposed to another."[13] This understanding leads him to define what are commonly termed "miracles," not in terms of "unnatural acts" which violate the laws of nature,[14] but as special or immediate acts of God, which are beneficial or religiously significant, in contrast to his ongoing work of creating and sustaining the world.[15]

This acknowledges that some events generally described as miracles, such as a particularly fortuitous sequence of events, do not contravene any known "laws" but may still be the result of the special working of God. He points out that our understanding of the "laws of nature" is constantly changing. An event that appears to be a miracle may be the working of a "law" which, as yet, we do not understand. Key to this understanding of "miracle" is that it is something that is both "beneficial" and "religiously significant." It is something that points the recipient towards God.

With increased knowledge of other cultures, it has become apparent that those in other times and cultures are no more gullible than those in modern Western society, and their views cannot simply be dismissed as the result of ignorance or superstition. Western rationalism, with its insistence on "scientific" explanations in terms of cause and effect, is not the only way of viewing the world. Even Western science has come to realize that there are many things which, at least at present, defy rationalistic explanation. All this has led to a broadening in perceptions and worldviews that affects openness to the possibility of miracles.

It would appear, then, that the answer a person gives to the question: "Can miracles occur?" is one which depends more on their presuppositions and worldview than it does on empirical evidence. Reports of miracles are like any record of past events: they cannot be "proven" in the usual sense, rather the evidence must be weighed and conclusions drawn. Ultimately it is a matter of faith—for the atheist and the agnostic as much as for the believer. It is a choice, an act of faith, to decide to believe we live in a closed system with inviolable laws where miracles cannot happen, just as it is a choice, an act of faith, to decide to believe there is a God, or at least some form of higher being who can, and perhaps even does, act in unusual and extra-ordinary ways in our world. I concur with Brown who writes:

> Left to her own devices, we would expect nature to behave normally. Nature could not do anything other than that. But if God is God, and if God is the author of nature, then occasionally, when it suits his purpose, we might have to reckon with God's doing things that we had never seen before.[16]

---

[13] Mark Corner, *Signs of God* (Aldershot: Ashgate, 2005), p. 14.

[14] Corner, *Signs of God*, p. 198.

[15] Corner, *Signs of God*, p. 15.

[16] Colin Brown, *That You May Believe* (Grand Rapids: Eerdmans, 1985), p. 32.

## B. The Historical Question: Did Jesus' Miracles Happen?

If it is conceded that miracles might indeed occur, this suggests the next question: Did Jesus' miracles, as recorded in the gospels, actually happen?

The gospels present Jesus as a person who was the subject of miraculous activity, particularly focused around his birth, baptism, transfiguration and resurrection. He is also depicted as someone who possessed supernatural knowledge and who performed miraculous deeds.[17] Their number is a matter of debate.[18] There are a number of criteria which can be used to assess historicity. These are:

1. The criterion of multiple attestation of sources and forms.
2. The criterion of discontinuity
3. The criterion of coherence.
4. The criterion of embarrassment.[19]

With respect to the criterion of multiple attestation, the evidence for the historicity of Jesus as a miracle worker is very strong. The arrangement of miracle stories in Mark's Gospel[20] suggests that the tradition of miracle stories existed in his sources. Mark includes blocks of miracle stories (Mark 1:21–2:12; 4:35–5:43; 6:30-56; 7:24–8:10) as well as miracle stories interspersed with other material (Mark 3:1-6; 8:22-26; 9:14-29; 11:12-14). The stories vary in length and tone. A few provide the names of people and places, but most do not. Even though Mark does not have a great deal of discourse material, he does include a small amount of material that presents Jesus speaking about his miracles (Mark 8:17-21; 9:28-29).

While "Q" is generally regarded as being a source composed predominantly

---

[17] See the Appendix for a listing of Jesus' miraculous deeds and the biblical references for them.

[18] It is difficult to gain consensus on exactly how many are recorded in the gospels because there is disagreement on such issues as: (a) what constitutes a parallel (e.g., are the stories of healing two blind men in Matt. 9:27-31 and Matt. 18:35-43 two accounts of the same incident or two separate incidents?); (b) what constitutes a miraculous deed (e.g., is the story of the coin in the fish's mouth in Matt. 17:24-27 a miraculous deed or a case of supernatural knowledge?); and (c) where is the borderline between the description of a miraculous deed and a summary statement regarding Jesus' miraculous deeds (e.g., are the descriptions of Jesus healing many people with demons in Mark 1:32-34 and Matt. 8:16-17 describing miraculous deeds or do they constitute summary statements?).

[19] C. Blomberg, "Concluding Reflections," in *Gospel Perspectives* (Sheffield: JSOT Press, 1986), pp. 445-51; René Latourelle, *The Miracles of Jesus and the Theology of Miracles* (New York: Paulist, 1988), pp. 53-69; J. P. Meier, *A Marginal Jew* vol. 1 (New York: Doubleday, 1994), pp. 619-31; and G. H. Twelftree, *Jesus The Miracle Worker* (Downers Grove: IVP, 1999), pp. 241-57 all include sections of significant length that apply the criteria for determining historicity for the overall evidence concerning Jesus as a miracle worker. Latourelle, Meier and Twelftree examine individual miracle stories in the light of these criteria.

[20] This is working from the assumption that Mark's Gospel was the first of the canonical gospels to be written, which is the consensus of the majority of scholars. Additionally, the traditional names for the gospels are being used without any presumption on the question of authorship.

of Jesus' sayings, it would seem to include at least one miracle story, that of the healing of the centurion's servant.[21] It also includes several sayings where Jesus' miracles are mentioned.[22] There are a small number of miracle stories that are unique to Matthew,[23] with a larger number that are unique to Luke.[24] This suggests that the sources that were unique to each gospel included miracle stories. John's Gospel appears to have been written independently of the Synoptic Gospels and provides a different theological perspective on miracles. While it does have miracle stories that are unique, possibly reflecting a separate tradition, it also includes miracle stories that have parallels in the Synoptics.[25] This implies that the miracle stories in John are not the fabrication of the author but extend to earlier traditions.

There is also evidence from extra-biblical sources that point to Jesus as a miracle worker. In his *Antiquities*, Josephus refers to Jesus as a "doer of surprising deeds."[26] While some of the content of the section appears to have been edited by later Christian writers because it includes some statements that a devout Jew would be unlikely to confess about Jesus, it is likely that the reference to Jesus as a worker of miracles is authentic. The word translated "surprising" is used by Josephus elsewhere to mean "miraculous."[27] Additionally, the Babylonian Talmud refers to Jesus as one who "practiced sorcery," [28] most likely a reference to healing. Although these statements are quite general, they do provide evidence that Jesus was reputed to have performed miracles and that this knowledge was not limited to his followers.

It can be seen that there is significant attestation from multiple sources, both biblical and extra-biblical. The principle of multiple attestation, however, also requires the inclusion of a variety of forms. Accounts of healings, exorcisms and nature miracles are presented in narrative form. Sayings about miracles include general biographical statements about Jesus,[29] rhetorical questions,[30] declarative statements,[31] miraculous knowledge,[32] and the mandate for Jesus' disciples to heal and cast out demons.[33] Not only is there support from multiple sources, but this support also comes in a variety of literary forms.

---

[21] Matt. 8:5-13 ‖ Luke 7:1-10. Some scholars view the healing of the mute demoniac (who is also blind in Matthew), Matt. 12:22-23 ‖ Luke 11:14, as a second example.

[22] Statements regarding exorcism in the Beelzebul controversy, Matt. 12:22-32‖ Luke 11:14-23; Jesus' reply to John the Baptist, Matt. 11:5-6 ‖ Luke 11:22-23; woes against cities who did not believe Jesus in spite of miracles, Matt. 11:20-24 ‖ Luke 10:12-15; Jesus' commissioning the disciples to perform miracles, Matt. 10:8 ‖ Luke 10:9.

[23] See Appendix for references.

[24] See Appendix for references.

[25] See Appendix for references.

[26] Josephus, *Ant.* 18.63-64.

[27] Josephus uses the same word to refer to miracles performed by Elisha (*Ant.* 9.182).

[28] *b. Sanh.* 43a

[29] Luke 13:32; Matt. 11:5-6 ‖ Luke 11:22-23.

[30] Matt. 12:27 ‖ Luke 11:19.

[31] Matt. 12:28 ‖ Luke 11:20.

[32] John 4:17-18, 21; 2:23-25.

[33] Mark 6:7, 13; Luke 10:8-9.

Additionally, the criterion of discontinuity provides support for the historicity of Jesus' miracles. There were stories about miracles in both Jewish and Greco-Roman literature, but there does not seem to have been any one person about whom there were so many stories.

A significant point of discontinuity between Greco-Roman literary sources and the NT is the length of time between the purported events and the writing down of the accounts. While there are differences of opinion as to the dating of Mark's Gospel, most date it no later that about AD 70, with some dating it possibly as early as the 50s. This means that Mark was written within a generation of the events it reports. This is to be contrasted with the reports of the first-century miracle worker, Apollonius of Tyana, about whom little is written until Philostratus produced a biography of him in the early third century. There are accounts of Jewish holy men from Galilee such as Honi the Circle-Drawer and Hanina ben-Dosa, which some commentators contend do provide a parallel with Jesus. However, such miracle workers only receive brief mention in the Mishnah, written approximately 200 years later. It is not until the fifth and sixth centuries that the traditions are more fully developed in the Talmuds.[34]

There is discontinuity between the manner in which miracles, particularly healings, are carried out. When Jewish prophets or Jesus' disciples performed healings, it was "in the name of God" or, in the case of those who came after Jesus, "in the name of Jesus." Other healers are reported using a range of incantations and talismans to effect healing. Jesus, however, performed healings in his own name. "I say to you . . ." (Mark 1:41; 2:11; 5:41) is a common statement on Jesus' lips.[35] Along with this is the emphasis on faith that is found in numerous gospel accounts of miracles but is largely absent from Greco-Roman or Jewish miracle stories.[36]

However, it is in the overall picture rather than the details of the miracle stories that the greatest discontinuity is found. As Meier concludes:

> The overall configuration, pattern or *Gestalt* of Jesus as a popular preacher and teller of parables, *plus* authoritative interpreter of the law and teacher of morality, *plus* proclaimer and realizer of the eschatological kingdom of God, *plus* miracle-worker actualizing his own proclamation has no adequate parallel in either the pagan or Jewish literature of the time.[37]

Furthermore, the criterion of coherence provides support for the historicity of Jesus' miracles. This criterion holds that when, by using other criteria, it is established that both what is reported of Jesus' words and what is reported of his deeds have a good chance of being historical, then there should

---

[34] Meier, *A Marginal Jew*, vol. 2, p. 624.

[35] Latourelle, *The Miracles of Jesus*, p. 59.

[36] Norman Perrin, *Rediscovering the Teaching of Jesus* (New York: Harper and Row, 1967), pp. 130-42.

[37] Meier, *A Marginal Jew*, vol. 2, p. 624.

be coherence between the two.[38] One example where this is quite clear is that Jesus' response to the accusations that he cast out demons by the power of Beelzebul is congruent with the accounts of his actions in casting out demons. Moreover, in his response to John the Baptist's query as to whether he was the one who was promised or whether another was coming, he pointed to his practical ministry, particularly the healings, but also to his proclamation of the kingdom of God.[39] This coherence is particularly noticeable in Matthew where a section composed primarily of Jesus, teaching (Matthew 5–7) is immediately followed by a section that focuses predominantly on Jesus' miracles (Matthew 8–9).

With regard to the criterion of embarrassment there is less support here for Jesus' miracles than there is for some of Jesus' teaching. After all, who would be embarrassed about the positive effects of Jesus' healing ministry? But it does seem unlikely that the church would invent the charge that Jesus' exorcisms were the result of him being in league with Beelzebul. This, at least, could be seen as a source of embarrassment.

A general consensus has been reached that Jesus did extraordinary deeds which he and others considered to be miracles. Meier argues that the evidence, particularly that of multiple attestation and coherence, indicate that "total fabrication by the early church is, practically speaking, impossible."[40] He goes so far as to claim:

> If the miracle tradition from Jesus' public ministry were to be rejected *in toto* as unhistorical, so should every other gospel tradition about him. For if the criteria of historicity do not work in the case of the miracle tradition, where multiple attestation is so massive and coherence so impressive, there is no reason to expect them to work elsewhere.[41]

There is, however, less consensus among scholars when it comes to the historicity of any particular miracle story. For some this goes back to the philosophical question of whether some types of miracles can happen and the presupposition that they do not. For others it is simply a matter of the quantity of the data being insufficient to make a determination based on the criteria for historicity alone. Many of the miracle stories in the gospels are short and do not have significant corroborating data, therefore it is not possible to "prove" their historicity. The lack of corroborating evidence does not necessarily mean the account is unhistorical. In Blomberg's words, "Multiple attestation enhances the case but single attestation in and of itself does not detract."[42] Twelftree further points out that "we cannot move from '*un*proven' to '*dis*proven.'"[43] The overall evidence for Jesus as a miracle worker is

---

[38] Meier, *A Marginal Jew*, p. 1.176.

[39] Matt. 11:2-6 ‖ Luke 7:18-23.

[40] Meier, *A Marginal Jew*, vol. 2, p. 630.

[41] Meier, *A Marginal Jew*, vol. 2, p. 630.

[42] Blomberg, "Concluding Reflections," p. 446.

[43] Twelftree, *Jesus The Miracle Worker*, p. 250.

sufficiently strong that, barring a preconception to the contrary, it becomes possible to at least consider the possibility that specific miracle stories go back to historical events.

## C. The Literary Question: What Did the Evangelists Intend When They Included the Miracle Stories in the Gospels?

In the study of the gospels, there has been increasing interest in the particular theological perspectives of each of the evangelists, and this has flowed over into examination of their individual interests in and use of the miracle stories.

One way of understanding the evangelists' intent when they included the miracle stories is to examine the words they use to describe miracles. The most common word used of miracles in the Synoptic Gospels is δύναμις (*dynamis*). While its basic meaning is power, strength, or might, it can also be used, in the plural, with the meaning of mighty or powerful deeds, in other words, miracles.[44] It is related to the verb δύναμαι (*dynamai*) meaning "to be able," "to be capable," suggesting that these powerful deeds are the work of God who is "capable," "powerful." With the use of this word, the focus is on the event as an expression of God's power rather than the event for its own sake.

A word frequently used in the NT is σῴζω (*sōzō*) meaning "to save."[45] It is used in all four gospels of eschatological salvation, but in Luke and Mark, and to a lesser extent Matthew, it is also used of healing. In each case it is the healing of the whole person that is brought about in response to faith. In the gospels physical healing is an expression of eschatological salvation.

The most common word for miracle in John's Gospel is σημεῖον (*sēmeion*), a sign or a corroborating or authenticating mark.[46] For John, Jesus' miracles testify to Jesus' identity (John 3:2; 7:31). The appropriate response to "signs" is belief (John 2:11, 23; 4:53; 9:38). The word also appears in the Synoptics, but typically in condemnation of those who seek such "signs" as proof.[47]

Another commonly used word is ἔργον (*ergon*), "work." While it is used in a general sense of Jesus' ministry in the Synoptics, it is linked more specifically with Jesus' miracles in John. Like "signs," Jesus' "works" bear witness to the fact that he has come from the Father.[48]

There are several other words that are used occasionally including θαυμάσια (*thaumasia*), "amazing things" (Matt. 21:15), παράδοξα (*paradoxa*), strange or remarkable things (Luke 5:26), and τέρας (*teras*), a wonder or marvel. This last word is used only in the plural combined with σημεῖα, and always negatively,

---

[44] O. Betz, "Might: δύναμις," in C. Brown, ed., *New International Dictionary of New Testament Theology*, volume 2 (Exeter: Paternoster, 1976), pp. 601-06.

[45] J. Schneider and C. Brown, "Redemption: σῴζω," in *NIDNTT*, vol. 3 (1978), pp. 205-16.

[46] O. Hofius and C. Brown, "Miracle, Wonder, Sign: σημεῖον," *NIDNTT*, vol. 2, pp. 626-33.

[47] Matt. 12:38-39; 16:1-4; Mark 8:11-12; Luke 11:16, 29-30; 23:8-9.

[48] John 5:19-24, 36-37; 10:25, 32, 37-39; 14:10-11.

either in the sense of wonders produced by false messiahs (Matt. 24:24; Mark 13:22) or in the sense that the Synoptics use σημεῖα of the signs that people seek yet refuse to believe.[49]

From this it can be seen that the more sensational words, such as θαυμάσια, παράδοξα or τέρας, are only used rarely or in a negative sense. The words that dominate are "mighty deeds," "signs," "works" and cognates of the verb "save." The picture that these words build up is that Jesus' miracles are done in the power of God, in the service of God, as pointers towards God, and as expressions of God's salvation, not simply to produce spectacular events.

Another way of coming to an understanding of the gospel writers' intentions regarding the inclusion of miracle stories is to examine how each writer structures their gospel and how the miracle stories fit within that structure.

## 1. Mark

Mark's Gospel can be divided into two parts. The majority of the miracle stories are included in the first half (Mark 1:1–8:26) and only three are narrated in the second half (Mark 8:27–16:8). This reflects the interplay of key themes in Mark: power and authority in stark contrast to suffering and death. Jesus is presented as a powerful miracle worker and authoritative teacher as well as the suffering Messiah who gives his life for many. Jesus' power and authority are dominant in the first half, while his suffering and death are dominant in the second half.

The first group of miracles focuses on Jesus' ministry in Capernaum. They follow shortly after the accounts of Jesus' baptism, empowering with the Spirit, temptation by Satan (Mark 1:9-13), and Mark's general summary statement of Jesus' ministry (Mark 1:14-15), and are introduced with an additional summary statement highlighting Jesus' authoritative teaching (Mark 1:22). The miracle stories themselves highlight Jesus' authority over demons and illness. Also introduced in this section is the theme of the "Messianic Secret"[50] which draws attention to the fact that a view of Jesus as a powerful Messiah is incomplete without a view of him as the suffering Messiah.

The narrative then moves into a section which includes a series of healing miracles that draw attention to Jesus' interaction with his critics, in particular, the Jewish leadership. Jesus' claim to have authority to forgive sins (Mark 2:10) and his claim to have authority over the Sabbath (Mark 2:28; 3:4), both linked with healing miracles, anger the Jewish leadership which conspires to destroy him (Mark 3:6). This section culminates with the charge that he casts out demons by the power of Beelzebul (Mark 3:22). While these stories

---

[49] John 4:48, cf. Matt. 12:38-39; 16:1-4; Mark 8:11-12; Luke 11:16, 29-30; 23:8-9.

[50] The label "Messianic Secret" has been given to a theme that is particularly dominant in Mark's Gospel. Jesus instructs his disciples and evil spirits not to divulge his identity and tells people who have been healed not to tell others.

expand the focus of Jesus' authority and power, they also hint at the final culmination of Jesus' ministry in suffering and death which results in salvation for people and victory over the powers of evil (Mark 3:4, 6, 23-26).

Following a section of teaching in parables, Mark recounts four astounding miracles: calming the storm (Mark 4:37-41), healing the Gerasene demoniac (Mark 5:1-5), healing the hemorrhaging woman (Mark 5:48-51), and raising Jairus's daughter (Mark 5:22-24, 38-42). In the preceding discussion of the significance of parables Mark noted the privileged position of the disciples. The miracle stories that follow feature the presence of the disciples; in fact for two of them only disciples are present. The section concludes with the disciples being sent out to do what Jesus had been doing, namely, proclaiming that all should repent, and casting out demons and healing people (Mark 6:6b-13). Jesus' power and authority is extended to his disciples. But also included in this section is a reminder of the other side of the contrast: in his hometown of Nazareth, Jesus is rejected and ministry is limited by unbelief (Mark 6:1-6a).

The martyrdom of John the Baptist (Mark 6:29), another reminder of suffering and death, introduces a series of miracle stories dominated by two accounts of feeding large numbers of people (Mark 6:30-44; 8:1-10). The theme of bread, symbolic of messianic blessings and the eschatological banquet, runs right through this section, as does the theme of the disciples' failure to understand. Mark's commentary on the disciples' reaction to the miracles emphasizes their astonishment, lack of understanding and hardness of heart, and is pointedly contrasted with the Syro-Phoenician woman's faith. This section ends with the account of the blind man whose sight is restored in two stages (Mark 8:22-26). By placing this story at the central point of the Gospel, Mark makes it symbolic of the disciples' process towards understanding. So far the disciples have been able to come to terms, at least to some degree, with the concept of Jesus as the powerful Messiah, but as the account of Peter's confession and his reaction to Jesus' prediction of suffering and death show, they have not yet been able to grasp the concept of Jesus as a suffering Messiah (Mark 8:27-33).

This marks a turning point in Mark's Gospel. From here the prediction of Jesus' suffering and death becomes increasingly more explicit. Between here and Jesus' final approach to Jerusalem, only one miracle story is narrated, that of the healing of the epileptic boy (Mark 9:14-29), which again emphasizes the ineffectiveness and lack of understanding on the part of the disciples.

There are only two more miracle stories in Mark's Gospel. Their positioning gives them a symbolic meaning in addition to the significance of the stories in their own right. The restoring of sight to Bartimaeus who then follows Jesus "on the way" (Mark 10:46-52) functions prophetically. Eventually the disciples will "see." They will understand that Jesus is both the powerful Messiah and the suffering Messiah, and they will follow him. This is in contrast to the final miracle story, the cursing of the fig tree (Mark 11:12-14), which is the only miracle story with a negative outcome. Because it is interwoven with the account of Jesus cleansing the temple, it functions as a prophetic commentary on those who have rejected Jesus, particularly the Jewish leadership.

Mark's use of the miracle stories reinforces his presentation of the two aspects of Jesus as Messiah: his power and his weakness. The Christ of powerful deeds humbles and empties himself.

## 2. Matthew

Matthew uses many of the same stories as Mark, but the way he structures his Gospel gives them a different emphasis. In chapters 8–9, he narrates a series of miracle stories, including a number from the first half of Mark, though in a different order, as well as several that are not in Mark. This follows the discourse section (Matthew 5–7) commonly known as the "Sermon on the Mount." Almost identical summary statements occur prior to the Sermon and following the collection of miracle stories (Matt. 4:23; 9:35). Just as the Sermon concludes with a statement that the people were amazed at Jesus' teaching so too the series of miracle stories concludes with a statement that the people were amazed (Matt. 7:28-29; 9:33). These two sections are tied together in such a way that Jesus' teaching and deeds cannot be separated. The miracle stories function as support for Jesus' teaching.

In the teaching there is an emphasis on Jesus being the fulfillment of the law and being able to interpret that law authoritatively. This theme is continued in the series of miracle stories. In the first story the man cured of leprosy is told to go and show himself to the priest as Moses commanded (Matt. 7:4). Part way through the series is an explicit statement regarding the fulfillment of prophecy in which Isa. 53:4, part of a "Servant Song," is quoted (Matt. 8:17). The section concludes with reference to Jesus' compassion on the people because they were like "sheep without a shepherd" (Matt. 9:36). "Shepherd" is a common word in the OT and is used in a number of places, especially Ezekiel 34, as a metaphor for rulers and leaders.

Two more miracle stories are included in Matthew 12, again linked to the fulfillment of prophecy and the amazement of the crowds.[51] Although it was present in the previous sequence, the rejection by the Jewish leadership and the accusation that it is by the power of Beelzebul that Jesus is able to perform such miracles, is presented more strongly in this section.

Following another discourse section, Matthew includes a series of miracles that Mark used to focus on the disciples (Matthew 14–15). Matthew uses these miracles to focus on discipleship, but, unlike Mark, does not emphasize the failure of the disciples to understand. Instead the role of the disciples is given a higher profile and their responses to the miracles are depicted more positively. Yet even here there is mention of their lack of faith, and in other sections there are additional references to their failings with respect to miracles.[52]

---

[51] Matt. 12:18-21, cf. Isa. 42:1-4; Matt. 12:23.
[52] Matt. 14:31; cf. 8:26; 16:8; 17:20.

A key element in Matthew's use of the miracle stories is the focus on faith. Statements such as "let it be done for you according to your faith" and "your faith has made you well" are common.[53] Twice non-Jews are particularly commended for their faith (Matt. 8:10; 15:28). While Matthew's descriptions of the miracles tend to be briefer than Mark's, the dialogues between Jesus and those who are the beneficiaries of the miracles tend to be longer, especially when they involve the issue of faith. Matthew uses the miracle stories to encourage the on-going faith of his readers.[54]

## 3. Luke

Luke follows the same basic outline as Mark and Matthew, but has his own emphases. In the sequel to his Gospel, Luke describes his first book as being about "all that Jesus did and taught" (Acts 1:1; cf. Luke 24:19). The sequence of verbs is significant. While Matthew gave priority to Jesus' teaching, Luke brings Jesus' deeds to the fore.

Luke includes many of the miracle stories from Mark, though notably does not include any material from Mark 6:45–8:27. Luke shares one miracle story with Matthew, possibly emanating from the "Q" source. Luke contains a number of miracle stories not found in any other gospel. His account of Jesus' ministry can be divided into three sections: ministry in Galilee (Luke 4:14–9:50), the journey to Jerusalem (Luke 9:51–19:44), and the final week including the passion (Luke 19:45–24:53). The majority of the miracle stories occur in the first part, and while there are fewer miracle stories in the second part, they are still prominent. There is only one miracle story in the final part, namely, the healing the high priest's servant's ear (Luke 22:50-51).

Luke introduces Jesus' ministry with the incident in Nazareth where Jesus reads from Isaiah:

> The Spirit of the Lord is upon me, because he has anointed me to bring good news to the poor. He has sent me to proclaim release to the captives and recovery of sight to the blind, to let the oppressed go free, to proclaim the year of the Lord's favor (Luke 4:18-19; cf. Isa. 61:1-2).

Jesus' comment, "Today this scripture has been fulfilled in your hearing," along with the Luke's placing of this incident at the beginning of his account of Jesus' ministry, indicates that Luke intends his readers to interpret that ministry in the light of this prophecy regarding his empowerment by the Spirit. The miracles are to be seen therefore as the result of the work of the Spirit. But miracles are also an expression of "good news to the poor," or good news that consists of release, healing, and freedom. When John the Baptist's disciples bring John's query as to whether Jesus is the one who was promised, Jesus replies in similar terms: "Go and tell John what you have seen

---

[53] Matt. 9:29; 8:13; cf. 9:22; 15:28.

[54] See R. H. Fuller, *Interpreting the Miracles* (London: SCM Press, 1963), p. 82.

and heard: the blind receive their sight, the lame walk, the lepers are cleansed, the deaf hear, the dead are raised, the poor have good news brought to them" (Luke 7:22). And as Luke continues his account in Acts, this same understanding is expressed when Jesus' ministry is summarized as: "God anointed Jesus of Nazareth with the Holy Spirit and with power; he went about doing good and healing all who were oppressed by the devil, for God was with him" (Acts 10:38).

Thus the miracles are presented as integral to salvation history. While Mark makes a clear distinction between healings and exorcisms, Luke frequently merges the two. Healing is often expressed as deliverance. The miracles are evidence of the fall of the kingdom of Satan, but, more importantly, they are evidence that "the kingdom of God has come to you" (Luke 11:20). When the disciples return from their mission and are amazed that even the demons submit, Jesus says to them, "Do not rejoice that the spirits submit to you, but rejoice that your names are written in heaven" (Luke 10:20). The focus is primarily on the positive outcome of salvation history.

While the miracles are, in a sense, "proofs," they are not universally accepted. This is unambiguously expressed in the parable of the Rich Man and Lazarus where Jesus comments: "If they do not listen to Moses and the prophets, neither will they be convinced even if someone rises from the dead" (Luke 16:31).

Similarly there was initial amazement in Nazareth (4:22), but this sentiment quickly turned to anger. However, this rejection meant that the prophecy that Jesus would bring good news to the "poor" becomes more explicitly fulfilled as Jesus turns to those who are outcast: the sick, lepers, tax collectors, women, sinners, and non-Jews. It is these people who respond positively.

Like Mark and Matthew, Luke highlights the place of faith on the part of those who are healed, but he also depicts faith as the means by which the significance of the miracles is appropriated. For example, it is the one leper out of the ten who returns to give thanks who is commended for his faith. The proper response, as this man demonstrates, is to praise God (Luke 17:11-19).

Luke focuses on Jesus' miraculous deeds, but not for the sake of the deeds themselves. They are subsidiary to salvation. In the words of R. H. Fuller: "The healings, exorcisms and raising from the dead are all signs that Jesus is the prophet-Messiah sent from God: in him the salvation of God is present in history."[55]

## 4. John

Just as John's Gospel as a whole is quite different from the Synoptic Gospels, so too is his approach to the miracle stories. The Gospel can be divided into two parts: the "Book of Signs"[56] and the "Book of Passion" or the "Book of

---

[55] Fuller, *Interpreting the Miracles*, pp. 85-86.

[56] John 1:19–12:50. The label "Book of Signs" is also sometimes used to denote a possible

Glory."[57] John has fewer miracle stories than the Synoptics, only seven in the first part.[58] They tend to stress the desperate situations in which Jesus chooses to act, as well as the power of Jesus' word in overcoming overwhelming obstacles and producing astonishing results.

John describes the miracles as "signs" and "works." Thus they both point to Jesus' relationship to the Father and the power and glory of Jesus himself. Each miracle story is associated with a discussion that uncovers it meaning. Rather than focusing on the kingdom of God, as the Synoptics do, these discussions focus on eternal life, Jesus' relationship with his Father, and Jesus' glory. This different focus is perhaps why there are no accounts of exorcisms in John. Such an omission would seem to be deliberate, as it is unlikely that the writer would have been unaware of exorcism stories.

The first "sign" that John presents is the turning of water into wine at the wedding in Cana (John 2:1-11). The placement here serves a similar function as the Nazareth narrative does in Luke: it is a summary of Jesus' ministry. He turns the water set aside for Jewish purification rites into wine for celebration, symbolic of the messianic banquet and the presence of the Messiah who fulfils the law (Isa. 25:6). The statement, "You have kept the good wine until now," is not simply part of the narrative of the event, but functions as a theological statement to the effect that in Jesus the "good wine" has now come. This understanding is reinforced by the following pericope where Jesus cleanses the temple and by implication challenges the way in which the conventional religious order functions. The miracle at Cana reveals Jesus' "glory," yet Jesus' "hour" has not yet come. "Glory" and "hour" are both words that John frequently associates with Jesus' death. The story as a whole, then, functions symbolically. Jesus is the Messiah who fulfils the law of Moses and brings salvation through his death.

John continues the series of "signs" with healing the official's son at Capernaum, healing the man at the pool of Bethsaida, feeding the five thousand, walking on water, healing the man born blind, and concludes the sequence with raising Lazarus.[59] Each "sign" to some degree presents Jesus as giver of "life."[60] This theme is brought to a climax with the raising of Lazarus. Apart from the passion narrative, this is the longest narrative in the Gospel, and unlike the previous "signs," which are frequently followed by an explanatory narrative, this one has an explanation intertwined with it.[61] This

---

source the writer of John's Gospel may have used. It is argued that this source contained a collection of accounts of Jesus' miraculous deeds, and is the source of the miracle stories unique to John.

[57] John 13:1–20:31. This section focuses on the last week, the passion and the resurrection narratives, hence the label "Book of Passion." But John frequently refers to Jesus' death as him being "lifted up" or "glorified," hence the title "Book of Glory."

[58] There is also one miracle story in the second part. It occurs in chapter 21, which is likely to be a postscript added at a later stage in the composition history of the Gospel, and so functions differently from those miracles recounted in the first part.

[59] John 4:46-54; 5:1-9; 6:5-13; 6:9-21; 9:1-41; 11:1-44.

[60] Meier, *A Marginal Jew*, vol. 2, p. 798.

[61] Twelftree, *Jesus The Miracle Worker*, p. 214.

miracle also forms a bridge to the "Book of Passion." John presents this event as the direct trigger for the Jewish leadership's final decision to get rid of Jesus (John 11:45-53). Thus it points forward to Jesus' death and resurrection.

Response to Jesus' "signs" is mixed. Some people respond with faith.[62] Others react with unbelief, which often results in a plot to get rid of Jesus.[63] Still others see the signs simply as wonderful events (John 4:48; 6:2, 30). Belief based on signs is encouraged: "Believe me that I am in the Father and the Father is in me; but if you do not, then believe me because of the works themselves" (John 14:11; cf. 10:38). However, this faith based on miracles is only a starting point. It is a faith that goes beyond the signs that John wants to encourage: "Blessed are those who have not seen and yet have believed" (John 20:29). Engendering such belief is, in fact, the author's purpose in writing:

> Now Jesus did many other signs in the presence of his disciples, which are not written in this book. But these are written so that you may come to believe[64] that Jesus is the Messiah, the Son of God, and that through believing you may have life in his name (John 20:30-31).

It can be seen that each of the gospel writers uses the miracle stories in different, though not mutually exclusive, ways. Mark presents Jesus as both powerful Messiah and suffering Messiah. Jesus' miracles cannot be taken in isolation from his death. Matthew uses the miracle stories as support for Jesus' teaching and as evidence that he fulfils prophecy. Jesus' teaching and his deeds go together. Luke sums up Jesus' ministry as "good news for the poor" and uses the miracle stories as demonstrations of the healing, release and freedom that is inherent in this "good news." Jesus' miracles are integral to salvation history. John presents the miracle stories as "signs" that point to Jesus, his relationship with the Father, and the eternal life that is available through Jesus. While they have different emphases, each evangelist has the same basic purpose: to present Jesus in such a way as to cause people to respond in faith. The miracle stories are part of the way in which they do this.

## D. The Theological Question: What is the Significance of Jesus' Miracles?

To the extent that the gospels reflect Jesus' life, his actions and his words, they are a window to Jesus' own understanding of the miraculous deeds he

---

[62] John 2:11, 23; 4:50, 53; 6:14; 9:38; 11:25-27, 40, 45.

[63] John 5:18; 6:66; 9:24; 11:46-53; 12:37.

[64] There is a textual variant associated with the verb "believe." Some manuscripts, which the NRSV follows here, have an aorist subjunctive which may put the emphasis on initial "coming to believe." Other manuscripts have a present subjunctive, which carries the nuance of ongoing belief. The overall context of John does not make a sharp distinction between the two. The context here, whether the original is understood to be an aorist or a present tense, suggests that the phrase "that you may believe" is not exclusively initial belief or ongoing belief, but is inclusive of both.

performed. Thus it is to the evangelists that we must turn for guidance in coming to an understanding of the significance of Jesus' miracles for us today.

The miracle stories are interwoven throughout each gospel account of Jesus' life and ministry, though to a lesser extent in the final days before his death. In their accounts of his death, the miracles Jesus performed during his life are overshadowed by the miracle of which Jesus was the subject, that is, the resurrection. Therefore if we are to come to an understanding of who Jesus was and the significance of his life, we must come to an understanding of the miracles in the light of the resurrection. It is in the light of reflection on the resurrection that the evangelists present their accounts of Jesus' life, including his miraculous deeds.

There is a general consensus among scholars that Jesus' miracles are presented as indicators of the presence of the kingdom of God. The exorcisms and the defeat of Satan that they implied (particularly the implication that Jesus is the "stronger man" who has defeated the "strong man," Satan; Matt. 12:22-29; Mark 3:22-27; Luke 11:15-22), together with the healings and the fulfillment of prophecy they implied, seem to indicate that, in some sense, Jesus understood the kingdom to be already present (Matt. 11:4-5; 12:28). However, many of the references to the kingdom suggest that it has only "come near" (Mark 1:15). The kingdom in its fullness is still to come. Nevertheless, the miracles are meant to lead people into the kingdom. The miracles present Jesus as the embodiment of its power and grace.

The miracles also point to Jesus' identity as the eschatological Messiah who brings salvation. The miracles are a concrete, visible sign of holistic salvation. Physical, emotional, social and spiritual restoration and freedom were prophesied as being part of the age to come. In the miracles, Jesus is presented as the bringer of that salvation.

The power through which Jesus performs miraculous deeds is depicted as being the power of God. His relationship with God is portrayed as unique, expressed both in his use of the word *Abba* (Father) to refer to God (Mark 14:36), and in his repeated insistence that his works are the works of his Father (John 5:36; 10:25, 32, 37). In the miracles God's power is at work.

In each of the gospels this presentation of Jesus is implicit both through Jesus' teaching and his miraculous deeds. However, it is only through the passion and resurrection narratives that this becomes explicit. Jesus' followers, especially in Mark, are characterized as having a partial appreciation of his identity and the significance of his deeds during his life. However, it is only with the resurrection, and the theological reflection triggered by it, that Jesus is fully revealed as the inaugurator of the kingdom of God, the divinely appointed bringer of eschatological salvation and the agent of God's power.

Such a presentation requires a response. The response in Jesus' own time was mixed. Some responded with unbelief and hostility, others with faith and acceptance. Those who responded to an encounter with Jesus with faith were able to enter into a transforming relationship with him. It is this sort of faith response that the writers of the gospels want to elicit from their readers.

412

# E. Conclusion

We return to the questions that were posed at the outset. To the philosophical question "Can and do miracles occur?" the answer (whether positive or negative) cannot be proven, at least not in the usual sense of a "proof." Yet if one remains at least open to the possibility, and does not automatically on the basis of preconceived ideas reject the concept of miracles out of hand, then it is possible to have an openness regarding the answers to the questions below.

The evidence regarding the historical question "Did Jesus' miracles occur?" is strong. While there is insufficient evidence to "prove" that any specific miracle occurred exactly as it is reported in the gospels, the overall evidence that Jesus did perform miraculous deeds, especially healings and exorcisms, is weighty indeed. If the overall evidence for Jesus as a miracle worker is accepted, then it becomes possible to consider that individual miracle stories may go back to real events.

Examination of the gospels themselves provides answers to the literary question, "What did the gospel writers intend when they used the miracle stories?" The evidence strongly suggests they intended the miracle stories, along with Jesus' teaching, to be indicators of the inauguration of the kingdom of God, evidence of Jesus' relationship with his Father, and testimony to a decisive juncture in salvation history. Ultimately they called their readers to respond to Jesus in faith.

The final question, a theological one, "What was/is the significance of Jesus' miracles?" is one which continues to be open to interpretation. If the first two questions are answered in the negative, then it becomes difficult, if not impossible, to consider the evangelists' interpretation of the significance of Jesus' miracles as legitimate. Some other explanation must be found. If, however, the first two questions are answered in the affirmative, or if Jesus' miracles are at least regarded as possible, then it also becomes possible to consider that the evangelists' interpretation of those miracles is reasonable. Today's readers of the gospels generally, and the miracle stories in particular, are faced with the same choice that the original readers, and in fact the original witnesses to Jesus' ministry, were faced with. They may choose to respond with scepticism and unbelief, or they may choose to respond with faith and acceptance, both of Jesus' deeds and words, and of Jesus himself.

## Appendix: Miracles of Jesus Recorded in the Gospels

The layout of the following table begins with the miracle stories in Mark, along with parallels in the other gospels. This is based on the view of the majority of scholars that Mark's Gospel was the first of the canonical gospels to be written. The table then lists those stories that are common to Matthew and Luke, that is, those likely to have come from "Q," and finally lists those stories that are unique to Matthew, Luke, and John respectively.

| | Mark | Matthew | Luke | John |
|---|---|---|---|---|
| Man with an Unclean Spirit | 1:23-26 | | 4:33-35 | |
| Peter's Mother-in-Law | 1:30-31 | 8:14-15 | 4:38-39 | |
| Many with Demons | 1:32-34 | 8:16-17 | 4:40-41 | |
| Man with Leprosy | 1:40-42 | 8:2-4 | 5:12-13 | |
| Paralytic Man | 2:3-12 | 9:2-7 | 5:18-25 | |
| Man with a Withered Hand | 3:1-5 | 12:10-13 | 6:6-10 | |
| Calming a Storm | 4:37-41 | 8:23-27 | 8:22-25 | |
| Gerasene/Gadarene Demoniac(s) | 5:1-5 | 8:28-34 | 8:27-35 | |
| Raising Jairus's Daughter | 5:22-24, 38-42 | 9:18-19, 23-25 | 8:41-42, 49-56 | |
| Haemorrhaging Woman | 6:48-51 | 9:20-22 | 8:43-48 | |
| Feeding Five Thousand | 6:35-44 | 14:15-21 | 9:12-17 | 6:5-13 |
| Walking on Water | 6:48-51 | 14:25 | | 6:19-21 |
| Syrophoenician/Canaanite Woman's Daughter | 7:24-30 | 15:21-28 | | |
| Deaf Mute Man | 7:31-37 | | | |
| Feeding Four Thousand | 8:1-9 | 15:32-38 | | |
| Blind Man at Bethsaida | 8:22-26 | | | |
| (Epileptic) Boy with an Unclean Spirit | 9:17-29 | 17:14-18 | 9:38-43 | |
| One/Two Blind Men (Bartimaeus) | 10:46-52 | 20:29-34 | 18:35-43 | |
| Withered Fig Tree | 11:12-14, 20-25 | 21:18-22 | | |
| Centurion's Servant | | 8:5-13 | 7:1-10 | |
| Blind Mute Possessed Man | | 12:22 | 11:14 | |
| Two Blind Men | | 9:27-31 | | |
| Mute Man with a Demon | | 9:32-33 | | |
| Coin in Fish's Mouth | | 17:24-27 | | |
| Miraculous Catch of Fish | | | 5:1-11 | |
| Raising the Widow's Son at Nain | | | 7:11-15 | |
| Mary Magdalene | | | 8:2 | |
| Crippled Woman | | | 13:11-13 | |
| Man with Dropsy | | | 14:1-4 | |
| Ten Men with Leprosy | | | 17:11-19 | |
| High Priest's Servant | | | 22:50-51 | |
| Water into Wine at Cana | | | | 2:1-11 |
| Official's Son at Capernaum | | | | 4:46-54 |
| Man at Pool of Bethsaida | | | | 5:1-9 |

|  | Mark | Matthew | Luke | John |
|---|---|---|---|---|
| Man Born Blind |  |  |  | 9:1-41 |
| Raising Lazarus |  |  |  | 11:1-44 |
| Another Miraculous Catch of Fish |  |  |  | 21:1-11 |

## Bibliography

Betz, Otto. "δύναμις." In *New International Dictionary of New Testament Theology*, volume two, edited by C. Brown, pp. 601-06. Exeter: Paternoster, 1976.

Blackburn, Barry L. "Miracles and Miracle Stories." In *Dictionary of Jesus and the Gospels*, edited by Joel B. Green, Scot McKnight and I. Howard Marshall, pp. 549-60. Downers Grove: InterVarsity Press, 1992.

Blackburn, Barry L. "The Miracles of Jesus." In *Studying the Historical Jesus: Evaluations of the State of Current Research* in Bruce Chilton and Craig A. Evans, eds., pp. 353-94. New York/Leiden: Brill, 1994.

Brown, Colin. *That You May Believe: Miracles and Faith Then and Now*. Grand Rapids/Exeter: Eerdmans/Paternoster, 1985.

Collins, C. John. *The God of Miracles: An Exegetical Examination of God's Action in the World*. Wheaton: Crossway Books, 2000.

Corner, Mark. *Signs of God: Miracles and their Interpretation*. Burlington/Aldershot: Ashgate, 2005.

Geisler, Norman L. *Miracles and the Modern Mind*. Grand Rapids: Baker Book House, 1992.

Geivett, R. Douglas, and Gary R. Habermas, eds. *In Defence of Miracles: A Comprehensive Case for God's Action in History*. Downers Grove: InterVarsity Press, 1997.

Hacking, Keith J. *Signs and Wonders Then and Now: Miracle-working, Commissioning and Discipleship*. Nottingham: Apollos, 2006.

Hofius, Otfried, and Colin Brown. "σημεῖον." In *New International Dictionary of New Testament Theology*, volume two, edited by C. Brown, pp. 626-33. Exeter: Paternoster, 1976.

Hume, David. *Enquiries Concerning the Human Understanding and Concerning the Principles of Morals*. Reprinted from the Posthumous Edition of 1777 and edited with Introduction, Comparative Table of Contents, and Analytical Index by L. A. Selby-Bigge. London: Clarendon Press, 1975.

Kistemaker, Simon J. *The Miracles: Exploring the Mystery of Jesus's Divine Works*. Grand Rapids: Baker, 2006.

Latourelle, René. *The Miracles of Jesus and the Theology of Miracles*. New York: Paulist Press, 1998.

Lewis, C. S. *Miracles: A Preliminary Study*. New York: Macmillan, 1947.

Schneider, J., and Colin Brown. "σώζω." In *New International Dictionary of New Testament Theology*, volume three, edited by C. Brown, pp. 205-16. Exeter: Paternoster, 1978.

Stanton, Graham. "Message and Miracles." In *The Cambridge Companion to Jesus*, edited by Markus Bockmuehl, pp. 56-71. Cambridge/New York: Cambridge University, 2001.

Swinburne, Richard, ed. *Miracles*. New York/London: Macmillan/Collier Macmillan, 1989.

Twelftree, Graham H. *Jesus the Exorcist: A Contribution to the Study of the Historical Jesus*. Tübingen: Mohr (Siebeck), 1993.

Twelftree, Graham H. *Jesus the Miracle Worker*. Downers Grove: InterVarsity Press, 1999.

Evelyn Ashley

Twelftree, Graham H. "The History of Miracles in the History of Jesus." In *The Face of New Testament Studies: A Survey of Recent Research*, edited by Scot McKnight and Grant R. Osborne, pp. 191-208. Grand Rapids: Baker Academic, 2004.

Wenham, David W., and Craig L. Blomberg, eds. *The Miracles of Jesus*. Gospel Perspectives, volume 6. Sheffield: JSOT Press, 1986.

# 17. The Titles of Jesus

*Van Shore*

## A. Gospel Christology

At a critical juncture in his ministry, Jesus asked his disciples who they and the people thought he was (see Mark 8:27-30; Matt. 16:13-20; Luke 9:18-20). Various answers were given. The titles listed in Mark 8:28-29—"John the Baptist," "Elijah," "one of the prophets," the "Christ"—are not by any means the only ones conferred upon Jesus in the New Testament (NT).[1] No one of these titles by itself could do justice to all the aspects of his person and mission. Each of them reveals only one particular aspect of the wealth of conviction about Jesus that is found in the NT.[2] What follows in this chapter is an examination of three titles, namely, Messiah, Son of Man, and Son of God. The meaning of each will be illuminated by drawing comparisons and contrasts between their usage in the gospels and in Second Temple Jewish texts.[3]

Christological titles might be regarded as faith formulations emerging within the life of the earliest Christian communities. The content of two of our

---

[1] When it comes to the various designations the following are some examples in the New Testament: "Son of God," "Messiah," "Logos," "God," "Lord," "Son of Man," and others that may not necessarily be adjudged as titles, namely, "Teacher," "Healer," "Servant of God," "Prophet," "Shepherd," "Bread of life," "Wisdom of God," "Light of the world," and "Lamb of God." Especially significant is the confession of Jesus as Lord, which is particularly prominent in the Pauline corpus. See Douglas McCready, *He Came Down From Heaven: The Pre-existence of Christ and the Christian Faith* (Downers Grove: InterVarsity Press, 2005), pp. 55-64.

[2] Over recent decades there has been a proliferation of monographs focusing on the titles of Jesus. For example, see Colin Brown, *Jesus in European Protestant Thought, 1778–1860* (Durham: Labyrinth, 1985); Bruce Chilton and Craig Evans, eds., *Studying the Historical Jesus: Evaluations of the State of Current Research* (Leiden: Brill, 1994), pp. 33-74; Gerald O'Collins, *Christology: A Biblical Historical and Systematic Study of Jesus Christ* (New York/Oxford: Oxford University Press, 1995), pp. 234-35; Charlotte Allen, *The Human Christ: The Search for the Historical Jesus* (New York: Free Press, 1998); Stanley E. Porter, *The Criteria for Authenticity in Historical-Jesus Research: Previous Discussion and New Proposals* (Sheffield: Sheffield Academic, 2000), pp. 28-62; Donald Hagner, "An Analysis of Recent 'Historical Jesus' Studies," in Dan Cohn-Sherbok and John Court, eds., *Religious Diversity in the Graeco-Roman World: A Survey of Recent Scholarship* (Sheffield: Sheffield Academic, 2001), pp. 81-106.

[3] This prehistory has its locus in Jewish theology, in the Old Testament (OT), and Second Temple Jewish literature.

three titles, Messiah and Son of God, was shaped by what the earliest communities, looking back and reflecting on the life of Jesus of Nazareth, believed about him. The Synoptic Gospels set out to narrate an event of the past, namely, Jesus' unique history, which had fundamental significance for the evangelists and the communities addressed by them.[4] In fact, the closing statement of John 20:31 that "these things" have been written that you might believe "that Jesus is the Messiah, the Son of God, and that through believing you may have life in his name," could be applied to all four gospels. But all the gospels, John included, emphasize the fact that before the first Easter the disciples were struggling to understand Jesus' vocation and mission. But in the post-Easter context, faith in Jesus came to be expressed confessionally and is articulated in the reporting of Jesus' life in the gospels. These writings show that history (the reporting) and the *kerygma* (the proclamation about Jesus) have become inseparable.

The number of confessional statements about Jesus is not great, but they are placed strategically in the Synoptics. These include: Peter's confession of Jesus as the Messiah (Mark 8:29; Luke 9:20), which in Matt. 16:16 is expanded into a confession of Jesus as the Messiah and Son of God; the confession of Jesus as the Son of God by the Roman centurion at the cross (Mark 15:39; Matt. 27:54)[5]; and the disciples' confession of Jesus as the Son of God, recorded only in Matt. 14:33 and which is associated with the story of Jesus' walking on the water. By contrast, no where in the gospel tradition is "Son of Man" bestowed on Jesus honorifically. Douglas Hare observes that "Son of Man" is rigidly restricted to sayings attributed to Jesus and is, conversely, absent from all NT statements about his significance. "It is inexplicable," he writes, "why no relic of the alleged confessional use of the 'son of man' has been preserved in the resurrection narratives." The phrase, he concludes, "does not represent the christological confession of the primitive community."[6] Rather the title occurs in Jesus' own, often oblique, pronouncements of what the Son of Man is doing or will do at the end of the age, or, most tellingly, will suffer. For example, the Son of Man, Jesus says, is homeless (Matt. 8:20); he has authority to forgive sins (Mark 2:10); he will be rejected (Mark 8:31); he will be betrayed (Mark 9:31) and handed over to the Gentiles to be killed (Mark 10:33); he will be raised from the dead (Mark 9:9); he will come again in great glory (Mark 14:62) and in eschatological judgment (Matt. 25:31-33). Moreover, Jesus' employment of the term in the gospel narratives does not evoke any objection or controversy, unlike the use of other titles such as Messiah, Son of God, and Son of David.[7]

---

[4] See Martin Hengel, "Eye-witness memory and the writing of the Gospels," in Markus Bockmuehl and Donald Hagner, eds., *The Written Gospel* (New York/Cambridge: Cambridge University Press, 2005), p. 70.

[5] According to Luke 23:47 the centurion exclaims: "Certainly this man was innocent."

[6] Douglas R. A. Hare, *The Son of Man Tradition* (Philadelphia: Fortress Press, 1999), p. 243.

[7] In Mark's Gospel, the high priest's cry of "blasphemy" seems to be in response to Jesus' affirmative response to the question whether he is "the Messiah, the Son of the Blessed One" (Mark 14:61). The term "Son of Man" (Mark 14:62) appears to function both as a self-

## B. Jesus' Self-Understanding and the Nature of the NT Evidence

Our knowledge of Jesus is primarily indirect because he seldom spoke directly about himself and we have no documents from his hand. In the decades between the ministry of Jesus and the composition of the four gospels, the record of what Jesus had said and done circulated in oral form.[8] The emergence of the four gospels in the last third of the first century is a crucial development. More than one factor was responsible for the writing down of the traditions about Jesus, not least the fact that the generation of eye-witness disseminators of Jesus' work and words began to die out. Moreover, the experience of the risen Christ within the community shaped perceptions of Jesus' ultimate identity and significance, and these, as we noted above, are brought to speech in the gospels.[9]

In the context of NT Christology, the following line of enquiry by Oscar Cullmann illustrates one way in which various titles have been analyzed. He grouped the individual titles into four categories which represent specific stages of salvation history.[10] Cullmann admitted that this scenario involved an unavoidable schematic classification. Each title is related not only to one of these four categories but also to others where appropriate.[11] Thus he refers to titles which denote Jesus as Prophet, High Priest and Servant in the context of his public ministry. From the perspective of eschatology, the titles Messiah and Son of Man find their significance. The titles Lord and Savior refer to his present work. The titles Logos (the Word), Son of God, and God refer to his pre-existence.[12]

---

designation and as part of the allusion to the scene in Dan. 7:13-14 where a humanlike figure receives divine vindication.

[8] Knowledge about the historical Jesus must stand or fall on the data revealed in the gospels about the adult Jesus during the last three or so years of his life. There are some apocryphal materials from the early Christian tradition and some sources external to the NT. See Wilhelm Schneelmelcher, ed., *New Testament Apocrypha*, 2 vols. (Louisville: Westminster John Knox Press, 1991).

[9] See Marcus Borg and N. T. Wright, *The Meaning of Jesus: Two Visions* (San Francisco: HarperSanFrancisco, 1999), p. 5: "The gospels contain two kinds of material: some go back to Jesus, and some is the product of early Christian communities. To use an archaeological analogy, the gospels contain earlier and later layers. To use a vocal analogy, the gospels contain more than one voice: the voice of Jesus, and the voices of the community."

[10] Oscar Cullmann, *The Christology of the New Testament* (Philadelphia: Fortress Press, 1963). Judicious treatments are also provided by Ferdinand Hahn, *The Titles of Jesus in Christology* (London: Lutterworth, 1969); Willi Marxsen, *The Beginnings of Christology: A Study of Its Problems* (Philadelphia: Fortress Press, 1969); C. F. D. Moule, *The Origins of Christology* (New York/Cambridge: Cambridge University Press, 1977); David F. Wells, *The Person of Christ: A Biblical and Historical Analysis of the Incarnation* (Westchester: Crossway Books, 1984), pp. 67-81.

[11] Cullmann, *Christology*, p. 9: "a mutual assimilation of meanings and connotations may have taken place in the consciousness of the first Christians."

[12] In referring to Cullmann's division of his field into the earthly, the future, the present, and the pre-existent, Hendrikus Boers in his "Jesus and the Christian Faith: New Testament Christology Since Bousset's Kyrios Christos," *Journal of Biblical Literature* 89 (1970), pp. 450-56, writes on p. 452: "[B]y assuming that the foundation of NT Christology was the activity of Jesus in these four areas he [Cullmann] interprets the primitive Christian formulations of faith in

Furthermore, Cullmann's analysis of these titles contains the following claims about Jesus' self-understanding. The baptism of Jesus, where the divine voice addresses him as "my Son, the Beloved" (Mark 1:11), initiated in him the consciousness of being called to accomplish the will of God and the awareness that he had been appointed to bring about the forgiveness of sins, redemption, through his death in fulfillment of the Isaianic prophecy regarding the Suffering Servant.[13] Because Jesus' first recorded public utterance concerned the kingdom of God (see Mark 1:15), kingship and "Sonship" are to be viewed as inseparably related in his message. Inherent in the title Son was the notion of the uniqueness of the relationship between the Father and the Son, and also of the unity of the Father and the Son in the carrying out of the Father's will.

More recently, Ben Witherington III has argued that, even though it has been traditional to commence with the direct evidence of the titles of Jesus, in some ways the *indirect* evidence of Jesus' self-understanding is more convincing than the direct evidence. He notes that, except for the Gospel of John, the key to assembling a portrait of Jesus is not found primarily in the way Jesus refers to himself. Rather, it is found in what he does and in what those actions both individually and as a group represent. Hence, as much as names, titles and appellations evidence some relation to a definition of Jesus' identity, they nevertheless produce confusion between being and doing, role and relationship.[14] James D. G. Dunn issues a similar *caveat* in his observation that a person is the sum of the roles he fills and of the relationships of which he is part.[15] The question that Jesus asks his disciples, "Who do you say that I am?" indicates, in relation to identity, that relationships were formative for him and that his self-awareness might properly be confirmed by his closest followers (Mark 8:27-30; Matt. 16:13).

What's in a name? In antiquity, it was often and widely assumed that a name, and especially an appellation or self-chosen identification, revealed something significant about character. Quite intentionally this process is very

---

Christ as merely the articulation of an already underlying Christology. Thus, even Cullmann's discussion of the historical development in the use of the various titles becomes the mere explicating of the details of an already presupposed Christology."

[13] In its description of the messianic figure who will come from the tribe of Levi, *T. Levi* 18:4-8 has uncanny parallels to the accounts of Jesus' baptism (Matt. 3:13-17; Mark 1:9-11). *T. Levi* is not easy to date because it underwent lengthy editorial development (second century AD). It may have been influenced by the Gospel of Mark, but it nonetheless represents traditional Jewish perspectives.

[14] See Ben Witherington III, *The Many Faces of Christ: The Christologies of the New Testament and Beyond* (New York: Crossroad Publishing, 1998), p. 25. J. D. G. Dunn, "Messianic Ideas and Their Influences on the Jesus of History," in James H. Charlesworth, ed., *The Messiah Developments in Earliest Judaism and Christianity* (Minneapolis: Fortress Press, 1992), pp. 365-81 comments: "I have become increasingly persuaded that the best *starting* point for study of the main body of the Synoptic tradition is to view it as the earliest churches' memories of Jesus as retold and reused by these churches. . . I regard the earliest tradents within the Christian churches as preservers more than innovators, seeking to transmit, retell, explain, interpret, elaborate, but not to create *de novo*" (p. 371).

[15] J. D. G. Dunn, *Jesus Remembered: Christianity in the Making* (Grand Rapids: Eerdmans, 2003), p. 615.

different from title or honor recognition as evidenced in the following:

> The Jews answered him, "Are we not right in saying that you are a Samaritan and have a demon?" (John 8:48).

Name-calling functioned as a powerful social weapon. John's intention clearly is to cast the Jews as opponents of Jesus, as outsiders, thus creating distance between them on the one hand and Jesus and his disciples on the other. Furthermore, names could be viewed not merely as distinguishing labels in antiquity but also as badges of honor or dishonor. What is evidenced in the following two examples from the Synoptic Gospels is that power was established flowing in a particular direction from one person to another in the process of naming a social relationship.

> Simon Peter answered, "You are the Christ, the Son of the living God." And Jesus answered him, "Blessed are you, Simon son of Jonah! For flesh and blood has not revealed this to you, but my Father in heaven (Matt. 16:16-17).

> And a voice came from heaven, "You are my Son, the beloved; with you I am well pleased" (Mark 1:11).

The significance of the naming of Jesus in both incidents is couched in the language of transcendent disclosure. Ben Witherington aptly observes that the titles of Jesus, such as Son of Man, Son of God, Lord, and Messiah, "represent claims to honor, and yet they are relational in character."[16]

We now turn to an examination of the titles Messiah, Son of Man and Son of God. These three will be discussed chiefly in relation to Mark's Gospel.

## C. Messiah

Christ, Χριστός, is the title or term most frequently applied to Jesus in the NT. Yet the term "messiah" is not often found in biblical and Second Temple Jewish texts. In the Hebrew Bible the term was applied predominantly to a king, but also to a priest, and occasionally to a prophet. Technically the Hebrew *mashiah* and its Greek equivalent Χριστός mean "anointed" or "anointed one" (cf. John 1:41). Used as a noun, "anointed one" refers to the patriarchs (twice), high priests (six times), Cyrus, the Persian king (once), and Israelite kings (twenty-nine times). The term can also be used of a murdered high priest (Dan. 9:26), a prophet (Isa. 61:1), and even of the whole people of Israel (Hab. 3:13; Ps. 28:8; 84:10; 105:15). In these texts the term denotes those invested, usually by God, with power and leadership. However, the term is never applied to an eschatological figure. In OT prophecies of the rule of

---

[16] Ben Witherington III, "The Christology of Jesus," in M. A. Powell and D. R. Bauer, eds., *Who Do You Say That I am? Essays on Christology* (Louisville: Westminster John Knox Press, 1999), p. 7. See also Jaroslav Pelikan, *The Illustrated Jesus Through the Centuries* (New Haven: Yale University Press, 1997), pp. 9-23.

God to come there is no reference to a "Messiah." Nevertheless, the promise expressed in 2 Sam. 7:12-17 that David would never lack a descendant to sit on his throne, one that would last forever, created an expectation, especially in turbulent times, that God would raise up a king, a "son of David," who would restore David's kingdom. We begin to encounter such expectation in Jewish texts of the first century BC in response to the disintegration of the Hasmonean dynasty that had begun in the mid second century so promisingly with the Maccabean revolt and the assertion of Jewish independence.

The notion of a charismatically endowed descendant of David who would break the yoke of the heathen rulers is well-expressed in *Psalms of Solomon* 17, probably written soon after Jerusalem had been captured by the Romans in 63 BC:

> But we hope in God our savior, for the strength of our God is forever with mercy. And the kingdom of our God is forever over the nations in judgment. Lord, you chose David to be king over Israel and swore to him about his descendants forever, that his kingdom should not fail before you. But because of our sins, sinners rose up against us, they set upon us and drove us out (17:3-5).
>
> See, Lord, and raise up for them their king, the son of David, to rule over your servant Israel in the time known to you, O God. Undergird him with strength to destroy the unrighteous rulers, to purge Jerusalem from Gentiles who trample her to destruction (17:21-22).
>
> (trans. R. B. Wright, *Old Testament Pseudepigrapha*, vol. 2, pp. 665, 667.)

This "son of David," this king to come, is hailed as "Lord Messiah." He will purge Jerusalem of Gentiles and apostate Jews, punishing them for their arrogance, scattering the nations, and ruling in righteousness with God's blessing.

It is undeniable that such hopes were fuelled by further Roman incursions into Judea in particular and the whole of Syria in general. Josephus mentions several messianic pretenders, such as Judas the Galilean, who founded the so-called "Fourth Philosophy" in AD 6 at the time of the census of Quirinius (*J.W.* 2.118-19) when direct Roman rule was imposed on Judea. The historian notes that the act of Judas breaking into the armories at Sepphoris was part of his "zealous pursuit of royal rank." In their study of periodic first-century messianic ferment, Richard Horsley and John Hanson observe that:

> . . . there were several mass movements composed of Jewish peasants from villages or towns such as Emmaus, Bethlehem, Sepphoris—people rallying around the leadership of charismatic figures viewed as *anointed kings of the Jews*. These movements occurred at the time when Jesus of Nazareth was presumably born.[17]

---

[17] Richard A. Horsley and John S. Hanson, *Bandits and Messiahs: Popular Movements at the Time of Jesus* (Minneapolis: Winston Press, 1985), p. 117.

At the outbreak of the Jewish War in 66 a royal, messianic figure briefly emerges. Menahem, the leader of the *sicarii*, appears in Jerusalem in royal robes, only to be killed in a fracas with rival groups (Josephus, *J.W.* 2.444-48). His followers withdrew to Masada. The second Jewish War (AD 132–135) was led by Simon bar Kosiba who was hailed by Akiba, a leading rabbi, as Bar Kokhba, "son of a star" (cf. Num. 24:17), and as king and Messiah.[18] Bar Kokhba gave the rebuilding of the temple destroyed in AD 70 such a high priority that he had a representation of it stamped on his coins. For him, temple and kingship were inseparably related.[19]

The expectation of *Psalms of Solomon* 17 is clearly of a messiah who is human. This contrasts with *4 Ezra* 13–14 (c. AD 100; which postdates the NT gospels) and *1 Enoch* 37–71 (c. first century BC) which anticipate the coming of a pre-existent, almost divine figure. The functions and attributes of the Messiah are by no means clear in extant pre-AD 70 Jewish documents.[20] In some Second Temple eschatological texts there is no expectation of an end-time anointed one, while others appear to expect more than one as in several texts from the Qumran corpus and the *Testaments of the Twelve Patriarchs* which both expect a priestly and a Davidic messiah.[21] Messianic ideas and titles were fluid and often related to each other, as is evidenced in 1 *Enoch* 48 where "Son of Man," "Messiah" and "Elect One" are used interchangeably to describe a single person and his functions as God's agent fulfilling his redemptive purposes. The phenomenon of late OT and Second Temple messianism resists reduction to a coherent system. In the first century AD, we can conclude that, where the coming of a Messiah was expected, there was no consensus about what he was expected to do, when he was expected to come, and what his coming would mean.[22]

The NT gospels all affirm that Jesus should be recognized as the legitimate bearer of the title Χριστός. Witherington notes that most scholars accept that Jesus was crucified under the placard "the king of the Jews," and that the early church was unanimous in calling Jesus Χριστός as a virtual

---

[18] S. van der Woude, "Messianic Ideas in Later Judaism," in G. Kittel and G. Friedrich, eds., *TDNT* vol. IX, (Grand Rapids: Eerdmans, 1964–1976), p. 523.

[19] Simon was hailed as the Messiah in spite of his non-Davidic descent. This might best be explained by the current political situation in Palestine. The Bar Kokhba incident offers confirmation that even in the second century AD messianic expectations were not fixed.

[20] See John J. Collins, *The Apocalyptic Imagination: An Introduction to the Jewish Matrix of Christianity* (New York: Crossroad, 1984), p. 110.

[21] See, for example, 1QSa 2.11-15; *T. Iss.* 5.7-8. Arthur L. Moore, *The Parousia in the New Testament* (Leiden: Brill, 1966) identifies five different possible "Messiahs—God himself, Messiah (king representative), Servant of Yahweh, Son of Man (whether corporate or individual) and Son of God" (p. 10). See also William Horbury's article, "Jewish Messianism and Early Christology," in Richard N. Longenecker, ed., *Contours of Christology in the New Testament* (Grand Rapids: Eerdmans, 2005), pp. 3-24.

[22] There was no limit to the ideas current in first-century Judaism concerning the Messiah. James M. Scott, *Adoption as Sons of God* (Tübingen: Mohr [Siebeck], 1992) writes: "If there is one thing New Testament scholars have learned from their Jewish colleagues in recent years, it is to show great caution in expressing generalizations about messianism or the Messiah in pre-Christian Judaism" (p. 294). See also James H. Charlesworth, "From Messianology to Christology: Problems and Prospects," in *The Messiah*, pp. 3-35.

second name for him.[23] Although identifying Jesus as Messiah became the central way of defining the ultimate religious significance of Jesus in early Palestinian Christianity, it must be underscored that the manner in which he carried out the role did not fit conventional Jewish expectations.[24]

The link between Messiah and kingship is reinforced in the opening chapter of Matthew's Gospel. Matthew intentionally arranges the names in his genealogy to underscore the point that Jesus is the Messiah, descended in unbroken lineage from king David (Matt. 1:1, 17). The genealogy also functions in an apologetic manner. In Jesus' day there was at least one person who aspired to the title of king, Herod Antipas, and one did not lightly, even by implication, issue a direct challenge to a son of Herod the Great.[25] And yet, this is precisely the sort of context within which one can understand the crowd's reaction to Jesus as reported in the Fourth Gospel: "When Jesus realized that they were about to come and take him by force to make him king, he withdrew again to the mountain by himself" (John 6:15). So where messianic expectations are expressed, they form part of a larger story told and lived by Jews in Jesus' day. In effect, the expectation of the emergence of a king was the focal point in many scenarios of national liberty.

When we turn to Mark's Gospel it is conspicuously evident that Mark also believes that Jesus is the anointed one, the Christ, and the Son of God (1:1). But the designation he reveals to have been on Jesus' own lips most frequently throughout his narrative, if not exclusively, is "Son of Man." This phrase is linked particularly to the tasks Jesus must undertake first in Jerusalem and then at the eschaton when he returns in judgment (14:62). Mark reveals not only that Jesus' preferred self-reference was Son of Man, but that the church's confession of Jesus as the Messiah and Son of God is vindicated by climactic disclosure incidents in his narrative. In Mark 8:29 there is some glimmering of comprehension that breaks through for Peter, but it immediately becomes clear that for him partial insight is still blended with misunderstanding that will require further, and painful, correction.

In fact, one could make an excellent case that the Markan narrative is especially centered on these three titles—Messiah, Son of God and Son of Man—and that they function as a thread tying together the christological reflections of this Gospel. Titles are revealed to the reader early (1:1); revealed privately to Jesus at his baptism; known by demons and spirit beings;

---

[23] Ben Witherington III, *The Jesus Quest: The Third Search for the Jew of Nazareth* (Downers Grove: InterVarsity Press, 1997), p. 213. On the use of the term Christ in the gospels refer to Larry Hurtado, "Christ," in J. Green, S. McKnight and I. H. Marshall, eds., *Dictionary of Jesus and the Gospels* (Downers Grove: InterVarsity Press, 1992), pp. 106-17; Ben Witherington III, "Christ," in G. Hawthorne, R. Martin and D. Reid, eds., *Dictionary of Paul and His Letters* (Downers Grove: InterVarsity Press, 1993), pp. 95-100

[24] See W. C. van Unnik, "Jesus the Christ," *Sparsa Collecta: The Collection of Essays of W. C. van Unnik*, part 2 (Leiden: Brill, 1980), pp. 248-68. Van Unnik proposes that "for the early Christians messiahship did not consist in the outward activity of a king but in a person who possesses the Spirit of God" (p. 266).

[25] See the discussion in Doron Mendels, "Pseudo-Philo's *Biblical Antiquities*, the 'Fourth Philosophy,' and Political Messianism of the First Century C.E." Charlesworth, ed., *The Messiah*, pp. 261-75.

revealed to Peter, James and John on the Mount of Transfiguration, but are clearly not understood and not believed by Jesus' adversaries at his trial; and finally affirmed at the point of Jesus' death by the centurion, a Gentile. What is clearly evident is that the title Χριστός appears at crucial junctures in Mark's narrative structure. But when Jesus first publicly acknowledges the title, in Mark 8:27-30, the evangelist stresses that Jesus immediately qualifies it by speaking clearly of his impending rejection, suffering and death as the Son of Man (8:31). The confession of 8:30 is qualified again in 9:31 and 10:32 in order to make clear to his hearers that Jesus is to be a suffering Messiah and, as Son of Man, must go up to Jerusalem and die there.

Jewish messianic expectation, according to the evidence available, had no place for a suffering, much less a crucified, Messiah. Jesus radically interprets the content of Peter's confessional language. However, Peter's momentary insight will only be sustained if he is able to grasp the necessary revelation that God's redemptive purposes can only be fulfilled through the suffering of the Messiah and Son of God, Jesus. Similarly, in Mark 14:61-62, Jesus does not reject the question of the high priest, "Are you the Χριστός?" but accepts that he is indeed the Messiah, the Son of the Blessed One. But he immediately transposes the discussion to his preferred form of self-identification, namely, Son of Man. But who, among the Council, would believe that Jesus, totally alone and powerless, was a credible Messiah let alone the portentous Son of Man?

How distant this picture is from the militarism of *Psalms of Solomon* 17 or of the abortive messianic movements reported by Josephus. If Jesus accepted the appellation "messiah" he is at pains to re-define just how he proposes to express that destiny. This extends to actions as well. Jesus is recorded entering Jerusalem, not on a horse, the bearer of a conquering king, but on a donkey. According to Matt. 21:4-5, this was to fulfill Zech. 9:9: "your king comes to you . . . riding on an ass." Jesus is a king, yes, but of a kingdom that does not conform to any conventional human conception, and especially to any Jewish hopes that a Davidic messiah might restore the integrity of the nation and drive out Romans and apostates alike.

Temple and messianism are closely linked in the gospels. In Mark 11:15-17, which records Jesus' casting out of the money-changers and his commandeering the space to teach, is to be understood as his taking control of the temple as its lord (cf. Mal. 3:1). His prediction of its overthrow in Mark 13:2 is bound up with his own vindication, both as a prophet and as Messiah. When his prophecy of the temple's destruction comes to pass, that event will demonstrate to those who witness it that Jesus was indeed the Messiah who had authority over temple and cult. Mark 13:2 and its parallels thus make explicit the meaning of Mark 11:15-17.[26]

Jesus believed he was Israel's Messiah. He believed he would win the

---

[26] As Achtemeier, "Gospel of Mark," in David N. Freedman, ed., *The Anchor Bible Dictionary*, vol. 4 (New York: Doubleday, 1992), p. 553, writes that "Jesus' public confession in Mark points to the equivalence of the three titles used 'Messiah,' 'Son of God' and 'Son of man' with their common element the reference to kingly power."

messianic victory over the real enemy and would build the true messianic temple by taking Israel's destiny upon himself and by going to the cross. Mark's insight is that Jesus, as suffering Messiah, was actualizing the prophetic hope of the return of the Lord God to Zion (see Isa. 40:3; Mark 1:3). In Jesus the Christ, God was acting to rescue Israel, fulfilling the covenantal promises to Abraham, and inaugurating a new creation, namely, a new people of God from among Jews and Gentiles, who would believe in Jesus as Messiah and constitute the body of Christ in the world.

## D. The Son of Man

With the exception of the term "the kingdom of God/heaven," there is no phrase more common in the Jesus tradition and across the gospel sources than "Son of Man." It is the unanimous consensus of early Christian memory that Jesus used this title of himself.[27] Broadly speaking, for the last 150 years, scholarly controversy has focused on two principal interpretations of the title, namely, that Son of Man refers to a human or to a heavenly figure.[28] Traditionally, among Christians "Son of Man" has been understood as an expression of Jesus' humanity and therefore as a counterpoise to his status as Son of God, a title that denotes his divinity. This development can be dated to the early second century, as can be seen in Ignatius of Antioch (Ign. *Eph.* 20:2). But the reference to "one like a son of man" coming with the clouds in Dan. 7:13 was always a problem for either view since that figure appeared to be have both human and divine attributes. The publication of *1 Enoch*, a book long known in the Ethiopic church, in the first half of the nineteenth century provided access to an important Jewish witness to the title.[29] Before considering any study of the use of the phrase in the gospels, we must deal with use of the phrase in exilic and Second Temple texts.[30] We turn first to the book of Ezekiel,[31] before proceeding to Daniel and *1 Enoch*.

In the opening chapter of Ezekiel the voice that the prophet hears as he lies prostrate and overwhelmed addresses him directly as "son of man," which the NRSV translates quite appropriately as "mortal" (see, e.g., 2:1; 3:1; 4:1). God will consistently use this expression when addressing Ezekiel. The epithet is a conventional Hebrew idiom, *ben 'adam*: the noun *'adam*, "human

---

[27] The Greek title υἱὸς τοῦ ἀνθρώπου occurs 82 times in the gospels. If one counts the parallel sayings only once, there are 51 occurrences. See Joachim Jeremias, *New Testament Theology* (London: SCM Press, 1971), pp. 259-60.

[28] See William Horbury, "The Messianic Association of 'the Son of Man,'" *Journal of Theological Studies* 36 (1985), pp. 34-55. Horbury provides a concise review of the twentieth-century discussion (pp. 34-36). See also, Geza Vermes, *Jesus in His Jewish Context* (Minneapolis: Fortress Press, 2003), pp. 81-90.

[29] See Delbert Burkett, *The Son of Man Debate: A History and Evaluation* (New York/Cambridge: Cambridge University Press, 1999), pp. 13-31.

[30] See James H. Charlesworth, *Jesus within Judaism* (New York: Doubleday, 1988), p. 42: "I am persuaded that Jesus knew and was influenced by Daniel and *1 Enoch* 37–71, even if it was via the traditions that flowed to, or through, or from these apocalypses."

[31] This term occurs some ninety-three times in the book.

being," designates a class; *ben*, "son of," specifies a member of that class. However, different nuances are proposed for the usage of this phrase. Greenberg believes that designating Ezekiel as "mortal" serves to distinguish him from the divine beings that he sees not only in chapter one but also in chapters 8–11 and 40.[32] However, the following should also be noted. In Ezekiel's day, Israel is experiencing divine judgment. The prophet's script of lamentation, mourning and woe is intended to confront his audience. He wants the exiles to come to terms with their failures and transgressions. Ezekiel's task will entail a remolding of the very foundations upon which Israel's theology was constructed. To do so, he must engage in the daunting transformation of tradition. We see Ezekiel at this work already in his account of God's advent and claim upon his life (Ezekiel 1–3). The appearance of Yahweh's glory in Babylon shatters expectations because the people had sought to make of God a permanent, protective presence in the land of Israel. A mere mortal, Ezekiel, is called to model the necessity of discerning God's word for the times and for fashioning the nation's theological inheritance into a form that can both survive the collapse of old ideas and support God's new work into the future. In that future every divine word will be fulfilled and the people will acknowledge that a prophet, one like a son of man, *and* his Lord have been among them.

The repeated designation of Ezekiel as "son of man" should be juxtaposed with the Son of Man tradition associated with Jesus of Nazareth. To interpret the carrying out of God's will by Ezekiel in his day as "son of man" is to see with new eyes the Son of Man tradition in the gospels. Ezekiel's status was defined not so much by his status as a prophet but rather as a mortal, a son of man. Fundamental to Jesus' awareness as Son of Man is that God's redemptive purposes can only be achieved through his being willing to lay down his prerogatives and status (cf. Phil. 2:5-8). In fact, it is in the scandal of the cross, and, in the foolishness of the wisdom of that cross, that God's glory finds its clearest expression—in one who suffers and dies, in a mortal. "We beheld his glory," the Fourth Evangelist confesses (John 1:14), and that glory was revealed in the weakness of human flesh.

John Bowker argues that the use of son of man in Ezekiel, Psalm 8 and the Targums make explicit the "chasm between frail, mortal man and God himself."[33] This supports my view that the title serves the gospel references well where the suffering, frailty and ignominious death of the Son of Man is in view. Maurice Casey, with support from Geza Vermes, also captures something of the sense of the inherent creaturely weakness, mortality and humility that are denoted by the title "son of man."[34]

---

[32] Moshe Greenberg, *Ezekiel 1–37* (Garden City: Doubelday, 1983), pp. 61-62. Cf. W. Eichrodt, *Ezekiel: A Commentary* (Philadelphia: Westminster Press, 1970), p. 61. Eichrodt, citing Ps. 8:5, observes that the title son of man emphasizes Ezekiel's humanity and creaturely weakness. Note also Job 25:6 in which "a son of man" occurs in parallel with "a mortal."

[33] John Bowker, "The Son of Man," *Journal of Theological Studies* 28 (1977), pp. 19-28.

[34] Maurice Casey, "Aramaic Idiom and the Son of Man Problem: A Response to Owen and Shepherd," *Journal for the Study of the New Testament* 25.1 (2002), p. 20.

Vermes argues from later rabbinic usage that "son of man" that was used not only to refer to "a human being" but also, and most importantly for Vermes, as a circumlocution for "I."[35] E. P. Sanders agrees, contending that the saying of Jesus—"the Sabbath was made for humans, not humans for the Sabbath; so the Son of Man is Lord even of the Sabbath" (Mark 2:28)—means that Jesus, in speaking of the Son of Man is referring to "humankind" and that the saying means "a human being is Lord of the Sabbath." Yet, when predicting his own death in Mark 8:31 Jesus, as Son of Man, is using a circumlocution for speaking about himself.[36] Maurice Casey, who has established himself as one of the most authoritative voices among the present generation of NT scholars on the meaning of Son of Man, agrees with Vermes that the phrase could be used to refer to humankind but disagrees that it could denote a speaker.[37] It should also be noted that the views advocated by Vermes and Sanders have been vigorously challenged by P. Owen and D. Shepherd on the ground that neither of the usages they espouse is attested at the time of Jesus.[38]

The term "son of man" occurs in Daniel (see 7:13-14) in which "one like a human being" (lit. "son of man") (NRSV) appears, coming on the clouds of heaven. This imagery is the model for Jesus' statement about the coming of the Son of Man recorded in Mark 13:26 and 14:62. In Daniel, the one like a son of man approaches the Ancient One and is presented to him. To him is given "dominion and glory and kingship" to be exercised over the nations; nations that will serve him. The son of man in Daniel 7 explicitly refers to an individual who represents faithful, beleaguered Jews, the "saints of the Most High." Their vindication and triumph only occurs only after they have been given into the power of the fearsome fourth beast (see Dan. 7:17-18, 23-27). John J. Collins argues that, as the human being was the climax of God's creating activity and was given dominion over the rest of creation, so Israel, as the climax of God's universal redemptive purpose, will be given dominion over all other nations.[39] Furthermore, the kingdoms of the world, which will serve the one like a son of man, are represented by fantastic beasts while the faithful of Israel, by contrast, are represented by a human-like figure. Hence, the hope of the reign of the son of man is identical with the anticipated reign

---

[35] Vermes, *Jesus*, pp. 82-84.

[36] E. P. Sanders, *The Historical Figure of Jesus* (London: Penguin Books, 1993), p. 246.

[37] Maurice Casey, *Son of Man: The Interpretation and Influence of Daniel 7* (London: SPCK, 1979), pp. 224-27. Casey was followed in turn by Barnabas Lindars, who argued somewhat similarly for an intermediate sense between the generic (a human being) and personal reference—an idiomatic generic sense (a man in my position). See his *Jesus the Son of Man: A Fresh Examination of the Son of Man Sayings in the Gospels* (London: SPCK, 1983), pp. 23-24. See also P. Owen and D. Shepherd, "Speaking up for Qumran, Dalman, and the Son of Man: Was *Bar Enasha* a Common Term for 'Man' in the Time of Jesus?" *Journal for the Study of the New Testament* issue 81 (2001), pp. 81-121, esp. pp. 84-88.

[38] P. Owen and D. Shepherd, "Speaking up for Qumran," p. 121.

[39] See the discussion in John J. Collins, *Daniel* (Minneapolis: Fortress Press, 1993), pp. 281-94. He notes a connection between the dominion given to the son of man in the Daniel vision and the supremacy of humankind asserted in Genesis 1 and 2 by the granting of dominion over the beasts (Gen. 1:28) and the man's authority to name them (2:19-20).

of Israel, the saints (7:27), over its oppressors. Daniel 7 is a reflection therefore on Israel's national destiny in the context of the saints' harassment by their Syrian overlords.[40]

The following question arises with respect to the son of man expression in Daniel 7. When the seer wants to say "like a human being," he uses the Aramaic *keĕnosh* (7:4). Why, then, is the expression "like a *son* of man" (*ben keĕnosh*) chosen in 7:13? The answer may have to do with the shifting context of the vision. Daniel's vision has taken the reader to the heavenly court where one would expect to see, not a human being, but the *bĕne ĕlohim*, "the sons of God," before the throne of God. However, the surprise of Daniel's vision lies in the fact that in heaven he sees a *son of man*, rather than one of the *sons of God*, approaching the Ancient One.[41] Thus while the translation "like a human being" is not incorrect, it fails to capture the nuances of the context that led the writer to adopt the particular expression "son of man" on this occasion.

In the section of *1 Enoch* called the *Similitudes* (chs. 37–71) the Son of Man is clearly of great importance. We are told of his righteousness and familiarity with divine secrets (46:3), his victory over the mighty of the earth and judgment of the wicked (46:4-8; 62:9; 63:11; 69:27-29), his preordained status in God's plans (48:2-3, 6; 62:7), his pre-existence (48:6), and his redemptive role on behalf of the elect (48:4-7; 62:14). In addition, this figure, as we have already had cause to remark, is the same one described in these chapters as "the Chosen One" (or the "Elect One") and as the "Messiah" (or the "Anointed One"): identical functions are attributed to all three figures (see 49:2-4; 51:3-5; 52:4-9; 55:4; 62:2-16).

This figure acts as judge on God's behalf ("in the name of the Lord of the Spirits," *1 En.* 55:4), and in that capacity sits upon a throne closely associated with God: "on that day the Chosen One will sit on the throne of Glory" (45:3). The meaning here is not that the Son of Man rivals God or becomes a second god but is seen rather as performing the eschatological functions associated with God, and is therefore God's chief agent. G. W. E. Nickelsburg[42] rightly underscores the link between the Son of Man as eschatological judge in the *Similitudes* (see especially *1 Enoch* 62–63) and in the sayings about the eschatological role of the Son of Man in the gospels (see, e.g., Matt. 25:31-46; Mark 13:26-27).

The conception of the Son of Man as divine agent is well seen in *1 Enoch* 46, where, employing imagery from Dan. 7:9-14, the writer pictures the Son of Man/Chosen One in a heavenly scene where he is prominently associated with God, possesses an angelic aspect, is privy to all heavenly secrets and who will remove kings from their thrones and mighty ones from their comfortable seats.[43] The Son of Man is God's chosen agent of eschatological deliverance,

---

[40] See Collins, *Daniel*, pp. 309-10.

[41] See Owen and Shepherd, "Speaking up for Qumram," esp. pp. 118-20.

[42] G. W. E. Nickelsburg, "Books of Enoch," *Catholic Biblical Quarterly* 40 (1978), pp. 411-18.

[43] It is worth noting that the first reference to the Chosen One as Son of Man is in this passage, where the influence of Dan. 7:13-14 is apparent.

a figure next to God in authority, who acts as God's chief representative on earth.[44] But before we conclude that this compelling vision expresses a common expectation of the coming of the Son of Man, Morna Hooker cautions us that, according to the evidence, first-century Jews were not expecting an eschatological Son of Man from heaven.[45]

The Son of Man sayings in the Gospel of Mark attribute authority to him in contested matters such as forgiveness of sins (2:10) and lordship of the Sabbath (2:28). Other sayings predict the rejection and vindication of the Son of Man (8:1; 9:31; 10:33-34). At the *parousia* of the Son of Man there will be a manifestation of his glory (8:38; 13:26). In Mark 13 the Son of Man gathers the elect (13:27). In all four gospels "Son of Man" is used only by Jesus except in John 12:34, where the Jewish crowd enquire of Jesus, "Who is this Son of Man?" With justification Ragnar Leivestad, among many other scholars, observes that Son of Man is a characteristic feature of Jesus' distinctive "voice." Therefore, he argues, we can "substitute the appropriate first-person pronoun for 'the son of man' in the sentences with no difficulty."[46] As in the Synoptics, so in the Fourth Gospel, "Son of Man" is essentially a synonym for "I," and does not therefore represent a claim to an established title.[47] The variation between the first person pronoun and "son of man" in parallel sayings in the gospel narratives in the NT is a clear indication that in the early Jesus tradition these two expressions were accepted as interchangeable.

Blessed are you when people hate you, and when they exclude you, revile you, and defame you on account of the Son of Man (Luke 6:22).

Blessed are you when people revile you and persecute you and utter all kinds of evil against you falsely on my account (Matt. 5:11).

[H]e asked his disciples, "Who do people say that the Son of Man is?" (Matt. 16:13).

[H]e asked his disciples, "Who do people say that I am?" (Mark 8:27).

---

[44] One must keep in mind that some have insisted that the manlike figure of Dan. 7:13-14 was intended by the writer as only a symbol of the "saints of the most high": so Morna Hooker, *The Son of Man in Mark* (London: SPCK, 1967). Other scholars, such as Christopher Rowland, *The Open Heaven: A Study of Apocalyptic in Judaism and Early Christianity* (New York: Crossroad, 1982), take the figure to be a genuine heavenly being.

[45] See Hooker, *The Son of Man in Mark*, p. 91.

[46] Ragnar Leivestad, "Exit the Apocalyptic Son of Man," *New Testament Studies* 18 (1971–72), pp. 243-67 (p. 256).

[47] The basic data concerning the usage of Son of Man is that it occurs approximately 81 times in the four gospel narratives: 14 in Mark; 30 in Matthew; 25 in Luke and 12 in John. Suffice it to say that Son of Man appears frequently in the gospels, but only on the lips of Jesus, and does not occur elsewhere in the NT as a confessional claim or expression of significance.

In the Fourth Gospel, in place of the passion predictions of the Synoptic Gospels which state that the Son of Man must suffer,[48] John has drawn attention to specific aspects of the suffering and death of the Son of Man. The one word that enlightens our understanding of this expression relates to Jesus being "lifted up" (John 3:14-15; 8:28; 12:32-34). It refers both literally to Jesus' crucifixion and symbolically to Jesus' exaltation. When Jesus is lifted up, exalted in the abject humiliation of the cross, his identity is revealed for all who can see. Paradoxically, the cross is a revelation of both Jesus as Son of Man and of the one true God who sent him. Divine identity is unveiled. This is reinforced all the more by what the Johannine Jesus says:

> When you have lifted up the Son of Man, then you will realize that I am he, and that I do nothing on my own, but I speak these things as the Father instructed me (John 8:28).

Of the sayings in the Fourth Gospel, it is "the lifting up of the Son of Man" (John 3:14-15; 8:28; 12:32-34) that surpasses the Gospel's seven "I am" declarations (John 4:26; 6:20; 8:24, 28, 58; 13:19; 18:5). This is so because the sayings about lifting up the Son of Man juxtapose the exaltation with the humiliation of Jesus on the cross, and serve to disclose his divine identity in that event. In the Fourth Gospel, John records that when the Greeks come and ask to see Jesus, he realizes that the hour has come for him to be glorified. It is now the time for him to be lifted up so that he can draw all people to himself (John 12:23-24, 32). The lifting up will not only reveal his identity but also humankind's destiny. All people will be drawn to him in the most comprehensive salvific sense. Therefore the Johannine Son of Man sayings refer to the integral relationship between Jesus, indeed Jesus as God, and God.

At the end of Jesus' life, as all through the ministry, Jesus is still using "Son of Man" of himself. As Christianity moved in widening circles into the non-Jewish Hellenistic world, the title Son of Man became not only mysterious but incomprehensible, and was therefore jettisoned. Other titles, such as Lord, became central; and new titles such as high priest, as in the letter to the Hebrews, were applied to him to meet particular needs.

However, even though Son of Man disappears in the NT completely as a reference to Jesus, apart from Acts 7:56 (though note also Rev. 1:13; 14:14), this only enhances the claim that this enigmatic title was his chosen self-designation. The very obscurity of the title allowed him to define his "mission and his message."[49] It is also clear, in my view, that for Jesus the title took on all that was signified by its use in the OT, especially in Ezekiel, Daniel 7, and in *1 Enoch* 37–71; from the focus on mortality and weakness in Ezekiel, to heavenly representative of the people of God in Daniel whose destiny is to

---

[48] With concrete details of his rejection and death there is the probable reference to Isaiah 53 as an expression of the prophetic destiny Jesus must fulfill.

[49] This point is well made by Russell Morton in his article "Son of Man," in Craig A. Evans, ed., *Encyclopedia of the Historical Jesus* (New York/London: Routledge, 2008), pp. 593-98 (p. 598).

exercise authority over the nations, to eschatological judge and divine agent for the redemption of the world in *1 Enoch*.

## E. Son of God

Divine sonship was a familiar category in the Hebrew Bible and in Second Temple Judaism that shaped the religious vocabulary of first-century Christian communities. In what appears to be an archaic use of the expression in the Hebrew scriptures, the heavenly hosts are referred to as "sons of God" (Gen. 6:2-4; Deut. 32:8; Job 1:6; Ps. 29:1; 89:6). Though in a number of cases the Septuagint translates the phrase as "angel(s) of God" (see, e.g., Deut. 32:8), this is not a consistent practice (as in Deut. 32:43). In references to the Davidic king, the language of divine sonship is both prominent and influential (see 2 Sam. 7:14; Ps. 2:7; 89:26-27).[50] From the Ancient Near Eastern perspective, the king could be called "son of God," or even, for that matter, "god." In 2 Samuel 7, the relationship between the king of Israel and God is described as a father-son relationship. God is the father of the "king," his "first-born." This designation takes on a different nuance when it is used of Israel as the people of God; Israel is called "son" and God is "Father" of the nation.

The use of "son of God" for the king was influential in Second Temple Judaism and in early Christianity. "Son of God," for example, is found as a messianic title at Qumran.[51] Nathaniel says to Jesus, "Rabbi, you are the Son of God! You are the King of Israel" (John 1:49). This messianic usage with respect to divine sonship did not connote divinity, but it certainly confirmed a special status and relationship to God. This is also evidenced in extra-canonical literature where the titles "sons" and "firstborn" of God are given to righteous individuals (Wisd. 2:18; 5:5; Sir. 4:10; *Pss. Sol.* 13:9; 18:4) and to Israel collectively (Exod. 4:22; Deut. 14:1; Isa. 1:2; Jer. 3:22; Hos. 1:10; 11:1; Wisd. 12:21; 16:10). The common denominator in all these cases is that the title son of God denoted someone specially related to or favored by God. In the case of the king, the status was much more formal; he represented God and God's rule to his people. But in its broader reference the expression is more indicative of someone who closely reflected the character of God, who fully performed God's will.[52]

---

[50] On divine sonship, see John J. Collins, *The Scepter and the Star: The Messiahs of the Dead Sea Scrolls and Other Ancient Literature* (New York: Doubleday, 1995), pp. 154-72. Some scholars suggest that Israel took over the Canaanite concept of an assembly of gods under the supremacy of El, and that these "holy ones" (see Deut. 33:2; Ps. 89:5, 7; Dan. 4:17; Zech. 14:5) could also be called "sons of god" (see Job 1:6; 2:1; 38:7).

[51] See 4Q246 where the future king is designated "Son of God" and "Son of the Most High." Note the discussion and commentary in J. A. Fitzmyer, "The Aramaic 'Son of God' Text from Qumran Cave 4 (4Q246)," in *The Dead Sea Scrolls and Christian Origins* (Grand Rapids: Eerdmans, 2000), pp. 41-61.

[52] J. D. G. Dunn argues that the theological logic is clear from Sir. 4:10 and Matt. 5:45/Luke 6:35. See, *Jesus Remembered: Christianity in the Making*, vol. 1 (Grand Rapids: Eerdmans, 2003), p. 711. "To be compassionate to the orphan and widow is to be like a 'son of

From the opening words of Mark's Gospel, Mark affirms that Jesus is the Χριστός and the Son of God (1:1). This affirmation of Jesus as "Son" is repeated in 1:11 and in several instances thereafter. In Mark, the portrait of Jesus is emphatically paradoxical. The Jesus who is the beloved Son (1:11) and David's Lord (12:35-37), and who will receive glorious vindication by God (14:62), is also the Son of Man who came "to serve, and to give his life as a ransom for many" (10:45). In fact, only through and after Jesus' obedient death can the truth about him be perceived clearly and then correctly proclaimed—hence the value of the centurion's testimony, "Truly, this man was God's Son" (15:39). The only human figure in Mark to refer unequivocally to Jesus' divine sonship does so in light of Jesus' death he has just witnessed. Ironically, the character in question is in charge of carrying out the execution.

Matthew's high view of Jesus is evidenced in three specific areas. First, although Matthew employs a number of terms for Jesus, it is widely agreed that Son of God and other expressions of Jesus' divine sonship—"my/his Son" (2:15; 3:17; 17:5; 21:37), "the Son," (11:27; 21:38; 24:36; 28:19)—are central to all that Matthew intends to affirm.[53] When Matthew employs the words of Hos. 11:1, "out of Israel I have called my son," he is identifying Jesus as God's Son and thus as the embodiment of Israel, the true, obedient Son (Matt. 2:15). Since the phrase Son of God in this period functioned as a messianic title, it did not carry in and of itself the overtones of divinity that later Christian theology would associate with it.[54] Second, much more frequently than the other evangelists, Matthew uses the Greek word προσκύνειν (to worship) to describe the reverence people offered to Jesus. Thus the magi come to "worship" Jesus (Matt. 2:2, 8, 11); in the account of Jesus walking on the water, the disciples "worship" him as the Son of God (14:33; contrast Mark 6:52). Jesus refers to himself as "the Son" and to God as "my/the Father" (Matt. 11:25-27). Third, Jesus' own intimate relationship with God as Son is the cause of his celebration of God's handing over "all things" to him such that he becomes the mediator of revelation about God (Matt. 11:25-27).

One of the striking aspects of the Fourth Gospel is the frequency with which Jesus refers to himself as God's Son, both to the disciples and to the wider public. In the Synoptics, however, Jesus' only overt public reference to himself as the Son of God is in the scene where he responds to the high priest's question (Mark 14:61-62/Matt. 26:63-64/Luke 22:70). However, in the Fourth Gospel, Jesus, as God's Son, declares his obedience to God (5:19, 30) and claims to be intimately associated with "the Father," who loves "the

---

God,' to act with uncalculating generosity and love even to the enemy is to model oneself on God."

[53] See J. D. Kingsbury, *Matthew: Structure, Christology, Kingdom* (Philadelphia: Fortress Press, 1975). In the more extended temptation narrative in 4:1-11, Jesus' divine sonship is explicitly mentioned twice (4:3, 6) and is probably implicit in the third temptation (4:8-10).

[54] See N. T. Wright, *The Challenge of Jesus: Rediscovering Who Jesus Was and Is* (Downers Grove: InterVarsity Press, 1999), pp. 107-08; Raymond E. Brown, *The Death of the Messiah*, 2 vols. (New York: Doubleday, 1994), pp. 520-47, esp. pp. 534-44.

Son" (5:20), and has given him power to raise the dead and to be the judge of all (5:21, 25-27; 17:2). The Johannine Jesus expects all people to honor the Son just as they honor God (5:22-23). He also declares his conviction that belief in the Son is the basis for eternal life and a share in the resurrection on the last day (6:40). In addition, in the story of the raising of Lazarus, Martha acclaims Jesus as "the Messiah, the Son of God" (John 11:27), an affirmation which anticipates that recorded in 20:28 as the crowning confession of the Gospel. Hence, the two christological titles "Messiah" and "Son of God" reflect a provenance in Jewish and biblical traditions which further suggests that the historical origins of Johannine Christianity is to be sought in Jewish-Christian circles of the second half of the first century. The Fourth Gospel presents Jesus' divine sonship as unique (1:14, 18; 3:16). Whereas those who come to believe in Jesus are given "authority to become children of God" (1:12), Jesus alone is the Son to whom God has given all authority and who has uniquely shared in the divine glory from "before the world was made" (17:1-5). For this very reason, the attribute of glory is attributed to both God and to Jesus.

As much as the Fourth Gospel distinguishes the Father and the Son it just as consistently affirms an unprecedented link between them and attributes to Jesus, the Son, participation in divine attributes and status. As is characteristic of most references to pre-existence in the NT, the Johannine prologue links Jesus specifically with the moment of creation as the one through whom all things came into being (John 1:1-3; cf. 1 Cor. 8:6; Col. 1:15-16; Heb. 1:2). By attributing the key role in creation to the one through whom redemption also comes, the text reflects belief in the connection between redemption and creation—between God and Jesus, and between Father and Son.

This reaches its climactic moment in the crucially important prayer of John 17. Jesus' appeal for divine vindication may be intended to refer to the pre-existent and heavenly status ascribed to him in the Prologue: "So now, Father, glorify me in your presence with the glory that I had in your presence before the world existed" (17:5). This approximates to the wording of the Prologue's "the Logos was with God" (1:1-2). As Raymond E. Brown has rightly observed, when the Prologue claims that the word was God, this is almost certainly meant to anticipate and correspond to Thomas's acclamation "my Lord and my God" (20:28).[55]

## F. Conclusion

The Christian tradition has unanimously pointed to Jesus Christ as the answer to the question of where God has revealed himself in a definitive way. Jesus of Nazareth is the person, honored with the titles Messiah, Son of Man, and Son of God, in whom the promises of the God of Israel intersect with the human quest for meaning and fulfillment.

---

[55] Raymond E. Brown, *The Gospel According to John I–XII* (Garden City: Doubleday, 1966), p. 5.

The very terms Messiah, Son of Man and Son of God, which witness to his distinct identity and role, demonstrate the conviction that Jesus found his identity and carried out his role precisely in service of and obedience to the one God of Israel. With respect to his status as Messiah, Jesus of Nazareth does not fit the conventional expectation of this role, as we saw above: as Messiah Jesus suffers and dies. In the Synoptics, Jesus as Son of God is clearly linked with the inauguration of the kingdom of God. Jesus' references to himself as Son in the Fourth Gospel are used in the context of affirming his own obedience as well as the authority given to him by the Father. This unity of the Son of God with the Father lies in the Son's dependence upon the Father in all that he says and does. So complete is this unity that Jesus is said to exercise the divine prerogatives of judging and giving life; but they are divine prerogatives granted to him by God, his Father. As Son of Man, the term which Jesus used self-referentially, he sums up in himself all that that term, however opaquely, had come to denote—from the frail and all too mortal one who spoke the word of God, to heavenly representative of the beleaguered faithful, to exalted revealer of divine secrets and eschatological judge—in exilic and Second Temple Jewish texts.

As we have seen, the ideas which are encapsulated in the three titles are complex. "Messiah" and "Son of God" emerge out of and attempt to articulate the meaning of the words and acts of Jesus. "Son of Man" is his self-designation, enigmatic and ambiguous. The convergence and mutual reinforcement of these titles—Messiah, Son of Man and Son of God—in the one person, Jesus of Nazareth, underscores his uniqueness in the unfolding purposes of God.

## Bibliography

Bauckham, Richard J. *God Crucifed: Monotheism and Christology in the New Testament.* Grand: Rapids: Eerdmans, 1998.

Borg, Marcus, and Wright, N. T. *The Meaning of Jesus: Two Visions.* San Francisco: HarperSanFrancisco, 1999.

Broadhead, Edwin K. *Naming Jesus: Titular Christology in the Gospel of Mark.* Sheffield: Sheffield Academic Press, 1999.

Brown, Raymond E. *An Introduction to New Testament Christology.* New York: Paulist Press, 1994.

Burkett, Delbert. *The Son of Man Debate: A History and Evaluation.* Cambridge/New York: Cambridge University Press, 1999.

Charlesworth, James H. ed. *The Messiah: Developments in Earliest Judaism and Christianity.* Minneapolis: Fortress Press, 1992.

De Jonge, Marinus. "The Earliest Christian use of Christos: Some Suggestions." *New Testament Studies* 32 (1986): 321-43.

Green, Joel B. and Turner, Max, eds. *Jesus of Nazareth Lord and Christ: Essays on the Historical Jesus and New Testament Christology.* Grand Rapids/Carlisle: Eerdmans/Paternoster Press, 1994.

Hare, Douglas R. A. *The Son of Man Tradition.* Philadelphia: Fortress Press, 1999.

Horsley, Richard A., and Hanson, John S. *Bandits, Prophets and Messiahs: Popular Movements at the Time of Jesus.* Minneapolis: Winston Press, 1985.

Hurtado, Larry. *Lord Jesus Christ: Devotion to Jesus in Earliest Christianity.* Grand

Rapids: Eerdmans, 2003.

Lindars, Barnabas. *Jesus Son of Man: A Fresh Examination of the Son of Man Sayings in Light of Recent Research.* London: SPCK, 1983.

Longenecker, Richard N., ed. *Contours of Christology in the New Testament.* Grand Rapids: Eerdmans, 2005.

Marshall, I. Howard. *The Origins of New Testament Christology.* Downers Grove: InterVarsity Press, 1990.

McCready, Douglas. *He Came Down From Heaven: The Pre-existence of Christ and the Christian Faith.* Downers Grove: InterVarsity Press, 2005.

Moule, C. F. D. *The Origins of Christology.* New York/Cambridge: Cambridge University Press, 1977.

Neusner, Jacob, William Scott Green and Ernest S. Frerichs, et. al., eds. *Judaisms and Their Messiahs.* New York/Cambridge: Cambridge University Press, 1987.

Powell, Mark Allan, and Bauer, David R. eds. *Who do you say that I am?: Essays on Christology.* Louisville: Westminster John Knox Press, 1999.

Rowland, Christopher. *Christian Origins: From Messianic Movement to Christian Religion.* Minneapolis: Augsburg Publishing House, 1985.

Witherington III, Ben. *The Many Faces of the Christ: the Christologies of the New Testament and Beyond.* New York: Crossroad Publishing, 1998.

Wright, N. T. *The Challenge of Jesus: Rediscovering Who Jesus Was and Is.* Downers Grove: InterVarsity Press, 1999.

# 18. The Passion and Resurrection Narratives

*Ian K. Smith*

The passion and resurrection narratives form the climax of each of the gospels. They bring together many Old Testament (OT) themes, much of the teaching of Jesus, and are to be read in the light of messianic expectations of the Second Temple period. It is through the events of the passion and the resurrection that Jesus fulfills for Israel her vocation of being a light to the nations. When the full import of this is understood, as evidenced in the Acts of the Apostles, God's covenant with Israel is freed from its geographical locus in Jerusalem to go to the ends of the earth. Jerusalem therefore becomes not only the place from which the New Testament (NT) church spreads; it is the place of the fulfillment of the gospel tradition.

## A. The Triumphal Entry

The passion narratives in the Synoptic Gospels are normally understood as beginning with the Last Supper (Matt. 26:1; Luke 22:1; Mark 14:1). Prior to this, each Synoptic Gospel records Jesus' triumphal entry to Jerusalem and his visitation upon the temple, which resulted in its cleansing from misuse for financial gain (Matt. 21:12-17; Mark 11:12-19; Luke 19:45-48). In each account, the evangelist records how this visitation marks the end of the old covenant. In Matthew and Mark this is seen in the withering of the fig tree, a tree that is often used to symbolize Israel (Jer. 8:13; Hos. 9:10; Mic. 7:1); in Luke there is the incident of Jesus weeping over Jerusalem as the city did not recognize the day of its visitation (Luke 19:41-44). The narrating of Jesus' entry to Jerusalem is replete with many OT references (e.g. Zech. 9:9; Ps. 118:26) which leaves the reader in no doubt that this is the arrival of Israel's messianic king.

Other royal overtones from the Second Temple period can also be detected in the triumphal entry. In 167 BC, Antiochus IV, the Seleucid king, had defiled the Jerusalem temple by sacrificing unclean animals (2 Macc. 6:5) to Olympian Zeus (2 Macc. 6:2) on an altar erected over the existing temple altar (1 Macc. 1:59).[1] This desecration was one of the events that led to the Maccabean revolt. The success of the revolt eventually curtailed the influence

---

[1] Bruce M. Metzger, *The New Testament: Its Background, Growth and Content* (Nashville: Abingdon, 1965), p. 20.

of the Seleucids and led to the re-establishment of religious freedom for the Jews. The purification of the temple after its desecration, which occurred in December 164 BC, is still celebrated by Jews in the feast of Hanukkah. Prior to this rededication of the temple, Judas Maccabeus, the one who had led the revolt, entered Jerusalem as a messiah-like figure. This entry is described in 2 Macc. 10:7 (NRSV) as follows:

> Therefore, carrying ivy-wreathed wands and beautiful branches and also fronds of palm, they offered hymns of thanksgiving to him who had given success to the purifying of his own holy place.

The similarities between the entry of Judas Maccabeus to Jerusalem and that of Jesus are plain, as is the fact that each of them proceeded to the purification of the temple: the former from its defilement by Gentiles, the latter from its defilement by the people of Israel. The major difference between the entries, however, is that the Maccabean purification of the temple was in order that it might return to its former function; Jesus' purification of the temple was so that it might be replaced. The crucifixion and resurrection of Israel's Messiah will surpass all that the temple signifies (John 2:19-22).

Mark (14:3-9) and Matthew (26:6-13) begin their respective accounts of the passion narrative with Jesus being anointed for burial[2] by a woman placing nard on him, a potent fragrance from a root found in India.[3] The extravagance of the act is seen not only in the value of the nard (a year's wages), but also in the fact that the container is cracked, thereby disallowing the retention of any of the perfume for a later date. This extravagance is juxtaposed with the venue of the event: the house of a leper. Whether Simon was a leper who had been healed by Jesus, or whether he still suffered from the disease, the stigma and ritual uncleanness is not a concern for Jesus. The venue and the instrument of the anointing (a nameless woman) alert the reader that the kingdom of this messiah has values that are paradoxical with respect to societal norms. The placement of this story as a frontispiece to the passion narrative appears to be intentional. The actions of this woman are not recorded merely for historical curiosity; they convey theological significance about the nature of the kingdom of God and the significance of the death for which Jesus is anointed. Throughout the gospel narratives, it is at the intersection of the historical and theological perspectives that significance is determined.[4]

---

[2] This is probably a different event from that which is described in Luke 7:36-50, though there may be literary borrowings between the two stories. Note also the Fourth Gospel's placement of the story before the triumphal entry (John 12:1-11). See Ben Witherington III, *Women in the Ministry of Jesus: A Study of Jesus' Attitudes to Women and their Roles as Reflected in His Earthly Life* (Cambridge: Cambridge University Press, 1984), pp. 110-13.

[3] Ben Witherington III, *The Gospel of Mark: A Socio-Rhetorical Commentary* (Grand Rapids: Eerdmans, 2001), p. 367.

[4] See Joel B. Green, *The Death of Jesus: Tradition and Interpretation in the Passion Narrative* (Tübingen: Mohr, 1988), p. 2: "[T]o claim for it [the crucifixion] historical *certitude* hardly begins to answer the question concerning its historical *significance*. Indeed, only to treat Jesus' death as an historical incident is to be left with Cleopas and his companion on the

The historicity of the crucifixion is well-attested.[5] Due to the barbaric nature of this form of execution and the fact that the victims were usually slaves, the literary world did not often refer to it.[6] However, some records remain, the most detailed of which are those within the four canonical gospels. The Roman historian, Tacitus, who died in AD 120, wrote:

> [Nero] punished with the utmost refinements of cruelty, a class of men, loathed for their vices, whom the crowd styled Christians. Christus, the founder of the name, had undergone the death penalty in the reign of Tiberius, by sentence of the procurator Pontius Pilatus, and the pernicious superstition was checked for a moment, only to break out once more, not merely in Judea, the home of the disease, but in the capital itself, where all things horrible or shameful in the world collect and find a vogue.
> (*Ann.* 15.44, trans. John Jackson)

Similarly the Jewish historian, Josephus, who died in c. AD 100, is reported to have written:[7]

> About this time there lived Jesus, a wise man, if indeed one ought to call him a man. For he was one who wrought surprising feats and was a teacher of such people as accept the truth gladly. He won over many Jews and many of the Greeks. He was the Messiah. When Pilate, upon hearing him accused by men of the highest standing among us, had condemned him to be crucified, those who had in the first place come to love him did not give up their affection for him. On the third day he appeared to them restored to life, for the prophets of God had prophesied these and countless other marvellous things about him. And the tribe of the Christians, so called after him, has still to this day not disappeared.
> (*Ant.* 18.63-64; trans. Louis H. Feldman)

---

Emmaus-road in puzzlement."

[5] "*He was crucified under Pontius Pilate*. It would be no exaggeration to say that this event is better attested, and supported by a more impressive array of evidence, than any other event of comparable importance of which we have knowledge from the Ancient World." A. E. Harvey, *Jesus and the Constraints of History* (Philadelphia: Westminster, 1982), p. 11.

[6] Martin Hengel, "Crucifixion in the Ancient World and the Folly of the Message of the Cross," in *The Cross of the Son of God* (London: SCM Press, 1986), pp. 91-185, esp. pp. 114-30. See also L. L. Welborn, *Paul, the Fool of Christ: A Study of 1 Corinthians 1–4 in the Comic-Philosophic Tradition* (London: T. & T. Clark, 2005), pp. 129-47.

[7] There is the probability of later Christian interpolations in this text. See Hans-Ruedi Weber, *The Cross: Tradition and Interpretation* (London: SPCK, 1979), pp. 14-15; John P. Meier, *A Marginal Jew: Rethinking the Historical Jesus*, volume one (New York: Doubleday, 1991), pp. 59-61; Steve Mason, *Josephus and the New Testament* (Peabody: Hendrickson, 2003), pp. 172, 213-48.

## B. The Last Supper

The significance of the crucifixion is best determined by Jesus' own interpretation of the events as anticipated at the Last Supper.[8] It is generally held that the Last Supper was part of the annual celebration of Passover[9] (which was celebrated on Nisan 14), which, by the time of Jesus, had been combined with the Feast of Unleavened Bread (which continued until Nisan 21).[10] Passover celebrated the liberation of Israel from Egypt and Unleavened Bread commemorated how the Israelites ate only unleavened bread on the eve of the Exodus (Exodus 12; 23:15; 34:18). This combined feast was a restatement of Israel's identity. During Passover, the population of Jerusalem would increase dramatically, although few take seriously Josephus' estimate of 2,700,000 pilgrims (*J.W.* 6.425-26); Sanders' estimate of 300,000-500,000 seems more reasonable.[11] The gathering of such a large crowd during the Roman period could provide the occasion for civil disturbance, hence Pontius Pilate, who was normally stationed at Caesarea, and many of his soldiers were in Jerusalem.

At the time of Jesus, the Passover was no longer a meal shared in haste (Exod. 12:11), but had evolved into a banquet involving the purchase of an unblemished lamb and other foods.[12] It was celebrated in family units, and Jesus expressed his eager desire to eat this meal with his disciples (Luke 22:15). Four cups punctuated the meal, each of which had significance. The first cup was used to bless the day, and was followed by herbs dipped in sauce. Prior to the second cup, the youngest son would ask why this night was different from other nights. In reply, the head of the family would tell the story of the Exodus and give an exposition of Deut. 26:5-11. In the light of this the meal was an act of remembrance of and thanksgiving for God's faithfulness in the liberation of an oppressed people. The singing of a psalm and the drinking of the second cup follow this. The head of the family would then take unleavened bread, bless it, break it and hand it to the others, which would be followed by the meal and then the third cup. The drinking of the fourth cup happened after the singing of a psalm at the conclusion of the meal, although it is unclear whether the fourth cup was part of the Passover at the

---

[8] Martin Hengel, "The Atonement," in *The Cross of the Son of God* (London: SCM Press, 1986), pp. 187-263. For a view that counters that of Hengel, see Green, *The Death of Jesus*, pp. 320-23.

[9] For a discussion about the association of Passover with the Last Supper see M. Casey, *Aramaic Sources of Mark's Gospel* (Cambridge: Cambridge University Press, 1998), pp. 219-52.

[10] For details on the reckoning of Passover within the Jewish calendrical system(s) of the first century see J. Nolland, *The Gospel of Matthew: A Commentary on the Greek Text* (Grand Rapids: Eerdmans, 2005), pp. 1042-46. For a combination of the two festivals see 2 Chr. 35:17 and Josephus, *Ant.* 14.21; 17.213.

[11] E. P. Sanders, *Judaism. Practice and Belief 63 BCE–66 CE* (London: SCM Press, 1992), pp. 126-28.

[12] For more detail on the practice of the Passover as referred to in the New Testament see J. B. Segal, *The Hebrew Passover: From the Earliest Times to AD 70* (London: Oxford University Press, 1963), esp. pp. 33-37, 241-47.

time of Jesus.[13]

Jesus reinterprets the symbols of the Passover in the light of his impending death. In Luke 22:17 there is reference to Jesus taking a cup and giving thanks for it, which is probably a reference to the first cup of the Passover meal. In Luke 22:19 there is mention of the distribution of the bread, which is representative of Jesus' body, and in the following verse there is another cup, which is clearly the third cup of the Passover. This cup is the new covenant in Christ's blood, a statement that is rich in OT allusions. In Exodus 24 the significance of blood in sacrifice is seen in the sprinkling of half of it on the altar (24:6) and the other half on the people (24:8), thereby binding God to his people. At the Last Supper Jesus is declaring that God will bind himself to his people by virtue of his sacrifice on the cross. Jesus' death becomes the inauguration of a new covenant (Jer. 31:31-34) and the Lord's Supper a celebration of this inauguration.

Each of the canonical gospels allows the reader to feel the suffering whereby this new covenant is inaugurated. The failure of old Israel is emphasized by Jesus' abandonment by his disciples in their flight from Gethsemane (Matt. 26:56; Mark 14:50), in the denial of Peter (Matt. 26:69-75; Mark 14:66-72; Luke 22:55-63; John 18:15-18, 25-27) and ultimately in the betrayal of Judas (Matt. 26:14-16, 47-50; Mark 14:10-11, 43-45; Luke 22:3-6, 47-48; John 18:2-3).[14]

## C. Arrest and Trial

In contrast to the faithlessness of old Israel, Jesus is seen as one, who, as Israel's Messiah, fulfills Israel's obligation of covenant faithfulness. Through emotional and physical anguish, Jesus continues to be faithful in the Garden of Gethsemane, whereby the reader receives an insight into his humanity. With angelic assistance (Luke 22:43, cf. 1 Kgs. 19:5-8; Ps. 91:11-12; Dan. 3:28; 10:16-19), Jesus is portrayed as a faithful Israelite at prayer, dependant upon the wisdom of God as evidenced by the words, "if you will. . ." (Luke 22:42). There are similarities between this prayer in Gethsemane and the Lord's Prayer: at Gethsemane Jesus uses the address πάτερ (Father) (Matt. 26:39), he prays that God's will be done, and he exhorts the disciples not to fall into temptation (Matt. 26:41). Jesus' request for God to grant him a reprieve does not show a lack of faith; there are many similar requests in the OT for God to change his mind, which are made in the context of trust in divine sovereignty (e.g. Exod. 32:10-14; 2 Sam. 15:25-26; 2 Kgs. 20:1-6). It is not from the pending crucifixion *per se* that Jesus asks to be delivered; the cross has been the object of Jesus' intentional journey to Jerusalem (Luke 9:22; 13:33; 22:22, 37; 24:7, 26, 44; Acts 1:16; 17:2-3). Jesus prays to be delivered from "the cup," a reference to the cup of God's wrath, a common

---

[13] I. Howard Marshall, *The Gospel of Luke: A Commentary on the Greek Text* (Grand Rapids: Eerdmans, 1978), pp. 797-98.

[14] Witherington, *The Gospel of Mark*, p. 376.

OT allusion (Ps. 11:6; 75:8-9; Isa. 51:17, 19, 22; Jer. 25:15-26; 49:12; 51:57; Lam. 4:21; Ezek. 23:31-34; Hab. 2:16; Zech. 12:2). This cup is poured out upon Jesus when he cries: *Eloi, Eloi, lama sabachthani* (My God, My God, why have you forsaken me?) (Mark 15:34). It is this separation from the Father that causes Jesus the greatest foreboding, as it is the ultimate abandonment. Subsequent to the prayer, Jesus finds his disciples sleeping (Luke 22:45). The events of the day are taking their toll; it is a picture of total exhaustion. It is at this point of emotional and physical weakness that Jesus is arrested and taken to the house of the High Priest. The fact that the arrest is effected at night, under the cloak of darkness (Luke 22:53), gives the reader a hint of the injustice of the forthcoming trial.

It is difficult to reconstruct the order of the events around the trial at the High Priests' houses.[15] John mentions that Jesus was led first to the house of Annas before going to the house of Caiaphas (John 18:12-14, 24). Matthew also states that Caiaphas was High Priest (Matt. 26:57). Luke, however, clearly states that Annas was the High Priest in Acts 4:6 whereas in Luke 3:2 both Annas and Caiaphas are associated with the office of High Priest. Knowing something of the historical background, however, helps overcome these apparent inconsistencies. Annas was Caiaphas' father-in-law (John 18:13) and had been High Priest from AD 6–15, when Valerius Gratus, Pontius Pilate's predecessor, had deposed him in favor of Caiaphas. As a Gentile overlord had deposed Annas, many Jews would still have regarded Annas as the real High Priest. This would account for the reason why Luke sees both Annas and Caiaphas as High Priest(s) in Luke 3:2.

The most likely synthesis of the accounts concerning Jesus' Jewish trial(s) is suggested by the nineteenth-century commentator Godet[16] who argues that there were three trials: (1) a brief encounter with Annas, which was an inquiry where no judgment was made; (2) the meeting with Caiaphas; (3) the trial before the Sanhedrin. The trials before Caiaphas and the Sanhedrin mirror one another because the official decision came before the whole body, which replayed the Caiaphas meeting.[17] As High Priest, Caiaphas chaired the Sanhedrin.[18] This reconstruction accounts for why neither Matthew nor Mark records anything about Annas, as no decision was made at his house. Luke's lack of mention of Annas' house may be an example of literary compression. It is unclear whether Peter's denial took place at Annas' or Caiaphas' house.

Regardless of the locations, the trials are shown as displays of Jesus' strength in the face of formidable opposition. By contrast, Peter's denial to a

---

[15] For a comprehensive account, see David R. Catchpole, *The Trial of Jesus: A Study in the Gospels and Jewish Historiography from 1770 to the Present Day* (Leiden: Brill, 1971), pp. 153-218.

[16] F. Godet, *A Commentary on the Gospel of Luke*, volume 2 (Edinburgh: T. & T. Clark, 1870), pp. 311-12.

[17] D. L. Bock, *Luke*, volume two (Grand Rapids: Baker, 1996), pp. 1779-81.

[18] See Philip S. Alexander, "Jewish Law in the Time of Jesus: Towards a Clarification of the Problem," in Barnabas Lindars, ed., *Law and Religion: Essays on the Place of the Law in Israel and Early Christianity* (Cambridge: James Clarke, 1988), pp. 44-58, esp. pp. 46-49.

powerless servant girl (Luke 22:57, 60) is a display of weakness and faithlessness. The words of his denials may have reminded the initial readers of the gospels of the formula for expulsion from the synagogue: "I have never known you" (cf. Matt. 7:23).[19] The irony of what happens with Peter is not to be missed; simultaneously, with Jesus being condemned as a false prophet, his prophecies about Peter's denial are coming true![20] This, however, is not the end for Peter: his three denials will be matched by the threefold commission in John 21:15-17. Matthew recounts Judas's remorse and suicide at this point in the narrative (Matt. 27:3-10; cf. Acts 1:18-20) as he seeks to reverse as much as possible of what he has done. Unlike Peter, who finds restoration through repentance in life, Judas' attempted solution is in remorse and suicide. The question of whether Judas' remorse was also true repentance is best left to God; it is an issue upon which the text is silent.

Jesus' desertion by his disciples means that he faces his trial alone. It appears that the Sanhedrin in Jerusalem had significant power and functioned as the highest Jewish court. It met in Jerusalem, probably on the Temple Mount, and regulated the running of the temple. Apart from being a law-court, the Sanhedrin, along with the High Priest, also acted as the representative of the Jewish people in dealing with the Romans. The Sanhedrin was a sizable body of about seventy members.[21] The right to sentence a person with capital punishment, however, had been removed from this court, as Josephus attests, once Judea became a Roman province.[22]

The primary charge that is brought against Jesus is his claim regarding the destruction and the renewal of the temple. Hooker points out that Mark chooses the word ναός (sanctuary) here, not ἱερόν (temple), his usual word for temple, indicating that the charge may have referred to the inner sanctuary, thereby adding to its gravity.[23] It is the lack of response that precipitates the second charge. Jesus is asked whether he is the Messiah, the son of the Blessed One (Mark 14:61). As the "Blessed One" is a circumlocution for "God," this brings together the claims to messiahship and to deity. First century messianic expectations did not necessarily associate the coming messiah with the Son of God,[24] but Jesus' affirmation of his identity in the language of ἐγώ εἰμί (I am) and of "Son of Man" categories (Mark 14:62), reminiscent of Ps. 110:1 and Dan. 7:13, brings together these two roles. This is a clear provocation to his accusers.

The trial of Jesus now moves from the Jewish authorities to the Romans under Pontius Pilate (Luke 18:32 cf. Luke 23:1; John 18:28). Due to the

---

[19] Marshall, *Luke*, p. 842; H. L. Strack and P. Billerbeck, *Kommentar zum Neuen Testament aus Talmud und Midrasch*, volume 1 (München: Beck, 1956), p. 469.

[20] Witherington, *The Gospel of Mark*, p. 386.

[21] Alexander, "Jewish Law in the Time of Jesus," p. 48.

[22] *J.W.* 2.117. See also E. Mary Smallwood, *The Jews under Roman Rule: From Pompey to Diocletian* (Leiden: Brill, 1976), pp. 149-50.

[23] Morna Hooker, *A Commentary on the Gospel according to St. Mark* (London: A. & C. Black, 1991), p. 358.

[24] N. T. Wright, *The Challenge of Jesus: Rediscovering who Jesus was and is* (Downers Grove: InterVarsity Press, 1999), pp. 74-75.

deposition and exile of the Herodian ethnarch (*J.W.* 2.93), Archelaus, in AD 6, Judea had come under direct Roman rule by a governor, appointed by the Emperor, and accountable to the Roman legate for Syria. Pontius Pilate served in this role from AD 26–36. Both Philo and Josephus refer to Pilate, describing him as a stern and even cruel leader, which may complement the gospels' depiction of him as a weak, accommodating and indecisive man.[25] Jesus' trial before this Roman governor becomes the "handing over" to the Gentiles mentioned in Matt. 20:19 (Mark 10:33; Luke 18:32). The irony of this should not be lost: the messiah's role was deliverance from Gentile oppression that Israel might be a light to the nations, but this is achieved through his subjection to a Gentile court. This trial took place in the headquarters of the governor, the praetorium (John 18:28). There is debate about whether the praetorium refers to the Antonia Fortress, North West of the temple complex, or to Herod's palace.[26] In the trial before Pilate, the charges are more civil and political than religious: they focus upon subversion, as evidenced in the alleged discouragement of the payment of taxes to the emperor, and the pretence of being a king (Luke 23:2). Pilate seizes upon the second charge relating to Jesus' royal status (Mark 15:1-2; Luke 23:3; John 18:33).

When Pilate learns of Jesus' association with Galilee, he refers the case to Herod Antipas, who was in Jerusalem for the Passover. Unlike Judea, Galilee was not under direct Roman rule;[27] it was situated within the tetrarchy of Herod Antipas, the son of Herod the Great. Antipas (often called 'Herod' in the NT [Matt 14:1-12; Mark 6:14-29; Luke 3:1, 19-20; 9:7-9; 13:31; 23:6-15]) ruled Galilee as a client (as tetrarch). The careful reader of the gospels will know that Herod was not warmly disposed towards Jesus. Not only was Jesus a threat to Herod's authority, but Herod had already been instrumental in the death of Jesus' cousin, John the Baptist (Mark 6:14-29), and on one occasion the Pharisees warned Jesus of Herod's desire to have him killed (Luke 13:31). Furthermore, there was enmity between Herod and Pilate (Luke 23:12). Pilate is motivated less from political courtesies and more from a desire to share the responsibility for any decision regarding Jesus' execution. Herod, however, agreed to Pilate's summons, more concerned with the theatrics of Jesus' miracles than with justice (Luke 23:8). Jesus, however, does not reply to Herod's questions (Luke 23:9).[28]

The final phase of Jesus' trial is punctuated by Pilate's attempts to effect Jesus' release (Luke 23:13-25). Pilate finds no grounds for Jesus' execution (Luke 23:22). Jesus is flogged (John 19:1), a punishment which could produce

---

[25] See Jean-Pierre Lémonon, *Pilate et le gouvernement de la Judée: Textes et monuments* (Paris: Gabalda, 1981); B. C. McGing, "Pontius Pilate and the Sources," *CBQ* 53 (1991), pp. 416-38; H. K. Bond, *Pontius Pilate in History and Interpretation* (Cambridge: Cambridge University Press, 1998); Warren Carter, *Pontius Pilate: Portraits of a Roman Governor* (Collegeville: Liturgical Press, 2003).

[26] Witherington, *The Gospel of Mark*, p. 389; *BDAG*, p. 859.

[27] Alexander, "Jewish Law," p. 46.

[28] This may be seen as a fulfillment of Isa. 53:7-8, and/or the most appropriate response to this travesty of justice.

death as the *flagellum* had pieces of lead, bone and even hooks tied in it that could tear the flesh. Pilate seeks to use the governor's custom of releasing a prisoner chosen by the crowd at Passover (Matt. 27:15). We know of this custom of a Passover pardon only through the gospel accounts, and so no extra detail can be supplied.[29] The injustice of Jesus' death is again underscored by the crowd's choice of Barabbas, a known insurrectionist who had committed murder and thereby deserved capital punishment (Luke 23:19, 25). This release of Barabbas results in a later indictment from Peter in Acts 3:13-14.

Jesus is mocked for his regal claims. He is dressed in a bright robe and a crown of thorns is placed upon his head (Luke 23:11; Mark 15:17-20; Matt. 27:28-31). There is some dispute about the significance of the robe due to the uncertainty of its color. In Mark 15:20 and John 19:2, the robe is described as purple (πορφύρα) whereas in Matt. 27:28 it is described as scarlet (κόκκινος). Both colors represent status: purple representing royalty and officialdom, whereas scarlet, or red, was the color of a Roman soldier's cloak. Nolland suggests that just as a reed was symbolic of a scepter (Matt. 27:29), so the officer's cloak was representative of the royal color of purple.[30] The thorns, which formed the crown that was placed on Jesus' head, were probably the rachis of the leaf that grows at the base of a date palm frond (probably the *Phoenix dactylifera*).[31] When placed upon Jesus' head, these thorns would form a caricature of a radiating crown, which in other "coronations" may have represented the light rays that were meant to emanate from the heads of divinities. In this case, however, it is an example of mockery and sheer brutality. Jesus is ridiculed, spat upon and led away with a significant military escort.

## D. The Crucifixion

As a means of execution, crucifixion was particularly cruel: both in its physical act and in its public humiliation. No standard practice can be established, although it can be determined that the victim was flogged beforehand and was required to carry the crossbeam (*patibulum*);[32] a vertical stake was permanently fixed in the ground at the site of execution. The victim's feet were tied or nailed to the upright gibbet to which was also attached a piece of wood that served like a small seat (*sedecula*) which partially supported the body's weight.[33] The cross beam would then be raised by forked poles and placed either at the top of the upright or across the upper portion of the upright. A tablet specifying the crime was hung around the

---

[29] Lémonon, *Pilate*, p. 191.

[30] Nolland, *The Gospel of Matthew*, p. 1182.

[31] See H. St. J. Hart, "The Crown of Thorns in John 19.2-5," *JTS* 3 (1952), pp. 66-75; C. Bonner, "The Crown of Thorns," *HTR* 46 (1953), pp. 47-48.

[32] "Every criminal who goes to execution must carry his own cross on his back" (Plutarch, *Mor.* 554 A/B).

[33] Carson, *The Gospel According to John* (Grand Rapids: Eerdmans, 1991), p. 608.

accused as a public deterrent. The condemned person was then nailed or bound to the cross with arms extended, raised up. The victim faced death with all organs intact and with relatively little blood loss. Death came slowly, sometimes over several days as the body succumbed to shock, exhaustion and asphyxiation. In order to breathe, it was necessary for the person to push with the legs and pull with the arms. The small seat (*sedecula*) would prolong the agony as it partially supported the body's weight. Muscles would ache from exhaustion, but collapse would mean asphyxiation. Roman citizens were exempt from this form of execution due to its brutality. Josephus described it as "the most pitiable of deaths" (*J.W.* 7.203). The brutality of execution was a way of keeping public order throughout the Roman Empire, especially in troublesome areas such as Judea, whose history was punctuated by accounts of insurrectionists being crucified.[34]

Executions were typically located outside the city walls. Despite the custom of requiring the condemned to carry their own crossbeams (Plutarch, *Mor.* 554A; see n. 32 above), we are told that Simon of Cyrene was compelled to assist Jesus (Matt. 27:32; Mark 15:22; Luke 23:26). This may have been a concession due to Jesus' extreme weakness from the previous flogging. Whether Simon was a Gentile or a Jew is uncertain. Simon is a Greek name and Cyrene was the capital of the Roman province of Cyrenaica (Libya), which had a significant Jewish population (Josephus, *Ag. Ap.* 2.44). Luke mentions devout Jews from Cyrene in Acts 2:10 and a Cyrenian synagogue in Acts 6:9. In Luke's Gospel in particular, there is an emphasis on the call to deny self and to follow Jesus (Luke 5:11, 27, 28; 9:11, 23, 49, 57, 59, 61; 18:22). Hence Simon's action of cross bearing is portrayed as a living parable of the nature of Christian discipleship (Luke 9:23; 14:27).[35]

Jesus' identification as Israel's Messiah, acting on behalf of Israel, means that there is a causal link between the rejection of Jesus and the resultant destruction of Jerusalem in AD 70 by the Romans. Israel would not escape the fate of her Messiah. The women who followed Jesus to the cross were told not to weep for what was happening to Jesus, but for would happen to them in the wake of the crucifixion (Luke 23:28-31). The association between the death of Jesus and the destruction of Jerusalem also makes sense of the lesser to greater argument of green wood and dry wood (23:31): if crucifixion is what happens to a "living tree," who is faithful to God, what will happen to the faithless nation of Israel?[36] It is for this reason that, in each Synoptic Gospel Jesus' prophecy of the fall of Jerusalem (Matt. 24:1-51; Mark 13:1-36; Luke 21:5-36) immediately precedes the passion narrative.

As the crucifixion proceeds, there are three cosmic signs. The first of

---

[34] Josephus gives several accounts of crucifixion being used to suppress opposition to the Romans in Judea, e.g. *J.W.* 2.75, 241, 253, 306, 308; 3.321; 5.289, 449-51.

[35] See B. K. Blount, "A Socio-Rhetorical Analysis of Simon of Cyrene: Mark 15:21 and its Parallels," *Semeia* 64 (1993), pp. 171-98, in which Simon is portrayed as a cross-bearing disciple whose action is to be emulated.

[36] Wright, *The Challenge of Jesus*, pp. 85-86; Joseph A. Fitzmyer, *The Gospel According to Luke*, volume 2 (Garden City: Doubleday, 1985), 1498-99.

these is darkness, which recalls an eschatological motif from the judgment imagery of the day of the Lord (Amos 8:9; Joel 2:10; 2:30-31; Zeph. 1:15), whose darkness is like the mourning for the loss of an only son (cf. Amos 8:9-10). The darkness is not a solar eclipse as Passover always coincided with a full moon. The gospels do not tell us whether this was a natural phenomenon (e.g. dark cloud, dust storm) or supernatural. The significance of the event is clear: it conveys God's displeasure. In Exod. 10:21-22, the plague of darkness signifies that God's curse rests upon the land. At the crucifixion this curse is borne by Israel's Messiah in an act of atonement for the sins of many (Gal. 3:13).

(2)

The second cosmic sign is that the curtain in the temple was torn (Mark 15:38; Matt. 27:51).[37] There were two curtains in the temple: one that protected the Holy of Holies (Lev. 21:23; 24:3; Josephus, *J.W.* 5.219) and the other that separated the temple from the outer court (Exod. 26:37; 38:18; Num. 3:26; Josephus, *J.W.* 5.212). It is difficult to decide which curtain was torn. The fact that ναός (sanctuary) is used indicates the possibility that it is the inner curtain, however the public nature of the phenomenon could require that it was the outer curtain.[38] The tearing of the curtain signified the end of the temple's dominant role as a sacred symbol. It was not so much a picture of Gentile access to the Holy of Holies, for this temple would soon be destroyed, its fate being inextricably linked to that of Jesus. It is more an image of the glory of God coming out of the temple. Painter points out that at the beginning of Jesus' ministry the heavens were rent and the Spirit came down upon Jesus. Here, there is the opposite, for as Jesus cries out that he is forsaken by God the temple veil is rent and the Spirit of God leaves the temple thereby ensuring the temple's doom.[39] Subsequent to this, the place of worship is neither Jerusalem-centered nor temple-based; worship is focused on the risen and ascended Jesus (cf. John 4:21-24). (3)

The third cosmic sign is the shaking of the earth, a sign of God's coming judgment (cf. 2 Sam. 22:7-8; Nah. 1:6). The raising of the holy ones is unique to Matt. 27:52-53. Although many exegetical issues remain concerning this passage, the relationship between it and the resurrection of the valley of dry bones in Ezekiel 37 is clear (esp. Ezek. 37:12). This is both the re-establishment of Israel and the manifestation of eschatological realities,[40] which will result in a new Heaven and a new Earth (cf. Isa. 65:17-25; Rev. 21:1-5).

---

[37] See M. De Jonge "Matthew 27.51 in Early Christian Exegesis," in G. W. E. Nickelsburg and G. W. MacRae, eds., *Christians Among Jews and Gentiles: Essays in Honor of Krister Stendahl on His Sixty-Fifth Birthday* (Philadelphia: Fortress Press, 1986), pp. 67-79 for different understandings of the rending of the curtain.

[38] Marshall, *Luke*, p. 875.

[39] John Painter, *Mark's Gospel: Words in Conflict* (New York: Routledge, 1997), p. 207. See also William L. Lane, *The Gospel According to Mark: The English Text with Introduction, Exposition and Notes* (Grand Rapids: Eerdmans, 1974), pp. 574-75; E. Best, *The Temptation and the Passion: The Markan Soteriology* (Cambridge: Cambridge University Press, 1990), pp. 98-99.

[40] Nolland, *The Gospel of Matthew*, p. 1214.

The normal Roman practice was to leave the bodies of those crucified on the cross to be devoured by vultures.[41] This practice, however, was offensive to Jewish sensibilities as the Mosaic law insisted that someone hanged on a tree should not remain there overnight (Deut. 21:22, 23), for such a person, who was under a curse, would desecrate the land. This would be doubly offensive if it happened on the Sabbath, hence the haste to remove Jesus from the cross. When there was a reason to hasten death, the legs of the one being executed would be smashed, thereby causing asphyxiation.[42] At the point where the soldiers intended to smash Jesus' legs, it was discovered that he was already dead, so the soldiers pierced his side (John 19:31-34). The flow of blood and water from the wound has been given various interpretations. On medical grounds, some have argued that the issue of blood was from the heart and clear fluid from the pericardial sac.[43] Others have seen sacramental[44] and theological allusions.

There is a sense of vindication of Jesus even prior to the resurrection. In Luke 23:47, the centurion declares Jesus to be δίκαιος (righteous), a terrible finding with respect to an executed criminal! In Mark and Matthew the centurion confesses that Jesus is the Son of God (Mark 15:39; Matt. 27:54). In his death, Jesus has embodied all that he has taught through his life: he has taken up the cross, turned the other cheek, prayed for those who persecuted him, allowed his persecutors to take his tunic and his cloak as well. He has fulfilled the ethic of the kingdom, of being perfect even as his heavenly Father is perfect (Matt. 5:48). As Israel's Messiah, he has fulfilled Israel's vocation and thereby forgiveness and blessing is available to Israel, and through her to the nations.[45]

## E. The Burial

Jesus' death is followed by burial, which is organized by Joseph of Arimathea, a rich (Matt. 27:57) member of the Sanhedrin (Mark. 15:43) and a

---

[41] Carson, *The Gospel According to John*, p. 622.

[42] See N. Haas, "Anthropological Observations on the Skeletal Remains from Giv'at ha-Mivtar," *IEJ* 20 (1970), pp. 38-59. Haas discusses an archaeological find of fifteen ossuaries in 1968. This find includes the bones of a man who had been crucified, whose legs had been fractured at the point of death. Concerning him, Haas comments: "the left tibia and fibula were broken by a simple, oblique, dentate-serrate line. . . the fracture on the right tibia bone (the fibula being unavailable for study) was produced by a single, strong blow. This direct, deliberate blow may be attributed to the final 'coup de grace.'" Haas, "Anthropological Observations," p. 57.

[43] See Carson, *The Gospel According to John*, p. 623.

[44] See Rudolf Bultmann, *The Gospel of John: A Commentary* (Philadelphia: Westminster, 1971), pp. 677-79; Raymond E. Brown, *The Gospel According to John*, volume two (Garden City: Doubleday, 1970), pp. 946-53; Martinus C. de Boer, *Johannine Perspectives on the Death of Jesus* (Kampen: Kok Pharos, 1996).

[45] N. T. Wright, *Jesus and the Victory of God* (London: SPCK, 1996), p. 596: "Unlike his actions in the Temple and the upper room, the cross was a symbol not of praxis but of passivity, not of action but of passion. It was to become the symbol of victory, but not of the victory of Caesar, nor of those who would oppose Caesar with Caesar's methods. It was to become the symbol, because it would be the means of the victory of God."

disciple (John 19:38). Nicodemus, also a member of the Sanhedrin (John 3:1), assisted Joseph (John 19:39). The involvement of these two members of the Sanhedrin in Jesus' burial raises questions about their participation in the earlier unanimous decision of the Sanhedrin to have Jesus put to death (Mark 14:64). Luke comments that Joseph had not consented to the decision and action of the Sanhedrin (Luke 23:50-51). Were they absent from the meeting? Had Nicodemus repented of an earlier decision? On such issues the text is silent; these men are now seen as a faithful remnant within rebellious Israel.

Criminals were normally not placed in family tombs for fear of desecrating others who were buried there. All deceased persons were buried outside the city. After taking Jesus' body down from the cross, it was wrapped in strips of linen accompanied by myrrh and aloes. Myrrh was a fragrant resin used by the Egyptians for embalming, and aloes a powder from eaglewood (similar to sandalwood and therefore aromatic). The Jews did not embalm bodies as was the custom in Egypt, hence these spices were to offset the smell of rotting flesh. Joseph placed the body in a tomb, hewn from a rock. Luke notes that it was a tomb where no one had previously been laid (Luke 23:53); reminiscent of a comment that is also made of the colt that had not been ridden prior to the triumphal entry (Luke 19:30). Such comments give the impression of that which is untainted and intended for sacred use.

## F. The Resurrection

The burial of Jesus is followed by the absolute climax of the gospel narratives, the resurrection. The main biblical accounts of Jesus' resurrection are Matt. 28:1-20; Mark 16:1-8; Luke 24:1-12; John 20:1-29 and 1 Cor. 15:3-11. The resurrection tradition was a part of the apostolic church's view of Jesus as evidenced in much of the NT teaching such as Rom. 4:24-25; 10:9; Phil. 2:9-11; 1 Thess. 1:10; John 3:14; 8:28; 12:32, 34; Heb. 9:12-24; 1 Pet. 1:3; 3:18. In these passages, the resurrection of Jesus is not just a single detached article of faith assuring the Christian of life after death; it is woven into the very structure of Christian doctrine and lifestyle. It informs christian teaching about baptism, justification, ethics and the future hope for the cosmos. The discovery of the empty tomb on the first day of the week led to Christians regarding Sunday as a special day, a celebration known as the Lord's Day (Acts 20:7; 1 Cor. 16:2; Rev. 1:10; Justin, *1 Apol.* 67; Irenaeus, *Frg.* 7).

The OT references to resurrection focus more on the hope for Israel than on the hope for the individual. Although some OT passages do refer to the resurrection of individuals (e.g. Job 29:25-26; Ps. 49:15; Isa. 26:19; Dan. 12:1-3), the major OT thrust deals with the post-exilic renewal of Jerusalem, the raising and revivification of Israel (Hos. 6:1-2; Ezek. 37:1-14) and the "new heavens and new earth" (Isa. 65:17).[46] Such a resurrection was therefore

---

[46] N. T. Wright, *The New Testament and the People of God* (London: SPCK, 1992), p. 332: "As such, 'Resurrection' was not simply a pious hope about the new life of dead people. It carried with it all that was associated with the return from exile itself: the forgiveness of sins, the re-establishment of Israel as the true humanity of the covenant god, and the renewal of all

envisaged as the culmination of history in a number of eschatological scenarios (Dan. 12:1-3; *1 Enoch* 51; Rev. 20:4-6). This is seen in Jesus' encounter with Martha, who, following the death of Lazarus, answered Jesus' question about the resurrection (John 11:23) with an affirmation of belief in the resurrection at the last day (John 11:24). Jesus, however, points to the presence of the eschatological reality of resurrection through his own presence (John 11:25) within history. In the resurrection, we see the fulfillment of God's promises to Abraham, which results in the blessing of the nations. Christian worship is no longer tied to the temple; it is focused on the resurrected and ascended Christ.

There is significant diversity between the different resurrection accounts. All the gospels agree that Jesus died and was buried, that the disciples were not ready for his death and they were therefore overcome with confusion. They agree that the resurrection took place on the first day of the week (Matt. 28:1; Mark 16:1; Luke 24:1; John 20:1), that the women's visit is the first step in disclosure, that the stone being rolled away is the first physical clue, and that the resurrection is affirmed by angels. The gospels affirm that Jesus appeared to a variety of people after the resurrection, that the reports of the resurrection were doubted, that no one witnessed the resurrection itself, and that Jesus' resurrection body was tangible. The end result of these events is an unshakeable belief in the resurrection.[47] Differences include the wording of the angelic resurrection announcement (Matt. 28:5-6; Mark 16:6; Luke 24:5-6), John's description of the role of Mary Magdalene (John 20:1), the reference to an earthquake (or not) (Matt. 28:2), and the angel of the Lord rolling the stone away (which is unique to Matt. 28:2-4). This diversity is probably evidence of many resurrection accounts to which the evangelists had access. Readers of the NT can therefore rejoice in the wealth of traditional material concerning the resurrection rather than feel compelled to harmonize the accounts.

A belief in resurrection was foreign to the Greco-Roman culture of Jesus' times. There were many Greek views about life after death, but none claimed a somatic and physical resurrection.[48] The most influential Greek view of immortality is that of Platonism. Plato taught that the soul has three functions: the rational, the spirited (courage) and the appetitive (bodily desires and affections). He likened these to a charioteer (the rational) with two unequally yoked winged horses: one good (the spirited) and one bad (the appetitive)

---

creation." .

[47] See for example W. L. Craig, *The Son Rises: The Historical Evidence for the Resurrection* (Chicago: Moody, 1981); G. E. Ladd, *I Believe in the Resurrection of Jesus* (Grand Rapids: Eerdmans, 1975); Alister McGrath, "Resurrection and Incarnation: The Foundation of the Christian Faith," in Andrew Walker, ed., *Different Gospels: The New Edition* (London: SPCK, 1993), pp. 27-42; T. F. Torrance, *Space, Time and Resurrection* (Edinburgh: Handsel, 1976), pp. 39-45.

[48] See A. Oepke, "ἀνάστασις," *TDNT*, vol. 1, p. 369. Oepke argues that ἀνάστασις was understood by the Greeks in two ways: (a) resurrection is impossible; (b) resurrection (or resuscitation) may take place as an isolated miracle. However, he argues that the idea of a general resurrection at the end of the age is alien to the Greeks.

(*Phaedr.* 246 A-D). The rational component of the soul is preexistent (*Tim.* 69–70) and eternal (*Republic* 10.611B) and is adversely affected by its association with the physical and mutable world. The soul therefore has relations both with the physical and transient world and with the unchanging ideal world. The elements of the physical world (e.g. fire, water) can pollute the soul and the soul can rule bodily desires (*Tim.* 86B). After death, the soul must do penance for earthly misdeeds in a state of bodiless existence that leads to successive rebirths and eventual release of the soul to the divine (*Phaedr.* 249 A-B). This purification leads eventually from this cycle of rebirth and enables the soul to find release from somatic pollution in the realm of the divine.[49] Similarly Aristotle argued that that which distinguished humans from other forms of life (plants, animals) was the intellect, hence immortality was reserved for the active intellect.[50] Pythagoras believed in the transmigration of the soul, which was necessitated by the soul's defilement through earthly birth. This defilement demanded expiation to be paid to Persephone, the goddess of the underworld, by successive incarnations and deaths, with intervening periods of reward and punishment, before the purified soul could be released from the cycle of rebirth.[51] Greek mystery religions also asserted a form of life beyond the grave as evidence in the Eleusis cult and the Dionysiac mysteries.[52] None of these views, however, equated to a Hebrew belief in somatic resurrection. Hence when Paul addressed the council of the Areopagus (Acts 17:22-34) concerning the resurrection of the dead, he was faced with both mockery and with cautious curiosity.

The Hebrew belief in resurrection was not universal. The most significant difference within Judaism at the time of Jesus was between the Sadducees who denied the resurrection (Acts 23:8; Josephus, *Ant.* 18.16-17; *J.W.* 2.165) and the Pharisees and Essenes who affirmed it. It is the Pharisees, however, who represented popular Judaism (e.g. *1 En.* 22:13; 51:2; 2 Maccabees 7; *Pss. Sol.* 3:12; 15:12-13; *2 Bar.* 30:1; *Ps.-Philo* 3:10). Central to this Hebrew understanding of resurrection was the idea of Sheol—the place of the dead. The issue was whether God would raise a person from Sheol, where the dead lived even as "shadows." Resurrection was therefore not the continuation of "spiritual" life *after* death, as if death were a non-event, but as N. T. Wright has argued, it was always somatic and referred to as "life after life after death."[53]

The exact chronology of the first Easter Sunday poses difficulties. The names of the women who visited the tomb are recorded differently. Matthew

---

[49] M. J. Harris, *From Grave to Glory: Resurrection in the New Testament* (Grand Rapids: Zondervan, 1990), pp. 38-39.

[50] Harris, *From Grave to Glory*, pp. 38-40.

[51] J. A. Philip, *Pythagoras and Early Pythagoreanism* (Toronto: University of Toronto Press, 1966), pp. 151-71.

[52] See Craig S. Keener, *A Commentary on the Gospel of Matthew* (Grand Rapids: Eerdmans, 1999), pp. 705-10.

[53] N. T. Wright, *The Resurrection of the Son of God* (Minneapolis: Fortress Press, 2003), p. 31 (emphasis his).

names Mary Magdalene and the other Mary (Matt. 28:1); Mark mentions Mary Magdalene, Mary the mother of James, and Salome (Mark 16:1); Luke mentions Mary Magdalene, Joanna, Mary the mother of James "and the others with them" (Luke 24:10); John mentions only Mary Magdalene (John 20:1). Thus the one woman who is mentioned in all the gospels is Mary Magdalene. There is confusion about what happened upon Mary's arrival. John says that when Mary discovered that the stone had been removed from the tomb's entrance, she ran to Peter and the "beloved disciple," reporting the theft of the body of Jesus. Upon her report, both disciples ran to the tomb. The "beloved disciple" believed upon seeing the empty tomb (20:8) while Mary stood outside weeping (20:11). When she looked again in the tomb she saw two angels seated where Jesus' body had been. At this point, however, she still believed the body had been stolen (20:13). Jesus appeared to her (20:16) and she told the disciples of the appearance (20:18). This account seems at variance with those of the Synoptic Gospels in which there is an immediate angelic announcement on Mary's first visit to the tomb (Matt. 28:5-7; Mark 16:6-7; Luke 24:5-7). There are several attempts to solve this apparent discrepancy including the possibility of Mary making two trips to the tomb, or the more likely suggestion that John 20:1-10 and John 20:11-18 are two accounts of the same event, the former from the perspective of the "beloved disciple"; the latter from the perspective of Mary.[54]

Other literary factors should also be noted when looking at the different accounts. The events surrounding the resurrection do not form a sequence in which one event is dependent on a former event, at least not to the same extent as is the case in the passion narrative where the crucifixion is dependent on the trial and the trial is dependant on the arrest.[55] That which all accounts affirm, however, is the physical resurrection of Israel's Messiah. This news is attested by women, despite the disqualification of the testimony of women who, according to Josephus, could not be trusted "due to the levity and temerity of their sex" (διὰ κουφότητα καὶ θράσος τοῦ γένους αὐτῶν [*Ant.* 4.219]).[56] It was the women, however, who were at the cross, who came to anoint the body with burial spices, and became witnesses to the resurrection. It is they who provide continuity of witness throughout the passion and resurrection narrative.

There are several post-resurrection appearances which show the fulfillment of Israel's vocation in its resurrected Messiah. Jesus' disciples needed to be convinced that the resurrected one was the same Jesus who had been crucified (Mark 16:6). Therefore Luke emphasizes the senses of touch and sight, and even the event of Jesus eating food (Luke 24:39-43). John also stresses the reality of the resurrection in the encounter with Thomas (John 20:24-29). The relationship between the encounter with Jesus and the need for

---

[54] Four "solutions" are outlined by Bock, *Luke*, volume two, pp. 1886-88.

[55] See a discussion of this in Brown, *John*, volume two, p. 971.

[56] Note the discussion on the credibility of the women's testimony concerning the resurrection in R. Bauckham, *Gospel Women: Studies of the Named Women in the Gospels* (Grand Rapids: Eerdmans, 2002), pp. 257-310.

faith is underscored. Faith was always to be the response of Israel to God's revelation (e.g. Gen 15:1-6), and this is no different after the resurrection.

The significance of the passion and resurrection as the fulfillment of God's purposes for Israel is most clearly seen in Jesus' meeting with two men on their way to Emmaus (Luke 24:13-35). These two appear to be among those who did not believe the testimony of the women who witnessed the empty tomb. Their encounter, however, is not just with an empty tomb but with the risen Jesus. The emphasis of Jesus' discussion with them is that the passion and resurrection are the fulfillment of all the OT Scriptures. Each of the three sections of the Hebrew Bible—the Law, the Prophets and the Writings (here referred to as the Psalms, a significant section of the Writings)—is shown to find its fulfillment in Christ (Luke 24:44).

The resurrection therefore results in the re-establishment of Israel and the inauguration of Gentile mission. This re-establishment is recorded in different ways in the gospels. In Matthew, the Great Commission is the re-establishment of Israel as it becomes the means whereby the nations will be blessed (Matt. 28:19). In Luke we read that the Gentile mission is the direct result of the death and resurrection of the Messiah: "The Christ will suffer and rise from the dead on the third day, and repentance and forgiveness of sins will be preached in his name to all nations, beginning at Jerusalem" (Luke 24:46-47). The reconstitution of Israel finds further fulfillment in Luke's second volume, both in the commission of Acts 1:8 and in Pentecost (Acts 2). In John the reconstitution of Israel can be seen in Jesus breathing the gift of the Holy Spirit upon his disciples (John 20:21-23) and in their commissioning. The gospel is now released from its Jerusalem-focus. The Messiah has acted for Israel in his death and resurrection. Sins are forgiven and Israel is redefined as those who are buried with Christ (in baptism) and raised with him to newness of life (Rom. 6:1-4; Col. 2:12). The death and resurrection of Jesus therefore fulfills God's promises to Israel. The blessings of the covenant God are appropriated through the faithfulness of Israel's Messiah. Israel is released from its geographical limitations and redefined as those who gather around the resurrected Christ. In the crucifixion and resurrection, therefore, Jesus acted as Israel's Messiah, and through his faithfulness fulfilled all that the former order was unable to achieve.

## G. Conclusion

The three major OT offices of prophet (1 Kgs. 19:16[57]), priest (e.g. Exod. 40:13; Lev. 7:35; Num. 35:25) and king (e.g. 1 Sam. 9:9; 1 Sam. 16:1-3; 1 Kgs. 1:34) were all fulfilled in Jesus. Jesus fulfilled the role of Israel's prophet by embodying the perfect revelation of God the Father in his exemplification of the teaching outlined in the Sermon on the Mount: on the cross he turned the other cheek, loved his enemies and prayed for those who persecuted him. As priest, he offered atonement for the sins of Israel. With the forgiveness of

---

[57] The anointing of Elisha is the only example of the anointing of a prophet in the OT.

sins and the bestowal of blessings by God, a new age dawned, a new covenant which had been foretold in Jer. 31:31-34. As king, Jesus conquered the power of sin as evidenced in death, in guilt and in the realm of the principalities and powers.

This fulfillment involved both vocation and location, particularly with regard to the offices of priest and king. The vocation of the priesthood was to make atonement on behalf of the people; the location of this activity was seen primarily in the tabernacle and later in the temple in Jerusalem. Similarly, the vocation of the king was seen in the exercising of the rule of God and the conquest of enemies on behalf of the people, the clearest example of which was David's conquest of Goliath; the location of this was focused in the king's palace in Jerusalem. Hence in the Second Temple period, these offices were tied to a specific geographical location: Jerusalem. This is now all surpassed through the death and resurrection of Israel's perfect Messiah.

The cross and the resurrection, therefore, become the fulfillment of all that preceded them and the inauguration of all that would follow. The focus of God's covenant rule was no longer upon lesser "messiahs" of the old covenant; the locus of this work was no longer focused on physical Jerusalem, but upon Jesus and the Heavenly Jerusalem, the place of his rule (Heb. 12:22-23). It is not surprising, therefore, that by the time the reader comes to the end of the canonical gospels, that the climax of each of these books is the crucifixion and the resurrection. The new covenant is inaugurated by the resurrection of Jesus and the consequent gift of the Holy Spirit. The new covenant sees release from the ongoing centrality of Jerusalem and the beginning of the Gentile mission.

## Bibliography

Best, Ernest. *The Temptation and the Passion: The Markan Soteriology*. Cambridge/New York: Cambridge University Press, 1990.

Blount, Brian K. "A Socio-Rhetorical Analysis of Simon of Cyrene: Mark 15.21 and its Parallels." *Semeia* 64 (1993): 171-98.

Brown, Raymond E. *The Death of the Messiah*. 2 vols. New York: Doubleday, 1994.

Catchpole, David R. *The Trial of Jesus: A Study in the Gospels and Jewish Historiography from 1770 to the Present Day*. Leiden: Brill, 1971.

Craig, William Lane. *The Son Rises: The Historical Evidence for the Resurrection*. Chicago: Moody Press, 1981.

Green, Joel B. *The Death of Jesus: Tradition and Interpretation in the Passion Narrative*. Tübingen: Mohr (Siebeck), 1988.

Harris, Murray J. *From Grave to Glory: Resurrection in the New Testament*. Grand Rapids: Zondervan, 1990.

Hengel, Martin. *Crucifixion in the Ancient World and the Folly of the Message of the Cross*. Philadelphia: Fortress Press, 1977.

Ladd, G. E. *I believe in the Resurrection of Jesus*. Grand Rapids: Eerdmans, 1975.

Lémonon, J.-P. *Pilate et le gouvernement de la Judée: textes et monuments*. Paris: Gabalda, 1981.

McGrath, Alister. "Resurrection and Incarnation: The Foundation of the Christian Faith." In *Different Gospels: Christian Orthodoxy and Modern Theologies*, edited by Andrew Walker, pp. 27-42. London: SPCK, 1993.

Torrance, Thomas F. *Space, Time and Resurrection*. Grand Rapids: Eerdmans, 1976.

Weber, Hans-Ruedi. *The Cross: Tradition and Interpretation*. Grand Rapids: Eerdmans, 1979.

Wright, N. T. *The Resurrection of the Son of God*. Minneapolis: Fortress Press, 2003.

# INDEX OF ANCIENT PEOPLE

Herod Antipas, 3, 15, 25, 83, 85, 88-91, 99-100, 116-17, 136, 205, 244, 260, 424, 444
Herod Philip, 85, 89
Herodias, 85, 89-90
Hezekiah (King), 18
Hillel, 129
Honi the Circle Drawer, 150, 402
Hyrcanus I, 6-7, 122, 135, 145-46
Hyrcanus II, 81-82, 135, 136

Ignatius of Antioch, 186-87, 204-5, 426
Irenaeus, 187-88, 194-95, 197-98
Isaiah, 161, 176
Isis, 73

Jaddua, 131
Jairus, 302
James (Apostle), 184, 227-28, 293, 425
James (the Just, brother of Jesus), 102, 147, 153, 213, 217, 347
Jason (High Priest), 131-33, 148
Jason of Cyrene, 139
Jehohanan, 20
Jerome, 216-19
Joanna, 452
Joazar, 98
John (son of Mattathias), 3, 6
John (Apostle), 184, 425
John Chrysostom, 355
John Mark, 264
John of Patmos, 232,
John the Baptist, 25, 70-71, 88, 90, 122, 205, 218, 235, 258, 269-70, 274, 276-77, 295-96, 313-14, 321-22, 329, 335, 337, 341-45, 347-49, 384, 403, 406, 408, 444
John the Presbyter, 264, 293
Jonathan (High Priest), 101, 150
Jonathan (son of Mattathias), 3, 6, 134, 139
Joseph (father of Jesus), 15, 219-20, 223-24, 306-7, 314
Joseph (son of Jacob), 139
Joseph of Arimathea, 340, 448-49
Josephus, 14, 122, 124, 127-28, 130, 137-38, 141, 143-44, 147, 149, 150, 253, 439, 443-44, 446, 452
Josiah, 142
Judah, 333-34
Judas (Iscariot), 284, 441, 443
Judas (son of Hezekiah the bandit), 149
Judas Maccabeus, 3, 6, 81, 134-35, 139, 438
Judas the Galilean, 98, 117, 145, 149, 150, 333, 422
Julius Caesar, 91-92
Justin Martyr, 188, 191, 193-95, 197-98

Juvenal, 112

Levi, 221

Mani, 215
Marcellus, 97
Marcion, 190-91, 193, 195, 198
Marcus Ambibulus, 97
Marcus Aurelius, 188
Malthace, 85, 87
Mariamme I, 85-86, 136
Mariamme II, 85
Mark (the evangelist), 235-36, 263-66, 268, 293
Mark Antony, 16, 82, 91
Martha, 322, 434, 450
Marullus, 97
Mary (mother of James), 452
Mary (mother of Jesus), 13, 112, 162, 219-20, 226, 306-7, 313
Mary (sister of Martha), 322
Mary (the "other"), 452
Mary Magdalene, 231, 450, 452
Mattathias, 3, 6, 134
Matthew (Apostle), 225, 293
Matthew (the evangelist), 265
Menahem, 423
Menelaus, 131, 133
Moses, 6, 141, 143, 152, 174, 281, 392

Nathan, 369
Nathaniel, 432
Nebuchadnezzar, 330
Nehemiah, 130
Nero, 92, 101-3, 304, 439
Nicodemus, 322, 351, 449
Nicolaus of Damascus, 141

Octavian. See Augustus
Onias III, 132-33, 139
Origen, 216-19

Papias (Bishop of Hierapolis), 56, 192, 234-35, 263-65, 275, 293
Parmenio, 131
Paul, 53, 143-44, 152, 184, 209, 211-13, 263, 269, 314, 347-48, 451
Peter (Simon), 11-12, 184, 194, 209, 225-28, 235-36, 263-65, 268-69, 271-73, 281, 284, 286, 293, 297, 300-301, 311, 321-22, 339, 347, 406, 418, 424-25, 441-43, 445, 452
Petronius the Centurion, 222
Phasael, 135-36
Philip the Tetrarch, 3, 83, 85, 88, 99-100, 117

# INDEX OF PLACES